PASSION AND CRIMINALITY

A LEGAL AND LITERARY STUDY

BY

LOUIS PROAL

ONE OF THE PRESIDING JUDGES
AT THE COURT OF APPEAL OF RIOM (PUY-DE-DÔME)
LAUREATE OF THE "INSTITUT"

TRANSLATED FROM THE FRENCH

BY

A. R. ALLINSON M.A. (Oxon.)

PARIS

CHARLES CARRINGTON

13 FAUBOURG MONTMARTRE

TRANSLATOR'S FOREWORD.

FEW more important Works have been published of late years than Louis Proal's *Passion and Criminality*. It is a book that appeals at one and the same time to the specialist in Psychology, Ethics, Criminology and Insanity, and to the general reader.

M. Proal is a well-known authority on all questions connected with Crime, its causes and motives, its various forms and manifestations, its frequency and distribution, and its *The Author's Weight and Standing.* proper punishment, and the author of other valuable and interesting works, throwing light on these vitally important subjects. He holds a high position in the legal profession in France, being one of the Presiding Judges at a French Court of Appeal, and having previously held very responsible official and judicial appointments in other parts of the Country, especially in the South. All this has afforded M. Proal unrivalled opportunities of observation ; and indeed the most cursory glance through his books must show what an enormous mass of invaluable information he has gleaned from many different sources—from cases in which he has acted as Advocate or Prosecutor, or presided as Judge, from confidences made to him as *Juge d'Instruction*, from Reports of Criminal Trials, from Official Records of Suicides, etc., etc. Moreover, this wealth of detail is marshalled in the most admirable order, each argument adduced and each conclusion arrived at being supported by a series of apposite facts in illustration, the whole set forth in that clearly ordered and lucid style that seems the birthright of every educated Frenchman.

Passion and Criminality is a truly wonderful book. No doubt the reading is often sad and painful, but it is never dull. No doubt *The Book is true to Life.* the facts are often distressing and humiliating to our ideals of what humanity should be, and throw a lurid light on some of the social arrangements and the boasted civilization of modern Europe, but they are authentic. The impression is ever present of a writer of great original acumen and powers of observation, who is thoroughly acquainted with all aspects and intimacies of his subject —a subject of enthralling interest to all concerned with the progress of mankind, and one displaying some of the most curious and little realised secrets of the human mind in health and still more in disease.

For Good or Evil.   Nor is the Statistical side of M. Proal's labours unimportant. Every Chapter teems with valuable information as to the frequency and distribution of Passional Crime and Suicide in France, and supplies quite indispensable data both for the student of contemporary French life, and for the Comparative Statistician who would bring into focus the social phæ-nomena of France and those of other countries, in order to take a comprehensive view of the whole and arrive at trustworthy conclusions as to the general trend of social evolution for good or evil. This cannot but be of especial, and indeed paramount, interest to Englishmen at a moment when their Country is confronted with the same problem of a diminishing birth-rate and threatened stagnation of population, which has for twenty years past caused so much anxiety to French Politicians and Sociologists.

The Author's Literary Brilliancy.   Then again there is the literary side. Here M. Proal displays a wide and extensive knowledge of the Literature of his native land, especially that of the great classical period of French poetry and prose, and again and again aptly illustrates facts and incidents of criminality and criminology by pertinent quotations from Corneille, Racine, and the rest. Nor is his acquaintance with more modern writers deficient; he mentions constantly and quotes freely from Chateaubriand, Lamartine, George Sand, Alfred de Musset, Théophile Gautier, and the like, not to mention Flaubert, Barbey d'Aurévilly,

Guy de Maupassant, Zola himself. At the same time our Author's own personal bias in favour of the more correct and academical writers of the earlier period, as against the "morbid, anæmic, hysterical"—to use some of his own epithets—Novels, Plays and Poems of the Romantic School, is evident enough. All the Works originating in the impulse of the "Romantic" revival of 1830 and onwards, he clearly regards as without exception showing more or less manifest traces of nervous derangement and diseased mental conditions on the part of their authors. Any way the literary aspect of the book is far from being the least attractive and suggestive. M. Proal's discussion of *Werther* in particular and other books, such as Jean Jacques Rousseau's, of the same period and tendency, in their bearing on suicide, being profoundly interesting, and, indeed, a masterpiece of its kind.

As throwing light upon contemporary society in France, its special circumstances and peculiar dangers, and involved in these conditions the future of the French Nation, *Meaning to the English Reader.* apart altogether from the more general aspect of the Work as dealing with the Psychological, Ethical, Criminal, and other problems affecting mankind at large, *Passion and Criminality* cannot fail to be intensely fascinating to readers of the present day. In many respects France leads the van of progress in Europe; and, to a large extent, other countries must look to her as the mirror reflecting their own future development in many directions of social change and evolution. She is their model in much that is excellent, their warning as to certain social perils to be avoided.

From all points of view, Legal, Statistical, Literary, Social, whether limited to France or looked at more generally as affecting *The Problems of Life.* directly or indirectly all civilized nations, *Passion and Criminality* marks an epoch. It will be read with deep interest by students, while affording both amusement and

instruction to all who care to be introduced to a wealth
of curious information bearing on social life and problems,
and a profusion of unexpected and often pathetic side-
lights on the dark places of contemporary civilization in
town and country among a neighbouring people.

PREFACE.

THE study of Crime as determined by Passion is forced
upon the attention of Moralist and Magistrate alike by the
large number of victims, active and passive, it is responsible
for from year to year. Love, which occupies so considerable a place in Life and Literature, claims ever more and
more importance in the Annals of Crime and the Statistics
of Suicide. While Poets and Novelists extol the beauties
and virtues of Love, it is the shame and despair and
criminality incident to the same passion that Magistrates
have every day occasion to note. What is it but Passion
that drives so many men desperate, turns so many into
madmen or murderers? What else is it brings so many
unfortunate and guilty beings to the Morgue, the Mad-
house, and the Criminal Assize? In Love's dramas, which
may so easily become dramas of the Law Courts, we may
say with Racine:

> "Partout du désespoir on rencontre l'image,
> On ne voit que des pleurs et l'on n'entend parler
> Que de troubles, d'horreurs, de sang prêt à couler."[1]
>
> (BÉRÉNICE.)

If Poets do well to represent happy love under the
lineaments of a young and lovely woman, full of life and
joy, not less faithfully may Students of Crime portray
unhappy love in the guise of a dread Fate holding the
Shears, or a Fury with brandished sword in hand. In
very deed Love makes many self-immolated victims,—by
drowning and charcoal fumes, by the rope and the pistol.
Love has ruined many a fine intellect and broken many a
heart. Moreover, where unhappy lovers do not resort to

[1] "Everywhere we meet the image of despair; naught is seen but tears,
naught spoken of but grief and horror and blood about to flow."

suicide, or go mad, or die of chagrin, it is no uncommon thing to see them kill the object of their affections. Who shall count the cups of poison, the dagger thrusts and revolver shots Love is responsible for?—who reckon up the vitriol thrown under its promptings and the nooses it has tied?

It is no mere collection of crimes of passion I propose to compile ; my subject is the Psychology of the lover whom passion drives into crime, of the mistress whom desertion drives into despair, of the man whom jealousy or a mistaken sense of honour makes a murderer, or disappointed love a suicide. These studies do but sum up the long series of observations I have made, both on the Bench and in my Chambers as a *Juge d'instruction* and *Procureur de la République*, where I have enjoyed so many opportunities of cross-questioning those accused of crimes arising from passion, of studying their character and the motives of their aberrations, of reading the documents left behind by suicides, or composed by murderers in their own defence.

Not a few difficult problems of psychology and moral responsibility are involved in suicide and crime, the results of outbreaks of passion. How many questions must needs arise from the study of those emotions which lead so many thousands of men and women, young men and maidens, to madness, suicide and crime !

How comes it that affection may turn to hate, and lovers become the bitterest foes,—that the transition is so easy from love to loathing, from the transports of the most exalted tenderness to the frenzies of the most savage anger? How is it so fond a feeling may grow so cruel and lead to the commission of so many barbarous murders by poison and strangulation, and the infliction of such appalling wounds? Whence comes the cruelty of love and the ferocity of jealousy ? Why does the jealous lover strike the very woman he adores ? Why does he pierce with dagger thrusts the very bosom on which he has lain, and disfigure the very features he has just been covering with kisses? Why does the woman whom her lover has deserted burn out the eyes that moved her soul to love, and send a bullet through the heart she was so fain but now to feel beating beneath her hand? How is it love may grow so venomous as to put knife and pistol into the hand of lovers and husbands, who after having sworn eternal affection, tear each other's eyes out at the domestic hearth, and in the very conjugal bed? Why does this passion, capable as it is of producing heroes, so often manufacture only cowards and murderers?

To end our string of questions, why does love if unrequited make people so unhappy they must needs kill themselves? How is it that lovers, who might very well live together, prefer to die together?

Such are the chief psychological problems I propose to study. It appears to me to be an inquiry not devoid of utility to investigate why love, which should serve as the foundation of society and family life, so often becomes a malignant power, destructive alike of the family and of society.

I hope further that this study of crime as determined by passion, indispensable as it is to the student of Morals and Criminality, may also be found interesting by the Critic of Literature, whose delight it is to verify in the great Tragic poets the exact portrayal of the passions of humanity. The object of the Stage being the entertainment of the spectator by an imitation of life and a mimic representation of its passions, the depicting of Love, its aberrations and its crimes, is the main thing aimed at. There are few Tragedies that do not contain murders and suicides from love. In the *Andromaque* for instance there is a murder, that of Pyrrhus, and two suicides, those of Oreste and Hermione. In *Bajazet* there are three murders,—of Bajazet himself, of Roxane, and of Orcan, and a suicide, that of Atalide. It is a regular butchery. Most of the heroes of the Stage are really Criminal Court heroes. Literature copies Crime, —the crime of passionate outbreaks, just as Crime of the same type copies Literature. To ascertain therefore whether the literary portrayal of crime and passion is faithful or no, it is no idle task to compare the love-sick murderers of the boards with those that appear at the bar of the Assize Courts. While determining the Psychology of the "woman scorned," of the jealous lover and murderer, I intend to inquire concurrently how far my judicial observations coincide with the characters of Hermione, Roxane, Phèdre, Médée, Cléopâtre, Oreste, Pyrrhus, Mithridate and other heroes of the great Classical Drama of France.

It has been maintained by some that it is useless to look for psychological truth in Dramatic poetry: "Shall we never learn," writes M. Stapfer, "Philistines that we are, vain professors of Morals and History, to taste poetry in its pure state, in all its complete and unsophisticated absurdity?" This Critic admires the poetry Corneille has put into the rôle of Cléopâtre, while holding at the same time that the character is false, and that no trace of human verity is to be found in the part. I am of a diametrically opposite opinion, and believe the chief beauty of Corneille's and Racine's plays to consist in the psychological verisimilitude of the characters they draw.

In the course of the present study, I shall frequently have occasion to show that Corneille's psychology is no less acute and delicate than Racine's. Corneille is not only a Politician and a Philosopher, he is a Psychologist to boot, and one of the most perspicacious. He is stinted of his due meed of praise by such as are content to admire the vigour of his thought and the splendour of his verse, complaining the while of the coldness of his delineations of Love. Corneille possessed the heroic spirit, but he united with it the tenderest of hearts, and this tenderness he has instilled into his Tragedies. "What greater tenderness," says a good judge, La Bruyère, "can there be than that lavished in the *Cid*, in *Polyeucte* and in the *Horaces*?" The Critics are wrong, I maintain, and specially so M. Larroumet, in attributing to Racine exclusively the gift of portraying passionate love; we find it in Corneille too, equally precise and equally faithful, and it may be, conjoined with an even more penetrating analysis. Racine is not invariably as soft and tender as they make out, and Corneille is more tender and more passionate than he is described. He married for love at a time when Racine contracted a union of mere convenience. The poet of reason and high heroism, he showed himself less reasonable than his rival, and succumbed to new passions at a mature age; his head was ever ready to be turned by love. I shall show by means of numerous examples borrowed from some of the less well-known pieces of Corneille that every shade and delicacy, every refinement and subtlety, of Passion has been described by him with an admirable truth and precision unsurpassed by Racine himself.

Those cries of love, anger and revenge that Corneille and Racine put in the mouths of their *dramatis personæ* are not mere "authors' stuff," but veritable exclamations of Mother Nature; so true are they to life that I have often heard the very same in the mouths of persons accused of crimes of passion. By virtue of the resemblances I shall bring out between the dramas of Literature and those of the Law Courts, the fact will once more be made manifest that the first and highest quality of genius is psychological verisimilitude. After all that Commentators have written on the Drama of Corneille and Racine, I trust this new light thrown on them by the reports of the Criminal Courts will not be without its interest. It will be seen that simple Nature suggests to the desperate or jealous lover, to the forsaken mistress and the wronged husband, though entirely lacking in intellectual culture of any sort, cries of passion bearing an astonishing likeness to those of Hermione, Médée, Roxane and Phèdre, of Oreste and Othello, in the plays. Their exclamations of grief and love bear a simpler, a less elegant form, it is true, but also not unfrequently one impressed with a more striking and tragic note, from the very fact that they are not, as in plays and romances, overlaid with a flood of rhetorical embellishment. I shall quote numerous examples of this, all proving how untrue is the criticism of Schlegel on Racine, when he

b

writes: " The essence of Racine's muse was gallantry ; the
major part of his Tragedies were composed merely to depict loveable, and above all, loving women." The essence
of Racine's muse was Love, which is ever the same at
bottom among small and great alike ; his heroines are not
invariably loveable and loving women such as Bérénice or
Aricie ; some of them are fierce and passionate beings, a
prey to all the pangs of love and jealousy, such as Hermione, Roxane or Phèdre.

But side by side with the Drama of Corneille and
Racine, which is a school of Psychology, exists a Literature of sentiment and the senses, which glorifying passion, suicide and crime, its results, is a veritable school of
sensuality, ever teaching the pernicious lesson that suicide
and crime are justified as flowing from an overmastering
emotion. I intend in the following pages to bring home
the responsibility resting on this class of Literature by a
record of the suicides and crimes, *literary, romantic* and
naturalistic, due to its evil influence.

CONTENTS.

CHAPTER I.

SUICIDE AS DETERMINED BY PASSION.

CHAPTER II.

DOUBLE SUICIDE AS DETERMINED BY PASSION.

CHAPTER III.

HATE AN INCIDENT OF LOVE.

CHAPTER VI.

ADULTERY ON THE PART OF THE WIFE.

CHAPTER VII.

ADULTERY ON THE PART OF THE WIFE (*continued*).

THE FORGIVING HUSBAND—THE AVENGING HUSBAND.

CHAPTER VIII.

ADULTERY ON THE PART OF THE HUSBAND.

CHAPTER IX.

CAUSES OF THE FREQUENCY OF SUICIDES AND CRIMES ARISING OUT OF PASSION.

CHAPTER X.

SUICIDE DETERMINED BY PASSION AND THE CONTAGION OF LITERATURE AS AFFECTING IT.

CHAPTER XI.

CRIME DETERMINED BY PASSION AND THE CONTAGION OF NOVELS OF PASSION AS AFFECTING IT.

CHAPTER XII.

CRIME DETERMINED BY PASSION AND THE CONTAGION OF PLAYS OF PASSION AS AFFECTING IT.

CHAPTER XIII.

RESPONSIBILITY IN CASES OF CRIME DETERMINED BY PASSION.

CONCLUSION.

MEANS OF DIMINISHING CRIME DETERMINED BY PASSION.

PASSION AND CRIMINALITY

CHAPTER I.

SUICIDE AS DETERMINED BY PASSION.

"Ariane ma sœur, de quel amour blessée
Vous mourûtes aux bords où vous fûtes laissée?"[1]

CHILDREN are seldom known to die of grief, to kill themselves or go mad, on the death of their parents, — irreparable though the loss be. Similarly sorrow caused by the death of children or of husband or wife produces but a small crop of suicides and cases of madness. For instance in the year 1890 there were in all France only 67 suicides due to the loss of children, of husband or wife, and of parents. The total of suicides caused by disappointed love and by jealousy on the other hand reaches a very much higher figure,—amounting to about 500 annually.

Again to this total of self-inflicted deaths must be added a not inconsiderable number of lingering deaths and instances of madness determined by love sorrows. As the result of an unreciprocated passion for a woman they have only known a short time, whom very likely they would soon have learned to hate, had they married her, whose loss in any case they could supply, we see unhappy lovers fall into a state of languor and depression, dangerous at once to health and reason. Their countenance expresses sadness and deep dejection ; their gaze is indifferent to their surround-

[1] "Ariane, my sister, wounded by what love didst thou die on those shores where thou wast forsaken?"

ings, and fixed in a stony stare, either lifted to the
sky or lowered to the earth; they speak little, eat little,
and sleep less. This state of prostration, checking
nutrition as it does, leads to a rapid wasting away.
Amnon, the son of David, we read in the Bible (2 Samuel,
ch. xiii.) conceived so violent a passion for his half-sister
Tamar, "that he fell sick" for her; he refused to eat and
grew thinner and thinner. This sort of dejection is well
described by Racine in *Phèdre*; the sufferer can neither
sleep nor eat, and seeks out dark and lonely spots, the
better to weep at her ease, exclaiming :

"Je ne me soutiens plus, mes forces m'abandonnent." [1]

Her nurse, watching her, sees with terror that she is dying
in her arms of a disease she hides from her, the disease
of love. This disease, so often turned into ridicule, may
indeed be a "sickness unto death." The grief of disappointed love *is* sometimes fatal, especially in the case
of a young girl. When relatives, noticing her deep-seated
melancholy, ask her the reason, she answers, "she has a
fatal grief." The adjective is no mere metaphor, but the
exact expression of her feeling; she knows that the
gnawing grief at her heart is leading her step by step to
the tomb. Every sorrow is able to kill, but love's sorrows
above all others. Love then is no idle game, but a stern
reality not to be trifled with.

Not sensual love only, such as Phèdre feels, may bring
about this state of dejection. Love the most pure, if without hope of return, or balked by relations, may produce
the very same despair in the most chaste of maiden
bosoms. Many forms of wasting sickness, resulting in
death, arise from nothing else than an unhappy love
affair. In his notice on Millevoye, de Pongerville relates
how the Poet sought the hand of a young female relative
in marriage, with whom he was deeply in love and who
reciprocated his affection. The girl's father rejected his
demand, in spite of his child's prayers, unwilling to marry

---

[1] "I faint and fall, all my strength deserts me."

her to a penniless poet. The girl's heart broke with grief, and she wasted away and died. Her death, which overwhelmed Millevoye with sorrow, was the first cause of his characteristic melancholy. Another poet, Alfred de Musset, who possessed a nature of feminine susceptibility, well understood the influence of grief and disappointment on a girl's heart:

"Savez-vous ce que c'est qu'un cœur de jeune fille?
Ce qu'il faut pour briser ce fragile roseau,
Qui ploie et qui se couche au plus léger fardeau?" [1]

The greater the purity and tenderness of the unhappy soul, the more imminent the risk of despair where a young girl is concerned, when forsaken by her *fiancé* or when her relatives are opposed to her union with him. Stricken to the heart, she is left dizzy and amazed, stunned and paralysed by the pain; her natural craving to love and to be loved is balked, and her whole being broken. If in place of the adored being whom in the innocence of her maiden fancy she had endowed with the most entrancing qualities, she sees quite another man appear, a hard-hearted, barren-souled fellow who plays her false, the blow is so heavy it may easily destroy life or sanity; the victim dies of love and grief, like Ariane in the play.

The young man, whose love is balked or not returned, experiences the same sufferings; he grows sombre, pensive and silent, and no longer wears his usual air. A mother relates how after passing the evening with her son at the house of friends, she saw him, on leaving, so sad and preoccupied that she followed him trembling, in dread of some catastrophe. Suddenly her son kissed her; then pushed her away with the words, "Farewell, mother, leave me alone now," and drawing a pistol from his pocket, drew the trigger and shot himself dead.

Absorbed in his own thoughts, the unfortunate lover

---

[1] "Dost know the nature of a maiden's heart? dost know how little it needs to break that tender reed, that bends and droops beneath the lightest load?"

loses all taste for work. If he is a working-man, he neglects his trade; if a man of education, he loses the love of study. The Poets, those faithful observers of human nature, have noted this characteristic trait. In his Idyll of the "Harvesters," Theocritus makes one rustic say to another, "Why! what ails you? you cannot plough a furrow now, as once you could; you cannot cut the corn." The other replies, "I have no spirit left to sow the field before my own door."—A similar observation is made by Virgil in his *Eclogues* and in the *Æneïd*: "Ah! Corydon, unhappy Corydon, what madness has come over you! your vine remains half pruned on yonder leafy elms. Why will you not to work?" (Eclogue II.). Dido cannot sleep or busy herself any more with her usual occupations, when she sees Æneas is thinking of forsaking her; she neglects the oversight of her army and the building of her Palaces.—Werther notices the same thing in himself: "'Tis a fatality, William; all my activity has degenerated into a restless indolence. I cannot bear to remain idle, yet I find it impossible to do anything" (Letter xxxviii.)—After his rupture with George Sand, Alfred de Musset longs to set to his work afresh, but has no strength left for the task; he can do nothing but dream of his faithless mistress, whose image is engraved in his memory and flesh and spirit. Unable to work, he abandons himself to his grief, eating out his heart in sorrow; watching the blood flow from his wound, his food bitter thoughts and tender, cruel memories, he slowly dies of love, he grows indifferent to life and fame, and lets his genius languish.

I borrow next from various criminal actions sundry observations of a like kind. A father, whose daughter, a girl of sixteen, had fled from home to follow a young man, whom her family would not allow her to marry, said in reply to judicial interrogatories: "My daughter had no more heart for her work; she is a good workwoman, yet she was obliged to begin what she was doing again and again."—A master said, speaking of a workman of his who ended by committing suicide: "He was now quite

unable to work.   Seeing him so pensive and melancholy,
I was struck by his sombre looks and I asked him what
he was thinking about.   He replied, "I am thinking of
her."   I have myself known a case where a young lover,
being unable to work in consequence of the one idea
that paralysed his energies, was refused the girl whose
hand he had asked for ; the latter's family judged him a
hopeless idler and sent him about his business, whereas
the poor fellow's sole and only crime was to be too deep
in love.   His despair led to suicide.—"I cannot work any
more," writes another workman who had been disappointed
in love, "my head is half mad ; I must give up my
work."—A young work-girl, who lately committed suicide
at Marseilles together with a young man she wished to
marry, because the latter's mother was opposed to the
match, had struck her companions by her dreamy, dis-
traught and self-absorbed looks.   One of her friends,
speaking of her to me, said : "She was wrapped up in
her own thoughts ; if you spoke to her, it was an evident
effort to her to answer, and she seemed to be waking
out of a dream."   Finding an account in a newspaper of
a young girl's suicide, she exclaimed, "A happy woman,
that!"   Death has no terrors for a girl suffering from
balked or slighted love ; it may even be said to have
attractions for her.

Love in fact longs for death, when it cannot satisfy its
craving for union, for complete fusion, for one common life.
I read in a farewell letter to his father written by a student,
driven desperate by his mistress's unfaithfulness, that
death was calling to him, luring him on, and had an
irresistible attraction for him.   Corneille has noted the
fact in the lines :

> "L'amour au désespoir ne peut craindre la mort ;
> Dans un pareil naufrage, elle ouvre un heureux port." [1]

These pangs of unhappy Love arise from an imperious

---

[1] "How should despairing Love fear death ?   In such a shipwreck of the
soul, death is a happy harbour of refuge."   *La Toison d'Or*, Act iii. Sc. 5.

craving for union that fails of satisfaction. Love is *unitive* by nature, St Thomas says ; its tendency is towards the closest union, it desires the most absolute and never-ending possession of the beloved object, an eternal conjuncture. Love would fain be one and one only, he merged in *her*, and she in *him*. "The loved one is in the lover," St Thomas says again, "and the lover in the loved one. Body, heart and soul, each feels the need to be absorbed and assimilated in the other." No one has described this craving for union with more truth and vigour of language than Bossuet : "In the transports of human passion," he says, "who does not know that lovers will bite and almost devour each other, and would fain become incorporate in each other's bodies in all ways, and as the Poet[1] wrote, seize even with the very teeth what they love, to possess the same, to feed on it, be one with it, live in it."[2] This fierce craving for union being unsatisfied, lovers feel a sense of aching incompleteness and pain at the enforced separation.

"To separate lovers is by itself a sore punishment," Corneille says. Plato accounted for this suffering of love separated from the beloved object by a myth, which contains a deep psychological signification. He says that Man was at first created *androgynous*, that is, uniting in himself both sexes. These were subsequently separated, and each half is ever seeking to regain the other half from which it has been sundered. Love is the pursuit of that part of ourselves which we lack. Man is happy, if he find his *half*, unhappy if he cannot find it, or cannot be united with it. So long as he fails to meet with it and possess it,

---

[1] The poet is Lucretius ; vv. 1072-1081.

[2] *Meditation on the Gospel.* Words of Our Lord during the Last Supper, first part, 24th day.—This need of union is true of Divine love no less than of human : "We may say," writes Bossuet in another place, "that the Divine Spouse, seeing the soul fulfilled with love of him, communicates himself to it, gives himself to it, embraces and draws it within himself. . . . We may say further with St Bernard that this embrace, this kiss, this Divine contact and conjuncture, is not in the imagination, nor in the sense, but in the most spiritual part of our being." (*On the Union of Jesus Christ with His Church.*)

he is incomplete; and suffers accordingly till his being is made perfect.

"Man is an imperfect creature," Pascal says; "he must needs find a mate to be happy." It is in this sense the Bible says it is not good for man to live alone. The people expresses the same philosophical idea as Plato, when it calls the woman man's "better half." I have found the same expression occurring in the letters of unfortunate lovers who have killed themselves in despair. "Life is unendurable to me," wrote one of these, "because I am robbed of the half of myself." The two parted halves crave to be rejoined in one whole. To "make but one" is the aspiration of all true lovers. If they were asked, "What you crave, is it not to be so closely joined in one as to make separation impossible,—to make but one?"—they would answer unhesitatingly in the affirmative. (Plato, *Symposium*.)

What specially characterizes the psychological condition of the lover is this fixed notion; he dreams only of one person, whom he longs to possess, he sees only *her*, he speaks little, that he may ponder the better of *her*, if he does speak, it is of *her*,—the sole and only object of his thoughts. The intellectual shrinkage produced by love leads to a correspondingly exaggerated estimate of the beloved object.

Corneille has very accurately noted this characteristic of love, how it becomes a fixed idea, a sort of possession. Pulchérie, discoursing of her love, says to Justin :

> " Léon seul est ma joie, il est mon seul désir,
> Je n'en puis choisir d'autre et n'ose le choisir ;
> Depuis trois ans unie à cette chère idée,
> J'en ai l'âme à toute heure, en tous lieux, *obsédée*." [1]

Falling in love at a mature age with Mlle. Duparc Corneille notes in himself this same *possession*, and seeks a cure :

[1] " Léon is my only joy, the only desire of my heart ; I cannot, nor I dare not, choose another. For three years wedded to this cherished thought, my soul is *possessed* by it at every hour, in every place." Act iii. Sc. 2.

> " Puissé-je, malgré vous, y penser un peu moins,
>   M'échapper quelque jour vers quelques autres soins,
>   Trouver quelque plaisir ailleurs qu'en votre idée,
>   En voir toute mon âme un peu moins *obsédée*." [1]

It is all very well to urge a lover to admire the beauty of another fair one, bidding him :

> " Comparez-lui l'objet dont vous êtes blessé,
>   Comparez-en l'esprit, la façon, l'entretien,
>   Et lors vous trouverez qu'un autre la vaut bien ! " [2]

He is incapable of examining other women, and comparing them with the one he loves. The day his mind finds liberty enough to institute such a comparison, love will be near its end. But so long as it lasts, he can direct his thoughts to none but the one beloved object.

A young man, to whom a plan of marriage was proposed in order to divert him from an unhappy love affair, answered in these words : " I have a high esteem for the young lady you would have me marry, but I can never love her ; *the other* is ever before my eyes, I am sick of love for her."—All very well for Charlotte to cry to Werther : " Cannot you find in the whole world another woman able to satisfy the wishes of your heart ? " Werther only answers there is for him in all the world no woman but Charlotte.—I read in the official account of a suicide how friends, by way of consoling a comrade who had been unfortunate in love, would tell him : " Think no more of her ! there are plenty of other pretty girls in Marseilles." " Nay ! " answered the unhappy lover, " there is but one girl in all Marseilles I can love, the rest are nothing to me."

The ill-starred lover rejects all consolation ; he buries

---

[1] "Could I, in your despite, but dream something less of my passion, escape for an hour to some other preoccupation, find some pleasure elsewhere than in the thought of you, see my whole soul something less *possessed* of this one idea."

[2] " Compare with her the source of your wound, compare her wit and mien and conversation, and lo ! you will find another in no way inferior to your own beloved !"   Corneille, *La Veuve*, Act ii. Sc. 2.

himself in his grief and would rather not be cured. He
seeks out lonely places that he may concentrate his
thoughts on the loved one ; he finds her image in his
soul and takes delight in a contemplation that only serves
to still further increase his passion. Or else he carries
with him into his solitude the portrait of his mistress,
holding it for ever before his eyes to feed them on her
" counterfeit-presentment."

The attempt is often made, and rightly, to induce the
patient to travel, in order to distract his mind and help
him to get rid of the one idea that possesses him ; and
this means is sometimes efficacious.[1]   But more often than
not, the sick man hugs his malady and refuses to apply
the remedy ; he will not leave home, he would rather not
be cured. A young man suffering from unhappy love
replied to his friends, who begged him to follow Tele-
machus' example in the island of Calypso and sail away :
" No ! " he said, " it is impossible for me to leave her ; my
feelings simply overmaster me."

Separation from the beloved object is not always
successful in driving away the fond memory by which
the unhappy lover is possessed ; far from inducing forgetfulness, absence may merely serve, by reason of the pangs
of separation and the tears it sets flowing, to make the
desire of fruition more violent than ever. I have known
victims of this species of *possession* return from a long
journey without being cured, and presently commit suicide
or kill the loved one who refused to favour their suit.
Year by year we see young soldiers join the Regiment
with sore hearts, because they have left behind in their
native village a girl they love. Separation does not
invariably calm their grief ; some of them grow sombre
and silent and avoid their comrades' society. Eventually

---

[1] In his notice on Béranger, Paul Boiteau tells how this means was successful in the poet's case. The latter, desirous of curing himself of a violent
passion which had attacked him when well on in years, had with his usual
excellent good sense, recognised the fact that separation was the most effectual
remedy, seeing that the presence of the person loved invariably increases the
strength of love.

they are found hanged, or drowned, or their brains blown
out by a pistol shot.   Love sorrow may survive separation
many years or even to the last day of life.   A young
woman of twenty-two, who had wished to marry her
cousin whom she dearly loved, having been married by
her relatives to another man, remained all her life plunged
in so deep a despair that, widowed eventually, she could
find no consolation, and ended by suffocating herself,
crying : " I long to die, I long to die."   (January 1897.)
It is a mistake to say Time cures all griefs ; there are
some griefs Time cannot heal.   Love sorrows are all the
more difficult to bear for young people from the very
fact that they are not yet broken in to suffering, and have
no knowledge of the great sorrows of life.

Lovers are themselves aware of their psychological condition, characterized as it is by the presence of one fixed
idea.   A young man under accusation, who had killed his
fiancée because she broke her troth, said in answer to
questions : " Her conduct turned me into something like
a madman.   Still I cannot say I *am* mad ; only I had the
fixed idea the girl was to become my wife, and I could not
drive it out of my head.   I was urged again and again to
forget her, to dismiss the notion altogether, but it was
impossible."—In another case, the friend of a man who
had committed a murder out of disappointed love, spoke
in similar terms : " His projected marriage had grown into
a *fixed idea* with him ; he was ready to talk of his passion
to anyone who would listen.   Under the fatal influence of
this fixed idea, which would seem to have to some degree
disturbed his intellect, he must in my opinion have made
the murderous attempt he did."

In some instances parents are so alarmed at the change
wrought in their child's character as a result of thwarted
love, that they suppose him to be ill (as indeed he is), and
call in the doctor.   In a murder case, where a young man
had killed his *fiancée*, who had broken off the engagement,
cross-examination revealed the fact that the accused, in
the agonies of the deepest despair, used to beat his head,

crying out : " I have an idea in my brain that tortures me ;. that's where the mischief is." Possessed by the image of the girl he loved, he could neither sleep at night nor work by day ; [1] he was constantly getting up in the night, walking about his room, getting into bed again, then once more rising, unable to find a moment's repose and complaining of violent headaches. The physician who was called in by the parents found him to be suffering from congestion of the brain ; from the first he had a presentiment the young fellow would come to no good,—and as a matter of fact he ended by killing the girl. Once a lover in his despair falls into this condition of prostration succeeded by exaggerated excitability, anything may happen ; according to circumstances and the bent of his character, he may resort either to suicide or murder, or both. Sometimes we hear these despairing lovers cry out, " This thing must end ! "—for they feel themselves that this state of excessive tension cannot last. Friends and neighbours are conscious of calamity brooding in the air, and the actual conclusion is very often suicide or murder or both together, or else madness.

Among the common people simple folks are still to be found who firmly believe witchcraft to be responsible for such like catastrophes. Some few years ago, the Criminal Court of the Bouches-du-Rhône had to deal with an offender, who had killed a young woman, because, as he said, she had made him ill by taking away his sleep, his appetite and his taste for work ; I have had the "dossier" of papers connected with the case in my hands. The unfortunate young man was condemned to fifteen years' hard labour !—I have also known mothers accuse their daughters' seducers of having used magic arts to turn them mad with love ; they believed them to be "bewitched." Again, the father of Desdemona is quite unable to explain otherwise than by the intervention of sorcery the love his daughter, young, beautiful, bashful, proud and

---

[1] Plato has noticed these tortures of unhappy love : " He cannot sleep by night, nor stay still by day." (*Phædrus.*)

rich, feels for Othello, a man of years, poor and a foreigner, and "black as soot" into the bargain. He cannot fathom the motives that have led her to quit the paternal roof to follow after this man to all appearance so ill fitted for the part of a seducer ; he asks him if he has not thrown a spell over the girl by means of love potions and arts magic.

Even when it is not a disease, love is a passion that is by its very nature exclusive and absorbing. M. Maillet holds that Ambition presents a yet more exclusive character ; but I do not agree with him. No doubt Ambition is absorbing, but not to the same extent as Love. "The thoughts of my sin so absorb me," said David, "that my eye can see naught else." [1] The man who is deeply smitten with love can think of one thing only :

"Aimer est tout son but, aimer est tout son bien." [2]

Dominated by this one fixed idea, intelligent men grow stupid. They have only a single thought left, that of their passion ; to this they make everything else sub-servient, indifferent alike to fortune and the pleasures of society, of pride and of ambition :

"Son arc, ses javelots, son char, tout l'importune." [3]

All they care for is solitude, that they may ponder undisturbed over the object of their passion ; they think only of the individual they are enamoured of, they seek out every opportunity of meeting and seeing her. Girls who are pursued by these ardent lovers declare they

---

[1] Masillon's analysis of this state of mind evinced much penetration when he said, speaking of Love : "It is distinctive of this passion to fill the whole heart to overflowing. . . . The lover can think of nothing but his love ; it possesses and intoxicates him to the exclusion of everything else. Every object recalls its fatal images, and rouses its unholy desires ; society, solitude, presence, absence, objects the most indifferent, occupations the most serious, the holy sanctuary itself, the blessed altars of God, the awful mysteries of Religion, all recall its memory." (Sermon on the "Prodigal Son.")

[2] "To love is all his aim, to love is all his bliss."

Corneille, *Andromède*, Act i. Sc. 4.

[3] 'Her bow, her darts, her car, all stir his heart."

cannot take a step without encountering them in their path. This obstinacy, this *possession* of all the faculties, lasts sometimes for a number of years ; no matter how often shown the door, they return to the attack again and again, never wearying of the one idea they have in their heads, their love. A working man of Marseilles who had asked in marriage a sailor's daughter and had been refused, commits a series of acts of savage nocturnal violence, for which he is condemned to four years' hard labour. After undergoing his punishment at Noumea, he returns to Marseilles on the expiration of the five years, as fiercely in love as at the moment of his leaving the place. He starts out to find the girl, discovers her living as the mistress of another workman and kills her on her refusing to have anything to do with him.

The ill-starred lover neglects his business, his friends and even his kinsmen :

> "Et quand on aime bien et qu'on voit ce qu'on aime,
>   Peut on songer à des parents ? " [1]

Pascal, that profound observer of the passionate emotions, has also observed : " I entirely agree with the man who declared that in love we forget fortune and family and friends. . . . What makes men go so far in love is this, that they imagine themselves to need nothing else whatever but what they love ; their whole mind is full of this, and there is no room for any other thought or anxiety."

If Love can make children forget their parents, it also on occasion will make parents forget their children. Fathers allow their children by a first marriage to be ill-treated by their second wife or by their mistress; in their case paternal love is stifled under their passion for the woman they are enamoured of. I find in a letter to his second wife from a working joiner who had married again the following expression : " From one who is ready to die for you and who loves you better than his life, for I would have sacrificed my little girl for your sake."

[1] " When a man loves ardently and sees what he loves, how can he think of kinsfolk ? " *Psyché*, Act iv. Sc. 3.

It is the concentration of every thought on one single object which makes the joy of reciprocated love so great and the pangs of unhappy love so poignant. The imagination, entirely absorbed in a single object, pictures under enormously exaggerated proportions the bliss and the unhappiness resulting from the possession or the loss of the person beloved. He is persuaded he could no longer live without her:

"Hors de votre présence, il doute s'il peut vivre." [1]

And in actual fact, sometimes the lover is made so miserably unhappy by the loss of the loved one that he dies of the blow. In the letters of unfortunate lovers who put an end to themselves, we often meet with this thought: "Without you life is unbearable. I would much rather die."

It is this same concentration of thought on one single object again which accounts for the empire the woman exercises over the man who is enamoured of her.

There is a large element of illusion in love, whether happy or the reverse, serving to exalt the merits of the beloved object by the addition of quite imaginary perfections. The lover is convinced there exists no other woman prettier, or more sweet and lovable, than the one he loves,—yet she is very often plain. The official reports of suicides which I have consulted often enclose, along with letters written by the despairing lover, the photograph of the woman for whose sake he has done the deed. And the woman is seldom possessed of any remarkable charms of person. It is by no means always fine eyes, whether black or blue, straight cut noses and regular features, that trouble men's heads and set hearts aflame. A woman in love is, on her side, no less firmly persuaded of her lover's superiority. Everybody knows the "loci classici" in Lucretius, Horace and Molière describing the blindness of Love, which lends entirely imaginary good qualities to the object of affection, transforming positive defects into

[1] "Deprived of your presence, he doubts if he can live."

merits. "Passion spreads a veil over their mistress's faults; nay! does more, it changes them into beauties; the polypus on Agna's nose is no defect in Balbinus' eyes."

But let Love be flown, and the lover is astonished he can no longer find in his former mistress the high qualities that once charmed him so. It is not that she is changed; the alteration is in himself. The ardour of desire as yet unsatisfied contributes greatly to this process of idealization, which often comes to an abrupt end after fruition.

The lover has ever before his eyes the image of the loved one, which follows him everywhere and never leaves him. He sees it everywhere; as Corneille says:

"Tout ce que je voyais me semblait Curiace." [1]

The presence of the beloved object embellishes Nature, brightens the horizon, warms the very air he breathes. The lover lives enveloped by her image, brightened and warmed by the sunbeams of her eyes. The fond feelings that swell his heart make him find the flowers more lovely, the rays of the setting sun and the light of the moon more beauteous, the songs of the birds more tuneful. The days of their love-making are those when poets and painters are able to delineate best and most emotionally the charms of Nature, the cheerfulness of morn and the sadness of evening, the softness of night and the silent peacefulness of the fields. It is just because the image of the beloved object peoples the world and makes it beautiful, that when this is lost the world is left desolate, and seems a desert. After Bérénice's departure, the East appears an empty waste to Antiochus:

"Dans l'Orient désert quel devient mon ennui!" [2]

The East is but Bérénice personified; Bérénice gone, nothing is left. For the man who is deep in love, the universe is but the woman he loves.

"Un seul être vous manque et tout est dépeuplé." [3]

---

[1] "All I beheld, methought, was Curiace."
[2] "In the desert East, what weariness of soul is mine!"
[3] "One being is taken from you, and all is left desolate."—Lamartine.

His horizon is so limited, the World is simply the dwelling-place of the one he adores; apart from her, it has no existence, universal Nature is nothing to him. His love is fortunate,—the World wears a radiant smile ; unfortunate,—and all Nature frowns. This Earth, which seems a Paradise to him who loves and is loved again, becomes a sepulchre or a hell, when he loses the loved one or is hindered from wedding her. Already frantic with love, he grows frantic with despair, and longs to quit a world where he suffers so sorely. The tomb has no terrors for him, for what is existence to him henceforth but a living death? When he announces to his friends his intention to have done with life, these refuse to take his words seriously, for they have no true conception of his sufferings. Parents again, who are sometimes admitted by their sons into the secret of their projected suicide, attach no importance to the confidence ; having outgrown the age of love and lost the recollection of the high-strung emotions of earlier years, they do not realize the young man's despair and the fatal attraction the idea of suicide exercises over him. A young girl when disappointed in love, very rarely lets her parents know of it ; she is afraid to confide her despair to them, she would like to spare them the pain of seeing her unhappiness, and carefully conceals her scheme of putting an end to herself.

A man in pain would be ever asleep, if he could ; in waking, he regrets the time of respite during which he ceased to feel his agony. His sum of energy once exhausted, he longs for death as for an eternal sleep, that he may suffer no more. In the written documents left behind them by suicides, I have again and again found this same cry of suffering, this craving for rest : " My pain is more than I can bear ; I am going to sleep, I am going to seek forgetfulness of my sorrows in death." It is excess of suffering that is the determining factor of suicide. " Oh ! fair and cruel girl, who deserve not to be loved," cries a shepherd in Theocritus, " I am here to make you my last present, the noose that is to end my days, for I am fain to encounter your scorn no more, and I am away whither you send me, to a land where Love can give no further pain, where is oblivion of all sorrows."—I am mad with grief," exclaimed an unhappy lover before putting an end to his life. . . my tears hinder me from writing more."—" I am sorry to quit this world," writes another in his despair ; "still I am happy to think I shall find rest in eternal sleep."—" The eternal repose of the tomb seems infinitely sweet to me . . . my pain is greater than I can bear," are the words of yet another ill-starred lover before killing himself. —A young workwoman, an embroiderer by trade, who had been unable to marry the man of her choice, wrote before ending her days : " Life has been for me nothing but one huge sorrow; may my death be the awakening to true happiness ! "—" How soundly I shall sleep ! God grant my hand fail me not ! " writes one desperate man.—Another unhappy lover prefaces his death with the words : " I am wretched on these shores, and I am away to see what lies on the other side."—" I admit I am an arrant coward, but my suffering is more than I can bear, and I am at the end of my endurance," writes a domestic servant, who empties two chambers of a revolver into her body, because she cannot obtain fulfilment of a promise of marriage that had been made her.—Another woman whose lover had forsaken her, writes : " My agony is too great, I can endure my life no longer ; my poor head cannot bear the pain of desertion any more."

The lover, whose love is not reciprocated, is so terribly unhappy for this reason, that he has concentrated all his thoughts, all his desires, all his plans, all his hopes on one single being.   This being failing him, what is left ? "Everything is ended," he cries ; "to live without you is an impossibility.   My only hope is to find peace and quietness in a better world."—In her love letters to Bothwell, Mary Queen of Scots again and again gives expression to this thought, that she cares for life for his sake only, that his love is the sole and only stay of her life and that without him all she could wish for would be instant death.   The instant her passion meets with an obstacle, she exclaims: "Alack! would I were dead!"

Grown-up men know there are greater sorrows in this world than love disappointments; but young folks imagine no pangs can be keener than those of thwarted love, or a projected marriage broken off or even merely delayed. The fear of seeing a marriage drop through, which after all is only deferred, may be sufficient to determine an access of despair ending in self-destruction. To give a recent instance: a young man of twenty-eight is anxious to marry a girl he is in love with. The girl's family, without refusing his suit, require the young man to put in his period of military service first. He consents to this and prepares to join his regiment, but his parents now raise objections; eventually the youthful lover, in despair at seeing his marriage postponed, commits suicide.—A young workman without a penny of property, is eager to marry, but his family urge him strongly to put some money by before entering on housekeeping, telling him the nightingale does not begin singing till it has built its nest. He however is for marrying before having made his nest, and kills himself because his parents advise him to put off his marriage.

Talent and genius are no preservatives against suicide from disappointed love; indeed they may even be described as predisposing causes. The greatest writers of the Nineteenth Century, Goethe, Chateaubriand, Lamartine, George Sand, Alfred de Musset, etc., all felt the temptation of suicide. Léopold Robert *did* put an end to himself in consequence of ill success in love. Poets, Musicians, Painters, feel keenly the pangs of unhappy love from the very fact of their high degree of sensibility.

Women of equivocal character are by no means incapable of feeling love sorrows acutely, even to the extent of leading them to commit suicide. Not a year passes but the Quartier Latin is the scene of sundry tragedies of the sort. "I am a poor girl without family or fortune," wrote a young woman who had been forsaken by a student of medicine ; " I have had to bear much sorrow and dreadful suffering ; I am sick of life, and I have made up my mind to kill myself. I am taking the opportunity of M——, being away to take some acetic acid from amongst his drugs." This she swallowed, lay down on her bed and so died. When Parisian students at the end of their course seek to break off connections likely to stand in the way of their plans of settling down and making a name for themselves, it is not an uncommon occurrence for the rupture to provoke a fit of despair leading to suicidal results.

Then again, there are many women of unstable equilibrium, mentally incapable of being crossed, who after making a scene with their lover, suddenly throw themselves out of window or jump into the River. Sudden impulses of this sort towards suicide are of frequent occurrence among a degenerate type hereditarily, among hysterical and neurotic subjects. Plenty of examples may be found in the Works of Doctors Magnan, Legrain, Dagonnet, Féré, Legrand du Saule, Garnier.

Speaking generally, suicides of women are less numerous than those of men. There are a crowd of good reasons to account for the difference. Religious and family feeling, fear of death, tolerance of suffering, avoidance of excess, dread of scandal, are all sentiments more fully developed in the female than in the male sex. Besides, a woman is better protected against the temptation to commit suicide by the sense of shame, which makes her dread the exposure of the Morgue and the inevitable medico-legal examinations. It is well known how an epidemic of suicide which appeared among the women of Miletus was stayed by a law ordering that every woman who killed herself should be exposed naked in the public Market-place. Nevertheless, under stress of acute disappointment in love, the most timid young girl will put an end to herself with as much determination as the bravest man ; grief will make her oblivious of everything, religion, family, weakness, shame, timidity, fear of death itself. "Women," says Plutarch, "have ordinarily nothing in common with Mars ; but for all this the frenzy of love drives them to the commission of reckless deeds entirely repugnant to their natural disposition and to self-sought death."

While, taking the total number of suicides, the figure representing those of women is four or five times less than that of men, we yet find an almost identical number of female and of male suicides consequent upon thwarted love. Thus for instance, in the year 1889, of 247 suicides due to disappointments of the affections, 123 were men, 124 women ; in 1893, of 333 suicides, there were 164 men and 169 women.

Moral suffering is more especially acute with delicately organised natures, endowed with keen sensibility and vivid imagination,—and these are just the qualities in which women excel. Besides this, Love being the chief business of her life, she has nothing else to console her disappointment such as the acquisition of power and influence, the winning of honours and wealth,—all important safety valves where men are concerned. For a while she will struggle against her grief and force herself to take an interest in the affairs of every day, but this battle against mental suffering very quickly wears out her strength.

Among young girls and women who are led to commit suicide by disappointments in love, a certain number of those who put an end to themselves in Paris come from the provinces. Forsaken by their lover or finding themselves pregnant, they fly from home to hide their shame in Paris. "I can never get over my grief," cries a girl of twenty on the eve of committing suicide. "I have come to Paris. The only favour I ask is to be buried without inquiries as to my family."

Suicide due to thwarted love was of much less frequent occurrence in former days. Schopenhauer reckoned the total at only half a dozen per annum for the whole of Europe. "It is not in Novels only that Werthers and Jacobo Ortis are to be found ; every year Europe might supply a half dozen of instances."[1] In his Treatise on Suicide written in 1822, Dr Fabret says that in 1818 there were eighteen suicides attributed to the effects of amorous passion. Now in the year 1893, for example, there were in France no less than 333 cases of suicide from disappointed love, and this figure must be further increased by a number of suicides arising out of jealousy. It is difficult to arrive at the precise number, inasmuch as the Statistics published by the Ministry of Justice make the mistake of confounding in a single category suicides determined by jealousy, dissipation and ill living. For instance in 1892 the total of suicides due to these three factors rose as high as 137.

Why in the society of to-day are there more suicides from love than in former times? Is it because there is more love? Obviously not. The reasons for the increase must be sought in the non-satisfaction of the craving for love by way of marriage, which day by day grows less frequent, in the ever-growing number of irregular liaisons, ending in eventual rupture, in the precocity of the rising generation in matters of love and dissipation, in the development of nervous diseases and of alcoholism, in weakening of the will power and excessive excitation of the sensibility, in novel reading and morbid over-stimulation of the imagination, in the decay of belief in Religion with its prohibitions of suicide.

To arrive at the exact total of suicides caused by love and jealousy, we must add in also a certain number set down to intemperance. Of the 927 cases coming under this head in 1892, I am convinced that in a very considerable number of instances the real cause of the intemperance and consequent suicide was some unhappy love affair. Despairing lovers very frequently rush into intemperance to stifle their grief. Men end miserably as sots, because in earlier days they could not marry the girl they loved or because they were betrayed by their mistress, and so tried to drown their sorrows in wine and alcohol

[1] Schopenhauer, *Reflexions*, p. 73 (Paris ed., F. Alcan).

" To stupify my wits," writes Werther to his friend, " I have for some time now got into the habit of allowing myself, starting with a glass of wine, to presently finish off the bottle " (*Letter LXVII.*). Intoxication is like sleep, it brings forgetfulness. We know how Alfred de Musset, to console himself for his rupture with George Sand, adopted habits of intemperance. His god-mother (Mme. Jaubert) having reproached him for his folly, the unfortunate and still inconsolable poet wrote to her to excuse his glass of absinthe,

> " Qui pendant un quart d'heure étourdit ma misère . . .
> Dans ce verre, où je cherche à noyer mon supplice,
> Laissez plutôt tomber quelques pleurs de pitié." [1]

Again it not unfrequently happens that unhappy lovers rush in their despair into dissipation, as others take to drink, to stifle their grief. Not a few girls moreover after being forsaken by their lovers, hurry out of recklessness, wretchedness or despair into evil living, yet without being able to forget their first love. " Since Louis left me to rejoin his regiment," wrote a young girl who had already made several attempts at suicide and who ended by smothering herself with charcoal fumes, " I have been guilty of numberless follies, which he will never forgive. Write and tell him of my fatal determination. You will cut off a lock of my hair and give it him as a remembrance of me."

Again we find included in the Statistics of the Ministry of Justice a large number of suicides under the extremely vague heading of "domestic troubles." For instance in 1890 there were 1097 such. The officials who draw up the formal reports of suicides make use of this phrase whenever they are ignorant of the precise nature of the trouble which brought about the suicide, and which the family wish to keep secret. I have devoted special study to these

---

[1] " Which for a brief half hour stifles my wretchedness . . . in this glass, wherein I seek to drown my torment, rather let fall some drops of pitying tears."

reports, and I have come to the conclusion that a number of suicides classed under the category "domestic troubles" ought properly speaking to be set down to disappointed and unfortunate love.

We see then that Love unreciprocated or otherwise balked is responsible for a large number of victims; this living principle becomes a principle of death, when it is left unsatisfied. Nor is it only unfortunate love that leads to suicide; the mere craving for love if it fails of satisfaction may bring on a profound melancholy ending in suicide. A young man of timid, morbid disposition, devoured by the need of loving and being loved, may suffer so acutely from the aching void in his heart as to eventually kill himself in sheer despair. " I deliberately choose to put an end to myself; I suffer so, because no one loves me," writes a young workman, a brass-founder, and consumptive. A young workwoman of Paris, seventeen years of age, leaves her father's house one morning as usual on her way to the workshop, after kissing her mother and brothers affectionately; her face wears an untroubled look, and there is absolutely nothing to point to an impending catastrophe. Yet she has just written a letter to her parents, which she is now on her way to post, before throwing herself into the Seine, which runs thus : " My dear parents,—to-morrow morning you will receive a letter, giving you full particulars of my death. Courage. I die of want of interest in life, and this terrible feeling must be my excuse and my claim to forgiveness. It has been the curse of my life. I felt myself attacked by a mysterious malady that was bound to bring me to the grave. Courage, dear parents,—courage, if for nothing else, for the sake of your dear little ones, who will have a brighter destiny than their sister. My dead body will be found in the Seine."

Moreover, every year thwarted love is the predisposing cause of a certain number of religious vocations, more particularly among young girls who have been betrayed and forsaken. These turn to God and wed Him,—for is not the Religious life a chaste form of wedlock? God becomes "the beloved consort," as Bossuet himself names Him in his letters of pious exhortation and advice addressed to Religious Women.

Spouse of God, the maiden who takes the Veil becomes at the same time mother of the orphaned and the poor. Nunneries are well worthy the respect of all, inasmuch as they afford young girls who cannot marry satisfaction of that imperious craving to love and to be loved which under other circumstances calls so urgently for marriage and motherhood.[1] These human feelings, spiritualized by the Divine Love, beget the marvels of charity, and give happiness to thousands of noble creatures, who but for the Religious life would miss it altogether. Alfred de Musset who, in spite of all his loose living, possessed a vivid intuition of the needs of the human heart, clearly recognized the truth that nowhere else is so much love to be found as in Religious Houses :

> "Cloîtres silencieux, voûtes des monastères,
> C'est vous, sombres caveaux, vous qui savez aimer."[2]

Nor is it women alone that pass from human love to love Divine, like Mlle. de la Vallière who became Sister Louise de la Miséricorde ; men of tender and emotional natures turn priests, when they lose their *fiancée*, as did the Abbé de Rohan, Lamartine's friend, or throw themselves enthusiastically into the Divine Love, when the age for human love is over. Enough to recall the names of St Augustine, Pascal and Racine, to see how easily high-souled lovers merge into religious mystics. " Racine," Mme. de Sévigné said, " loves God as ardently as he used to love his mistresses."

Over and above lovers who resort to suicide because they are unable to marry the one they love, there are also,

---

[1] Ch. Nodier, writing in 1803 his *Méditations du Cloître* (Meditations of the Cloister), demanded the re-establishment of Religious Houses, in order to save men from suicide.

[2] " Silent cloisters, vaulted monasteries, 'tis you, ye dark and sombre halls, that best know how to love."

exceptionally, young men, and still more young women, who put an end to themselves in order to escape marrying against their will; they prefer death to an antipathetic marriage. When a girl commits suicide to avoid marrying, it is because she is anxious to wed another husband than the one her friends desire her to. At first she appears resigned to her family's wishes, but as the wedding day comes nearer and nearer, her heart rises in revolt, her aversion to the man they would force upon her increases and on the eve of the fatal day she kills herself. So it is with Monime in the play, who loves another, and rather than marry Pharnace or Mithridate is for stabbing herself to the heart, tries subsequently to hang herself, to

" Faire un affreux lien d'un sacré diadème,"[1]

and after that plans to poison herself, when her previous attempt fails.

To give one or two examples of suicide on the part of young women whose inclinations have been thus thwarted. A girl who had been deeply affected because she could not marry the man she was fondly in love with, in consequence of her parents' opposition, was plighted by them to another young man. As the wedding-day came nearer, she grew more and more nervous and agitated ; compelled to take to her bed, she showed evident signs of a wish to put an end to herself. The physician who was called in gave her a draught to calm her nerves. Left alone with her sister, she had recourse to various pretexts to get her out of the way ; not succeeding in this, she went to the window under the pretext of the room being too hot, and suddenly springing over the sill threw herself out.— Another instance : a girl living in the suburbs of Paris, being on the point of contracting a marriage she disliked with an officer in the Army, went to town one day to visit a relative ; she seemed in excellent spirits, and presently asked her relative to go into the garden to gather her some roses. Thus left alone in the house, she shot herself

[1] " To make an ill-omened cord of a sacred diadem."

dead.—This type of suicide is very uncommon among young
men, who are much less often constrained by their family
into a marriage contrary to their wishes. Still examples
do occur, such as the following : a Parisian shop-assistant,
in love with a woman of the same place whom he could
not marry, makes up his mind to a provincial marriage.
He leaves the city, but the very day before his wedding,
returns to Paris and blows his brains out, after writing
the following letter : " I choose to end my life by my
own hand. Why ? Mystery. No one will ever know.
Farewell, father, mother, family and friends. Forgive me.
Farewell. Louise, forgive me. Be happy." I myself
noted the case of a young man who killed himself, to
escape marrying a cousin, whom he had seduced indeed,
but had now ceased to care for. He was a clerk of
twenty-three, living at Marseilles with an uncle, who was
in business. He had run away from the cousin, leaving
her at her country home in the Department of the Loire
in a condition of pregnancy. The girl wrote to him to
remind him of his promises. This letter he showed to
his uncle, who told him, "As you have deceived the girl,
you are bound to make it good. Go and marry her ; I will
give you the necessary leave of absence." Hearing this,
the young man left his uncle with the words : " Well and
good ! I know now what I must do," and went away to
kill himself.—A working man of sixty-one, who had been
living for years with a mistress, who was now sixty-two
years of age, had at last, yielding to her importunities,
promised to marry her ; when his mistress claimed the
fulfilment of this promise, he hanged himself rather than
keep it.

Most cases of female suicide determined by disappointments in love are those of young girls. Still, instances
do occur of married women, repulsed by men they are
running after, putting an end to themselves, in a fit of
despair. This is what Phèdre does in Racine's play,—
hanging herself because she is scorned by Hippolyte.

Then again the desire for marriage, if remaining unsatisfied, may lead to acute despair in the case of women living under irregular circumstances and suffering from the fact. In Paris especially, where this equivocal form of *ménage* is so common, when the mistress begins to see the number of children increasing fast, she feels an eager desire to regularize their status, and her own, a desire the lover does not always share. Hence bickerings, household differences and much mental suffering, ending in some instances in the woman's suicide. In very exceptional cases also shame at her degraded condition and the impossibility of escaping it may lead a fallen woman to commit suicide, even when she has no child, if she belong to a well-connected family. "My dreams proved impossible of realization," wrote a young woman in this situation, who had hoped to rise above her shame by marrying her lover; "I shall be a dead woman when you get this letter. The man I thought worthy of me has deceived me, and I die of the blow. Pity and forgive me. Tell papa and mamma of my death." She then proceeded to smother herself by means of charcoal fumes.—Another mistress, before meeting her death in the same way, wrote to her lover, who obstinately refused to marry her: "All I ask you is to leave me your photograph, when you bury me. A long farewell from your loving mistress, who had hoped to be your wife." Suicides of this kind, of mistresses anxious to become lawful wives, but driven to despair because they cannot succeed in restoring their good name by this means, are of pretty frequent occurrence in Paris. Such women are hungry for respect and consideration and perfectly well aware of the fact that a fallen woman's rehabilitation is worked out not by Love, as the Novelists would have us believe, but by marriage and the proper performance of the duties it involves. It is the world's scorn makes them suffer; to recover its esteem is the great object of their ambition.

Women of pleasure also occasionally commit suicide. Courtesans are capable in very exceptional cases of so fond an attachment as to lead to their death. La

Fontaine, in *La Courtisane amoureuse*, shows how a woman of this class can still sometimes be susceptible of a disinterested love. He represents her as saying with touching humility:

> "Constance vous adore,
> Méprisez-la, chassez-la, battez-la,
> Si vous pouvez, faîtes-lui pis encore ;
> Elle est à vous." [1]

We give a copy of a letter written quite lately by a woman of pleasure, who put an end to her own life: "You know, dearest, that without you my life is unendurable, above all since I have lost my poor little girl. Farewell, I loved you true. My wish is that you may be happy."

The sort of mistresses for whose sake men kill themselves have little resemblance to those I have just been describing; more often than not they are creatures only worthy of contempt. We see intelligent men fall deeply in love with women quite unworthy of their affection, which is only increased by the scorn they cannot but feel for them. Once a man allows his senses to govern him, the more he despises a woman, the more he loves; like the Chevalier Desgrieux, who goes on loving Manon,[2] in spite, nay! perhaps because of her infidelities towards him, he says:

> "Je t'aimais d'autant plus que je t'estimais moins." [3]

Blinded by passion, cheated by the modest exterior and angel face vicious women often possess, unhappy and infatuated young men adore to madness contemptible creatures who drive them to despair. When proofs of unfaithfulness accumulate, they weep and lament like children, without having the strength of mind to break off the connection. If they do try to end the liaison, the shame of which they feel, they soon come back again, in

---

[1] "Constance adores you, scorn her, repulse her, beat her, do what worse you can to her ; she is yours in spite of all."

[2] *Manon Lescaut* by the Abbé Prévost.

[3] "I loved you all the more, the less I could respect you."

the vain hope of inspiring an exclusive attachment in
their fickle mistress's bosom.   But this reconciliation is
short-lived, fresh disputes arise, and a final separation
takes place.   Instead of looking upon the termination of
so degrading an attachment as a happy release, they feel
the parting so acutely as to come back once more, to beg
another reconciliation ; and if this is refused, they kill
themselves, crying :

> "Vous lirez dans mon sang à vos pieds répandu
> Ce que valait l'amant que vous avez perdu." [1]

They hope such a proof of love as this will make their
mistress remorseful.   But no!—all the woman sees in her
lover's death is an act of homage due to her beauty ; her
self-conceit is pleasantly tickled at having inspired so fine
a frenzy of despair, and she is much obliged to the unhappy
man for having offered so striking and public a testimony
to the power of her charms, for of course the Papers will
not fail to entertain their readers with this drama of love
and suicide, which will confer a flattering celebrity on the
heroine.   There are even coquettes ready to find pleasure
in pushing men who love them to despair, and owing them
a grudge if they do not kill themselves.

Love without respect is common enough.   Catullus
loved Lesbia without respecting her.   Cynthia's treacheries
failed to cure Propertius of his love.   The Emperor Justinian
chose his wife Theodora from a house of ill-fame.   Desgrieux adored Manon ; Jean-Jacques Rousseau loved
Thérèse, and so on and so on.

Plenty of men prefer love without respect to respect
without love.   Every day we see husbands forgiving their
wives, not out of any magnanimity or philosophical
tolerance, but out of simple weakness.   Quite lately in
Paris, a husband, Agent for a Commercial house, surprising
his wife *flagrante delicto* in a lover's arms, takes steps in
the first flush of his indignation to procure a Separation ;

---

[1] "You will read in my blood shed at your feet what worth the lover was
that you have lost."   Corneille, *La Galérie du Palais.*

yet the day he receives notice to present himself, along with his wife, before the Magistrate, he feels he has not the strength of mind, so fondly does he love her still, to see her again without taking her back, and ashamed of such weakness shoots himself through the heart. It cost him less pain to kill himself than to go on living without taking an adulterous woman back into his arms!

I found one day while examining the report of a criminal trial an expression, trivial indeed but highly expressive, which renders excellently at once the violence and the physical origin of this love which survives all proofs of unworthiness in the object: "I have you in my blood, darling, in my very skin."

Women likewise very often separate love and respect; they love men they do not respect, while they do not care for others they do esteem.

> "Je vous estimai plus,—je l'aimai davantage." [1]

Clarissa Harlow in Richardson's Novel loves Lovelace. Don Juan is loved by Elvira, Charlotte, "a thousand and three" other women.

If Love is irrational, the reason is that while not without a psychical side, it is yet closely bound up with the senses and has a corporeal origin. It is a passion quite as much physiological as intellectual, capable of being developed by food, perfumes, temperature, a whole host of physical conditions. External charms determine it far more than moral qualities, and this without any consciousness on the part of the lover, who believes himself all the time to be affected by the mental and moral attributes only of his *inamorata*. Deep down lurks the instinct of reproduction, a fact which lovers plunged in ecstatic reverie often fail to observe; when their heart is pure, they have no very clear conception of their real feelings, and imagine themselves to have none but ethereal desires, aspirations for the union of twin souls, and the like, while

---

[1] "I esteemed you the more,—I loved him the better." Corneille, *Médée*, Act. ii. Sc. 6.

really and truly it is a case of Dame Nature inspiring them, without their knowing it, with the craving for a physical union whose object is the reproduction of the species.

> "Ces délires sacrés, ces désirs sans mesure,
> Déchaînés dans vos flancs comme d'ardents essaims,
> Ces transports, c'est déjà l'humanité future,
> Qui s'agite en vos seins." [1]

Nature in her desire to secure before all else the continuance of the species, has multiplied the motives of sexual attraction, making Love dependent on the colour of the eyes, the abundance of the hair, the delicacy of the skin, the shape of the nose and a hundred other minutiæ. . . . " If Cleopatra's nose had been shorter," Pascal says, "the face of the whole World would have been changed." A mere nothing, a smile, a gesture, are enough to kindle a passion that stirs the universe." " The eyes," writes Pascal in another passage, "have the greater share in this."— " The emanations of beauty," Plato declares, "enter the soul by the eyes, the most subtle of the organs of sense." *Ex aspectu nascit amor*,—" Love springs from the eyes." A look from them captivates the heart, a smile is the determining factor of a man's life.

Reason has nothing to do with the blossoming of Love ; it is some quite trivial motive, something at once futile and mysterious, that brings passion to a head :

> "Souvent je ne sais quoi qu'on ne peut exprimer
> Nous surprend, nous emporte et nous force d'aimer." [2]

As the virtuous Pauline says to Sévère :

> " Un je ne sais quel charme encor vers vous m'emporte." [3]

The rapidity with which "love at first sight" often

---

[1] "Those sacred longings, those ineffable cravings, let loose within your frame like eager swarms, those transports of desire, 'tis already the humanity of a future day that stirs your bosom."—Madame Ackerman.

[2] "Ofttimes a mysterious something that none can express surprises us, carries us away and forces us to love."   Corneille, *Polyeucte*, Act ii. Sc. 6.

[3] " A mysterious charm once more impels me towards you."

springs into existence is yet another proof to show it is
not reason that determines it, but certain external qualities
visible at the first glance.   Virgil, Racine, Shakespeare,
have all described this commotion produced by a look,
the *lightning stroke* of love, as it is called :

"Ut vidi, ut perii, ut me malus abstulit error." [1]

Virgil, *Eclogue*, viii.

"Je le vis, je rougis, je pâlis à sa vue." [2]   Racine, *Phèdre.*

From the instant of the first glance they exchange,
Romeo and Juliet feel they belong to each other.   Both
men and women are at times struck down with love, as
one is struck down by a disease.   Dr Féré quotes one
case in his book, where the lightning stroke was determined
in the French King, Henri III., by an impression of the
olfactory nerves (*L'Instinct sexuel*, p. 129).[3]   The strong
stimulus the sense of smell may exercise over the genital
sense is well known ; and this is why, ever since Jean-
Jacques Rousseau, who was intensely sensitive to the
exciting influence of perfumes, erotic novelists so often
attribute the fall of their heroines in part to the scent of
flowers.

It would appear difficult then to share the opinion of
Pascal, who holds that the Poets have erred in depicting
Love as blind, inasmuch as according to him it is always
reasonable.   "It is ill done to have robbed Love of the
title of Reason," he says ; "the two have been quite
unwarrantably contrasted one with the other, seeing that
Love and Reason are but one and the same thing."   As
a matter of fact, so little is Love the same thing as Reason,
so near akin is it to Unreason, that we say of a man
deeply in love that he is *mad* with love, that he loves *to
distraction.*   Love is so subversive of reason, that a man
of sense is recognised to be in love, when he begins to
commit follies ;

[1] "I saw, I was undone, in an instant a fatal frenzy carried me away."

[2] "I saw him, I blushed red, I grew pale at sight of him."

[3] *L'Instinct sexuel.* ("The Sexual Instinct.") Evolution. Dissolution.
Paris, F. Alcan.

" L'amour et la raison sont ennemis jurés." [1]—(*La Veuve.*)
" Vouloir que la raison règne sur un amant
  C'est être plus que lui dedans l'aveuglement." [2]

The Poets then have not done wrong to represent Love
under the guise of a boy with a bandage over the eyes.
It is this blindness that accounts for the follies, suicides,
murders and crimes of every kind Love is responsible for.
While it costs some their reason, others lose life and yet
others honour. Unless Love brought about a species of
blindness, should we see so many young men ruin, dishonour and even kill themselves for the sake of unworthy
mistresses,—so many young girls sacrifice their good name
and expose themselves in unlicensed intrigues to the chance
of a pregnancy that may bring them to shame, abortion,
infanticide or suicide, and hurry them from the arms of
their parents to the bar of a Criminal Court or the slabs of
the Morgue,—so many married women become adulteresses
or even poisoners,—so many mothers forget their children
to fly with a lover, who is often a contemptible scoundrel,
and will forsake them in their turn,—so many men turn
cowards, traitors, swindlers, thieves, forgers, murderers, to
satisfy the caprices of a mistress who will one day betray
them, and maintain at the price of crime a precarious hold
over a woman, neither prettier nor more agreeable than
the rest of her sex? How many times do the Magistrates
whose office it is to question criminals hear the latter
exclaim: "Ah! women! women! It is the love of women
has been our ruin!" Some years ago, questioning a young
man of education and intelligence, who had just been condemned to death for theft and murder, I asked him how
he had come to such a pass. "'Tis love of women has
brought me to this," was his unhesitating answer.

Love blinds men so completely it can render the wisest
of them fools, humble the proudest at a woman's feet, rob
the strongest of their might, the cleverest of their wits, the

---

[1] " Love and Reason are sworn foes."

[2] " To imagine Reason sways a lover's mind, is to be further gone in blindness than he." Corneille, *Andromède.*

C

most prudent of their virtue. The most beautiful and high-born ladies suffer themselves to be seduced by men who are both ugly and vulgar.

This insane infatuation was symbolized in Antiquity by the legend of Pasiphaé, who albeit she had a king for her husband, became madly enamoured of a bull. The wild passion Mary Stuart conceived for Bothwell is familiar to all readers of history, though the latter was ill-favoured and brutal and often ill-treated her, to the point of making her wish for death, yet without curing the Queen of her infatuation. So great was her attachment that she used to say, "she would give up without a moment's hesitation France, England and her own country, and follow Bothwell to the end of the world clad in a white petticoat rather than be parted from him."[1] Her correspondence reveals her submitting to her lover's wishes even to the extent of doing a crime at his orders. When Bothwell bids her seek out the King her husband and entice him into a lonely palace, where it will be easy to murder him, she goes on the vile errand. Women enamoured of men unworthy of them themselves recognize this unworthiness, but they say like Mary Tudor in *Victor Hugo*: "I know quite enough all you are going to tell me, that he is a villain, a coward and a wretch; I know it as well as you do and blush for it, but I love him,—what would you have me do?" These attachments to vulgar fellows, actors, mountebanks and the like, often arise from physiological reasons. In all ages great ladies have been found frantically in love with men of the people, Bohemians, servants. Already in the eighteenth century Gilbert wrote:

> "J'aurais pu te montrer nos duchesses fameuses
> Tantôt d'un histrion amantes scandaleuses
> Fières de ses soupirs obtenus à grand prix,
> Elles-mêmes aux railleurs dénonçant leurs maris."[2]

---

[1] Mignet, vol. i., p. 316.

[2] "I might have shown you our high-born Duchesses, now shameful mistresses of an actor, proud of his sighs won at such a price, themselves denouncing their husbands to the mockery of their lovers."

Mountebanks and acrobats, like the gladiators of old, frequently inspire with a mad passion not only women of vicious life, but even virtuous and modest girls belonging to respectable families. Here is an instance: a certain Matracia, condemned to death some years ago at the Assize Court of the Department of the Bouches-du-Rhône and executed at Marseilles, an acrobat, was already a man of fifty-four, and a widower, having killed his first wife by his cruelty (in a scene of furious jealousy he had bitten her nose off and then exposed her in a state of nudity at the window), when he seduced a pretty girl of Marseilles of twenty-two, belonging to a highly respectable family of watchmakers. He had carried her off and married her in spite of all the precautions taken by her family. Some time afterwards, the acrobat having killed for some quite trivial motive his mother and sister-in-law, whom he had never forgiven for the opposition they had shown to his marriage, his wife who was an eye-witness of this double murder, still madly in love with him, followed him in his flight, all covered as he was with the blood of her mother and sister, without taking the time even to raise the unhappy victims from the ground where they lay dying, stabbed by the ferocious ruffian.

Beauty is not a *sine qua non* for the excitation of this amorous fascination. The Comte de Chamilly, who inspired the pious authoress of the *Lettres portugaises* with so violent a passion, was so dull and heavy a fellow, "that to see and hear him," Saint-Simon declares, "no one could ever have believed him capable of inspiring so extravagant a love as that which is the soul of these famous *Lettres portugaises.*"

Plain women may nevertheless inspire violent love. I have myself seen a curious case of a husband who was madly in love with his wife who was a hunchback and a cripple. When the latter ran away from him, he wept scalding tears like a child and fell fainting under the severity of the blow.

"Tout est mystère dans l'amour.
Ce n'est pas l'affaire d'un jour
Que d'épuiser cette science." [1]—(*La Fontaine.*)

Love claims its victims at all ages, but more especially among the young. Love has its age, in spite of what Pascal says, who holds that "love is ageless, it is always being born afresh." But in exceptional instances it may spring up in the heart of a man of ripe years or even in that of an old woman ; Mme. du Deffant was seventy when she conceived a violent passion for Walpole. But, except in rare and exceptional cases, Love is the passion of youth, as ambition is that of maturity.

When a young girl commits suicide, it is almost invariably owing to an unhappy love affair. Suicides of young people are very frequent as the result of thwarted affection. For many years past the number of such suicides has been on the increase.[2] For instance, in the year 1892 there were, from various causes, 87 cases of suicide of minors under sixteen, and 475 of minors between the ages of sixteen and twenty-one, whereas in 1880 these figures stood at 55 and 267 respectively. Suicides for love on the part of minors are not classified separately in the statistics published by the Ministry of Justice, but since perusing, as I have done, all the official reports preserved in the Bureau of the Public Prosecutor of the Department of the Seine, I am convinced that these represent a considerable figure out of the total number.

The precocity of young people of the present day in matters of love and licence has produced a corresponding precocity in suicide. Cases of suicide for love occur at sixteen, fifteen and even earlier ages. The fierce emotions of love and jealousy are too strong for children of this

---

[1] " All is mystery in Love. 'Tis not the business of a day to exhaust this science."

[2] The total of suicides which had for a long period followed an upward course, fell again in 1893. It increased again in 1894, but once more fell in 1895, the date of the latest statistics available. In the latter year it decreased from 9,703 to 9,253.

tender age, and shatter them ; unable to bear the pain, they kill themselves. But persons of mature and even advanced age also commit suicide from the same motives. Men of fifty and sixty lay violent hands on themselves because they are repulsed by young girls whose affections they try to win. Women of forty and fifty seek a voluntary death, because they are scorned by young men with whom they have fallen in love. Quite lately a woman of forty-two was found hanged on a tree in the Wood of Clamart, with a letter in her pocket declaring the motives of her desperate act. It ran as follows :

" I am forty-two years of age, and an unhappy and desperate woman. My lover has left me. Ah! if only I had known him when I was twenty, I should not be putting an end to myself to-day.

" I wish to be buried just as I am, without being un-dressed, or exposed at the Morgue, not to shame my family, which is very respectable.

" I was not born vicious, but I had no trustworthy support to rely upon. I was considered pretty ; the downward path was rapid, and I followed it only too quickly. May I be forgiven.

" Alas and alas! I loved him fondly, he has such a good heart! Had they not made me appear so vile in his eyes, he would have rehabilitated my good name.

" Farewell to all my family. Forgive me. Peace to my ashes. 'Tis wrong to despise the dead ; they have paid their debt to society.

" How bitterly I suffer! I might be already dead."

To make quite sure of success, the unhappy woman had drunk nitric acid before hanging herself.

Some further examples. A seamstress of thirty-three, very respectable and industrious, falls suddenly in love with a young locksmith of the same neighbourhood ; she hopes he will come and propose for her, but he never does, and she poisons herself.—A man of forty, possessed apparently of everything needful for happiness, excellent health, a handsome fortune, several country houses, ex-

periences the most acute grief at his failure to marry a
young lady he is in love with. He never leaves off repeating to his mother, who lives with him : "I am terribly
unhappy! I cannot bear my life any longer;" till one
evening, after supping with his mother, he goes up to his
room and there kills himself.

Suicide resulting from disappointed love is as a rule
premeditated ; the idea becomes more and more persistent
as the mental agony increases. A struggle ensues between
the longing to escape the pain which has now grown unbearable on the one hand and the instinct of self-preservation and the family affections on the other, motives still
attaching the sufferer to life.

"Jeannette mine, I am going to blow out my poor
brains. Don't think I do so in a moment of temporary
insanity ; I have made up my mind long ago. Good-
bye! I have only another quarter of an hour to live; it
is now a quarter past eight, at the half-hour all will be
over.

" Accept my last kiss.

" I tremble, but I am not afraid."

In a number of letters and documents left behind by
suicides, I find this confession of nervous trembling, which
indeed is manifested plainly enough by the handwriting,
which becomes more and more irregular towards the last
words. The desperate man whose letter I have quoted
just above, fighting against this trembling, declares he is
not afraid ; while others avow the terror to which they are
a prey. Finishing a letter to his parents, a young man
who is on the point of killing himself out of disappointed
love, adds : "I must bid farewell, for I begin to tremble ;
in these my last moments I am afraid, and I believe it is
for the first time in my life."—In some cases there is much
hesitation as the supreme moment approaches, and intending suicides will wander all day long about the banks
of the river before finally throwing themselves into its
waters.—Some women are strong enough to offer a long
resistance to the temptation to commit suicide, and only

yield to it after several months' time. Others give in sooner, after a vain struggle extending over weeks or days. Yet others succumb to a sudden access of despair ; after some scene of jealousy and recrimination, women of a nervous temperament suddenly throw themselves from the window or into the water. Take an example. A young student was living with a young workwoman, when he received a visit from a former mistress. A violent quarrel broke out between the two women, and the student in order to calm them, told them he loved them both, but that henceforth, to prevent all jealousy, he would see neither the one nor the other. So far were these words from restoring peace, that one of the two instantly declared she was ready to sacrifice herself and rushed towards the door to hurl herself down the stairs. The young man darted after her, caught her up and made her come back again. But meantime the other work-girl pushed a chair to the window, climbed over the balcony and threw herself into space. Suchlike cases of jumping out of windows are very common in Paris, especially after quarrels between lovers and on the part of jealous women. These women, after threatening their husband or lover that they will throw vitriol in their face, will suddenly turn their fury on themselves and hurl themselves out of the window.

Suicides by charcoal fumes, by hanging and fire-arms are more premeditated than those by drowning or jumping out of window, for they require more preparation beforehand. At the same time the presence of a weapon within reach may suddenly rouse the idea of suicide, as in the following instance. A young man of wealth is anxious to marry a poor girl, a match his family are strongly opposed to ; to overcome their objections, he threatens to kill himself, though without any intention of doing so really, and flourishes a pistol about to frighten them. In the course of the interview, he flies into a passion, grows exhausted by his own violence, and finally quits the room angry and exasperated at the refusal he has met with. At this moment feeling the revolver in his pocket, he pulls it out and shoots himself.—Suicides of young men are, I believe, less deliberate than those of young girls; they are very often done on the spur of the moment, as in the following case. A young man says to his mistress: "You wish to leave me?" "You really wish to leave me?"—"Yes!" the woman replies, "I want no more of you." Instantly the young man takes out a razor and cuts his throat.

The general belief is that anyone who survives an attempted suicide feels no desire whatever to begin again. Nevertheless we see plenty of instances where unhappy lovers, even young girls sometimes, when rescued from death, refuse all remedies, openly express regret that their lives have been saved, and repeat their attempt at the first opportunity. They display remarkable energy too in accomplishing their purpose. One such, after drinking poison, hangs himself to hasten his death; the rope breaks, but he only begins again. These determined suicides repeat their attempt by the most varied methods or sometimes by the same over again. If hanging or poisoning fail, they light a brazier of charcoal; if this fail, they jump into the river; if they are rescued from a watery grave, they try poison again. A seamstress who had twice already attempted to poison herself, but had been brought back to life, took poison for the third time and refused to drink an antidote.

A young shop-assistant who killed himself by means of charcoal fumes, left the following behind him: "I have tried to poison myself, but without success; perhaps I shall have better luck to-day."—A young girl, who had already tried to drown and poison herself, makes yet another attempt, after first writing this note: "When you read this letter, I shall be dead. This time I do not mean to fail. I hoped you would return; I waited till ten o'clock, the hour at which I am now dissolving the poison I am going to drink. My sufferings will soon be over; buy flowers for my grave. 'Tis my birthday; good-bye!" She had just swallowed the poison, when her lover came in; showing him the phial she had emptied, she cried: "Look! I have kept my word." A few hours later she breathed her last.—After trying to hang herself in her diadem or head-band, Monime exclaims in Racine's play :

"D'autres armes sur toi, sauront me secourir."[1]

A woman of pleasure throws herself into a river, in despair after a love disappointment. Rescued by a soldier, she takes him for her lover, but after a while returns to her intention of committing suicide and puts it into execution.

Intending suicides seek such means of killing themselves as are most rapid and involve the least possible amount of pain. Afraid of failure and dreading to survive the attempt, they sometimes resort to several methods in succession ; very often they take poison first and then proceed to smother themselves with charcoal fumes.

The instruments of suicide differ according to sex. Women who are so ready to avenge themselves on rivals by disfigurement, dread wounds for themselves which have the same effect ; they prefer such modes of death as avoid convulsive spasms at the moment of dissolution and mutila-tion of the person. Wishing to preserve their beauty even in death, they generally shrink from using fire-arms, which disfigure the face.

In 1888, out of 597 suicides by means of fire-arms, 563 were men, and only 34 women. Women prefer charcoal fumes, drowning, hanging or poison. A woman who poisoned herself had previously written to one of her friends, begging her to come as quickly as possible and see to her funeral, to save her from the inquisitive eyes of strangers, because she said she hated people to see her looking ugly.

The charcoal brazier appeals to women as a means of suicide, as being handy and allowing them to wait death lying on their bed.

Drowning is another of their favourite methods ;

"Dans la profonde mer Œnone s'est lancée."[2]

---

[1] "Other arms you wear may yet avail to help."
[2] "Into the deep sea Œnone has thrown herself."

In Antiquity, the Leucadian rock from which unhappy lovers threw themselves into the sea is remembered to this day. Horace tells us how despairing suicides used to leap by crowds into the Tiber from the summit of the Fabrician Bridge. In our day the bridges of the Seine, the Rhône and other rivers have taken the place of the Leucadian rock and the Fabrician Bridge for intending suicides who do not live by the sea. Rivers, the waters of which are clear and rapid, seem to tempt those bent on self-destruction more than streams having a slow and turbid current ; where the choice is open, they select the former. Thus at Lyons more suicides take place in the Rhône than in the Saône.

Women who feel a repugnance to water resort to hanging or poison. Many poets make their heroines die by hanging. In a tragedy of Euripides Leda hangs herself, and Sophocles describes Jocasta as perishing by the same means. In *Mithridate*, Racine represents Monime as attempting her life by hanging.

> " Et toi, fatal tissu, malheureux diadème,
> Instrument et témoin de toutes mes douleurs,
> Bandeau, que mille fois j'ai trempé de mes pleurs,
> Au moins en terminant ma vie et mon supplice,
> Ne pouvais-tu me rendre un funeste service ? " [1]

The motives deciding women to make use of poison are the same which moved Cleopatra, who after instituting a number of experiments upon her slaves in order to study the effects of various poisons, eventually chose the bite of an asp, on the ground that this was followed neither by convulsions nor pain at the last moment. Parisian suicides, both men and women, very often employ cyanide of potassium, which is used in the workrooms to clean jewellery with. Opportunity determines the choice of this poison, the fact that it is ready to the workwomen's hand.

---

[1] "And thou, fatal web, unhappy diadem, instrument and witness of all my griefs, fillet that binds my brow and which a thousand times I have wetted with my tears,—couldst not now at least, when I am ending life and sufferings together, couldst not render me this last dismal office?"

There is a fashion in ways of suicide as in everything else. In Tacitus' day men opened their veins; and the Roman Historian mentions with scorn the case of a victim of proscription who had drowned himself in the Tiber. One form of suicide is deemed noble, another common and vulgar. For some years now the pistol has been adopted by women more frequently than it used to be, having been brought into vogue by several much-talked-of instances of double suicides committed by this means. But women always find the disfigurement caused by fire-arms repugnant to them; a girl who killed herself together with her lover by means of a pistol, writing to one of her female friends to announce her intended suicide, declared, " The thing that grieves me, is to spoil my face." Occasionally after taking poison a woman discovers she has not drunk a sufficient dose, so lays hold of a pistol to make an end. I have also verified some cases of suicide by fire-arms occurring in a carriage. Here is an instance. On October 31st, 1896, a young woman of twenty-five, elegantly dressed was seen crossing the Pont de Solférino in Paris, her face exhibiting evident signs of grief; presently she hailed and got into a passing cab. The vehicle had barely advanced a few yards when the driver heard an explosion; on descending from the box, he found the young woman lying on the seat of the cab and vomiting blood. She had just aimed a revolver bullet at her heart, after partly unfastening dress and stays. " Kill me, put an end to me," she cried repeatedly to the crowd which had collected; "put me out of my pain." She was conveyed to a hospital, but refused to answer any questions, only saying: " Let me die in peace; I would rather die." It was not long before she breathed her last. She was a country governess; and the following letter was found upon her : " Dearest, I love you too fondly, and would have you all to myself. I have struggled till I can no more. I am ill and broken-hearted. All reasons urge me to leave you ; love me and forgive me, farewell ! "

Men hesitate between different forms of suicide, seeking

the one that will cause them least pain ; some will first of all determine to drown themselves and direct their steps to a river, then presently change their mind and go home and hang themselves.   Fire-arms are the weapons preferred by men, especially by sportsmen and soldiers, who always have a gun or a revolver handy.   Young men often go in for suicide by shooting after a scene of mad dissipation. Sailors prefer drowning.   In sea-port towns this last method is common among all classes of society.   If a sailor does choose the pistol, he goes to the sea-shore to kill himself.   The following is a case in point, where the unhappy lover announced his intention in a letter he left behind conceived in these terms : "Three o'clock in the morning. I have slept soundly, and night bringing re-flection, I have determined to kill myself on the pier, beside the sea on which I have spent half my life."

Thoughts of dress by no means desert a woman when she is making her preparations for suicide.   A girl adorns herself for death as for a fête day.   When Cleopatra had resolved to seek a voluntary death, she had her hair dressed, donned her finest raiment and placed the Crown Royal on her head.   Nor are young work-girls less vain than the Egyptian Queen ; they wish to be pretty even in death, in the first place to please themselves, and secondly, to make the faithless lover sorry for what he has lost.   When a poor girl commits suicide in consequence of an engagement broken off or a promise of marriage forgotten, she puts on to die in the costume she had got ready for her wedding day or fondly dreamed of wearing on that occasion ; she dons the white frock, which very often she has embroidered with her own hands, and throws the veil over her head, then lies down on her bed of death as on a nuptial couch, fain to be as pretty when dying as she had dreamed to be fair in church and at the dance for the man who has scorned her.   A girl who was found dead dressed in a white wedding-dress and holding a book of devotion in her hands, had traced these lines before killing herself by means of charcoal fumes : " I want M. G."

(the man who had jilted her) "to see me as I lie dead."—
Another young girl, who had drowned herself, had been
careful to write down what her wishes were as to the way
they were to dress her and to point out the place where
she had put the wedding veil she had bought.—Another
girl of sixteen went out to get flowers, saying to a neighbour on her return: "Do you see my bouquet? but you
don't know what it is for." The woman paid no particular
attention to the remark at the time; but the same evening
when the girl's lover came back from the factory, he found
his sweetheart stretched dead upon her bed, dressed in
white and surrounded by flowers.—Moreover when a
young girl commits suicide, she is filled with thoughts
of her funeral. A work-girl of nineteen finding herself
pregnant threw herself in despair from a fourth floor
window. Throughout the day preceding her suicide the
neighbours were struck by her melancholy looks and
nervous trembling. She spoke repeatedly of death, saying
that if she were to die, at any rate she would have white
funeral trappings. This wish for a fine funeral is constantly found among women under similar circumstances.
I have noted the same thing in the case of a Magistrate,
who confessed to having eagerly desired the red gown
that it might be laid over his coffin, as also in an Officer
of high rank, who before' putting an end to himself, took
off his ordinary clothes in order to don his uniform.

In the choice of the garments she assumes for her death,
women are influenced by fond recollections connected with
the articles in question. "I wish them," wrote a work-girl,
"to put on me the hat that lies on my table."—"I wish,"
said another young girl, "to be left in the same clothes
I shall be wearing at my death; my lace frock, it will be
almost the identical costume I used to wear when I knew
M——; I beseech them to let me keep it on for that
reason."—Virgil had noticed this trait as characteristic of
women who commit suicide from despair at disappointed
love; he describes Dido as putting on and mournfully
gazing at the garments she had worn when she was happy.

" Ce lit, ces vêtements si connus à ses yeux,
Suspendent un moment ses transports furieux.
Sur ces chers monuments, ce portrait et ces armes
Pensive, elle s'arrête et répand quelques larmes." [1]

I found the same tender recollections that moved the
Queen of Carthage, actuating a Parisian workman for
the garments which recalled the best days of his life.
Having lost his wife by consumption, he killed himself a
month afterwards by means of charcoal fumes, and was
found dressed in the clothes he had worn on his wedding-
day.   He had placed on his bosom wrapped in newspaper
the necktie and shirt studs his wife had given him on that
day.—A lover deserted by his mistress begged before
killing himself that the ring he wore might be left on
his finger as a souvenir of the faithless one.—" I wish,
Lottchen," writes Werther, when informing her of his last
wishes, " I wish to be buried in the clothes I am now
wearing.   Your hand has touched them ; they are sacred."
(*Letter LXXVIII.*)

Lovers again often desire to have buried with them
objects that have belonged to their beloved, her photograph, the love letters they have received from her.
Women put these letters in their bosom.   They ask likewise for flowers to be placed on their tomb, a rose or a
bunch of violets in their hands.

Despairing lovers as a rule wish to die on the same
spot where they have loved.   I have found this desire
expressed in the letters of simple working-men, so natural
is it.   The places that witnessed their love remain graven
on their memory, and they love to call up the image of
them.

To kill herself, a woman will choose the spot where she
has been happy, the bed where she has lain beside him
she loved.   In Sophocles' play of the *Trachiniæ*, Deianira
enters the chamber of Hercules to kill herself there ; after

---

[1] " This bed, these garments so familiar to her eyes, suspend for an instant
the transports of her frenzy.   Pondering on these fond memorials, his portrait
and his arms, she tarries and sheds some tears."

throwing her husband's garments on the nuptial bed, she lays herself on the same spot, crying : " Oh ! nuptial couch, farewell for ever.   You will never more see me rest here." Like the heroine of the Greek poet, to-day as of old,— for is not the human heart ever the same?—women often come to die in the room, on the bed of their lover, in his absence ; if they find the door locked, they get in if needs be by breaking it open or climbing in at the window.   When unable to enter the old room they once occupied, they will die outside its threshold or somewhere near at hand. " I am dying near you," wrote a forsaken woman, who had come to a house close to her lover's residence to kill herself there. . . . " I send you a thousand kisses before I die.   I love you still.   My last thoughts and my last tears are for you."

A country girl jilted by her *fiancé*, drowned herself in the fountain which had been witness to the oaths of eternal affection which they had exchanged, but which she alone remembered.—Men whose imaginations are less romantic and their sensibility less delicate, do not attach the same importance to their choice of the spot where they propose to lay hands on themselves.   Most usually the unhappy lover prefers to kill himself at the feet or outside the door of his mistress.

> " Le désespoir le fit courir
>   A la porte de l'inhumaine . . .
> J'espérais, cria-t-il, expirer à vos yeux." [1]

He hopes to melt her heart or stir a feeling of remorse. But the woman who has ceased to love, after uttering a scream of physical terror at the horrid sight, steps over the corpse and away to her pleasures.   She has no wish to weep over a dead man, she much prefers laughing with the living.

Women who have been forsaken also sometimes experience the desire to go and kill themselves at the feet of their faithless lover.   " I have many a time told you I

---

[1] " Despair made him hasten to the cruel one's door. . . . I hope, he cried, to die before your eyes."

shall never have another lover but you," writes a girl who
has been jilted.   I will wait for you at X——, and
ask you whether you wish me to come back with you.
If you say yes! you will make me very happy; if no!
I intend to die at your feet." Jealous wives who have
run away or have been turned out again often come to
put an end to themselves before their husband's house;
they wish to make him a witness of their death.

Suicides from love are much less frequent in the country
than in towns.   Though the agricultural population is
much more numerous than the industrial, two or three
times more suicides are found among the latter than among
the former.   Thus in 1880, 23 cases of suicide resulting
from disappointed love were noted committed by persons
engaged in agriculture as against 66 by individuals belonging to the industrial classes, in 1890, 35 as against 88,
in 1891, 44 as against 139.   The reasons are obvious.
Peasants, who read few novels, hardly ever go to the
theatre or hear passionate music, develop their muscles
rather than their nervous system by the manual labour
they accomplish in the open air; they are calmer, more
judicious, better balanced than the men of cities; the
peace of the open country enters into their hearts and is
an anodyne to their sorrows.   In large towns on the
contrary the feverish activity there prevalent, the sedentary
life, the abuse of highly-spiced reading, the taste for erotic
music and literature, the habit of theatre-going, the over
refinements of civilization, all tend to develop sensuality
and sensibility at the cost of quiet reasonableness.

Then again in all large cities, Paris above all, the
conditions under which women live are going from bad
to worse, marriage becoming more and more difficult for
them and longer and longer postponed, irregular liaisons
growing more frequent and giving rise to constant ruptures.
Paris has been called the hell of horses, the purgatory
of husbands, and the paradise of women;[1] but to judge

[1] This was a proverbial saying as long ago as the seventeenth century.
In his *Suite du Menteur* (Act ii. Sc. 1), Corneille makes Lyse say :

by the number of the last-named who commit suicide there, it is more of a hell than a heaven for them.   As a matter of fact, of the whole number of suicides for love in Paris, the proportion of women exceeds that of men. Indeed, suicide on the part of women forsaken by their lovers is growing so common in that city that within the last two or three years a girl of seventeen, wishing to poison herself in consequence of a disappointment in love, begged one of her female friends to get her some poison, and the latter made no sort of difficulty about doing so. As the quantity provided was insufficient, the intending suicide despatched another friend to a druggist's to obtain some more.   The two friends stood by quietly while she swallowed the poison, looking upon the thing as quite a matter of course, and calmly watched her dying struggles without a thought of calling in a doctor.   About the same date (July 1897) four young women stifled themselves all together in one room with charcoal fumes, saying they were tired of existence and wanted to be rid of the troubles and vexations of their life.   Among them was a young workwoman, who was pregnant and had been forsaken by her lover.

The writings left behind them by suicides deserve particular attention, inasmuch as they enable us to diagnose accurately the moral character of suicide and discover whether it is or is not a form of criminality.   According to some writers on crime, suicide and homicide are to be referred to one and the same physiological and psychological condition ; they are, so these thinkers maintain, only different forms of the same degeneracy, the same immorality.   I believe myself, on the other hand, that if there are some suicides as guilty as murderers, there are others that should inspire a profound feeling of compassion, nay ! even in certain cases sympathy and

> " Il est riche et de plus il demeure à Paris,
>   Où des dames, dit-on, est le vrai paradis."

—" He is rich and what is more he lives in Paris, where they say is the true Paradise of ladies."

D

esteem,—though without this in any way implying approbation of their conduct. Can anyone regard as an act of immorality the suicide of a workman who, betrothed to a girl he loves and who loves him, kills himself on discovering himself to be consumptive, with the words : " being threatened with tuberculosis and being unwilling to marry under these circumstances, I think it better to kill myself"? The motives of suicide are so complex and varied, and differ so widely in different instances, it is impossible to judge all cases by the same standard. Some kill themselves from cowardice, others from devotion.

Doubtless among suicides are to be found criminals, madmen, fanatics, men of morbid, nervous, hysterical organization and weak mind, but also refined and tender hearts,—hearts too tender, too sensitive. Such as kill themselves for disappointed love may be of morbid constitution and over-tender susceptibility, but they entertain none of the anti-social sentiments characteristic of the criminal ; they are but victims of their unsatisfied cravings after love and tenderness. This tenderness shines in the most touching light through all they write ; their letters are full of delicate, disinterested, lofty feeling, for their parents and family, their friends, and even for those who have occasioned their present despair. As a rule they bear no grudge for the cruelty, indifference and treachery that have caused them such agony. To the last they express nothing but love towards those who love them not, they wish nothing but happiness for those who have wrought their misery. The woman who is killing herself because she has been forsaken, cannot bring herself to hate the faithless wretch who is responsible for her death. The lover who is committing suicide because he has been betrayed, pardons with his last breath the woman to whom he owes his doom. I have before me a very large number of letters written by persons who have put an end to themselves for love ; as I cannot quote them all, I will copy a few only as examples of the rest :

" My darling Alice," writes a sailor to a girl who had

refused him; "let me call you so for the last time, for when you receive this letter, I shall be a corpse. The heart that beat only for you will be pierced by a bullet.

"I shall not fail, my hand will be steady; the grief I suffer assures me of this, for I shall be rid of this and my life together.

"All I take with me is a lock of hair and some flowers —memorials of happier days.

"Be happy, Alice; this is my only wish for you, and receive the last kisses of one who loved you so well, he dies for your sake."

"From the first day I saw you would not be my husband," writes a woman who had been engaged in an irregular liaison of which she was ashamed, "I have had but one thought, to die! If I cannot be your wife, at least I will end my present pain. I forgive you from my heart, and my last thought will be for you."

Among a thousand letters I have read, I have only once met with bitter words directed against the faithless lover, and in that case we must add that the woman had thought of killing him before putting an end to herself. "If I do not succeed in killing M——," she writes, "I ask that he may be confronted with my corpse, if I die. Death inspires the meanest wretch with sentiments of awe and terror, and I want him to feel some remorse at any rate for his villainy." The letters of women deserted and of disappointed lovers who commit suicide invariably end with words of love and forgiveness. The only angry expressions occasionally found are addressed to stern parents who have opposed their union and so led to their despair. "I shall kill myself within the hour, and you will have my death on your conscience," writes a young man to the father of the girl who had refused him.

Despairing lovers do not forget their parents when dying by their own hand; we constantly find them writing to aunts or cousins, begging these to come and console their grief and live with them. A young girl wrote to her friend :

'I beseech you, directly you hear of my death, hasten to my father" (she was an only daughter); "comfort him, make him understand it was better for me to die, as I could never have endured my pain; if I had lived, I should have fallen into some wasting sickness or a brain fever. . . . Let no one accuse my father or my brother of want of foresight. When M—— showed too marked attentions towards me, they did say some words of warning, but I promptly reassured them, for I did not at that time foresee myself that the attachment then just beginning would assume such proportions later on. Both felt confidence in me, for the past was a guarantee for my future conduct; hitherto I had manifested so little susceptibility to love, they thought me superior to all feminine weaknesses; my cheerful, but at the same time haughty, disposition made them feel quite secure." The same young girl, writing directions for the distribution of various souvenirs among her female friends asked that one of these should be given a little frame of black velvet which hung at her bed's head and contained her mother's hair. "She can put into the same frame," she writes, "her own much regretted mother's hair. . . . We both felt the same fond affection for our dear lost ones; she will understand me perhaps better than anyone, for God has tried us both with the same bereavement."

These two or three letters I have quoted, full as they are of tender and refined feeling, are amply sufficient in my opinion to prove that the unhappy beings who kill themselves for love, so far from being criminals, are more often than not good-hearted and affectionate creatures, only too loving and too sensitive. It is the very excess of their love and tender-heartedness that makes the grief of not being loved or of not being united to the object of their passion intolerable to them; it is the craving for affection, eating out their hearts with unsatisfied desire, that plunges them in despair and disgusts them with life. To this excess of sensitiveness they join a lack of sufficient will power. They feel too keenly and suffer too acutely, without possessing the force of mind to bear the suffering. They are creatures of too *emotional* an organization, often sufferers from neurasthenia and hysteria.   A man of sound organization and strong will may meet with a great sorrow, but he will bear up against it and not kill himself ; a man of ill-balanced temperament, excessive sensitiveness and feeble will, is crushed under the weight of sorrow and shirks the pain by committing suicide.   The thought of suicide soon becomes a fixed idea, a "possession by the Evil One," in persons of degenerate type hereditarily ; it is a symptom of mental debility.   Notions of suicide are very common in hysteria, and it is now well known that hysteria affects men as well as women, and is not, as was long supposed to be the case, an exclusively feminine complaint.   In one word, a physiological predisposition must be present over and above a disappointment in love to determine suicide.

CHAPTER II.

DOUBLE SUICIDE AS DETERMINED BY PASSION.

"Et jusque dans la tombe il est doux de s'unir." [1]—CORNEILLE.

THE analysis I have attempted of Love in the foregoing chapter has clearly shown the fact that lovers experience a craving to be one, "the twain to make one flesh," to adopt the powerful language of Scripture. Unless this craving is satisfied, unless they can be united and live always together, they are so unhappy they prefer death to separation. Unable to be united in life, they are fain to be joined together in death ; they say with Corneille :

> "Si l'hymen n'a pu joindre nos corps,
> Nous joindrons nos esprits, nous joindrons nos deux morts." [2]

When a lover who has lost his betrothed kills himself, it is that he may rejoin her in the tomb ; he thinks death will bring them together once more ;

> "Et si dans le tombeau le ciel permet qu'on aime,
> Dans le fond du tombeau je l'aimerai de même." [3]

To go on living, when she is dead, seems an impossibility to him ; he must follow her even in the grave. This longing for union in death has been described by Ovid in the suicide of Pyramus and Thisbé. Pyramus believing mistakenly that Thisbé is dead, betakes himself to the tree they had designated for their tryst, carrying with him

---

[1] "Yea ! even in the tomb 'tis sweet to be united."

[2] "Though Hymen could not join our bodies, yet will we unite our souls, our two deaths, in one." Corneille, *Œdipe*, Act ii. Sc. 4.

[3] "And if Heaven but suffer Love to flourish in the tomb, in the depths of the tomb I will love her as fondly as ever."

Corneille, *Pulchérie*, Act iii. Sc. 2.

Thisbé's veil, which he kisses and exclaims: "Now, dear and holy veil, be dyed with my blood too." Thisbé coming to the trysting place finds Pyramus' dead body, and kills herself in her turn. "Unhappy Pyramus," she cries, "the love you bore me has undone you. Ah well! my arm shall be as brave as yours and my love shall fear death no more than yours has. I will follow you to the tomb; I will be at once the cause and the companion of your death. Alas! nothing but death could have separated us, and even death shall not divide us!" Separation is the greatest of all griefs for lovers. They long to be together, and never part; they want a close, a lasting, an eternal union; failing it, they grow despairing and die together, their craving to be together still expressing itself in the wish they formulate in their last written words, to be buried in the same grave.

This longing for union in the tomb I have found in all the letters and documents I have examined of those whom Love has driven to suicide; they express it under many different forms, and repeat it over and over again, in their anxiety to induce their relatives to respect their wishes. The impossibility of union in this world or of a complete, final and immutable possession of each other, is at the bottom of all their grief and despair; accordingly they find their only consolation in the thought that their bodies will lie side by side in the same grave.

A young married woman of twenty-six, who had made up her mind to die with her lover, but survived the wound received, told me a short time since that her lover kept repeating, while engaged in the preparations for their suicide, how grieved he was to think they would not be laid in the same grave; the young woman's relatives possessing a family vault in a cemetery at Marseilles, he was afraid they would wish to keep their daughter's corpse in their own tomb.—When Dr Bancal and Mme. X—— were making their plans to die together, they wrote to a friend of both of them, begging him to unite them after death on one and the same bier. Mme. X—— told him:

" Pray be so good as to come to the house directly you receive this letter, you will find us dead . . . do not grieve for us, we shall die very happy . . . you must lay us on the same bier." Bancal for his part had written to his friend: "I am most anxious to be beside my dear mistress, that our bones may mingle together; the thought of this gratifies me inexpressibly."

"La mort même, à ce prix, la mort a sa douceur." [1]

Lovers dying together constantly write to their parents in such terms as these: "Do not part us! if you still love your son a little, I trust you will respect his last wish, which is to be buried with the woman he loves."

The longing to be joined in the tomb with the loved one is so natural a one, we see it expressed no less by queens than by work-girls, by artisans as by princes, and that at all epochs,—for is not the human heart ever the same? Cleopatra after the defeat of Antony, in the petition she addresses to Octavius, begs to be interred by her lover's side: "Do not refuse me," she prays, "a tomb by his side, and that dying for him, I may at any rate dwell with him in Hades." Going to kneel on her lover's sarcophagus, she cries to him: "Thou wilt not suffer thy wife to be dragged alive behind the victor's car of triumph. No! thou wilt rather hide me by thy side, and take me to be with thee in this tomb."

Abelard writing to Heloïse, after he has entered the cloister and made her do the same, concludes his letter by expressing the wish that she may have herself buried beside him in the same tomb. "I hope and trust," he tells her, "that, when you have accomplished the time of your life, you will be buried by my side." And—for he is as full of vanity as love,—he adds, "My tomb will be the more famous for it."

In the *Cyropædia* (bk. vii., ch. iii.), Xenophon, describing the despair of Pantheia at the death of Abradatas, relates

---

[1] "Death itself, at this price, death has a sweetness of its own."
Delille, *Æneid*, Bk. iv.

how she has his body brought in, then stabs herself and dies with her head resting on her husband's bosom ; before striking the fatal blow, she had directed her nurse to wrap in the same shroud her husband's corpse and her own.

Poets have not failed, when depicting the death of lovers, to assign them this longing to be united in the same grave. Tasso in his *Jerusalem Delivered* represents Olindo, who dies with Sophronia, as saying: " As thou hadst to die, it makes me happy to be the companion to share thy death, since I could not share thy life. I weep for thee, but not for myself,—for am I not dying by thy side ? "—When Romeo comes to Juliet's tomb to kill himself upon it, he cries to Paris : " If you have any vestige of pity left, open the tomb and lay me by Juliet's side." This craving to be reunited in the tomb with the loved one must needs be a cry of Nature's own prompting, for I have found it expressed in a letter written by a joiner of Aix who, inconsolable at the loss of his wife, committed suicide in his despair. Writing to his children, he says :

" I am leaving you to rejoin her I have always loved ; divide what I leave behind amongst you, as brothers should ; do not let selfishness make you quarrel ; remember what your mother used to say, ' why be illconditioned ? we have such a short time to be in this world,'—good words worthy of so good a woman. . . . My last wish, if you can get it granted, would be to put my body in your mother's grave, that is to say, to take me from my coffin, open hers and place my body on hers ; I shall be near her then.

" Farewell, children, farewell all ; in dividing, you will put aside for my little Jeanne 160 francs.

" YOUR FATHER."

In *René*, when Amélie is bidding farewell to her brother, she says to him : " Ah ! if only the same tomb could one day reunite us ! but no ! I must sleep alone."—In the *Elective Affinities*, Charlotte has Edward laid by the side of Ottilia, although she is not his wife : "They have suffered enough," she says, "to have won the right to rest together."—Quite lately in a criminal case that made no little noise in the world, we have seen a married woman consent with a similar generosity to her husband's being buried beside his mistress, for whom he died.

When a pair of lovers kill themselves, they not only find consolation in the thought that they are about to be united in the tomb ; each of them is likewise made happy by seeing that the other loves so ardently as to prefer death to separation,—a knowledge that sweetens death.

A girl who committed suicide in Paris on August 31st, 1897, along with a young man she wished to marry, on the refusal of the latter's family to consent to the match, wrote thus : "As I have no hope of marrying him, why! I prefer to die with him. Death will make us one for ever, and I shall be happy. Above all let no one touch my engagement ring."

The numerous judicial documents I have consulted as well as the personal inquiries I have made, all point to the light-heartedness, the astonishing gaiety of spirits, with which lovers prepare as a rule for their double suicide. The mother of a young man, who last April committed suicide together with the girl he was violently in love with, told me how her son had been in the habit for some months before the fatal event of continually singing snatches of opera composed *a propos* of situations analogous to his for heroes of the stage who wish to end their life.

A young girl told her lady friend of her intention to commit suicide with a smile on her face ; pointing to an article of dress, she said : "What a pity! I shall never wear it, for I am going to die to-morrow." The Doctor Bancal mentioned a little above, writing to a friend, said : "We have not more than six or seven hours to live, but we are as calm as if we were going to rest to wake up to-morrow morning in each other's arms." In a letter to his mother he expressed the same idea : "I look upon eternity with as much delight as if I were gazing at one of those fair scenes of Nature I have sometimes enjoyed so highly." Witnesses who saw them the day before their suicide were struck by their high spirits ; the butler stated that when he saw them, he could not help exclaiming : " How merry they are to-day ! " Madame X—— sang while making her preparations. During the week preceding their death, the two lovers went every night to the theatre.—A married woman, who had made up her mind to die with her lover, but survived the attempted suicide, assured me she went to sleep quite peacefully, knowing all the while that during the night her lover was to kill her and then himself.—Chambige stated that when on the way in a carriage with Madame Z—— to the villa where they were to put an end to themselves, they were both of them in great spirits, and that he could not refrain from singing the aria from Faust, " All hail my latest morn."

In the majority of instances a plan for double suicide is arranged long before the event ; in several cases of the sort I have noted that the pistol used had been bought a month or several months beforehand. In the Bancal case, already twice referred to, Madame X—— wrote : " It is now a month since our plan was determined on ; we were to have waited till to-morrow, but fearing my family might succeed in discovering where I was living, I asked my dear Prosper if he would put it twenty-four hours sooner. This request he did not refuse, and to-night we cross Charon's ferry."

In the papers they leave behind, lovers, more particularly women, enter into the most minute details, completing all their preparations with remarkable coolness. Bancal had had a locket made for his mother containing some of his hair and some of " his darling's," with a farewell letter in these terms : " I die as I have lived without knowing what I ought to believe or not to believe. . . . I do not need your pity, I have lived more in ten days and tasted more happiness than one man's life can well contain." His mistress two days before the suicide had sent off a box containing articles of dress, etc., for her daughter ; on the paper in which the things were wrapped up, she had written : " For Léonie, a black frock, three pairs of gloves, a locket containing her father's hair, my own and her sister's, and a silver thimble." She wrote to her daughter's schoolmistress to ask her to take special care of her : "Talk to her very often, I beg you, of her father, but make her forget her mother, if possible."—Only a few minutes before starting with Chambige to kill themselves together, Mme. Z—— wrote a merry letter to a female relative.

Another thing showing their coolness is that very often lovers, before killing themselves, sit down to a meal to which they do full justice. It might be supposed their appetite would fail at such a moment, but no! they eat with a surprising gusto and light-heartedness. It is not unlikely that in some instances they may drink also to excess to give themselves an artificial stimulus, as is the case in a great many suicides due to the most widely different motives. Still I do not think that the mental condition of lovers who kill themselves together is really at all like that observed in desperate men who are afraid of death at the very moment of inflicting it on themselves and often seek " Dutch courage " in the bottle. Lovers who commit suicide look death in the face with calmness, almost with satisfaction.

When the notion of dying together has once entered two lovers' heads, it grows into a fixed idea, absorbing all their thoughts and making them forget everything else,—parents, children, honour, shame. Mothers rush upon death, forsaking the sweetest of children and giving themselves up to their lovers with a quite extraordinary cynicism. Mme. Z——, who was a Society lady of the highest consideration, and a mother who loved her little ones, was found quite naked lying beside Chambige, with whom she was ready to die after giving herself to him. Yet she was perfectly well aware that her state of nudity would be noted by the officers of Justice, when they came to draw up their reports as required by Law. That sentiment of shame which was so powerful among the women of Miletus that it arrested the epidemic of suicide, had been totally obliterated by passion in the case of Madame Z——. Young girls belonging to respectable families and possessing parents whom they fondly love, leave all to fly to the lover who awaits them, that they may kill themselves together. The mother of a girl who had committed suicide along with a young man because the latter's family were opposed to the match, told me with tears: "My daughter had always been a model of filial piety and goodness (this was true,—impartial witnesses, quite unconnected with the family, have told me she was a beautiful character), and had never occasioned me the smallest pain; gentle, tender, pious, she was all love and delicate attentions for my husband and myself; and yet she left us to go with that young fellow, knowing her conduct would plunge us into the most horrible despair. She was sincerely religious and a child of Mary, yet she consented to have intimate traffic with the villain, for I am certain he defiled her before killing her."

At the same time the most pure and exalted love may sometimes exist, especially among girls, without any desire for sexual relations. Indeed signs indicative of virginity are occasionally noted in girls who have elected to die with their lovers. One of these, being threatened by her parents that they would put her in a nunnery, committed suicide along with her lover, and at the post-mortem the doctors ascertained her to be a virgin.

Every year a certain number of young men called to the colours commit suicide when the time comes for starting to join their regiment, because they cannot bear separation from their *fiancée* or their mistress; in some cases they decide to die with them. One R—— was engaged to a girl at Lyons when he was obliged to leave home to perform his military service; the separation was extremely painful to him, but he resigned himself for the time being. Some months later he obtained a few days' furlough, which he spent with his *fiancée*. But when the moment arrived for returning to the regiment, the two lovers found they could not bear to part and resolved to die together. The poor girl was found with two wounds in the right temple caused by revolver bullets, lying beside her lover who was dead. She gave the following account of what had happened: "We had not the heart to part, when his furlough was expired, and so we determined to die together. He told me: 'I will shoot you through the head and then blow out my own brains. You, if you are still alive, must do as I did.' Léon fired one shot at me, and two at himself. As I was not killed, I took the revolver and put a second bullet into my head. I then fainted away. Regaining consciousness, I lay for two hours on my lover's body, folded in his arms." The lovers had previously written a letter to make known their last wishes. This letter, begun by the young man and finished by his companion, ran thus: "I am killing myself so as not to part from my little wife; I suffer too much when I am away from her. We wish to be buried together." The girl had added: "We do not wish our bodies to be surrendered to the Doctors. We wish to be buried together, just as they are found."

Another instance occurred some few months ago at Marseilles. A young man had enlisted in the Marine Infantry, but when the moment for departure came, so violent was his despair at leaving his *fiancée* that he conceived the idea of dying with her, and won her consent to the plan. He announced his purpose to his parents in the following letter: "As you are no doubt aware, I have gone off with Yvonne. Unable to endure separation from her, I failed to join the colours. At this moment I am put down on the roster as a deserter. When you receive this letter, we shall both be dead by our own act." They went to an hotel, where they supped and spent the night. Next morning they had breakfast at half-past ten and afterwards withdrew to their room; a minute or two later two explosions were heard. A rush was made to the spot, when the girl was found stretched dead on the bed, while the young man lay in the death agony on the floor in a pool of blood.—When a young soldier asks leave of absence to visit his family, but really to see his *fiancée* or his mistress, he is unable sometimes to return to the regiment on the expiration of his furlough, preferring to die with his beloved, whom he induces to share his determination. "My dear parents," wrote a young soldier, "we cannot bear to part, and have made up our minds to die together. We cannot live apart, and it is to end the pain we feel in separation that we put an end to ourselves."—Double suicide again occurs sometimes on the soldier's return from military service. The girl who is left behind by her lover on his departure to the army, becomes a prostitute ; the lover, ignorant of the evil life she has been living, takes up with her again, but the first day he learns the truth, he either breaks off the connection or else asks her to die with him.

So impatient are lovers in their desires that a mere delay in the execution of a projected marriage may throw them into violent despair. Quite lately the corpses of a young man of twenty-eight and a girl of nineteen were found in the Seine closely bound together ; they were to have been married in a short time, but a difficulty having arisen causing a postponement of the wedding-day, they preferred to die together. The following letter was found on the young man, written to him by his *fiancée* : "My own L——, I love you, and I swear by all I hold dearest in the world I will be yours for life and for death,—Your wedded wife that is soon to be."

We even see lovers who have already enjoyed each other's favours committing suicide, and this not only when they are in danger of being parted, but merely because they cannot see each other more frequently, because their possession of each other is incomplete, and inadequate to the ardour of their desires. This may happen when one of the lovers is married, and can only be with the other on rare occasions. I saw an interesting example of this at Marseilles not long ago. Here is the tale as told me by a young married woman of twenty-five, who had wished to die along with a young painter of twenty-six but who survived the attempt on her life : "My husband being very rough and unkind to me, I fell in love with B——, whom I used to see passing my house, and who manifested a very ardent affection for me. Our interviews took place at long intervals at an hotel in the suburbs of Marseilles. These my lover found much too 'few and far between'; he longed to be with me day and night and felt it bitterly when we had to part. I could see him as he passed before our house, and this was enough for me and gave me patience. But it was far from satisfying him, and he felt our separation keenly, and the rarity of our meetings; he besought me to leave my husband and fly with him, but the dread of shame held me back. At last, in despair at the obstacles that kept us apart, he proposed that I should die with him, and I agreed. He was to shoot me and afterwards kill himself. To this end we met at an hotel and spent the night together. While I was asleep, he fired a pistol shot into my temple—where you can still see the mark. I felt I was wounded and fainted. Presently I recovered consciousness, to find myself bathed in blood and to see my lover lying stone dead on the bed. He had shot himself in two places. I deeply regret he did not succeed in killing me."

A fortnight later, the same woman, now restored to calmness, having been visited by her mother and sisters, and freed from the hold her lover exercised over her, expressed quite opposite sentiments in an interview I had with her. She now repented the folly she had committed, and said : "Ah! if it were to do over again, and he asked me to die with him, I should tell him, if you want to kill yourself, why! go and do it, but I have not the slightest wish to follow your example." All she thought of now was her husband, her only wish to be reconciled to him, get his forgiveness and have him pay her a visit; and she asked me again and again with evident anxiety whether he would soon be coming to see her.

Schopenhauer could not understand how two beings who love each other and can find perfect happiness in their love, do not prefer to break altogether with social conventions and undergo any sort of shame rather than forswear life and the bliss of living together. Yet it is very easy to understand how married women or unmarried girls, though violently in love, may still recoil before the disgrace and shame of eloping with their lover, and how seeing his consequent despair, they may end by consenting to the idea of dying with him. In such a case the lover exercises a sort of fascination over his mistress; if she hesitates, he speaks of killing himself only, and succeeds by means of this threat in overcoming her scruples; if he dare not ask her in so many words to die with him, he lets her guess his plan of killing himself, that she may conceive the notion of sharing his suicide. Vanity, jealousy, selfishness, all unite with love to make him eager for this double suicide; if she survived him, the husband or someone else might get her again; by sacrificing her life for him, she flatters his pride, for is she not affording him the very highest proof of affection? In one word, since he must die, he feels a keen delight in dragging another along with him to end in his arms life and grief at once. This state of mind on the part of the lover who is fain to kill himself and drag along the same road the woman he loves, because they are kept apart by insurmountable obstacles, is the same which Jean-Jacques Rousseau assigns to Saint-Preux in the walk he takes with Mme. de Wolmar at Meillerie on the shores of the Lake of Geneva. Saint-Preux is violently tempted to hurl himself and Mme. de Wolmar with him into the waters of the lake below; this temptation he succeeds in overcoming, but many lovers yield to it. In suchlike cases, a married woman, rather than fly and live dishonoured, prefers to tread the path of death by her lover's side.

E

Again the fear of disgrace decides many a young girl not to survive her fall, but rather to die with her lover. Here is an instance I noted some months ago at Marseilles, completing the information collected by the Commissary of Police by details I gathered from the relatives of the unhappy pair. A young clerk of twenty-nine was desirous of marrying a girl of his own age with whom he was violently in love, and who was of irreproachable character and belonged to a highly respectable family. His mother however, thinking him too young to marry, refused her consent. The young people continued to see each other and walk out together, but the girl, who was as good as she was pretty and charming, remained unsullied in spite of all her love. More and more eager to marry, the young man did all he could by prayers and threats to force his mother's consent, but without avail. He then urged the girl to consent to an elopement, so as to compel his mother to agree to the match. Loving her parents dearly and fearing the scandal that must ensue, she was long in making up her mind ; eventually she yielded to her lover's prayers and left the paternal roof with trembling steps, scarce able to stand, but hoping soon to return on her lover's arm. After taking her to an hotel, the young man wrote to his mother, telling her he had carried off his *fiancée*, that she had given herself to him, that he must marry her now, and beseeching her to give her consent. The mother refused. He wrote to her again, declaring that his betrothed, seeing herself dishonoured, was for killing herself and begged for death at his hands as a favour, but that he had not the courage to kill her ; he besought his mother for her consent for the last time. The latter again refused. Hereupon the two lovers, driven to the alternative of disgrace or death, chose the latter ; the young man first shot his mistress with a revolver and then himself, both dying the following day. When the room was entered and the young man asked for an explanation of the tragedy, he repeated several times over, " It had to be," and these were the only words he was able to articulate. Letters written by this pair of despairing lovers previously to their suicide leave no doubt as to the reason for their self-sought death; the girl was anxious to escape shame and the young man to avoid scandal. We give the letter she wrote to her family:

"My dear Parents,—Forgive your Jeanne the act she is about to commit. But, loving without hope of a happy issue, she prefers to die with him she loves rather than live without him. I kiss you all; my last thoughts are with you.

"Your little Jeanne who loves you dearly and believes you will forgive her."

Besides this, she had written a special letter to her mother:

"My good, kind Mamma,—I have waited till to-day to die. I still hoped, but my darling boy's mother having entirely refused to listen to reason, we are forced to die. Better to die than to live an object of the world's scorn, amid the ironical smiles of friends and neighbours. This would be an unparalleled torture to me, and the fear of it has largely contributed to my determination to end my life.—Dear mother, forgive your child all the pain she is giving you. How I wish I could have made you happy; but there, what would you have? No one can command their fate, and I have always had a presentiment I should end thus.

"Farewell for ever."

The young man on his side had addressed the following lines to his family:

"Dear Mother and Brothers,—Forgive me. I die in despair. I love without hope of a happy issue, and dread the scandal that threatens me. Pray for me."

He had also composed a letter to the girl's parents to the following effect:

"You will no doubt curse my name, when you learn the death of your darling Jeanne; yet, forgive me, we loved each other so fondly the idea of separation was too grievous to be borne."

Parents are sometimes responsible for the suicide of their children, because very often they oppose their projected marriage from motives of worldly interest. The young man's family do not consider the girl rich enough, or *vice versâ*. On August 11th, 1897, in Paris, a young man of twenty and a girl of seventeen who had been brought up together and loved each other, seeing that the young man's relations were opposed to the match on the ground of the young woman's not being sufficiently well off, simultaneously leave their families, install themselves at an hotel, and put an end to themselves after writing the following letters :

"My dear Mother," writes the young man, "we are about to die by our own hands ; we love each other so fondly, we would rather die than see our dearest wishes balked. Perhaps now you will leave off saying bad things of one who has never been more than a dear friend to me, for though we have been three days together now, she has never given herself to me. Awaiting death that will so soon have us for its own, I declare once more what I have so often told you, that she is a good woman. The nearer we come to our deaths, the more I am convinced you have treated her unjustly.

"My good mother, I forgive you, for at the bottom of your heart you loved your son but too well, and would fain have had him marry a rich wife.

"We have just addressed a heart-felt prayer to God to grant us courage and keep our hearts from failing.

"Your son who has always loved you truly."

The girl also wrote on her side to her mother :

"My dear little Mother,—when you read these lines, I shall be already dead ; but you must forgive me, for though I have behaved so ill, you love me too well to leave me in doubt of your forgiveness. It is eleven years to-day since my father died, and by a strange coincidence, 'tis on the very same day I am going to rejoin him in another world. It was not to have been to-day, but on Sunday our courage failed us. Yesterday death would not have us ; to-day I hope to die, for it is terrible to live on only to endure never-ending pain.

"True it is, a good girl should not allow herself to do what I have done, but disgusted with my life, loving and being loved, as every creature longs to be, I forgot myself so far as to follow my lover and to court death along with him. Forgive me.

"Before dying, we have just been praying to God that He may to-day give us courage to die ; and if I go to Heaven (for I believe in God), I will pray for you.

"Your daughter who loves you and sends you her last kisses. Farewell, darling mother."

The sound of shots being heard, a rush was made to the room occupied by the young couple, when the girl was found stretched on the bed, the death rattle in her throat and her head pierced by a pistol bullet, and lying near the bed the young man with a wound in the head and a prey to extreme nervous agitation, covered with blood, weeping, wringing his hands and crying : "Oh ! my father who seest me ; oh ! my God, who art with him : is she dead?" On being questioned a few moments later by the Commissary of Police, he said : "My companion is named X—— ; we were brought up together, she lives near me. We wished to die. It was with her own hand she shot herself with a revolver in the head. I was lying by her side. I took the weapon from her and fired two shots at myself. I felt I had done it ineffectually ;" both bullets in fact had gone round, instead of penetrating, the skull and lodged between the bone and the scalp.

Esquirol cites a case of double suicide on the part of the son of a French *Juge de Paix* and a young girl his relatives refused to allow him to marry. The two lovers sought the Forest of Saint Germains, where the young man proceeded to blow out the girl's brains, afterwards hanging himself from a tree with her shawl.

The refusal of parents to consent to their son's marriage with a girl less rich than himself, was the cause of another double suicide which occurred in Paris quite lately. The parents, in order to disgust their son with the match, had spoken ill of the girl in question. Learning this, she wrote to the young man's mother: "To show you I am not a woman that goes with all men, as you say, I intend to die with my Léon, for I love him and I could not go on living without him. . . . You were for marrying him to a girl he does not care for; but on Monday, instead of coming for her engagement ring, she will arrive to see him dead. Léon is yours no more, he belongs to me now, as you would not agree to let us be happy together in this world.

"It is to you he owes his death. You can never have really loved him, to act as you have.

"We both wait for death with the utmost calm. While I am writing to you, my dear boy is busy stopping up all the cracks that might admit the air. We have only one fear,—that we may fail in our attempt."

At the foot of the letter the young man had added: "I make a point of telling you that it is not my little wife you are to blame, if I die; I asked her myself to die with me. . . . I let you think I would agree to marry Marie, to get you to leave me in peace. But it is not Marie I love, 'tis my little Berthe I adore; *she* is *my wife*, since yesterday, for did I not buy her her wedding-ring yesterday evening, and I forbid anyone to remove it from her finger. I think you will respect the last wish of a dead man." Then he wrote yet another message to his father, begging him to have them buried together: "I say this to you, father, for my Berthe, as well as I, loved you dearly. Farewell, my dear father. With these letters was yet another, written by the girl to her mother: "Mother mine, for I'm not afraid to call you so still, you told me I would never dare to kill myself. Well! you see now we are not afraid to die together. I write you these lines as the braziers are being lit."

Men who believe themselves forced into suicide by illness or want of success in life, persuade their wives or mistresses to die along with them. In these cases, the suggestion of suicide comes very near to being actually

criminal, as was recognised by a man deeply in debt who
wrote: "Having made up my mind to have done with
life, I am filled by the wild idea of not leaving this world
alone.   I feel myself as if I were being driven into crime."
—A girl of twenty, who had wished to die with her lover,
but survived the attempt she made on her life, gave the
following account to the Commissary of Police who had
discovered her lying wounded beside her lover's corpse:
"Last Sunday, my lover informed me that, having submitted to a medical examination, he had been found to
be suffering from a venereal disease, which he had contracted with another woman; he declared he could not
live under such conditions and that he wished to kill
himself.   On Tuesday he was for starting to throw himself under the wheels of a train; I thereupon consented
at his suggestion to join with him in putting an end to
ourselves by means of charcoal fumes.   After stuffing up
the doors and windows, we lighted in the middle of the
room a little stove we had removed from its usual place;
we also prepared a decoction of poppies, of which we
drank a glassful.   We then retired to bed, and yesterday
(Wednesday) we awoke still alive, having vomited during
the night; we were ill all the succeeding day.   At mid-
day to-day we resumed our purpose of suicide.   Léon,
who had meantime purchased a revolver, lay down on the
bed next the wall with me outside him nearer the edge;
he then fired a shot into my head, and I fell fainting.
When I came to, I saw that Léon had shot himself also.
I took the weapon from his hand, and fired two shots at
myself, but without reaching a vital spot."

A celebrated novelist, who is at the same time a
perspicacious moralist, M. Ed. Rod, in his last romance
le Dernier Refuge (The Last Resort), has shown a married
woman who dies along with her lover long after flying
from her husband's roof.   The lovers kill themselves
because Society turns its back on them, because the duties
they have violated take their revenge by making their
life unbearable from remorse, because, especially to the

woman who has preserved a strong sense of self-respect, the disesteem she feels herself surrounded by, seems more intolerable even than death. Double suicide, of married woman and lover, is the consequence of their false position.

It is not only in novels that we find unfaithful wives and their lovers driven to double suicide, nor is it solely in the higher ranks of society that this takes place. Quite lately a countrywoman, who had deserted her husband and children to follow her lover to Paris, ended by killing herself along with him. She announced her reasons for coming to this determination in the following terms: "Fate has so willed it for both of us; we must die, death is our only road to freedom. Dear children, I cannot draw back now, I dare not break my oath. We have suffered grievously; we ask God for pity and forgiveness."

Some few months ago, a married man, who had left his wife to live with his mistress, killed himself by means of charcoal fumes along with the partner of his guilt. In the letter they left behind, the two lovers declare themselves forced to take this step, adding: "We love each other, and we would rather die together than part."

"We regret nothing, for what has our love brought us but unhappiness?

"We ask one favour only,—to be buried side by side." The husband had also written a letter to his wife, begging her to forgive him.

In the notorious cases of Bancal and Chambige already referred to, we see married women committing suicide together with the lover within a few hours or a few days at farthest after their flight from the husband's roof. The mistresses of these two men, intoxicated by their guilty passion, but still alive to their sense of honour, unable to endure the only alternatives left them in the false position they have placed themselves in, viz., separation or public disgrace, abandon themselves to their lover, then seek for death as the only means of escaping shame and remorse.

According to the account given by the student Chambige, —a perfectly true one in my opinion, Mme. Z—— would seem to have said on the way to the villa where the lovers put an end to their lives : " I will give myself to you, but you must swear by all you hold most sacred to kill me immediately afterwards. . . . Only promise me to place in my right hand the rose you plucked this morning and then kiss me." After yielding to his embraces,[1] she claimed the fulfilment of his promise to kill her with loud cries : "You are a craven," she told him again and again, "kill me at once ; you promised to kill me immediately my dishonour was accomplished." Then with her own hand she pointed the revolver at her right temple, and thinking the aim bad, adjusted it afresh, ordering her companion to draw the trigger.

Madame X——'s state of mind closely resembled that described by Balzac in his *Femme de trente ans* (A Woman of Thirty) and by Dumas père in *Antony*. In the Bancal case, the two lovers killed themselves some days after Mme. X——'s flight from her husband's house ; but the plan of this double suicide had been settled a month before that date. Before flying with Dr Bancal, Mme. X—— had made him swear to kill himself along with her. Nor had her conscience been awakened only after the sin had been committed ; deadened as this was by the intoxication of a passion which made her find a fierce delight in courting ruin, in sacrificing everything to her love, she had yet enough sense of right and wrong left to dread the scandal that must inevitably ensue and to prefer to die rather than survive her sin.

M. Sighele believes that the idea of a double suicide originates in most cases with the woman ; but this proposition appears to me to require qualification. It is correct enough when a married woman is in question, who hitherto of unblemished virtue, yields to her lover's wishes on condition of dying with him afterwards, that she may not survive her shame. In such a case it is quite true ; the woman seeing herself disgraced eagerly demands death to cover her dis-

---

[1] The subsequent medico-legal examinations clearly established the fact that repeated acts of sexual intercourse had preceded death.

honour, while the lover, having given his promise to die only to gain possession of his mistress, regrets his bargain, once he has satisfied his passion. Returning to a calmer state of mind and body, and not having the same urgent reasons as the woman for wishing to die, he would fain live on to enjoy the continued possession of his mistress's person.

Still M. Sighele's statement is true enough where it is a question of a woman older than her lover, whose affection she is afraid of losing. This was so in the much-talked-of attempt at double suicide on the part of Lamartine with Mme. X——, with whom he had fallen in love at Aix-les-Bains. This lady who was an invalid and married, being summoned to rejoin her husband, and foreseeing that, exceeding Lamartine as she did in age, she would soon lose his affection, moreover, being devoid of any religious belief, had been the first to suggest the idea of their dying together.

In another instance of double suicide cited by Dr Brierre de Boismont and appealed to by M. Sighele in support of his proposition, it is again a married woman older than her lover that is concerned, and possessed of great influence over him. She was thirty-nine, the young man twenty-six, when they committed suicide, the young man having been only sixteen at the time when the woman, then twenty-nine, had conceived a violent passion for him, which she induced him to share. I have noticed yet another double suicide of a married woman " of a certain age," who detected in the very act of adultery with a lover younger than herself, not knowing what would become of her, determined to die with her lover and persuaded him to adopt the same resolution.—In the Bancal case, again the woman was married and older than her lover, for Dr Lombroso is mistaken when he says Dr Bancal's mistress was a girl.—In the Chambige case likewise the woman was the older of the two ; she had many white hairs. In a recent instance of double suicide which occurred in Paris, it was again the woman who first conceived the idea of dying ; she was a woman of twenty-four, mistress of a young man of nineteen. She had already lived for several years with another lover, who had gone away to perform his military service, leaving her with a child on her hands. This soldier being now due to return almost immediately with the intention of renewing his previous connection with his former mistress, the latter terrified at the prospect and unable to make up her mind to leave her new lover, with whom she was deeply in love, preferred to die along with him. She asked a neighbour to take charge of her little girl, bought a quantity of charcoal, lit it and lay down on the bed by her lover's side, where they were both found dead next morning.

When a woman who wishes to commit suicide cannot induce the man she loves to share her resolution, she calls him a coward, torments him with reproaches of every sort, and when she finds he is not going to take the plunge, arranges her own suicide in such a way as to involve his death along with her own, without his knowing anything about it beforehand. This is what a woman did lately in Paris, having kindled a brazier of charcoal without her lover's knowledge. To remove all suspicion, she showed herself particularly merry on going to bed with him, kissed him with more than ordinary affection, and spent half-an-hour in reading a novel before going to sleep. The lover awoke in the morning half stupefied, to find his mistress lying still and cold beside him.

In some very exceptional cases, excessively jealous lovers cause their mistress so much pain by their continual suspicions, reproaches and complaints, that at last the latter, indignant at being doubted, wearied of unfounded charges and generally disgusted with the wretched life they lead, proposes that they should die together, in order to prove to the lover the sincerity of her love. The lover agrees, and they proceed to kill themselves. I have noted a case of this kind as occurring lately in Paris.

When the lover of a married woman, jealous of the husband, wishes to die along with his mistress, if he does not succeed in inducing her to agree to the scheme or fails to bring her to the point of putting it into execution, he usually kills his mistress without her consent in the paroxysm of his jealous agonies, and then puts an end to himself. One L——, a man of thirty-six, a widower and the father of a young daughter, had entered into criminal relations with a friend's wife, herself the mother of four children. The lovers were unable to see each other often, and suffered much at the deprivation. L——, being of a very jealous disposition, became intensely unhappy, and judged death to be preferable to the life he was leading. At an interview his mistress accorded him at his request, he described his sufferings to her and his wish to die, and besought her to adopt the same resolution. He succeeded in persuading her and got her to sign a letter in which the two lovers announced their intention of committing suicide together. But just as they were about to carry out their plan, it occurred to them that the pistol they had provided was too small, and they went out to buy another of larger bore. Once in the open street, the woman saw the folly of her conduct, and changing her mind fled to her own home to escape from her lover. The latter hurried in pursuit; finding the entrance barred, he climbed over the gate, darted up the stairs, overtook the woman in her bedroom and shot her with a revolver; seeing her fall, he fired a second shot at himself which killed him on the spot. When his body was raised, it was noticed that he smelt of absinthe, which he had drunk to excite his courage to the commission of the act he had already determined on. He had had the strange notion of writing a letter to his mistress's husband in these terms : " Forgive two unhappy beings who have long adored each other and who would rather die than live apart. We are a pair of cowards. Forgive us, and care for our children." In another letter addressed to one of his relatives, he wrote : " Being unable to have lawfully the woman I love, I prefer death to the life I lead now. Do not blame, only pity me. I am a coward to abandon my little girl, but I cannot go on living ! "

Still, apart from these exceptional cases, I believe the idea of dying together to originate rather with the man than with the woman. The one that imposes his will is the stronger, the more energetic, the one that yields to suggestion is the more nervous and impressionable; and surely it is woman that best answers the latter description, as it is the man that excels in strength of will power. In *Hernani* it is the lover that makes the suggestion of dying together to the woman : " Weep no more, rather let us die ! " Cases often occur where a man who is ardently attached to a woman but parted from her by insurmountable obstacles, tortured by separation and the fear of seeing her fall into the arms of another, longs to die himself and to kill the object of his passion, dissimulating what really amounts to murder under the form of double suicide, to which he almost forces the woman to consent. To give an example : a young girl in the Department of the Basses Alpes had entered on an intrigue with a workman, a hatter ; her family having discovered this, were anxious to break off the connection. Learning their intention, the lover in despair at the thought of losing his mistress, made her sign a paper in which the girl and himself expressed their determination to die together. Some days later, he went to see his mistress, and after kissing her, said : " Thérèse, we must die, the time is come ; " with these words he fired three shots at her with a revolver, killing her on the spot, then four more at himself, but without inflicting any serious wounds.

When young fellows, of idle and dissipated habits, disappointed in their plans and crippled with debt, do like Tony Auray and Soularue and commit suicide together with their mistress, it is the lover who driven to self-slaughter drags the woman along the same road out of jealousy, to prevent her ever belonging to another man. M. Sighele cites the case of Tony Auray in support of his thesis, but it really tells against him ; as a matter of fact, the accused confessed he had killed his mistress before committing suicide, that other men might never have her. The girl in question was only fifteen, and had eloped with him from her parents' house under promise of a brilliant future. After leading a merry life with her for some months, when he had exhausted all his resources and squandered the inheritance his father had left him, he turned his thoughts, like Rolla, in Alfred de Musset's poem, to suicide. He shot her five times in the head, while she was asleep; at the first shot she awoke, and turning to her lover, called upon him by his name, "Tony!" Undeterred, he fired again and again, and presently a bullet pierced both lobes of the girl's brain. He then discharged the sixth shot into his own mouth, wounded himself in five places with a sword-cane, and finally leapt from the window into the street.

In these cases of double suicide imposed by the lover on the mistress, we ought—if we are to call things by their real name—to speak of the lover as preluding his own suicide by what is nothing more nor less than a murder.

But how does a lover having special reasons of his own for desiring death, succeed in communicating the wish to his companion, who has not the same motives for thinking of suicide? The mystery is accounted for by the community of ideas and sentiments which exists between two lovers deeply enamoured of each other, and by the ascendancy the more passionate or the more energetic exercises over the other. If a mere prolonged and almost exclusive contact between two individuals, a mere living together, is very often sufficient to make them think the same thoughts, desire the same objects, grow alike, how can this intercommunication of ideas and feelings fail to be yet more rapid and more intense between two lovers absorbed in each other? What one wishes, the other wishes,—they say so themselves in the papers they leave behind. This is what I find in a letter written by two lovers who committed suicide together by means of charcoal fumes: "It is not a case of one dragging the other along with him;

it is by common consent we resolve to die together."
When one of two lovers has more ardour and passion
than the other, he easily acquires no small ascendancy
over his companion by the vivacity of his feelings and
the force of his language ; in one word, he dominates the
weaker vessel by sight, word and touch, silences scruples
and hesitations by a combination of prayers, threats and
sophistry, and ends by getting his idea of a double suicide
accepted, representing it to be a noble, sweet and poetical
thing to die together. This form of suggestion produces
an especially powerful effect on nervous, impressionable
natures, such as readily obey other and more dominating
personalities. This suggestibility again is further increased
by the state of exaltation and excessive stimulation of
senses and imagination which is characteristic of lovers
under the empire of passion. I have noted one very
remarkable case where double suicide was suggested by
a man to his mistress, and not without effect, although
the latter had ceased to care for him and was thinking
of marrying another man. He besought her to come and
see him for one last interview, and on her coming expressed
so vehemently his grief at losing her and his fixed purpose
to kill himself, that he actually persuaded her to die with
him (July 1897).

Suicide may also be mutually suggested by women to
each other in virtue of community of feelings and sufferings. The four young women who died together by
charcoal fumes at Paris on the 8th July 1897, thus
mutually suggested the idea to one another, telling each
other they were tired of life and had better all die together. The first notion of committing suicide came from
the mistress of the establishment ; her sister, who was
deeply attached to her, said, "If my sister dies, I will do
the same." Their two workwomen, one of whom was
pregnant and had been deserted by her lover, determined
to follow their example, after partaking of a meal together,
during which they excited one another by singing songs.
The four girls lay down on the same bed, where they were

found smothered by the fatal fumes next morning. The neighbours had heard the sound of loud laughter till one o'clock in the morning.

A work-girl of twenty, suffering from the pain of a broken engagement, attempted to commit suicide, but was prevented in time. Under the influence of disappointment and unhappy circumstances, she became the mistress of a workman of her own age, with whom she went to live. She formed a close friendship with another workwoman of thirty, who lived in the same house with her lover; this woman was ill and disgusted with life, and was often heard to say she only wished she were dead. Her complaints found a ready echo in her young friend's bosom. The two women made up their minds to die together; they lay down on the same bed and were found dead under the influence of charcoal fumes, leaving each of them a word of farewell to her lover: "I kiss you for the last time," said one; "I love you dearly," said the other, "but I would rather make an end of it all."

Sometimes a passionate, romantic friendship arises between young women, which produces the same despair as love and the same wish to die together. To give an instance; a work-girl of eighteen, who had been married for some months, had formed a close friendship at the workshop where they were employed with a companion three years her junior. One day (in May 1897) the husband on his return home found his wife and her young friend lying insensible on a sofa, having made an attempt to kill themselves by means of charcoal fumes. The younger girl was dead; the wife was still breathing, and was eventually brought round. Questioned as to the motive for her attempted suicide, she said: "My friend and I were unhappy. Having lost her parents, she had been placed in an establishment supported by public charity, but not liking it, she had been entrusted to the care of an aunt who put her to work in the same workroom with me. Many a time she spoke of putting an end to her life. For my own part I felt myself overwhelmed by a grief

I could not account for; I had left off eating, and was very often in tears. Then by common agreement we decided to commit suicide. We chose asphyxiation by charcoal, and stretched ourselves on a sofa to wait for death. . . . It is impossible for me to tell you precisely the motives that drove me to suicide; my husband is very kind to me, and lets me want nothing. It was not my friend who urged me to the step. It was just an act of pure madness on the part of both of us."

The romantic character of this double suicide comes out still more clearly in a letter the married woman had written before her attempt to kill herself: "Unable to live one without the other, we prefer to die together. We are happy at the thought.

"I die of disappointment and life-weariness. Berthe does not regret her aunt. I *do* regret my parents, and beg of them to forgive me. I beseech my husband also to be good to my little girl.

"Before entering on our last sleep, we ask to be buried side by side. We should love to have flowers on our grave."

Nothing is so contagious as the idea of suicide. It would seem as though ideas were like fruits; a sound apple put beside a rotten one does not make the latter sound, but a rotten apple put beside a sound one spoils it. Similarly morbid ideas are communicated with extreme facility, so much so that semi-madmen and alcoholic patients very often affect those surrounding them by way of suggestion. It is notorious that the habit of alcoholism frequently inspires ideas of suicide; in fact many sufferers of this kind end by killing themselves. Nor is it at all uncommon for them to induce their wives or mistresses to share their ideas of self-slaughter. For instance: in May 1897 at Paris, the police found a man lying dead, smothered by charcoal fumes, beside his wife, who was still breathing. The latter told the following tale: "On Sunday my husband spent his whole week's wages on absinthe. Monday, he showed signs of suicidal intentions, and would not let me do any work. Next

F

day he ordered me to buy a bushel of charcoal and borrow a brazier, which we kindled after papering up the doors and windows, and writing a letter he dictated." In this letter they said: "We have but one wish, to be united in the same coffin."

A jealous man, who is weary of his life, kills the woman he is in love with and then himself. The jealous woman who has ideas of suicide often succeeds in making her lover share them too, as in the following instance. In April 1895, a man and a woman were found in a bedroom at an hotel lying dead from charcoal fumes and closely embraced in each other's arms. The woman having recovered consciousness, related how, although married and the mother of six children, she had been the mistress of the man stretched beside her, who was likewise married and the father of a family; she went on to say that they had chosen to die together in order to escape the vexations involved in their false position. She stated further that the initiative had been taken by her lover. But as a matter of fact the judicial enquiry established the fact that it was she who had urged the commission of the act; jealous of the lawful wife and failing to induce her lover to break with her, she had made up her mind to suicide, so great was the pain this sharing of his affection occasioned her, and had succeeded in getting her lover to adopt the same resolution. She had gone to find him at his work and had taken him to the hotel to die there along with her. It was further shown by the enquiry that neither the woman, mother of six children as she was, nor the man, though father of a family, had felt any hesitation about abandoning their little ones, and that they were both happy and content to die. The woman had left the following lines: "I regret nothing I have done, do not weep for me; I only ask one thing—my children's forgiveness." The lover's letter ran thus: "I ask pardon with clasped hands of my two children. I quit this world quite happy and without regret."

When in the Middle Ages, under the empire of enthusiastic faith, a call to the religious vocation took the place of suicide, a man who entered the cloister in despair at disappointed love sought to draw the object of his passion there as well. When Abelard decided to go into a monastery, he forced Heloïse to take her vows before he had pronounced his own.

M. Sighele is of opinion that, in all instances of double suicide from love, " the one who decides the other to commit suicide is hardly ever the actual, material author of his own and his companion's death ; it is the weaker of the two, the one that did not originally wish to die at all, but was over-persuaded to this extreme course, that first strikes down the loved one and then commits suicide." " Here we have," he adds, " an instance of specialization of function ; in every suicidal, as in every criminal, double partnership, one plans, the other does." I have not myself noticed anything of the kind ; in almost all cases, the woman, afraid of failing in her purpose or disfiguring herself, begs her lover to kill her before putting an end to himself. I have never yet known a case of double suicide where the woman first struck down her lover and then proceeded to kill herself. This only happens when a woman commits a murder out of jealousy or revenge, and then puts an end to herself from remorse, but then this is not a case of double suicide at all. The one who carries out a double suicide with fire-arms is almost invariably the lover ; the reason is plain enough, and is given by Mme. Z——, when she says to Chambige : " You will kill me and yourself afterwards ; you are a man, and should be braver than a woman." The woman does not possess courage enough to kill her lover with his consent and then turn the weapon upon herself. In an exceptional instance, a woman of great energy of character, who wished to kill herself along with her lover, said : " The idea that vexes me is that of disfiguring myself ; but no matter, if Ferdinand's courage fails, I will take the pistol, place it under my chin and so blow my brains out. When Ferdinand sees me dead at his feet, he will not have the courage to endure life any longer."

Death by means of charcoal fumes and drowning give lovers the means of dying together without the necessity for one of the two to preface his own suicide by the murder of the other ; after kindling a brazier, they merely lie down on the bed in each other's arms, or else throw themselves simultaneously into the water. Instances are also known where lovers provide themselves each with a pistol, to the trigger of which is fastened a ribbon ; the young man pulls the ribbon of the girl's pistol, while the latter does the same to the man's, both firing at the same moment at a given signal.

The lover whose hand does not shake at firing several revolver shots at his mistress, is less firm when he turns the weapon upon himself; he does not fail to hit his mistress in a vital spot, but he often does so in his own case. Then very frequently the instinct of self-preservation asserts itself, his excitement cools and he has no wish left to start afresh ; "We wished to die together," one lover explained; "but I was unfortunate, I failed in my first attempt, and I had not the courage to fire a second shot at myself." It is just because the lover not unfrequently bungles the attempt on his own life and is afraid to try again, that Justice, confronted by the dead girl and the lover whose attempt on himself has been ineffectual, requires the latter to give an account of his conduct. On the other hand, I have known a case where the lover killed himself, but failed where his mistress was concerned.—If the woman survives her wounds, she never forgives the lover who has recoiled at the last moment for his lack of determination. Lately, a master at the College of P——, though at the time a man of thirty-seven, married, and the father of a family, had entered into relations of intimacy with a married lady of thirty-two, the mother of a little boy. Not being able to continue the intrigue, the lovers decided to kill themselves, the man with a pistol, the woman by means of a strong dose of laudanum. The latter drank the poison, but her life was saved by the energetic measures taken to counteract its effects. Learning afterwards that her lover had not kept his promise of shooting himself, she conceived so violent an anger against him that she bought a bottle of sulphuric acid and threw it in his face.

A woman, even when quite a young girl, when she has once made up her mind to die with her lover or her *fiancé*, is more obstinate in her purpose than a man; she begins afresh her attempts at suicide, when the first have failed. A girl who had chosen to die with her *fiancé* because her family were opposed to the match, after receiving a pistol shot in the head which only inflicted a slight wound, besought her companion to shoot her again.—But the most striking example of a woman's extraordinary tenacity of purpose when once she has resolved to die with her lover is that of Mme. X——, Dr Bancal's mistress; for seven long hours the lover was engaged in bleeding, hacking, poisoning his mistress, giving a dose of poison after using the bistoury, returning once more to the bistoury after the poison, without Mme. X—— expressing a single regret or manifesting any desire for the butchery to cease; it seemed as though it were a pleasure to her to receive death at her lover's hand. Corneille, who has expressed with such marvellous perspicacity every feeling of the human heart, makes Créuse say, speaking to Jason:

> " Laisse-moi le bonheur d'expirer à ta vue ;
> Souffre que j'en jouisse en ce dernier moment." [1]
> *Médée*, Act v. Sc. 5.

The two lovers had selected a strange mode of death, they had formed the project in fact of opening their veins and bleeding to death. I copy the account given by Dr Bancal before the Court of Assize:

" It was during the night of the 23rd, 24th, that L—— asked me to end her days, saying : ' We must begin.' I

---

[1] " Leave me the bliss of dying as I gaze on thee ; suffer me to enjoy that sight at this last moment of my life."

answered : 'We have plenty of time.' She returned : 'But you forget you told me it would perhaps be a long business . . . ; we must begin.' I opened two veins in her legs, and she lost a great deal of blood, . . . and fainted away. On her recovering consciousness, I asked her whether she wished 'to go on living, and she said 'No!' I spoke to her of using my bistoury, but she told me she did not wish her heart pierced with cold steel. I then asked her if she would drink some acetate of morphia, which I had brought with me. To this she assented ; I divided the poison into two portions, of which I gave her one and swallowed another glassful myself, . . . I then opened the artery in her left arm. While this was doing, day broke ; I asked her a second time if she wished to live, and again she said 'No!' and begged me to get done with it. 'You spoke to me of a means, employ it,' she said ; 'we must make an end, make an end !' I gave her a cut with my bistoury, but it was not strong enough ; I gave myself one also. We remained so some moments, thinking our last hour was come. L—— presently revived : 'I do not feel myself to be dying,' she said, 'we must begin again ; try to make this the final one. . . .' I struck her a second blow, and she said : 'Ah! that is a good one !' and pressed my hand. After that, she never stirred again. I then cut myself three times with my bistoury ; I lost blood, but I did not succeed in killing myself. I plunged the instrument three times more into my open wounds, and turned it round and round, without any better success." When at last the room was entered, Mme. X—— was found dead, and Dr Bancal lying bathed in his blood. When compresses were applied to his wounds, he endeavoured to tear them off, declaring he wished to die ; he would not allow them to remove his mistress's dead body, crying repeatedly he was going to join her soon. Some days afterwards, while his wounds were being dressed, he introduced his finger into one of them to tear it wider open. Again during the course of his examination, he twice over tried to kill himself.

The incredible obstinacy with which Dr Bancal strove to kill his mistress, the courage with which the latter submitted voluntarily to these murderous operations, are both to be accounted for by the amorous exaltation which intoxicated them. A state of amorous, as of any other kind of exaltation, mystical or political, supplies a special energy that makes pain unfelt. It even makes it sweet and pleasant to die by the hand of the person loved.

"Oh! qu'un coup de poignard de toi me serait doux!"[1]   HERNANI.

This strange cry, that would seem to be the utterance of a maniac, is yet a natural enough one in the mouth of a passionate lover.

It might well seem that if there is one profession more than another that should cure the spirit of romantic exaltation, it is the medical. Nevertheless, Dr Bancal is not the only doctor who has chosen to die together with his mistress. There was a notorious case at Berne in 1864, in which a Dr Demure and his *fiancée* poisoned themselves, simultaneously.

In fact no profession is a safeguard against this amorous delirium, so akin to positive madness, when passion has once reached its paroxysm, and so closely connected with suicide, when it is thwarted.

> "Même l'homme du peuple et le moindre garçon,
> A qui certes jamais Zénon ne fit leçon,
> Même la jeune fille, humble enfant qui s'ignore,
> Qui se sentait dresser les cheveux hier encore
> Au seul mot de mourir, tout d'un coup enhardis,
> Ils vont oser régler ces apprêts si maudits,
> Méditer longuement, d'un œil plein de constance,
> Le poison ou le fer, leur unique assistance."[2]

---

[1] "Oh! how sweet would be a dagger thrust from thee!"

[2] "Even the common man, and the meanest lad, whom Zeno certainly never taught the lesson of Stoicism, even the young girl, poor ignorant child, who but yesterday would feel her hair rise on end at the mere name of Death, in an instant grown courageous, are bold to make their dismal preparations for suicide, and weigh deliberately, with unflinching eye, poison or the steel — their only hope of aid." Leopardi, *translated* by Sainte-Beuve.

CHAPTER III.

HATE AN INCIDENT OF LOVE.

"The only implacable hatreds are those of Love."
PROPERTIUS, II. viii. 3.

I HAVE described in the two preceding chapters how Love frequently paves the way to Despair and Death, whether voluntary or involuntary. I intend to enquire in the present one in what ways Love may be changed into Hate, and how this loving Hate may lead directly to the murder of the beloved object. "I hate and I love," Catullus says; "you will ask me perhaps how this can be; nay! I cannot tell you, I only know it is so, and suffer in the knowledge." What is the explanation of this love, instinct with hate? Why is it that magistrates, when questioning women accused of having killed their lover, constantly hear them plead in excuse: "I should never have killed him, had I not loved him"?

La Rochefoucauld was right when he said: "If we judge Love by the most of its effects, it has more kinship to hate than to friendship." Love it is, in very deed, that strikes the savage blow, love that kills by steel and fire; the lover knifes the object of his affections, the mistress shoots her lover or throws vitriol in his face. Thus Love is very near akin to hate and hate to love. It may even be said there is ever something of hate in love and of love in hate. A jealous man loves and hates at one and the same time; he is tender at once and brutal; he overwhelms the person loved with caresses, longing all the while to strangle her. Tortured by jealousy, lovers quarrel and make it up again with kisses, love and hate; a prey to the most contradictory emotions, they pass from love

88

to hate, and from hate to love. Reproaches, recriminations and bitter words form part of the tenderest passion, even when reciprocated, making it at once sweet and bitter.

Love is so near a neighbour to hate, that the lover hates the woman he adores, if she resist his wishes, nay! sometimes hates her after she has yielded to his desires. Amnon, son of David, we read in the Bible, deeply enamoured of his sister, "forced her and lay with her. Then Amnon hated her exceedingly ; so that the hatred wherewith he hated her was greater than the love wherewith he had loved her."[1] In the love affairs of monarchs, so near is love to hate, that there is a very small interval between adoring and murdering the beloved person. The loves of King Henry VIII. ended in the disgrace of Catherine of Aragon, the decapitation of Anne Boleyn, the repudiation of Anne of Cleves, the decapitation of Catherine Howard.

What a strange mixture of love and hate was displayed in the tragic liaison between the poet Alfred de Musset and the great novelist Georges Sand! Loving madly and hating furiously, they part with screams of fury only to come together once more with a burst of tenderness. This torment they renew again and again, finally coming out of this duel of the affections, mangled and sore with hard fighting, weeping, groaning and broken-hearted, filled with an imperative need to confide to the public their sufferings and grievances, in verses dripping tears and novels full of gall and bitter sobs! The life these lovers led together was so grievous, that after the rupture of their relations Georges Sand wrote to Sainte-Beuve saying she would rather blow out her brains than begin afresh the existence she had known with Alfred de Musset. After a reconciliation which preceded the final separation, she had already written to her lover: "Shall we go and blow our brains out together at Franchard? 'twill be the quickest way to end it." And some days later on, Alfred de Musset himself, not less weary of the life he led with his capricious mistress, at once adoring and despising her, reminded her

[1] 2 Samuel, xiii. 14, 15.

of this projected suicide, writing to her in these words:
" . . . If you are for renouncing life . . . remember the
oath you swore me, and do not die without me." [1]

Simultaneously with the first inception of a passion
arises the possibility of a tragedy, a suicide, a murder.
At the instant a man and a woman engage in an idyll of
love, they very often, quite unawares, are raising a question
of life and death ; and if they were not blinded by love,
they might well ask themselves :

> " Mais qui sait ce qu'il doit ordonner de mon sort,
> Et si je viens chercher ou la vie ou la mort ? " [2]

Indeed it is no uncommon thing to see a love idyll
transformed into a tragedy. In his essay on *Bajazet*, La
Harpe says in the course of a severe criticism of the
piece : " Idylls should not be made the preludes of
murders." But this literary dictum rests surely on an
incorrect observation of the psychological facts ; as a
matter of fact love idylls do frequently end in sanguinary
dramas. Love, the principle of life, is often a principle
of death to boot. When Dante in the *Inferno* goes down
into the second circle of hell, he sees there " more than a
thousand shades . . . that Love hath sent out of life."

It was not without good reason that the Greeks, who
assigned to Venus (Aphrodité) the most pleasing and
poetical epithets, gave her also one grim and horrid title,
that of the " murderous Venus." [3] The records of our Courts
of Law attest the fact that no name can be better justified.
Every day the Correctional Tribunals and the Assize
Courts have before them men who have struck, insulted,
killed women they loved, and women guilty of the same
violence towards their lovers. In several cases of the
sort, I have noted the fact that the lover had killed
or tried to kill his mistress a few moments after having

---

[1] Marieton, p. 194.

[2] " Yet who knows what may be ordained me by fate, and if I am to find
life or death ? "

[3] Plutarch, *De Amore*. The Romans spoke of *Saevus Amor* (Cruel Love).

had intimacy with her.   It is the most violent affections
that are followed by the most ferocious hatreds.

Without actually resorting to crime, lovers constantly
make each other suffer, as if they were mortal foes.   When
still in the period of ecstatic passion, they could not credit
a possible to-morrow of hate and anger ; yet after a few
weeks' time, we often see them tormenting and torturing
one another.   Taught by experience, Georges Sand was
so well aware of the truth that love will often change to
hate, that at the very beginning of her new liaison with
Dr Pagello, she wrote to him : " I love you, because you
please my fancy ; it may be I shall find myself forced to
hate you before long."

Why does Hermione have Pyrrhus, whom she loves,
murdered ?   Why does Roxane cause Bajazet, whom she
would fain marry, to be strangled ?   Why does Othello
smother Desdemona, whom he adores ?   La Bruyère has
supplied a word of explanation to account for this strange
mixture of love and hate that fills lovers' hearts : a lover
longs to make all the happiness, or if this cannot be, then
all the unhappiness, of the one he loves.   " To love is to
love oneself ; a man loves in order to be happy, for his
own sake, for the bliss he hopes to win from the object of
his affections.   The lover loves the loved one, as the
wolf loves the lamb." [1]   The fact is he is more preoccupied
with his own happiness than with the happiness of the
individual he loves,—a truth which has been finely expressed by Corneille in the following verses :

> " Vous-même qui brûlez d'un amour si fidèle,
> Aimez-vous Domitie ou vos plaisirs en elle ?
> Et quand vous aspirez à des lieux si doux,
> Est-ce pour l'amour d'elle ou pour l'amour de vous ?
> De sa possession l'aimable et chère idée
> Tient vos sens enchantés et votre âme obsédée. . . .
> C'est par là qu'elle seule a droit de vous charmer,
> Et vous n'aimez que vous quand vous croyez l'aimer." [2]

---

[1] Plato.

[2] " Nay ! you yourself who burn with so faithful a love, do you love Domitia
or but the joys you find in her ?   And when you aspire to such fond regions,

Happiness on the part of the person loved is a torment, an insult, for the lover, if he is not the author of it, and does not share it ; he will cry with Phèdre :

" Non, je ne puis souffrir un bonheur qui m'outrage. " [1]

What drives the jealous lover mad, is the thought of the happiness his mistress is about to enjoy with his rival, and it is to hinder that happiness he kills her.

The same sentiment dominates the forsaken woman ; she might perhaps resign herself to her abandonment, if she were not tortured by the thought of her lover's coming happiness with another woman. She kills him to prevent his tasting this felicity ; she cannot bear him to be happy except through herself. The eighth of August 1891, the Assize Court of the Department of the Bouches-du-Rhône adjudicated on the case of a married woman of thirty-five, who had fallen in love with her cousin, a young man of twenty-five, himself married and father of a child. She commenced by sowing dissension between him and his wife, subsequently poisoning her own husband that she might belong entirely to her lover. Soon however she began to notice a progressive coldness on the part of her lover ; he felt regret for having treated his wife as he had done, and was anxious to make it up with her. She made desperate efforts to prevent any such reconciliation ; then presently, when she was convinced her lover was going to escape her, rather than see him happy with his wife and child, she poisoned him. The lover suffers positive pain at the happiness of the loved one when it comes from another, and longs accordingly to turn it into unhappiness; he would rather see the woman he loves unhappy or even dead than happy with another. There are only a very few lovers of a gentle, timid disposition, individuals in whom

is it for love of her or of yourself? The flattering and tender thought of possessing her holds your senses bewitched and your soul enthralled . . . herein alone has she power to charm you, and all you love is yourself, when you think you are loving her." Corneille, *Tite et Bérénice*, Act i. Sc. 3.

[1] " No ! I cannot endure to see a bliss that is an outrage to me."

the psychical side of love is better developed than the physiological, who kill themselves, expressing a wish meantime that the girl who has refused to marry them, or the mistress of whom they are jealous, may be happy with another.   They say like one of the characters in *Psyché*:

> " Vivez, belle Princesse, et vivez pour un autre ;
>   Nous le verrons d'un œil jaloux,
> Nous en mourrons, mais d'un trépas plus doux
>   Que s'il nous fallait voir le vôtre.
> Et si nous ne mourons en vous sauvant le jour,
> Quelque amour qu' à nos yeux vous préfériez au nôtre,
> Nous voulons bien mourir de douleur et d'amour." [1]

In the first chapter of the present work, I gave a certain number of instances of unfortunate or jealous lovers who die of love and grief or kill themselves in despair, desiring all the while that the object of their passion may be happy with another.   To the cases there adduced, I may add another of quite recent date.   A young man, twenty-nine years of age, belonging to a highly respectable family, being in love with a girl of a coquettish and fickle nature, tormented by jealousy, but without the courage to break off the connection, preferred to commit suicide after breakfasting for the last time with her.   After the meal he had two letters delivered to her, one for her relations, the other for herself.   Then he took a carriage to the Bois de Boulogne, and quitting it on his arrival, went off and shot himself dead with a revolver.   This is a copy of the letter he wrote to the girl he loved :

" MY DEAR LOUISE,"

"Farewell !   I ask but one thing, your forgiveness.   My only fault is to love you too much, my dear ; I am unable to ensure your happiness.   But, dear little woman, do not be cast down ; you are young and pretty and clever, you

---

[1] " Live on, fair Princess, and live for another ; we shall look on him with a jealous eye, we shall die at the sight, but by a gentler death than if we had to behold yours.   And if we do not die, while saving your life to enjoy some love that we see you preferring to our own, yet would we right fain expire of grief and love."   *Psyché*, Act ii. Sc. 4.

have every gift to win love, and you will certainly find
some one less dull than I am, who will understand you
better ; he will not love you so well, but he will amuse you
far more.   Then, my dear, two men at once,—'tis surely
one too many.   No doubt, if I saw you indifferent to your
friend the *avocat*, I should not grieve, but every time you
mention him, your face is wreathed in smiles.   No ! dearest,
he is not indifferent to you, you like him ; well, then! I am
one too many.   So I am dying for you, to make you
happy.   Your happiness is all I wish, darling little girl.
In return I only ask your forgiveness.   You will know
there is one man on earth who loved you very sincerely,
and he has never played you false.   Farewell, farewell,
Louise, you are my only love, and my last.   Farewell, I
give you a thousand kisses.   Excuse my scribble ; but
remember my last day is come, and in my present state I
cannot write better.   Farewell, I die for you, Louise.
Farewell."

Men who kill themselves to work the happiness of the
woman they love, but who do not love them, are few in
number.   No doubt to love is to wish the happiness of the
person loved, but on condition of sharing it oneself, of
being its author, to wish in fact one's own happiness as
involved in the possession of the beloved object.   The
natural cry of passion is Médée's : "*I, I* alone, and I am
satisfied."

The effects of Love vary according to the character of
those experiencing it.   All men do not love after the same
fashion, because they have not the same temperament, the
same disposition.   There are several sorts of love.   The
love that comes more from the heart than from the senses
still remains tender and resigned, if it is unfortunate ; it
suffers " more in sorrow than in anger " ; it is rarely
tempted to resort to murder ; if it dees feel the temptation, it escapes it by suicide ; it would rather die than kill,
and dies forgiving.

The love that kills and poisons and inflicts pain is sensual love. This it is that fills men with hate and spite and vindictiveness. In brutal natures, physical love becomes phrenzy at the smallest opposition, and leads to the commission of the most savage acts of violence. The man grows mad to satisfy his sexual desires ; he seizes the knife to strike the woman that resists him, just as the male among brutes uses his claws and teeth to subjugate the female to his appetites or punish her resistance. In order to possess a woman who resists or even one who merely asks delay before yielding, we see men threaten her with a knife, level a revolver at her, squeeze her throat till she is all but strangled. The craving to possess is sometimes so violent, mere delay is cause enough for an outburst of fury. I knew the case of a young man who killed his *fiancée* because she refused to let him have her before marriage. The girl's mother having remarked to him "that he would have her at Easter," he replied, " Easter is too long, I cannot wait." Another young man killed the girl he loved and whom he had asked in wedlock because she answered she was still too young to marry.

Murderers from love express their craving to possess by the cry, " I *must* have her." "By force or fraud I *must* have her ! " said one murderer of this kind. " I *must* have her, even if I should go to the scaffold for it," cried another lover who had been shown the door. So much is this seemingly trivial phrase the natural cry of sexual passion, that the greatest of Christian orators, Bossuet, makes use of it in the pulpit : " 'Twill perhaps be but a glance," he says. . . . " But beware. . . . A fire darts from vein to vein. He *must* have her ; he *must* win her. But it is adultery ; what matter for that ? " The phrenzy of the man who murders the woman who resists him arises from the violence of the craving, which is impatient to be satisfied and irritated at every obstacle it encounters.

The ferocity of the murderer from motives of love comes not only from the violence of his passion, but also from the exasperation due to wounded self-love. A man who is repulsed by the woman he is enamoured of, is as deeply hurt in his pride as in his affections, and his chagrin easily grows into an implacable hate, greedy for revenge. "You struck this poor girl in the most cowardly and treacherous way," a judge of the Court of Assize said to a prisoner in the dock, "you wished to kill her?" "Yes!" replied the accused, "because she would not love me, because she scorned me." *The Judge*: "You wanted to revenge yourself for her disdain?" *The Accused*: "Yes! for her disdain, which has driven me mad."—The workman Laffargue, whose crime of passion inspired Stendhal with so strange an admiration, had some days before he murdered his mistress, put the following question to an ex-gendarme of his acquaintance, making as though it were a case that interested one of his comrades: "What would you do, if you were attached to a woman, and she would not see you any more, but left you in the lurch?" "Why! I would console myself with another," answered the gendarme philosophically. "You talk mighty fine," retorted Laffargue; "that's all very well in theory, but in practice it's not so easy, I can tell you." "All a mistake," replied the gendarme; "if your friend will look close, he will find all his grief of mind comes from offended self-love." Laffargue thought a moment, and then exclaimed: "True enough, self-love does play the chief part in the matter."

Love is more cruel in men than in animals, because, if vanity increases the pleasure of possession, self-love wounded by disdain largely augments the pain of rejection and the desire for vengeance. This simple explanation of crime as the result of passion, which occurred to the mind of a plain gendarme, yet escaped the sagacity of Stendhal, who is accounted by Taine, I know not why, the greatest psychologist of the Nineteenth Century. Oreste, Pyrrhus, Hermione, Roxane, Médée are victims every one of them quite as much of self-love as of love. Racine, who as a psychologist is of a very different order of penetration to Stendhal, depicts Oreste as "ashamed to have uttered so many useless vows," as dreading to become "the bye-word of Epirus," like the young lover who, rejected by the girl he wants to marry, kills her out of vexation, exclaiming, "People will say she would not have me!"—Hermione is proud and haughty; offended and humiliated by the scorn of Pyrrhus, she boils with rage, when told that Pyrrhus disdains her:

> "Qui vous l'a dit, seigneur, qu'il me méprise?
> Jugez-vous que ma vie inspire du mépris?"[1]

She suffers cruelly in her pride from Pyrrhus' disdain. How this scorn of his will avenge Oreste for the indifference she shows to him!

> "Quelle honte pour moi!   Quel triomphe pour lui!
> Est-ce là, dira-t-il, cette fière Hermione?
> Elle me dédaignait, un autre l'abandonne."[2]

Unable to sit still under the blow of this humiliating neglect, she thinks that "her repute" requires her to exact vengeance;

> "Si je le hais, Cléone, il y va de ma gloire."[3]

Chimène has the same cry for revenge, and almost all Corneille's heroines, whose pride impels them to claim vengeance, and the thought of their wounded honour.

> "Il y va de ma gloire, il faut que je me venge,"[4]

exclaims Chimène; and again in *Pulchérie*, Irène declares:

> "Après deux ans d'amour, il y va de ma gloire,
> L'affront serait trop grand."[5]

When Médée is hesitating whether she shall exact vengeance on Jason or no, it is the remembrance of the affront she has received and the fear of becoming the

---

[1] "Who told you, my lord, that he scorns me? Think you my life inspires him with contempt?"

[2] "What shame for me! What triumph for him! Is yonder, he will cry, the proud Hermione? She scorned me; another now forsakes her."

[3] "If I hate him, Cléone, 'tis due to my repute I should."

[4] "'Tis due to my repute; I must avenge myself."

[5] "After two years of love, 'tis a question of my good repute, the insult would be too unbearable."

laughing-stock of her enemies, that kindle her anger afresh and reawake the thirst for revenge.

"Ah, me!" she exclaims in Euripides' tragedy of Medea, "unhappy victim of my untameable pride. . . . Should I become a mockery to my foes by leaving my enemies unpunished? Up, up, Medea, prepare your plans. . . . You must never be a laughing-stock in the eyes of Sisyphus and Jason."

What is it but pride wounded by Bajazet's indifference that inspires Roxane with her longing for revenge? This Sultana, who calls on Bajazet to marry her, and offers herself to him, the crown in one hand, the rope in the other, breathes only vengeance when once she sees herself disdained:

> "Qu'il meure! Vengeons-nous." [1]

The woman who has been forsaken suffers moreover in her self-esteem at the thought that her enemies and her rival will laugh at her abandonment. This is the feeling that stirs Hermione when she says to Pyrrhus:

> "Vous venez de mon front observer la pâleur,
> Pour aller dans ses bras rire de ma douleur." [2]

Nor is it only the kings and queens of tragedy that commit crimes of passion as much from wounded self-esteem as from disappointed love. The most commonplace criminals, mere working men and women, are not less susceptible in this direction, not less easily wounded in their pride by the scorn of the one they love. It is beyond belief how great is the part played by self-love in amatory crimes committed by men of the people; it may be their susceptibility is even more acute than that of better born folks.

It is now some years ago that I was present at the trial of one Silvy at the Assizes of the Department of the Bouches-du-Rhône. He was a young farmer, who had one

---

[1] "Let him die; we must have vengeance."

[2] "You come to note the pallor of my brow, to return to her arms and make merry at my pain."

night made his way into his sister-in-law's bedroom, with whom he was deeply smitten, and with savage fury dealt her four stabs with a knife in the throat, the bosom and the arms, all because the young woman, another man's wife and the mother of three small children, had refused to yield to his wishes. Cross-examination brought out the fact that the young murderer was afflicted with a repulsive disease, and had been excessively wounded in his self-esteem by the disgust he inspired in his sister-in-law's mind.

It is with this same desire of exacting vengeance for the scorn of the woman who repels their advances that rejected lovers do not limit themselves to killing their victim; they slander her into the bargain, falsely pretending they have received her favours, in order to salve their humiliated self-esteem. I was myself on the bench at the trial in the Assize Court of the Bouches-du-Rhône of a certain Sicard, who was for ever persecuting with prayers and menaces a young girl named Amélie B——, the daughter of a popular and highly respected railway employé. At the instance of the girl's parents, the Commissary of Police had Sicard summoned before him and represented to him how unreasonable were his endeavours to force the girl to listen to his offers of love. Wounded in his self-love, Sicard answered to the effect that she had not always scorned him, but had several times come to see him. This was an odious calumny, for an autopsy of the girl's dead body, held subsequently, proved her a virgin. Still under the domination of the violent chagrin the girl's disdain occasioned him, Sicard proposed to a printer that he should publish in his paper some verses he had written and in which he had the effrontery to allude to the favours he had never actually received. On the printer's refusing, he flew into a violent passion and threatened to smash his presses. Anxious at any price to overcome the girl's resistance, he showed her a bottle of sulphuric acid and a loaded revolver, threatening to use them if she persisted in her rejection of him. A few days later he bought two large-bladed kitchen knives, lay in wait for Amélie at the door of the workroom where she was employed and called on her to stop. On her refusal to do so, he gave her three knife thrusts in the back, and the poor child fell dead, after uttering two loud screams.

The accused in this instance was a common scamp, a conceited, quarrelsome, dissipated fellow. It was different with the two elders who calumniated Susannah, in order to avenge themselves for her disdain ; for they were both of them Judges respected for their wisdom. The story is very old, but it might well have happened yesterday, so striking is the actuality of its details. The two old men, who had conceived a violent passion for Susannah, used to be constantly meeting in the neighbourhood of her abode, but took good care not to confess to one another the motive that brought them thither, each hoping to achieve success before the other. One day, however, their secret slipped out ; after walking a while underneath Susannah's windows, they went away, each his own way, to dine. Each made what haste he could to return to his post of observation, and meeting afresh without an excuse to account for their presence in the same spot, they were constrained to mutually avow their passion. The sequel is familiar to all. Daniel, who displays all the acumen of a trained examining magistrate of our own day, questioned them separately, proved the existence of contradictions in the accounts given by the two judges, and confounded the calumniators of Susannah's good name. Nowadays, no less than two thousand years ago, the slanderers of a good woman who resists attempts on her virtue, are often functionaries of high rank, who having the woman in their service and under their orders, revenge themselves for her rejection of their proposals by evil insinuations. In other instances, we find men who have been repulsed by a married woman they are enamoured of, intentionally rousing the husband's jealousy in order to sow dissension between the couple, and so make the wife unhappy.

Similarly women who see themselves repulsed by men

they love do not hesitate to employ calumny as a means of revenge for the slight.   History is full of accounts of such acts of female vengeance.   Racine has not failed to attribute this trait to Phèdre; as soon as the wife of Theseus realizes with certainty that she cannot induce Hippolyte to share her guilty passion, furious at the affront, she accuses him to his father of having wished to ravish her, instilling her evil insinuations with an essentially feminine artfulness:

> ". . . La fortune jalouse
> N'a point en votre absence épargné votre épouse,
> Indigne de vous plaire et de vous approcher,
> Je ne dois désormais songer qu'à me cacher." [1]

When a magistrate questions a woman who has avenged her lover's desertion of her by murdering him, he often receives the reply: "I had too much pride to submit to such an affront; honour required me to exact vengeance." The prouder a woman's character, the more exasperated is she at the scorn she has had to put up with, the more does she dream of vengeance.   A woman who loves fondly, but has little pride, suffers bitterly at her lover's defection, but she does not think of punishing him.   Such is the case with Bérénice and Mlle. de la Vallière, women of gentle, modest, unassuming disposition, ready for suffering and self-sacrifice.   Médée, Hermione, Roxane, on the other hand, are greedy for vengeance, because they are full of pride.   Even in crimes proceeding from love, it is true to say with Holy Writ that "pride is the root of all evil."

The opposite sentiments of love and hate are so inextricably commingled in the heart of a forsaken woman, or of an unhappy and jealous lover, that often they cannot tell themselves what their real feelings are, and exclaim with Hermione:

---

[1] ". . . Envious fate has not in your absence spared your spouse; unworthy to please or even to come near you, I ought henceforth to think of naught but to hide my face."

"Ah ! je ne puis savoir si j'aime ou si je hais ! " [1]

In very truth, they love *and* hate at one and the same time. When a maiden who has been forsaken reminds her faithless lover of his promises of marriage and beseeches him to keep them, she is a prey simultaneously to anger and affection, she curses and covets him all at once, she menaces him with death, fondly loving him all the while. The letters she addresses to him are full of tenderness and violence, of appeals of love and threats of death.

St Thomas and Pascal supply the explanation of these self-contradictory emotions, declaring,—the former, that anger is a form of concupiscence, the latter, that concupiscence is at bottom only a sort of hate. Plato had long before noted the fact that concupiscent love quickly gives place to hate.

Hermione has Pyrrhus assassinated, the man she loves and hates at one and the same time. Oreste, who in his conversation with Pylades, had been able to read his own heart and recognize the truth that his transports of hatred against Hermione were in essence but an outburst of feelings of tender love, does not display the same sagacity in reading the heart of Hermione. He proves himself a very short-sighted psychologist when, fresh from the murder of Pyrrhus at Hermione's orders, he comes to her to claim the promised recompense. Hermione overwhelms him with reproaches for having executed the very commands she had laid upon him. She has no recollection in fact of having ever given him such orders :

"Mais, parle ; de son sort qui t'a rendu l'arbitre ?
Pour quoi l'assassiner ? Qu'a-t-il fait ? À quel titre ? " [2]

---

[1] " Ah, me ! I cannot tell whether I love or hate ! "
Compare also Rotrou's lines :

" Hélas ! que résoudrai-je en cette peine extrême ?
À peine je la hais que je sens que je l'aime."
(" Alas ! what decision can I come to in this agony of pain ?
Scarce do I hate her but I feel I love her still.")

[2] " But, speak ; who made you the arbiter of his fate ? Why kill him ? What has he done ? What right had you ? "

Then, when Oreste reminds her of her injunctions, she chides him for having failed to read her thoughts, for having believed in the hate of a frenzied lover's heart. Oreste had showed himself an abler psychologist, when to the cry of Hermione :

> "Ah ! ne souhaitez pas le destin de Pyrrhus,
> Je vous haïrais trop," [1]

he replied with an acumen beyond his wont :

> "Vous m'en aimeriez plus." [2]

Roxane has Bajazet slain only because she loves him and was fain to marry him. Médée herself, implacable Fury as she is, cannot refrain from telling Jason, on whom she is about to exact so terrible a vengeance :

> "Je t'aime encor, Jason, malgré ta lâcheté." [3]

When Pyrrhus is for wreaking vengeance on Andromaque who repulses him by doing her son to death, she cannot believe in the possibility of such cruelty, and says to Céphise :

> "Crois-tu que dans son cœur il ait juré sa mort ?
> L'amour peut-il si loin pousser la barbarie ?" [4]

Yes, truly ! love sore humiliated by the scorn of the beloved one is capable of inspiring the most barbarous acts. Is it possible to conceive more hateful words than those addressed by the son of Achilles to Hector's widow : "Wed me, or I take your son's life." This revolting bargain underlies all he says :

> "Je n'épargnerai rien dans ma juste colère,
> Le fils me répondra des mépris de la mère . . .
> . . . Allez voir votre fils . . .
> Madame, en l'embrassant, songez à le sauver." [5]

---

[1] "Ah ! desire not Pyrrhus' death, I should hate you too exceedingly."

[2] "Nay ! you would love me better for it."

[3] "I love you still, Jason, spite of your cowardice."

[4] "Think you in his heart he has sworn his death? Can Love push its barbarous cruelty so far ?"

[5] "Naught will I spare in my just anger ; the son shall answer to me for

The most tender and passionate lover turns into the most implacable enemy of the woman who repulses him ; he declares he cannot live without her, that he loves her and her only, that he is ready for any and every sacrifice to please her; yet, if she will not assent to his offers of marriage, he fires pistol bullets at the head and bosom of the woman he was so eager to wed, and plants a dagger in her back. In 1887, the Assize Court of the Bouches-du-Rhône adjudicated in the case of a young shoemaker, who had murdered under circumstances of exceptional cruelty a young and charming girl, with whom he was violently in love, because she refused to marry him, being already engaged to one of her cousins. The refusal deeply exasperated the young man. After first writing her a series of passionate love-letters, which were returned to him, he ended by sending threatening letters ; he notified her that he would kill her, adding, "when all is said and done, I shall only get twenty years." Meeting her one day, he threw himself upon her, and passing an arm round her neck,—while the unhappy girl begged him in a broken voice for Mercy ! Pardon ! Pity !—he stabbed her in the back with his shoemaker's knife. As she still continued her course, running away with the knife buried in her flesh, he darted after her in pursuit, crying, "What ! aren't you dead yet ?" Catching her up at last, he struck her a second blow, stretching her dead at his feet.

I could tell of a hundred similar crimes. Nor are suchlike deeds of cruelty committed only by men of the common herd, whose violent passions, inadequately modified by education, recall those of primitive savagery. Here is the account of a crime of love wrought in the full light of the seventeenth century by two men of the highest quality, the Abbé and the Chevalier de Ganges. Deeply smitten by the charms of their sister-in-law, the beautiful Marquise de Ganges, whose portrait Mignard painted, and furious at finding their suit rejected, they agreed together

the mother's scorn . . . Go see your son . . . and lady ! as you kiss his cheek, think how you may save his life."

to exact vengeance for the slight she had put on them.[1]
They forced their way at night into her bed-chamber,
the Chevalier sword in hand, the Abbé holding in one hand
a pistol and in the other a glass full of poison. With one
voice, their hearts swelling with rage and their eyes darting
fury, they cried to the Marquise : "You must die ! choose
between fire, steel and poison." After vainly beseeching
her brothers-in-law to spare her life, the Marquise, seeing
the Abbé's pistol and the Chevalier's sword pointed at her
breast, took the poison which the Abbé offered her. When
she had swallowed it, the murderers waited there for some
minutes to give the poison time to produce its effect, and
prevent anyone bringing aid to their victim. These two
assassins, who were condemned to be broken alive on the
wheel, belonged to most exalted society, and were men of
wit and intellect, more especially the Abbé. Only the
exasperation of disappointed love had turned them into
fiends.

These examples, which I might easily multiply, show
very clearly what we ought to think of that admiration for
crimes of passion which Stendhal brought into fashion.
A crowd of novelists, dramatic authors and even critics
keep reiterating that the man who does not love to the
pitch of crime cannot say he loves at all, that true and
genuine love does not stick even at murder. This piece of
literary sophistry is so widely prevalent as to be found
in the works of two authors, not less sensible as a rule
than witty, Jules Lemaître and Alexandre Dumas *fils*.
In an analysis he gives of a play of Maurice Bouchor's
called *Michel Lando*, the famous critic thus expresses himself: "Suppose that Michel loves for good and all—in
other words, as true lovers do, to madness and crime ; for
this, as you know, is what genuine love implies." [2] Dumas
fils, who has written so many witty and wise things, and
some rather outspoken ones, about love, says in his turn:

---

[1] The poet Gilbert wrote a "Heroical Epistle" on this tragedy of love,
which had an extraordinary degree of notoriety in the seventeenth century.

[2] *Journal des Débats*, 4th Jan. 1892.

"He who does not love like Des Grieux,[1] that is to say, if need be, to the pitch of committing crime or braving dishonour, cannot say that he really loves."[2]   I am myself persuaded, on the contrary, that true Love is inconsistent with criminality, that murder from motives of amorous passion proves nothing but the violence of a man's cravings and the exasperation of his wounded self-esteem. That savage cry of frenzied passion, "She balked my will, I struck her dead," which always evokes, I cannot tell why, an ardent quiver of sympathetic emotion in the spectators, even the female portion of them, of *Antony*, is habitually the utterance of men in whom the Magistrates of Justice note only coarse sensuality, monstrous selfishness, excessive excitability, savage cruelty. The love that kills is of the same type as the love that commits rape ; it is as a rule the appanage of natures compounded of mud, and blood, and evil pride. If it were true that the commission of murder or acquiescence in dishonour were the necessary proofs of a genuine passion, that none can love ardently without killing, without wielding revolver or dagger, we should have to allow true love to be the exclusive prerogative of scoundrels ; for it is no uncommon thing to find the criminal record of murderers from love showing previous convictions for offences against the common law. Indeed, if it were really needful to riddle a woman with knife thrusts in order to become a hero of romance, we should have to award the cobblers the blue ribbon of Love,—at any rate in Provence, where I have had opportunity to observe them,—for it is they who are most frequently guilty of crimes of violence from love, just as it was the shoemakers who, in Paris during the Commune, committed the greatest number of acts of brutality.

Passionate love does not involve killing either others or oneself. But if we must compare homicide and suicide as proofs of true love, I should not hesitate to declare suicide to be more a mark of deep affection than murder.

---

[1] Hero of the Abbé Prévost's famous novel *Manon Lescaut*.
[2] A Dumas *fils*, *Entr' actes*, 3rd Series, p. 238.

Murderers from amorous passion are, as a rule, the most selfish, the most sensual and the most excitable of men in love.   Lovers who die of grief or kill themselves in despair are truer and better men than those who turn their rage on others.   The gentle, tender-hearted woman who, like Bérénice or Attalide, would rather suffer herself than cause others pain, loves better and more truly than the proud virago who, like Hermione or Roxane, does not hesitate to plunge into crime ; so great and noble is her love it enables her to forgive the very man who makes her suffer, and to desire for her faithless lover a happiness she can never share with him.

CHAPTER IV.

SEDUCTION AND DESERTION.

"'Tis sport for you, but death to us."

DESERTION involves every form of pain and suffering for a woman,—loss of the object of her love, scorn of her beauty, preference accorded to her rival, public disgrace made yet more poignant by the dread of seeing her rival and the world at large mocking her grief. "When I am in sorrow in my convent," said Mlle. de la Vallière, after Louis XIV. had forsaken her and showed his preference for Mme. de Montespan, "I will remember all they have made me suffer."

The woman who loves and is loved is proud and happy in the affection she inspires. Her self-respect is flattered by the passionate feelings displayed toward her ; preferred to all other women by the man she prefers to all others of his sex, she sees in this preference a homage to her beauty, sweetness and charm. The love she inspires increases her value both in her own eyes and those of all her friends ; knowing herself loved, she finds additional reasons for loving herself. On the other hand, when a woman is forsaken, what heartrending pangs must her affections endure, what wounds her vanity undergo![1] To believe herself beautiful and to be scorned, to think herself beloved and to be forsaken, what agony for a woman's self-esteem ! To lose the love that was her joy and pride, that satisfied at once her craving for tenderness and her

---

[1] When Catherine de Médicis laid proposals before Elizabeth of England, then thirty years of age, of a union with her son Charles IX., a boy of fifteen, the Queen replied she was too old for so young a monarch, who would neglect her. "I would rather die," she said, "than see myself scorned and forsaken." Mignet, *Marie Stuart*, vol. i. p. 179.

lust of power, what a bitter downfall of all her dreams!
In very truth, desertion is not only the loss of the object
of a woman's affection ; it means also the scorn of the
lover, and her humiliation in all her neighbours' eyes.
The death of the man she loves would be far less cruel
than his unfaithfulness. If she lost him by death, she
could at least find some consolation in weeping over
his grave ; time would change her sorrow into a gentle
melancholy.

But when the loss of the beloved one is aggravated by
his preference shown to a rival, what "a sorrow's crown of
sorrow" is here ! Her wretchedness is augmented by the
slight inflicted on her beauty, the ingratitude of her faithless
admirer, the triumph of another woman. Her sufferings
are all expressed in the heart-broken cry of Phèdre on
learning she has a rival :

> " Œnone, qui l'eût cru ? J'avais une rivale,
> . . . Ah ! douleur non encore éprouvée." [1]

This bitterness of the forsaken woman grows into rage
and fury at the thought that the being she adores and who
scorns her, loves another, that he is happy with her and in
her affection. She experiences the feeling Racine attributes
to one of his heroines :

> " Votre mort (pardonnez aux fureurs des amants),
> Ne me paraissait pas le plus grand des tourments." [2]

" The bitterest of all torments," Corneille tells us in one
of his less successful pieces, pieces in which nevertheless
many fine lines are to be found :

> " (C'est) voir en d'autres mains passer tout ce qu'on aime,
> C'est un malheur encor plus grand que le trépas." [3]

To these grievous sufferings common to all women for-

---

[1] " Œnoné, who could have credited it ? I had a rival, . . . Ah ! bitterness beyond all bitterness yet endured !"

[2] " Your death (forgive the fierce transports of loving hearts), your death
seemed not to be the bitterest of all torments."

[3] " Is to see all one loves pass into other hands ; 'tis a grief even bitterer
than death itself." Corneille, *Agésilas*, Act i. Sc. 3.

saken by those they love, must be added yet others in the case of a young girl who has been seduced and then deserted after receiving promises of marriage. Such a one suffers in her honour no less than in her love, and more than in her pride ; what drives her to despair, is not solely the treachery of her *fiancé*, but the loss of her good name as well.

A large number of young girls allow themselves to be seduced under promise of marriage to follow, and are then abandoned by their lovers. Poetry, novels and the stage have cast such a glamour over seduction, without giving a thought to the consequences resulting to the victim and her offspring, that many young fellows dream only of winning the aureole of Don Juan, and have no hesitation in making promises of marriage they never intend to fulfil. Public opinion, which is extremely hard toward the woman who has fallen, being on the other hand very indulgent for the author of her seduction, the employment of this form of deception is held to be quite a matter of course. I remember to have read in the report of a trial the following answer given by a seducer who was asked by the judge if he had promised marriage : " Of course I promised to marry her. How else do you suppose one sets about seducing a girl ? " Especially in the country, a sympathetic feeling springs up by reason of neighbourhood and association between a young man and a girl who work together or in near proximity to one another. In course of time the attachment becomes closer and closer, and the unscrupulous youth, eager to enjoy the girl's favours without incurring the responsibility of fatherhood, promises marriage, declaring he loves her only, and will never have any other wife. The girl resists at first, and waits to be formally asked in marriage, but her lover gives her a string of different excuses for putting off doing so ; he says his parents have not as yet made up their minds to give their consent, that they do not consider her well enough off, but they are old people, he adds, and when they are dead, he will be able to fulfil his promise. To overcome the final

scruples of the credulous girl, he talks of his ardent love,
declares how wretched he is, and goes through the comedy
of an intended suicide.

> " Il dira qu'il se tue . . .
> Mais Clarisse aime mieux le sauver et mourir." [1]

At last, believing in the sincerity of the love he manifests
for her, she ends by giving way. This proves her undoing,
for she will very soon find herself abandoned, especially if
pregnancy follows. The seducer takes her to a neighbouring town for her accouchement, and there, after slipping a
few coins into her hand, he tells her brutally to "get out of
it how you can. Don't talk to me of marriage. It is all
over between us; so don't rely on me any more." The
unhappy girl may weep, and beg, and pray, demanding
the fulfilment of the promised marriage that is to save her
good name and give her child a father; it is all to no
purpose. The seducer flies before the threats of binding
him to the marriage he has promised and the onerous
duties of a father; he remains callous to the grief and
shame of the woman he has made a mother, and often
leaves her entirely unprovided for. The period of pregnancy
passes in tears and loneliness. When her child is born, the
poor girl, who is now a mother without being a wife, tries
in vain to touch her betrayer's heart, to rouse in him the
paternal instinct; she tells him about the child and its
pretty ways and its likeness to its father; she beseeches him
to come and see it, but he refuses, and speaks of it coldly,
as if he were doubtful of his being its father at all. Sometimes, however, carrying on the comedy, he pretends an
affection for the child he does not really feel, and protests
his purpose of eventually recognizing it as his own and
marrying the mother, but always finds some excuse or
another for putting off the fulfilment of his fine promises.
"Who makes the child, should provide for it," says an
axiom one of these unhappy mothers without being wives

---

[1] "He will say he means to kill himself . . . But Clarisse would sooner
save him and die herself." Alfred de Musset.

reproduced almost word for word unconsciously in a letter written to her seducer, which I have beneath my eyes : " As you had the spirit to make it, have the spirit to provide for it." But your seducer, with all his fine bold spirit for the first, has no stomach for the second.

In cases where the mother abandons the child she has borne under such circumstances, it ʼs rare for her to be the first to conceive the idea of doing so ; it is the lover who advises the step, who urges the child's being put in the Foundling Hospital, much preferring to keep his resources for the supply of his own pleasures.

Of girls thus seduced and forsaken, some kill themselves in despair, others kill their lovers, some do both.

Those who end in suicide invariably forgive their faithless betrayer ; before their death, they write to bid him farewell and assure him of their unaltered love for the last time. " I bear you no grudge," writes one of them ; " I bid you farewell, my dearest, and kiss you a thousand times over, and our dear boy as well. I entrust you with the charge of my dear mother's tomb ; do not neglect it nor mine either." " Farewell ; be happy ! " writes another forsaken woman. " May you not be troubled by the thought of me, to remind you how I loved you. . . . My dream was to have been happy with you, but you would not ; you lied to me, and your lies were my death-blow. I would fain have lived to love you ; but no ! you would not. I die loving you fondly. I leave you my hair, which you must keep in memory of me."—Yet another writes to the man who has deserted her : " From the first day I saw you would never be my husband, I had only one thought, to die. If I cannot be your wife, at least I shall end my pain."

Nothing can well be more touching than these last farewells, replete with tender forgiveness, which they murmur in the very death agony. I read in a letter written by a girl to her faithless lover : " I love you still, and forgive you. Farewell, death is working in me."—Here is another letter written by a young woman of twenty-three to her lover, who had deserted her after making her the mother of a little girl.

" My beloved Louis, as your mind is made up about me, the best thing I can do is to die. Loving you dearly, I would fain end my sufferings.

" I send you my little girl's portrait and my own. Keep them, my dearest Louis, in memory of your Emma, who loved you to distraction.

" Louis, come to my funeral. I wish the last person to kiss me before they put me in the hearse to be you, my darling.

" Take good care of our little girl and kiss her lovingly for me. If she should ask you what I died of, tell her it was of loving too fondly.

" I am poisoning myself with cyanide.

" Farewell, my own Louis ; forgive all the vexation I am causing you.

" Farewell for ever. My fondest kisses for you and for our child.

" I would like my grave to be always covered with flowers ; come and visit it every Sunday with our child."

Even the woman who has been forsaken and driven to infanticide by her desertion, frequently forgives the villain who has ruined her ; she cannot force herself to curse the man she still loves in her heart of hearts. Thus Marguerite in *Faust*, in prison for the murder of her babe, still dreams of the lover she cannot help regretting, and throws herself into his arms when he reappears. Some unhappy girls under these circumstances go so far in their beautiful tender-heartedness as to write at the time of committing suicide to their relatives to make excuses for the seducer : " I pray you do not be angry with him," writes a poor girl to her sister ; " it is no fault of his if he has ceased to love me, while I love him still. I forgive him from the bottom of my heart."—True we find in some letters from the victims of desertion complaints and re-proaches such as these : " Why did you deceive me, why abandon me so cruelly ? why cause me such bitter pain ?" Yet these same complaints, these cries of agony, invariably conclude with words of love and forgiveness : " Still I send you my last and most ardent kiss," writes a poor deserted creature before committing suicide by means of charcoal fumes. In the letter of farewell she addresses to her lover before killing herself, the woman who has been betrayed and forsaken will very likely begin by styling him "wretch," but she always ends by telling him of her unabated love and full forgiveness. A young woman, deserted by her lover who had concealed his new address from her, having succeeded in discovering the latter, makes her way in his absence into his rooms and after tearing up his photograph which she finds on the chimney-piece, sits down to write the following letter: "Léon, you are a cur; I have found where you live at last. I thought till to-day you were doing it to try me. Still you know I love you all the time, so I think it best to kill myself. Forgive my doing it in your house. I love you. I adore you. No woman will ever love you like me. I kiss you for the last time." Then seating herself on a chair at the foot of the bed, she seizes a revolver she had brought with her and shoots herself through the heart.—"Already you have the death of two women on your conscience; remember the 17th December 1896" (the day of her suicide), writes another desperate woman.—Yet another letter: "When you receive this letter, I shall have ceased to live. I cannot live without you, still less know that you are with another woman. I might have been such a happy woman with you; but alas! you would not let me."—"I cannot live without you," writes a young Spanish woman; "I bid you farewell. I give you a thousand kisses, for I have loved you well. Farewell then, my own G——. Forgive me for giving you the trouble of having me carried to the Morgue, for that is all I have to expect. Still I should have dearly loved to die on your bed, my G——. If you love me a little, remember the happy hours we have spent together. Ah! well, as such is my destiny, I am going to die, your lover still."

This characteristic of the forsaken woman, who forgives the faithless one and chooses rather to suffer and die than to pain and kill, is depicted by Racine in Bérénice; she too forgives, and thinks of ending her own life. Titus has guessed her intention :

> "Vous cherchez à mourir ? et de tout ce que j'aime
> Il ne restera plus qu'un triste souvenir." [1]

As I have never yet found in the many letters I have read from women who have been deserted and have killed themselves in despair anything but words of love and forgiveness for the faithless lover, I cannot but ask the question whether Virgil is not guilty of an error in psychology in attributing to Dido, after her suicide, feelings of hatred towards Æneas, who meets her in the Shades.

> ". . . Didon garde un farouche silence,
> Se détourne en fureur de l'objet qui l'offense,
> Et ses yeux, d'où partaient des regards courroucés
> Demeurent vers la terre obstinément baissés." [2]

This persistence in hate on Dido's part seems to me inconsistent with the character of women who kill themselves, but always forgive the wrong-doer; nor does it justify the comparison Racine draws in the Preface to Bérénice between the Queen of Carthage and the woman deserted by Titus, inasmuch as the latter forgives, while the former does not. Dido's character is rather that of a woman who slays her betrayer than of one who kills herself, for she is animated by a vindictive fury against Æneas, and utters threats and imprecations more violent than those of Hermione against Pyrrhus ; her only regret is she did not burn all Æneas' ships, have all his comrades massacred, his son slain, and his body served up at a banquet. The character we have here is more that of Médée than of Bérénice.

The character of the woman who, when forsaken, kills

---

[1] "You are fain to die ? and of all I love, naught else will remain but a mournful remembrance."

[2] ". . . Dido keeps a grim silence, turning in fierce anger from the loathed object, and her eyes, that darted angry looks, remain obstinately fixed on the ground."

herself, is completely different from that of the woman who under like circumstances kills the author of her wrong.

The first is a meek, tender-hearted victim who suffers in silence, complains with discreet and gentle moderation, and yielding more and more to the melancholy that overwhelms her, fades, sighs, and dies with forgiveness on her lips. The second is a fury, screaming, stamping, tearing her hair, threatening, striking and destroying. The mother of a girl who had been deserted and had killed her lover told the examining magistrate that her daughter during the two days preceding the murder, had screamed, wept, stamped, and torn out hair by handfuls. The mother added that she had used every endeavour to calm her, but that nothing she said made any impression on her. A woman in the transports of rage does not appreciate reasonable advice; she cries with Phèdre:

"Sers ma fureur, Œnone, et non pas ma raison,"[1]

and with Hermione:

"Tant de raisonnements offensent ma colère."[2]

The particular prisoner I have been referring to, had been so annoyed by the persevering efforts of her mother to bring her to a better frame of mind, that she turned her anger against her and repulsed her savagely.

The girl who has been forsaken by her lover would often resign herself to her fate, if the latter did not proceed to marry another woman; clinging to the hope of wedding him some day or at any rate drawing him once more to her side, she would meanwhile seek consolation in the love of her child. "Though you will not marry me," she says, "at least do not wed another; do not compel me to see you with another by your side." Seeing she is going to lose him for ever and be left alone, forlorn and disgraced, while her lover is happy with another woman, frantic with pain, tortured by jealousy, heedless of life and indifferent

---

[1] "Assist my passion, Œnone, and not my reason."
[2] "So many arguments of reason but chafe my anger."

to what may become of her, to the suffering she is about
to inflict and the scandal that must follow, she grasps a
revolver or seizes a cup of vitriol in her mad desire of
vengeance.

Some few years ago, vitriol was the favourite means of
revenge among women who had been betrayed. Nowadays
they, frequently use the revolver as well, a weapon they
are beginning to wield with great dexterity. Not long
ago at Marseilles a girl said to her lover, who was thinking of leaving her in the lurch : " If you were to leave me
for another woman, I would put a bullet in your head."
Instead of one, she put four into his head, as a matter of
fact, exhibiting a remarkable mastery of her weapon.

Often it is after the publication of the lover's marriage
with another woman or even during the marriage ceremony
at the town hall or in church, that the woman who has
been betrayed takes her vengeance. The picture her
imagination draws of the pretty scene, at which she had
dreamed of herself appearing in her white dress, happy,
charming and proud, on her bridegroom's arm, but where
now a hated rival is to usurp her place, brings her passion
to the boiling-point. Hermione in the play can contain
herself no longer when she hears Cléone's account of
Pyrrhus' marriage :

> " Je l'ai vu vers le temple où son hymen s'apprête
> Mener en conquérant sa nouvelle conquête,
> Et d'un œil où brillaient sa joie et son espoir,
> S'enivrer en marchant du plaisir de la voir." [1]

In a transport of jealousy, she exclaims :

> " Le perfide ! Il mourra ! " [2]

" Directly I heard of my lover's marriage with another
girl," said a young woman of Istres, near Arles, brought
up on a charge of murder, " my exasperation was so

---

[1] " I saw him lead towards the temple where his wedlock is preparing, like
a conquering hero his new conquest, and his eye beaming with joy and hope,
grow intoxicate as he walked with the delight of gazing on his bride."
[2] " Perfidious wretch ! He shall die."

intense I formed the design of killing him. I loaded a
pistol, disguised myself in men's clothes, and went out one
evening and posted myself at a spot where I knew he
must pass. As soon as he came, I fired my pistol at
him."—In Provence, no less than in Italy, a young girl
will often disguise herself as a man in order to strike a surer
blow at the lover who forsakes her, borrowing her father's
or her brother's clothes. Dr Lombroso, who notes the
fact, is wrong in his explanation of it, believing as he does
that she finds a pleasure in the masculine disguise.[1] The
girl disguises herself thus simply and solely to escape
recognition, though she but seldom succeeds in doing so,
her voice and gait almost invariably betraying her.

Sometimes it is during her pregnancy that the woman
who has been betrayed and deserted takes vengeance on
her lover, hurling a cup of vitriol in his face with the
words: "I want to leave *you* a keepsake, as you have
left *me* one of you."—One woman on trial for this crime,
who had inflicted horrible burns on her lover's face, said
to him, pointing to her belly, "Well! you've got that, and
I've got the rest."

If some forsaken women seek secrecy in avenging themselves, there are others who exact their revenge in the
full light of day and before all the world. Some years
ago a young woman of Marseilles fired several revolver
shots at her lover in one of the most crowded streets;
on the passers-by running up at the sound of the explosions, she told them with a quiet, but concentrated
fury: "It's nothing; I've merely killed my lover."

One of the motives determining a girl who has been
forsaken to employ vitriol as her means of revenge, is the
wish to disfigure her lover, in hopes of making his intended
marriage with another woman an impossibility. "I had
no intention of killing him," said a young woman on her
trial, "I only wanted to disfigure him. My hope was that,
if I spoiled his face, his *fiancée* would no longer have him,
and then that he would come back to me and marry me."

[1] Lombroso, *La Femme Criminelle*, p. 493 (F. Alcan, Paris).

Another young woman from the district of *Mireille*,[1] who had burnt out her lover's eyes, gave me a similar answer in cross-examination : "Now he is blind, my rival will refuse to marry him ; but I, I love him still, and I will make him forget everything."

Girls who have been betrayed and deserted do not always confine themselves to disfiguring the faithless lover ; not unfrequently they kill him, but yet it is but seldom, when they appear in the dock, that they fail to win the jury's commiseration by the pitiful tale of their wrongs and sufferings. A poor child in this plight told her story in the following words : "In despair at finding myself repulsed by the man who had made so much of me in former days, indignant at his cowardice, frantic at the thought of my pregnancy and his refusal to restore my good name by marriage, I determined on revenge. I bought a pistol ; I started to pursue him, and meeting him at last, shot at him. I went home again like a mad-woman, not knowing whether I had hit him, and hardly aware of what I was doing. . . . I know I deserve punishment, but the man has robbed me of everything, good name and happiness ; he has brought shame on me and desolation on my family, he has ruined all my hopes ; life is henceforth worthless to me."

Nor is it always young men that seduce girls ; a considerable proportion are ruined by men of greater age, but at the same time of greater dexterity and boldness, who abuse the authority they hold over them as proprietors of shops and masters of houses, nay! even by relatives, uncles, and brothers-in-law. Some years ago I was present at the trial of a case of murder committed by a young Corsican girl on her uncle, who had seduced, and then deserted her, after making her a mother. The whole affair is so dramatic in its details and offers so much that is of interest to psychologist and moralist, that I am going to recount the story *in extenso*.

[1] Maillanne, district of Mistral, is some few miles distant from Saint-Rémy, near Arles. It was to Saint-Rémy that Gounod resorted to compose the music of Mireille.

A military officer of high rank living in Paris with his family was short-sighted enough, being without fortune, to inspire his daughter, whom he idolized, with luxurious tastes, and had had her taught many accomplishments, such as riding, singing, skating. His brother, a rich merchant of Nice and a married man without children, having come on a visit, proposed to take his niece back with him to Nice for a while, and the father agreed to his doing so. The uncle started homewards with the girl, who was pretty, bright and lively, while his wife was no longer either young or pretty. He was not long in succumbing to the charm of her youth and beauty, and fell desperately in love with her. The poor child, spoiled as she was by her uncle who took care to satisfy all her luxurious tastes, and appreciating keenly the affection he showed her, but without understanding its true character, was defenceless against the assaults made on her virtue. Finally the uncle, abusing her faith in him and her inexperience of life, succeeded in overcoming her last scruples, telling her he only asked her for the sacrifice of her modesty, not of her good name, which he would safeguard in the eyes of the world. In fact, like Tartufe, he promised her,

"De l'amour sans scandale et du plaisir sans peur," [1]

without fear, that is without fear of a child to follow. But the scandal came, the pregnancy she had so much dreaded declared itself. Afraid his brother would blow out his brains for him, he overpersuaded his niece to tell her father it was she who had made the first advances. "If you love me," he said, "you should sacrifice yourself for me;" and the girl, to save her lover whom she was already passionately attached to, now her senses were once awakened, agreed to the sacrifice ; instead of accusing her uncle of his baseness, she excused him, casting all the reproach on herself and meekly bowing her head beneath a father's curse.

[1] "Love without scandal and pleasure without fear."

So terrible was the blow for the latter, who in his double capacity as a soldier and a Corsican, had the most exalted ideas of honour, that he was utterly broken down and overwhelmed by his child's dishonour, and in a very short space of time was dead of grief. His wife threw herself in despair from the window of the house where they lived, and was killed.[1] Some weeks after the death of her father and her mother's suicide, the girl gave birth to a child. The uncle at once separated it from its mother and put it out to nurse in another country, in the neighbourhood of Turin, using every means to alienate the young mother's affection from her child. Unable to succeed in this, he proposed to find her a husband and provide her with a rich dowry; but the girl refused. Presently quarrels occurred, and the uncle turned his niece out of the house, telling her he intended to send the child to the Hospital for Foundlings. This purpose of his exasperated the young mother beyond all bounds : " Let him abandon me, if he will," she cried, " but to abandon my child,—this I will never put up with." Soon the thought of killing herself or else the man who was for deserting her and her boy took possession of her, and she purchased a revolver. Her uncle knew of this, but made no attempt to take the weapon from her, hoping she would blow out her brains in a fit of despair. However the wished-for suicide did not come about. After hesitating for a while between suicide and murder, she decided finally to kill her uncle. Learning he was staying temporarily at an hotel in Marseilles, she sought him out there. Then, her hands behind her, her hair tossed back, her eyes blazing and lips trembling, the girl advanced on her uncle, challenging with words of fire : " Look at what you have made of me," she cried ; " you have dishonoured me, taken my all, killed

[1] Such suicides of parents as the result of grief and chagrin at a daughter's dishonour are not uncommon. I have even seen a case of a girl of fourteen committing suicide by charcoal fumes because she could not bear any longer to look on at her elder sister's bad life and the pain it caused her parents ; she died with the words, "The dead are the happiest," on her lips.

my father and mother with grief; now you abandon me,
and wish to abandon our child. Look me straight in the
face as I look at you." Her uncle only shrugged his
shoulders, telling her she was behaving like a play-actress,
and for his part he did not care for romances. This cold
ironical answer increased the girl's exasperation; she
drew her revolver and fired several shots at her seducer
who fell to the ground. As he lay there, the Corsican
fired off all the remaining chambers of her revolver point
blank at him, screaming, "Die, die!" Then in an instant,
when she saw the blood pouring from his wounds, her
anger vanished, and pity and love regained their empire;
she threw herself fondly on the wounded man, wiping his
brow, covering his face with kisses, pressing his hands and
exclaiming, "Forgive me! forgive me! no! dearest, you
must not die! You are only wounded, I will not have
you die."

However, the uncle did die of his wounds, and the poor
girl was brought up before a jury of the Department of
the Bouches-du-Rhône. While in prison, during the preliminary examinations, she wrote the following letter to
a worthy priest:

"Monsieur l'Abbé,—In the shipwreck of my feelings
and my life, to whom should I appeal if not to you who
are a priest and whose pity should be infinite, like God's?
Besides, are you not the only person who on hearing of
the terrible event, experienced feelings of pity and forgiveness? I know how you alone understood my sufferings;
you alone were not surprised, for had you not foreseen
a catastrophe. Only it was not what might have been
expected; instead of killing myself, I killed another, I
killed the man for whose sake I had given up and
abandoned everything. You did not reject me, when in
spite of all your prayers, I refused to renounce my guilty
love.[1] . . .

---

[1] In his study on the Romantic Drama (*Le Drame Romantique*, p. 207) M.
Nebout finds fault with Victor Hugo for having attributed to Blanche a persistent love for the King who has dishonoured her; is it possible, he says, that

"I am going to entrust to you what I hold dearest in the world; this man in dying has carried away all with him, happiness, the sun, the light of day, but he has left me a child, my consolation for future days, if I have strength to go on living. . . . If it is my fate to quit my prison presently, I would accept any form of work, and my child once more in France and by my side, I might yet enjoy a relative happiness, for to have the little one by me is still to have something of his father, whose image he is. . . . If I am condemned to remain always in prison, or at any rate for many years, I am resolved in that case to escape my punishment. As then I could be of no use to the child, it would not be shirking my duty to have done with life. In this case I leave my child to you.

"You remember, Monsieur l'Abbé, when to wean me from this affection, you told me to picture him to myself as dead and decomposed. Then I would not see him otherwise than as handsome and fascinating, as he was, and now it is all ended, and I have him continually before my eyes all bloody and disfigured.

"Ah! if only I had obeyed you the last time I went to see you and you begged me to bring you my revolver! If I had not had it to my hand, I should never have gone

---

a girl should love the vile seducer who has stolen her honour and should wish to save him? Yes! it is quite possible; Victor Hugo has not exceeded the bounds of truth, as we see from the case of this Corsican girl, who, seduced by an uncle many years older than herself, ended by loving him passionately. More than this, there are girls, who after being seduced by their own father, and after at first loathing the foul seducer who has taken advantage of them, end by loving him passionately. This is a fact I have verified in several criminal cases. To account for the phenomenon, we must remember that love springs from sensual gratification when once the senses are awakened. Alfred de Musset writes:

"Amour, fléau du monde, exécrable folie,
    Toi, qu'un lien si frête à la volupté lie." . . .

("Love, scourge of the world, hateful folly, that so fine a tie unites to lust. . . .) Of course all girls who have been betrayed do not feel love for their seducers; indeed most of them loathe and detest them. Their sentiments vary according to temperament, education and character. Nothing is falser than rash generalizations.

so far as I did. You told me, some time ago, how you
never thought so edifying a first communicant as I was
was destined to suffer herself to be led astray by a false-
hearted villain. What would you say now I have a man's
death to lay to my charge?

"Monsieur l'Abbé, pray that I may be acquitted."

Women experience as a rule more pleasure in revenge
than men. The widow Gras, urging her accomplice to
join her in her vengeance, told her, "The cause of my
ruin was one ——, and I want to revenge myself on the
vile wretch. . . . You see what pain I suffer; well! make
him suffer a little of the same, and I think I shall be
better after that."

According to her character, her education and the nature
of her love, she wreaks her vengeance with the most far-
sought or the most perverse refinements of cruelty. She
is quite capable of resorting to suicide, simply and solely
to cause her betrayer remorse. A young woman who had
been forsaken wrote to her lover: "I am capable of any
violence, even of suicide, to cause you remorse and disturb
you in the course of your pleasures." Generally speaking,
anger stirs the most evil feelings of her nature. The very
woman who was good-natured, fond and devoted, when
she was loved, becomes ill-conditioned and treacherous,
when betrayed. She cannot bear the idea of the man who
has forsaken her being happy, respected by society and
surrounded by friends; she does all she can to rob him of
his good repute and alienate his friends, to make him suffer
in his pride, his person and his feelings; she studies his character, in order to strike him in the tenderest place, seeking
out the most cruel and abominable forms of revenge and
the best adapted to wound him deeply. "I love him and I
loathe him," wrote one; " if he forsakes me, I will dishonour
him,—him and his family." How abominable was Medea's
vengeance! To kill her own children, in order to make
the father suffer cruelly! Nor is such diabolical vengeance
untrue to nature; a woman's revenge is capable of going
even so far as this. For do we not often see women ready to

wreak their resentment on a faithful husband by sacrificing, if not the life, at any rate the interest, honour and happiness of their children? To cause their husband pain of mind, they torture him in his feelings as a father, sowing dissension with poisoned words between him and his children, and stirring the latter to acts of insubordination and violence against their father. There is a touch of Medea in all such women.

Torturing the father in order to make the husband suffer is an essentially feminine type of vengeance. Men much more rarely practise this horrid form of revenge. Still an instance occurred some months ago, where a certain Deblonder, in order to punish his wife, who wished to get a divorce and marry another man, killed their two little girls by way of lacerating the mother's heart.—This horrid notion of making a father or a mother suffer in the children is no mere literary invention imagined by poets,—a character in Shakespeare, seeking a means to make an enemy suffer, notes with regret that he has no child, saying he only wishes he had, that he might punish the father in the child. I find the same abominable idea in the mouth of a prisoner at the bar, a woman who had yielded to her thirst for vengeance; "I wanted to make him suffer, not by striking him, but his son." Some years since the Assize Court of the Department of the Alpes-Maritimes tried a woman who, having become mistress to a young man, was entrusted with the education of a child her lover had had as the result of a previous liaison; on his forsaking her, she avenged the father's faithlessness by strangling his child.—Yet another example. A married woman had abandoned her husband to live in a foreign country with a lover. A female child was the result of the connection. In a short time the mother forsook her lover and the child. But eight years afterwards, meeting her lover again, she wished to renew the old life with them; he refused however, and to punish him, she determined to make him suffer in his rôle of a father. She made it up with her husband and bribed him to claim as his own his wife's child in virtue of

the maxim of *is pater est* . . ., and the Courts were obliged
to admit the validity of this legal fiction. The true father,
frantic with grief, refused to have his child torn from him,
and set off with her for America. He was condemned to
three years' imprisonment for contumacy in illegally kid-
napping the child after the Court's decision.—In 1889, in
the Department of Vaucluse, a woman to avenge herself
on her rival poisoned her children. Domestic servants also
have been known, after dismissal, to wreak their spite on
their masters by poisoning their children. Anarchists at
the present day urge domestics to revenge themselves on
their masters by corrupting the children entrusted to
them.

This is nothing less than a return to the ferocious habits
of primitive mankind. The peoples of those days were
accustomed to punish their foes in the persons of their
children; and attributed the same atrocious form of revenge to their deities. In retaliation for an insult of
Niobé, Apollo and Diana slew her fourteen children.

In Corneille's *Rodogune*, Cléopâtre presents a cup of
poisoned wine to Antiochus and Rodogune, and on seeing
them hesitate, drinks first herself to dissipate their fears,
happy to die along with them rather than miss her vengeance. According to M. Stapfer there is no shadow of
truth in the character of the woman who declares :

"Tombe le ciel sur moi, pourvu que je me venge ! " [1]

I do not agree with him ; I am certain the craving for
revenge in a jealous, proud and spiteful woman's heart
may be so fierce and so blind as to suggest the idea to her
of making sure of her vengeance by her own death, and
inspiring the cry :

[1] "Let heaven fall on my head, if I may but get revenge ! " This cry
which seems so improbable to M. Stapfer, is the natural exclamation of a
woman eager for revenge ;

"Que je me perde ou non, je songe à me venger "

(" Whether it involve my ruin or no, my only thought is for vengeance "), says
Hermione, equally indifferent to her fate, if only she may satisfy her
vengeance. Act. iv. Sc. 5.

" Il est doux de périr après ses ennemis." [1]

Besides, we should remember that Cleopatra is not only a revengeful, jealous and self-seeking woman, but also an Asiatic mother, who has had her children brought up far from her side, and only calls them to her to be the instruments of her ambition and her anger.

No doubt women who in their desire of vengeance do not hesitate to kill their own children are unnatural mothers, Furies. But if *all* women are not Furies, *some* are; thirst for vengeance pushed to the limit of ferocity is an integral part of feminine human nature, or rather of some representatives of the sex. Médée, Camille, Cléopâtre, the Queen of Syria, Hermione, Roxane, are Furies; they know it in their own hearts, and call themselves by the name.

> " Tu ne revois en moi qu'une amante offensée,
> Qui *comme une Furie* attachée à tes pas
> Te veut incessament reprocher son trépas," [2]

says Camille in *Horace* (Act iv. Sc. 5).

Roxane, again, addressing Bajazet bids him :

> " Ne désespère pas une amante en *furie* . . .
> Dans ton perfide sang je puis tout expier." [3]

Hermione also is a Fury ; Pylades advising Orestes to fly from her says :

> " Quoi ! votre amour se veut charger d'une *furie*? " [4]

In fact, anger, jealousy, revenge may change a woman into a Fury who heretofore seemed entirely incapable of violence.

The female imagination is every day inventing new forms of vengeance. A woman of light character, who had deserted her children, came to ask her husband's permission

---

[1] " 'Tis sweet to die after one's enemies."

[2] " You see in me only an injured lover, who *like a Fury* dogging your steps, will unceasingly upbraid you for her death."

[3] " Drive not to desperation one whom love betrayed has made a *Fury* . . . 'tis easy to avenge all my wrongs in your traitorous blood."

[4] " What ! will your love burden itself with a *Fury*?"

to see them again. The latter refused, telling her she was unworthy to do so; "you rob me of the sight of my children," answered the woman; "well! when my turn comes, I will rob you of the sight of them."—"You mean you will kill me," retorted the doomed husband.—"No!" she replied, "I will make you suffer worse than that, I will blind you." And so she did, some days later; while the husband was playing with the children, she came in suddenly and threw vitriol in his eyes. The children might easily have been injured, for a nurse who was standing beside them received splashes of the corrosive fluid, which burnt her clothes. The woman shared the sentiments of Médée, who said to her children:

> "Il me prive de vous et je l'en vais priver . . .
> Il ne vous verra plus." [1]

To give herself the satisfaction of revenge, the woman who has been abandoned accepts unflinchingly the scandal and punishment that ensue upon her deed. A forsaken woman, maturing the design of blinding her lover, (a design she afterwards carried out), declared she had no fear of the penal consequences of the act, that supposing she were condemned to five years' imprisonment, she would willingly undergo them for the satisfaction of wreaking her vengeance.

To punish her rival and disfigure her beauty is for such a one a still keener pleasure. Atalide, aware that Roxane is even more deeply exasperated against her than against Bajazet, has good reason to say as she does to the latter:

> "Elle aura plus de soif de mon sang que du vôtre." [2]

Indeed Roxane is at first for pardoning Bajazet, and says to him:

> "Ma rivale est ici; suis-moi sans différer;
> Dans la main des muets viens la voir expirer." [3]

---

[1] "He robs me of you, and I am going to rob him of it . . . he shall never look on you more."

[2] "She will be even more athirst for my blood than for yours."

[3] "My rival is here; follow me without delay; come to see her die at the hands of the mutes."

Against her rival is primarily directed her craving for revenge; when she thinks presently of putting Bajazet to death as well, she desires to afford Atalide the sight of his death, to make he sufferings greater :

"Quel surcroit de vengeance et de douceur nouvelle
Que de le montrer bientôt pâle et mort devant elle." [1]

A jealous woman always seeks some refinement of cruelty in her vengeance. Thus Phèdre longs to add to the pleasure of killing her hated rival, the further satisfaction of having her slain before the eyes of Hippolyte :

"Je vais faire expirer ma rivale à tes yeux." [2]

In *Horace*, Camille winds up the imprecations she launches against Rome, which she detests like a rival, by these verses that will express the intensity of her hate and the delight she finds in revenge :

"Voir le dernier Romain à son dernier soupir,
Moi seule en être cause et mourir de plaisir." [3]

Before wreaking her vengeance, a woman relishes the thought of it in imagination, just as she feasts her eyes on the sight of it, when it is accomplished. A young woman of twenty-two, who had just killed her rival with a pistol bullet, gloated over her death agony, stepping back slowly from her side with a look of pleasure in her eyes, as if relishing her revenge; on her face could be read the satisfaction she felt at giving her a coffin for a bridal bed, and she might have been thought to be repeating Médée's line:

"Et pour lit nuptial il te faut un tombeau." [4]

This thought of the bridal bed that was not to be for her, had tormented her fancy; her fury had been kindled at the notion of seeing her rival enter it, and she was now

1 "What a heightened spice of vengeance and fresh satisfaction, to show him anon pale and dead before her eyes."
2 "I am about to slay my rival before your eyes."
3 "To see the last of the Romans sighing his last sigh,—I to be sole cause of the nation's ruin and *die of joy* at the thought."
4 "And for bridal bed you must have a tomb."

I

overjoyed at having made this impossible by shooting her dead.

When a woman who has been abandoned for another, disfigures her rival, it is not only that she wishes to make the marriage she abhors impossible; over and above this, she takes a tigerish pleasure in robbing her of her beauty, in making the woman ugly that her lover found prettier than herself, in covering with horrid sores the mouth that smiled at him, in burning out the eyes that inspired his love and expressed her preference. Knowing her rival's happiness at being thought beautiful and her pride in her lover's admiration, she longs by spoiling her face to end the odious superiority she claimed over her. Once disfigured, the hated rival will cease to be formidable, she who was an object of desire will become a sight of horror and loathing; she will be humiliated, and her humiliation in its refinement of malice will heighten the joy of vengeance.

There are even women who, whilst disfiguring their rival, make a point of sparing their sight, so that their victim may suffer more from seeing her own ugliness.

Revenge in such cases is, as a rule, long premeditated. Under the influence of despair, the forsaken woman shuts herself up alone, and concentrates all her thoughts on her grief; losing her sleep, she racks her brain day and night, pondering over the treachery she has met with. After forming her plan of vengeance, she hesitates to carry it into execution, especially where she still loves the lover or husband who has deserted her. This period of hesitation is faithfully portrayed in the answers given under examination by a girl of Saint-Rémy, guilty of throwing vitriol in her lover's face: "After making up my mind to revenge, I could not finally decide to put my purpose into execution. ... One day, whilst I was talking to L——, my mother came into the room, and said: 'You can see he's only laughing at your tears.' These words kindled my anger afresh; I asked my mother to withdraw, and turning to my lover I said: 'Remember what you promised me;

beware of my vengeance.' As he made no answer, but began to yawn, I added : 'I see I only weary you; goodbye for the last time, I shall not come to see you any more." Exasperated by his attitude of insulting indifference, the girl resumed her projects of vengeance, but she still hesitated to execute them, not having the heart to disfigure the man she loved, when some while afterwards she met her lover in the street and he pretended not to know her. Then at last, wounded beyond bearing by the insult, she went home hurriedly, disguised herself in men's clothes, armed herself with a bottle of vitriol she had procured long beforehand, and went and threw its contents in the villain's face.

The notion of revenge is a sort of demoniacal possession, that little by little fills the woman's mind and more and more dominates her whole being. According to circumstances, this persistent idea that pursues her day and night is alternatively welcomed and rejected for a certain number of days, weeks or months. A struggle rages between love and hate, reason and passion. But gradually her powers of resistance fail her, as she learns to gloat more and more complacently over the idea of revenge, till one day after many falterings and repeated alternations of loathing and forgiveness, a final incident, a casual meeting, the sight of her rival, a fresh insult, ends by firing the mine.

I borrow from the diary of a young woman accused of a crime of this kind, named Marie B——, the passages below showing how in the agonies of desertion, she passed from the stage of despair and thoughts of suicide to that of projected murder, and after many delays and hesitations to its actual realization.

"*November.*—I think I am going mad. Better a thousand times to die, but not before I have avenged my wrongs. The measure of your iniquities is full. Beware ; you know not, Léon, what pain and remorse you are preparing for yourself.

"*December.*—He is thinking of marrying. If I were not a Christian woman, I should kill him.

"*April*.—My little girl is dead. I long to die, but first to revenge!

"*June*.—He has come back, but I can see he does not love me any more. I mean to kill him.

"*July*.—I could have killed him, but I did not. I am going to put away my pride once more and ask him to come back; but if he refuses, I shall be pitiless, I swear I shall.

"*November*.—I cannot bear another woman to be the mother of *his* children, and so he must die.

"*13th December*.—I have written to him, and he has not answered. How insulting !

"I suffer beyond bearing; I would rather die, but he must die first.

"*19th December*.—I have seen him, but I could not get near him. I shall find my opportunity some day, Léon, and your life will be the price of the agonies I suffer."

On January 1, she writes on the back of the photograph of the lover who has forsaken her : L. R. condemned to death by me, Marie.

Next day, she writes : "He is still alive. My strength failed me. Twice I pressed the trigger in vain. I had no blood left in my veins, for in spite of myself I love him still.

"*3rd January*.—To-day I am going to try for death. May it overtake us both !

"*5th January*.—All day long I have sat in a carriage before his door, without gaining anything except the knowledge that a woman, tall, slender, and wrapped in a fur cloak, went into his house at half-past five and came out again at nine.

"I suffer too horribly; I must have your life, Léon. I trust I shall do better to-morrow."

On January 7, in the evening about nine, Marie B—— carried out the plan of murder she had first conceived more than a year before, and fired three revolver shots at her lover, but without doing more than wounding him. She was arrested, and declared next day she was sorry she had not killed him.

In her examination before the "Juge d'Instruction," she said : " I am going to tell you the whole truth. Will you be able to comprehend me ? I do not understand myself. You will see how the most different and apparently the most contradictory feelings fought for the mastery in my heart.

"I love the man, and at the same time I despised him, and even to-day, after having tried to kill him, I think I love him still. I am ashamed to talk to you in this way, but the truth is I am appalled at the injury this man has done me, by inspiring a love that even contempt has not been able entirely to kill. My head is a chaos."

The account this poor girl gave of the combination of love and hate, of tenderness and contempt, that tossed her heart and made a chaos of her mind, the analysis she gave of her hesitations and changes of mind, alone suffice to prove the small amount of psychological perspicacity displayed by Schlegel in his criticisms on Racine. He expresses surprise that Phèdre, after trying to melt the heart of Hippolyte, should in an instant pass from the most abject love to the most furious anger, and be able to declare :

"Je le vois comme un monstra effroyable à mes yeux."[1]

He cannot understand Phèdre's repeated alternations of purpose, planning to die in the first act, then abandoning her intention on hearing of Thésée's death ; in the second act endeavouring to pierce her heart with Hippolyte's sword by way of a piece of stage effect, in the third act again talking of dying without giving effect to her project, in the fourth returning to the same resolution, and eventually executing it in the fifth. Phèdre, he says, is for ever irresolute, she alternates between the most contradictory feelings ; in the fourth act she is on the point of asking pardon for Hippolyte, then suddenly changes her mind directly she hears of the latter's love for Aricie

[1] "I see him like a horrid monster before my eyes."

and now breathes nothing but vengeance.[1] These ever-lasting changes of mind and sudden breakings of purpose are, according to Schlegel, untrue to nature and moreover inappropriate in Tragedy. " If tragic necessity," he says, " requires us to depict criminal characters while making them in a certain way interesting, let them at any rate be of heroic mould, and do not let continual feebleness and vacillation render them unequal to the situations in which their own passions have involved them."

It is impossible, I think, to display greater ignorance of the effects of passion. Schlegel's literary criticisms are a tissue of psychological misconceptions. What really characterizes the mental state of the woman who has been forsaken, as it does that of the jealous lover, is the rapid and reiterated change from love to hate, from hope to fear, then back again from hate to love and forgiveness, from despair to hope, till the moment when, after many hesitations, this condition of unstable equilibrium ends in an explosion of anger or despair, in murder or suicide, or both these at once.

Not to see that Phèdre, after trying to touch Hippolyte's heart and failing, must needs be filled with a sudden passion of anger at the announcement, " Aricie has his heart! Aricie has his plighted troth!" is to understand nothing whatever of the effects of love and jealousy, and therefore to show oneself a very poor literary critic, for there can be no real criticism without psychology.

There never yet was a desperate woman frenzied by the indifference and treachery of her lover but is drawn hither and thither betwixt the desire for revenge and the love she still bears him in the midst of her indignation.

> " On a peine à haïr ce qu'on a bien aimé,
> Et le feu mal éteint est bientôt rallumé."[2]

---

[1] Schlegel, *Comparaison entre la Phèdre de Racine et celle d'Euripide*, p. 32. ("Comparison between the Phèdre of Racine and the Phædra of Euripides.")

[2] " 'Tis hard to hate the man one has fondly loved, and the fire but half extinguished is quickly rekindled." Corneille, *Sertorius*, Act i. Sc. 3.

The female heart, stirred by contradictory feelings, alternates between one and the other; hence those sudden changes of mind and purpose that make the tragedies of Racine and Corneille so moving, because they are so true to life. The woman though ready to curse the man she loves, hesitates at first to make him suffer when she feels the desire for revenge; presently, if some fresh affront is put upon her, her anger reasserts itself and she renews those plans for murder she had before rejected. In her famous monologue in the fifth act Hermione expresses vividly the alternations and hesitations of her wavering resolution :

"Et prête à me venger, je lui fais déjà grâce." [1]

Then no sooner has she resolved to forgive him than her anger returns as she thinks of Pyrrhus' scorn :

"Non, ne révoquons pas l'arrêt de mon courroux ;
Qu'il périsse." [2]

Roxane, who has all the fire of the South added to a Sultana's pride, hesitates long before putting Bajazet to death. She invents a thousand pretexts for delaying her vengeance ; first she gives up her project, then presently resumes it, a prey alternately to anger and affection, her threats of death succeeded anon by exclamations of the fondest love :

"Bajazet, écoutez ; je sens que je vous aime." [3]

This is genuine psychological insight.

Unwavering characters, consistent throughout, such as Schlegel asks, are not true to human nature, and least of all to feminine human nature.

The special characteristic of passion and particularly of jealousy is to destroy consecutiveness of ideas and firmness of purpose, to make the mind inconsistent, irresolute and full of self-contradictions.

[1] "And all ready to avenge my wrong, I am already by way of forgiving him."
[2] "No ! let us not revoke the resolve of my angry heart ; he must perish."
[3] "Hark, Bajazet ! I feel I love you still."

The very same alternations of resolve that Schlegel makes
a ground of reproach against Racine, are found equally in
Corneille's *dramatis personæ*, the reason being they are a
part of human nature.   Médée herself whose character is
so powerful, alternatives betwixt vengeance and pity :

> "Mais quoi ! j'ai beau contre eux animer mon audace,
> La pitié la combat et se met à sa place ;
> Puis cédant tout à coup la place à ma fureur,
> J'adore les projets qui me faisaient horreur.
> De l'amour aussitôt je passe à la colère . . .
> Je n'écoute rien et mon âme éperdue
> Entre deux passions demeure suspendue." [1]

What a knowledge of the human heart !   And yet the
literary critics persist in declaring Corneille could not
depict love and analyze jealousy !

Similarly, unfortunate or jealous lovers oscillate, like
women, between love and hate ;

> "Tous mes moments ne sont qu'un éternel passage
> De la crainte à l'espoir, de l'espoir à la rage," [2]

says King Antiochus in *Bérénice*.

So Pyrrhus is for ever wavering between his love for
Andromaque and his craving to be avenged for the slights
she puts on him ; he is turn and turn about fond and
furious, a humble suppliant and a threatening tyrant.   Mark
the same vacillation in Mithridate.   Frenzied with jealousy
he cries :

> "Non, non, plus de pardon, plus d'amour pour l'ingrate . . .
> Immolons en partant trois ingrats à la fois . . . ;" [3]

anon his anger fades away, pity and love resume their
sway :

---

[1] " But no ! 'tis in vain I excite my fury against them ; pity joins fight with
it and drives it back.   Then once more giving my wrath its way, I adore the
very schemes that but now made me shudder.   From love I pass in a moment
to anger. . . . I hearken to no word of reason and my bewildered soul hangs
in suspense betwixt two passions."

[2] " All my existence is but an everlasting passage from fear to hope, from
hope to rage."

[3] " No, no ! no more forgiveness, no more love, for the ungrateful wretch
. . . ; let us make an end and sacrifice three monsters of ingratitude at
once. . . ."

"Mais quelle est ma fureur? et qu'est-ce que je dis?
O Monime, ô mon fils! Inutile courroux."[1]

A woman who has been forsaken and who is for revenge
makes her preparations long ere she strikes the final blow.
She buys the instrument of her crime beforehand, and
studies the time and place most favourable for its execution; she abandons her purpose, then returns to it afresh,
traversing a cycle of the most opposite emotions. In
yielding to her anger, which is raised to fever heat by the
desire of retaliation, she thinks she can only recover some
little calmness of mind after her vengeance is satisfied.
And as a matter of fact, at the moment when she dis-
charges her pistol or throws her cup of vitriol, she does
experience a species of relief and relaxation of tension;
she is avenged and she relishes her revenge. In the
excessive excitement in which she is, she may occasionally
remain for several hours, or even for several days, without
regretting the wounds she has inflicted, the death she has
dealt. But before long a reaction ensues, and she is
bitterly sorry for what she has done and manifests the
deepest penitence. Marie B—— said to the "Juge d'Instruction": "The day I fired the shot, I experienced, I
confess, a species of satisfaction and relief of mind." On
the day following her attempt to murder her lover, she
said to the Commissary of Police: "I do not know how
serious M. G——'s wounds are, but I intend to repeat my
attempt, as soon as ever I get an opportunity. I have sworn
to kill the man, and I shall do anything and everything to
succeed." But some days later her anger subsided, love
and remorse filled her heart, and on the "Juge d'Instruction" remarking to her that her hatred of her former lover
must have been very deep-seated not to have sooner
yielded to remorse, when she saw the man she had loved
fall by her hand, the accused answered: "I was still
labouring under extreme excitement of mind; I had
suffered so terribly!"—Another young girl, who had

[1] "But what means my fury? and what is it I am saying? Oh! Monime,
oh! my son! How useless is my wrath!"

thrown vitriol in her lover's face and had relished her
vengeance at the time, declared some days subsequently :
" I feel the most lively regret for what I have done : I
would give my life that it should never have happened."

Goethe, who spent his life in loving and abandoning a
great number of women, without a thought of right and
wrong and absolutely callous to the grief of those he
forsook, has none the less drawn in *Faust* a striking picture
of the agonies of a girl who has been betrayed, who
believing herself to be on the high-road to happiness, has
rushed headlong into calamity and shame. " Dost remember, Marguerite, the days when thou wert wont to
come and kneel before the altar ?   Then thou wert full of
innocence. . . . Marguerite, what hast thou done ?   What
crimes are thine !   Dost come to pray for thy mother's
soul, whose death is upon thy head ?   Seest thou what
blood is this on the threshold ?   'tis thy brother's ; and dost
not feel stirring in thy bosom an unhappy being that e'en
now presages thee fresh pangs ? "   In that abode, where
of old were only sweet flowers and pious prayers, is naught
now but tears and blood, because the seducer has passed
that way.

CHAPTER V.

JEALOUSY.

"Jealousy feeds ever on suspicion. 'Tis a passion that is always seeking after new subjects of disquietude and fresh torments, and it becomes a form of madness the instant it passes from doubt to certainty."—LA ROCHEFOUCAULD.

THE essential characteristic of love is its desire for exclusive possession, its violent disinclination to share its bliss. So natural indeed is the feeling that it is seen among savage no less than among civilized peoples. This universality of the sentiment is a strong argument against the condition of sexual promiscuity which some writers on sociology attribute to primitive mankind. Every man is fain to have sole possession of the woman he loves, and dreads a rival's robbing him of his privileges. This apprehension makes men anxious and suspicious; tormented with doubts and fears, they grow sombre and preoccupied, absorbed in one fixed idea that gnaws their heart. A prisoner who stood accused of a crime he had committed out of jealousy, said that "something was always tearing at his brains."

The jealous lover or husband takes alarm at every trifle, and spends all his time in manufacturing motives for suspicion. When he is shown the groundlessness of his fears, he admits his mistake, but the next moment is at his old work again, a victim to doubts and apprehensions of every sort. Tossed about from one notion to another, now reassured, now a prey to fresh anxiety, he knows not what to think; he spies upon his wife and employs others to watch her smallest actions. He distorts her most trivial doings, and puts an ill interpretation on the most insignificant:

> " Un regard, un sourire, un instant d'entretien
> (Lui) semble un ennemi qui (lui) ravit son bien." [1]

I have noted myself in a number of instances of murder committed from jealousy, that nothing so exasperates a jealous man as to see the woman he is in love with laughing with someone else ; her merriment is in his eyes not only a sign of understanding between the pair, but he thinks they are deliberately making fun of him.

Corneille who has given a powerful delineation of jealousy, which he knew well, and this not merely from observation of others but from his own personal experience, represents the hero of one of his dramas as saying :

> " Tout ce qui l'approchait voulait me l'enlever,
> Tout ce qui lui parlait cherchait à m'en priver.
> Je tremblai qu'à leurs yeux elle ne fût trop belle,
> Je les haïssais tous comme plus dignes d'elle." [2]

Your jealous man would have no one so much as look at the woman he loves, or her look at any one. When Louis XIII. fell in love with Mlle. de Hautefort, " he would fain," says Cousin, " have had no man speak to her, no man even cast eyes on her with any particularity." A jealous husband hates his wife going out of doors and displaying her beauty to others ; he prefers to keep her shut up and isolated in the depths of the country. Alceste who is jealous urges Célimène to retire to the country. A workwoman whose husband had tried to murder her from motives of jealousy, told the examining magistrate that the latter would never let her go out to do her household errands. At a ball to see a rival's arm encircling the beloved one's waist, his eyes fixed on her face, his mouth inhaling her breath, is a veritable torment to a man of jealous disposition. In society, where savoir-faire, self-

---

[1] " A look, a smile, an instant's talk, he deems a foe that robs him of his rights." Delavigne, *L'École des Vieillards.*

[2] " All that came near her seemed eager to take her from me, all that spoke to her to be seeking to rob me of her. I trembled lest in their eyes she should appear too fair, I hated all men as better worthy of 'her than myself." Corneille *Pulchérie,* Act ii. Sc. 1.

respect, pride, all teach control, the jealous man conceals his pain and avoids making a scene. But at dances frequented by men of the humbler classes, who are not such complete masters of their feelings, jealousy is responsible for many a scuffle. Not long ago a carpenter of a jealous nature, seeing his *fiancée* at a dance, accompanied by her mother and her two sisters, required her to withdraw; unable to persuade her, he went away in a passion, fetched two guns and took ambush till the end of the ball. Directly he saw the women on the threshold of their house, laying one gun on the ground, he put the other to his shoulder and fired at the group. He wounded his *fiancée* and killed her sister, a girl of fifteen; the mother's life was saved by her daugnter who, seeing the murderer raise his weapon, threw himself in front of her to protect her with her own body.

The most tender lover, once he is bitten with jealousy, may quickly turn savage and brutal; having suffered himself, he would fain have others do the like, his misery makes him ill-conditioned, and he proceeds to insult, threaten and bully the woman he really loves all the while. In his jealousy he longs to strike her, his hand itches to be at her. In the households of working men in towns, and farm folk in the country, jealousy leads to a perfect rain of blows. To slap his wife's face is the first thing that occurs to a jealous husband in the lower classes. To return the blow is no less natural and inevitable on the part of the wife In a few hours' time we find the pair taking away the smart of the blows they have exchanged with a series of fond caresses, certain all the while very soon to begin the same quarrels and reconciliations all over again. In higher circles the very man who would not have dreamt of striking a woman with a flower, will let jealousy mislead him into beating her with a walking-cane, or if he does succeed in commanding his temper, he will regret he cannot copy the habits of commoner folk who settle accounts with their womankind by means of a big stick or a resounding slap:

"Que vous êtes heureux, vous en qui la nature
Agit sans aucun art et règne toute pure . . .
Gens du peuple, artisans, portefaix et vilains,
Vous de qui la vengeance est toujours en vos mains." [1]

A jealous lover who suspects his mistress of unfaithfulness tries to force her to confess a fault she has never been guilty of. He threatens her, even strikes her, to tear an admission from her, promising pardon if she will confess; then when the woman, who without having been actually untrue to her honour, admits an imprudence of behaviour that is open to misconstruction, he seizes on the admission to beat her worse than before.

Jealousy being in a general way a proof of love, it has been said that the woman who is its object never fails to excuse it. Molière makes one of his female characters say:

"Fi! ne me parlez point pour être vrais amants
De ces gens qui pour nous n'ont nuls emportements. . . .
Un amour si tranquille excite mon courroux,
C'est aimer froidement que n'être point jaloux." [2]

It is perfectly true that a woman will excuse much in the man who loves with jealous transport. Mary Queen of Scots, for instance, always loved Bothwell, who all the time made her suffer keenly from his jealous temper; "from the very morrow of her bridal, she had been for aye in tears and lamentation, her husband not suffering her to have liberty to look at any man whatsoever, or for any to look at her." Jealousy may very well win forgiveness for the cruelty and pain it is responsible for, when these are tempered by subsequent reconciliation and an augmentation of tenderness; but in the majority of instances, a jealous man does not inspire love, he is harsh and tyrannical, an unbearable and odious despot. The husband

[1] "How happy you, in whom Nature acts untrammelled by art and reigns in entire simplicity . . . common folk, workmen, porters and churls, you can always find vengeance in your own sturdy hands."

Campistron, *Le jaloux désabusé*.

[2] "Bah! talk not to me, as true lovers, of folks who feel no bursts of passion. . . . A love so uneventful moves my spleen; 'tis to love coldly never to be jealous."

who at first inspired fond affection in his wife's bosom by his passionate vehemence, soon loses her love through his strange suspiciousness and violent temper ; the suspicious watch he keeps, the doubts he expresses, the reproaches he loads his wife with, all make him odious. The time comes when jealousy turns the conjugal home into a hell, and the unhappy woman, for ever insulted and beaten, grows weary of such a dog's life and takes refuge with her parents. "Since my marriage, seven years ago now," a woman declared in a Court of Law, "not a day passes without my hnsband picking a quarrel with me out of jealousy and threatening me with violence. He told me once, 'I am going to buy a brace of pistols, and hang them by the bedside; I shall kill you and myself afterwards.'"— Another jealous husband used to keep a great Arab knife under the mattress of the bed where he lay with his wife. The latter, driven to desperation by these terrible threats, ended by going back to her parents. The husband went after her, and displayed so much regret and affection that she was touched and returned once more to her married home. But the former scenes of jealous fury having very soon broken out again, the woman lost patience and petitioned for a judicial separation. While the suit was still in progress, the husband killed her in a fit of resentment.

In another case a poor wife who had been insulted and beaten by her jealous husband at last took refuge in a neighbour's house, to escape his cruelties. The husband attempted to force the door in order to get his wife back, but finding himself unable to do so, he set fire to the house, declaring he meant to have her dead or alive. La Fontaine cites with a rather childish degree of admiration the similar case of a lover,

> "Qui brûla sa maison pour embrasser sa dame . . .
> J'aime assez cet emportement,
> Le conte m'en a plu toujours infiniment ;
> Il est bien d'une âme espagnole
> Et plus grande encore que folle." [1]

---

[1] "Who burned down his house in order to embrace his lady fair. . . . I

There is no degree of violence jealousy does not make men commit. A large number of women are horribly ill-used by jealous husbands and lovers ; they are kicked and cuffed on the face, belly and legs, their teeth broken and their earrings smashed. When justice holds an enquiry and the woman's body is examined who has been beaten by her jealous husband or lover, it is often found black and blue all over with blows. When these jealous brutes are striking their victims, they forbid them to scream out or make any complaint, and use any cries or protests they may make as a pretext for further violence. Many women are afraid to complain, and if the neighbours notice the marks of blows on their face, they invent various excuses to account for them. Some, tired out with being for ever beaten, commit suicide along with their children ; only a short time since the body of a young woman was recovered from the Seine, and her little girl rescued alive, whom she had dragged in along with her. The following letter was found on her: "My dear parents, since the day I was married, I have never been happy ; every day I am beaten. I cannot bear the life any longer. It is very wretched to be forced to kill myself along with my little Marie."

When a criminal from jealousy is brought before the Correctional or Assize Court, we sometimes hear counsel attempting to disprove the fact of the jealousy, on the ground that the victim was of unblemished conduct and afforded the accused no motive for the feeling. But the entire absence of motive is no reason for denying the existence of jealousy. A woman's virtue is no safeguard against suspicion ; a husband may be jealous of the most virtuous wife. A husband of fifty-nine, intensely jealous of his wife, who herself was fifty-one and had borne him ten children, stabbed her in fifteen places with a dagger, though she had never given him the slightest cause for jealousy.—The jealous husband is always com-

like his ardour well, and the tale has always pleased me vastly ; 'tis a true Spanish soul, great-hearted more than mad."

plaining of his wife's indifference ; even when he is loved,
he does not believe he is, and suspects his wife's fidelity
to him on the most trivial pretext. A young woman who
had already been shot at several times by her husband,
told the examining magistrate she had married her
husband for love, but that on the wedding night, having
felt some hesitation about yielding to his wishes, she had
awakened his suspicions and that from that time forth
she had been subjected to his brutality.

The husband who experiences doubts as to his being
really the father of his children, suffers such distress of
mind that he is quite capable of planning to escape his
pain by death ; " All I wish," wrote a husband to his wife,
before putting an end to his own life, is for you to be
happy, as well as the child that bears my name, but about
whose paternity I am not so sure. I love it all the same,
but I have neither strength nor courage to rear it." In
other cases a jealous husband will kill his pregnant wife,
to get rid of the child that is to be born. In 1860, in
the *arrondissement* of Digne, a husband lying in bed by
his wife who was with child, got up, seized a gun, fired
at her point blank and killed her. At the same date, at
Draguignan, a young husband of only twenty-two fired
at his pregnant wife and his mother-in-law, who were
seated on the threshold at the door of their house. The
wife fell wounded and gave birth to a still-born child, the
mother was not hit, but the son-in-law furious at having
missed his aim endeavoured to beat out her brains with
the butt end.

Not that jealousy is confined to the fear of losing the
physical possession of the beloved object. I do not
believe it is true to say, "we should readily forgive the
woman we love a thousand adulterous impulses, always
provided they have not been carried to accomplishment." [1]
He would be a person of little delicacy of feeling who
should be content with his physical possession, but quite indifferent to his possession of the heart. Jealousy is at one

[1] A. Dumas *fils*, *Affaire Clémenceau*, p. 142.

K

and the same time physical and moral, it extends to the possession of a wife or mistress's thoughts no less than to the mere possession of her body. However, men do not all feel jealousy in the same way. In some, a small minority, it is more moral than physical; in others it is rather physical than moral. Moral jealousy may lead to suicide, but not to murder. Here is an instance. A man of thirty once was married to a school teacher, whom he loved passionately; without suspecting his wife's behaviour, he did not believe she loved him and thought another man possessed her heart. The idea caused him such intense suffering that he ended by blowing out his brains. This example shows that jealousy is not confined solely to the dread of losing the physical possession of a woman, and that the mere doubt of continuing to hold her affection may drive into suicide a husband who yet has undisturbed physical possession. I have myself noted such delicacy of feeling in a plain workman, a leather-dresser. The man in his early days, before he was married, had been guilty of a misdemeanour for which he had been tried and convicted; this fact he concealed from his wife, whom he loved to distraction. However the latter at last found it out and was deeply chagrined by the knowledge. Hereupon the husband, fearing he had lost her love, killed himself with a revolver shot in the head.

It is physical jealousy that is responsible for acts of violence against others. Nay! more, the character of this jealousy often shows itself in the very nature of the acts committed. A husband, after strangling his wife, burned her sexual parts. Another individual who was brought before the Courts, wishing to revenge himself on a girl who would not listen to his suit, enticed her into a trap, lifted up her petticoats and threw a corrosive fluid over the lower parts of her abdomen. In his *Affaire Clémenceau*, Dumas *fils* makes the husband conceive the notion of punishing the lover in the part where he had sinned.[1] The

[1] Valerius Maximus cites instances of two Roman husbands who mutilated the partners of their wives' adultery, Bk. VI. ch. i. no. 13.—Horace mentions

very same vengeance which the Canon Fulbert practised on Abelard, was carried out a few years since in the *arrondissement* of Brignoles. By a refinement of cruelty the husband forced his wife by threats of death to perform the amputation on her lover with her own hands. In the Fenayrou case again the husband compelled his wife to take part in his revenge; Mme. Fenayrou stated that her husband, when informed of her infidelity, told her: " I will forgive you on one condition only, viz., that you help me in my vengeance; if not I shall kill you, your children and you." These threats he repeated every day; at last terrified and desperate, I consented "to save my children's lives." After the lover's murder, her husband returned her wedding wreath and ring, which he had taken from her, telling her, "all is now forgotten." More recently a young Provencal woman, thirsting for vengeance on her lover who was giving her up in order to marry, gave him a last assignation, and while they were together performed an amputation on him with a razor that made him incapable of marriage.

Moreover the circumstances under which the jealous person strikes his victim, sometimes reveal his state of mind and feeling; he kills his mistress after giving her a last assignation, after passing the night with her. Tacitus in the *Annals* (Bk. xviii. § 46) relates one of these dramas of love and jealousy, which are by no means uncommon in our own day. Octavius Sagitta, madly in love with a married lady named Pontia, bought her favours and later on the determination of the husband's rights. But, once free, Pontia being attracted by the allurements of another and richer match, refused her hand to Sagitta. The latter wept tears of despair and disappointment and threatened the false woman with every punishment; finally he asked and obtained the favour of passing some hours by her side. Then, after giving her proof of his love, seized

similar cases, Sects. 1, 2.—The ancient Hindus and ancient Egyptians had those guilty of seducing women mutilated. Manu. viii. 352; Diodorus Siculus, Bk. I. § 78.

with a sudden fit of jealousy, he stabbed her to death with
a dagger to prevent her ever belonging to another.—Some
years since, in Provence, a young woman of twenty killed
her lover under almost identical circumstances, because he
was contemplating breaking off his liaison with her, in
order to marry.   Masking her anger, she asked for a
final meeting, which was granted her.   The pair of lovers
spent the night together.   Early next morning, while the
man was still asleep, his mistress struck a dagger into his
body, exclaiming as she did so : " Mine, or the tomb's ! "
Similar crimes are committed by lovers, who strangle their
mistress, that they may suffer from no more doubts about
their fidelity.   It is the same sentiment Racine gives to
Mithridate :

> "Tu sais combien de fois ses jalouses tendresses
> Ont pris soin d'assurer la mort de ses maîtresses." [1]

The police, especially at Paris, occasionally find women
of pleasure strangled in bed, these crimes having for
motives either theft or jealousy.   A child of eleven, sleeping in a room next to that where his mother was spending
the night with a lover, one night heard the death-rattle in
the poor woman's throat ; he got out of bed and saw the
lover seated on the bed, strangling his mistress out of
jealousy.   The murderer seeing himself surprised, rushed
upon the boy, carried him back into his own room, locked
him in, and took to flight.   Next day the woman was
discovered dead by strangulation.—I myself heard a girl
who had killed her lover, much older than herself, relate
how the latter had made her promise under oath to consent
to a surgical operation on the day when, by reason of
advancing years he should no longer be able to continue
his relations with her.   "You are much younger than myself, dear !" he had told her; "You will still be young
when I am an old man, and I shall be jealous.   Give me
your oath then, you will never be another's.   I know you

---

[1] "You know how many times his jealous fondness has taken good care to
assure the death of his mistresses."

will keep your word ; promise me to submit to an operation that will destroy the woman in you."

The history of Abelard offers an interesting case of jealousy and its workings. After undergoing the mutilation, he was left a prey to intense jealousy. Fearing Héloïse's beauty and her habit of love should make her seek, or find unsought, a second lover, he made every endeavour to separate her from the world by giving her to God. He urged upon her that decorum required her to retire to a Nunnery to escape the world's curiosity, and found no peace till he had succeeded in persuading her to enter a religious house and bind her lips by vows—a consummation he hurried on by every means in his power. It was only when he saw his precious treasure behind the lofty walls of the convent and its barred doors that he adopted in his turn the monastic life, having taken good care to remain free so long as Héloïse was the same.

The man who marries a widow or a divorced woman is exposed to the risk of feeling retrospective jealousy in regard to the former husband, his pain arising from the thought of his wife having once belonged to another. In fact he is jealous of her past life. Her exclusive possession in the present and the future is not enough for him ; he would like the same exclusive possession to have held good in the past likewise. It is no uncommon thing to see workmen and farm hands marrying young women who have been seduced by some other man and who have had a child by him. Nor is it out of generosity, or from any wish to conform to the *ideas of Mme. Aubry,* that they marry them. More attracted by the dowry than sensible to the point of honour, they think themselves safe against any possible feeling of jealousy ; yet often after marriage this sentiment awakes into life. The husband, exasperated by the thought of the past, cannot look without indignation at the child that is not his and is constantly reminding him of the odious incident of former days. I find in the official account of a judicial case the following declaration by

a woman suffering from wounds inflicted by her jealous
husband, who afterwards committed suicide: "Jealousy
made my husband completely lose his head. Not long
before I had had my two children fetched from the
country; they are not his, but he had adopted them
when he married me last year. Their being there redoubled his retrospective jealousy. To-day on his rising
at 5 o'clock he remained standing by my bedside, caressing
my face and hair. All of a sudden, happening to stretch
out my arm, I touched something cold ; it was a revolver.
Before I could grasp hold of it, my husband fired two
shots at me, then turning the weapon against his own
body, killed himself."

This sort of retrospective jealousy on the part of the
husband with regard to the child of a former husband or
previous lover will sometimes culminate in the murder of
the child by the husband in complicity with the mother.
The child becomes the cause of incessant quarrels between
the pair ; and the mother comes at last to leave off loving
a being that, however involuntarily, makes her suffer so
much. Little by little she goes from indifference to dislike and joins in the hatred her husband feels against the
child out of jealousy.

Again marriage with a former mistress is frequently
troubled with scenes of jealousy, for the husband, remembering the light behaviour of the mistress, cannot help
doubts as to the firm foundation of the wife's virtue.

A young girl courted by a jealous lover, when she sees
the latter gloomy and preoccupied or else furiously
angry and offended at quite innocent words and actions
on her part, does not take the threats he launches at her
seriously. But a married woman, having more experience
and therefore better realizing the gravity of the menaces of
a jealous husband, often has a presentiment of the fate
awaiting her. This she announces to her relations and
friends ; "my husband will kill me," she declares, "one day
I shall be found dead ;" and her prediction is justified by
the event.

A jealous man who has lost possession of a woman, or fears to lose it, tormented by the thought of her lying in another man's arms, becomes a downright madman; he openly utters threats of death against his rival, entirely unable to control the violence of his words; "I will cut his belly open, I will tear his guts out," a husband screamed, gnashing his teeth the while. Dr Lombroso, and before him Dr Despine, have cited this absence of all prudence as a proof of mental obliquity; these men, they say, who in their jealousy are entirely unable to restrain their passion and publicly proclaim their purposes of revenge, are not made like other folks. But surely these threats are easily accounted for. The mouth speaks out of the fulness of the heart; few men and still fewer women can govern their anger.

> "Tu veux que je me taise et que je dissimule ;
> Nérine, porte ailleurs ce conseil ridicule,"[1]

cries Médée, a prey to jealousy and a thirst for vengeance, incapable either of concealing or dissembling her fury. No doubt a jealous man or woman who meditates violence, would be acting more sagaciously if he went about his preparations in secret; but passion abhors anything like prudence and reasonableness.

Passion having once reached its paroxysm, the jealous man, drunk with vengeance, becomes insensible to scandal or any other penalty that awaits him; a veritable frenzy, an absolute madness seizes him. A jealous husband brandishing a dagger he meant to use on his wife, was heard exclaiming he would kill her, kill her, if he had to go to the hulks for it. Jealous husbands turn into frantic madmen and go on slashing at their wife or rival till the knife breaks in their hands. One husband gave his wife twenty-four blows with a dagger. Another, after killing his, cut up her body into little bits, the better to assuage his vengeance. These jealous savages strike their victims blow after blow on every part of the body, breast, head,

---

[1] "You ask me to be silent and dissemble my wrath; Nérine, this is no occasion for so insensate a demand."

arms, trunk, limbs. We see women receive ten, twelve, fifteen, twenty, knife thrusts. A working-man of forty-six after a scene of jealousy, seizes a knife and plunges it time after time into his wife's breast, arms, legs, head, after throwing her on the floor, then casts himself on the bed and deals himself five blows in the region of the heart.— Another woman receives fifteen stabs with a dagger in the back, left breast, right breast, shoulder, belly, wrists. Very often a jealous husband will grasp his wife by the neck or hair and deal her a first blow with his knife, while she is still on her legs ; then on his victim dropping, he will kneel on her body, gashing her with reiterated stabs.

When a jealous husband is for punishing the lover or supposed lover of his wife, we see him provide himself with several weapons, a gun and a dagger, or several guns and several pistols ; he has never enough weapons to carry out his murderous purpose with. Often, after emptying his revolver, he throws himself upon his victim and strikes, and strikes, till the weapon breaks in his hand. A husband who had killed his wife's lover, said : "Yes! I fired off the six chambers of my revolver at her ; if there had been a dozen, I should have emptied them all." One prisoner, who had rushed knife in hand at his mistress, who had deserted him, and had stabbed her in eighteen places, said to the Court: "I laid in like a madman, I struck till I could not lift my hand." The wrong done him by an unfaithful wife or a successful rival being prodigious in his eyes, the jealous husband, intoxicated with fury, cannot satisfy his craving vengeance except by striking blow upon blow ; he would like to kill the offender over and over again. It is not one death he would make his rival suffer, but a thousand. "Though she had had as many lives as drops of blood in her body," Othello cries, "they would not have sufficed to quench my thirst for vengeance."—"When Aubert fell at my feet with his face to the ground, after the blow with a hammer I had dealt him," Fenayrou states in his examination, "I turned him over and holding him under me, face to face, looking straight into his eyes, I said to him : 'You miserable thief, you have robbed me of my honour, but I have got you at last ! You have tortured my heart, and your own heart shall pay for it ; " and so saying, I plunged the blade of a sword-stick into his body near the heart, turning it about to try and reach a mortal spot."—Other jealous husbands recoil at the thought of murder, not out of humanity, but in order that their victim, surviving his wounds, may suffer more long-drawn agonies. One such told his wife, before striking, " I did not give you life, and I will not rob you of it, but I mean to maim you for life."

When a jealous man is in the paroxysm of his fury, woe betide the relative or friend who is for intervening to protect the victim ; the madman turns his anger upon him at once. A daughter having endeavoured to save her mother from the violence her father was going to offer her, the latter began by striking his daughter twelve times with a knife, and then threw himself on his wife and dealt her fifteen slashing blows.

On being questioned after his arrest as to the crime he has just committed, the jealous malefactor replies that he was blinded by passion, that he was no longer master of his actions, that he did not know what he was doing. These explanations contain a large element of truth,—a fact however which in no way destroys moral or penal responsibility, though it may extenuate it. At the moment of striking his frenzied blows, the offender has the frantic look of a madman or a savage beast ; an eye-witness said of a jealous husband who had just fired at his wife, " he looked like a wild cat." Moreover observation shows that the man whom jealousy makes a murderer is marked by a congested condition of the brain, a blood-red face and eyes starting out of his head. He is described as seeing red, for he is blinded by excess of blood. An eye-witness said, describing a husband who had just killed his wife and afterwards attempted suicide : " His face was purple ; you would have thought he had a stroke of apoplexy." *Ora tument ira, nigrescunt sanguine venae* (" The face is

swollen with rage, the veins show dark with blood "),
writes Ovid.   In another case, a spectator spoke thus of
the murderer : " His face was extraordinarily red, in such
a state as I had never seen before."   Another added
further : " The blood had so run to his face, he could not
see ; the blood blinded him."—In women under the influence of jealousy, on the contrary, we do not remark the
same physiological phenomena ; they are pale rather than
red, all a-tremble, and the eyes especially bright.   Some
women, after firing a couple of shots from a revolver,
swoon away, while others are seized with a fit of trembling.   A girl who had just fired off two chambers of a
revolver at her lover came all pale and trembling to ask a
neighbour for a drink of water ; so agitated was she, they
had to hold the glass to her lips.

The man who has killed the woman he loves out of
jealousy is happy just at first at having satisfied his anger,
but very soon he bursts out sobbing and crying, " Wretch
that I am ! I have killed the woman I loved !"—A husband
who had just murdered from this motive the wife he
adored, when arrested and taken to the police office, spent
his time in weeping and lamenting, and covering with
kisses his victim's photograph, which he had drawn from
his pocket.—Another jealous husband, who had struck the
most furious and savage blows at his wife, presently threw
himself on her dead body, weeping and crying out in
despair.—These instances, which I could readily multiply,
show how true the picture is which Shakespeare has
drawn of jealousy in the case of Othello, who fondly
kisses Desdemona before smothering her.   The dramas of
the great poets of the world are but reproductions of the
tragedies of the Courts of Law.   I read in the report of a
criminal trial how a jealous husband, after firing five shots
with a revolver at his wife, without heeding the supplications of his victim, who besought him to spare the mother
of his children, afterwards overwhelmed her with marks of
tenderness and led her to an inn, where her wounds might
be attended to.

In the majority of cases, the jealous husband makes
no effort to escape, but surrenders himself as a prisoner,
saying to the police at the gendarmerie, " I come to give
myself up; I have just killed my wife." Still I have
known a case where the husband denied his guilt and
declared his wife had committed suicide; but the statement was in direct contradiction to the medical evidence,
as well as discredited by the affirmation of a witness who
had heard the wife cry out, " I am killed."

When the murderer from jealousy does not give himself
up to justice, he very often puts an end to his own life.
This is what Othello does, who dies kissing Desdemona
whom he has just murdered; " I gave you a kiss before
killing you," he cries ; "now that I kill myself, I cannot,
no ! I cannot refrain from dying with my lips on yours."
—The murder of Zaïre is followed by the suicide of
Orosmane. After having Pyrrhus put to death, Hermione
throws herself on his corpse and kills herself; Pylades
tells Oreste how he has seen her

> " Un poignard à la main sur Pyrrhus se comber,
> Lever les yeux au ciel, se frapper et tomber." [1]

Nor is remorse the only motive that impels the man
whom jealousy makes a murderer to commit suicide
afterwards. Apart from the wish he entertains to escape
justice, he puts an end to himself, that he may no more
be separated from the one he loves ; she being dead, he
longs to die too. On the other hand, if she survive her
wounds, he wishes also to live. As the by-standers were
hurrying to snatch her revolver from the hand of a woman
who had just fired at her lover out of jealousy, but had
missed her aim, she answered instantly : "Nay! Never
fear, I shall not kill myself, as I have killed him."

In these cases the suicide of the murderer follows
immediately on his victim's death ; it is a suicide of
overmastering impulse. But in other cases, the suicide

[1] " A dagger in her hand bend o'er Pyrrhus, raise her eyes to heaven,
then strike the blow and fall."

is as much premeditated as the murder. Determined to avenge her wrongs, the jealous woman forms the deliberate design of killing herself, after doing the same to her false lover;

"De ma sanglante mort ta mort sera suivie," [1]

declares Roxane.—A woman who had shot her lover, said under examination, "I wanted to kill him, but I was no less anxious to be rid of my own life."

Very frequently also the idea of suicide will arise in the mind of a victim of jealousy before that of murder; he is so unhappy he turns his thoughts to death, but wishes not to die alone. "I am going to die," said one such, but first I mean to kill her, I do not choose she should survive me, and as I cannot be happy with her, I must sleep the eternal sleep along with her."—"When I bought this revolver, it was with the intention of committing suicide," said another at his trial, "but before that I wanted to kill my mistress; I was too unhappy for anything."—Yet another told the same tale, "I long to die, but I mean her to die first."

The lover of a married woman may suffer so greatly from the necessity of sharing with the legitimate husband as to prefer suicide, and in that case he will be moved not to make the woman die along with him, but rather to kill the husband before putting an end to himself. I have myself noted an instance of the sort. A witness said, speaking of a jealous lover who before killing himself, had tried to murder his mistress's husband, "the fact is he was tired of life."—Again, the husband who is a prey to jealousy and unhappiness, may be seized with a disgust for existence and turn his thoughts to suicide as a relief, but unable to resign himself to the idea of his wife surviving him, he kills her first and himself afterwards. A jealous husband who had failed in the attempt on his own life, after having killed his wife, said: "My wife never loved me; I thought it best we should both of us

---

[1] "My bloody death will be followed by yours."

die together ; I fired two shots with a revolver at her and three at myself."—Nay ! a jealous husband may actually push his egoism so far as to kill his wife, if he himself falls ill and thinks he is going to die. In 1895, at the Assize Court of the Alpes Maritimes, a prisoner was tried, who being excessively jealous of his mistress and knowing himself to be seriously ill, said to her : " I am attacked by mortal sickness, but before I die, I shall kill you ; " and a few days afterwards he actually did so.—A jealous lover who murders his mistress, and then attempts his own death, will sometimes pretend he only killed her at her own desire ; he declares it to have been a double suicide, in fact, whereas it was really a case of murder and suicide. —Other instances occur where jealous husbands or lovers, who have been unsuccessful in business, being at the end of their resources and seeing ruin staring them in the face, kill themselves and their wife or mistress at the same time, that they may not leave them behind them unprotected. — Military men also, sick of the service and attacked by home-sickness, sometimes kill themselves and persuade their mistress to die along with them.

In July 1895 at Paris an electrician tried to kill his mistress from jealousy and afterwards committed suicide. He left letters behind him intended to lead to the belief of a double suicide : " We made up our minds long ago, Louise and I, we wished to marry one another, but her father is opposed to the match, and once said he would sooner see her dead than married to me ; his wish is about to be accomplished. How is it all to end ? I cannot tell, for Louise does not possess the courage to take her own life, and *I* cannot kill the woman I love so madly." Some days later, he adds : " Louise's father having seen us together, made a terrible scene, and Louise told me she dared not go with me any more ; so at last we must make an end." He struck his mistress several blows with a dagger in the breast and body, then shot himself in the mouth with a revolver. The neighbours, on running to the spot, found the man dead, but the woman still breathing. She was able, before expiring, to relate how her lover had struck her from motives of jealousy, adding that she had made all the resistance she possibly could. A witness confirmed her statement, declaring he had heard cries of help! murder!

A jealous woman on the other hand who falls ill and allows thoughts of suicide to master her, though she endeavours to induce her husband to share them, does not as a rule succeed, and lacking the courage to kill him, confines herself to simple suicide. "Over and over again in the course of her illness," says one husband, "my wife expressed the intention of committing suicide and proposed that I should tie us both up and that we should then submit to death by charcoal fumes. I agreed to this, in order to calm her, and for the time being she was satisfied. Then later on I talked her out of the scheme. However, yesterday morning, being seized afresh by her suicidal notions, and perceiving she could not induce me to die with her, she put an end to her life."

When jealousy arises between friends or relations, it straightway transforms them into implacable foes. In 1860, in the neighbourhood of Draguignan, two farmers lived together in the utmost friendship; they were always together, and each of the pair had made a will in the other's favour. Unfortunately they both fell in love with the same person. One of them won the fair one's favours and told his friend, who for his part had concealed his passion. The latter, maddened by the revelation and a prey to a frenzy of jealousy, proceeded to denounce his friend to the young woman's father, in order to put an end to the liaison. The other, on hearing of this piece of treachery, was violently angry and determined to avenge himself first and then commit suicide. He lay in wait for his former friend in the fields and stabbed him with a knife; this done, he swallowed poison, and death not coming quick enough, wounded himself mortally in the lower part of the body.

On learning the fact that his son Xiphares is loved by Monime, Mithridate cries in a passion of wrath:

"Ah! fils ingrat, tu vas me répondre pour tous ;
    Tu périras ! . . ."[1]

Nor is it on the boards only that suchlike scenes of jealousy occur between father and son, who are in love with the same individual, ending either in the murder of the son by the father, or in that of the woman. I have myself known a father, who was jealous of his own son, fire a pistol shot at the latter. In another case, a certain R—— attempted to kill a young girl he was violently in love with, and whom his son was equally attached to. The girl, who was merely wounded, gave the following account before the examining magistrate : "R—— told me he loved me with all his might, that in his eyes I was the most perfect woman in the world, that he had laid hands upon the photograph of myself I had given his daughter, my friend, and covered it with kisses every day, that he loved me madly, wildly, though he knew quite well he ought to do nothing of the kind. On hearing these words, I was so much agitated I began to tremble; he then came close to me as if to reassure me, but in reality to kiss me." This father who was so jealous of his son even grew jealous of the friendship existing between the girl he loved and his own daughter, whom he treated with such violence of language that she thought seriously at one time of drowning herself. He once more renewed his declarations of passionate love to the young woman he was enamoured of, and finally seeing she remained insensible to his ardour, because she loved his son, he fired a pistol shot at her. The Assize Court condemned him to ten years' imprisonment.

The main part of the observations I have made as to masculine jealousy are equally applicable to feminine. It may even be said that women are even more jealous than men. More even than vanity, more than love of dress,

[1] " Ah ! ungrateful boy, you shall answer for all ; you shall die ! . . ."

more than the love of mastery, jealousy is the dominant characteristic of feminine human nature. Only, in women jealousy is less often physical than it is with men. On the other hand, there is still more self-love in feminine jealousy than in masculine. Unable in the majority of cases to pursue either honour or power, knowledge or wealth, they set their pride and pleasure on pleasing, on making themselves loved, concentrating every thought on love. "Two pretty women may scarce be friends," said the great preacher Fléchier. Steadfast friendship, frequent enough between men, is rare among women; they are too jealous of each other. If jealousy is the main-spring of Racine's Tragedies, this is merely because Racine applied to the stage the observations he had made with regard to the women of the Court of Louis XIV. Hermione is jealous of Andromaque, Roxane is jealous of Atalide, Phèdre is jealous of Aricie, precisely as Mlle. de La Vallière is jealous of Mme. de Montespan, Mme. de Montespan jealous of Mlle. de Fontanges, and so on and so on.

There is little difference between the jealousy of great ladies and that of women of commoner clay. True, the latter come more readily to blows and open insult; but these battles royal and fierce bursts of passion are not unknown in the history even of princesses and queens. Elizabeth of England, learning that Miss Bridges was engaged in an intrigue with the Earl of Essex with whom Her Majesty was deeply smitten, had her summoned before her, overwhelmed her with reproaches and actually struck her.[1] The same queen, jealous of Lady Howard, whom she saw dressed out in a magnificent costume, made her take it off.—The daughter of Gustavus Adolphus, Queen Christina of Sweden, the monarch who called Descartes to her side and to whom Pascal dedicated his arithmetical machine, was not a whit less violent than the work-girl of to-day who throws vitriol in her lover's eyes. It is well known how she had her former favourite Monaldeschi put to death, because he had preferred a rival to herself;

[1] M. La Ferrière, *Deux Drames d'amour*, p. 253.

she laughed while they were cutting his throat before her eyes, and when Mazarin urged her not to come to Paris after the murder, she replied : " As for the action I have taken concerning Monaldeschi, I tell you, if I had not done as I have, I should not go to rest to-night without doing it, nor have I any reason to repent of my proceedings."

These rivalries between women find expression in mutual recriminations, fisticuffs, pistol shots or vitriol throwing. Sometimes the fury animating two rivals is so great it is impossible to bring them face to face before the *Juge d'instruction* or in Court. A married woman, who had been wounded by her husband's mistress, had an attack of fever on hearing that the *Juge d'instruction* was going to confront her with her rival. When a rivalry arises between a married woman and her husband's mistress, it is generally the former who, strong in her sense of right, strikes her unworthy rival. At the same time it is no uncommon thing to see the mistress, carried away by jealousy, seeking a quarrel with the lawful wife and telling her : " One or other of us is evidently superfluous."

It is the jealousy she feels with regard to her husband's first wife which so frequently makes the step-mother harsh and cruel towards the children of the previous marriage. The sight of these motherless beings, which should of rights inspire her with a tender compassion, irritates her as recalling the memory of one who before her time held so large a place in her husband's affections.

> " Des droits de ses enfants une mère jalouse
> Pardonne rarement aux fils d'une autre épouse." [1]

In fact the hatred the cruel step-mother exhibits towards the children of the first marriage is really only jealousy against the first wife. The same jealous dislike is also felt sometimes by men towards the first husband of a widow

---

[1] "Jealous of her children's rights, a mother seldom forgives the sons of another wife."

they have married, and the offspring of the earlier marriage.
Pyrrhus experiences it towards the son of Andromaque,
fearing Astyanax may too vividly recall the dead Hector,
and Andromaque admire in the boy "*his* eyes, *his* mouth,
and precocious signs of *his* gallantry." This jealousy on
the part of the step-mother often finds expression in acts
of cruelty. I will quote only one example, taken from a
recent judicial case ; a step-mother strangled her husband's
twelve-year-old daughter by a former marriage, and threw
the body into a well.—Sometimes children resort to suicide
to escape the brutality of their step-mother. I have even
noted the suicide of a young man of twenty, who hanged
himself, to avoid witnessing the ill-treatment his step-
mother practised on his younger brother.—If a step-mother
thus tortures the children of her husband's first marriage
it is because jealousy tortures her, driving her sometimes
even to the point of suicide. One man, who had been left
a widower with a little girl, had placed his child in an
educational establishment and married a second time.
When subsequently the girl, on the completion of her
education, returned to her father's home, tall, pretty and
the image of her dead mother, the new wife who had
replaced the latter, was so filled with jealousy that in a
spasm of fury she swallowed a phial of laudanum.

From the most trivial motives, women of a nervous
temperament, a prey to jealousy, take poison, smother
themselves with charcoal fumes, throw themselves out of
window, because their husband or lover, as the case may
be, has come home late, because he seems careless of their
love, because he refuses a kiss, or praises another woman,
and the like. I have myself known suicides due to every
one of these childish grievances. A jealous woman's
imagination exaggerates every trifle, puts an unnatural
construction on every incident, invents imaginary wrongs
to torment herself with, provokes fits of senseless despair
or baseless anger. The frequent quarrels that break out in
households and end in the suicide of the wife, generally owe
their origin to jealousy. After a more than usually violent

scene, the jealous woman opens a window, climbs over a balcony railing, and hurls herself into space, or else sets about her preparations for a death by charcoal fumes, after writing to her husband, " As we cannot get on together any longer, farewell! do not be angry with me.   It has to be."

A jealous woman longs to absorb her husband's every thought; she cannot witness without chagrin the affection he bears his friends,—they rob her of a share of the heart she would have entirely her own.   The wife of a man of letters may feel jealousy towards his books, which deprive her of a part of his time, and provide him with a happiness independent of her; the books are rivals,—she will endeavour to draw her husband from his studies, to bring him nearer to herself, to have him all her own.   A jealous wife cannot bear her husband to experience a single joy she does not share, she hates to share his heart and his time with anybody or anything.   Jealousy of the kind is no sign of a tender, loving, passionate heart, it is but a craving of her pride and spirit of domination; to fill her husband's thoughts so that he neglects his friends and his work, to keep him dominated, subjugated, absorbed by his love for her, is a delightful satisfaction to her self-love. A woman may also be jealous of her husband's good looks, not solely because it exposes him to the chance of other women being taken with him, but because it gives him a superiority over her, which humiliates her, and is liable to make him cold and disdainful towards her.   A woman who felt this jealousy of her husband, said on his being attacked by small-pox : " I hope with all my heart he may be disfigured ; he was too handsome altogether."

More particularly in the case of a wife who is older than her husband and who is now getting on in years, does jealousy assume an exceptional degree of intensity.   To see her hair whitening, her face wrinkling, her eyes growing dim and her teeth failing, while her husband still possesses his dark locks, fresh complexion, bright eyes and good teeth, and is quite able still to charm other women, gives her atrocious pain.   If to this is added the desertion of

her husband or merely the dread of this, which alone is
sufficient to cause her horrid suffering, we see her, under
the stimulus of an excessive and abnormal nervous excitement, now beg and pray her husband on her knees not
to forsake her, now threaten to kill him first, and herself
afterwards. Often these scenes of jealousy end in suicide
or else the murder of the husband and the suicide of the
wife. The woman buys a revolver, without precisely
knowing what she means to do with it; then one day,
after yet another scene, she turns the weapon against
herself or else against her husband.

In periods of Revolution, while men are led by ambition to denounce those whose place they covet, women
denounce other women of whom they are jealous. Under
the Terror jealousy laid low, as the result of treacherous
denunciations, more than one woman's head on the
scaffold ; and the authoress of the denunciation, the better
to relish her vengeance, never failed to take her place in
the first row to enjoy her rival's punishment.

There are mothers who are jealous of the youth and
beauty of their own daughters, sisters, and sisters-in-law
are jealous of each other. The Memoirs of Mlle. de
Rémusat tell us how jealous the sisters of Napoleon I.
were of Josephine. The mother who makes a match
for her son is often jealous of her daughter-in-law. Nay,
more! there are mothers who out of selfishness and pride,
would fain monopolize all their children's love and are
jealous of the affection they display towards other relatives
or even towards their father. Lastly, but more exceptionally, a woman may push her jealousy so far as to
be angry at seeing her husband showing more attention
to her children than to herself. I have even known
an instance of suicide proceeding from such a motive ;
a woman who thought her husband did not love her
enough, noticing that at table he would pass a dish to
his son before offering it to her, cried out in a burst of
senseless jealousy, "Enough of this!"—and opening the
window of the room sprang out into space.

Not that the women who complain the most bitterly of not being loved are themselves such as love the most ardently. Not only may there be in feminine jealousy more of egotism and self-love than of true passion, but there may actually be jealousy without love at all. Speaking of Count Almaviva, a libertine from sheer ennui and jealous out of mere vanity, Suzanne says to the Countess: "But why so much jealousy?"—"As with all husbands, my dear, simply out of pride," answers the Countess. The same observation applies, in very many cases, to female jealousy. A woman, though she cares little for her husband, does not therefore the less desire to be loved. This love flatters her vanity; she is irritated and offended, if she has to go without it, being robbed of it by another woman. Women who deceive their husband, may yet kill him out of jealousy. We give an instance. A widow of forty had relations with a young man, who however broke off with her because he learnt she had not been faithful to him; wounded at the slight, she tried to poison him. The young man taking his meals at an hotel along with other boarders, she slipped unperceived into the kitchen, and managed to throw a large quantity of arsenic into the pot-au-feu. Five persons suffered from vomiting in consequence. Then constituting herself nurse of the young man, who was one of the invalids, she attempted to give him a poisoned cooling-draught.

Jealousy may break out between father and son, mother and daughters, and lead to these monstrous crimes. Sons kill their father, daughters their mother, out of jealousy. Some years since, the Assize Court of the Bouches-du-Rhône tried the case of a young girl, who had killed her mother from jealousy, her lover being an accomplice in the act. Yet this girl had been brought up in a convent, where she had attracted attention by her peculiar piety. I found among the documents relating to the case a number of letters written from the convent, in which the school-girl in training there described the happiness she felt in hearing the Church music and witnessing the noble ceremonies of Religion. She had even thought of taking the veil. The Lady Superior of the convent where she had begun her religious noviciate wrote in the following terms to her mother: "Marie loves her dear father and her mother more than I can tell. When she speaks of them, all her being burns with ardour. . . . Oh! my dearest Madam, assure M. B—— with all confidence that Marie loves him fondly, and that nothing but the Will of God is strong enough to extort such a sacrifice from her. Tell him Our Lord is grateful to him for having given him his daughter for bride. . . . You are happy, most happy in never having suffered one impure breath of the wicked world to stain this tender flower, which has touched the sacred heart of Jesus. And indeed he loves his little Marie well and makes her very happy; she feels never a shadow of regret for having given up all that young girls desire and hope."

Some months later, having left the convent at her parents' order, she became the mistress of her mother's former lover. Jealous of the latter, she conceived a violent hatred of her. The mother having fallen ill, she longed for her death; then, on her recovery, she plotted with her lover to kill her, jealousy turning her into a parricide. Her lover asked her hand in marriage, and was refused; furious at this, he said to the girl: "Will you be mine?"—to which she replied, "Yes! I will."— "Well, then! only one way remains, we must get rid of your mother." At first the girl made sundry objections, but soon, dominated by the hatred inspired by her jealousy of her mother, she agreed to the plan of murder. "Feeling as I did the most ardent love for Léon," she declared to the *Juge d'instruction*, "I experienced a fierce passion of jealousy towards my mother." We reproduce the account she herself gave of the murder: "Léon began by striking her with his fists, and trying to strangle her, but as she resisted, he was obliged to take a kitchen knife. The creature would not die; she resisted fiercely and pushed Léon away, even after she had received two knife thrusts in the throat. He struck her on the mouth and broke two of her teeth; then my mother having got possession of the weapon, Léon called to me to fetch a big cheese knife; I got it and gave it him, and he plunged it in her throat." Further examination revealed the fact that, while the victim was struggling, her daughter had kicked her; and when she was dead, the accused had trampled upon her body. The two lovers carried the corpse down into the cellar and set to work to cut it into pieces, to make it unrecognizable. They divided the four limbs from the trunk, and attempted to cut off the head, but without success. Next day they went and threw the body into the sea. On coming back, they went to bed and indulged in sexual intercourse. In a letter she wrote to the *Juge d'instruction*, the accused added: "I cannot account for my having done what I have, I who would not have stayed by a dead person for all the wealth in the world."

I am bound for the sake of completeness to say something of the horrible scenes of jealousy caused by fathers who abuse their own daughters. It is a revolting subject, yet I cannot pass it over in entire silence. There are mothers who tremble when they see their husband kissing their daughters. Some to save their children's honour, actually give information to the law; others, terrified by the threats and violence of their husbands, do nothing to prevent these monstrous acts, but suffer agonies of grief at such a state of things. Among the many cases of this kind I have had before me, I remember one father who had abused his two daughters and had got them with child. He would say, "I did not bring girls into the world for other men to enjoy." The mother, who was aware of his abominable doings, dared not denounce him to the police; she only made up her mind to do so when she saw him beginning attempts on the third daughter, who was now growing up. Another father told his two daughters: "Though they should send me to the hulks for it, I am determined to give you each a child."

These incestuous relations are often accompanied by
jealousy. A father, who had abused his daughter, was
seized with jealousy and endeavoured to get her shut up
in a Penitentiary, laying a false charge of immoral
conduct against her.—Another girl, a victim to her father's
lubricity, was forced in order to avoid exciting his jealousy,
to be always badly dressed, with her hair in slovenly
disorder; her father forbade her to pay the smallest
attention to her toilet. For fear she should attract the
attention of a young man, who came to ask her hand in
marriage, he kept her shut up indoors, prevented her
speaking to the neighbours or leaving the house to look
for work. Eventually however he agreed to her marrying,
on condition of her going on with her relations with
himself. · But he became jealous of his son-in-law, and
compelled his daughter to come back to him, taking
her furniture away from her.—A father who abuses his
daughter and becomes jealous of her, invariably opposes
her marrying. One father who had at last consented to
his daughter's marriage, forced her to submit to him on
her very wedding-day, immediately after she had put on
her wedding costume for the religious ceremony. In
another case, the accused was a retired gendarme, who
exceedingly jealous of his daughter whom he had abused,
had stabbed her with a knife. Some time previously, he
had wished to kill a young man who had given the girl
his arm for a walk. Among girls who are the victims of
these monstrous acts, but dare not complain, some suffer
so terribly they end in committing suicide. I have known
the case of one such who killed herself in despair along
with her mother, to escape these incestuous outrages. It
has been said that "every man has in his heart a sleeping
swine"; and the swine often awakens with horrible results.
We may even go so far as to say there is no brute so foul
and cruel as to rival man in lubricity and cruelty. Fathers
are found ready to procure abortion in their daughters, to
strike them, to trample their bodies to bring about this
result. Nor are these monstrous passions only of modern

date ; they have always existed. Jousse relates how a President of Commission ("President aux Enquêtes") of the Parliament of Paris, Aimar Rauconnet, convicted of incestuous intercourse with his own daughter, was confined in the Bastille, where he committed suicide, foreseeing the sentence of death to be pronounced upon him. De Thou, who mentions the circumstance in his History (Bk. xxiii.), says he was a man of much reading and deep learning.

Jealousy depending largely on temperament, and temperament on climate, it is in the South, among the people of Provence and Corsica, among Italians, Greeks and Spaniards, that I have noted the most cruel and outrageous crimes inspired by jealousy. Under a sky of flame men's passions are fiercer than under one of ice. Fiery love is more often than not but the outcome of fiery suns. The heart is hotter in the South, because the blood is hotter there ; *Ut est genus Numidarum, in Venerem præceps* ("As is the race of the Numidians, headstrong in passion"). Love is more ardent and sensual, and *pari passu* jealousy more violent, in Provence, in Italy, in Spain than in Northern lands. Amongst Northern nations, imagination and day-dreams often play a greater part than the senses. Jealousy and the point of honour form the stock-in-trade of the Spanish stage, simply because these are the most prevalent and the strongest emotions in Spain. To fully understand the nature of jealousy among Southerners, I propose to give a few instances borrowed from recent trials.

In a comedy entitled "The Shorn Maid," Menander brings on the scene a love-sick and jealous captain, who cuts off his mistress's hair in a fit of jealousy. A certain Matracia, brought up before the Assize Court of the Bouches-du-Rhône on a charge of murder, had practised the same act of jealous violence on his wife, a woman of uncommon beauty ; he cut off her hair, and exposed her in a state of complete nudity at a window. In another fit of jealousy he bit her in the face, tearing out her nose with his teeth.

Some years since, at Marseilles, the sailors on board a Greek ship, hearing shouts of pain coming from their captain's cabin, hurried there to find him stretched on a bed with a wound in the groin from which the intestines protruded. His mistress had that moment stabbed him with a knife, because in the course of the day he had kissed a Greek woman. Often no more than this is needed to rouse the jealous fury of a Provençal, an Italian or a Greek woman. A woman of the South will punish her lover in the most horrible way merely because she has seen him talking to another; for this reason alone quite lately, at Marseilles, a woman poured a bottle of vitriol over her lover, as he lay asleep, drenching him from head to foot; in spite of the cries of pain he uttered she went on emptying the corrosive liquid onto his body to the last drop.

In the neighbourhood of Toulon, a young married man, by name S——, being constrained to break with his mistress, one R——, killed her, that she might never be another man's. The woman, who resided with her father, was on her side passionately attached to her lover; to use the expression of a witness in the case, she was infatuated with him and was ready to tear out the eyes of any one who should stand in the way of her love. Intensely jealous of the lawful wife, she repeatedly provoked very animated scenes with her. Outraged by her husband's faithlessness, the wife complained to her father, beseeching him to put a stop to it. Deeply grieved at his daughter's sorrow, the father conceived so fierce a hatred against his son-in-law's mistress that, again to follow a witness's phrase, "his eyes jumped out of his head" when he spoke of her. As the result of his representations, he extracted a promise from his son-in-law to break off the connection and restore to his wife her peace of mind; but still dreading a change of sentiment, he formed the plan of getting rid of the mistress during a walk by the sea, and proposed that his son-in-law should join in the plot. The latter rejected the idea, but promised, in order to make the rupture final, to leave the country and take his wife with him; later still, he abandoned this design, being now firmly convinced his mistress would follow him wherever he went. Hereupon the father-in-law returned to the charge, and ended by getting the other to see the necessity of killing the mistress; the lover acquiesced in the project, because he wished, when breaking with her, to have the certainty she would never belong to another man. To strike the blow when she was in her father's house was plainly impossible; she must be enticed into the fields, into some lonely spot. Acting on his father-in-law's advice, S—— invented a tale, promising his mistress he would elope with her at night and quit his wife for ever. R——, surprised at this right about face, felt some suspicion just at first, but this soon yielded to her love, and she made her preparations for flight. One night, in the face of a terrible storm, she left her father's house and joined her lover, who was waiting for her. Fearing and suspecting nothing, proud and happy to be flying with him, she allowed him to lead her to a lonely place where the father-in-law was waiting, concealed behind a rock. The instant he saw her, he sprang upon her and stabbed her several times over, but without killing her. The lover then joined in to help him finish her. After a terrible struggle with the two murderers, the woman fell dead, gashed with twenty-four knife thrusts.

Here is the account of a murder due to jealousy as given by the accused himself, who was blind. "Exasperated at my wife's ill conduct, I made up my mind to kill her; I bought a knife, after feeling it well to make sure it had a good point. In the night I grasped my wife by the neck, (she was sleeping by my side), and planted the knife in her throat. She only gave one cry, for she was only a little wren.[1] I waited by the bedside for two hours,[2] to

---

[1] A Provençal expression signifying anybody as small and frail as a little bird.

[2] The fact came out under examination that during these two hours the murderer sat quietly smoking cigarettes.

make sure she was dead, and as soon as I felt she was cold, I came away here to give myself up."

When an Italian workman is bitten by jealousy, he seldom fails to treat his rival or else the woman who has rejected him to menaces of death of this kind: "I will tear your skin off you, I will! I will cut your throat open!"—and he does cut his victim's throat according to promise. There are Italians who will out of sheer jealousy bleed women like sheep, or kill a man as readily as drink a glass of wine; they have a habit of heating the blade of their dagger red-hot in the fire, after rubbing it with a clove of garlic, to give the steel a keener temper. One Barbiéri, deeply enamoured of a young woman whom he wished to make his wife, although she was ten years his senior and was engaged to another man, threatened her with death; he showed a comrade a shoemaker's knife, telling him it was poisoned, and saying in a few days' time he would be the talk of the neighbourhood if the girl persisted in her refusal. She was the daughter of an innkeeper and obliged to talk to the travellers and boarders who frequented her father's establishment; yet the Italian would look at her savagely whenever he saw her speaking to other young men. "Some day or another I shall kill her," he would say.—"Why! you're mad," a witness told him.—"You're quite right," he answered; yet a few days afterwards, he had his knife sharpened and cut the poor girl's throat.— Another Italian, deeply in love with his brother's wife, fired several shots at her with a revolver as she was putting her children to bed; he wounded her and killed one of the latter.

Murders arising out of amorous passion are frequent among Italians, just as are political and anarchical assassinations, and murders where gain is the object. According to the Statistics published by the Ministry of Justice, there were in Italy in 1890, 3628 persons accused of wilful murder and of inflicting blows and injuries resulting in death; in 1891, 3944; in 1892, 4408; in 1893, 4336. Writers tell us that the progress of civilization has brought about a decrease in crimes of violence; I fail to verify this decrease from the Italian statistics.

If the Italian is guilty of a greater number of murders from motives of jealousy than the man of other nationalities, it is not to the "energy" of his character we must attribute this homicidal fury, but rather to the vindictiveness of his temperament and his excessive excitability. An Italian will often kill a man on the most trivial provocation; to avenge an insult, a witticism, a slighting remark, he will strike a passer-by or a companion dead; in different parts of the country, he uses knife, razor, shoemaker's knife or revolver. Three quarters of the murders and assassinations tried before the Assize Courts of the Departments of the Bouches-du-Rhône, Var, Alpes-Maritimes and Basses-Alpes, are committed by Piedmontese, Tuscans and Neapolitans. I have known Italians kill a passer-by who merely asked them not to sing so loud in the street, —kill an inn-keeper who turned them out of a drinking-shop,—kill an awkward dancer who trod on their foot at a ball,—kill a creditor who claimed payment of his debts, —kill a comrade who splashed them inadvertently with mud, and so on. It is incredible to what a pitch the Italian workman will carry his excitability. Quite lately at Toulon a working baker—an Italian—was called a "stale loaf" by a fellow-workman, with whom he had a trifling disagreement; two days afterwards, he shot him with a revolver to avenge the taunt, and declared in his examination that the insult he had received thoroughly deserved the punishment he had exacted. I could quote a hundred similar instances.

This fierce, murderous vindictiveness has always been observed as an Italian characteristic, at all periods of history. Most of the great artists of the Renaissance were continually taunting each other and fighting it out with fists and sticks and knives, for some dispute of the work-room, some rivalry in love, sometimes for even slighter causes. Caravaggio was for killing a cook because he had sent him up a badly seasoned dish of artichokes. The

Italian language has a special word to signify a violent man, one who is ever ready to take up the knife; he is called *uomo di cotello,*—"man of the knife."

The Spaniard, like the Italian, is quick to avenge himself on a rival or a woman of whom he is jealous, being no less touchy and proud. Here is a recent instance of Spanish excitability. Two workmen, shoemakers, one a Frenchman, the other a Spaniard, were working together; the Spaniard began to sing; the Frenchman criticized him; the Spaniard remarked that Spaniards were as good singers as Frenchmen, and on his companion making an uncivil retort, hurled his cobbler's knife at him, which remained sticking in his side, so that the victim had to pull it out himself. At his trial, on the judge asking him why he had given his comrade a wound that might easily have killed him, the Spaniard answered: "He treated me with disrespect." When jealousy combines in a Spaniard with a character of this proud, touchy sort, there is no act of savage vengeance it may not lead him to commit.

Among the savage peoples of hot countries, jealousy on the part of the man is so violent that women in some cases disfigure themselves in order to be less liable to rouse their husbands' jealousy, who may kill them in a fit of passion.—In the East, the women are kept in confinement, and never go out without veils which hide the face, because the men are always suspicious of their fidelity. The holy Legislator of the ancient Hindus "assigned to women love of their bed, of sitting still and of fine clothes, concupiscence, anger, bad inclinations, the wish to do evil and perversity of temper." (*Laws of Manu,* ix. v. 17.) So Manu would counsel the husband to watch his wife "night and day . . . in order to preserve his line," and to chastise her, whenever she committed any fault, "always on the posterior portion of the body." (*Laws of Manu,* viii. v. 299, 300.)—The founder of the Mussulman Faith had likewise but a low opinion of feminine virtue; he asks "whether we must count as God's child a being that grows up absorbed in embellishment and dress." (Koran, xliii.

17.) In Eastern lands, men despise women, and keep them confined to the house, where they are strictly watched by eunuchs. It is notorious how common are dramas of jealousy in the harems. Such a drama forms the subject of Racine's Tragedy of *Bajazet*.

In Switzerland, on the contrary, murders proceeding from jealousy are, like other crimes of amorous passion, of very rare occurrence. Two years ago, when visiting the Gaol of Lausanne, in which are confined the prisoners of the whole of Canton Vaud, undergoing sentences of more than a hundred days' detention, I found, out of 208 men and 20 women, only a single prisoner who had committed (fifteen years before) a crime of passion ; this was a husband who had killed his wife from jealousy. The Director of the Prison told me that not a single case of feminine vengeance had been known in the whole of Canton Vaud for a number of years.—But every rule has its exception, and we may occasionally find among Northern peoples temperaments as passionate as any of the South. Christina of Sweden, daughter of Gustavus Adolphus, known as the " King of Snow," used to say of herself : " My impetuous temperament has given me no less marked an inclination for love than it has towards ambition." Two romantic writers of the most passionate natures, Jean-Jacques Rousseau and Mme. de Staël, belonged to Swiss families.

Jealousy is capable of inspiring the most cruel instincts in a man of a hitherto good-natured and generous disposition. An honest working-man, who had strangled his mistress out of jealousy, said to the *Juge d'instruction* in the course of some reflexions on his past : " Till now nobody has ever had anything to say against me, and to-day I am a murderer ! This is what passion has made of me."—Othello was good-natured, loving and generous ; Cassio says of him, " He had a noble heart." Ludovico adds, breaking in :

> " O thou Othello, that wert once so good,
> Fall'n in the practice of a damned slave
> What shall be said of thee ? "—

to which Othello replies :

> "Why, anything ;
> A murderer, if you will."—

A good workman, and a man of excellent reputation,—a shoemaker once more, brought to trial in February 1892 for the murder of his wife whom he had killed out of jealousy, thus related the circumstances : " I struck my wife a violent blow with my shoemaker's knife, as she was sitting on a chair beside the bed and beginning to undress. Holding her by the hair with one hand, I struck her in the throat, from which a perfect torrent of blood instantly spouted out. The blow was so violent, my wife could not utter a single word and fell from her chair on to the ground, moving her arms and legs about."—*The "Juge d'instruction"* : " The doctor noticed the fact, and so did we that your wife's neck had been forcibly constricted by means of a scarf in which you had made a slip knot."—*The accused :* " As my wife continued to move a great deal, in spite of the enormous quantity of blood she was losing, being half mad I conceived the idea of cutting short her sufferings by tying a cravat round her throat. After a few minutes I found she had ceased to stir."—It came out in the course of further examination that the following day the murderer had gone to work at the establishment of a master shoemaker and there used the very knife with which he had killed his wife.—Euripides noted long ago how love may drive men, hitherto good-hearted and generous, into crime : " Love, indomitable Love," sings the chorus in the *Antigoné* . . . "the man possessed of you is a prey to madness. You even pervert the hearts of just men, to drag them to their undoing."—To win the hand of Hermione, Oreste turns murderer. Jealousy will transform into criminals men who have been honourable and upright hitherto.; it puts the fatal weapon in their hand and incites them to vengeance.

Jealousy leads to a large number of murders, as well as of woundings and acts of violence. The total of murders due to jealousy, as given in the statistics of the Ministry of Justice, is not complete ; it only includes cases where the criminal has actually been accused and brought up for trial. But a large number of such murderers kill themselves after despatching their victim; and so prosecution being rendered superfluous by the death of the criminal, these murders followed by suicide are not included in the general statistics. Besides, a large number of acts of violence inspired by jealousy, without involving death, cause broken health, serious mutilation, blindness, or the loss of a limb, sometimes a shock to the brain resulting in insanity. But all such cases do not come before the Criminal Courts ; a large proportion are dealt with by the Correctional Police.

Murders determined by jealousy are sometimes premeditated, sometimes the outbreak of a sudden fit of the passion. A jealous husband who had strangled his mistress told the *Juge d'instruction* that on going to bed with her in the evening to pass a last night by her side, he had hidden on a chair the rope he intended to use next morning ; this he had taken care to rub with soap to make it more slippery. The mistress noticed the rope intended for her, but she paid no heed, thinking her lover had bought it to hang himself with. The man had in this case long premeditated his crime. Three days before, in the course of a dispute he had with his mistress, he took her by the throat, saying : " One day when I hold you this way, you won't talk quite so much." The quarrel ended, he was observed to be plunged in a deep reverie, and on being asked what he was thinking about, he replied : " I am thinking of her ; I have given her three days more to live." And three days afterwards he strangled her.

On the other hand murders of this kind are often enough quite unpremeditated ; the thing comes so suddenly the man is astounded at his own crime, cannot understand how he came to do it, and even finds difficulty in recalling the exact circumstances. Perhaps a husband, catching his

M

wife *flagrante delicto,* strikes and kills her in a sudden access of blinding rage. Perhaps a lawful wife, confronted unexpectedly with her husband's mistress, cannot contain herself, and springs upon her hated rival. Or perhaps it is a husband, who, meeting his wife's lover in the street, and surprising some signs of mutual understanding between the guilty pair, on noticing a gleam of love and pleasure on his wife's face, leaps furiously at the lover and strikes him down. In other cases, a husband, on receiving from his wife's lips a cynical avowal of the wrong she has done him, loses his head and kills her on the spot.

The satisfaction of every passion affords pleasure just at first, however certain to cause regret subsequently. A jealous man, like a forsaken woman, finds in the vengeance exacted a genuine feeling of content, that makes the most severe pain a matter of indifference. A husband, who had killed his wife's lover, on being confronted with the corpse looked at it with an air of satisfied anger and said, turning to the magistrate : "*I* care nothing for the scaffold."— Another man, who had killed his mistress in a fit of jealous fury, exclaimed in his delight at being avenged: "What care I about going to Cayenne for twenty years ; I was determined to kill her."—A mother, whose daughter had been killed by a young man who had wished to marry her, indignant at the indifference displayed by the murderer in presence of his victim's dead body, asked him fiercely: " Are you satisfied now, you monster ? "—" Yes ! " returned the murderer, " I am satisfied ; 'tis you who are to blame for your daughter's death, because you would not let her marry me."—This indifference to pain and suffering is sometimes kept up by murderers from love till the hour of their trial, at which they refuse the indulgence offered them by the Court, and ask for death, that they may be buried beside their victims. But in such cases this indifference to pain springs from love and remorse, which have succeeded to the outburst of rage and jealousy.

Some writers on Criminology have supposed this indifference to pain and the satisfaction the victim of jealousy experiences, to be proofs of an abnormal moral state. No doubt the satisfaction of revenge resembles the feeling of relief a neuropathic patient is conscious of on the accomplishment of an act, the idea of which has long possessed his thoughts; it is a relaxation of his whole being, an indefinable sensation of relief. But this satisfaction experienced by a man in the accomplishment of his revenge does not constitute a moral anomaly; it is so keen a gratification, it has been called the pleasure of the Gods. Revenge is so natural a passion that Classical Mythology attributed to the Gods the most atrocious acts of this kind. If the Gods were so vindictive, what wonder if men are the same under the empire of jealousy. Anger strains the nerves and inspires a craving for revenge, that causes positive pain so long as it remains unsatisfied. This pain ceases on the accomplishment of the act of vengeance, it brings about a discharge of the electricity the nerves were charged with; and this relaxation of the nerves constitutes a real relief. Moreover, if we observe during their confinement criminals of jealousy who have found satisfaction in revenge, we note sudden reversals of behaviour, changes of ideas and sentiments, which show them to be constituted like other people; the majority display remorse for their crime. How many husbands who after killing their wives declared themselves happy in knowing themselves avenged, break out of a sudden into sobs and manifest the most lively repentance!

The mistake committed by Drs. Despine and Lombroso and the Criminologists of their school, is that of paying exclusive attention to the language held by persons accused of crimes of violence at the moment of their commission; they omit to observe criminals after their crime, under examination, at a time when their attitude and sentiments have widely changed. The very same persons who at the moment of committing their crime or soon afterwards, cynically declared they felt no sort of regret, that they were glad to have satisfied their vengeance and were indifferent to pain, express very different sentiments under examination. Then we hear them say: "I now deeply regret what I have done; at the present moment I realize the fact that I have done wrong and am sorry for it, though at the time I was mastered by my anger."—When the neighbours came running up at the cries of a woman who was strangled by her jealous lover, the latter said to them, pointing to the spot where he had thrown his victim: "She is yonder! She is dead, and I killed her; I am glad, and now I can die." If they had stopped there, without studying the murderer's character during the days following the crime, he might undoubtedly have been adjudged differently constituted from other men and the victim of moral anomaly. But, a few days later, the same criminal told the *Juge d'instruction*: "I am now sorry for what I did; if the crime were to do again, I should not do it."—Moral madmen exist, I am well aware; but then they are either insane or degenerate. Doubtless among those guilty of crime, there are degenerates suffering from moral madness, but all criminals are not degenerates.

CHAPTER VI.

ADULTERY ON THE PART OF THE WIFE.

"Happy, peaceful marriages! Happy the woman, whose bed is chaste."—EURIPIDES.

ADULTERY, which forms the mainspring of literary dramas, is not less fertile in judicial dramas; it is responsible for countless crimes and suicides. Never a session of the Court of Assize or a sitting of the Tribunal of Correctional Police at Paris occurs, at which one or more cases of adultery do not come up for judgment, and one or more murders resulting from them,—whether murder of the adulterous woman or her companion in guilt by the husband or that of the husband by the adulterous woman or her accomplice. A man, and still more a woman, who thought themselves to be merely indulging in an act of folly in committing an adultery, often find themselves led on to deeds of criminality, which they did not for an instant foresee at the beginning, and the world, that loves to make merry over conjugal mishaps, soon ceases to laugh, when it learns they have ended in an act of marital vengeance or a murder of passion.—A wife's adultery is not merely for the husband the heaviest possible blow to his honour, the shattering of all his dreams of love and happiness, the origin of painful suspicion as to the paternity of his children, the beginning of a scandal or else the resigning himself to a painful cohabitation with a woman he can no longer trust, it is often also the declaration of open war between the two and between the husband and the lover, the breaking out of a struggle at the domestic hearth, before the eyes of

children, relatives and servants, fought out with pistol
shots and knife thrusts, followed by a *cause célèbre* and an
appearance before the Assize Court.

According to Plutarch, adultery was unknown in Antiquity among certain peoples. Among the inhabitants
of the Island of Chios "in the space of 750 years, there
is no record of any married woman having ever committed
adultery or of any unmarried girl having been deflowered."
—According to Tacitus, instances of adultery were very
rare among the Germans ; their women lived "enveloped in
chastity. No one among this people makes light of vice ;
to be corrupt or to corrupt others is not styled the way of
the world . . . a woman is allowed once and once only to
form the hope and vow of being a bride, . . . in the being
to whom she unites her lot, it is not so much, as it were,
the husband she loves, as marriage itself."

On the other hand among the nations of the East
adultery was very frequent, and the legislator had so
little confidence in women's virtue as to account her guilty
of adultery on the slightest indications. According to
the *Laws of Manu* (viii. v. 256) proof of adultery followed
from the undermentioned facts, "being attentive in little
things to a woman, sending her flowers and perfumes,
toying with her, touching her ornaments or dress."

In modern days adultery and the crimes arising out
of it are growing more and more common. In France
especially, the number of adulteries has more than doubled
in the last ten years, in fact it has almost trebled ; 711 in
1883, it grew to 1657 in 1891, 1781 in 1892, 1813 in 1893,
1973 in 1894, and 1964 in 1895.[1] The advance is un-
interrupted. Between 1826 and 1830, the average of
adulteries was 53 a year. The law re-establishing divorce
has had the effect of multiplying the number of adulteries
fivefold.

We are bound moreover to remark the fact that the
total of adulteries brought before the Courts is insignificant
as compared with the number of those committed. The

[1] Report of the "Garde des Sceaux," *Journal Official* of 9th Nov. 1897.

great majority of these offences remain unknown to the husbands; and even where they are aware of them, the most part refraining from laying any complaint,—in this following the advice given by Bishop Carnus, the friend of Saint Francis de Sales, to an unfortunate husband who consulted him: "Believe me, my friend, it is better to be called Cornelius Tacitus than Publius Cornelius."

The causes leading to adultery on the part of the woman are very numerous and very complex. The chief are: disproportion in age, a marriage reluctantly entered upon, an education not suitable to the surroundings in which the wife is called upon to live, ennui, curiosity, vanity, exaggerated love of luxury and dress, romantic sentimentalism, lengthened absence of the husband, temperament, awkwardness and roughness of the husband at the commencement of married life, excessive novel reading and indulgence in sentimental music, bad advice and evil example of women already corrupted, etc., etc.

§ 1.—*Disproportion in age.*

The man who, being already of mature age, marries a young girl, wilfully runs a great risk of playing the part of an unhappy husband. Molière and C. Delairgne have both depicted the sorrows of an old man wedded to a young girl; the *Annales judiciaires* frequently become the repository of the fact that such a husband is likely very soon to regret his infatuation. In the course of judicial proceedings, adulterous wives sometimes declare in the most outspoken and cynical terms the reason of their ill behaviour; a woman, who ended by poisoning her husband, was in the habit of answering his remonstrances thus: "I am young, you are old, I have no child, so I take my fling."

I have myself been acquainted with the case of a wife who poisoned her husband, now getting old and incapable of properly satisfying her, that she might marry a younger man.

Women married to old men take young men as lovers;

these they choose among their daily companions, among kinsmen, neighbours, among their husbands' employés, sometimes even among their servants; and it is not uncommon to find them inciting their lover to rid them of their old husband. I read in the account of a criminal trial how a woman in bed with her lover urged him in the following terms to kill her husband, a very old man: "If you were a man, you would get up this instant, go into the country where my husband is at present and finish him. . . . I shall never be happy till I am rid of him." The lover went where he was told, and the woman was soon rid of her old husband.

In another case, a wife accused of murdering her husband, pleaded as the determining motive of her crime the disproportion in age existing between her husband and herself: "My husband," she said, "was twenty-five years older than I; we had had no proper connexion with one another for years."—Women who declare themselves *misunderstood*, who find their duties repugnant to them and declaim against Law, Society and Marriage in the name of so-called philosophical principles, have as a rule only grievances of a quite commonplace physiological nature to reproach their husband with,—grievances arising from a too marked difference in age.

Still disproportion in age does not invariably prevent the birth of love and even of very ardent love. I have myself had occasion to observe in a young woman of nineteen brought up for trial an ardent passion for a lover of sixty. Some few years ago in the neighbourhood of Aix a Captain of Artillery on half pay, seventy-six years of age, and his young wife of twenty-six, determined to die together, utilizing the fumes of burning charcoal for the purpose,—the husband to escape intolerable physical pain, the young wife so as not to survive her husband whom she adored. In a will she had made, the wife begged her brother to have a little tomb built, "where I long," she wrote, "to lie beside my dear husband." The pair were found still breathing, but a few days later the husband died. Frantic with grief, the young widow went to the tomb of her septuagenarian husband and there shot herself with a revolver; she was found dead, her right temple pierced by a ball, her face pressed to the ground and holding in her hand a revolver with five chambers still loaded. This instance alone is sufficient to show the critics are wrong, when they reproach the famous novelist, M. Zola, with describing an impossibility, the love of a young girl for an old man. Other similar examples I could quote, prove that M. Jules Lemaître and F. Sarcey are justified in thinking the dramatic author and the novelist may without exceeding the bounds of probability put back considerably the limit of age within which a man can love. In the *École des Maris*, Ariste who is no longer young makes Léonore love him and marry him, paying no heed to the jests about "an old man's love," of which she is made the subject. Sometimes also young men are found stirred by a wild infatuation for quite old women. It is not long since a married man of thirty-two committed suicide along with a woman twenty-five years his senior.

But such cases of mutual love between individuals of disproportionate age are after all exceptional. The love of a young girl for a man of mature years is very rare and never lasting. We cannot conceive a septuagenarian, sexagenarian, or even quinquagenarian Romeo.[1] A young girl who marries an old man may sometimes be moved by the words of love she hears for the first time and mistake for love what is really only the wish to get married. A

[1] Corneille who could not guard himself against love at a mature age, was ashamed of the fact, when at fifty he became enamoured of Mlle. Duparc; in *Pulchérie*, he makes the Senator Martien say:

> " L'amour dans mes pareils n'est jamais excusable ;
> Pour peu qu'on s'examine, on s'en tient méprisable,
> Ou s'en hait et ce mal qu'on n'ose découvrir,
> Fait encor plus de peine à cacher qu'à souffrir."
>
> (Act ii. Sc. 1.)

" Love in men of my age is never excusable. The slightest self-examination and you feel yourself contemptible ; you hate yourself, and the blow you dare not reveal, gives even more pain to hide than to endure."

girl of fifteen, who had been induced by a widower of forty-one to fly with him, told the *Juge d'instruction* that the fond words and promises of marriage the man had addressed to her had made a most profound impression on her mind. " The idea of marriage," she said, " never left me now, and under the sway of this overmastering thought, I ceased to be either industrious in my work or respectful towards my parents."

More often than not these disproportionate marriages end badly. History is full of instances of marriages made unhappy by too great a discrepancy of age between the contracting parties. Sophie Monnier,[1] who became Mirabeau's mistress, was sixteen when she married the Marquis de Monnier, a widower and sixty. When the Duc de Longueville married Mlle. de Bourbon, " he was old (forty-seven), she was very young and as lovely as an angel," as Mademoiselle put it ; the unhappy issue of the match is familiar to all.

I never understand why we give the name of " marriages of reason " to these unions (really so unreasonable) between two persons of disproportionate age. Reason condemns such marriages. A truly reasonable marriage is a love match between a pair whose ages are concordant. In Roman Law, according to the Lex Papia, great discrepancy of years was a sufficient obstacle to marriage.[2]

If husbands too far advanced in life are, as a rule, predestined to conjugal mishaps, those of too youthful an age are also sometimes failures. In the first case, adultery on the wife's part is to be feared ; in the second, it is the husband's conduct that gives cause for anxiety. The Marquis d'Entrecasteaux, President of the Parliament of Provence, who cut his wife's throat on the night of the 30th

---

[1] After her liaison with Mirabeau, she was on the point of contracting a marriage with a gentleman of family who was deeply in love with her ; death having taken him from her, she committed suicide.

[2] *Traité du Mariage*, by Astruc, Professor of French Law at the University of Toulouse, p. 131.—According to the old Genevese laws, a man who exceeded sixty could not " take maid or woman in marriage less than half as old as himself." A man of sixty therefore could not marry a woman of less than thirty.

31st May 1784, so as to be able to live freely with his mistress, has left a record written by himself of the imprudence his parents were guilty of in marrying him so young. "My parents," he wrote from his prison, "married me very young, for I was wedded at eighteen. . . . This, according to what they said, was to protect me against the passions of youth; but they failed to consider that these passions being as yet undeveloped, what they did was to imprison them up within me in bonds they put upon me, rather than to guard me against their assaults. The more closely they were confined, the more violent was their explosion, and the more terrible their effects."—In these too early unions the husband is liable to weary very quickly of his wife, to neglect her or to leave her at home to seek more adventurous pleasures abroad; sometimes even, finding her interfere with his freedom, he endeavours to get rid of her by criminal means. One young husband accused of a crime of this sort, had driven his wife from home at first and afterwards murdered her, declaring when he dismissed her: "I married too young, I want to have some fun now; later on I intend to take my wife back." —Too youthful a husband cannot rule his house or govern his wife, he is feather-brained, reckless and jealous. Here is an instance taken from the records of the Law Courts. A young workman of nineteen married a girl of his own age; before long he quite wore out his wife with his fits of jealousy and brutality. At last the girl losing all patience returned to her mother's house and petitioned for a divorce. Then the husband, broken-hearted at her leaving him, and exasperated by her action, besought his wife to come back to him; on her refusing, he bought a pistol, waited his opportunity, and stretched her dead by a shot from a revolver, after which he turned the same weapon against himself.

§ 2.—*Forced Marriage.*

When a girl cannot marry the young man she loves or fancies she loves, but is forced by her parents to marry someone else, this marriage seldom turns out happy. The young woman always regrets the man she would fain have married, and often gives herself to him, when circumstances bring them together. In *Polyeucte*, Pauline who has been unable to wed Sévère, the man she loves, and has been obliged by her father to take Polyeucte as a husband, succeeds by virtue of sound sense and right feeling in driving away the memory of "that perfect lover," who once filled her heart, and thoughts and aspirations, and to love her husband from a sense of duty and from admiration of his noble character. But Paulines are rare. Corneille's heroine even hesitates to see Sévère again at her father's orders declaring :

"Mon père, je suis femme et je sais mes faiblesses . . .
Il est toujours aimable et je suis toujours femme." [1]

She trembles for her virtue, for she already feels her old predilection awaking afresh :

"Dans le pouvoir sur moi que ses regards ont eu,
Je n'ose m'assurer de toute ma vertu." [2]

Of less heroic mould than Pauline who has strength to master her desires, many a woman, married against her wishes by her parents, cannot bring herself to love her husband ; she becomes the enemy of the man they have made her marry,[3] and her relatives are responsible for any faults she may commit.

"Et qui donne à sa fille un homme qu'elle hait
Est responsable au ciel des fautes qu'elle fait." [4]

At the same time even a love match does not invariably safeguard a woman against adultery. After six months

[1] " Father, I am a woman and I know my weakness . . . he is still loveable and I am still a woman."

[2] " In view of the dominion his looks have over me, I dare not be confident of all my virtue."

[3] *Hostis est uxor invita quæ ad virum datur.*—" The wife who is given an unwilling bride to a man is his enemy." Plautus.

[4] " And he who gives his daughter a husband she detests, is responsible to heaven for the faults she commits. Molière, *Tartuffe.*

of marriage, Mary Stuart was disgusted with Darnley, whom she had married for love.—Mme. Weiss, who tried to poison her husband, had married him with the utmost enthusiasm : " It was," she tells us, " with an exquisite joy, an ineffable tenderness, I learned his intention to marry me ; I spent the night on my knees in an outpouring of gratitude to God." Her family setting their faces against the marriage, she followed the man she loved to Algeria, and was married to him eighteen months later ; after giving him two children, she gave him a dose of poison. Women of fickle disposition and high-strung imagination, readily forget their first love, and answer, when their husband reminds them of former days : " You want me to love you still ? What would you have ? I cannot do it, I don't love you any more." A husband's calm and monotonous affection is not enough for them, they crave a new love, something ardent and passionate.—A doctor, who had seduced a young girl and then married her out of love, was abandoned by her, after she had made him the father of eight children. " I loved the woman fondly," he declared, " she possessed every means of charming, beauty, amiability, wit, artistic susceptibility ; her voice was adorable, her intelligence of a high òrder. I was dazzled and subjugated the first time I saw her."

A woman who previously to marriage deceived her relatives is very likely later on to deceive her husband. Rosine, who allows herself to be seduced by Lindor, once made Comtesse d'Almaviva, listens to Chérubin's suit and becomes a "guilty mother." A man, who had abducted his wife from her parents' house and had cause subsequently to regret it, said during his trial to the examining magistrate : " What are you to expect from a girl who ran away from her family ? "—The advice of Desdemona's father to Othello was similarly conceived : " Watch her well, Moor, keep an open eye on her outgoings ; she hath deceived her father, and may well do the like to thee." The experience of the Courts of Law confirms the observation of the great English psychologist ; among adulterous

wives, who do not stick at crime to rid them of their
husbands, we find women who have married for love
and deceived their parents and relatives to run away
with the object of their choice.

§ 3.—*Education disproportionate to the Social Condition
and Education of the Husband.*

Not only ought the ages of married people to be well
suited, but their tastes, sentiments and education must
be well matched also. A wife whose education is superior
to that of her husband, feels an inevitable repugnance to
the tie which binds her to a man who is her inferior ; the
love her husband shows her does not touch, it only annoys,
her. Vanity plays an important part in every woman's
love ; to love her husband, she must be proud of him,
find satisfaction for her vanity in his wit, his talents, his
social position. The most solid qualities of heart and
character are not enough to ensure a husband's being
loved ; if he wounds his wife's self-esteem by want of
personal distinction or vulgarity of manner, if his wife
finds him common, coarse, unworthy of her, she is not
far from being unfaithful to him, and indifference and
contempt lead by a rapid transition to downright dislike.
It is extremely difficult for a woman to love a husband
whose manners and conversation make her blush. It is
not long ago that the Assize Court of the Department
of Corrèze had occasion to condemn a woman who had
put the muzzle of a revolver to her husband's ear during
his sleep, and pressing the trigger with a firm hand had
lodged a bullet in his head. The motive for her act was
simply a deep dislike she had conceived against him. He
was a good and worthy man, but she despised him, and
had deceived him, being his superior in intelligence, education and family standing.

Mere external qualities are often better appreciated than
moral ones by women of small intelligence. To a husband
possessed of a good heart and a sound brain, they will prefer

a silly, chattering drawing-room fop, the sort of insipid, sugary creature who gives much thought to his clothes and is great at small talk. If they receive attentions from a man of *distinction*, holding a brilliant position or possessed of the aristocratic affix, they will fall straight into his arms from sheer silly vanity,—like Mme. Bovary in Flaubert's novel, who, married to a village doctor, is flattered at the idea of being M. Rodolphe de la Huchette's mistress. The aristocratic "de" and titles of nobility simply fascinate them. A provincial beauty of middle-class origin and a vain disposition, living in a country village, has a poor chance against the assaults of a gentleman from Paris, who seems to her everything that is *distingué*. This *distinction* often consists in a woman's eyes simply and solely in the good cut of a man's clothes. In a trial for murder, where a husband had killed his wife's lover, I heard the woman with my own ears admit she had been seduced in the first instance by a common bully's fine clothes.

§ 4.—*Romantic sentimentality.*

Women who expect too much from marriage, who imagine in the exaltation of their fancy it is going to bring them infinite happiness, heavenly bliss, experience inevitable disillusionments that are liable to lead to no little mischief. Dreamers of impossible dreams, they are astonished to find their husband does not possess all the perfections they fondly imagined ; expecting a bliss the mere thought of which draws soft tears from their eyes, they are shocked that marriage does not ensure unlimited happiness, and conceive a grudge against husband and marriage generally for their disappointment. They feel wretched with a husband they think too grave and cold ; failing to understand their companion, they consider themselves "misunderstood" by him, and look out for some "hero of romance" to appreciate them and bring them the happiness so fondly desired. These dreams of infinite love and perfect happiness, so irreconcilable with the stern realities of life, are suggested by the reading of too many novels or a mystical sentimentalism that overstimulates the fancy. From mystical reverie to amorous exaltation is but a step. In fact the two states may be said to lie so near each other as to be practically indistinguishable; romantic souls make love into a religion, while mystics turn religion into amorous ecstasy. One and the same phraseology serves to express love and sensuous mysticism. Mme. de Staël, relating the double suicide of a German lady and her lover, an officer and a poet, which occurred in 1811 at an inn at Potsdam, tells us how the two lovers, in the letters and documents they left behind, compared their reciprocal murder to the Sacrament, and had left a Service Book of the Lord's Supper open beside them. The woman, who had forsaken her little girl to join her lover, had written saying she would watch over her from on high. I have had occasion in several different legal cases to note the fact that women guilty of crimes of passion had in their earlier years undergone crises of mysticism. The same observation had already been made by Flaubert in *Madame Bovary*; he declares the adulterous heroine had when a girl based her religious feelings on a high-strung mysticism, small acts of pious devotion, and the pleasure of attending imposing ecclesiastical ceremonies and hearing beautiful church music.

§ 5.—*Platonic Love.*

Religious feeling is a safeguard against adultery, but always on condition it is genuine and does not degenerate into sensuous mysticism; for sentiment leads a woman to Platonic love, and Platonic love to another and less ethereal sort. No matter what illusions it may flatter itself with, love craves possession, and possession of the heart alone is not sufficient. It cannot remain for ever intellectual, and anyone who yields to it, thinking to continue master of his senses, may aspire to be an angel, but is on the way to becoming a devil instead. His heart may be full of high and noble aspirations, but he soon and inevitably drops into very prosaic realities.

Romantic women are very apt to be seduced by the illusion of Platonic love. Lord Byron, relating the Platonic love of Julia for Don Juan,—a quaint tale that ended in a very commonplace way,—exclaims very wisely : " Oh ! Plato, your accursed fancies, your system, assigning an imaginary virtue to the undisciplined heart of man, have paved the way to more immorality than all the long list of Poets and Romance writers." How many women have been caught in the snare of protestations of Platonic love, such as one I find among the documents in connection with a criminal case, addressed by a young man to a married woman: " I would prove I pay you a worship more pure and holy than ever maiden rendered to her Madonna. . . . Does not such humility then deserve one kiss as its reward?—a sister's kiss, if you will, a kiss on the brow." We know pretty well what comes of this sort of kisses.

Again romantic women are often seduced by the melancholy of dark heroes of melodrama who recount their sorrows to win consolation at fair hands. When their sadness is genuine, they exaggerate it, well knowing its power over the sex, and that pity leads to love. This, for instance, is what the student Chambige did with Mme. X——, a romantic spirit, who found life sad and repulsive, though she had the happiness to possess fine children, and who marvelled at the resignation the friends of her own sex displayed in face of the dreary conditions of life. He told her a long story about his mental griefs, a story that touched the young woman's heart, and soon led her from pity to a tenderer emotion. To stifle her scruples of conscience, she told him she would be no more than a sister to him, but before long, after a fainting fit he had, she declared her love for him in less fraternal terms, telling him she loved him because he had felt and loved deeply. Indeed two hearts that have suffered much feel themselves naturally drawn to one another. Here is a

N

letter I found among the papers of a woman who committed suicide in consequence of a love tragedy: "He suffered, and I suffered, atrociously; behold the mystery that brought us together!"—A man who was brought to trial for having fired off a revolver at his former mistress out of jealousy, told the *Juge d'instruction* it was the woman's sad, woe-begone look that had first attracted him.

Pity for undeserved misfortunes is often the prelude to love. Confident in the propriety of so generous a feeling, the woman thinks she may yield to it without remorse, but little by little the sentiment grows more tender and grows into passionate love. Virgil and Shakespeare, those two excellent observers of the human heart, have depicted this transition from pity to love in the hearts of Dido and of Desdemona. The account Æneas gives the Queen of his battles and disasters makes a profound impression on her. She owns as much to her sister:

> " Quelle intrépidité !   Quels revers !   Quels combats
>   Ont éprouvé son cœur, ont signalé ses bras ! . . .
>   Mon âme en l'écoutant se sentait alarmée. . . ."[1]

In the same way, it is while listening to the adventures, combats and hardships of Othello, that Desdemona is first stirred to pity, and then to love. "I told her all my story," says Othello . . .

> " Wherein I spake of most disastrous chances,
>   Of moving accidents by flood and field,
>   Of hair-breadth 'scapes i' the imminent deadly breach,
>   .   .   .   .
>   And often did beguile her of her tears
>   When I did speak of some distressful stroke
>   That my youth suffer'd. . . .
>   She loved me for the dangers I had pass'd,
>   And I loved her that she did pity them."
>
>   (*Othello*, Act i. Sc. 3.)

---

[1] " What gallantry !   What calamities !   What encounters have tried his heart, and signalized his arms ! . . . My heart, as I listened to his tale, felt itself alarmed. . . ."

§ 6.—*Ennui.*

Ennui constitutes a grave danger.   The woman who is its victim is tempted to seek some stirring emotion, some adventure, by way of distraction, to find amusement in unlawful love.   Virtuous hitherto, she begins to regret she has always been so.   Licensed affection seems insipid, guilty love poetical,[1] while weariness of the austere pleasures of family life, curiosity, the wish to extend her knowledge, *libido sentiendi* (Pascal), the hope of a happiness greater than any she has experienced heretofore, awake in her a craving for unknown and untried pleasures. She feels herself tempted to give ear to those who, seeing her sad, are eager to offer consolation ; at first she listens out of mere coquetry, from the want of anything better to do, to cheat the ennui that is eating her heart out, presently she is caught in the trap and one fine day finds herself assailed by the same passion she has inspired. Solitude, good for people who love the country, is bad for those who are only bored there.   Few women really love the country, while many are in the latter case.   A woman wrote in a letter addressed to the *Juge d'instruction* : "Idleness and the ennui I feel in the country, added to the bad advice of one of my female friends, were my undoing."   It is ennui, and nothing else, that throws the Queen into the arms of Ruy-Blas.

§ 7.—*Temperament.*

A romantic woman, who seems dominated by the longing to find a twin soul, is ready enough to put down to an impulse of the heart what is really only an impulse of the senses.   When she yields to the fascination youth exercises over a woman of mature age,

---

[1] An American lady caught in the act of stealing in one of the big Parisian shops, at the very moment she had 70,000 francs in her pocket, when questioned as to the motive for such apparently unaccountable behaviour, (for she was perfectly well able to have bought the articles she stole), made the following reply : "There is such an exquisite pleasure in stealing,"—the pleasure, in fact, of forbidden fruit.

she dissimulates her love under the cloak of fraternal or maternal sentiment; she lavishes on the youth she is enamoured of, a store of advice and counsel, directs his conduct, calls him her dear boy, and likes him to address her as his little mother.[1]

This love of a woman of ripe age for a man younger than herself has been often represented on the stage; we find it in *Henriette Maréchal* by the brothers Goncourt, in *La Crise* by Octave Fruillet, in *Les Effrontés* by Émile Augier. It is seen again in the case of some famous women—for instance in that of the Duchesse d'Albany, who was fifty-one at the date of Alfieri's death, whom she replaced by the painter Fabre, a much younger man than herself,—in Diane de Poitiers, who after being the mistress of François I., held the position with his son,—in Queen Caroline of England, who was proved to have committed adultery with the courier Bayami, and in many other instances. Magistrates often meet in the course of their duties in connection with civil or criminal trials with cases of adultery on the part of the farmer's wife with a young farm labourer, of the shop-keeper's with one of her husband's employés, of the notary or barrister's wife with a clerk, of the superior officer's wife with a young subaltern, of the Procureur or Judge's wife with her husband's Substitute, and so on. I once had occasion to prosecute a young labourer who from motives of jealousy had burnt his mistress's crops, a rich widow whose lover he was. He might have applied to himself a bad verse of Racine's on Pyrrhus:

"Brûlé de plus de feux que je n'en allumai."[2]

It is a physiological craving far more than any impulse of tenderness that as a rule urges a woman to adultery

---

[1] Such was the case with George Sand, who was thirty at the beginning of her liaison with Alfred de Musset, then twenty-three, as also of Mme. de Warens with Rousseau. G. Sand used to style Alfred de Musset her son, while he spoke of himself as her darling boy. This combination of maternal sentiment and sensual love is a sort of incest, and G. Sand touched the truth when she wrote to de Musset: "You are right, our kisses were incestuous."

[2] "Myself consumed with more fires than I kindled."

with an inferior, an employé of her husband's or a domestic servant. Empresses, like Theodora and Messalina, gave their favours to athletes. In Roman Law there were special enactments against women who surrendered themselves to their slaves. Old French Law punished with very severe penalties adultery committed by a valet with his mistress, or with his lord's wife. Muyart de Vouglans quotes a decree of the Parliament of Paris condemning a servant to be hanged for having committed this crime with his mistress, in spite of the fact that the latter had lured him on by indecently exposing herself before him. Fournel cites the case of a lady of quality, who caught in adultery with a waggoner, was condemned to the gallows in 1567, along with her accomplice. Another jurisconsult, Bruneau, mentions a magistrate's wife who was convicted of adultery with her farm tenant, and another lady of quality convicted of the same offence with her husband's clerk.

Female Don Juans are to be found as well as male. There are women who fly from one intrigue to another with the greatest ease, feeling no repugnance for difference of education and social position ; in pursuit of an ideal they never attain, under the spur of sensual inquisitiveness and the love of variety, they are for ever seeking new experiences, and disciples rather of the naturalistic than the idealistic, indulge in ever fresh adventures as fancy prompts them. Seducers are not all of the sterner sex.

Plutarch tells us that the Romans in returning from a journey, used to warn their wives of their near arrival to avoid the risk of exposing them to an unwelcome surprise. I have had occasion myself to note in several criminal cases, that the husband who remains too long away runs the danger of being forgotten and betrayed. Just at first the wife who is left behind alone, indignantly rejects the solicitations addressed to her, but little by little as the time draws out, her resistance weakens ; and before very long the husband's letters are not welcomed with the same delight, her replies become less frequent, less warm and less affectionately worded. In proportion as her heart grows cold towards the absent one, it warms to the sighs of the suitor on the spot.

Husbands who are compelled by their calling to remain away from home for months at a time, are exposed to the risk of finding on their return their wife to be pregnant or the mother of a child that is none of theirs. I have just been looking into a case against a woman named Marie Bapt, who having become enceinte during her husband's absence, poisoned the infant she gave birth to, because her husband refused to rear it. "I am a great criminal," she declared to the *Juge d'instruction* in reply to his questions, "and I deserve to be punished ; but I was driven to the crime, for my husband would not keep the child he was not the father of."

Other cases of adultery arise out of convenience of opportunity, a fine audacity on the seducer's part, a sudden surprise of the senses :

> " Une femme d'honneur peut avouer sans honte
> Ces surprises des sens que la raison surmonte." [1]

All women however do not possess Pauline's coolness in getting the better of these surprises, which indeed may overtake even women who love their husband ; taken unawares by an audacious, unforeseen assault, paralyzed by stress of feeling, they yield actually against their inclination, and when their shame is consummated, cannot account for a weakness they bitterly regret. I have myself seen in an assize trial how a woman who really loved her husband yielded to a sudden surprise of this sort, and afterwards experienced such violent remorse for her sin, that her health gave way under the strain. Day after day she bewailed her fault in secret, shutting herself up in her room to weep the more freely. One day her husband discovered her in tears and asked what was the reason of her distress ; on this she confessed everything, ready to

---

[1] " An honest woman may avow without shame these surprises of the senses which reason masters."

expiate her offence and even finding a certain solace in the admission of her guilt and the craving she felt to suffer punishment for it. So terrible a blow was this revelation to the husband that he fainted away on hearing it ; when he came to his senses again, he burst into tears, first cursing his wife, then presently forgiving her. After several days of cruel torture for both, he turned her out of the house, and she went back to her parents. A month later, he finally forgave her and took her back. Then, still a prey to fierce anger against his wife's betrayer, he started out to kill him.—In another murder trial where the husband had killed his wife's lover, the woman confessed she had given herself repeatedly to a friend of her husband's, though she loved the latter all the while, and was quite unable to account for her weakness. This is the *cruel enigma* M. Bourget has analyzed in a novel bearing that title, and in the criminal case I have mentioned the riddle was even more cruel than in the work of fiction, for it involved a woman hitherto of unblemished virtue, while the book deals with one who is the mistress of several lovers. A strange riddle indeed,—the conduct of a woman who loves her husband, feels remorse for her offence, and yet repeats it ! A woman may feel remorse, have right feelings towards her husband, and yet yield to the promptings of the senses; she is sorry for her fault because of its consequences and the grief it causes her husband, yet she does the same again. So in Homer, Helen is wasted with weeping, but all the time she never dreams of leaving her lover and going back to Menelaus.

When a husband is incapable of satisfying the passions of a Messalina, he runs not merely the danger of being replaced, but of being put out of the way into the bargain. Some years since the Assize Court of the *Bouches-du-Rhône* tried the case of a woman of thirty-seven, a veritable Messalina, who had debauched all the men of the hamlet where she lived, married men and bachelors alike.[1] She

---

[1] The passion of a dissolute woman is "a madness never reached at their coupling time by savage creatures and brute beasts." Aeschylus.

was married to a man of advanced age, who finding himself powerless to curb her ill-behaviour, had made up his mind to put up with it; yet she had conceived a violent grudge against him in spite of the fact that he did not interfere with her pleasures in any way. After two unsuccessful attempts to poison him, she had him murdered by one of her lovers at a country farm where he had gone to spend some days with his brother, to get in the olive harvest. Handing her lover a kitchen knife and a gun, she despatched him to the farm in question at dusk, giving him a detailed plan as to how the crime was to be done; "Now is the favourable moment," she said, "there is no moon; you can start without anybody seeing you. When you reach your destination, you must knock at the door under some pretence or other, and my husband or my brother-in-law will open it; you must lie down a short while beside them, and as soon as they are asleep again, you must strike; then you will set fire to the house, and so an end." The lover started, and carried out the double assassination in exact accordance with his mistress's instructions. The latter awaited his return all night with feverish impatience; at five o'clock in the morning, she went to his house and learned to her satisfaction that "all was finished," that her husband and brother-in-law had been murdered and consumed in the burning house. Nothing was found among the still smoking ruins of the farm except the calcined remains of the two corpses. When these bones were collected and placed on a cart to be carried to the cemetery, the woman, wishing to seize this opportunity for bringing home some of the farm produce, had two bags of olives loaded on the waggon, side by side with the chest containing the mortal remains of her husband and brother-in-law, mounting her thirteen-year-old boy on the equipage to drive. Under examination the lover related how he had bled the two old men to death, like a shepherd cutting beasts' throats.

The weakling husband of a depraved woman may fall sick, die of vexation or commit suicide as in the following instance: "My son," a mother says, "was married three months ago; it is now a fortnight since his wife went back to her own country; she is the cause of my boy's suicide, because he could no longer satisfy her,—she was so passionate. As late as yesterday he told me he felt exceedingly ill."

Still we must beware of generalizing from these isolated cases of insatiable sexual appetite in women ; the number of Messalinas in the world is far from being as great as novelists would have us believe. Sexual desire is much less powerful in women than in men ; the sexual passion is at once more violent, more aggressive and more brutal in the male. He it is who attacks and provokes, while his choice is determined more by physical than by moral qualities. Women on the other hand are, as a general rule, rather coquettish and vain than really sensual, more appreciative of tenderness, little attentions and acts of homage, loving looks and the like, than of manifestations of brutal passion. Her love is more psychical than physical, her choice governed rather by moral and intellectual gifts than by physical endowments. If she is guilty of adultery, she is more to blame than a man, because her sexual organization makes virtue easier to her than to him.

§ 8.—*Music.*

Danger lurks everywhere for a woman,—in the dissipations of society, in idleness, pleasure, parties, injudicious country walks, dances, operas, duets with music teachers or amateurs. The Romans feared the effects of music and dancing on women; Scipio Æmilianus called them dishonourable arts. No doubt this antique austerity was excessive, but are we not nowadays fallen into the opposite extreme, leaving women and even young girls freely exposed to the intoxication of love songs and erotic music ? Sometimes a young woman practising music with her teacher suffers what happened to Heloïse when Abelard was entrusted with her education. "The books were open before us," says Abelard, "but we talked more love than philosophy, and kisses were more frequent than sentences, my hand wandered to her bosom more often than to our books." Like Uncle Fulbert, the husband sees nothing, and the teacher cannot sufficiently admire his innocent simplicity.

§ 9.—*Pride of Beauty, Love of Dress.*

The love of pretty clothes is an essentially feminine passion. Rivalry in dress is often the cause of keen jealousy between women. Corneille, whose psychological genius I find pleasure in drawing attention to, has not failed to notice this trait in the psychology of Creuse, who is jealous of Médée's robe:

> "Après tout cependant, riez de ma faiblesse . . .
> La robe de Médée a donné dans mes yeux ;
> Mon caprice à son lustre attachant mon envie
> Sans elle trouve à dire au bonheur de ma vie." [1]

There are women ready to find consolation for the mourning they must put on in the thought that it will suit their complexion. In several criminal cases, I have seen the woman, taken red-handed in adultery and having narrowly escaped being shot, resume almost instantly her extreme preoccupation with matters of dress. This love of finery is responsible for the ruin of a large number of women, who let themselves be seduced, like Marguerite in *Faust,* by the offer of jewellery. When a vain woman, possessed by the longing to wear pretty frocks, has not the wherewithal, she seeks it in adultery. This forms the subject of Émile Augier's *Lionnes Pauvres.* The married woman descends to the level of the prostitute, or really lower.

When a vain woman is condemned to imprisonment, the

---

[1] "Yet after all,—laugh at my weakness, if you will . . . Médée's robe has dazzled my eyes ; my fancy, attaching my envy to its gloss, has other reasons too to find fault with the happiness of my life."

necessity of donning the gaol uniform which makes her look plain is more painful to her than the shame and disgrace. The loss of her beauty, and above all the cutting off her hair, sometimes occasions a degree of despair that ends in suicide.

The desire for elegance and becoming clothes, which is the natural appanage of every woman, is still further augmented by the habits of our own day. The passion of vanity has made the same strides among women as that of equality has among men. Just as every man busies himself with politics, and supposes himself quite capable of being a Counsellor General, a Deputy, a Senator, a Minister of State, without ceasing to be a hatter or a hairdresser, a mason or a street porter, so every woman, small shopkeeper's wife or working man's or what not, is fain to be dressed with as much elegance as the great ladies of society. Just as we find grocers, tailors, bakers, fishmongers, asking for posts out of all proportion to their claims, so we see women without a penny contract habits of luxury and expensive dress.

Beauty is another danger by attracting men's admiration, but poets and moralists have greatly exaggerated this risk. According to Propertius, "inconstancy is the attribute of every pretty woman." Ovid is of the same opinion : "Why take a beautiful wife, if you wanted a virtuous one? Virtue and beauty cannot go together."—"When a wife is faithful, 'tis a sure proof she is ugly," writes Seneca in his turn.[1] There is a great deal of exaggeration in these maxims ; beauty and virtue are frequently found together, and a want of beauty is not the best guarantee of female virtue. Plain women are not less inconstant than pretty ones ; if they are less sought after, they are all the more sensible to such homage as they do receive, and their self-love is more easily flattered. Receiving little admiration, they are all the more eager for it, and devour it greedily ; bitterly jealous of their fairer sisters, they seek to prove in this way they are not so entirely their inferiors, and think they

[1] *De Beneficiis*, iii. § 16.

are besting nature, that seemed to have refused them the gift of pleasure by denying them beauty. Seneca contradicts himself and refutes what he has said in the *De Beneficiis*, when he declares in his *De Matrimonio* that a plain woman will always throw herself at the head of the first comer. The world is apt to suppose the heroine of a love drama must always be a woman of remarkable beauty. This is quite a mistake ; very often she is of very ordinary good looks, often rather plain than otherwise. I have again and again observed this to be the case.

§ 10.—*Bad Advice.*

To the causes of depravation I have so far pointed out must be added bad advice on the part of women already corrupted, who take a malicious pleasure in communicating the taint to others. Just as a poor man is naturally jealous of a rich, and an unfortunate man of a prosperous one, so a ruined woman is jealous of the consideration an honest one enjoys, and cannot forgive her her good name. She longs to bring down to her own level the woman who now has the right to despise her, and so escape her contempt ; she wishes to humble her more virtuous sister, who crushes her with her airs of superiority,—a superiority that stirs her envy and dislike, and is a constant source of humiliation to her. It is by poking fun at marriage and making the husband appear ridiculous, by veiled confidences as to her own situation and its happy conditions, by excuses and sophistries she suggests, and instances she quotes, by meetings she contrives, and romantic novels she puts in her hands, that the woman of light character gradually weans her friend from her husband. Mme. d'Epinay relates in her Memoirs how this work of corruption was tried upon her by Mme. d'Ette, mistress of the Chevalier de Valory. A woman, who hitherto has remained true, is at first shocked by what is said to her ; but little by little under the influence of the mischievous sophisms she hears, her indignation diminishes, her reason is perverted, her scruples disappear, the attraction of the forbidden fruit awakens in her troubled fancy, and she ends by thinking perfectly natural a breach of her marriage vow that in the first instance revolted her beyond words. How often do magistrates hear this cry from women on their trial: " It was bad advice was my ruin ; my friends alienated me from my husband, telling me, one that he was too old for me, another that he was so plain and unfashionable, and so on. I cannot understand how I came to listen to them, for my husband was a kind, devoted, and loving man."

To sow discord in a household is an essentially feminine amusement. The woman of light character desirous of fomenting discord between her friend and the latter's husband, scarcely ever fails to persuade her that her husband is courting another woman. This she does to rouse her jealousy and get her to follow his example ; for a woman stung by jealousy is tempted to avenge herself by throwing herself at the head of the first comer. It is no uncommon thing moreover to see one or other of the husband's male friends employ the same tactics, telling the wife of real or supposed infidelities on the part of the husband, in order to stir her resentment, and then profit by it. Sainte-Beuve, as is well known, pursued this line of conduct with the wife of a famous friend. I have myself seen in a criminal case this treachery on the part of the husband's friend provoke the wife's adultery and this adultery bring about the murder of the false friend at the husband's hands. A certain A——, a married man, was the bosom friend of one C——, also married. The households lived in the same house and saw a great deal of each other ; A——, taking advantage of his friend's absence from home, used to come in sometimes in the afternoon to chat with C——'s wife, and informed her that her husband kept mistresses, and did not care for her at all. Mme. C——, who loved her husband, refused at first to believe these calumnies, but one day she was convinced and in a spirit of resentment and revenge gave herself to the author of them.

Nor is this sort of bad advice given only by friends and companions; women are often led astray by their female cousins, their sisters, or even their mother. From jealousy and dislike of their son-in-law, we see mothers-in-law countenance their daughter's adultery; they discover all sorts of defects in their son-in-law, and tell his wife of them. They say he is plain, undersized, ill-mannered, badly behaved, and express regret they did not give their child a more eligible husband, one like so and so, whose merits they point out specially and in detail. All this tends to turn the wife against her husband. Other mothers-in-law go even further; they directly encourage their daughter to take a lover, or at any rate refrain from blaming her, if they discover she has one. Juvenal long ago noticed the complaisance sometimes shown by mothers-in-law towards their daughter's lover. I have observed instances of the same thing myself. A retired officer in the Army, who had been guilty of serious violence towards his wife, when questioned as to the motives of his behaviour, gave the following reply: "Thinking to marry a well-brought-up girl, I found myself in presence of a second-rate actress, who took lessons in elocution from a former Associate of the Comédie-Française, and who had the most immoral instincts. More than this, her mother, who wished to keep her beside her, stirred her up against me to such a degree that even if I could have succeeded in combating my wife's natural propensity to behave badly, my efforts would have been continually thwarted by my mother-in-law's interference."—In another case, it was proved in evidence that a mother was in the habit of advising her daughter to take care of her beauty and not have too free intercourse with her husband, telling her, "You are much too good for him, my dear."—When a husband complains to his mother-in-law of his wife's bad behaviour, saying, "I am a good husband and father, you have nothing to bring against me; yet your daughter dishonours my name," the mother-in-law only answers with a smile.—The Governor of the Prison of Saint-Lazare told me he had often heard mothers

say to their daughters who were in confinement there :
" Make haste and get well, so and so is waiting for you."—
I have even known a mother advise her daughter to poison
her husband, telling her by way of encouragement that
she was herself no less determined to kill her own, and
pointing out to her how free and happy a double widow-
hood would make them.   " As soon as your husband is
dead," she told her, " I will kill mine too, and we will go
away and live together."   Some days later, she came again
to inquire whether her daughter had begun to administer
poison to her husband.   On the girl's telling her, " I dare
not do it ; if it came out, I should be undone,"—" You are
a fool," her mother replied, " no one will ever know ; what
is there to be afraid of ? "   Some time afterwards, coming
once more to see her daughter, she told her, " You are very
stupid not to have given anything to your husband yet, I
am sure ; well ! if you don't begin, I *shall*."   Spurred on
by these reproaches, the girl went out and bought poison
and gave her husband some.   During several days the
mother came regularly to ask after the invalid and inquire
how the poisoning was getting on.   She considered her
daughter was giving the poison in too small doses, and so
prolonging the sickness unduly ; she was impatient at the
long time her son-in-law took to die, and asked her
daughter repeatedly, " Come ! when am I to see you
in mourning ? "   She urged her to increase the quantities
administered, and begged her not to let herself be moved
to pity by her husband's sufferings.   Finally, she did not
forget, when his last moments were approaching, to have
a notary called in and get her son-in-law to make a will
in her daughter's favour.

Again, women of the lower classes are led to commit
adultery and even to murder their husbands by ill advice
given them by fortune-tellers and witches they consult.   A
young woman, whom one of the former, a woman who told
fortunes by the cards, had recommended to poison her
husband, so as to be more free, eventually after much
hesitation followed her advice, the woman having assured

her that if only she burned a candle to the "Good Mother" to secure the divine protection, her crime would never be found out.

These fortune-tellers, who abuse the confidence of women, girls and country folk, do an incalculable amount of harm, sowing discord in families, and facilitating seduction and adultery. I cannot understand why the Law does not endeavour to get rid of this social plague-spot; it could easily be done in many cases by applying Article 405 of the Penal Code dealing with the offence of "obtaining money by false pretences." Certain of impunity, these women ply their trade at markets and fairs in country places, while in towns they advertise their addresses in the newspapers. They have always been very numerous in Paris. In the Seventeenth Century, a sorceress was arrested by La Reynie who declared there were more than four hundred witches and magicians in that town, "who ruined great numbers of people, especially women and of all ranks of life." (*Le Drame des poisons*, p. 105.)

Adulteresses are always ready to combine dissoluteness and devotion. The Roman ladies used to visit the Augurs to consult them about their lovers. "Tell me, Janus . . . but dost answer suchlike questions? Have the Gods nothing more serious to attend to in heaven yonder? Truly your Olympus can have but little to do! One woman consults thee for a comic actor, another recommends to your divine care a Tragedian," writes the satirist Juvenal (Sat. vi.).—Women calling themselves Christians pray to heaven to secure the success of their guilty love. Aveline wrote to her lover, "This week I visited Notre Dame des Victoires, and had a candle burnt for the realization of our plans.—Mary Queen of Scots, writing to Bothwell, her lover, says: "Each of us is united with a faithless mate. Pray the Devil separate us from them, and God join us twain together for aye. . . . This is my confession of faith, and I am ready to die in the same. . . . I ask naught else of God Almighty, but only that you understand what I have in my heart, the which is yours." When

the Queen was planning her elopement with Bothwell, she
wrote to him : " I pray the good God we may soon see one
another in joyfulness."[1]—In a fit of despair occasioned by
the breaking off of her liaison with Alfred de Musset,
George Sand appeals to God, writing thus in her private
diary : " Ah ! give me back my lover, and I will be a pious
woman, and my knees shall wear out the church floor."—
The wife of a rich merchant of Marseilles, having become
the mistress of the youthful vicar of a suburban church,
listened anxiously in the morning for the sound of the bell
to tell her whether her lover's morning mass had taken
place at the usual hour.   The sacring bell not having rung
till later, she cried : " Yes ! he is a saint ! he would not say
his Mass before he had been to confess."   When the
accomplice of an adulteress is a priest, he will urge her to
fulfil all the customary outward acts of devotion, but
dissuade her from going to another priest for confession,
when she wishes to do so, in order to be able to com-
municate on some Holy Day ; he dreads lest confession
to a priest of the district may lead to the discovery of his
guilt.

Sometimes adulteresses go yet further, and unite piety
and crime.   In Mme. Gras' prie-Dieu were found filthy
books and a box of hashish compounded with cantharides ;
she appeared in Court with a huge rosary on her arm and
wrote hymns in prison.—A young wife who wished her
husband dead, on noticing that he had fallen ill, cried joy-
fully, " Ah ! if only God would. . . ."   But God having
shown Himself unwilling to rid her of her husband by a
natural death, she helped on his sickness by poison, praying
God to make it act as she wished and promising Him her
deepest gratitude in case of success.   " If only God could
have pity on me," she cried, " how I would bless His Holy
Name !   When he (the husband) groans, I praise the Lord
from the bottom of my heart.   Yesterday he was very ill ;
I really thought God was beginning to help me ! "

---

[1] Teulet, *Supplément au Recueil du prince Labanoff*, pp. 17, 18, 58.

§ 11.—*Intemperance.*

Intemperance in women is the prelude to adultery. The Romans long ago noticed the fact and used to say that "any woman who makes immoderate use of wine shuts her heart to every virtue and opens it to every vice." Valerius Maximus relates how a husband beat his wife to death to punish her for her intemperate habits, adding that "all men held she had justly expiated by an exemplary punishment her violation of the laws of sobriety."[1] We moderns are very far from such severity; our habits and laws are favourable to alcoholism, which has made alarming strides. Just as we very largely attribute to the progress of alcoholism the increase in the number of criminals, madmen and suicides, we are justified in holding intemperance responsible for the adultery of a certain proportion of women, especially among the working classes. Drunkenness, especially in Paris, works havoc in not a few households. In the Eighth Court of the Correctional Tribunal of the Seine, of which I was a member, we had every sitting to judge 8, 10, 12, 14 persons arrested on charges of drunkenness, and among these were women and even girls of 15, 16, 17 years old, who had already contracted habits of intemperance and were living a life of prostitution. The three other Correctional Courts of the Seine have an equally large number of cases before them. Drunkenness makes a woman, just as it does a man, violent, lustful and ill-conditioned. The married workman, who is a drunkard, beats his wife and children, and makes them endure all sorts of hardships, even including hunger; if a bachelor, he grows idle, dissipated and sometimes "bully" to some fast woman; he beats his parents, robs them and refuses to go to work. The workman's wife who gives way to drink, neglects her household duties, deserting her husband and children to indulge in a life of riot.

Alcoholism at the same time abnormally over-stimulates

[1] Valerius Maximus, Bk. XI., ch. iii., No. 9.

the sexual passion and diminishes the victim's power of resistance.

§ 12.—*Defects on the husband's side.*

Again, a wife's adultery is sometimes due to physical defects on the part of the husband or by a coarseness and want of delicacy that inspire her with disgust. The repugnance Mary Queen of Scots felt towards her first husband, Darnley, arose from that nobleman's bad breath ; she writes herself to Bothwell, " He hath well-nigh killed me with his breath, for 'tis stronger than that of your relation you speak of." Accordingly, whenever Darnley urged the Queen to share his bed, the latter, that she might pass the night alone, made a point of complaining of a pain in the side ; " I never go anigh him," writes Mary Stuart, "but the pain of my sick side doth seize me, so grievous is he to my senses."

Brutality on the part of the husband in the first days of married life is often enough to occasion in a woman of delicate susceptibilities a permanent dislike and repugnance. This is shown in the following extract from a judgment delivered by the Tribunal of the Seine : " Whereas the defendant X—— admits that from the time of her marriage with the plaintiff, she has consistently refused to fulfil her conjugal duty, alleging that from the very first her husband showed himself too impatient and did not employ all necessary precautions to spare the susceptibilities of a young woman absolutely ignorant of the obligations of matrimony." [1] Not a few husbands compromise their domestic happiness for ever by their impatience and coarse brutality on the marriage night.—Specialists in mental disease have even noted instances of insanity being induced in delicate women by the first conjugal assaults, which were more like rape than anything else. [2]—The wife who is disgusted by her husband's roughness shuts her bedroom door against

---

[1] *Gazette des Tribunaux*, 10th Jan. 1892.

[2] Paul Moreau de Tours, *Les aberrations du sens génésique*, p. 174. Pierre Janet, *Névroses et idées fixes*, vol. ii. p. 291. (F. Alcan, Paris.)

him, but it is not long before she opens it to a lover, who displays more tact than the other and spares her delicacy. Such is the situation Alexandre Dumas has described in Jane de Simérose in his *L'Ami des femmes*.

A coarse, ill-looking man is liable to suffer the fate of Vulcan, who was abandoned by Venus, because he was lame and dirty. Nevertheless, when husband and lover appear side by side in Court, we often find that merely from the physical point of view the former is in no way inferior to the latter, and that all lovers are not Adonises. Bothwell, who inspired so lively a passion in the breast of Mary Stuart, was an ugly man ; what seduced the Queen was his martial look, his bold bearing and energetic character. Helen of Troy, who left all to follow Paris, husband, child and country, said, speaking of her husband, "that she had no fault to find whether with his heart or his beauty."

Hypocrisy the concomitant of adultery.—The whole life of an adulteress is one tissue of falsehood, trickery and hypocrisy. Often she will profess the most religious devotion, in the hope her husband and the world at large will conclude so pious a woman to be incapable of anything wrong. The woman Fenayrou, after making up her mind to commit the crime she was brought to trial for, went to Confession and took the Sacrament. To cajole her husband, such a woman will simulate jealousy and charge the poor man with all sorts of imaginary wrongs ; she will avert his suspicions by hypocritical displays of fondness and tearful scenes of tenderness; Comedy and Tragedy are equally within her scope, and like a consummate actress she can assume every mask at will, the mask of conjugal affection, of jealousy, of melancholy, of piety, she can laugh and cry, melt with love or burn with anger, and at any moment sham a convenient attack of nerves. Not without reason the adulterous woman has been compared in character to the feline race,—the same apparent gentleness, same suppleness and grace, same treacherousness and even same cruelty, for the velvet paw is always ready to disclose its claws. To prevent her husband suspecting her lover, she will falsely accuse an innocent man of pursuing her, complaining of his marked attentions and declaring she has found means to recall him to proper sentiments, and the husband, touched by these confidences, cannot sufficiently admire his wife's goodness. These false charges against a man who has never gone out of his way to pay her the least attention, may easily lead to murder. Acting on the false information given him by his wife, a man demanded satisfaction from one of his friends ; when the latter refused to fight, the husband fired at him three times with a revolver.—To mask her guilty connection with a lover, a woman of this character will sometimes endeavour to get him married to a relative of her own, a cousin or niece, or else she will falsely accuse a perfectly innocent woman and make her out to be her *inamorato's* mistress.—In order to be free, she makes her husband acquire tastes that keep him away from home, and induces him to undertake useless journeys, the paramount importances of which she insists upon. Such are some of the wiles these unfaithful wives adopt to hide their guilty loves and mystify their husbands, and which form the staple of a thousand farces. The husband may watch his wife, invent secret locks and cunning chastity belts, buy a watch-dog to scare away enterprising lovers,—all is in vain; no precaution is of the slightest avail against feminine trickery. The woman never fails to find a way to meet her lover, to keep her secret and flout her lord and master. Comic writers, from Aristophanes and Molière down to the authors of contemporary farces, have only to observe real life to make their public laugh at the expense of Georges Dandin, bringing out the contrast it exhibits between the husband's unsuspiciousness and the woman's cunning.

When women are surprised by their husbands the moment after they have hidden a lover away somewhere, they will put on the most natural air in the world of astonishment and indignation at the suspicions they meet with, and fly into a passion with the man, calling him a madman to have dared suspect so virtuous a wife. In a case tried before the Assize Court I have known a woman, surprised by the husband, when the lover actually lay concealed in the bed, utter exclamations of astonishment and anger at the ridiculous jealousy of her husband, up to the instant when the latter pulling off the bed clothes sent the other scampering from the couch.—A woman who had poisoned her husband, a crime she admitted subsequently, threw herself with a pretence of the deepest sorrow on the man's body, when the Law ordered its exhumation. She screamed and tried to shed tears, putting her hands before her face, that the bystanders might not see her dry eyes.

Nuns in charge of female offenders in penitentiaries have often told me of their astonishment at the girls' falseness. One of them said to me: "The most abandoned are just the ones that affected the most virtuous sentiments; they act their parts so well, I am constantly deceived. Then when I see I have been made game of, I declare I will be less simple another time; but there! they are always able to cheat me again."

A married woman, afraid of her lover's giving her up and playing the comedy of a pretended suicide to keep him by her side, made a show of hanging herself, after writing him the following pathetic letter: "How you have made me suffer! I have sacrificed all to you for the last two years" (she had sacrificed her husband to him, having poisoned the poor man); "but I forgive you in memory of our love. You have been very cruel to me; you might have prevented my death and saved my children, but you would not. God's will be done! Pray Heaven you may not repent some day of your unkindness! Give one thought to a dying woman. Farewell! farewell!" She had written another letter to her aunt: "Before going back to God, (for indeed I think He will forgive me this desperate act), I entrust my children to you. . . . Poor little things, my heart bleeds for them, but it must

be done, I must be strong for their future happiness.
Alive, I could not help them as their father (whom she
had poisoned) would have done ; if I die, everyone will
pity them. . . . Be sure and tell them my last thought
was for them, that I love them above all else, for I sacrifice
my life for them." Eventually, the woman admitted under
examination that she was simply acting when she wrote
these letters, and that her attempted suicide was all a
pretence.

We may apply to such women the verses composed by
Alfred de Vigny after his betrayal by Mme. Dorval, who
had been his mistress :

> " Une lutte éternelle en tout temps, en tout lieu,
>   Se livre sur la terre en présence de Dieu,
>   Entre la bonté d'Homme et la ruse de Femme ;
>   Car la femme est un être impur de corps et d'âme." [1]

No doubt an adulteress, in the majority of cases, plays
some ingenious farce to hide her fault ; yet at times we
see her animated with such hatred of her husband that
she takes no pains to hide it ; she proclaims her sin with
her own lips with surprising effrontery, like the woman
who after trying to poison her husband, told a neighbour
on becoming enceinte : "You may tell my husband that,
if I have a child, it will most assuredly not be his."

A woman who wishes to break off her marriage in order
to wed her lover, lays snares for her husband to bring
about divorce ; she tries to make him insult or beat her ;
she refuses to let him fulfil his marital duties, in the hope
that he will enter into some irregular liaison that will
give her a pretext to claim separation.   In a case tried

---

[1] " A never-ending struggle, at all times and in all places, is fought out in
the world before God's eyes, between Man's good nature and Woman's wiles ;
for indeed a woman is a creature impure of body and soul alike."—But de
Vigny made the mistake of generalizing from one woman as if her baseness
were predicable of the whole sex, and summing up women in the cruel and
unjust line :

> "La femme, enfant malade et douze fois impure."

"Woman, that sickly child, foul with a thousand impurities."

on November 19th, 1895, it came out in the course of the
hearing that within a month after marriage, the woman
kept her favours for her lover and began to lay traps for
her husband. The latter was informed by the agency
employed, that his wife had given orders to have him
watched.

Divorce is favourable to adultery, as supplying a means
of breaking off one marriage and entering on another.
Very frequently an adulterous woman makes her lover
promise to marry her if she becomes free, and she is not
long before she finds a pretext for divorce. Of course the
Law does not allow an adulteress to marry the accomplice
with whom she has been caught sinning, but all she needs
is to avoid being surprised *flagrante delicto*. Not long
ago were found on the body of a married woman, killed
by her husband, the rough drafts of letters addressed to
a cousin, telling him she was going to appeal for a divorce.
—It is not long since we had to adjudicate on the case
of a husband who had fired two revolver shots at his wife,
whose evil life was notorious; the woman's answer was:
"I was going the pace, the sooner to get a divorce."—As
soon as a married woman has taken a lover, she goes
(often paying out of her husband's money) to consult a
lawyer as to the best way to procure a divorce. Before
cheating the Law, she begins by deceiving her lawyer,
telling him a string of falsehoods about the wrongs she
alleges herself to have suffered at her husband's hands.—
Clever women succeed in deceiving the Police and in
making them believe them to be the victims of their
husband's brutality, when all the while the real victim is
the husband himself. In the criminal records relating to
various women guilty of murdering their husbands, I have
found old Police reports describing them, as the result of
false information supplied by the women in question, as
victims of marital cruelty. To gain credence for the
brutalities they alleged, they would shout "murder" without any reason for doing so, so that the neighbours might
hear and report the matter to the Police.

To obtain a divorce, women will get false charges brought against their husbands of crimes against morality. Some years since, a lady living in a country house near Tours, induced her former governess to accuse her husband of a purely imaginary rape; this calumny she disseminated by means of the newspapers, so as to put pressure on the members of the Bench at Tours, who hesitated to prosecute the husband at her instigation. Above all it is among those of her own sex that an adulteress seeks compliant witnesses ready to trump up false charges against her husband and so lead to a divorce. One individual, who was urged to "bear false witness" in this way, but refused to consent, drew down on herself the following retort: "You're not half a woman, if you stand up for my husband."

Malevolence of women guilty of adultery; desertion of their children.—Novelists tell us "the voice of nature" always appeals to a mother's heart and teaches even bad women love and devotion towards their children. It is quite true many adulteresses continue to love their children when they have ceased to love their husbands. But it is no less true to say that "the voice of nature" does not always make itself heard by the woman who adopts a dissolute course of life, and that frequently an adulterous wife, on losing her love for her husband, feels her maternal affections diminish concurrently with her conjugal. Clytæmnestra, once guilty of adultery, ceases to love her daughter Electra. Mme. X——, who was ready to die along with her lover, the student Chambige, noticed the alteration that had occurred in her sentiments: "I am quite changed from what I used to be; I no longer think all day long of my children, I only think of you; it is horrible!" Absorbed in this delirium of her passion, the guilty woman has no time left to think of her children and attend to their health and education; if she is well-to-do, she hands them over to the care of servants; if poor, she leaves them to run the streets. I read in the report of a trial this

pathetic statement by an unfortunate husband : " My little
boy of five died of a sore throat, having caught a chill
while his mother was away keeping an assignation."—
In another case I find this statement made by the children
who were called as witnesses after a domestic tragedy :
" Since his marriage, our father never had a moment's
happiness, owing to our mother's bad behaviour ; she used
to neglect the house, and father, after his day's work was
over, was obliged to look after domestic matters."

An adulterous wife soon loses her children's respect.
Often she does not hesitate to let them see her *faux pas*,
and makes use of them to carry letters sending the father
out of the way and summoning the lover. Sometimes we
even find a mother compromising her own daughter, so as
to use her as a cloak for her adulterous doings.—Like
maternal affection, paternal love is also frequently destroyed
by adultery ; a father who keeps a mistress no longer has
the same respect for his children, nor the same fondness.
He also will sometimes employ them to deliver his love
letters, and is ready to ruin his children to satisfy his
mistress's caprices. Passion may even quench the sense
of pity ; fathers who are widowers have been known before
now to allow their mistress to domineer over and torture
their children.

Speaking generally, a woman loves or hates her husband
in her children ; these are more or less cherished according as the wife loves or hates her husband.[1]

---

[1] In the case of a large number of women, maternal love also increases or
diminishes, according as the mother has or has not suckled her children
herself. The preference a mother often shows for one of her children often
arises from the fact that she has suckled this one and not the others. I
have known the case of a woman who killed her little girl by her unkind
treatment, and who admitted she could not love the child because she had
not suckled it ; the same mother adored another child she had reared herself.
These facts prove that, with a large number of women, in whom education
and religion have not modified the original disposition, maternal love is rather
instinctive than intellectual, coming more from the womb and bosom than
from the brain and heart, contrasting herein with paternal affection, which is
more intellectual than instinctive. For the same reason the mother pays
greater attention to her children's bodies than to their minds, and feels their
misconduct less acutely than the father does.—Very often too a man loves or

Just as the wife who loves her husband is happy in discovering his likeness in the features of her children and exclaims with Andromaque :

"Voilà ses yeux, sa bouche et déjà son audace ;
C'est lui-même ; c'est toi, cher époux que j'embrasse,"[1]

so the wife who has ceased to love her husband finds no pleasure now in tracing his resemblance in her children's faces. Such a resemblance in fact becomes odious to her, and she loves her children less, because they remind her of their father. I have heard a mother tell her son, "Go away! you are so like your father." If a woman who is unfaithful to her husband has a child by her lover, this is the one she prefers.

As a rule mothers think their own children pretty and more attractive than anyone else's.

". . . Mes petits sont mignons,
"Beaux, bien faits et jolis sur tous leurs compagnons,"[2]

says the owl of its young ones. But the adulterous wife is an unnatural mother and no longer deems her children pretty. I find in the records of a criminal trial a characteristic remark made by a mother to one of her neighbours. Speaking of her daughter, she said, "You think her pretty, do you? well! for my own part I cannot bear to look at

hates his wife in his children ; thus the hatred the "*Ami des hommes*" bore towards his son Mirabeau arose mainly from that he felt against his wife. The working-man very readily cuts the connection with his children, when he has been divorced.   Still on the whole paternal love seems to me less dependent than maternal on that between husband and wife.

[1] "Look ! his eyes, his mouth and already his gallant boldness ; 'tis himself ; 'tis you, dear husband, that I kiss."
Médée expresses the same sentiment when she says to Jason :

"Souffre que mes enfants accompagnent ma fuite,
Que je t'admire encore en chacun de leurs traits,
Que je t'aime et te baise en ces petits portraits."

"Oh ! let my children go with me in my flight, let me admire you again in each of their features, let me love and kiss you in these miniature facsimiles."
[2] " . . . My little ones are sweet, handsome, well-made and pretty above all their companions."

her." Another mother said of her daughter, " I cannot endure the sight of her; when she cries, I want to kill her."—Yet these unnatural mothers, who bully and even kill their children, lavish the geatest care and fondness on their pet animals, their cats and dogs.   It is notorious that children are often treated cruelly by step-mothers and by their father's mistresses, who deprive them of food, air, and sleep, and beat them unmercifully.   The same atrocious offences are also occasionally committed by adulterous wives upon their own children.   Such women have really ceased to be either wives or mothers ; they have neither heart nor reason left, nothing but their sensual appetites ; they are no longer human beings, but brutes, resembling those animals that desert their young, beating and killing them to give themselves more freely to fresh embraces.   I myself prosecuted a woman who had abandoned her three little children in a shed, in order to indulge in dissolute courses ; she merely came once a day to toss them some bread through an opening in the wall.   When I visited the spot with the *Juge d'instruction* I found the children almost naked, lying in filthy straw stained with their excrements.   Hunger, cold, confinement, the hardships of every sort they had endured, had reduced them to a state bordering upon idiocy; one of them had his feet gangrened.

" The voice of nature " is silenced in the hearts of women that have succumbed to sensual, bestial passion.   Adulteresses are found ready to go on with their guilty amours while their children are on a bed of sickness.   In one case I saw tried, a mother gave an assignation to her lover on the very day her daughter died.—Another adulterous wife, when reproached by her husband for her conduct, threatened to kill her last born child, if he dared to have her watched.

> " Soevus amor docuit natorum sanguine matrem
>   Commaculare manus . . .,
>   Nunc scio quid sit amor." [1]

---

[1] "Cruel love taught the mother to embrue her hands with her children's blood . . ., now I know what love can do."   Virgil, *Eclogues*, viii.

If death surprises the sick child while the mother is hastening to a criminal rendezvous, the latter finds speedy consolation for her loss ; the deep mourning she must assume, with its long black veil, annoys her, so she leaves it off at the earliest possible moment or contrives to combine it with an elegant toilette.   The same indifference or positive dislike the adulteress sometimes feels towards her children, is also occasionally experienced by young women who are mothers without being wives.   To obtain greater freedom for their vicious propensities, they will strangle their children, poison them, dash in their skulls, throw them into ponds, rivers, the sea, or down privies,— and this not always directly after their birth, but at one or two years old, just when children are so charming, loving and loveable.

Filial piety may be stifled by habits of debauchery no less than maternal affection.   I have known an adulteress hurry away to an assignation while her father was in the very pangs of dissolution.   I have just been reading in some criminal records a number of letters written by her lover to a married woman, who had been obliged to leave Paris for the country to attend her mother who was dangerously ill ; she complains in every one of them how long her mother takes to die, thus preventing her from getting back to Paris,—in fact, she wearies for her mother's end, that she may the sooner see her lover again.   "What a horrid trade," she writes, "a sick-nurse's is!"—Once a woman has lost her sense of shame, she quickly grows capable of anything.   "Amissa pudicitia, mulier nihil abnuerit" ("Shame lost, a woman will stick at nothing"). This sentiment in a woman is the thread that keeps together the pearls of a necklace ; cut the thread, and all the pearls are lost ; do away with modesty, and all the female virtues fly away, conjugal affection, maternal love, filial piety, all disappear.   And the process of deterioration is a rapid one.   Looseness of conduct leads quickly to crime, abortion, infanticide, poisoning.   I have known the case of a young woman who had won a prize for good conduct when

a girl, yet within a few years' time appeared before a Court
of Justice charged with adultery and poisoning her husband.
The notorious Mme. Fenayrou had been quoted as a
pattern of virtue in the boarding school where she was
brought up; but taking to dissolute courses some years after
her marriage, she very soon developed into a criminal.

*Hatred of the adulterous wife towards her husband ; her
calumnies on his conduct.*—For the adulterous wife, the true
husband is the lover ; she speaks of herself as "his wife,"
while the husband is the obstacle, the stranger, the enemy.
But every obstacle must be removed, and every enemy
hated ; in proportion as the woman's love for her lover
increases, her hatred of her husband augments. One
woman on trial, relating how adultery had led her on
to poisoning, told the *Juge d'instruction* : "Yes! I am
guilty of the crime I am charged with ; my adulterous
connection with X—— was the cause of it all. When he
first asked me to be his, I rejected his proposal with scorn,
but I ended by yielding to his prayers ; I very soon
conceived a strong aversion to my husband." People
always hate those they have wronged ; the fault the
wife commits inspires her with an invincible repugnance
towards her husband. Under these circumstances, the
more gentle and affectionate the husband is, the greater
his wife's loathing and detestation.

An adulterous wife's hatred of her husband often
expresses itself in calumnies against his character,
calumnies uttered even in the presence of her children.
Feeling herself despised by her husband, she is jealous
of the respect and love the children show their father,
and she does all she can to deprive him of this consolation
by means of insidious slanders ; she complains to her
children of having been made unhappy all her life by
her husband's misconduct, painting him in the blackest
colours, and falsely accusing him of the most atrocious
vices. In some instances, I have known her accuse her
husband of wishing to kill her, to poison her, and she

sheds copious sham tears to move her children to pity
her wrongs. To make out the victim of her wickedness
to be a villain, to pose as a victim herself, when she is
the true villain all the time, to rob the father of the esteem
and affection of the children he adores, what a fine satisfaction for an evil-natured wife! The worst of it is, these
false-hearted misrepresentations almost invariably attain
their object, either because the husband is unsuspicious or
because he shrinks from confounding the woman's calumnies
by revealing her real character, out of consideration for his
children and a dread of wounding their feelings. This
confidence and generosity she takes advantage of to make
her husband suffer in his affections as a father, having
already tortured him in his love as a husband. I have
known such a one make her daughter believe her father
was suffering from a skin disease, in order to deprive him
of his child's caresses. All means are utilized to sow mis-
understanding between father and children. If she cannot
render the father odious in his children's eyes, she makes
a point of turning him into ridicule before them; when
she cannot get them to fear him, she incites them to laugh
at him. Her spite discovers a thousand perfidious ways of
wounding the husband in the father.

The unhappy husband, exasperated by these perfidies
and mockeries, sometimes ends at last by losing his head
and giving way to serious acts of violence, which call for
the intervention of the Law. A wife who had succeeded in
getting her husband to strike her and having him thrown
into prison in consequence, told her daughter: "Your
father has gone into prison with a black beard, he must
leave it with a white one." In another case a husband,
who driven to desperation had given his wife a blow which
proved fatal, exclaimed sadly: "She scorned me, and made
my children do the same!"

The husband tortured by suchlike calumnies, and in
despair at losing his children's love, the only consolation
left him, ends sometimes by committing suicide. To give
an instance,—a man of business in Paris poisoned himself

in the year 1895 with nicotine, after writing the following letter: "Not satisfied with dragging my name through the mud by her public liaison with M. X——, my wife has fled from home taking with her 3,500 francs and has instituted proceedings for a divorce against me. Now she forbids my son coming to see me, setting him against me by every kind of shameful falsehood and slander. I could bear everything till to-day, but I cannot endure the grief the loss of my son's affection causes me. I forgive my boy, who is young, and I think he will forgive my act of despair. But I hold my wife and her lover responsible for my death. She has robbed me of all,—my honour, my money, and the love of my son which consoled me for everything else." Other husbands, exasperated by their wives' persistent evil speaking, are filled with a fierce hatred that explodes some day and translates itself into murder; they go mad with anger. Some years ago in the neighbourhood of Tarascon, the wife of a farmer cultivating his own land was found murdered in her bed. She had been suddenly attacked in her sleep, the husband striking her with an iron pitchfork which was left sticking in her head. He declared to the *Juge d'instruction* that he had been driven beyond all bounds by his wife's calumnies, which had forced him to kill her.[1]

It is also by calumny that an adulteress avenges herself on any of her husband's relatives who say anything to her about her conduct. When her father-in-law or brother-in-law give her warnings of this kind, it is no uncommon thing for her to try to punish them by informing her husband they have endeavoured to seduce her.

> "Que ne sait point ourdir une langue traîtresse,
> Par sa pernicieuse adresse !"[2]

---

[1] In this case it was a dog that led to the detection of the criminal. The Law had been unable to discover who was guilty, till one day the Police were put in possession of the blood-stained clothes of the murderer, which had been buried in a neighbouring field and covered over with stones. It was the man's dog that attracted attention to them by scratching up the ground at the spot and howling. This discovery forced the husband to confess.

[2] "What calumnies will not a perfidious tongue invent out of its malignant cunning !"

Provocation to commit parricide.—But the adulterous wife does not invariably stop short at calumniating her husband and sowing discord between father and children ; she sometimes goes further, provoking acts of violence between them and even inciting the children to kill their father. In 1893, the Assize Court of the Bouches-du-Rhône adjudicated on a case of this kind.   A married woman, Vial by name, whose husband was a farmer near Aix and a hard-working, honest man, quitted her home again and again, forsaking husband and children to go after various lovers.   The husband, who was weak and good-natured forgave her every time, out of consideration for his children, and agreed to take her back again.   Far from showing gratitude for his clemency, the woman at each act of forgiveness only redoubled her hatred of her husband, and persistently spoke ill of him to the children, in order to alienate their affection from him.   He was really industrious and saving ; she made him out to the children to be idle and extravagant, and presently succeeded in making a quarrel between them.   One of the sons, a baker's apprentice, wished to buy an oven for himself on too hard terms, and his father did not approve the plan ; this occasioned the young man very keen vexation, which his mother took care to keep up and embitter still more. At her instigation he had a violent scene with his father, and threatened to leave his house, taking his mother and brothers with him.   A few days later, he put this threat into execution, and Vial on returning from his work in the fields, found his home abandoned by his wife and children, who had carried away everything with them. He then made his way to their new dwelling to get back the bed-clothes which they had carried off from his bed. His wife and son turned him out of doors and went up to a first floor window to hurl insults at him.   The son took his stand at the open window holding a pistol in his hand, and his mother behind him, urging him to use his weapon. She was heard to shout " Fire ! " and at the same moment the son discharged two shots at his father.   The latter

P

was wounded and took to flight, but his son, still at the invitation of his mother, rushed in pursuit, caught him up and fired at him twice again almost point blank.   The unhappy father received two balls, one in the left thigh, the other in the dorso-lumbar region.   In examination it was proved that the murder was premeditated on the part both of wife and son ; the son had bought the pistol with the intention of using it against his father, and the mother had given him the money for the purchase.

I have seen another case of parricide provoked by an adulterous wife, a woman of forty-seven, who, abusing the empire she possessed over her son of twenty, pursued him with continual solicitations to kill his father, whom she painted in the blackest colours for his benefit.   The young man resisted for some time, the idea of such a crime filling him with horror, but at last his mother succeeded in overcoming his scruples ; she procured him a gun to shoot his father with, and contrived means for his meeting him alone in the fields.   Following his mother's directions, the son came suddenly upon his father engaged in felling a pine-tree ; he took aim and stretched him stone dead at its foot.

It is often the best husbands that become the objects of dislike.   The husband who possesses every possible good quality when he is loved, is found to have every possible defect when this is no longer the case.   Just as love transforms defects into merits, hatred changes merits into defects.   If the husband is gentle and patient, his adulterous wife calls him a weak fool ; if he is careful and saving, she sets him down as a miser.   In the great majority of instances of the murder of a husband by an adulterous wife, I have found the husband to have been a good, hard-working man, devoted to his family, while the wife was lazy, greedy, extravagant and profoundly selfish.   I find among the documents relating to the poisoning of a husband by his wife this declaration made by one of the daughters : "My father used always to say, that when a man had children, he ought to save, and my mother would reply :

'I think more of myself than of my children.'" What a true confession! The adulteress really and truly loves neither husband nor children but only herself; in her abominable selfishness, she prefers pleasure to the family honour; she thinks only of herself, lives only for herself,—"I, I come first," she says, "the rest nowhere!"[1] This is why, if she has no children, she does not want any, and would rather be barren. She rejoices over her sterility, and if an incipient pregnancy declares itself, she plans to get rid of it. Alexander Dumas *fils* has noted this trait in the character of the adulterous wife in *La Femme de Claude*; in the novel mentioned Césarine desires to procure abortion. The midwives, who suppress as many infants as they bring into the world, do not limit themselves to giving assistance to unmarried girls who have been seduced; unfaithful wives also frequently have recourse to their treatment. In 1891, the Assize Court of the Var condemned on a charge of abortion Mme. de J——, wife of a naval officer, and for complicity in the matter her lover, the Mayor of Toulon.

Even when the husband, finding himself unable to put a curb on his wife's misconduct, makes up his mind to bear it quietly, the latter may still continue to cherish against him a dislike so violent as to make her desire and provoke his death. I have myself noted the case of a village Messalina who tried to poison her husband, and failing this, got her lover to kill him, although he was an old man, good-natured and quite resigned to his lot.

The ferocious hate an adulterous wife feels towards her husband finds an exact expression in the narrative Clytæmnestra gives in Aeschylus of the murder of Agamemnon; she recounts how "his dying convulsions send the blood spurting from his wounds; and the red dew of murder falls on me in dark gouts, dew as sweet to my heart as is the rain of Zeus to the fallows." Cassandra's

[1] This selfishness is found even, more often than might be supposed, in mothers of families who are not adulteresses, but who, merely in order to satisfy their love of luxury and dress, sacrifice the interests of their children. There are even married women who have a horror of the duties of maternity, and do not wish to have children.

murder, which followed that of Agamemnon, was likewise for the adulteress, "a soft, voluptuous joy that even yet gives zest to the delights of my love."

Other motives inciting the adulterous wife to the murder of her husband.—Hatred however is not the only motive that urges the adulterous wife to kill her husband; she wishes besides to put an end to her marriage, in order to live freely with her lover. A young woman of eighteen, who had been married against her will and who deeply regretted having been unable to marry a young man she loved, said cynically to two witnesses: "I left a suitor in the lurch who cried finely on my marriage day; but I mean to give my husband an eleven o'clock broth, to finish him off, so that I can then marry my old lover." What she wants is to bind the lover to her by marriage; and to do so, she must make herself a widow.

In most instances, before conceiving the idea of getting rid of her husband by poison, an adulterous wife begins by merely wishing for his death, without any notion as yet of causing it; if only her husband were to disappear, carried off by some accident or disease, she would be free! Free! a widow! what joy in the thought! When the Law seizes the letters an adulteress has written her lover, this homicidal sentiment is constantly found expressed: "Oh! how I long to be free! how I long to be rid of him!" She hopes some convenient sickness will come and give her her liberty, and if her husband falls ill, the homicidal idea that had already crossed her mind takes firm hold of her imagination and never leaves her: "If only he were to die," she tells herself, "I should be free to marry my lover." A great many adulterous wives content themselves with wishing for their husband's death, but others go further than this; they begin very soon to weary of the care they bestow on him, and if the sickness is prolonged, after noting with pleasure the progress it is making, they are tempted presently to hasten on its termination, which is to assure their freedom. At first they only desire the

patient's death, anon we find them preparing it, if it is
too long in coming of itself. When once the thought of
murder, long-cherished in the fancy, takes hold of an
adulterous wife's mind, it grows into a fixed idea, an
obsession of the intellect, which never again leaves her,
and sometimes betrays itself by compromising speeches
she cannot refrain from uttering. A husband whom his
wife had tried to poison, making a statement later on
before a Court of Justice, said the accused had been unable any longer to hold her tongue as to her wish to see
him dead, and had had the cynical effrontery to tell him
of it. "It was a fixed idea in her mind," he declared.—
In another similar case, a witness reported this cry of
impatience as uttered by an adulterous wife desirous of
her husband's death : "Will he never give out, the
creature!"[1] In connection with another criminal case, I
have even known a woman say to her daughter, speaking
of the latter's father, who was the best of men : "Ought
not a man like that to be shot and stretched dead on the
floor?"—"What would you do, if he were dead?" returned
the daughter.—"Why! then I should be my own mistress,"
was the mother's answer.

In some instances we find the mother-in-law sharing her
daughter's hatred against her husband so entirely as to
become her accomplice in the murder of her son-in-law.
Some years since in the *arrondissement* of Digne, a wife
plotted with her mother to poison her husband, and they
gave him a drink mixed with sulphur and phosphorus.
The attempt to poison in this way having failed, the woman
procured a gun and discharged it at her husband as he

---

[1] It is not alone in dramas of adultery that we see the criminal, watching his
victim lying on a bed of sickness, pass insensibly from wishing a natural death
to supervene to planning a violent end ; it is a psychological observation of
general application.   Before killing the widow Boyer, Vitalis seeing her struck
down by illness, began to wish for her death.   "If the good God would only
take her !" he said more than once to the girl who became his accomplice
later on.—"Ah ! yes," answered the latter, who had at first refused to
entertain the idea of committing the crime, but who afterwards felt the same
wish, and ended by helping her lover to second the disease in its effects.

slept; the shot carried away one of his ears without killing him.

The idea of killing her husband in his sleep often suggests itself to a woman's mind. When the sisters of Psyché persuade her that her husband is a monster, they bring her a lamp and a dagger to stab him with as he sleeps. Some few years since, in Provence, a woman, threatened with desertion on the part of her lover, took advantage of his slumbers to force a pair of scissors into his temple, using a flat-iron to drive them in with.

But poison is the means an adulterous wife most usually adopts when she wishes to get rid of her husband. This has always been the chosen weapon of such women; " *adultera, ergo venefica* " ("an adulteress, therefore a poisoner"), the Romans used to say. When Medea passes in review the different ways of avenging herself that occur to her, it is poison she chooses, " Many means," she soliloquises, " are open to me of doing them to death. . . . Should I set fire to their nuptial palace or plunge a sharpened sword into their heart? . . . Better to assail them by the direct road we women excel in and kill them by poison."

The Roman women, like the Greek, were skilled in the use of poisons. If we are to believe Livy, not a single case of poisoning came up for trial at Rome for many years.[1] But, after the submission of the Latins, the number of poisonings committed by women was so large, that the mortality among husbands was set down to an epidemic. The foremost citizens of Rome were dying fast, all of similar maladies and almost invariably with the same symptoms. A slave woman eventually came forward to reveal the fact to the Consuls that the city was being decimated by the perfidy of the women, and that a number of Roman matrons were manufacturing poisons. Acting

---

[1] *Livy*, bk. viii.—However the laws of the Twelve Tables contain a clause punishing the crime of poisoning.—Valerius Maximus records that Publicia, wife of the Consul Postumius Albinus, and Licinia, wife of Claudius Asellus, convicted of having poisoned their husbands, were strangled in virtue of a sentence passed by their parents and relatives. (Bk. vi., ch. iii., § 8.)

on this information, they caught some women in the act of preparing noxious drugs and discovered poisons hidden in several spots. Discoveries of the sort were made in the houses of twenty matrons, two of the number being ladies of patrician rank ; a hundred and seventy women were arrested in all.

According to Juvenal, whose Satires chronicle all the scandal of his day and are veritable judicial records, there were many women guilty of adultery and poisoning among his contemporaries. " Here we have," he writes in his first Satire, "a rich matron, who handing the mild Calene wine to her thirsty husband, mixes snake poison in the cup, and a second and more artful Locusta, teaches her less experienced neighbours how to carry the livid corpses of their husbands to burial undeterred by ill-report and thronging crowds." In his famous Sixth Satire the same author tells of other poisonings committed by adulterous wives : "Patrician or plebeian, all," he declares, "are alike depraved. . . . More destructive than the sword, luxury has burst upon us and avenges the world enslaved. . . . To-morrow, at break of day, each quarter of the city will have its Clytæmnestra. The only difference is that the daughter of Tyndarus, in frenzied desperation, brandished her murderous axe in both hands, whereas in our day the matter is quietly arranged with a small bit of a poisonous toad's intestine. Still the steel is there all the time, if the cautious Agamemnon has provided himself with an antidote in time."

Poisoning, common in Italy in the sixteenth century extended to France in the seventeenth. Nor was it only to open the way to inheritances that Brinvilliers and La Voisin kept open shop for the sale of poisons, it was likewise to end unwelcome marriages and pave the road to others. These women dealt in love potions as well as in poisons for inconvenient relatives. In July 1682, Louis XIV. published an edict for the punishment of poisoners, pushing severity so far as to regard as accomplices all who, possessing information " of anyone's having manufactured poisons or been asked for and delivered such," failed to denounce such persons to justice. A special Court was instituted to exterminate the whole class of men and women who dealt in poisons. But the King was so horrified at the appalling revelations that ensued that he stopped the proceedings and had a number of documents burnt, notably those concerning the case of Mme. de Montespan, convicted of having asked La Voisin for powders to win her the King's good graces and kill Mlle. de la Vallière, and later on to destroy Louis XIV., who had by that time deserted her, and Mlle. de Fontanges, her successor in the Royal favour. The latter died at twenty-two, firmly persuaded she had been poisoned. Among women found guilty of poisoning were even magistrates' wives. Louis XIV. connived at the flight of a large number of great lords and ladies compromised by these revelations. When Mme. Tiquet, wife of a Counsellor of the Parliament, was condemned in 1699 to be beheaded for having killed her husband, her family earnestly besought the King's mercy ; " However, the Archbishop of Paris represented to the King that the impunity this crime enjoyed was by way of making it extremely frequent ; that husbands depended for the safety of their lives on Mme. Tiquet being punished ; that already poisoning was very common and the Grand Penitentiary had his ears filled with continual confessions of women who accused themselves of having attempted their husbands' lives. This remonstrance decided the King to make a great and terrible example." When Mme. Tiquet was executed, her head after being severed from the body was left for some time on the scaffold, " no doubt in order that the sight might make a deep impression on the minds of the married women present at the said execution."

A case of wholesale poisoning, which compromised several women and was tried in 1868 before the Assize Court of the Bouches-du-Rhône, revealed the existence at Marseilles of regular manufactories of poisons for the use of adulterous wives. A fortune-teller and a herbalist,

a man named Joye, kept this establishment. They were
consulted by women as to their lovers' fidelity and the
best means of ensuring their continued affection; by
husbands as to the fidelity of their wives and the means
of making these love them; by mothers in search of a
son-in-law; by the owners of sick animals as to the way
to cure them by some charm or other. These swindlers
would begin by proposing to married women to rid them
of their husbands by throwing a spell over them. "You
must go to the churchyard," Joye declared; "take a nail
out of a coffin and invoke it in these words, 'nail, I invoke
you, hoping my husband will die.'" The woman would
hesitate at first, but before long she would come to see
the herbalist again and take the poison he handed her.
As soon as the poison had taken proper effect and ridded
the woman of her husband, Joye would call on the widow
to claim "the price of her work."—The fortune-teller on
her part, in order to try the woman's mettle who came to
consult her, would say: "The cards announce that someone very nearly connected with you must die soon, and
that his death would suit you very well." When she saw
that this notion was welcomed with satisfaction, she would
add more to the same effect, and finally slip the poison
into the woman's hand. She sold large quantities of it.
To obtain it, women of the lower classes often went so
far as to sacrifice the whole of their little belongings.

It was the professional rivalry existing between the
herbalist and the fortune-teller that eventually led to the
truth coming out. The herbalist having more customers
than the fortune-teller, the latter became jealous and angry
at his interference with her profits and denounced him
to a woman named Marino, whom another, Ville, her
husband's mistress was desirous of poisoning. This Ville,
who had already poisoned her husband, was now planning
to do the same to her lover Marino's wife, so that she
might marry him herself, quite resolved also to kill her
lover in the same way, if he should refuse to marry her.
Marino, being informed by his wife of the statements the

fortune-teller had made to her, wished to verify it, and went to see the herbalist, leading him to believe he was aware of his mistress's design and approved of it. " I am Ville's lover," he told him, "and I know all that has occurred. But you have only done half the business. I want to be able to live at my ease with Mme. V——; can you rid me of my wife?" On hearing these words, Joye looked the other steadily in the eyes, to make sure whether he was speaking sincerely; then after casting a glance around, he whispered putting his lips to his ear, " Are you a man?"—" If I were not," returned Marino, " I shouldn't be here. But I warn you, I don't wish my wife to suffer as long as M. Ville did." These words reassured the herbalist, who putting on a smiling aspect, added : " It was not I who looked after M. Ville, it was that cheating baggage Louise, who's hardly good enough to shuffle the cards and tell a fortune, yet must mix herself up in things she knows nothing about. She could not succeed in finishing M. Ville. So I came to the rescue, and with my white powder, settled his hash in a few days. Leave me alone, follow exactly the directions I'm going to give you, and youi wife won't give you much more trouble." [1]

To avoid arousing suspicion a wife who wishes to rid herself of her husband by poison, gives him small doses ; she poisons him slowly, but surely, dealing him his death drop by drop with a smile on her lips. When the unfortunate man, parched with the poison asks for a drink, she administers yet another dose in the cooling draught she gives him, quite regardless of his horrible sufferings. To baulk the doctor's skill, she will sometimes employ turn and turn about drugs that produce exactly opposite effects. If the medical attendant succeeds by appropriate treatment in re-establishing the invalid's health, the woman will begin her attempts afresh, doubling the doses this time.

Joye was condemned to life imprisonment with hard labour. After his condemnation, he asked for his diploma as a herbalist and a book of prayers, which had been taken from him.

Sometimes it is when in robust health that the husband is seized by a sudden, unaccountable sickness, at others it is in the course of an ordinary illness that his wife gives him poison, hoping that its effects will be confounded with those of the disease. It has been proved that cases of poisoning are more frequent during epidemics of cholera, because women take advantage of this and try to put down the symptoms really due to the poison to the account of the prevalent disease. This also gives them a pretext to at once get rid of the evacuations, so as to avoid their being analyzed.

It is no uncommon thing for a wife who poisons her husband to take advantage of the lengthened period of his illness to get the man she is slowly murdering to make a will in her favour. Indeed more often than not the husband never suspects his wife. Occasionally however he sees that his illness is no ordinary one, feels he is not nursed lovingly, that he is a burden, and that his death is a thing hoped for. If the woman notices these suspicions, she strives to remove them by acting a play of pretended love and wounded feelings ; she lavishes marks of fond affection on her husband and complains bitterly of his unjust suspicions, making such a to-do that the poor victim ends by excusing himself and asking pardon for having even suspected her. But the husband's relations, friends and children, struck by the wife's attitude and manner, are more clear-sighted ; they form suspicions, watch the woman and keep her away from the sick man's bed. It was to his friends' perspicacity, who had him removed and carried to an hotel that in a recent case the husband owed his life. A child whose father was poisoned by his mother, told his uncle " that he noticed how for some time his mother was not the same towards his father, that she did not seem to look after him well." Struck by her indifference, the child watched his mother in terror, and surprised her putting something suspicious in his father's medicine. Not daring to say anything, he determined to keep on the alert all night, but was overcome by sleep. He was awakened by the complaints his father was making to his mother about the draught she had just given him and which he declared had a bad taste.

In some instances the husband who feels his wife does not love him, has a presentiment of the fate awaiting him. " I shall die poisoned," he says to his family and friends ; " if I do die, have a *post-mortem* made, to make sure I have not been poisoned." He avoids taking drink and medicine from his wife's hand, and is observed to sit up in bed to examine the phials on the table by his bedside.

When the poison acts too slowly to accord with her wishes and the husband's health holds out, the adulterous wife, impatient to be left a widow, will sometimes forget all prudence and hasten on his death by large doses ; she wants to get done, and would rather run the risk of discovery than live any longer with her husband. She wearies to be free, and able to marry her lover, and in her blind impatience gives vent in spite of herself to her real feelings before the bystanders. " The thing must end ! " exclaimed one such woman to a neighbour, unable longer to contain herself, " I would rather die with my lover than go on living any longer with my husband." However, suchlike outbursts of annoyance and impatience are the exception ; more often the adulterous wife who poisons her husband masters herself sufficiently to hide her criminal acts under a veil of consummate hypocrisy. To prepare those about her for her husband's death, she makes a display of excessive grief, says she is broken-hearted, that science is powerless to save him. In her impatience to see him dead, she declares recovery to be impossible at a time when his condition is not yet by any means desperate. Finally, when the poor invalid does die, she manifests the deepest sorrow, crying, groaning and pretending to weep.

The accomplice.—The unfaithful wife will sometimes poison her husband without feeling any positive dislike to him, simply and solely in order to regain her freedom

and be able to marry again.   Mme. B——, recently condemned by the Assize Court of the Seine for an attempt
to poison her husband, did not hate him, indeed she used
to call him her "big brother," "her great boy."   Nor did
he interfere with her pleasures, but left her perfect liberty.
Still she wished him out of the way, that she might marry
afresh.   Nor was it enough for her to get a divorce; she
had already been divorced once, and a second would have
been a point against her, as a widow is more courted than
a *divorcée*.

The wife accomplishes the crime by herself, when the
lover refuses to join in the plot for murdering the husband.
But most often the poisoning is carried out with the complicity and co-operation of the lover.   When the husband's
death is carried through by the wife and her accomplice
together, sometimes the idea of the crime originates with
the woman, sometimes with the lover; now it is the
woman induces her lover to kill her husband, now the
lover that incites the wife to commit the crime.   Chateaubriand relates in his Memoirs that one of his ancestors,
having become the lover of a married lady, Jacquemine
de Boysirioult, killed her husband at the instigation of his
mistress, who had promised him her hand as the reward
of the crime.   Three months afterwards, he married his
victim's widow, but prosecuted for murder and found
guilty, he was beheaded on a scaffold at Rennes in 1574.

When it is the woman that urges her lover to kill her
husband, she resorts to every kind of ruse to suggest the
act to his mind, to rouse him to its accomplishment and
to overcome his last scruples.   If the husband is to be
shot down with a gun, it is she who studies the locality,
stations her lover in ambuscade in a favourable position,
and entices the husband thither to be shot at.   On the
day fixed for the deed, she lavishes her caresses on her
husband to lull his suspicions to sleep, on her lover to
excite his courage, encouraging her accomplice by her
words and picturing the happiness awaiting him when
once her husband is dead; if he hesitates, she reanimates

him by fresh caresses. In a case tried by the Assize
Court of the Bouches-du-Rhône,—it has been made into
a novel, like so many other judicial dramas,—the examination established the fact that the adulterous wife
had posted her lover armed with a gun at a spot where
he could conveniently take aim at her husband, and that
seeing him hesitating to pull the trigger, she kissed him
passionately to induce him to make up his mind.

In the course of the interviews that take place where
an adulterous wife and her accomplice are confronted before the *Juge d'instruction*, how often we hear the lover
declare to his mistress : " It was for love of you, to obey
you, that I have brought dishonour on my name ; *you* have
made me a murderer."

A lover who at his mistress's instigation had killed the
latter's husband and was on trial for the crime, told the
Juge d'instruction : " Yes ! it was I who did it, but she
forced me into it. . . . We gave him poison not once,
but ten times over.   The man's soul was nailed into his
body.   After that she badgered me to strangle him, to
throw him under a waggon ; last of all she gave me gun-
powder to shoot him with."   The murderer added that at
the instant of firing, his mistress came up and kissed him,
to give him courage.—When the widow Gras, after dressing in *grande toilette* to go to the Opera, hid her accomplice
in the dressing-room, where he was to await his victim, she
kissed him again and again, making him admire her pretty
costume and repeating : " Look how fine I am ! " and
promising to marry him as the price of his crime.—I have
even known a country woman make a will in favour of her
servant in order to decide him to kill her husband ; passion
not being a strong enough motive to make him a murderer,
she kindled avarice in his heart as well.   The lover threw
himself by his mistress's orders on her husband during his
sleep, to beat him to death, but the latter succeeded in
freeing himself from his hands and in felling the aggressor,
who prayed for forgiveness and promised to leave the
country.   The husband, a good-natured man, promised for

his part, so as to avoid scandal, not to lay any information with the Police. But the wife, furious at having failed, incited her lover to make a fresh attack on her husband.

When the lover, at his mistress's instigation, becomes the husband's murderer, the chief reason is always that he is jealous of him. To share his mistress with another man makes him suffer cruelly in heart and body and self-esteem.[1] The material picture of the other taking his share possesses his imagination, torturing and exasperating him beyond all bounds. He would have the woman belong to himself and himself only, and to put an end once for all to this odious partnership, which he cannot bear to think of, he yields to his mistress's instigations or himself takes the initiative in planning murder. " Be mine ! " he cries, " and mine alone, and for this become a widow." A woman who had poisoned her husband, at her lover's instigation, told the *Juge d'instruction* : " One evening as I was walking with my lover, he said to me, ' Loving each other as we do, if it were not for the fear of compromising ourselves, we would get rid of those two obstacles, I of my wife, you of your husband.' These words stuck persistently in my mind, and finding an opportunity of committing the crime, I did it so as to be his, to live with the man I loved so well, the man I loved better than myself."

With eyes fixed on the happiness awaiting them after the husband's death, hypnotised as it were by thinking ot it, the adulteress and her accomplice make plans for the future, while the poison is slowly but surely producing its effect. At the very time when she was poisoning her husband, Mme. Weiss was thinking over the furniture of the rooms she would occupy with her lover after her husband's death. The lover on his side, before his mistress had become a widow, sent her a railway ticket from Spain, so that she might come and join him there

[1] This jealousy of the lover towards the husband, when it does not translate itself into murder, may lead to suicide, so great is the pain of sharing the loved one's favours with another man. I have noted several cases of the sort.

directly it was all over. Nay! more, actually before the first dose of poison had been administered, he had ordered the cards that were to announce his marriage with the widow, and had already completed all the civil formalities necessary for the marriage.—In another case, an unfaithful wife, who was getting a revolver sent her from Paris to kill her husband with, ordered a black dress at the same time for mourning.—The impatience the lover experiences to be rid of the husband often shows itself in imprudent acts, which later on become pieces of presumptive evidence against him; during the husband's illness and its final stages, he is seen wandering about the house and even pushing his way indoors, to find out if the man is going to die at last and make room for him.

When the adulterous wife's lover is himself a married man, a double crime becomes needful to enable him to marry his mistress,—the murder of his mistress's husband and that of his own wife. To regain their freedom, the lovers resort to a twofold crime to get rid of the obstacles standing in the way of their union. The lover kills his wife, and the mistress her husband, or else the lover himself undertakes both crimes. Some years since, at Saint-Nazaire, near Toulon, a man of sixty-seven, being eager to marry his mistress, a married woman of forty, began by putting his wife out of the way. This once successfully accomplished, his mistress, equally impatient to regain *her* liberty, said to him: "Well! you have your riddance!... Now, when shall I get rid of my husband?" A few days later, she did "get rid of him," as she put it.—In other instances the lover commits both murders, as in the following case: A miller, after drowning his wife, not without suspicions on the part of his children, who all but caught him in the act, did not hesitate a few months later to kill his mistress's lover, in order to install the latter at his mill.

If the lover, after murdering his mistress's husband, hesitates to go further and kill his own wife, the mistress is far too jealous to let her live. When Mary Queen of

Scots formed the project in conjunction with her lover
Bothwell to assassinate her husband, the Earl of Darnley,
she claimed of her lover as the price of her complicity,
" for this my painful labour," the right to take the place
of his lawful wife; " the feigned tears (of Lady Gordon,
Bothwell's wife) ought not to be of so great a weight," she
writes to him, " as the trusty labours I do undergo, to the
end I may deserve to come into her place."

Among crimes of poisoning committed by adulterous
wives, I have had occasion to note one of peculiar atrocity
carried out with the complicity of a priest, the Curé of Les
Baux in Provence.[1]   " I am guilty of the crime laid to my
charge," the woman involved told the *Juge d'instruction* ;
" it was my criminal relations with the Curé D—— that
led me to it.   When he first asked me to give myself to
him, I indignantly refused, but I ended by yielding.   I
soon came to hate my husband. . . . When he was ordered
elsewhere, the Curé said to me : ' What will become of
you ? Your husband cannot keep you ; get rid of it all.'
' But it's not so easy,' I replied.   Seeing I was inclined
to listen, he added : ' If you were to give him a dose of
poison, it wouldn't be out of the way.'   ' But,' I objected,

<hr>

[1] I have the profoundest respect for Religion ; yet I do not hesitate to give
an account of this odious crime committed by a priest.   Anyone acquainted with
human weakness is not surprised to find some priests unworthy of their
calling, —was there not a traitor among the twelve Apostles ?   There are bad
priests, just as there are bad magistrates and bad soldiers.   Fléchier, recounting in the *Grands jours d'Auvergne* the crimes of some wicked priests,
said quite justly that Religion is in no way affected by the unworthiness of
some of its ministers.   What I do not understand is the excessive indulgence
of the diocesan authorities towards bad priests ; instead of expelling them
altogether, they are often content to remove them elsewhere.   This Curé of
Les Baux had previously earned an evil reputation in the post he had held
before coming into the South, but all that was done was to send him to
another.   When a priest is denounced for evil behaviour to his Bishop, the
latter makes enquiries among the neighbouring clergy, who being good men,
cannot bring themselves to believe in their colleague's criminal conduct, and
the Bishop for want of sound information cannot himself credit an accusation
the actual truth of which he has never verified.   The Bench of Magistrates
are the only persons aware of the real facts through information received from
the Gendarmerie, the " Juge de Paix " and the Police.

'the chemists won't sell it.'   The Curé retorted : ' Bah ! you're a goose ; doesn't every grocer sell vitriol and rat poison.'

"On my declaring I should never dare to come to Confession with such a crime on my conscience, he said at once, ' I will give you absolution.'   Still I could not make up my mind to commit the crime ; I told him again I should never dare to go to Confession, and he promised me absolution a second time.   From that date my husband's death was a thing decided.   The Curé warned me not to put in too much poison, to prevent a sudden death arousing suspicion.   At his advice I scented the mixture with orange flower water.   On the 6th of February I gave my poor husband his first dose of poison.   My husband complained of wind and pain in the stomach and colic, but he went to bed and fell asleep.   Next day I visited the Cure to tell him what I had done ; I said my husband was not very ill, and he exclaimed, ' The wretch has a stomach of iron. . . .'   When finally my husband died, the Curé told me if they exhumed his body, I must make great demonstrations of grief in order to divert suspicion."   The Curé admitted he might have felt a certain attachment to the woman, but always within the limits of a godly affection, declaring she had never had the honour of being his mistress, though he was quite aware she might have wished to be.   The woman answered : "·I was attached to you, it is true ; but you loved me too, passionately."   She stated that the Curé had promised her that so soon as her husband's death should have been forgotten, he would summon her to join him in his new place of abode and to take her again into his service, representing her if need be as his cousin.   She gave, moreover, this curious detail as to the beginning of their adulterous relations ; all the time the curé D—— was trying to inspire her with disgust at her husband, he kept urging her to lavish attentions on him so as to divert suspicion, and was constantly giving her money that she might be able to give him good things to eat ; " Now

go and buy the beast a nice cutlet," he would tell
her.

When the priest was confronted with his accomplice,
the interview was fertile in startling incidents, and Molière
might have learnt fresh traits of character from it to complete his portrait of Tartufe. The accused woman said to
the Curé: "You are the reason for my being here."—The
Abbé D——: "Unhappy woman! how dare you say such
a thing. Jesus Christ . . ."—The accused: "Yes! you
talk about Jesus Christ now, but you didn't think of Him
that day you threw me down on the sofa."—The Abbé:
"It is not true! I have not the smallest immorality to
reproach myself with in connection with you. Look, what
a position you have put one of God's ministers in!"—showing her his prisoner's dress.—The accused: "Don't talk of
God! You are unfit to wear a priest's robes after what
you made me do to my poor husband. He was not ill-
natured; but for you I should never have dreamt of killing
him."—The Abbé, turning to the crucifix: "God is still
my master, and Him I adore; He knows my innocence
and purity."—The accused: "You, innocent! . . . You know
very well it was by your advice I poisoned my husband.
You loved me, and I loved you; you wanted to carry me
away with you and I wanted to go,—that's what undid us!
. . . You deny it all, because you always told me one
should deny everything and stick to it, no matter what
proof they could bring against you. We are both of us
guilty; the only difference between you and me is that I
confess my crime, while you deny it insolently."—The
Abbé: "I pray God for your husband and for you,
Madame."—The accused: "The day you left for your new
post, you told me with tears, 'My poor Pauline, we shall
never see each other more!' and I cried bitterly too. If
only you would speak the truth, you must admit all this
is perfectly true."—After the interview the Curé said to the
officer who was taking him back to prison: "Poor woman,
if I could only talk to her alone in private for one minute,
she would withdraw what she says. I find she is *still* in

love with me." The Curé was right ; the woman loved him still. To melt her heart, he gave vent to groans and moans in the night which were heard even in the women's cells, and she got up to listen and was moved to tears. The Curé then got a message conveyed to his accomplice ; with the object of misleading justice, he accused another perfectly innocent man of the husband's death. On the day of the trial, the woman repeated her confession, giving the most precise details as to the priest's guilt ; then at the very end of the hearing, she asked permission to speak and to the amazement of all declared she was alone to blame. The Advocate-General, who was prosecuting, having gone to the prison to ask her explanation of this change of front, she told him she had wished to secure the Curé's acquittal, because she loved him still.

Marie Broyer, during her examination, wrote letter after letter to the *Juge d'instruction*, to exculpate her lover from a theft he was accused of.

As a general rule, the accomplice of an adulterous wife endeavours to extenuate his own guilt by throwing on her the chief share of responsibility On the other hand it is no uncommon thing to see the woman, more generous than the man, assume against all truth and likelihood the whole guilt of the crime and exculpate her lover entirely in order to secure his acquittal.

Suicide of the husband.—To rid herself of her husband, an unfaithful wife does not always need to murder him ; she kills him with sorrow and chagrin, more slowly but not less surely than if she had poisoned him. When the husband is a man of a resigned disposition, he will sometimes quietly die of grief. If the pain and indignation he feels are too excessive for him to bear, he ends it all by suicide. On the body of a house-painter found drowned in the Seine in August 1896 was found the following letter : " My death is the result of the grief my wife's misconduct causes me."—Another husband, before killing himself, wrote to his wife : " You always knew it, I have told

you over and over again, I am ashamed, bitterly ashamed,
of your behaviour."—The number of husbands who commit
suicide cursing, nay! rather still loving in spite of all, their
unfaithful wife, is greater than people suppose, even among
the Parisian working-men.   To give a few examples.   A
journeyman butcher, thirty-three years of age, in despair
at the misconduct and desertion of his wife, throws himself
into the Seine, the following letter being found upon him :
"My dear Jeanne, you have quite misunderstood me, I had
forgiven you, but you chose to begin again ; I wish you
well, but you will repent your conduct some day,—when
it is too late.   Farewell, farewell,—from one who loves
you and has always loved you."   Another workman,
rendered miserable by his wife's misconduct, commits
suicide after writing to her :   "As you cannot behave
reasonably, and you make me pass in the house for what
I am not, I prefer to die.   Kiss my little Madeleine for
me fondly, I shall never see her more.   I have cried
bitterly thinking of her.   What will become of her?"—
A day labourer writes : "I am killing myself because of
my wife's unfaithfulness.   I beg my brother to take care
of my little girl and be a father to her.   I have not
strength to write more, my powers fail me, for it is hard
for an honest man to come to this ; I must be brave."
—The working-men of Paris have many faults, but they
have also many high qualities, and notably much delicacy
of feeling and a highly developed sense of honour.   You
would scarcely believe how many good husbands there
are amongst them, whose honour is so deeply wounded
by their wife's unfaithfulness as to lead them to commit
suicide.   In a great number of judicial reports on cases of
suicide, I read statements like the following : "X—— was
a good workman ; for some time past he had had frequent
scenes with his wife, reproaching her for her loose behaviour ; he loved her dearly and was ashamed at her
light conduct, and had declared he would kill himself
some day."—"Dear little wife of my heart," writes another
unhappy husband, who had been deserted by his wife,

"these two or three lines will be the last you will ever receive from me, for I am going on a journey none ever return from. Think of me a little, and from the bottom of the tomb I will thank you for your thoughts. Farewell ; your husband who has never ceased to love you and who kisses you for the last time."—I have myself noted the case of a husband who, on his wife's deserting him, determines to kill himself by means of charcoal fumes. While he is engaged in his preparations, his wife rings at the door; but he will not open, for he loves her still and fears, if he sees her again, he will forgive her. Whilst awaiting death, he writes her a letter, urging her to reform.

The character of *Jacques* in George Sand's novel, who commits suicide to make room for another man, has been adversely criticised. Such a case is obviously exceptional ; but it does occur, as I have seen myself. A husband, and the father of one child, put an end to himself, after writing to tell his wife he was killing himself, because he could not win her love, and to enable her to marry again. He ended his letter with recommendations to bring up his child well.

The despair experienced by a husband deserted by his wife may lead to madness. To give an instance. A certain R——, a farmer and an honest hard-working man, was married to a woman whom he loved passionately, but who left him to go off with a lover. So great was his despair that his whole character underwent a change ; he was a different man, his neighbours said of him ; he gave up working, and had only one idea left, one subject of conversation, his wife's unfaithfulness ; he would burst out crying at meals and leave the table without being able to eat, tossing the plates in the air. His state of nervous tension was extreme : " I am undone," he would exclaim, " I am a dishonoured man." Presently, from excessive loquacity he passed into a condition of prolonged taciturnity ; not a word could be drawn out of him, and he sat hour after hour silent and preoccupied, buried in his own thoughts. Little by little the idea of vengeance took hold on his mind. Unable to wreak this on the young man who had carried off his wife, he determined to punish his father by burning his crops.   He was brought up for arson before the Assize Court, but acquitted by the jury.

It is notorious that the insanity with which Auguste Comte, the famous founder of Positivism, was attacked in 1826, was due to overwork, and still more to the grief caused him by his wife's bad behaviour, who forsook him to go off with a lover.[1]   Quite recently, a prisoner who had tried to kill his wife, admitted to me that the shock the discovery of the latter's adultery had given him had shaken the balance of his wits ; indeed it was proved in the course of the trial that as the result of this mental disturbance he had fallen sick, refusing either to eat or drink and remaining plunged in the deepest despair.   There is no doubt great moral suffering may lead to mental aberration.

Nor does an unfaithful wife, when abandoning her husband and children to follow a lover, content herself with disgracing them ; she robs both husband and children and strips the house, carrying away money and even the very furniture of the rooms.   I have known a woman, abandoning her husband and four girls, remove his furniture and the bed the children slept in,—and another who actually made off with the bed-clothes from her children's bed.   The husband, left along with his young family, struggles to overcome the grief and shame that stifle him, in order to hide their mother's wickedness from them ; to console them and himself, he redoubles his tenderness and devotion towards his children, but often sinks exhausted under the weight of sorrow and debt combined.   One despairing husband writes : " I married, a bachelor myself, Mlle. ———, a widow ; she left me on four several occasions, each time without money and in debt.   To pay these I sold part of my furniture.   I mean to have done with it all ; this will make her for the second time a widow."   Another husband writes : "Cheated and deceived by my wife, who has carried off my all, and unable to meet my obligations, I find myself forced to put an end to my

[1] G. Dumas, *Revue philosophique*, 1898, p. 33.

life."—Often the flight of the unfaithful wife involves the ruin of the family; the lover is not in all cases satisfied merely to gratify his passion, he urges the woman to empty her husband's strong-box and carry off his savings. Having taken the wife, he makes no scruple about taking the injured man's money too. All these reasons focussed in one, shame, grief, ruin, drive a certain proportion of unfortunate husbands to suicide. The fact that their children still remain with them does not always suffice to preserve them from despair. A stone-cutter, thirty-five years of age, on being abandoned by his wife, commits suicide by charcoal fumes, after writing to his two children who lived with him: "Farewell, children, forgive me; but I cannot live without your mother."—I have myself noticed the case of a working-man, who being abandoned by his wife and separated from his child whom the latter had taken away with her, was found dead, holding his child's photograph in his hands.—Lastly, the workman who has been abandoned by his wife, saddened and discouraged, often loses all his love of work, takes to drinking to drown his sorrow, and so comes to poverty and wretchedness. A working printer, forsaken by his wife and who a short while since tried to put an end to himself by means of charcoal fumes, gave the following answer to a Police Commissary who questioned him as to the motives leading to the rash attempt: "The act of despair I have been guilty of is due to the many griefs my wife has caused me ever since our marriage, and to extreme poverty as well."

To taste the happiness offered her by adultery, a wife breaks her husband's heart, sacrifices her children's honour, yet when she thinks she has it,—this bliss bought with the tears of her nearest and dearest,—often the cup of joy is dashed from her lips. The day comes when the woman who has forsaken her husband is in her turn abandoned by her lover, and having quitted the hearth and home where she was honoured and loved, she now finds herself without a home at all, and must choose between suicide and the life of an adventuress, if her husband refuses to

take her back again. She writes to him to express her
remorse and wish to resume their old life together; if her
husband makes no reply, she renews her prayers and
supplications, and ends by putting an end to herself in
despair. I have noticed quite lately the case of a school
teacher of the South-West of France, who having forsaken
her husband, a worthy man, a master carpenter by trade,
and two children of tender age, in order to follow her lover
to Paris, was in her turn abandoned by him and killed
herself in a cab with a revolver.

A wife who leaves her husband to go off with a lover
is particularly exposed to the risk of being in her turn
forsaken when she is older than her lover; here again
suicide is very often the epilogue to adultery. "My wife
left me on the 28th of January," a husband told a Police
Commissary, who was inquiring particulars of her suicide;
"she deceived me with a young man, who in due course
left her in the lurch. I am not surprised at her having
poisoned herself, for she had made three attempts previously to put an end to her life with petroleum or
phosphorus."

But a large number of unfaithful wives come to a less
tragic end; they finish by becoming prostitutes. *C'est le
premier pas que coûte* in adultery, as in other things. A
woman rarely stops short at the first offence; she always
goes on from a first to a second, from a second to a third,
and so from one lapse from virtue to another, soon arrives
at prostitution. Among "gay" women on the Police register
are a considerable proportion of married women.

When an adulterous woman is not forsaken by her lover,
she herself will look out for a successor to him. Adultery
has its disillusions no less than marriage, and these set
a woman longing for revenge; then, anxious to make
a better choice this time and find at last the ideal man of
her dreams, after playing her husband false for a lover,
she plays this lover false in favour of another. It is easier
for a woman to have no lover at all than to have only one.
Like the drunkard who seeks intoxication in bottle after

bottle, the adulteress is unfaithful to the lover that she may be faithful to Love.

A small minority of unfaithful wives are able to keep free of promiscuous gallantry, but even these very seldom find the happiness they had hoped for; instead of experiencing a more generous love than their husband showed them, they frequently meet with an affection at once more selfish, more suspicious and more brutal. The lover can feel but small confidence or respect towards a woman who has deceived her husband, so he is jealous and makes his mistress miserable. I have known cases where the woman was so unhappy as to commit suicide.

Nor is it always an easy thing for an unfaithful wife who has quitted her husband's roof to break the connection that has now grown hateful. The lover opposes her departure, telling her she belongs to him and has no right to leave him, and going so far as to bully her and even threaten to murder her. This is the beginning of the adulteress's punishment; her irregular liaison becomes a torment, aggravated by regret for her lost good name, and disgust and disappointment with herself and the world.

Some years ago, the Assize Court of the Alpes-Maritimes adjudicated on the case of a young woman of twenty-one, who finding herself unable to break off her connection with a lover who now only inspired her with dislike, ended by ridding herself of him by stabbing him with a knife, as he lay asleep by her side.

Moreover, there comes a time when the wife who has forsaken her husband's roof, begins to turn her thoughts to the man she has left. The husband who at close quarters was indifferent to her or even odious, regains his attractions when viewed from a distance; she appreciates him better now she has left him, and finds to her great astonishment she no longer dislikes him. I find among the official reports of suicides filed and classified at the Public Prosecutor's office of the Department of the Seine two letters from two women who had left their husbands, and were so deeply sorry for what they had done as to kill

themselves in consequence. The first, after trying in vain
to poison herself, ended her life by means of charcoal
fumes, leaving the following lines behind : " It is six
o'clock. My wits are wandering, and my sight troubled.
Death is not far off now. I always loved him. Since our
divorce, I have not had one happy day."—The other who
had also abandoned her husband, shot herself with a
pistol, after writing to her mother : " I am going to die.
Better leave this world than turn out ill. I declare to you
it hurts me sadly to die ; I am young, and I might perhaps
have been happy some day. But it is so dismal to live
always alone, without a friend. Bury me near my father,
I shall feel less lonely. I send you a big kiss, our last.
Think of me sometimes, and when you have time, bring a
few flowers to lay on my tomb. You will find my room in
great disorder, but for some time I have taken no interest
in anything."

Adultery may likewise become a torment and a punishment, even in cases where the wife has not left her
husband's roof, if the lover, whose unworthiness she has
realized, is determined to remain her master. Such a
master is a far harder one for a woman, a far more selfish
one, than the husband she used to complain of ; he orders
her about like a slave, and she obeys him for fear of
causing scandal. She used to picture herself reigning a
sovereign queen over a generous heart, and lo ! she finds
herself crushed under the most humiliating yoke. Sick of
suffering,[1] she sometimes chooses as the lesser evil to
avow everything to her husband, declaring : " Come what
may, I will confess my sin and expiate it ; my husband
must do what he likes with me. Anything is better than
the torment of continuing my connection with an unworthy
being ! "

These, the usual consequences of adultery, viz., the wife's
suicide, the family's ruin, poverty, drunkenness and death
of the husband, are all touched upon by Flaubert in his

---

[1] This situation, as we all know, has been put on the stage by E. de Girardin
and Alexandre Dumas *fils* in their play entitled *Le Supplice d'une Femme.*

famous novel of *Madame Bovary*. The heroine begins
with adultery and ends with suicide, dragging her husband
into poverty, wretchedness and intemperance. At the
time of the prosecution initiated against the great novelist,
the Imperial Advocate professed to find an offence against
morality in the scene of Mme. Bovary's suicide. I do not
share his opinion ; on the contrary the catastrophe of the
tale contains a powerful moral lesson, since it is an exact
representation of reality, summing up the disillusionment,
bitter disappointment and tragic end of the adulteress.

CHAPTER VII.

ADULTERY ON THE PART OF THE WIFE (*continued*).

"Thou shalt not kill."

The Forgiving Husband.—The Avenging Husband.

THE husband is always the last to hear of his wife's misconduct. He feels a natural confidence in the woman he has chosen, while his own self-esteem will not allow him to doubt of her faithfulness; besides, he believes the mother of his children incapable of an action that must dishonour them. But before long an anonymous letter, some speech of an indiscreet friend, the discovery of a letter, makes him aware of his calamity. In dramas of adultery as represented on the stage, authors frequently employ the machinery of letters which are lost and subsequently discovered by the husband to give rise to striking situations. And in so doing, they only follow what actually happens very often. Thus, for instance, I have myself come across a case like this: a woman writes a letter to her lover, but afterwards tears it up and writes another, throwing the fragments of the first into the grate; these the husband collects, puts together again and discovers in this way the proof of his wife's unfaithfulness. In another case, the wife on starting with her husband for a journey had left in her lover's hands a number of envelopes directed by a servant whom she had left behind in the house, in order that the husband, recognizing the maid's hand-writing might feel no suspicions. But the lover's letters came so frequently in the servant's envelopes, that the husband became suspicious, opened a letter and discovered the truth.

When a husband suspects his wife's fidelity, he often

makes use of a subterfuge in order to catch her, which almost always succeeds. He pretends he has to go on a journey, gets his wife to accompany him to the railway station or the railway omnibus, so as to make her feel sure he has really started, then gets out at the first station and returns to his house, where he discovers his wife in company with her lover.

The accomplice of the unfaithful wife is often the husband's bosom friend; and novelists and play-writers are perfectly accurate in representing it so. Opportunity makes the thief, with lady-killers as with cutpurses. Sometimes the would-be seducer constitutes himself the husband's friend for the express purpose of getting over his wife; he insinuates himself into the home circle, the more easily to attain his unholy purpose. Similarly it is often by her most intimate female friend that a married woman is betrayed, and it is the friend of her heart who robs her of her husband's love.

So long as he does not actually surprise his wife *in flagrante delicto*, the husband hesitates to credit his calamity, invites his wife to justify herself, readily believes her protestations of innocence and allows himself to be melted by her tears. Quick to take alarm, he is equally quick to cool down again. Molière, who pokes so much fun at the unfortunate husbands who are duped by their wives, himself played the part, by his own admission, of a duped and acquiescent mate. Being informed of his wife's uncontrollable passion for the Comte de Guiche, he made up his mind to upbraid her; "but her mere presence," he tells us, "made me quite forget my resolution, and the very first words she said in her defence left me so entirely convinced my suspicions were ill-founded, that I asked her pardon for having been so ready to believe evil of her."—I give an extract from the records of some legal proceedings, being part of a letter written by a married woman to her lover: "After blows and silly accusations come caresses and excuses, accompanied by the offer of a new frock."—Mary Queen of Scots,

writing to her lover Bothwell, tells him how her husband,
though he undoubtedly had the gravest reasons to suspect
her, would regain perfect confidence at the smallest mark
of hypocritical fondness she displayed towards him.   " Of
a sudden I do make him two or three pretty speeches,
whereat he is right glad and fears no more." Not that
it is out of generosity a husband is so forgiving; the fact
is he is smitten with his wife's beauty and a slave to his
own senses, because he is of a weak character and incapable of proper pride.   Love does not as a rule shine
much in dignity ; the great idea is, at all costs, to keep
possession of the person loved.   Few men are able to
kill love by contempt ; in most cases love survives in spite
of it.   I find among the records of a trial the following
letter from a married woman to her lover, showing very
clearly the weakness of disposition of some husbands and
their never failing readiness to forgive : "I got home
yesterday evening, and found the poor old boy half asleep
and half awake.   He had eaten nothing all day long.
The moment he saw me, he began crying like a child,
and said, ' If you have been deceiving me, confess, and
I will forgive you.'   I swore I had never deceived him
in my life."

Not a few husbands are like the Emperor Claudius, who,
writes Tacitus, "at one time would be furious at his wife's
immoralities, at another softened and tender-hearted at
the thought of their relations to one another and their
young children."   He would undoubtedly have forgiven
Messalina, if Narcissus had not made haste to have her
executed ; he had spoken of her as "poor Messalina,"
giving orders that she should appear before him to plead
her own justification.   Narcissus understood these and his
other words to imply that the Emperor's anger was cooling
and love was about to reawake, for when a husband invites
his wife to justify herself, he is already half-way to forgive
her and to credit her excuses and regret for the past.

There are husbands so feeble-minded that, after turning
their guilty partner out of doors, they will go and beg

her to return to their roof. Others, after taking an oath to punish the faithless wife who has left them and uttering terrible threats of what they will do, are only too eager to welcome her back, the moment she returns home ; the mere sight of her appeases their anger instantly.

When an unfaithful wife who has been driven from her husband's house wishes to obtain pardon and forgiveness, she tries to slip in again and take refuge in the marital bed, so as to lead up to a reconciliation. It was because he "feared the coming night and with it the associations of the conjugal bed," that Narcissus, to forestall a pardon on the part of Claudius, gave the order to kill Messalina without a moment's delay.

A more respectable motive for forgiveness on the part of the husband is the fear of bringing scandal on his children. Just at first, on learning his wife's unfaithfulness, he cries in a fury of rage and indignation, " I must kill her, I must kill her ! " But the remembrance of his children soon occurs to him and he restrains his passion. Husbands who have actually bought a dagger or revolver to kill their guilty wife with, will renounce their purpose for the sake of their children. I have even known the case of a husband who, though knowing himself to have been poisoned by his unfaithful wife, had yet refused to de- nounce her, preferring to die without a word rather than provoke a scandal that would be certain to recoil on his children. In some judicial proceedings I have just been examining, I find the following declaration made by a wife : " My husband having left me for a time to practise his trade of a knife-grinder in the country, I had relations with G——. Having become pregnant and dreading my husband's return, I wrote to him to say that I had yielded in a moment of light-headedness, and that I besought him to forgive me. When my husband came home, I threw myself into his arms crying bitterly and asked his for- giveness. He reproached me sternly, but ended by de- claring he was willing to keep me for the sake of our two children, refusing however to let me lie in at his house or to rear the child I was about to give birth to."—Another husband, P——, who killed his wife's lover and was brought to trial for the crime, had forgiven the woman, telling her that "if henceforth she would behave like an honest woman, looking after her children carefully and managing her house well, though he was quite certain three out of the five were the lover's, yet he would love them all and make no difference between them, seeing it was no fault of theirs if three of them did belong to another man."

When a husband forgives his wife, in the interest of his children, in order to avoid scandal, he very seldom gets any reward for his generosity ; for, as a rule, an adulteress's repentance is very much what a drunkard's oath is. One lapse from virtue leads to another. Penitence soon wears off, and bad habits resume their sway ; the mud she has once fallen into calls her back irresistibly to wallow in the same again, and no mere ephemeral remorse can wash away the effects entirely. The forgiving husband can by no means rely on his wife's remorse, or confidently expect any reformation. In many judicial cases where an unfaithful wife had been murdered by her husband, I have ascertained that the latter had already forgiven a first offence, which had then been very speedily followed by a fresh one of the same sort.

The great majority of adulteresses are incapable of appreciating the generosity of forgiveness ; all they see in it is a sign of weakness, and they think they can do with their husband what they please. A wife detected by her husband the moment after she had given him a poisoned draught, said to him : " You have forgiven me so often ; forgive me this once more."

Besides, many women are of such a heedless disposition and fickle character that anything like real repentance is out of the question. The Assize Court of the Department of the Seine adjudicated some few years ago on the case of a husband who had killed his wife after surprising her *in flagrante delicto*; it came out in the course of the proceedings that he had already forgiven her once. His wife, falling on her knees before him and weeping scalding tears, had promised to reform her conduct; but the very next day she was out buying "pencils" to paint her eyebrows with and only thinking of the most attractive toilet to please her lover. We see wives who have just escaped an attempt on their husband's part to shoot them almost immediately returning to their vicious mode of life. I remember observing the case of a woman who, after being caught *in flagrante delicto* with her lover by her husband, who fired several shots at her with a revolver, proceeded only a very few minutes afterwards to attend to the cares of her toilette with a calm and precision that astounded a police inspector, well used as he was to extraordinary sights. She plied her powder-puff, gazed in the looking-glass, and arranged her hair, as if she had entirely forgotten the awful drama that had just occurred.

The majority of adulterous wives stifle their conscience and feel but little remorse, or even if they do feel it, go on indulging their passion notwithstanding; they may regret the consequences of their wrong-doing, their husband's anger, the scandal that ensues and the reprobation of public opinion, but without experiencing any very keen sense of guilt or any very deep desire to alter their conduct. It is chiefly when their passion has cooled that they first begin to be really penitent. True, in some women of more delicate moral susceptibility, remorse may be deep enough to affect their health injuriously; but this is exceptional, though I *have* known instances. An unfaithful wife may fall ill of remorse, as the result of spending her days and nights in tears. I have also known the case of a woman of this sort who poisoned herself on learning that her husband had discovered her offence; she left on the dining-room table a letter to the following effect: "Regretting to find my husband is aware of my wrong-doing, I prefer to disappear, that he may excuse my fault. I hope he, his family and mine, will forgive me."—Another married woman who had fallen from virtue, discovering that her husband was aware of her unfaithfulness to him, put an

end to her life, begging that she might be buried far away
from the village where she had done wrong.—Dr Frend
speaks of an adulteress who, tortured by remorse and
unable for an instant to forget the sin she had committed,
which filled her whole mind with morbid persistency, used
to wash her hands and genital parts a hundred times a
day ;[1] like Lady Macbeth, she longed by this washing
and physical purity to regain the moral purity she had
lost.

An unfaithful wife who is a prey to remorse is urged by
her conscience to confess her sin to her husband, to humble
herself before him, to ask his forgiveness and do penance
for her offence. This confession is the first act of expiation
and relieves the strain of her feelings. But it is seldom the
avowal does not lead to some catastrophe ; either the
husband drives the traitress from his house and starts off
to challenge the lover, or else he forgives the penitent.
But such forgiveness is never lasting, and the house
remains divided against itself. Sometimes the discord
arising between man and wife as the result of the latter's
confession of her sin, ends in the woman's suicide. Here
is an instance. A wife had been guilty before her marriage
of a lapse from virtue which her husband, a man of a very
jealous disposition, at last forced her to confess. From
that moment reproaches and recriminations rained upon
the poor woman, alternate quarrels and reconciliations
followed each other unceasingly, and life soon became so
unbearable that she poisoned herself in sheer despair. She
had but just time before expiring to say one word to her
husband : "Kiss me."

Some writers, Beaumarchais in particular in *La mère
coupable*, have pictured the unfaithful wife as fainting with
grief and shame at the moment of making confession of
her fault to her husband. Such a thing may happen, but
I have never seen it. I *have* known the case of a husband
who swooned with grief on receiving his wife's avowal of
guilt.

---

[1] *Revue neurologique*, 30th January 1895.

The husband's vengeance.—When a husband, informed of his wife's unfaithfulness, gives a rein to his anger, he is affected in different ways. Sometimes he thinks only of killing the erring woman, without paying much attention to the lover; sometimes he turns his whole fury upon the lover, and spares the wife he still loves; sometimes he wreaks his vengeance on both of the guilty pair. In cases of discovery *in flagrante delicto*, as a rule he strikes the woman at the same time as her paramour.

Schopenhauer maintains that "honour requires only the punishment of the woman and not that of the lover.[1] On the contrary honour seems rather to demand the latter's punishment. We say of a husband who strikes down his wife's lover that he has avenged his honour. His honour is outraged at least as much by the lover's act as by that of the guilty woman. It is the thought of his honour that kindles in his heart an imperious craving for revenge against his wife's accomplice. "I will have his life," cries the wronged husband, "or he shall have mine. I must kill him ; he has dishonoured me."

Othello, when he has killed Desdemona, exclaims addressing his friends: "Call me, if you will, a murderer, but for honour's sake; I did everything for honour and naught for hate." Whenever, at various periods of history, husbands have ceased to hold their honour compromised by their wives' unfaithfulness, marital vengeance has been unknown. At the end of the Roman Republic, adultery on the part of the wife was accepted with complete indifference by the husband. "Lucullus," Montaigne writes, "Cæsar, Pompey, Antonius, Cato, and other noble Romans, were all cuckolds, and knew it without making an ado; there was only one silly fellow, Lepidus, in those days, who died of the pain of it."[2] The most famous Patrician dames of the period lived adulterous lives,— Mucia, Pompey's wife, Servilia, mother of Brutus, Valeria, sister of Hortensius, Claudia, wife of Lucullus, Tertiella,

[1] Schopenhauer, *Aphorisms*, p. 91, F. Alcan, Paris.
[2] Montaigne, *Essais*, Bk. iii., ch. v.

wife of Crassus, etc.; yet, according to Ovid, "never an adulterer pierced by the husband's sword dyed with his blood the waters of Styx." [1] At the same time this indulgence towards adultery is not so much a mark of gentleness of character as of contempt for women. The behaviour of Cato of Utica with regard to his wife Martia is characteristic; he lent her to his friend Hortensius, to have children by her, taking her back again after his friend's death, because the latter had made her his heiress. Hortensius, before procuring Cato's wife to be lent to him, had previously asked him for his daughter, who however was also already married, telling him : " it was honourable and useful to the common weal that a fair and honourable young woman in the flower of her age should not remain idle, letting her natural aptitude to conceive children go for naught, nor yet that she should trouble and impoverish her husband by leaving him more children than he had any use of." Such being the state of public morality, husbands did not think of killing their unfaithful wives, they were content to repudiate them. This is what the Roman Emperors, as a rule, did ; thus Scribonia was repudiated by Augustus, Livia Hostilia by Caligula, Plautia Urgulanilla by Claudius, Domitia by Domitian, Flavia Sulpitiana by Pertinax, etc.—In the Middle Ages the sentiment of conjugal honour grew more awake, and this combined with the violence of contemporary manners made acts of marital vengeance frequent. In the sixteenth century too husbands were prompt to stab unfaithful wife and accomplice together. After commending a certain number of ancient emperors and kings for having put away their adulterous wives without killing them, Brantôme [2] adds : " Nowadays none of our great folks do the like ; but the smallest punishment they do inflict on their wives, is to put them in perpetual confinement on bread and water, and there they do them to death, poison

---

[1] Ovid, *Ars Amoris.*

[2] *Dames Galantes,* First Discourse. See Brantôme, " Fair and Gallant Ladies," translated by A. R. Allinson, M.A.—C. Carrington, Paris, 1901.

them, kill them whether of their own hand or by the Law."
He quotes a large number of kings, princes, lords, who had
stabbed, poisoned or even strangled with their own hands
their guilty wives ; he protests against these butcheries
and urges unfortunate husbands to be content with repudiation, because, he says, God forbids murder, and
because women "are creatures more near resembling the
divinity by reason of their beauty." In the seventeenth
century manners were less brutal. In the eighteenth, not
only were they still further softened, but indulgence on
the husband's part became mere cynicism ; not merely did
he excuse, he actually authorized his wife's unfaithfulness.
The fashion of the time was not to love one's wife, to make
light of her fidelity and leave serious marriage to the
people and the Protestants.

In our own day, acts of marital vengeance have grown
very common. There are, it is true, and especially in the
Capital, husbands ready, like Cato, to lend their wives ;
there are even more husbands who live on their wives'
unfaithfulness than die of their misbehaviour. Suchlike
complaisant husbands were numerous at Rome ; "In this
way," Ovid writes, "a man may readily obtain great credit
at this price . . . and your house will be filled with fine
things that have cost you nothing" (*Elegy*, iv. 3). Nowadays
the feeling of conjugal honour has penetrated all classes ;
and the fear of ridicule unites with the former sentiment
to kindle the wrath of the outraged husband. In several
cases before the Courts, I have known the husband relate
how after the discovery of his disaster he thought everybody, as he passed in the street, was looking at him with
malevolent curiosity, and that his rival was mocking his
dishonour. In fact, the dread of being the object of
public ridicule was an important factor in exasperating
his anger.

When a husband first acquires proof of his wife's unfaithfulness, he either breaks out in fierce threats, or else
constrains himself to hide his resentment under a forced
calm, which is only the more menacing for the concealment.

His anger is concentrating, accumulating in his heart, till it finally explodes in furious rage ;—

"La douleur qui se tait n'en est que plus funeste." [1]

The frequency of these acts of marital vengeance may further be attributed to the increased frequency of adultery in modern times, as well as to the mistaken belief that a husband possesses the right to kill his wife, if caught in the act. The number of persons accused of adultery before the Courts rose in 1895 to a total of 1964. In his last report on the Administration of Criminal Justice, the "Garde des Sceaux" (Chancellor) writes: "Adultery still continues its continually progressive increase." [2]

Among legal misconceptions prevalent among the public, none is more widely spread than that which attributes to the injured husband the right to kill his wife and her accomplice, if caught *in flagrante delicto*. I have myself seen a husband who had murdered his wife's lover and tried to kill her, state under examination that he had the right of life and death over them. This strange mistake, the cause of so many murders, has been disseminated by the majority of writers, novelists, dramatic authors, critics, moralists, preachers, doctors of medicine, who have written on the subject of marriage. "The Law," says Dr Despine, "permits homicide as an act of vengeance to the injured husband." [3] Dr Letourneau commits the same mistake in the Preface he has written for a work of Dr Lombroso, *L'Homme criminel*. George Sand is guilty of the same error in her *Histoire de ma Vie* (5th Part, ch. x.). In his book *De L'Amour et de la Jalousie*, Stendhal denounces the savage tyranny of this barbarous code which secures to the injured husband the right to become a murderer without fear of consequences, and the same sentiment is repeated word for word in his work entitled *L'Amour*. Proudhon states his approval of the right

[1] "Indignation that is hidden is only the more deadly for its silence."
[2] *Journal officiel*, 9th November 1897.
[3] Despine, *La Science du cœur humain*, p. 98.

granted to the husband to kill an adulterous wife, though
at the same time refusing the lover the right to administer
so much as a fillip of the finger to his unfaithful mistress,
on the ground that the latter is free.[1]

Where is this mistake not to be found? It occurs in
the *Indissolubilité et Divorce* of the Père Didon, in the
Annales médico-psychologiques of May—June 1891, p. 441.
Not a week passes without my meeting with it in some
newspaper, review or book. In an article of the *Semaine
littéraire* of Geneva of October 23rd, 1898, M. Henry
Bordeaux expresses his indignation at the Code's according the husband the right of vengeance, and in the *Éclair*
of November 1st, 1898, M. Émile Bergerat does the same.
Saint-Marc Girardin, who was a Professor at the Sorbonne,
and a member of the French Academy, also believed the
Code to legalize marital vengeance; in his *Cours de
Littérature dramatique*, he wrote: "But then! suppose
the husband were to do what has often been done in
the world, a thing the Law has not thought good to
punish,—if he were to kill the lover?"

Above all it is our dramatists, anxious to reform the
Law without possessing any precise acquaintance with its
provisions, who have given most prominence and devoted
most vehemence to their protests against the supposed
ferocity of the Code in this particular. "Without going
into fuller detail," says the author of *Les Tenailles*, Mons.
P. Hervieu, "I think I am justified in maintaining that a
contract . . . which, in almost express terms, gives one of
the contracting parties and one only the right of life and
death over the other . . . cannot and ought not to be the
last word of Civilization, of Christian Morality and Social
Wisdom."[2] Taking his stand on this supposed right
granted by the Law to a husband to kill his wife,
Alexandre Dumas *fils* claimed the privilege of divorce;
he could not understand how the Law should permit the
husband to kill and yet refuse the right of divorce.

---

[1] Proudhon, *La Pornocratie*, pp. 203, 208.
[2] *L'Éclair*, August 14th, 1898.

"Poor Law," he said, "which is reduced, not daring to free man and wife by a divorce, to allow them by implication to free themselves by murder." "Can anyone conceive," he goes on, "such a contradiction, such an incredible deviation from justice, logic and common-sense, a law showing in one direction all the indifference and scepticism of the most corrupt nations, and in the other all the cruelty of the most barbarous peoples and savage tribes, actually below the law of the Quajaz, among whom a woman is put to death only on the second act of adultery." Further, with a really surprising illogicality, the same writer who declares the law ferocious, cruel and inconsistent, because as he holds it legalizes revenge, actually encourages the husband to employ this very right. In *Le supplice d'une femme*, Émile de Girardin and Alexandre Dumas *fils* are guilty of the same mistake ; in this play Dumont (the husband) says, addressing Alvarès (the lover) : "I have questioned the Law, and asked what means it afforded me ; I can kill you both, you and her." Similarly the *dénouement* of *Diane de Lys* depends upon the mistaken idea that the husband possesses the right to kill his unfaithful wife and her accomplice, when caught red-handed. In Scene 13 of Act iv., the husband refuses to fight the lover, declaring : "Why fight with you, when I have the right to kill you ?" So saying, he slays the lover, invoking his supposed right to do so. In *La Femme de Claude*, Alexandre Dumas again represents the murder of the adulterous wife as an act of justice accomplished in the name and with the sanction of the Law.

Not only are these two last mentioned plays founded on a misconception of the Law, but the same error was at the bottom of the campaign Alexandre Dumas conducted against the indissolubility of the marriage tie. Inasmuch as the Code, he argued, grants the husband the right of freeing himself by murder, why should it not accord him the right of gaining the same end by means of divorce ? It is surely contradictory to give the husband a right to dissolve his marriage by the revolver, and yet refuse him the privilege of ending it by divorce. But this contradiction which the famous writer saw in the Law, existed only in his own imagination. As a matter of fact, far from recognizing any right on the husband's part to kill his wife caught in the act of committing adultery, the Law punishes such a murder by from one to five years' imprisonment.

The mistake committed by Dumas and the authors who have followed him arises from the fact of their having misinterpreted through ignorance of legal phraseology the terms of Article 321, § 2, of the Penal Code, which runs as follows: " In the case of adultery provided against by Article 336, the murder committed by the husband on his wife, as also on the accomplice, at the moment when he surprises them *in flagrante delicto* in the conjugal domicile, is *excusable.*" Dumas, assigning to the word *excusable* the meaning it bears in ordinary parlance, supposed it to be synonymous with "justified," "legitimate." But in the language of the Law we must distinguish between an *excuse* and a *justifying circumstance.* An "excuse" diminishes culpability, a "justifying circumstance" abolishes it. So, for instance, provocation is an *excuse,* while lawful self-defence ·is a *justifying circumstance.* When the existence of an *excuse* is proved, says Article 326, if it is a question of a crime carrying the penalty of death or of life imprisonment with hard ·labour, the penalty shall be reduced to imprisonment for from one to five years.

Thus the contradiction Alexandre Dumas drew between the civil and the penal law has no actual existence,—*except* in his own writings. There we find it; the very man who revolts against the cruelty of the Code, which, according to him accords the husband a right to kill his wife, himself exhorts the husband of an unfaithful wife to murder, urging him in so many words to " kill her." In *L'Affaire Clémenceau* and *La Femme de Claude,* the husband kills the adulterous wife with a beautiful calmness ; you would say he was fulfilling a sacred duty, an act of piety in putting her to death. The dramatic author, so indulgent towards the courtesan, recognizes only one punishment for the unfaithful wife, — death. The husband, in his plays and novels, kills his wife as if she were a rabbit or some form of contemptible vermin.

It is on the faith of this supposed, but purely imaginary, contradiction between the penal law permitting, as they fancied, a husband to kill his wife and the civil law forbidding him to break his marriage under any circumstances, that many Deputies and Senators voted for the re-establishment of Divorce. M. Eugène Pelletan has himself been guilty of this common mistake ; the husband, he writes in his book entitled *La Mère*, p. 309, " can still kill his wife, and her lover ; the Penal Code gives him the right to do so." In view of the very small majority by which the re-establishment of Divorce was passed, the question may well be asked whether the vote was not due in part to this prevalent misconception.

The body of writers who with Alexandre Dumas proposed the re-establishment of divorce hoped that this measure would put an end to acts of marital revenge. Now that the husband, they maintained, will be able to repudiate his guilty partner, why should he resort to violence ? Having it in his power at any moment to serve her with a claim for divorce, he will no longer feel called upon to serve her with pistol bullets in the head. Practical experience however has not justified these expectations. The law of divorce has not saved unfaithful wives from the knife and revolver of their injured husbands. The total of divorces increases every year,[1] while no diminution is observed in

[1] Direct claims for divorce continue to advance in a regular progression, writes the Minister of Justice in his Statistics for the year 1894, published in 1895. From 3190 in 1886 they rose to 8673 in 1894. Of these 8673 claims, 2991 were initiated by the husband, 5682 by the wife.

The number of applications for legal separation declined at first after the re-establishment of divorce; it rose again however from the year 1890, in which it reached a total of 2041, subsequently rising by progressive stages to 2059, 2094, 2171, and finally 2405 in 1894.

It is among the working-class population that divorce is most common. It is less frequent among the commercial and industrial classes, but is making progress among persons of private means and those practising the liberal prothe frequency of marital reprisals. Husbands are more and more in the habit of getting rid of an unfaithful wife and her paramour by violent means, in spite of the facilities they now possess to end their marriage by divorce. Quite lately at Marseilles, in broad daylight, in the open street, an injured husband planted a knife in his wife's bosom. Another threw his out of the window.

True, juries constantly acquit husbands who have killed their unfaithful wives, but the Law is not responsible for these acquittals, the Law decrees a punishment for the murder of an adulterous wife ; it is for jurymen to apply it. Moreover, juries do sometimes condemn the husband who murders his wife under such circumstances. Here is an instance arising out of an affair that occurred at Cannes some years ago, at the very time Alexandre Dumas was residing there. A married couple, the D——s, lived on bad terms with one another, a consequence of a strongly marked divergence of tastes ; the husband disliked society, while his wife was devoted to evening parties, "at homes" and theatre-going. The chance of social intercourse introduced Mons. A—— to their acquaintance, and he soon became intimate. His marked attentions soon awoke Mons. D——'s suspicions, who before long acquired actual proof of his wife's unfaithfulness. The pair separated, but subsequently renewed their married life together and came to spend the winter of 1892 at an hotel in Cannes, where Mme. D—— occupied a bedroom and sitting-room on the *entresol*, while her husband, his mother and children were lodged on the first floor. On Feb. 17, the husband having found Mons. A——'s name on the hotel books, became suspicious ; he went and listened at the door of his wife's rooms, and thinking he heard his former rival's voice, went upstairs to fetch his revolver, and begging the manager of the hotel to go with him, threw open his wife's

fessions. It is also increasing in the rural districts. And nevertheless to make divorce still more frequent, writers of talent, Paul Hervieu in *Les Tenailles*, Paul and Victor Margueritte in their novels, propose to grant divorce by mutual consent or even at the wish of one only of the married couple.

door.   Inside he saw Mons. A—— trying to hide himself behind a sofa and fired three shots at him with his revolver at point-blank range.   Mons. A—— was carried to his room mortally wounded and died next day.   Arraigned before the Assize Court of the Alpes-Maritimes, the husband was condemned to a year's imprisonment.[1]

Divorce is as unavailing to put an end to marital reprisals as it is to feminine revenge, for it cannot prevent jealousy and passion.   At Mme. Panckouke's trial for firing three revolver shots at her husband's mistress, the Presiding Judge asked her : " Why did you not follow up your application for a separation ? "   " Because what I wanted," answered the accused woman, " was neither separation, nor divorce ; what I wanted was my husband."   During the course of proceedings in divorce, and after their termination, murderous dramas are not unknown ; when a husband, even after divorce, sees his wife in another man's arms, indignation and jealousy will sometimes master him so violently as to drive him irresistibly to acts of violence.

After first advocating the murder of unfaithful wives, the plays and novels of the day are now preaching the doctrine of forgiveness.   Midway between murder and forgiveness (which may well make the husband ridiculous), lies a solution of the difficulty, more accordant at once with the husband's' dignity and the respect he owes his partner's life, viz., separation with scorn :

" Ne peut-on se venger à moins qu'on n'assassine ? "[2]

Yes ! a man may avenge himself by scorn.

[1] His wife retired to a convent, whence she wrote numerous letters to her husband, asking for his forgiveness, and this was not refused.   She was not long in forgetting her lover's tragic end.

[2] " Cannot a man avenge his wrongs without resorting to downright murder ? "   Corneille, *Attila*.

CHAPTER VIII.

ADULTERY ON THE PART OF THE HUSBAND.

BASING their contention on the statistics of crime, some writers have maintained the thesis that women show themselves more often guilty of adultery than men; in 1886, for instance, 865 women were prosecuted and only 822 men; in 1887, 883 women and 843 men. But in this, as in other things, statistics do not reveal the whole truth ; they must be used with discretion and duly compared with the provisions of the Penal Code. In fact, we must never forget that men and women are not, from this point of view, on a footing of equality,—and never have been so. According to Manu, the Legislator of the Hindus, a woman ought to go on reverencing her husband as a god, even when he showed himself guilty of adultery (vi. 54, *Laws of Manu*).—Roman Law and old French Law did not allow the woman under any circumstances to charge her husband with adultery.—At the present day, according to Article 336 of the Penal Code, adultery on the husband's side only constitutes an offence if it has been committed with a concubine kept in the conjugal domicile. An isolated act of adultery does not constitute the keeping of a concubine ; to do so, it must take place under the conjugal roof. If these two conditions are not fulfilled together, a husband's adultery remains unpunished ; we may therefore say with truth that the majority of acts of adultery done by the man do not come under the surveillance of the Law at all. While quite recognizing the fact that adultery on the wife's part involves consequences altogether more serious than the same offence when committed by the husband, we may admit that the impunity accorded the husband in most instances offends against morality and the ideal of the equality of the sexes before the Law. Women are not entirely without justification in saying that, the laws being made by men, it has happened in more than one respect that they have been framed in men's own interest, without much heed being paid to the equality of the sexes. Cicero, who cannot be suspected of any leaning to *feminism*, observed even in his day that the Lex Voconia had been passed in the interest of the male sex, and was full of injustice towards women.[1]—Contemporary law-makers are applying themselves to the task of abolishing this inequality formerly set up by the Law between adultery on the part of women and of men. According to the new Penal Code of the Netherlands, "the penalty is imprisonment for six months at longest for any married person committing an adultery" (Article 241), this body of law making no distinction in this respect between man and woman.

Adultery will lead a man to commit the same acts of cowardice and cruelty as it will a woman. Dissipation extinguishes family feeling and destroys paternal affection. Fathers will ruin their children to satisfy a mistress's caprices, or desert them to follow a concubine, leaving their offspring in destitution. I have known the case of a father, who having lost a little girl by smallpox, forsook his two other daughters attacked by the same disease, to go off with his mistress. Abandoned to her own resources, the mother was forced to sell or pawn almost the whole of her furniture in order to nurse her sick children. On being reproached for his abominable behaviour, the unworthy father merely answered : " I have done extremely wrong, I admit; I was bewitched by my mistress." Another husband, a working-man, deserted his wife, leaving her the task of rearing seven young ones. The eldest boy, the only one able to work, helped his mother to supply the needs of his little brothers and sisters ; but one of the latter having fallen seriously ill, he was so heart-broken at the misfortunes of all kinds and the

[1] Cicero, *De Republica*, iii. § 10.

grinding poverty which had burst upon the unhappy family as a result of the father's desertion, that he put an end to himself. Meantime the father remained entirely insensible to all the calamities he had brought about by his ill-conduct.

In other cases fathers let their children be made martyrs of by their mistress. Valerius Maximus relates how Catiline, being desperately in love with Aurelia Orestilla and seeing that the son he had by a former wife was an obstacle to his marriage with her, did not hesitate to get rid of the youth by poison. "It was at his very funeral pyre that he kindled the hymeneal torch, and he offered as a wedding gift to his new wife the crime that abolished his paternity." [1]

The unfaithful husband is often rough and brutal towards the wife he no longer loves; he is for ever finding fault and ill-treating her. When a married woman is delivered of a still-born child, it is occasionally the husband's rough usage that is responsible for the catastrophe. A certain number of women ill-treated by their husbands commit suicide in despair.

The husband who forsakes his wife takes pleasure in deriding her grief; he listens to her reproaches with indifference, irony or even positive satisfaction; he is not at all sorry to see her tears, the sight of them is an amusement. If he does seem to be softened, it is because they awake in him a passing caprice of amorousness. Don Juan for a moment finds something piquant in Elvira's sorrow, but at heart he is purely indifferent to her sufferings. Alfred de Musset, who is partial to Don Juan, does not fail to note his cruel character:

> "Vous le verrez tranquille et froid comme une pierre
> Pousser dans le ruisseau le cadavre d'un frère
> Et laisser le vieillard traîner ses mains de sang
> Sur des murs chauds encor du viol de son enfant." [2]

---

[1] Valerius Maximus, Bk. ix., ch. i.

[2] "You will see him calm and cold as a stone push into the kennel a father's corpse, and let the greybeard drag his bleeding hands over walls yet warm with his child's ravishment."

Adultery less often drives the husband to homicidal acts than it does the wife; it is less liable to make him hate her. At the same time it is no uncommon thing to see unfaithful husbands load their lawful wife with insults and humiliations, and even end by murdering her, so as to be enabled to marry their mistress. Wives the best, the most gentle and patient, are often victims of their husband's brutality. The Duchesse de Choiseul, who was murdered by her husband, was a woman of admirable gentleness and goodness. The Marquise d'Entrecasteaux, whose husband, President of the Parliament of Provence, cut her throat with a razor during the night, was of so mild and gentle a disposition she was known among her friends by the name of Sister Angelica. Before gashing her throat three times with a razor, her husband had already tried twice over to poison her, besides throwing her down on the stairs of his house, at the time when she was with child. The Marquise, who was aware of his attempts to poison her, besought her physician not to divulge the facts : "Most excellent Doctor, the fearful torments I endured made you say I should have died of the effects of poison if you had not come promptly to the rescue. You said loud out, in my presence, that my husband was at the least very remiss not to try to find the guilty party. Do not say this again. I know the hand that was for destroying my existence, but to name it to you would be both needless so far as you are concerned and blameworthy on my part. As your habits of observation may have led you to guess the truth, I beseech you in your mother's name and by all you hold most sacred, never to reveal the things you saw and heard during the past night. You will not refuse this favour, dear and worthy sir, to an unhappy and dying woman, who must needs have much at stake to write you these lines by stealth and from her sick-bed,—to one who will for ever call herself your grateful and devoted well-wisher, the Marquise d'Entrecasteaux, née de Castellane, Marquise de Grimaud."

I have just instanced a President of the Parliament of Provence and a peer of France, of whom adultery made criminals. Adultery leads to murder in all classes of society. Just as adulterous Queens, like Mary Stuart and Jeanne de Provence, have not recoiled at the murder of their husbands, so Kings guilty of the same offence, such as David and Henry VIII. have done to death their lawful wives or the husband of the woman they coveted. When once a priest makes himself the accomplice of an adulteress, he becomes quite capable of helping the woman to poison her husband. When a husband murders his wife, we may say, almost for certain, that adultery is what has driven him to the crime. Sensuality makes men cruel. When Henry VIII. had Anne Boleyn beheaded,—and he had loved her fondly,—he had the moment of her execution made known to him by a cannon shot; this signal he awaited with impatience, and on hearing it hurried at once to Jane Seymour's lodging, to tell her the joyful news. Elizabeth of England, daughter of Henry VIII. and Anne Boleyn, gave a similar example of cruelty towards the Earl of Essex, who had been her favourite; she had a concert of music on the day of his execution. History attests on its every page the connection existing between cruelty and dissoluteness. La Voisin declared under torture, "that a great number of persons of all conditions and ranks had applied to her to procure the means of putting many individuals out of the way, and that dissoluteness was the leading motive of all these crimes." Dissolute kings have nearly always been monsters of cruelty, like Tiberius and Nero. In India voluptuous orgies were habitually accompanied with human sacrifices. In fact there is a close association between voluptuous passion and cruelty. Men affected with Sadism experience an irresistible craving to add cruelty to the other pleasures of debauchery. Criminals kill the women they have violated, not merely to suppress the evidence they might give against them, but still more because they find pleasure in shedding blood. This Sadism, a combination of cruelty with bestial debauchery, is sometimes committed on animals. To give an example. At Barles, in the *Arrondissement* of Digne, a farmer noticed again and again the death of a certain number of ewes, which, while perfectly well the night before, were found dead next morning in his fold. Thinking a spell had been cast over his flock, he went to the curé and asked him "to exorcise the spell" by his prayers. The mortality however continuing among his ewes, a neighbour of greater penetration than himself urged him to apply to the Public Prosecutor ("Procureur de la République") By the advice of this magistrate he had his sheep-fold watched at night-time by the "garde champêtre" (rural policeman), and this latter, himself carefully concealed, saw a young shepherd, a tall, sturdy young man, enter the building, seize a ewe by the neck and strangle it, while performing acts of bestiality upon its body.—Vacher, who murdered such a number of women, used to cut their throats after ravishing them.

Often it is with the domestic servants, or with his children's governess, that a husband has immoral relations. Among farmers in the country it is suchlike relations with the farm-maid that are most to be feared by the lawful wife. The maid, proud of her triumph, does not always leave the mistress in ignorance of it, and to make it more decided still, tries to get rid of the latter altogether. In towns, among families of a higher social position, it is a similar connection between the husband and the governess that is apt to endanger the life of the mistress of the house. The wife, feeling a presentiment of the fate awaiting her, might of course escape it by leaving her home, but she cannot bear to forsake her children and make way for a rival in her husband's affections.

Sometimes the husband is forced by his wife to turn the concubine out of the house, but he is not slow to find means to see her again ; his passion for her increases with absence, while his dislike to his wife grows in equal proportions. Then presently the notion of getting rid of his wife and taking back his mistress enters his head and becomes firmly lodged there. His words betray his secret thoughts in spite of himself, till his wife guesses them and questions him in terror as to what he means to do. "If you have no pity for me," she adjures him, "at any rate have some for our children." Finding his intentions suspected, the husband we might suppose would give up his ideas of murder; but it is seldom as a matter of fact that he draws back, and one day the wife is found dead, who only the day before was sound and well.

Not unfrequently the husband who has just killed his wife betrays himself by his own imprudence and the haste with which he calls his mistress to his side or proposes to marry her. His wife's dead body is hardly cold before he sets about marrying again. The mad passion urging him to this second marriage is such at times that, even if his crime is discovered, he feels no regret, provided he can get his new wife to follow him to New Caledonia or Guiana, our French convict stations. The Marquis d'Entrecasteaux, in the account he gave of his crime, declared that his passion, "far from being extinguished by the crime it had led to, seemed only to have gained fresh strength from it." Compelled to fly from justice and horrified at the ignominy he was involved in, he had several times thought of killing himself, but had always been dissuaded from the attempt by the hope of seeing his mistress once again. "The love that had made me a criminal and that even now doubled my torments, this same love prevented my ending them once for all. The hope of one day seeing again the woman who is the object of my passion could not indeed stifle my remorse, but it enabled me to bear all its horrors."

Each sex has its favourite means of carrying out its criminal intent. I have shown in an earlier chapter how women more usually resort to poison, while men as a rule prefer the knife or fire-arms. Still, just as we sometimes find a wife murdering her husband with pistol balls, so we occasionally see a husband making use of poison to rid himself of his wife.

The instruments employed vary likewise according to profession and occupation, as the criminal has a natural tendency to use the weapon he finds under his hand. Thus the druggist will employ poison; the waggoner will crush his wife under the wheel of his cart; the farmer will beat out her brains with a spade; the hairdresser will use a razor, the cook a kitchen knife. When it is a King who wishes to be rid of his wife, he does not kill with his own hands, but employs subordinates; if he desires to put a husband out of the way in order to take his wife, he despatches the unfortunate man to some post of danger. When David wished to get rid of Uriah, the husband of Bathsheba, he wrote to one of his generals: "Set ye Uriah in the forefront of the hottest battle, and retire ye from him, that he may be smitten, and die." (2 Samuel, ch. xi.)

Men are less clever actors than women. Still, even a man will play the deceiver in love, lavishing promises to gain the favours he covets, and then his passion once satisfied, forgetting them every one. He will cajole his best friend, to steal away his wife, his daughter or his sisters; cheat his wife, be she the best of wives and mothers, to hide his adulterous amours from her; play the comedy of tenderness, tears and protestations of devotion, at the very time he is planning her death.—An old man who is desirous of seducing a young girl resorts to the same artifices an old woman employs towards a young man; he poses as a father to her, in order to mask his love and avoid awakening her distrust. He endeavours to dissipate his wife's suspicions by surrounding her with fond attentions; if he decides to kill her with the blow of some heavy weapon, he entices her into an ambush artfully prepared beforehand; if he gives her poison, he displays the liveliest signs of affection in the very act. If he succeeds in killing her, he parades the profoundest grief. A husband who had just poisoned his wife, said to his mother-in-law, pointing to his face: "Behold the mark of my tears."

Suicide of the wife forsaken by her husband.—Nor does the husband, any more than the wife, invariably need to kill his partner, when he wishes to be rid of her ; in many cases it is enough for him to make her miserable and so drive her to a lingering death of grief or a sudden act of despair. The number of women forsaken by their husbands who die of sorrow or commit suicide is greater than is generally supposed. In my examination of the official records of suicides in the Department of the Seine, I have come across a not insignificant number of instances where married women have put an end to themselves when deserted or slighted by their husbands.[1] The letters left behind by them to explain their motives all revealed the deepest grief, but no trace of anger against the husband ; generally speaking, they forgive him, because they love him still, reserving all their indignation for the mistress, who has robbed them of their husband's love. One poor woman, deserted by her husband who left her to go off with a mistress, wrote thus before ending her life by her own act : "I am not angry with him ; on the contrary, I wish him every possible happiness. But I curse the name of the bad woman who has taken him from me. He little knows what grief his desertion causes me. He cannot know how much I loved him. My last thought is for him. Ah! if only I had died a year ago, what suffering I should have been spared !"—"My dear parents," writes another unhappy wife, "I am disgusted with life. My husband has left me. I know he will never come back. I loved him dearly. He has behaved badly. I would rather have done with it right off."—Women thus deserted

---

[1] Still the number of these suicides of wives forsaken by their husbands is smaller than that of suicides of husbands deserted by their wives, just as there are more suicides of widowers than of widows. Men find it harder to bear domestic griefs than women do. There are husbands (I have known such myself), who commit suicide to escape the continual quarrels due to their wives' ill-tempered disposition. "Unable to resign myself to live in constant variance with my wife," writes a working printer to the Commissary of Police, "I prefer the repose of death to such a life, which is a veritable hell." Death has fewer terrors for them than a woman who is always angry.

by their husbands sometimes put an end to themselves by means of charcoal fumes or else drown themselves along with their children.—I have myself known the case of a wife who, finding herself no longer able to please her husband owing to illness, committed suicide by charcoal fumes in dread of his suing for a divorce.

Nay! more, a wife who without being actually forsaken by her husband, yet sees a mistress better loved than herself, may experience a grief profound enough to lead her to commit suicide. An instance is afforded by a married woman, and the mother of a little girl, who suffered so bitterly from the knowledge that her husband kept a mistress that she wrote a letter to her parents to inform them of her intention to put an end to herself: "My dear parents, I am going to cause you great grief, but I cannot bear to live any longer. Life is a hell upon earth to me. Take great care of my little Julie. Tell her my last thought is for her. Be very good, little Julie, and think how sadly your mother suffered."

Just as a certain number of adulterous wives who have quitted their husbands are in their turn abandoned by their lover and end in suicide, so there is a small proportion of husbands who, having forsaken wife and children to go off with a mistress, who after a while leaves them in the lurch, are eventually driven to self-destruction. In their case remorse at having ruined their lives and sacrificed their family is added to the suffering caused by their mistress's unfaithfulness, and tends yet further to make them disgusted with life.—Some husbands, who have forced their wives to ask for a separation or divorce by reason of their ill behaviour, suffer so keenly from their loneliness as to choose death in preference. Such cases are rare, but still I have seen some. "I cannot bear up against the extremity of my suffering," writes a schoolmaster separated from his wife. "But you must know my last thought will be for you. Perhaps I am partly to blame; in any case, I shall have been well punished, and you will forgive me."

Vengeance of the married woman.—Acts of vengeance on the part of married women upon an unfaithful husband are much less frequent than those committed by women who have been forsaken by a fiancé or a lover. " Supposing your husband were to deceive you," asks one of the charactérs in a novel of a wife, "what would you do ? "— " I love him so ardently," answers the heroine, " I believe I should kill him and myself afterwards ; for to die after wreaking such a vengeance would be preferable to living a true wife with a faithless husband." Many wives hold suchlike language, but very few carry their threats into execution. Some in the first crisis weep and lament loudly and go almost mad with grief ; others, less violent but more deeply smitten, silently languish away in melancholy and disappointment ; others again, more high-spirited or because they have no children, claim a separation or a divorce. But the majority dread any public scandal ; more exasperated against their rival than against their husband, whom they still love, they await his return, seeking consolation meantime in the love of their children and in religion.

A married woman is more ready to forgive her husband's unfaithfulness than a husband is to forgive his wife's. For the latter, in spite of the pain it gives her, realizes that the offence in his case does not involve the same consequences as in hers. Moreover, she is anxious to spare the father of her children and avoid scandal.

It is chiefly against her husband's mistress that a married woman's anger is directed. Médée herself in Racine's tragedy,—and a strong substratum of love underlies her fury,—has no thought at the first but of punishing Créuse her rival. Jason she would fain spare ; she says to Nérine:

> " Jason m'a trop coûté pour vouloir le détruire,
> Mon courroux lui fait grâce . . .
> Qu'il vive et, s'il se peut, que l'ingrat me demeure,
> Si non, ce m'est assez que sa Créuse meure."[1]

---

[1] " Jason has cost me too dear for me to wish to destroy him ; my anger spares him. . . . Let him live, and if he can, let the thankless wight be thankless still ; if not, 'tis enough for me that Creusa dies."

As a rule a wife's anger is concentrated on the rival who is eager to supplant her in her husband's affection, and this anger, so ready to turn to downright fury, kindles the desire of vengeance. Then the married woman, no less than the girl who has been seduced and forsaken, will be ready to throw vitriol in her rival's face, to disfigure her for life. Then will she endeavour to catch her husband and his mistress *in flagrante delicto*, so as to make a marriage between them impossible, in the event of her own divorce ; for by the terms of Article 298 of the Civil Code, "In the event of divorce allowed in Law by reason of adultery, the guilty husband shall never be permitted to marry his accomplice." Some few years ago now, in Paris, a lady of society, desirous of annulling her marriage in order to marry her lover, who was the husband of one of her bosom friends, had initiated a petition for divorce, alleging acts of violence as having been committed upon her by her husband. On his own side the lover was ready to make every effort to break off his marriage and marry his mistress. Informed of their designs, the lover's lawful wife succeeded in surprising her husband and his mistress *in flagrante delicto*, with the object of rendering the marriage they were aiming at impossible ; she shot her rival five times with a revolver, besides stabbing her again and again in various places.

Examination before the *Juge d'instruction* brought out the fact that the lawful wife's fury was raised to white heat by this remark of her rival's, " *Your* husband! is he yours ? " This question, so strange and cynical in seeming, is explained by a well-known effect of love, which makes lovers believe themselves to belong to each other, even when by law they really belong to others. The beloved object seems to be the lover's actual property. Though Charlotte is married, Werther looks upon her as belonging to him ; "You are mine," he writes in a letter to her; "yes! mine, Lotchen, for ever. What of it if Albrecht *is* your husband ? This is but in the world's eyes, . . . you are mine, mine, yes! Lotchen, mine." The mistress of a married man in the same way claims that he, though another woman's husband, belongs to her and reproaches the lawful wife with stealing him from her, while he too holds she belongs to him, though he is not her husband in actual fact. Mary Stuart (who must often be quoted in psychological studies such as our own dealing with passion) when Darnley's wife, says, writing to her lover Bothwell, himself married to Lady Gordon, that he belongs to her and she to him, "for I may of a surety call you mine, who have won you by myself in true love;" she charges him "to keep himself for her to whom alone you do of rights appertain." Woe for her and for Bothwell if her lover, like a new Jason, should make of her but "a sweetheart of the second place," and force her to play the part of another Medea.—Love claims primary possession of the beloved object not only as against the husband but also against the father. When Agamemnon asks Achilles:

> " Et qui vous a chargé du soin de ma famille?
> Ne pourrai-je sans vous disposer de ma fille?
> Ne suis-je pas son père? Êtes-vous son époux?"[1]

the latter answers, in the name of his great love, like a hero of romance:

> ". . . Non, elle n'est plus à vous . . .
> Je défendrai mes droits. . . ."[2]

However it is between two women, each claiming to defend her rights and contending for a man's heart, that the most violent and tragic scenes occur.[3] This is why dramatists so often choose the rivalry of two women as the motive of a play. It is on her rival a married woman practises the most refined and humiliating acts her vengeance can suggest. Women of the lower classes have

---

[1] "And who charged you with the care of my family? Can I not, without your interference, dispose of my daughter's hand? Am I not her father? Are you her husband?"

[2] ". . . No! she is yours no more . . . I will defend my rights. . . ."

[3] *Homo homini lupus; mulier mulieri lupior,*—"Man is a wolf to man; but a woman is more wolfish to a woman," says the proverb; and if this is so, ealousy is the reason.

been known to apply manual chastisement to a rival, after
pulling up her frock as if she were a baby, while society
ladies have before now had a husband's mistress defiled
by their footman, while they feasted their eyes on the
spectacle of her humiliation. The rivalries of Queens,
which have provoked so many wars between nations, are
often nothing but rivalries between two jealous women.

Sometimes we find a married woman, to avenge her
husband's unfaithfulness, being unfaithful herself; "an eye
for an eye," she says, "and a tooth for a tooth; you deceived me, and I deceive you." Then in her blind anger
she will throw herself at the head of the first comer, be he
who he may, to make the author of her pain suffer in turn,
to render him ridiculous, and possibly also to bring him
back again to her side by rousing his jealousy. Corneille,
who has expressed with no less penetration than Racine
the feelings of the female heart, has faithfully represented
the thoughts of the woman who practises this form of
revenge in the following lines :

> " Je veux qu'il se repente et se repente en vain,
> Rendre haine pour haine et dédain pour dédain . . .
> Et pour le punir mieux,
> Je veux même à mon tour vous aimer à ses yeux." [1]

The wife who avenges her wrongs in this headstrong
fashion is false to her husband while loving him all the
while, yet gives herself to the first comer without any
affection for him at all.

"*Free Unions.*"—The large amount of sorrow, shame
and crime that are to be found in family life, and some
of which I have been recounting above, have inspired
certain Utopian thinkers with the idea of abolishing
marriage, in order to put an end to them once for all.
Adultery, they declare, and marital vengeance and murder
between husband and wife, would all disappear, if only

---

[1] " I would have him repent, and repent in vain, I would pay him back hate
for hate and scorn for scorn. . . . And the better to punish him, I would fain
in my turn love you before his very eyes."

union between the sexes were free. The argument is on a par with that of other theorists of the same kidney who propose, in order to put an end to theft to abolish property altogether.

If marriage has its victims, free unions have far more to show; in fact they are seldom peaceable and happy. The poets who have extolled free love in their verses have rarely known the joys of peace and quietness themselves. Ovid used to beat his mistress; Propertius longed for one who should show a gentle and peaceful disposition; the finest of Alfred de Musset's love songs are cries of despair.

To abolish marriage would not be enough to make lovers happy, for in "free unions" more quarrelling and violence take place than in lawful wedlock. It would seem at first blush that, in free unions, each of the lovers possesses a primary and inherent right to claim his or her liberty, so soon as ever life in common has become unbearable, that this rupture may be made by common consent, that a mistress's unfaithfulness, not involving the same serious consequences as a married woman's treachery, ought not to occasion the same despair, and that murder, under such circumstances is an absurdity, seeing each can recover independence without needing to resort to poison or pistol. But practice differs widely from theory. Passion does not stop to argue; and freedom in "free unions" exists more in appearance than reality. If one of the lovers wishes to recover freedom of action, the other does not; he thinks the being he loves belongs to him and will not allow her liberty to leave him. Such lovers usually have long quarrels before arriving at a final rupture; they part, come together again, and once more part. How many letters have I read like the following, which I borrow from the documents relating to a case of suicide: "It was after an argument with my lover," writes a young woman, "that I took the revolver and fired a shot at myself, which caused the wound you see near my eye; already the night before I had made up my mind to have done

with life and started out with the resolve of drowning
myself." How many ruptures of such relations are the
preface to scenes of violence and even of murder and
suicide, under circumstances resembling those recounted
by a young woman, anxious to regain her liberty, in the
following terms: "'As you will not be mine, you shall
never be other men's,' my lover declared ; with these
words he seized me by the hair and fired several shots
at me with a revolver, which however only wounded me.
I fell to the ground ; then thinking he had killed me, he
fired a shot at himself which stretched him stone dead."

It is not between married people only that love often
ends in mutual enmity and continual quarrels, without a
possibility of finding an escape in a rupture restoring
freedom to those concerned. There are galley-slaves of
free love quite as much as there are of marriage. Just
as there are married women who poison their husbands to
recover their liberty, so there are mistresses who poison
their lovers with the same object. I find the following
question and answer recorded in the records of a criminal
case as passing between the *Juge d'instruction* and a woman
accused of having poisoned her lover : "But why did you
not adopt the simpler plan of leaving him ?"—"I knew
him to be very violent," was the reply; "he had often
threatened he would kill me if I left him ; I went in terror
of his vengeance."

Similarly mistresses keep their lovers by their side by
making them believe them capable of throwing vitriol in
their eyes, if they dare to leave them ; lovers are afraid
to break off the liaison from terror of their mistress's
reprisals.

Unfaithfulness on the woman's part is more prevalent
in "free unions" than in lawful marriages. How many
coquettes keep several affairs going at once, taking a
delight in making their slaves feel their mastery by
humiliating tasks and exciting rivalries that often end
in fatal quarrels! A young man, the lover of such a
woman, who was killed in a duel with a rival, far from

lamenting his death, exclaimed in his dying moments:
"I am killed, I am going to die, but I am very happy!"—
so grievously had he suffered from his mistress's fickle
whims and the jealousy her other lovers caused him.

Domestic servants who are at the same time their
employers' mistresses not unfrequently follow the example
set them by unfaithful wives and poison their protector.
Once they have contrived to get a will made in their favour,
they are tempted to get rid of the testator, so as to marry
and enjoy their legacy with a younger man.

Forsaken lovers more frequently revenge themselves
on their mistress's unfaithfulness than do husbands in the
like situation, and the deserted mistress is likewise more
vindictive than the lawful wife. Besides, how many love
affairs end in the Police Court! how many times is the
Law called upon to bring former lovers to account for the
vilest of all offences, blackmailing.[1] How often do love-
letters preserved by discarded mistresses prove in their
hands effective instruments of extortion! Each lover has
his portfolio in the boudoirs of some of our frail beauties.

Last of all, the birth of a child, which tightens the
affection of a married pair, more often than not only
brings discord into "free" households, where the desire
is to remain childless. The lover shrinks from fatherhood,
and does not always resist the temptation to procure
abortion. If a child, that joy of the properly constituted
family, does appear in an *irregular* ménage, it is received
with indifference or even aversion on the part of the father,
who curses it for the responsibilities and expenses it
involves him in. Not only does he, to escape the burden,
very often force his mistress to submit to treatment to
procure abortion, but we even see him on occasion kill the
woman who is with child by him in order to get rid of
the offspring of her womb.

---

[1] This practice of levying blackmail has assumed appalling proportions. I
have actually tried and condemned a priest for roguery of this sort, who after
seducing a girl belonging to one of the most respected families of Vaucluse,
had subsequently extorted considerable sums of money from her relations by
threatening to make public the love letters he had received.

From this brief résumé of the acts of shame and criminality often occurring in "free unions," something else than the abolition of marriage is needed to bring about the suppression of crimes of passion.

Suicide, moreover, is much more common in "free unions" than under the conditions of legalized marriage. Far more acts of despair are found to occur among women forsaken by their lover than among married women deserted by their lawful husband.

CHAPTER IX.

CAUSES OF THE FREQUENCY OF SUICIDES AND CRIMES ARISING OUT OF PASSION.

"This passion hath won so great force and so much honour that they who should clip its wings . . . are the very folk that magnify it the most and idolize it."—PLUTARCH.

CRIMES of passion have always existed. Among all peoples and under every latitude, love, jealousy, anger, revenge, stir men's hearts; and everywhere like passions result in like crimes. In every country of the globe are to be found Clytæmnestras and Hermionés, Roxanes and Phèdres, Othellos, Romeos and Werthers. In the Ancient world as in the Modern, unfaithful wives have poisoned their husband with their lover's complicity, outraged husbands have killed their guilty wife, maids seduced and wives forsaken have wreaked vengeance on lover or faithless mate, and unhappy lovers have died of love or killed themselves in despair.

Such crimes then are no novelty; what is new is their frequency. And the disquieting thing from the point of view of public safety is the indulgence juries show towards this type of crime.

De Tocqueville expressed a hope that the progress of democracy would bring about greater regularity of morals and that disorders and crimes arising from amorous passion would go on decreasing in frequency.[1] His prognostications have not been verified. In former days magistrates had to note only a small number of crimes of this nature. For instance, in 1864 there was not a

---

[1] *Democracy in America*, 3rd Part, ch. xi.

single case of feminine vengeance in the whole Department of the Bouches-du-Rhône; at the present time within the same limits there is an average of eight to ten every year. It is the same everywhere. If energy consists, as Stendhal professed to believe, in burning out the eyes of a fickle lover, stabbing to death a woman who shows too much, or too little, resistance, France can never have counted so many men and women "of energy" as in our day. In his last published Report on the administration of Criminal Justice, the "Garde des Sceaux " (Chancellor) of France states that "crimes of violence, hatred and extravagant living have undergone a numerical increase." [1] This generation is witness to a recrudescence of hate, in love as in politics. Platform and press alike celebrate the beauty of hate; Of all hatreds," says M. Barrès, "the most intense, the most sublime, the queen of queens, is that exhaled by civil strife." [2] The spirit of enmity breathes everywhere; furious hate is the fashion of the time, even in love.

Stendhal was wont to reproach the upper classes of his day with their nervous dread of scandal, their excessive care for the proprieties and the externals of morality. He could hardly say the same to-day. The higher classes now compete, revolver in hand, with hairdressers, shoe-makers, coachmen, cooks and chamber-maids, in acts of passionate violence. It is past counting the number of Othellos and Hermiones, Orestes and Roxanes, that nowadays appear before the Assize Courts and Police Courts, in all classes of society. The society of to-day boasts of its tender sensibility, yet never before has passion been so vindictive, never has love stabbed so many breasts, broken so many heads, disfigured so many faces, blinded so many eyes. The arrows Mythology attributes to Cupid are in these days veritable poniards, keen knives, loaded revolvers, which are far from wounding hearts only metaphorically; blood flows in streams from the wounds they make, and

---

[1] *Journal officiel*, 10th May 1896.
[2] *Du sang, de la volupté et de la mort*, p. 85.

T

the spectator of these murderous dramas of love may well cry with Oreste :

"Dieux ! quels ruisseaux de sang coulent autour de moi." [1]

Nor yet at any previous period have so many suicides and double suicides for love been known. At Marseilles, in one single month and in the same *arrondissement*, I have myself noted no less than three double suicides due to amorous passion.

The chief reasons for this frequency of crimes of passion are : the excessive indulgence shown by juries towards this kind of crimes, the precocity of contemporary youth in the direction of dissipation and alcoholism, the depravation of mind due to the sophistries invented and disseminated by modern novels and plays, the increase of nervosity, and the inefficiency of the Law for the proper punishment of seduction.

Merciless to the thief, the modern jury is indulgent to the criminal of passion and, speaking generally, to all who are guilty of offences against morality,—often to the pitch of excusing such altogether.

All crimes for which love is responsible are readily forgiven now, though in former times judges were not nearly so indulgent in these cases. Tacitus recounts as a strange and shocking crime a murder committed out of jealousy by a Tribune of the People, Octavius Sagitta, and says the author of the crime in question was prosecuted by the Senate under the law dealing with murderers.[2]—Dante places in Hell the husband who killed Francesca da Rimini.—In the sixteenth century manners were rough enough, and yet De Thou tells us that, when Baleins, Governor of Lectoure, stabbed an officer who had violated his sister, the King of Navarre was horrified at Baleins' audacity and the enormity of his crime (Bk. ii.). The juryman of to-day is less horrified than was the King of Navarre at the audacity of murderers from love or

---

[1] "Ye Gods ! what torrents of blood flow round me."
[2] Tacitus, *Annals*, bk. xiii. § 44.

jealousy; in proportion as he shows himself more and more severe against theft, he grows more and more indulgent towards crimes of amorous passion. Juries in the Department of the Seine above all have an infinite compassion for forsaken women who punish their deserter by means of vitriol or the pistol. The women know it, and when they have a possible choice of exacting their vengeance in the provinces or in Paris, they always select the latter. The woman Panckouke, who might have killed her rival in the country, if she had so wished, waited till she had returned to Paris before striking the fatal blow. "Country juries," she declared, "are so stupid; Paris is the place where I will kill her." She did as she said she would, and just as she had foreseen, a Parisian jury acquitted her.

How comes it that juries are so ready to forget the suffering, wounds, even death of the victim, and constantly give verdicts of acquittal in favour of persons accused of crimes of passion? The reasons are manifold. So many novels and dramas have been written extolling the beauty of crime where Passion is the motive, descanting on the great-souled heroism of the murderer for Love, maintaining the sacredness of Prostitution and the rehabilitation of the soul by Affection, that public opinion has been led astray by these literary sophistries. A jury after all only reflects public opinion. If society at the present day is utterly anarchical and has even lost the power to defend itself, it is because politics and fiction (whether in novels or plays) have scattered sophistries broadcast on the world, and while diminishing the number of the duties incumbent on men and women, have correspondingly multiplied their rights. While revolutionary socialism claims the *right of insurrection* for the citizen, the *right of work*, the *right of credit and capital* for the working-man, the *right of enjoyment* for the poor man, our modern Romance, Poetry and Drama have invented the *right of suicide*, the *right of love* the *right of adultery*, the *right of vengeance* for forsaken lovers and outraged husbands, the *right of abuse* and the *right of board and lodging* at the public expense for poets. Every day we behold new claims made upon society. Authors and composers demand the *right of representation*, advocates the *right of unrestrained libel.* Not long ago at a sitting of the Eighth Chamber of the Correctional Tribunal of the Seine, I actually heard some milkmen claim the *right of watering*![1]

The claims urged to all these manifold rights have the effect of relaxing all social ties and abolishing all duties. The so-called *right of insurrection* does away with the duty of respecting "the powers that be." The *right of credit* dispenses with the duty of so acting as to deserve credit. The *right of suicide* cancels the duty of bearing the trials of life. The *right of capital* abolishes the duty of saving. The *right of maintenance* frees the poet from the duty of earning the price of his writings according to the ordinary law of supply and demand. The *right of love* releases from the duty of being true to the marriage vow. The *right of revenge* abolishes the duty of respecting the life of other men.

Sophistry is contagious, and readily impregnates a jury. Novels and plays have so extolled the nobility of crimes of passion and so eloquently justified revenge, that juries, quite forgetting the duty they have been summoned to fulfil, fail entirely to defend society, and pity, not the victims, but the authors of crimes of this nature. The French, less attached than the English, to their national laws, institutions and traditions, are more accessible to literary sophistries ; they worship talent to the pitch of idolatry. They forgive everything to the talent of the author in vogue at the moment, even when he puts into circulation paradoxes that are ruinous to society itself; the very same individuals who refuse their respect to the

---

[1] Anarchism completes the Rights of Man by claiming the *right of theft* and the *right of murder.*—Dostoieffsky in one of his Novels makes a member of the Secret Societies of Russia say : "Crime is not a form of madness, as Littré defines it, but a sound doctrine, almost a duty, in any case a noble act of protest."

wisest social institutions, will not venture on the smallest criticism of the fashionable Novelist of the day.

Then again, the impassioned appeals of the Defence exercise an enormous influence over half-educated persons, who know nothing of the tricks of oratory and fall ready victims to every theatrical effect and moving incident prepared beforehand to stir the Court.   Sometimes we actually see the jury, carried away by Counsels' eloquence, forget their judicial functions altogether and join the public in applauding, just as if they were at the Play.   An eloquent advocate, practised in the art of moving the heart of juries and putting their reason to sleep, can instil a doubt into their minds as to the most positive facts, call up interest and sympathy for the author of the crime, cause all the victim's sufferings to be forgotten, as well as all the claims Society has to be defended against evil-doers.[1]   He carries an acquittal by storm.   The power of rhetoric over untrained minds is such, that men accused of perfectly well-established crimes, listening to the sad tale of their unfortunate lot drawn by their Counsel, end by themselves entertaining doubts of their guilt.   A convict said to Dr Lauvergne : " Nothing in this world ever astonished me so much as my advocate's speech for the defence : I was all surprise, on returning to my cell after a sitting of the Court, to believe myself an honest man. Yes, sir, my Counsel had convinced me of the fact." Since the summing up has been done away with, which interposed an interval between the speech for the defence and the verdict and so allowed the jury to calm down and recover their common-sense, the decision is given under the influence of emotion produced by heated eloquence of a special pleader.   Juries transfer to the Palais de Justice habits formed in the theatre.   The public for its part flocks to the Assize Court with as much eagerness as to the

---

[1] It is this seduction exercised by rhetoric over the multitude that accounts for the ever-increasing number of advocates who are elected deputies.   The physician alone can rival the advocate in popularity, particularly when he pays his visits gratuitously.

theatre, bringing the same attitude of mind to bear and seeking the same gratification,—the titillation of its emotions. The Counsel for the defence and the Public Prosecutor strive to impress the jury, the former by theatrical effects, by showing the children, the parents of the accused, the latter by displaying the victim's blood-stained clothes and exhibiting various articles connected with the crime, the murderer's knife, or revolver, or what not. Criminal justice is nothing if not theatrical. This craving to dramatize everything, justice no less than politics, comes from our passionate addiction to the play-house. The theatre is often a criminal court, and con-versely, the criminal court is a theatre.

We can readily comprehend that a jury's feelings are stirred, when they have before their eyes a young girl, seduced by promises of marriage, forsaken by the lover who has made her a mother, carrying an infant in her arms, and speaking to them in the same sort of words as a poor child brought up for trial on a criminal charge used to the *Juge d'instruction* of Aix: "I feel the keenest regret for what I have done; but think of the state of mind I was in. After being seduced by my lover, who had neglected no means to bring about my fall, not only do I see myself abandoned by the man who had sworn to marry me, and who broke all his promises, but he was now on the point of destroying my last hope by marrying another girl. Nay! more, not content with dishonouring me, he is trying to overwhelm me with infamy by making out my child is not his. . . . I am not the first this wretch has ruined. I have learned since that he deceived another girl Marie B——, whom he abandoned after making her a mother as he did me."

It is both humane and just to consider every point that may mitigate the guilt of an unhappy woman who has suffered bitterly. When Dante met Francesca da Rimini in Hell, he said to her: "Francesca, thy calamities fill me with sadness and pity; they make me weep. . . . Alas! how many gentle thoughts and soft desires have brought

you to this mournful pass!" A jury then is equally in the
right to compassionate the misfortunes of a poor girl who
has been seduced and forsaken, and who, bodily strength
and courage alike exhausted, pinched with cold and hunger,
without means to feed and clothe her child, is tempted in a
moment of despair to an act of violence upon her seducer,
who now refuses her all help and threatens to have her
arrested. At sight of this wife who will have no husband,
this child who will have no father, pity is but natural,
when the poor girl in the dock tells the jury: " I am now
bitterly sorry for having entertained the fatal idea of
avenging my wrongs on Louis R——. I pity his present
condition, but if he is unhappy, I am deserving of compassion too. He dishonoured me. I am driven from my
father's house; my parents have told me plainly they will
never see me again. When I come out of prison, I shall
be without refuge or resources, I shall have a child to feed,
and I shall be reduced to begging my bread."

But it is not merely young and inexperienced girls that
exact vengeance on the seducer who refuses to give them
back the honour he has robbed them of; women who are
mothers without being wives, widows possessed of more
knowledge of the world than virtue, claim the right to
avenge themselves on young men they have themselves
led astray. Even loose women who have had children
before entering into relations with the young lover who
subsequently abandons them, or who simply give their
favours at the first meeting in the streets or at a public ball,
use the revolver or throw vitriol over their lovers of the
moment,—and still an indulgent jury acquits them. I will
quote, by way of example, a case lately adjudicated by the
Assize Court of the Bouches-du-Rhône, which ended in a
verdict for the accused. A Corsican girl had come down
from her village to Ajaccio, to prepare for an examination.
For the first year she conducted herself wisely, but during
the second she began to frequent the public balls. When
under examination for admission to the Post-Office Service,
she was caught copying and struck off the list of candidates.

Instead of going home to her friends, she remained at Ajaccio, on the look-out for adventures. She made the acquaintance at a public ball of an employé in the Post-Office and became his mistress; later on after a series of similar liaisons, a pregnancy declared itself. Her brother and uncle arrived to hunt up the lover and called upon him to marry his mistress. But in view of the proofs given them of the girl's general looseness of behaviour, they did not press it. Soon afterwards, the Post-Office official mentioned left Ajaccio, came to Marseilles and proposed to marry. His former mistress having heard of this bought a pistol, and practised the handling of the weapon ; then she came to Marseilles and killed her lover with a brace of pistol-shots. The jury acquitted her, although it came out as the result of cross-questioning that the girl was living a life of prostitution.

Suchlike unjustifiable acquittals increase the frequency of crimes of passion. Intending throwers of vitriol, before attacking their lover, inquire into the general result of prosecutions against other women who have done the like. If the verdict was in their favour, they are heard to declare : " Well, well ! if all I have to expect is a few days of preliminary confinement, I may surely give myself the gratification of punishing my false lover." Women are no longer satisfied now with throwing vitriol at the lover who has actually deserted them ; if they have reason to believe they are going to be left in the lurch, they resort to the vitriol bottle. In one single Department, that of the Bouches-du-Rhône, I find sixteen cases of vitriol throwing coming before the Assize Courts in the year 1879. Other cases of the same description, not resulting in any serious consequences, are dealt with by the Correctional Police. Nor do women deserted by their lovers limit themselves to throwing vitriol over the latter on their refusal to marry them ; there are some who, to punish the parents who withhold their consent, act in the same atrocious way to them. Some years ago at Sisteron, a woman so deserted threw vitriol over her lover's mother.

Women who throw vitriol take very little heed of people standing near their victim, they just pitch it broadcast. They do not injure merely the man they wish to punish ; the passers-by also often get splashed with the corrosive fluid.

It is a mistake to say that vitriol throwing was brought into fashion by the crime of the Widow Gras in 1896; it has long been practised in the South, especially in Provence. I had myself to deal with a case of vitriol throwing as long ago as 1870. The same year, in the same Department, another young woman, who had thus treated her lover, told the *Juge d'instruction* : "Realizing that I was not strong enough to knife him effectually, I made up my mind to throw vitriol in his face ; I had heard them say that other girls who had been abandoned had used this means of revenge." Next year, another act of the same horrid sort took place in the neighbourhood of Aix. A certain G—— had had, before his marriage, relations with a servant in his father's house ; his parents having noticed this, dismissed the girl and married their son. On his subsequently losing his wife, he renewed his liaison with his former mistress, who bore him a child, but some time afterwards he gave her up and proposed to marry again. The woman then determined on revenge, and threw a bottle of sulphuric acid right in his face. The victim lost his eyesight after enduring atrocious agony. The acid had been thrown in such quantities, that his clothes were partly burned off him and the stones forming the framework of the door disintegrated. The jury acquitted the woman.

The example of these female vitriol throwers has proved contagious ; men have taken to following it. Young men make use of this means of forcing the girl who rejects their addresses to become their mistress or wife. "If she will not do what I ask, if she will not marry me, I will burn her eyes out," is their cry. Sometimes they make use of the same threats towards the girl's parents. One young man, who was seeking the hand of a girl of his acquaintance, furious at being repulsed, told the young woman's father :

"Think well! marriage or death! Think well, there will be two funerals." He bought a gun and began by pointing it at the girl. She begged for mercy in vain; he blew out her brains with the words: "Next comes your father's turn."—Lovers who have been sent about their business revenge themselves on their mistress in the same terrible way.—Men who have tempted married women from their duty, threaten to throw vitriol in their faces, when they express a wish to return to their husband's roof. A man named Marais had enticed a young married woman from her home, but it was not long before she was sorry for her sin and sought to win her husband's forgiveness. Marais set himself against his mistress returning to her lawful husband and told her, "If you leave me, I will spoil your face,"—and he carried out his dreadful threat.

Habits of retaliation have become only too common. Girls are sometimes so terrified by the threats of vengeance addressed to them as to marry men they do not love, but who inspire them with fear. I have seen an even more extraordinary thing. A young workwoman wished to leave her lover in order to get married; but her lover declared he would kill her if she left him. Not daring to carry out her proposed marriage and not having the heart to remain with a man she no longer loved, she put an end to herself.

If juries continue to fail to support the Law and do not insist on human liberty and life being respected, people will more and more get into the habit of taking justice into their own hands, and we shall return to a state of savagery. It becomes a more and more common thing to see debtors wreak vengeance on creditors who sue them for payment,—robbers and poachers on police and keepers, —to see soldiers who have been punished use outrage and violence towards their officers whom they think over harsh, servants who have been dismissed punish their masters, and working-men their employer. A judge of the Tribunal of Aubusson was killed by a litigant, and another of the Tribunal of Apt wounded, while a *Juge d'instruction* of

the Tribunal of the Seine was not long ago shot in
the face by a woman calling herself a victim of the Law.
Anarchists blow up the houses inhabited by magistrates
on whom they wish to wreak their vengeance. Actors,
and still more frequently actresses, who have been hissed,
revenge themselves on their critics. A sculptor, J. F——,
annoyed at the report given by an expert in a commercial
dispute, sprang upon the latter, a graving tool in his hand,
and wounded him very seriously in the chest and abdomen.
At the Court of Algiers a former Préfet was condemned to
a term of imprisonment for having struck the Headmaster
of the School, after a heated interview in consequence of
his son not having passed an examination. Artists admire
the "noble attitude" of anarchists hurling bombs to avenge
themselves on the "bourgeois." Those who dare not at
present wreak their vengeance for fear of the Law, wait
for a revolution to take reprisals on society. For some
years past magistrates have been liable to receive a boot
at their head from the prisoner in the dock in revenge for
the penalties inflicted on the latter.

Revenge is the most antisocial of all passions, the one
that causes most blood to be spilt. It is for mutual revenge
that political parties proscribe each other. It is revenge
that in times of revolution sets the blood of priests, nobles,
citizens flowing. The men of the Terror used to call the
guillotine the people's vengeance. Politicians inspire hate
between different classes. Catholics persecuted the Jews
to avenge on their descendants the crime committed by
their ancestors in crucifying Jesus Christ. Protestants
persecute Catholics in revenge for the revocation of the
Edict of Nantes. Each party, as it triumphs in turn, is
for exacting reprisals on the beaten faction. Always hate,
always the spirit of revenge.

The manners and customs of Corsica show a tendency
to become acclimatized on the Continent of Europe,
because crimes of revenge are not repressed with adequate
severity. Now it ought to be recognized there is no
passion more difficult to eradicate than that of revenge,

when once it has become part of the habits of a nation and grown into their nature.[1]   The *vendetta* is kept up to this day among Corsican families; the banditti of that country are actually utilized in elections.   We saw quite lately at Aix a remarkable instance of this persistency of the *vendetta*.   A young soldier was found assassinated; the criminal was a compatriot, who had travelled to Aix on purpose to avenge a family feud dating back several generations.   His mother and sisters had accompanied him to help and encourage him in his act of vengeance, while a priest, who was a kinsman of the family, had come in person from Corsica to Aix to hire a lodging for the others.   At the trial the sister of the murdered man stated that out of her four brothers, three had been killed and the fourth was in hiding in the *maquis*.   This is the condition of things we should come to, if through excessive indulgence for crimes of passion, the right of revenge should ever become part of our moral code,—to the profit of the husband outraged by his wife's adultery, to the profit of the woman forsaken by her lover who says, "marriage or death," to the profit of the young lover pursuing the woman he loves with the threat, " Be mine, or I kill you! love or death."

In Switzerland, on the contrary, juries are extremely severe, too severe even, towards crimes arising out of amorous passion.   The only prisoner for a crime of this kind I found, in 1896, in the prison of Lausanne, was a husband who had killed his wife from jealousy.   In France he would have been acquitted; in Switzerland he was condemned to life-long confinement, and this only because the death penalty has been abolished in the Canton Vaud. Yet there were a number of extenuating circumstances telling in favour of this husband driven wild by jealousy, —his good antecedents, his penitence, the ill-behaviour of

---

[1] Lacenaire was ready to admit that all his crimes arose from the fact that he had never been able to overcome his craving for revenge.   " Yes, my dear M. R——," he said to his teacher, " I have at last overcome all my evil passions, except one,—revenge."

his wife. Between this Draconian severity and absolute acquittal, there is surely room for a judgment tempered with mercy.

Another cause of the frequency of suicides and crimes due to passion is the precocity of young people of the present day in dissipation. For instance, in 1892, there occurred 87 suicides of children under sixteen, and 475 of young people of both sexes of between sixteen and twenty-one. Now the majority of such suicides are determined by love disappointments, jealousy or dissipation. From 1835 to 1844, the average was only nineteen of suicides of minors under sixteen years of age.[1]

Never before has youth been so precocious as now in the matter of suicide and crime resulting from amorous passion. We hear girls of fifteen and sixteen exclaiming: "Ah! how weary I am of it all! how sick I am of my life! I wish I were dead." This overwhelming weariness of spirit arises nearly always from some disappointment in love. Such suicides on the part of young girls are of common occurrence among working people. The parents start in the morning for their work, leaving their little girl still asleep; on their return they find she has hanged herself or killed herself by means of charcoal fumes, and on enquiring into the reason for so fatal a despair, the existence of which had quite escaped their notice, they find it is disappointed love that has made death seem preferable to life to their child, who was playing only yesterday with her doll. The parents of a girl of fifteen find on coming home from their work that the child they had left the same morning quietly asleep in her bed is dead; questioning the neighbours, they are told how she was seen during the day making her way with a chair to the spot where she was afterwards found hanging dead, walking slowly with drooping head, deeply buried in her thoughts. The motive of her despair was a passion she had conceived for a young man who had fixed his affections elsewhere.

We even see boys of sixteen or seventeen kill themselves

---

[1] *Annales médico-psychologiques*, 1855, p. 61.

along with their mistresses, who are younger still. "A fortnight ago," says a father, "my boy (seventeen) told me he loved Maria V——, and that he was going to commit suicide with her. I paid no attention to his remark. Last Wednesday he left his home." The father of the girl makes a similar statement: "I learned," he says, "that my daughter used to go with a young man and that she declared she would commit suicide."

Quite young girls manifest the same precocity for murder arising out of amorous passion. The Courts have girls of fifteen brought before them for vitriol throwing.

Lads of fourteen, fifteen, sixteen, commit suicide from disappointed love or kill their mistresses from jealousy. This extraordinary precocity in suicide and murder arises from their equally extraordinary precocity in amorous dissipation and alcoholism. Taking mistresses as they do at an age when reason and will are as unformed and unripe as is their physical development, the violent impressions of love and jealousy are too powerful to be governed. Impotent to endure the disappointments of love, which are not of their age, they kill themselves. Impotent to master the transports of jealousy, they kill others. Little scamps of fifteen have mistresses of fourteen, and even sometimes more mistresses than one. We had to adjudicate in the Eighth Chamber of the Correctional Tribunal of the Seine on the case of a prisoner of sixteen who had two mistresses, one of fourteen, the other of fifteen. One of these childish mistresses having taken a ride on the wooden horses of a merry-go-round, he told her in a furious passion he "would cut her head off"; another time he gave a rendezvous in these words: "If you miss meeting me, I'll down you;" and the girl having failed to keep the assignation, he punished her by firing a revolver at her point blank.—Similarly, young girls still under age have on their side several lovers at once; hence quarrels arising out of jealousy, which end in suicide or murder. In the official report of the suicide of a lady's-maid, I find the girl had three lovers, a house-painter, a paviour and a

slater.   One of her lovers having refused to let her into
his room, she fired two revolver shots at herself outside his
door.   Girls who act as artist's models are as a rule very
depraved ; corrupted themselves by the loss of their
natural modesty, they do their best to corrupt their young
companions.

Children displaying such precocious passions are extremely
nervous and irritable, incapable of enduring the slightest
annoyance.   At the smallest disappointment of affection,
or the gentlest rebuke on the part of their parents for their
ill behaviour, they commit suicide.   I give several instances
taken from the official records of cases in the Courts of the
Department of the Seine.   A girl of eighteen was seen
talking to a young man in the street by her uncle, who remarked upon it to her and threatened to tell her father ;
a day or two afterwards the girl shot herself with a revolver.
Another still younger girl, of sixteen, on being scolded by
her father for the same thing, immediately left her home
and went off to drown herself.—" My daughter," declared
in another case a woman subjected to examination by the
Police Commissary, " my daughter had for some time been
much with an employé of the Telegraph.   I remonstrated
with her and begged her to break off the connection ;
within a few days from that time she went out and jumped
into the Seine."—The father of another girl of sixteen
makes a similar statement : " Discovering the fact that my
daughter was keeping up a correspondence with a young
man, I took occasion to reprimand her, as was only my
duty.   After dinner, I kissed her, as if nothing had
happened, taking no notice of her tears.   I started for
my afternoon's work, and on my return home was informed
she had thrown herself into the river."   I have noted a
large number of suicides on the part of young girls proceeding from a similar motive ; they will not give up
these precocious liaisons, and rather than submit to their
parents' rebukes, they give up life instead.   A certain proportion, still more deeply corrupted, desert their parents'
roof at fourteen, fifteen or sixteen to have fun, as they put

it, with men, and when the parents try to rescue them from a life of prostitution, or they suffer a disappointment in love, they put an end to their life by charcoal fumes or go off to drown themselves, declaring they are sick of living. A laundress of fourteen, who had formed a connection with a soldier, on being expostulated with by her parents, wrote to them in these words: "After the scene you have made, I see there remains only one thing to do, to have done with life altogether. My mind is quite made up this time; if you want to recover my body, you will find it in the Seine. Now, before dying, I only ask you one favour, not to hold X—— responsible for my death; he has nothing to do with it, it is I that have enough of life."

The precocity of young men, or rather boys, for suicide is still greater, for to habits of dissipation they add those of intemperance. The number of very young men who give way to drink is appalling. As long ago as the end of the Second Empire, V. Sardou, in his *Famille Benoiton*, drew attention to this tendency towards alcoholism in Farfan whom he shows on the stage intoxicated with absinthe. Since that date habits of alcoholism have greatly developed among young men. In a considerable proportion of official reports of suicides of young men I find included statements on the part of parents attributing their act to habits of intemperance and profligacy. "My boy, after a course of dissipation, put an end to his life by means of charcoal fumes," writes one father. Another states: "As the result of his heavy drinking, my son had grown very irritable and unable to endure a word of blame." Youths of the sort, who have fallen into habits of drunkenness and profligacy, cannot bear reproof or a disappointment in love. "I am bound to have a scene with my father, so I have made up my mind to have done with my life altogether," writes a youth of sixteen to his mistress. He was seen writing this letter with a smile on his face; a moment later he shot himself with a revolver. Schoolboys forsake their parents, after robbing them, and keep gay women, only to kill themselves later on, when they have exhausted their resources, or when their mistress leaves them for somebody else ; jealous in an instant, after some words with her or with a rival, they take a revolver and blow their brains out. I have noted the suicide of a little lad of fourteen, who killed himself because a young *danseuse* he wanted to elope with had refused to agree. At an age when they ought to be still playing marbles and prisoner's base, children kill themselves or even kill others in passionate despair. The Assize Court of the Department of the Aude tried a atrocious young scoundrel of eleven, who having failed to violate a little girl of his own age, struck her on the head and stabbed her. He confessed his crime with all the cynicism of a hero of melodrama : "Yes! it was I who killed Marie. She would not let me have my way, so I struck her on the head with a hammer. The hammer slipped through my fingers, and I drew a knife out of my pocket, and stabbed her twice in the throat." Two years ago, at Marseilles, a young man of nineteen emptied four chambers of his revolver at his grandmother, because she wished to dismiss a young maidservant he was in love with. Two youths who had murdered a young girl declared : "Though barely fifteen, we already loved women and loved them passionately,—so much so that, had we been obliged to live apart from them, we should have died of ennui and vexation." [1] On September 21, 1897, a young student committed suicide in Paris, after writing to his family to say he was killing himself, because having tasted all the pleasures of life, he could not expect any more satisfaction out of anything. Another young man put an end to himself, after enjoying the favours of a young cousin of his, with whom he was smitten. In the letter he left behind giving the reasons for his suicide, he writes that from the very day his cousin gave herself to him, he conceived a deep disgust for her and life in general. He says that, had she resisted him, she would have secured

[1] *Gazette des Tribunaux,* 30th September 1886.

his happiness, but that having once yielded to his desires, she might do the same to others, and from that moment he had taken a disgust at life.

This precocious development of the passionate impulses among young people of the present day arises from a too early familiarity with the theatre, from an immoderate reading of novels depicting Love (for the delineation of Love awakes the corresponding feeling), from the effeminate sensual education they receive. Parents allow their children to see, and read, and hear everything. A mother, whose son committed suicide at Marseilles, after killing the girl he was in love with, admitted to me she had been to blame in letting him read novels of every type and taking him to the theatre at too tender an age. The reading of fiction and theatre-going combined had, by exalting his imagination and sensibility at the expense of his reason, predisposed him to a romantic and tragic passion resembling those described and depicted in romances on the stage. To witness the representation of a Love drama is not an amusement for a child ; it cannot but over-stimulate the senses and imagination of a youth, just when the essential part of education is to fortify the reason and will, and delay the development of the passionate impulses. There is far too much hurry nowadays to treat children as if they were grown up, to initiate them much too early in the knowledge of good and evil. There is no sort of need to hasten by means of love scenes on the stage the awakening of passion in youthful hearts; Nature looks after all this. A crime of passion seen on the boards by children may even awake criminal instincts in them. Physicians of experience recommend keeping children and women apart from persons affected by nervous disorders, for these are contagious. Similar precautions should be taken to spare them the sight of persons under the empire of inordinate passion, that they may not be affected prejudicially by their example. Youthful brains should not be excited by the representation of high-strung sentiments, for fear they retain an impress capable of leading to the repetition on their own part of the same excesses. The sight of a person eating or drinking wakes the desire to eat and drink. The spectacle of a person intoxicated with love awakes the desire of experiencing a like passion. The high-strung sentimentality of plays and novels is communicated to the young reader and still more to the precocious theatre-goer.

It is not true to say children may read everything without risk, as Goethe maintains. " Even in the case of a mere child," he says, "there is no need to be too anxious about the influence a book or a play may exercise over him." [1] On the contrary, I am of opinion myself that parents cannot be too anxious as to the influence books have over their children. Men of mature age can defend themselves, though not always even then, against literary sophistries and impure pictures ; but young people, boys and girls, cannot. Vicious doctrines vitiate their mind, foul pictures befoul their imagination, depraved books deprave their character. Criminals often confess to having been ruined by unhealthy literature. One Aubin, who was condemned to death and executed at Douai in 1877, said when giving an account of his past life after his condemnation, that his precocious depravity had been due to reading bad books. " In spite of my parents' wishes, who confiscated and burned I do not know how many immoral and irreligious books of mine, I was for ever feeding on such literature, and experienced an irresistible craving to follow in the footsteps of these heroes of romance, whom I then looked upon as the leaders of elegance and high tone."

The young people of the present day are poisoned by the air they breathe ; newspapers, novels, operettas, popular songs of the café-concerts, everything they see, and read, and hear, presents to their eyes, ears and imagination images of too free a kind, all tending to stir precocious passion. I have before me the catalogue of a People's Library, in which are included, by way of forming our children's character, the *Pucelle* of Voltaire, *Les Amoureuses de Paris*, *La Nonne amoureuse*, *Les Viveurs de Paris*, *Filles*

[1] *Conversations of Goethe and Eckermann*, p. 268.

Lorettes et Courtisanes, L'Amoureux de la Reine, Les Drames galants, Une Femme de feu, Une Affolée d'amour, and a hundred other books of the same sort. I have seen girls of fourteen and fifteen come for these books to the library in question, which was founded by the most influential politician of the district, without the Inspector-General of Libraries finding a word to say against the choice of books forming the collection. Surely it would not be inopportune to remind this official that it is not in the school of obscene literature the youth entrusted to his care will learn the virtues it so much needs, that bad morals make bad citizens and bad soldiers, and that when the Roman armies were beaten by the Barbarians, obscene books were found in the possession of the vanquished soldiery.[1] A noble poet, H. de Bornier, who rightly believes that one of the greatest dangers a country can run is found in immoral reading, has written a play called *Le Fils de l'Arétin,* to combat this peril. In it Bayard, well aware of the havoc wrought by profligacy and obscene books among soldiers, says :

> "Maudites soient du ciel les œuvres de débauche ! . . .
> Moi soldat, je le sais, je sais que tel ouvrage
> En abaissant l'esprit, abaisse le courage ! "[2]

I have read somewhere that Prince Bismarck thought the same, and did all he could to keep the Prussian army from the danger of immoral reading.

If Society has a large share of responsibility for the deterioration of the young people of the day and the consequent frequency of suicide and crime arising out of amorous passion, parents are no less responsible in many cases, through their culpable weakness, for this precocity in profligacy and criminality. By accustoming their children to yield to every caprice, parents, and above all mothers, little know how utterly incapable their weak indulgence is making their children of resisting the

---

[1] Plutarch, *Life of Marcus Crassus.*

[2] " Cursed of Heaven be the works of profligacy ! . . . . As a soldier, I know that such stuff by degrading the mind, degrades the courage too ! "

temptations of passion. "An effeminate education," Plato says, "undoubtedly makes children peevish, ill-tempered and always ready to get angry for the most trivial reasons.[1] In the Vladimiroff trial, as in others, it was proved that the extreme nervous excitability of the authors of crimes of passion was due in part to the bad education they had received from weak and foolish mothers. Such maternal weakness arises not merely from excess of affection, but from defective intelligence and a perverse spirit of opposition against the father's authority and a regular piece of selfish calculation, so as to win over the children's love by a course of indulgence. Maternal weakness, producing as it does spoiled children, peevish, selfish creatures, unfit to bear the slightest cross and greedy only for pleasure, is rearing beings directly predisposed to such forms of suicide and crime as result from passionate impulse. Young people are never taught to endure ennui, disappointment or pain ; they must be for ever having amusement and enjoying themselves. But, to live one's life out, a man must know how to bear weariness and grief and pain.

> "Savoir souffrir la vie et voir venir la mort
> C'est le devoir du sage et tel sera mon sort."[2]

Young people often resort to suicide and crime of the type that forms the subject of the present work, *i.e.* suicide and crime arising out of amorous passion, from the most trivial motives, being incapable of tolerating the smallest resistance to their wishes. The Assize Court of Algiers tried a young man of nineteen, who being engaged to a girl of seventeen, killed her because she would not let him kiss her and generally showed too much self-restraint where he was concerned. I have heard women on trial for various crimes curse their mother's weak indulgence which had ruined them by gratifying all their caprices, and recognize the fact, when it was too late, that they would

---

[1] Plato, *Laws*, bk. vii.

[2] " To know how to endure life and see death's approach, this is the duty of the wise man, and such shall be my lot." Gresset, *Edward III.*

still have been good and happy women, if only they had listened to their father's good advice, which had formerly seemed too harsh to them on account of the contrast it presented to their mother's indulgence.

Further, I attribute the frequency of crimes and suicides of passion to the development of nevrosity. Diseases of the will and the nervous system are more frequent than of old. We have grown more sensitive, more impressionable. The reasoning powers are lowered, the will weakened, while sensibility has grown more acute. A host of different causes have determined the advances made by nevrosity. Modern life is more agitated than in former days, especially in our large towns, while the country is more and more deserted, where life is calmer, and the open air gives rest and refreshment to the mind. The excitement incident to life in large towns is further increased by the preoccupation of the struggle for existence, becoming every day more severe. In a study I published in the *Revue des Deux Mondes* of May 1, 1898, on suicides due to extreme poverty in Paris, I showed by means of the documents in the Public Prosecutor's Office of the Department of the Seine that a certain section of the Parisian population lives in constant dread of not being able to find work and so pay its rent. This anxiety shatters the nervous system. Poor women, too weak to endure the privations and hardships of life, are exposed to nervous disorders through excess of suffering. Excessive indulgence in pleasure, worldly preoccupations, long evenings in theatres and drawing-rooms, where the air remains unchanged, a luxurious, agitated yet idle life makes women of the world intensely nervous. On the other hand men equally find concentrated in the great towns every cause of fatigue and nevrosity,—keenness of competition, eagerness of professional rivalry, anxieties of business, and along with all this overtaxing of the moral and intellectual powers, everything conducive to physical over-excitement.

Again, work is not always carried on under conditions satisfactory for the nervous system. Sewing machines, electricity as applied to industry, the vibration of various machines, produce nervous disorders. Young women who work in badly ventilated workrooms, with insufficient food, soon become anæmic and nervous. The female staff in telegraph offices and telephone exchanges is specially liable to nervous troubles.

Reading for examinations and the overwork it involves leads to many cases of nerve weakness or neurasthenia. Failure often produces profound discouragement, fits of despair and even madness and suicide. I have myself seen some cases of this.

The alarming progress made by alcoholism in the last twenty years is well known ; and we know that the children of alcoholic parents are often nervous, irritable and badly balanced.

In the higher classes of society, the abuse of pleasures and of erotic music, the strain after over-wrought emotions, the craving for refinements of luxury and the table, weaken the will and unduly develop sensibility and sensuality at the expense of reason. In very many contemporary novels the heroines are neuropathic, just like the society ladies who have served the authors as models.

The great wars of the empire, in which so many of the strongest and most vigorous men of the nation died on the field of battle, yet further contributed to the enfeeblement of the public health and the nervous exhaustion of subsequent generations.

The mighty political and social commotions France has gone through during the last hundred years, Revolutions, the War of 1870, 1871, the Siege of Paris, the Commune, the progress of Revolutionary Socialism, losses of fortune and employment following on changes of Government, have shattered the nervous system of a large number of men and women who lived for years in the midst of terror and fierce emotions.

Such then are the chief causes that have made nervous disorders more common than formerly. But nervous patients are naturally predisposed to the commission of suicides and crimes of passion, because nevrosity renders passion irritable, morbid, uncontrollable, weakening at the same the will which alone could hold it in check.

Diseases of the will have increased in direct proportion as nevrosity has advanced. We note in many women a brilliant imagination, a bright and agreeable wit, but along with all this, a poor, weak will and a lack of vigour to strive and react against temptations in adverse circumstances. Want of will power becomes more and more frequent among men, even men of talent; a "strong man" is a more and more rare phenomenon. Such weakness shows itself everywhere in the management of the family, no less than in that of the Government. No one now understands the art of commanding, — or of obeying. General Jarras, Chief of the Staff in the Army of Metz, has left it on record that it was weakness of will, even more than want of intelligence, that made the Commander-in-Chief an incapable officer. He writes, " He possessed in no sense the energy necessary for command ; he did not know how to say 'I will !' and to be obeyed. To give a plain and precise order was an impossibility for him." Enfeeblement of character was an equally marked trait of Roman society at the period of the Decadence of the Empire. Such relaxation of will power is mainly due to two things, sensualism and scepticism ; to be strong, the will requires to be based on a sense of duty. It is the same spirit of scepticism and sensualism that makes passion morbid, irritable, liable at a moment's notice to be carried away into suicide or crime.

The insufficient provisions of our Law for the protection of girls against seduction is another determining cause of acts of feminine revenge. Young girls are not adequately protected in France. At thirteen, she is presumed to have given a free consent !—at thirteen ! The Law takes no sufficient account of the consequences of seduction. Merciless towards the victim, public opinion is very indulgent towards the seducer. In every literature manuals of seduction exist for the use of profligates.

If these villains were compelled to repair the wrongs they do towards the girls they seduce and the child they are,—or rather ought to be,—responsible for, they would be less eager to make "conquests," which might in time become burdensome. Prudence would impose some self-control on them, which Conscience is by itself powerless to dictate. Then, if there were fewer poor girls seduced, there would be fewer throwers of vitriol, fewer desperate women charged with abortion and infanticide.

True, the Law awards damages to the girl who has been seduced and become a mother, in reliance on a fictitious promise of marriage, but the reparation is inadequate. We must go further; what is wanted is a modification of the Law forbidding inquiry into the question of paternity. This reform is demanded by MM. Lecointa, Bérenger, Beaune, Poiton, Beudant, Rodière, Laurent, that is to say by magistrates and lawyers possessed of the practical spirit; it is no mere Utopia. —Again, why not modify the law requiring the recognition of a natural child to be made by an authentic act? Why regard as null and inadmissible the letters in which the natural father, writing to the girl he has seduced, acknowledges his paternity? Our code is old-fashioned, it wants reforming. While other nations are better at making reforms than revolutions, we French are best at the latter; we find it easier to overthrow a government than to modify a law. Our lawyers hate all innovations. No doubt the problem to be solved is a delicate one. I cannot here enter into the merits of the case; I must be content to point out the necessity for a reform which has already been accomplished by the legislators of other countries. In a body of law where every offence causing prejudice to another person involves a responsibility, whether penal or civil, it is not right that the seducer alone should be irresponsible, and suffered with impunity to turn out mother and child on the streets without succour or assistance. The man who makes the child should rear it. It is incomprehensible that the Law should punish

with death the crime of infanticide committed by a
mother driven to sin by shame, want and despair, and
at the same time acquit of all civil responsibility whatever
the moral infanticide the profligate father is guilty of by
forsaking his child. In a society where animals are protected, and very rightly, it is surely inconceivable that
the victims of seduction and their illegitimate children
should not enjoy the like privilege.

CHAPTER X.

SUICIDE DETERMINED BY PASSION, AND THE CONTAGION OF LITERATURE AS AFFECTING IT.

"Les premiers poètes, les premiers auteurs rendaient sages les hommes fous ; les auteurs modernes cherchent à rendre fous les hommes sages."[1]—JOUBERT.

MME. DE STAËL, writing down her reflections on suicide in the year 1812, declared that suicides were rare in France, and that in any case they could not be attributed either to melancholy of disposition or exaltation of ideas. The French character has changed greatly since that date; it has become melancholy :

> "Gaieté, génie heureux, qui fut jadis le nôtre,
> Rire dont on riait d'un bout du monde à l'autre,
> Esprit de nos aïeux, qui te réjouissais
> Dans l'éternel bon sens, lequel est né français,
> Fleurs de notre pays, qu'êtes-vous devenues ? "[2]

A host of reasons, social, political, religious, economic, physiological and literary, have transformed the National character. Suicide has become very common at all ages. The number increases in an alarming ratio :

From 1827 to 1830, there were on the average 1739 suicides a year, that is to say five suicides for every 100,000 inhabitants of the country.

From 1876 to 1880, the average number was 6259 yearly, seventeen suicides for every 100,000.

---

[1] "The poets and authors of an earlier day made fools into wise men ; our modern authors do all they can to turn wise men into fools."

[2] "Bright spirit of happy gaiety, that once was ours, laughing at all things laughable from one end of the earth to the other, merry soul of our ancestors that gladdened you with unfailing good sense, the native heritage of every Frenchman, fine flowers of our land, what has become of you ? "

In 1887, there were twenty-one suicides for every 100,000 of the population.

In 1895, the total rose to 9253, including 7288 men and 1966 women.

Suicide has become the disease of the century.

Not only are suicides much more frequent than among the peoples of Antiquity, but the motives determining them have changed. With the Ancients suicide was resorted to chiefly from political and patriotic motives, or on the termination of a war to avoid falling into the hands of the conquerors.[1] Suicides from love were not numerous.

Nowadays suicides, which have become much more frequent, are determined by habits of intemperance, disappointed ambition, loss of money, extreme poverty, jealousy, dissipation, love sorrows. Few kill themselves out of patriotism. In his book on Waterloo, M. Henri Houssaye relates how a French officer, in despair at being defeated, put an end to himself after blowing out his horse's brains; but instances of the sort are extremely rare.

Imaginative literature contributes not a little to increase the number of suicides, and we hear of *literary* suicides carried out in imitation of characters in fiction and plays.

In chapter x. of my book on *Le Crime et la Peine*, I have already treated in a general way of the influence of imitation on morality and criminality. I have shown that the tendency to imitation is an instrument of moral education on the one hand or of corruption on the other, according to the examples given. I propose here to point out the influence of the examples provided by novels and plays, which utilize suicide as a mainspring of their action.

I have repeatedly noticed that members of the same family have put an end to themselves in the same house,

---

[1] In this way the Teuton women, after praying Marius to send them to Rome "as a gift to the Vestal Virgins, declaring they would renounce all intercourse with men," but having failed to obtain the favour, hanged themselves the following night. If their husbands, writes Valerius Maximus, had had the same courage as their wives, Marius would never have won the day.

on the same spot, by the same means, with the same weapon and sometimes actually on the same day of the year and at the same hour. Often in the written statements they leave behind them, they themselves declare their suicide is an imitation of that of their father, mother, or some other relative. I read, for instance, in a letter left behind by a suicide, whose mother and an uncle had both put an end to themselves: " I do as my mother did." We see husbands announcing that they will kill themselves under the same circumstances as those surrounding their wife's suicide.

This fatal repetition of the same terrible acts can only be accounted for by the extraordinary power of the tendency to imitation, by the suggestions arising from the example and words of the previous suicide and the spot where the deed was carried out. All this proves there is such a thing as mental contagion, no less than physical and nervous contagion.

Mental contagion is also demonstrated by the inter-communication of ideas and sentiments that takes place among men in habitual intercourse with each other, by conversation between relatives and between friends; men reciprocally act and react on each other in the way of suggestion by their doings and words. It is in this contagious imitation that the explanation is to be sought of those epidemics of suicide that break out, particularly among women and soldiers in barracks, — that is to say among persons who by their sex and youth are specially impressionable.

After this, how can anyone doubt as to the influence exerted by author over reader, by literature over morals?[1] To be convinced of its reality, it is enough to remember how Writers mould their readers in their own image, how they make them participate in their own ideas,

---

[1] Still this influence is denied by some eminent critics, by Cuvillier-Fleury (*Dernières Études historiques et littèraires*, vol. i. p. 174), by M. Jules Lemaître (*Les Contemporains*, 4th Series, p. 165), by M. Faguet (*La Revue Bleue*, 25th Feb. 1893).

passions and sentiments. Voltaire made men Voltairians, Goethe Wertherians, Byron Byronics, Leopardi Leopardists, Lamartine Lamartinian Romantics, Hugo Worshippers of the great Victor, George Sand Sandists, Murger Bohemians, Baudelaire Baudelairians, Tolstoï Christian Socialists.

Philosophers have their disciples and school of imitators, —Saint Thomas Aquinas the Thomists, Luther the Lutherans, Calvin the Calvinists, Rabelais the Rabelaisians, Descartes the Cartesians, Spinoza the Spinozists, Kant the Kantists, Hegel the Hegelians, Renan the Renanists, Lacordaire the Lacordairians.

Everywhere we find imitation, in politics as in literature. In politics, some copy Brutus, some Cæsar, this man Catiline, that Robespierre, that other Danton ; even Marat has had his imitators. The historians and orators of the Republics of Athens and Rome have made republicans, even under the *ancien régime* at the end of the Eighteenth Century, and thus paved the way for the French Revolution. "Guard carefully," says Condillac addressing the republican youth of his day, "guard carefully those early feelings inspired in you by the perusal of Ancient History." Forgetful of the fact that political laws should be adapted to the character, traditions and temperament of each several people, the makers of constitutions have more often than not been mere plagiarists ; at one time it is the English Constitution they make an awkward copy of, at another they draw their inspiration from the Republics of Antiquity, at another they sit down to reproduce the institutions of Switzerland or the United States. It is this mania for imitation that has compromised in France the establishment of a form of government really adapted to the genius of her people.

National literatures again imitate one another. Our own, for instance, has been, turn and turn about, a copy of Latin literature, of Greek, of Italian, of Spanish, of English and German literature ; at the present moment it copies Russian. And these literary imitations are invariably accompanied by a corresponding imitation of tastes and manners. Whenever it has copied such and such a foreign literature, our literature has at the same time imbued the mind of its readers, and inoculated Society generally with such and such a feeling and sentiment,—the sentiment of order and discipline in connection with Roman literature, that of grace and beauty with Greek literature, wit and *finesse* with Italian, heroism with Spanish, melancholy with English and German, pity with Russian.

The books children read, and above all the books they read first, leave an ineffaceable impress on their minds. Nothing is more impressionable than a child's brain. We speak of it as being of wax, and receiving impressions as though graven on a soft surface; and these metaphors represent an actual physiological truth. First impressions are ineradicable; they become essential notions of the mind and lead to the actions of the future. The influence of early reading often lasts a lifetime and sometimes determines the direction of a man's whole career. Books of travel inspire boys with the taste for exploration; Jules Verne makes many travellers. Lives of navigators and books written by naval officers rouse in young readers a tast' for the sea; Pierre Loti makes many sailors. We see children of twelve, thirteen, fourteen, after reading a book of travels that has enchanted them, leave home and start away to visit the country that attracts their fancy. The fact has been noticed in the newspapers, and I have observed it myself in the course of my official duties, as being by no means uncommon. The central offices often forward at the request of parents to country police stations the description of children who have run away from home to see Paris, Russia, the coast of the Mediterranean, or some other country of which they have read fascinating accounts in some book.

The biographies of great Captains inspire a taste for war. The account of a fight described in the *Iliad* led Alexander the Great to throw himself into the career of arms. A man grows brave, a Roman of the Romans, as he reads Plutarch's *Lives of Famous Men*. Jean-Jacques Rousseau tells us how, when quite a child, fired by the tales of Plutarch, reading one day at table the story of Mucius Scaevola, he put his hand on a chafing-dish and kept it there, to represent the hero's noble deed. The history of Napoleon I. has led thousands to adopt a military career. The admirers of his genius, Béranger, Bathèlemy, Méry, and above all Victor Hugo, have made Napoleon popular and prepared the way for the Second Empire. The Tragedies of Æschylus fired the Greeks with patriotism and hatred of their Persian foes. "Every man," says Aristophanes, "who had ever read the *Seven against Thebes* burned to march forward to the fight." Tyrtæus' war-songs roused the martial spirit of another section of the same people. The *Marseillaise* breathed the very spirit of heroism into the men of the Great Revolution. Pious works are called *edifying*, because they edify, or build up, the moral man.

Every man, Bacon says, is born a debtor,—debtor to his father and mother, to his teachers, to the writers who have formed his mind. No one who has read and re-read Epictetus and Marcus Aurelius, Descartes and Maine de Biran, will ever say he owes nothing to books, or that Literature exerts no influence on morals ; he would be basely ungrateful if he did. Saint Augustine tells how a book of Cicero's, now lost, changed his heart.[1] "Are you vain," says Horace ; "then read thrice with respect such and such a little book and you are cured." . . . Do you feel some evil passion occupying your heart ; defend yourself against it by reading some good book that elevates the heart. "There are words and magic phrases, the virtue of which will soothe this frenzy and remove much of the evil." [2]

A good book does infinite good, just as a bad book may do an incalculable amount of harm. The greatest benefactors and the greatest enemies of mankind are books.

---

[1] *Confession of Saint Augustine*, bk. iii. ch. iv.
[2] Horace, *Epistles*, bk. i. Ep. i.

One little book, the Gospel, has renewed the face of the world. By its instrumentality, the poor have been suc-coured, the sick better tended, women more honoured, children more kindly treated, marriage has been purified, new virtues practised, the equality of men and the fraternity of nations proclaimed. Another book, the Koran, it is which preaches sensuality and cruelty to thousands of mankind, and is the greatest obstacle to the progress of civilization and the Mussulman peoples.

If there are books that inspire courage, patriotism and the sense of honour, there are others which predispose the soldier to cowardice, contempt of discipline and disgust with the conditions of military life.

A good pen is as powerful a weapon as a good sword. The word of a single man may avail more than a whole army. Francis I. admitted freely that the Bishop of Sion had done him more hurt than all Switzerland with its armies.[1] Louis XVIII. recognized that Chateaubriand's pamphlet against Napoleon I. had been more useful to him than a host of men.—There are pens sharper than daggers, styles more deadly than stilettos, inks that burn more fiercely than vitriol.

The influence exerted by Literature is greater in our own days than formerly, because it no longer finds the same counterpoise in social influences which were formerly more powerful than at present. The active effects of Religion have diminished, especially amongst the lower orders, the power of government is greatly weakened, and besides is not invariably on the side of traditional ideas, paternal and marital authority have less vitality from day to day. On the other hand, the influence of books, newspapers and the stage is continually growing greater.

This influence of Literature is particularly marked in the case of persons of nervous temperament, who gifted as they are with more than average sensibility, sympathize more readily with the writers. Nevrosity creates a special aptitude for mental contagion.

[1] Bayle, *Dissertation sur les libelles diffamatoires.*

X

Books then are the most powerful agents of civilization or corruption. With each of us there are certain authors (it may be one, or it may be more), who inspire our predilections and feelings. We make their thoughts our own, and model ourselves on them; our behaviour is based upon the ideas and images their books suggest, on the doctrines and examples they set before our eyes.

Books again it is that have taught us to love Nature, the woods, lakes and mountains. Peasants who live in the country do not as a rule appreciate its beauties; it is readers of Rousseau, of Chateaubriand, Lamartine, George Sand, who feel its charm the most. So great is the power of descriptive writers that they give a vogue to the particular district they delineate with loving care. Rousseau has done this with Switzerland, Clarens, the Lake of Geneva, the neighbourhood of Chambéry and the woods of Montmorency. Bernardin de Saint-Pierre has made all the world in love with the landscape of the Tropics, Chateaubriand has discovered the glories of the Virgin Forest and Savannahs of America, the beauties of Greece and Judæa. Balzac has taught us to admire Touraine, George Sand Berri and Brizeux, Chateaubriand and Renan Brittany, Flaubert and Maupassant Normandy, Mistral and Daudet Provence and Languedoc, Pierre Loti Iceland and Japan. Few of us can understand Nature without the help of the writers who have depicted her. Most people see her only through their recollections of what they have read. Watching a storm, Charlotte in Goethe's *Werther* exclaims : " Oh ! Klopstock ! "—because she remembers to have read a description of one in that poet. Tourists sailing at evening by moonlight on the Lake of Bourget, cannot refrain from crying on the name of Lamartine, and singing stanzas of his poem *Le Lac.* In a cultivated intellect literary reminiscences are associated with the events of everyday life, even under the most tragic circumstances. A desperate man (I have seen an instance), will start out to commit suicide, singing the air from Faust : " All hail ! my latest morn." In a case of murder, I found that the murderer had gone to the spot where the crime was to be committed, singing the air from *William Tell*: " To my good right I boldly trust." The better to adapt the verse to the means he proposed to employ,—his intention was to knock down his victim with a vigorous blow, he had added the word *arm* to that of *right*, and sang : " In my good right arm I boldly trust ! "

Clavière, one of the Girondists, repeated this couplet of Voltaire's, as he made his preparations for suicide :

> " Quand on a tout perdu, quand on n'a plus d'espoir,
> La vie est un opprobre et la mort un devoir." [1]

Lucan, after opening his veins at Nero's command, proceeded to recite the lines in which he had described a wounded soldier bleeding to death like himself.

Travels in the East were brought into fashion by Chateaubriand, Byron and Lamartine. Venice owes a part of its popularity to Lord Byron, George Sand and Alfred de Musset. We think of Mérimée, when we visit Corsica, of Théophile Gautier in Spain, of Victor Hugo on the banks of the Rhine.

Nor do literary reminiscences serve only to express pre-existing sentiments ; they are capable of creating new ones, of originating predilections and ideas we did not previously possess, of suggesting new lines of action. It may be questioned whether Nero, who was an artist run mad, (his dying words were " *qualis artifex pereo*,—Oh ! the loss to Art ! the loss to Art ! ") did not burn Rome down, moved by a literary reminiscence of the burning of Troy, for Tacitus tells us that according to a rumour, " but one universally believed at the very time when his capital was in flames, he had mounted the boards of his theatre and sung the destruction of Troy." The infamous Gilles de Rays, Maréchal of France, who was executed in 1440 for a long series of rapes and murders done to children, confessed that it was after reading Suetonius' account of the orgies of Tiberius and Caracalla that

---

[1] "When all is lost, and hope is gone, life is a disgrace and death a duty."

he conceived the idea of enticing children to his castle, polluting them and killing them afterwards.[1]

Lakes and seas have also their painters and poets. The Scotch poets have made men love the Highland Lakes, Byron the Lake of Geneva, Lamartine the Lake of Bourget, Victor Hugo the Ocean, Joseph Autran the Mediterranean.

Infidelity and Christianity are turn and turn about literary fashions. In the seventeenth century it was the proper thing to begin with love and end with religion. In the eighteenth, Voltaire brought hatred of revealed religion into vogue ; while Chateaubriand in the nineteenth made a drawing-room Christianity once more fashionable.

Feelings of sadness or gaiety, outbursts of passionate love or cries of despair and disappointment are often literary reminiscences. When youthful poets, believing themselves to be dying, asked a willow to be planted on their tomb, it was the recollection of an elegy by Millevoye or a poem by Lamartine that inspired the thought.

Authors themselves copy each other, even to the particular turn of phrase and the words used. For instance, in La Nouvelle Héloïse, Saint-Preux writes : " Seated at the feet of my beloved, I will pull hemp, and will wish for nothing else, to-day, to-morrow, the day after to-morrow, all my life long." Goethe borrows the sentiment, as well as its mode of expression, when he makes Werther say : "With you I wished in the old days to gather currants and shake plum-trees, to-morrow, the day after to-morrow, all my life."

Love being an instinctive, intensely personal passion, depending on the temperament and character of each individual, literary imitation would seem impossible in this case ; yet books do actually originate fashions of making love. At all periods of history we find lovers accommodating their actions to the fashion of love-making then in vogue in literature. A poet, a philosopher, or still more

---

[1] Jacob, *Curiosités de l'Histoire de France* ; Krafft-Ebing, *Psychopathie sexuelle*, p. 80.

often a novelist, creates a type of love which serves society for a model. Plato created *Platonic* love, Sappho Sapphism, Theocritus, Virgil, d'Urfé made *pastoral* love popular, the Troubadours *chivalrous* love, Petrarch and Dante *mystic* love, while Mlle. de Scudéry brought *preciosity* into vogue, Corneille invented *heroic*, Racine *passionate*, Rousseau *romantic* love, Chateaubriand, Goethe and Lamartine introduced *melancholy*, the Romantics *frenzy*, the Naturalists *realism* into love, and the Marquis de Sade *Sadism*.

In the Preface to *Mademoiselle de Maupin*, Théophile Gautier calls the man a fool who says literature influences morals; "books," he declares, "are the fruit of morals, good or bad—precisely as peas come in spring, without anybody's thinking of saying the peas make the spring come ; Boucher's little shepherdesses were painted and bare-bosomed, because the little *Marquises* of his day were the same." Doubtless pictures are painted from models, but in turn they become models themselves. Literature, I admit, is, if not the exact image of Society, at any rate a reflection of its manners, morals and aspirations; but Society in its turn becomes the image of Literature. There is a mutual action and reaction of Society upon Literature and Literature upon Society. Society acts upon Literature by providing it with models ; Literature reacts upon Society by giving it types which in their turn are copied. There is a reciprocal exchange of ideas between writers and the public. Imaginative writers, who as a matter of fact exercise very little imagination, seek their types in the world at large, while in their turn readers seek their models in books. Young men and women in especial feel in the highest degree the influence of novels and romances. The fair readers of *Astrée* adored shepherds, planned sheep-farms, longed to buy a flock to drive a-field in the meadows. In the côterie of Mlle. de Rambouillet, love was conducted after the fashion of the characters in *Clélie* and *Cyrus*. After the *Cid*,

"Tout Paris pour Chimène eut les yeux de Rodrique ;"[1]

---

[1] "All Paris for Chimène had the eyes of Rodrique."

all the young men were in love with Chimène,—they would fain love like Rodrique, and the women like Chimène. As a reaction against the free delineations of love Brantôme, Régnier, Marot had brought into vogue, d'Urfé, Mlle. de Scudéry and Corneille purified love and made it chivalrous. Doubtless the manners of society were not so pure as the maxims of *Clélie* and the *Cid*, but their ideal was to approximate to them.

With the licentious Romances of the Eighteenth Century, Love grew frivolous. Marivaux teaches women to *marivaudize*, as Petrarch had taught them to *petrarchize*. With Florian, pastoral life came into fashion again, and once more great ladies might be seen dressing as shepherdesses, building dairies and *florianizing*, as it was called.

After the publication of the *Nouvelle Héloïse*, every woman wished to be Julie, and every man Saint-Preux. Notwithstanding all his genius which, one would think, should have saved him from imitating others, Napoleon I. borrowed from Jean-Jacques Rousseau the expression of his love, as he had in his youth borrowed his republican ideas from him. He too in his early days was an imitator of Saint-Preux. He copied Rousseau's style, borrowed his expressions and turn of phrase.

Goethe brought in the fashion of dreamy, melancholy love. This melancholy, which Goethe communicates to his contemporaries and indeed all his readers, was by his own admission an echo of the melancholy of Shakespeare's heroes.[1] The youth of Germany was at that time deeply penetrated by the charm of gloomy reading and a passionate love of English literature, "the melancholy, sombre impress of which affects the minds of all who cultivate it. . . . Hamlet and his soliloquies were spectres

---

[1] *Memoirs of Goethe*, p. 203.—Montesquieu is mistaken in attributing the "spleen" of Englishmen exclusively to the dismal and foggy climate of their country ; in other countries as foggy as England, for instance Holland and the Lyonnais, the same tendency to melancholy and suicide is not observed. It is rather to Literature, to the imitation of Hamlet and other heroes of Romance and the Stage, that English "spleen" must be attributed.—It is from English Literature also that Voltaire seems to me to have borrowed the theory of

that haunted all men's brains." Young men in Goethe's day would recite on any and every occasion the chief passages of Hamlet, which they knew by heart, and arrogated to themselves the right to be as melancholy as the Prince of Denmark, though they had neither father to avenge nor guilty mother to bear with, and had never seen a ghost in their lives. *Werther* only put into words the morbid condition affecting the youth of Germany, misled by a silly imitation of Hamlet, himself a morbid character, almost a madman, haunted with the idea of suicide; the mine was ready, it was Goethe's Story that fired the spark and brought about the explosion.

It is well known that in *Werther* Goethe has described an episode of his own youth and that the tragic end of the hero of the romance was borrowed from an incident of which he was a witness. One of his friends, Jerusalem, deeply smitten with love for a married woman, killed himself in despair. The friend in question was a victim of his reading; on his table was found a copy of a tragedy of Lessing's, *Emilia Galotte*, a circumstance Goethe did not fail to reproduce in the history of *Werther*. According to Kestner, Jerusalem "used to devour great numbers of novels and admitted himself there was hardly a romance he was not acquainted with." His suicide deeply impressed Goethe. M. E. Rod refuses to believe he ever really thought of killing himself; still he has himself put it on record in his Memoirs that he tried to commit suicide. He pondered long as to the form of death he had better choose, passing in review in succession, hanging, drowning, fire-arms, the opening of a vein; "after much reflection," he writes, "on different kinds of suicide, I found none more

suicide he has developed in his *Orphelin de la Chine*. Idame proposes to Zanti to die with him, declaring:

> Les mortels généreux disposent de leur sort. . . .
> Un affront leur suffit pour sortir de la vie,
> Et plus que le néant ils craignent l'infamie."

"High-minded mortals are masters of their fate. . . . An affront is enough to make them quit this life, and more than death they fear dishonour."

noble than that adopted by Otho, Emperor of the Romans."
Every night he would lay a very handsome poniard by his
bed-side, and before extinguishing his candle, would try to
drive it into his breast; unable to succeed in this attempt,
he ended by laughing at himself, and to complete his cure,
resolved to embody his feelings in a romance. He got
relief by turning reality into poetry. Unfortunately his
friends "supposed themselves bound to turn poetry into
reality and now and again put a bullet through their
heads." *Werther* led to a veritable epidemic of suicide,
which we may call Wertheritis. So many were the victims
of the Tale that a Protestant pastor spoke of Goethe as a
murderer. Mothers wrote to the author to reproach him
for having driven their sons to suicide.

The son of a woman of letters, Mme. von Hohenhausen,
shot himself at Bonn after reading *Werther*, several
passages of which he had underlined. His mother in
despair wrote a letter to Goethe, which all writers might
well take to heart: "Ye men whom God has gifted with
genius," she told him, "men who should of rights be the
teachers of the human race, God will require an account
of the use you have put your talents to." At Halle a
copy of *Werther* was found in the pocket of a shoemaker's
apprentice, who had committed suicide by throwing himself from a window into the street. Mlle. von Lasberg of
Weimar believing herself to be deserted by her fiancé,
threw herself into a river; she had a *Werther* on her at
the time.[1]

To realize the extraordinary influence this Romance
exercised over a great number of readers whom it led on
to suicide, we must remember the fact that the notion of
suicide is essentially infectious, that it is disseminated
with great rapidity by the sight or merely by the account of
acts of a similar kind, and that it is readily communicated
by young people to one another. Here is a recent instance
of suggestion in the direction of suicide taken from the
official records of a case preserved in the Central Police

[1] Mezières, *Goethe expliqué par ses œuvres.*

Offices of the Department of the Seine. A young man employed in a merchant's office, indignant at a scolding his master had just given him, conceives a sudden disgust for life and starts off for the Seine to drown himself. On his way thither he meets two of his friends, clerks like himself but in another office. He tells them of his determination, and paints in the blackest colours the miseries of life. His comrades listen to him at first with interest, presently with a more lively sympathy; little by little, as he goes on, they realize and approve his resolution and finally make up their minds to adopt it too. Then all three proceed to throw themselves into the river. I leave the reader to draw for himself the psychological conclusion from these facts and to understand how little man, quite rightly defined by the Idealists as a free being endowed with reason, is reasonable in practice, and how he is really robbed of his freedom by the influence of a word, a suggestion. To give one more example. A girl of seventeen decides to drown herself for some trivial reason; before starting to carry out her intention, she writes the following lines: "I am going to kill myself, because I am tired of my life; finding myself superfluous in the world, I am going to find my lost sister who drowned herself like me last year, in the month of May." Her sister had drowned herself in May 1896, so she is going to drown herself in May 1897!

When once the notion of suicide has sprung up in the brain, and has not been instantly rejected, it makes a lodgment there, grows into a fixed idea, a possession of the spirit, to struggle against which becomes more and more difficult. Here is a recent instance, again borrowed from the official report of a case of suicide, to which I find the following letter appended: "I am so weary of life, a notion has come to me to destroy myself; ever since that day I have been troubled in mind and unable to get rid of the idea; on the contrary, the further I have gone, the heavier has it grown to bear. I went to see a priest at the Jesuits' College, and he said a mass for me on several occasions. I have taken to wearing the scapulary, and my Confessor has given me much good advice, but God alone knows what is to become of me. I have lived for the last six years in chronic disgust at the life of my kind; I have sought to distract my mind in every way, and have done whatever my companions did, but my heart was not in it. Unable to continue in such a state, I now make up my mind to end it all."—To give another instance. A young man of twenty shoots himself through the heart with a revolver, after writing a letter to his parents in these terms: "My dear parents, forgive me the sad resolve I have adopted, but life has been a burden to me for a long time. I have always been subject to black thoughts that make my life unbearable. I have struggled against them till now, but at last I have lost all hope and have made up my mind to die."

If the temptation to suicide is so difficult to resist for neuropaths, whose number is so great, when it takes root in their mind without any of the prestige of poetry, it is easily comprehensible how forcibly the fancy of young people must be struck by the perusal of a novel, in which suicide is depicted in the most attractive colours, as an act of heroism, a sign of passionate and romantic love. Goethe told Eckermann towards the end of his life, that he re-read *Werther* only once and had taken good care not to look at it again, because its perusal made him feel ill at ease, and he feared a return of the mental agonies he had described in that work; he compared it to a battery of fire-bombs.[1]

Werther was translated into all languages, and fired the fancy of young people not only in Germany, but in neighbouring countries as well. When Bonaparte started for Egypt, he took with him a copy of *Werther*. The disease became epidemic. It spread to Italy, naturally

[1] M. Ed. Rod, who published not long ago in the *Revue des Deux Mondes* a remarkable study on Goethe, appears to me to have made a mistake in stating that Goethe always had an undoubted predilection for this Romance of his early days. Mme. de Staël had, on the contrary, written long before in *L'Allemagne*,—and rightly,—that Goethe attached little value to the book.

the land of gaiety rather than of melancholy. Foscolo wrote the Romance of *Jacobo Ortis*, in which subject, form and catastrophe are similar to those of *Werther*. The name *Jacobo Ortis*, under which the book was published, was that of a young man who had committed suicide at Padua. Foscolo's hero, like Werther, kills himself in consequence of disappointed passion ; he loves a married woman, and unable to be hers, plunges a dagger in his heart, firmly persuaded he has a right to destroy himself. Murders, it is true, are frequent enough in Italy, but suicides are rare, and we may well look upon the suicide of Jacobo Ortis as a literary imitation of Werther.

Italians, lovers of life and its pleasures, whom the beauty of climate and sea invite to enjoyment, are little given to melancholy ; yet they have had a great pessimistic poet in Leopardi,—

"Sombre amant de la mort, pauvre Leopardi." [1]

But it was above all in France that *Werther* spread the shadow of its melancholy. Napoleon was touched by it in his young days and dreamed of suicide. "One day, leaving the crowd of my fellow-men," he wrote on May 3rd, 1788, " I enter the house to dream alone and give myself up to all the keenness of my melancholy. Which way does it point to-day ? The way to death. In the dawn of my days, I can still hope to live long ; what frenzy leads me to desire my own annihilation ? Doubtless the question,—what to do in this world ? As I am bound to die, is it not all the same if I kill myself ? " A host of poets celebrated "divine melancholy." M. Legouvé represented it under the guise of a pensive maiden, "a cypress before her and *Werther* in her hand"; Mme. de Staël in *L'Allemagne* penned an enthusiastic panegyric of Goethe's Romance, and commended suicide in her work on the Influence of the Passion (*L'Influence des Passions*) ; [2]

---

[1] "Gloomy lover of Death, poor Leopardi."

[2] At a subsequent date she regretted this panegyric and wrote her Reflections on Suicide (*Réflexions sur le Suicide*) to counteract it. In this latter treatise

Sismondi wrote a defence of self-destruction, which others applied in practice. Suicides became so frequent that Charles Nodier wrote in 1803 : "The pistol of Werther and the headsman's axe have decimated us." He too, after he had intoxicated himself with the perusal of German Romances, wrote *Le Peintre de Salzbourg*, "a diary of the emotions of a suffering heart," and a poem entitled *Le Suicide et les Pélerins*, in which he prays "the Father of Nature" to forgive the man who seeks to find a refuge in death.

In 1818, several young men, united by the bonds of a very close intimacy, Ampère, Sautelet, Jules Bastide, Albert Stapfer, used to meet to read *Werther*, *René*, *Obermann* and *Manfred* together. When circumstances separated them, they used to exchange the impressions made on them by this melancholy reading. Ampère writes to his friend Bastide : "Alas! there are times when I feel, like Werther, that God has turned away His face from man, and given him up to misfortune, without help or stay. Man is put on earth only to bear weariness and pain." In another letter he describes the bitter, fierce despair that filled him on reading Byron : "My dear Jules, all last week the sense of a curse was upon me, round about me, within me. I owe this to Lord Byron; I have read *Manfred* through twice running in English. Never, never in all my life, has any work crushed me like this. It has made me ill." Ampère cured himself of this mental sickness by Science and Faith ; but his friend Sautelet, a favourite pupil of Cousin's, died of it at thirty. He wrote to one of his friends : "It is hardly possible to live a double life, to act and to think at the same time ; I feel, as I said I did in the summer, that man is set in the world for action, and yet I cannot abandon the other. You have

she explains how the Germans, having no political life but being trained mainly by books, derive from these circumstances a habit of analysis and sophistry, a predilection for the far-fetched, that is injurious to masculine directness of conduct. She hopes Germany, recovering her national independence, may be able to get rid of her morbid sentimentality and her *literary* suicides.

no idea of the bad thought that just now flashes through my mind; it is, that I should like to blow out my brains, to put an end to my doubts. If in a year or two life does not look clearer to me, I will end it. I will carry out this idea I have had of my *Werther de la vérité*, or *The True Werther*" (a work he was contemplating). "Perhaps this would be a piece of folly, perhaps a great action. I leave you to judge."[1]

We cannot play with suicide with impunity, any more than we can with love or madness. We may bring on madness by pretending we are mad, and we may end by killing ourselves, if we go on coquetting with the idea of suicide. This is precisely what happened to Sautelet. For eighteen months he had amused himself by saying laughingly he was going to kill himself; his friends chaffed him about it, and he joked about it himself. Then, he left off talking about it, and six months later, he destroyed himself on the night of 12th, 13th May 1830, after attending to a number of minute details of type-setting and printing for the number of the *National* that was due to appear next day, and of which he was editor and proprietor.[2] Armand Carrel states that a large number of other suicides took place at the same time as Sautelet's.

A few years later, two famous painters committed suicide, Gros in consequence of disappointments, Léopold Robert through an unhappy love affair. A sculptor, Antoine Moine, a compatriot and friend of Jules Janin, also put an end to himself. "Disillusion seized him," says Jules Janin, "and with it weariness of everything; he ceased to care for the art that was his very life, he forgot all, even the young wife, who loved him so dearly,

[1] I borrow this letter from the Preface Sainte-Beuve prefixed in 1833 to the second edition of *Obermann*. He added to it the following remark : "How many episodes like that we have just sketched, how many poems, dim, un-heard of, involved in a strange fatality, occur every moment round us in the lives of noble beings !"

[2] On May 14, 1830, the *National* was signed A. Thiers, Editor-in-Chief, "signing the journal provisionally in place of M. Sautelet, deceased."

even his son, who already shadowed forth the high hopes he realized later on, and he died as Léopold Robert had died. Surely it is a crime and a great one to give such examples to survivors. Gros gives example to Léopold Robert, Léopold Robert points the way to Antoine Moine. Cannot they understand, these impatient spirits, that all men are jointly responsible for one another?"[1] The same author, Jules Janin, gives an account of another, very curious, suicide, that of a wig-maker of Courbevoie, by name Molard, who had been thrown off his balance by reading the Preface to *Cromwell*. He committed suicide by means of charcoal fumes, after penning the following note: "Farewell, my friends in Politics and Literature. . . . Farewell, all good neighbours, . . . down with the *Vêpres Siciliennes* (Sicilian Vespers) and long live *Cromwell*!"[2]

René contributed quite as much as *Werther* itself to propagate the melancholy that leads to self-destruction. In his *Défense du Génie du Christianisme*, Chateaubriand states that he originally wrote the Story to combat "the special tendency of young men in this Century, the tendency leading straight to suicide," with the idea of inspiring repugnance "for these criminal fancies"; but contrary to his intentions, he only disseminated the disease more widely, which he had meant to stay. *Renés* swarmed everywhere. Chateaubriand was in despair at the effect his Romance had produced on young people and was sorry he had ever written it. "If *René* did not exist," he said subsequently in the *Mémoires d'outre-tombe*, "I would not write it now; if it were possible to destroy it, I would do so. A whole tribe of *Renés* in poetry and prose has sprung up. . . . There is never a lad leaving school but dreams himself to be the most unfortunate of mankind; never an urchin of sixteen who has not already exhausted life. . . . I do not know what the *Renés* who have followed me have found to say to get into closer

[1] Jules Janin, *Histoire de la Littérature dramatique*, vol. i., p. 34.
[2] *Ibid.*

touch with insanity." By way of repudiating some of his responsibility, Chateaubriand added truly enough that he was not the first who had inspired young men with the taste for morbid melancholy. "Jean-Jacques Rousseau was the first to introduce among us these dreams, at once so culpable and so disastrous. By separating from his fellow-men and giving himself up to his own thoughts, he has led a host of young men to think it a noble thing to throw oneself into the *dim abyss* of life. Subsequently the story of *Werther* further developed the same poison. The author of the *Génie du Christianisme*, feeling bound to include in the scope of his apology some pictures to strike the fancy, has made a point of denouncing this new form of vice and depicting the fatal consequences of an inordinate love of solitude."

By developing among young men a taste for dreaminess and solitude, the literature of imagination has inspired them with a disgust for action and a consequent disgust for life. Solitude, an excellent thing for the philosopher and the man of religion, is often perilous for a young man, because it allows him to concentrate his thoughts on himself. "Solitude is bad for a man who does not share it with God," Father Louis says justly to René; "it doubles the powers of the soul at the very time it robs them of all opportunity for their exercise." In places of religious retreat contemplative souls find "in God wherewith to fill the void they feel within themselves," but young men who without faith plunge into solitary meditations, "will mistake hatred of mankind for the elevation of genius, will repudiate all duty human and divine, will feed the isolation on the idlest fancies, and will sink deeper and deeper into a scornful misanthropy, the sure end of which is madness or death." [1]

Werther, René and similar books have been bad models for young people, and have inoculated them with morbid melancholy and suicidal mania. Seeing this same melancholy has inspired Goethe, Chateaubriand, Byron, Lamartine,

---

[1] Chateaubriand, *Défense du Génie du Christianisme.*

and George Sand with the finest literary productions of the Nineteenth Century, we feel almost bound to think the reasons for the sentiment must all spring from elevation of soul and nobility of heart.

But melancholy often arises from very prosaic causes, sometimes even physiological ones, especially with the young. That a grown man who has known the great griefs of life should be sad and melancholy is natural enough; we should be surprised if he were not. But in young men who like René, Raphaël, Werther, conceive a disgust for life and dream of suicide, the weariness that consumes them and which they dignify with the name of melancholy, comes only from want of work to do, from repugnance for action in general, or for some trade or profession they deem unworthy of their genius, from inordinate self-conceit, and above all from an ardent desire for love that is not yet sated. The void they complain of is nothing but the wish to press a woman in their arms; Werther who can analyze his own feelings, has no difficulty in discovering the cause of all his sadness. "Alas!" he exclaims, "this void, this terrible void I feel in my bosom! I often think . . . if you could once, only once, press her to your heart, you would be cured." The reason for the melancholy afflicting the hero of Charles Nodier's *Peintre de Salzbourg* is the same as in Werther's case; like Werther, he is in love with another man's wife and his pain comes from the impossibility of enjoying her favours.

No less does the melancholy of René proceeed from the vivacity of his amorous desires. "Having never yet loved, I was overwhelmed with a superabundance of vitality. At times I would blush unexpectedly and feel as it were torrents of red-hot lava coursing through my veins; at others I would utter involuntary cries, and night was divided between restless dreams and sleepless watchings! Something was wanting to fill the abyss of my existence; I would go down into the valley and climb the mountain, summoning with all the strength of my aspirations the object of a future flame. . . . Ah! if I could but have made another partake the transports I experienced! Oh! God, if Thou hadst but given me a woman according to my desires.   If as to our first father Thou had brought me an Eve, a part of myself. . . . Celestial Beauty! I would have fallen down and worshipped Thee! But alas! I was all alone!" It was above all else this craving of unsatisfied desire that threw him into a secret languor, a profound disgust with life, and inspired him with the determination to escape his weariness and disappointment by a self-sought death.

René is Chateaubriand himself, who was attacked in his youth by a deep-seated melancholy. The lonely life he led at the Château de Combourg, the severe education he received there, his habit of walking and dreaming in the woods, the misfortunes of his boyhood, the contemplation of the crimes of the Revolution and the overthrow of society, exile, poverty, all undoubtedly contributed to his melancholy, but these causes are not sufficient by themselves to account for it.   Chateaubriand possessed in the highest degree the sensibility and imagination belonging to the artistic temperament, and these qualities made him eager for happiness, love and fame, and left him for ever dissatisfied with the reality, because his dreams so far surpassed it in allurement.

The chief cause of this precocious melancholy arose from the intensity of his craving for love, which sprung up in flames of fire in his ardent temperament and high-strung imagination.   "For lack of an actual object for my affections," he tells us in the *Mémoires d'outre-tombe*, "I evoked by the magic of my vague but fierce desires a phantom that never left me.   I combined a woman of my own out of all the women I had ever seen. . . . This enchantress followed me everywhere invisible to all eyes; I used to converse with her as with a real, living being. . . . Pygmalion was less fondly enamoured of his statue. . . . This delirium lasted for two whole years, during which the faculties of my nature reached the very highest point of exaltation. . . . I showed all the symptoms of a violent passion; I grew hollow-eyed and thin, and could not sleep; I was absent-minded, sad, ardent, and shy. My days passed in a strange, wild, senseless fashion, that yet was full of delicious pleasures. . . .

"The gales of Boreas only brought me sighs of voluptuous desire, the murmur of the rain invited me to slumber on a woman's breast. The words I said to this woman would have given back sensibility to a greybeard and warmed the marble of a tomb. Knowing nothing, knowing all, at once virgin and a lover, Eve in innocence, Eve after the fall, the enchantress by whom came my madness was a wild combination of mystery and passion. I raised her on an altar and fell down in adoration before her. The pride of being loved by her yet further increased my love. Did she walk, I threw myself on the ground to be trodden under her feet or to kiss their imprint. I trembled at her smile, the sound of her voice stirred my heart, I shuddered with longing if I touched what she had touched. The air breathed from her wet mouth penetrated me to the marrow of my bones and circulated in my veins in place of blood. . . . I knew not which existence was real and which not; I was a man and not a man; I became a cloud, a wind, a sound. . . . I stripped off my very nature to melt and be absorbed in the maiden of my desires.

"Of a sudden struck with my own foolishness, I would throw myself on my bed and roll about in my agony, watering my couch with bitter tears that no one saw, and that flowed In sorrow for an empty abstraction." Then Chateaubriand would rise and go wandering through the woods a prey to senseless agitation nearly allied to despair, feeling neither the chill nor the damp of the night, but plunged in gloomy reveries, until at dawn he heard the bell that rings for departed souls. At this he would ask himself for what he had been sent into the world, and if it were not better to leave it in the freshness of morning than to finish out the day's journey under the burden and heat of the day.

·"The red of desire," he goes on, "arose in my cheeks; the idea of ceasing to exist grasped my heart with a sudden joy. . . . The last glimmer of reason escaped me. . . . I had a fowling-piece the old and well-worn trigger of which often went off at half-cock. This gun I loaded with three balls and went to a spot retired from the main avenue. I cocked the weapon, put the muzzle in my mouth, and knocked the butt on the ground. I repeated my attempt several times, but the gun would not go off, and now the appearance of a game-keeper prevented my carrying out my resolution at any rate for the present. It was a fatality unwished for and mysterious, and I came to the conclusion my hour was not yet come."[1]

René's attempted and Werther's actual suicide are not, as they have often been called, philosophical suicides; they are suicides determined by passion. Werther kills himself because he loves a woman who is another man's wife; René wishes to die because he presses in his arms only the phantom of a woman.[2] Never has the madness of love inspired more burning pages than these of Goethe and Chateaubriand; in both Writers love assumes a sensuous and mystic character we find again in the authors of the Romantic School, and suicide puts on a poetical and religious guise that makes its delineation most dangerous for young people.

[1] *Mémoires d'outre-tombe*, 1st Part, bk. iii.—It is impossible not to compare this morbid state of the imagination in Chateaubriand with the nervous disorder his sister Lucile (the Amélie of *René*) suffered from. She too had a high-strung imagination and a morbid sensibility. She went mad eventually and killed herself. Sainte-Beuve, *Nouveaux Lundis*, vol. iii. p. 19. Chateaubriand states in the *Mémoires d'outre-tombe* that his sister was afflicted with the mania of persecutions; "She had besides," he writes, "the same form of mania as Rousseau, without being proud of it like him,—she thought everybody was conspiring against her."

[2] Sainte-Beuve writes: "René begins where King Solomon finishes, with satiety and disgust." (*Chateaubriand et son groupe*, vol. i. p. 354.) It seems to me, on the contrary, that René begins with the most ardent desire, and that his melancholy arises chiefly from the thirst which consumes him, and which he would fain satisfy. It is unsatisfied sexual desires that tempt him to suicide. Physicians who have written on sexual psychopathia have noted the association of the sexual cravings at the age of puberty with a voluptuous inclination to suicide. (See Krafft-Ebing, *Psychopathia sexualis*, p. 80.)

Chateaubriand so clearly felt the danger himself, that he adds in his *Mémoires d'outre-tombe* : "Any who may be troubled by these pictures and tempted to copy these extravagancies, any who may cling to my memory by reason of my empty fancies, should remember they are listening but to the voice of a dead man."

Nor is it in *René* only that Chateaubriand has described the suicide of passion ; in *Atala*, in the episode of Velleda in *Les Martyrs*, we find the same picture repeated. In his Romances, the most ardent love is always associated with the idea of death, and assumes a character at once sensuous and mystic. This mystic sensuousness of Chateaubriand recalls that of Solomon, who "spake three thousand proverbs, and his songs were a thousand and five," says the Bible,[1] and who, nevertheless, "loved many strange women, together with the daughter of Pharaoh, women of the Moabites, Ammonites, Edomites, Zidonians and Hittites ; . . . and he had seven hundred wives, princesses, and three hundred concubines." Seven hundred and three hundred make as nearly as possible Don Juan's thousand and three.

In Chateaubriand as in Rousseau and Goethe the need of loving was so strong, it was even directed to the fictitious beings he had himself created ; he loved them as if they had been real. So Rousseau was in love with Julie. While writing Goetz von Berlichingen, Goethe was smitten with Adelaide's charms ; he tells us so himself in his *Memoirs*. At the end of his *Vie de l'Abbé de Rancé* Chateaubriand relates how he spent all his life in company with Atala, Cymodocé and Velleda. Balzac in the same way, by dint of describing the "splendid" courtesans of his Novels, fell under the spell of their charms ; while from living constantly in thought in the society of the great ladies of the Seventeenth Century, Cousin had at last become their devoted lover and admirer.

In *Atala*, Chateaubriand has conceived the strange notion of depicting a Christian suicide ; a young girl kills herself to escape violating the vow of virginity her mother

---

[1] 1 Kings, ch. iv. 32; xi. 1, 3.

had sworn for her. Her language, Christian though she is, resembles Phaedra's, " feeling as it were a divine being that stayed me in my awful longings, I would fain," she says, "this divinity had been annihilated, if only clasped in thy arms, I might have fallen from abyss to abyss amid the ruins of God and the world; even now . . . must I say it? even now that Eternity is on the point of absorbing my being, at the moment when I am to appear before the inexorable Judge, when, to obey my mother, I see, and see with delight, my virginity destroy my life, alas! alas! by a horrible contradiction I bear with me the regret, the pain, that I have never been thine!"[1] The whole motive of this Romance seems to me false. A Christian maiden poisoning herself that she may not yield to love, is an impossible, a chimerical creation; if she is a true Christian, she cannot contemplate suicide, which her faith forbids her to commit; if she feels the fierce temptation Atala expresses, she yields to it.

Atala's suicide is not likely to find imitators among the fair readers of the story. There is little fear of this; Atala will tempt none to suicide. I cannot say as much of Velleda's. The idea of a proud and passionate woman, who destroys he. 'f after yielding to love rather than survive dishonour, is romantic in the highest degree, and has seduced many writers of Romance who have imitated it in fiction, and without a doubt many women too who have copied it in real life.

[1] Joubert has written on this subject: "Chateaubriand assigns to the passions he describes an innocence they do not possess, or have only possessed once. In Atala the passions are muffled in long white veils." I do not agree with Joubert; it seems to me that Atala's love is not an innocent passion, but a sensual one, in no way resembling Virginie's. Nay! more, in *Atala* as in *René*, love is complicated with incest; Atala is the daughter of Lopez, adoptive father of Chactas. The imagination and the senses of the two lovers are fired when they discover they are brother and sister. Atala "was seized on her side with confusion and delight;" Chactas after exclaiming, "Oh! my sister! oh! child of Lopez! daughter of my benefactor!" adds, "'Twas too much for our hearts, this fraternal bond that came to us and united its affection to our love." . . . "Atala no longer offered anything but a feeble resistance, and I was coming very near the moment of my happiness," when a storm sprung up very opportunely and the lovers were met by Father Aubry.

Chateaubriand had felt the influence of Rousseau and Goethe ; in his turn he exercised a considerable influence over Lamartine, Victor Hugo, Alfred de Vigny, George Sand and even Byron, whose genius had more than one point of resemblance with his own. Byron like Chateaubriand loved the woods, the sea, travel, independence, solitude, he would copy the wolf that dies without a cry, he compares himself to the desert lion, " The lion is alone, and so am I," he exclaims in *Manfred* ; like Chateaubriand, he bewails the shortness of life and the necessity of death : " To die, ah ! me, to die ! to go the way all have gone and all will go one day ! To go back to the nothingness I was before I was born to life and the pain of living ! " In the notice he published on Byron, Sir Walter Scott depicts him " sad, melancholy, smiling externally, heart-torn within, letting a shadow of gloom mingle even with his wildest fits of exultation." Alfred de Musset calls him " That great inspired prophet of melancholy." I have no wish to deny the noble side of this melancholy :

" Les cris du désespoir sont ses plus doux concerts ; "[1]

but at the same time it is impossible not to recognize that its causes are not all of them impersonal or of a very elevated nature, that his despair is made up largely of wounded pride smarting under his critic's attacks, of a spoilt child's peevishness, whining at his inability to satisfy all his caprices, of his never satiated thirst for pleasure, of the bitterness he finds in every enjoyment, of the hostility shown him by the society in which he lives and which drives him into voluntary exile, of his political disappointments, and above all of the humiliation he felt so keenly of dragging his club foot about with him. Sir Walter said, after reading *Childe Harold* : " A poem of great merit, but one that does not give one a high opinion either of the heart or the character of the writer. Vice should be a little more humble, and needs impudence almost as great as the talent possessed by the noble Lord

[1] " Cries of despair are its least harsh accords."

to seriously ask us to pity him for the weariness and disgust of life he has contracted in the society of his boon companions and his mistresses."

Sick of life and eaten up with ennui, Byron as everybody knows sought a heroic death ; he would have nothing to say to suicide, but longed for a soldier's death, as he declares in some fine verses written a few days before his end :

> " If thou regret'st thy youth, *why live*?
> The land of honourable death
> Is here :—up to the field, and give
> Away thy breath !" [1]

" So lived and died this great, but unhappy man," writes Taine ; "the malady of the Century has had no more illustrious victim. Around him like a hecatomb lie the others, wounded by the grandeur of their talents and the intemperance of their desires, some drowned in stupor and intoxication, others exhausted by pleasure and labour, these hurried headlong into madness or suicide, those crushed down in impotency or laid low by sickness."

There was no small admixture of affectation in Lord Byron's melancholy, and a good deal of literary imitation ; a great admirer of Goethe, his wish was to unite in himself the two types of Faust and Mephistopheles. He posed as a combination of Don Juan and Satan, doubting and making mock of everything in heaven and earth. If I were writing a purely literary study, it would be my business to bring out the nobler side of his poetic genius, but in a Work in which I am merely inquiring into the effects of imaginative Literature on manners and morals, I am bound to record that Byron's influence over young men was far from beneficial. Spending his life in the search for voluptuous and gloomy emotions, he has been the accredited prophet of that cult of *self*, which has found so many disciples in literature and so many imitators in society ; he has represented sceptical doubt and wilful perversity

---

[1] From lines headed "On this day I complete my Thirty-Sixth Year," and dated Missolonghi, Jan. 22, 1824.

as being signs of intellectual superiority, contempt for humanity and ordinary life as the inevitable result of experience. Young men, women, poets, all who live by the imagination, were enraptured with Byron, and young men adopted him as their model, even in costume, and poets copied him. After the publication of *Lara, Childe Harold, Manfred*, a host of writers *Byronized*, just as a number were found to *Wertherize* after Goethe's Romance first saw the light. Byron complained bitterly of this spirit of imitation; "what will ruin our glory," he wrote to Moore, "is admiration and imitation. . . . The rock of danger for the coming generation will be the number of models and the easiness of imitation." Byronism became a literary fashion, and passed into the manners of the time.

Lamartine, George Sand, Alfred de Musset, all felt Lord Byron's influence. The perusal of the *Corsair, Lara, Manfred*, made a profound impression on Lamartine, stirring his imagination to its depths. "This poetry intoxicated me," he declared, "it was a second Ossian for me." He composed a *Second Canto of Childe Harold's Pilgrimage*, and Musset addressed him in the following verses :

> "Vous avez lu *Lara, Manfred* et le *Corsaire*,
> Et vous avez écrit sans essuyer vos pleurs ;
> Le souffle de Byron vous soulevait de terre,
> L'Écho de son génie en vous avait gémie." [1]

In one of the finest of his *Méditations*, Lamartine, while admiring Byron's genius, protested against his scepticism and blasphemous expressions, but he had not yet reached that condition of religious resignation, when he too was seized with disgust of life and a craving for death under circumstances I will recount directly.—George Sand was even more impressed than Lamartine by the pessimistic poetry of Lord Byron.—Alfred de Musset fell under the

---

[1] You have read *Lara, Manfred*, and *The Corsair*, and you have written without drying your tears ; the inspiring breath of Byron lifted you from your feet, the echo of his genius had resounded in you."

same influence, for all his protests against the slur of plagiarism :

> " On m'a dit l'an passé que j'imitais Byron,
> Vous qui me connaissez, vous savez bien que non ;
> Je hais comme la mort l'état de plagiaire,
> Mon verre n'est pas grand, mais je bois dans mon verre." [1]

Quite true ! Musset does drink from his own glass ; the glass is pretty enough, but the liquor he pours into it is in very truth a Byronic vintage, at any rate in his earlier poems, flavoured with Parisian wit. Franck, Rolla are close kinsmen of Manfred.

Among the psychological causes of this suicidal type of melancholy it remains to name the abuse of analysis and reflection. " I have thought too long and too deeply," says Byron, "until my brain labouring and boiling in its own vortex became an abyss of flame and fancy." Stenio says, addressing Lélia : " Do you not personify, with your beauty and your melancholy, your world weariness and your scepticism, the excess of sorrow wrought by thought?" It is a piece of sophistry to say with Rousseau that "the man who thinks is an animal spoiled." Thought is the noblest attribute of man, the chief cause of his superiority to the brutes. It is the man who never thinks that is an animal, yes ! and an idiot or an imbecile. But, if we must think, we must act as well, and the man who is entirely absorbed in his thoughts, loses by degrees all taste for action and active life, he deems himself a superior being, because he scorns practical duties ; his misanthropy comes simply from his pride. Father Souël then was quite right when he said to René : " I see a young man obstinately devoted to chimeras, who hates the world and who has thrown off the burdens of society to give himself up to useless dreams. A man is not superior to his fellow, my dear sir, merely because he views the world under an odious light. People hate their fellow-men and life in general

---

[1] " I was told last year I imitated Byron ; you who know me, are aware this is not so ; I hate like death the sin of plagiarism—my glass is not a big one, but 'tis my own I drink from."

only for want of seeing far enough. Extend your view a little, and you will soon be convinced that all these evils you complain of are pure fancies." From the day when the melancholy dreamer experiences a real sorrow, which delivers him from his imaginary griefs, he thinks no more of suicide. "Strange circumstance," says René, "I no longer desired to die, from the moment I was really unhappy. My grief had become a preoccupation that filled all my days."

Another abuse we must mention in addition to this of reflection and reverie, is the abuse of books, which supply a false experience in anticipation of the real, and explode too soon the illusions of youth. "The large number of examples before our eyes," writes Chateaubriand, "the multitude of books that treat of man and his sentiments, make young people clever without experience. They are disabused before they have enjoyed; desires remain, but all illusions are gone. . . . They are left to live with a full heart in an empty world, and before they have made good use of anything, they are completely disillusioned."[1] A prey to this disgust with life and all it has to give, a young man seeks only solitude, and loses his energy in useless reveries.

It is impossible to say how many young men fell victims to the Romances of Goethe and Chateaubriand and the Poems of Byron.

"Ils ne mouraient pas tous, mais tous étaient frappés"

—"All did not die, but all of them were smitten"—with the malady of the Century. Some, like Molé and de Tocqueville, found healing in politics, others, like Ampère, in science, others again, like Ballanche and Senancourt, in religious faith. Study, hard work, the practice of a profession, belief, are the best specifics against melancholy. But amongst artistic souls, that live in reverie without any diversion from external everyday occupations, melancholy made worse ravages. Under the influence of

---

[1] Chateaubriand, *Le Génie du Christianisme*, 2nd Part, bk. iii. ch. ix.

Werther and *René* and Byron's poetry, the greatest poet of the Nineteenth Century, Lamartine, and the greatest novelist, George Sand, were attacked by a gloomy melancholy that drove them both to the length of attempting suicide.

" I remember," Lamartine says, " to have read and re-read *Werther* in my early days, and the impression this work produced on me has never been effaced or cooled. My mind was inoculated with the melancholy of the great passions by this book." [1] Like Goethe, he was no less moved to enthusiasm by *Ossian.* All imaginations of the time, including even Napoleon's, had been stirred by this influence, and Lamartine spoke of it thus in *Jocelyn* :

> " Ossian ! Ossian ! lorsque plus jeune encore
> Je rêvais des brouillards et des monts d'Inistore,
> Quand tes vers dans le cœur et la harpe à la main,
> Je m'enfonçais l'hiver dans des bois sans chemin." [2]

From Literature this love for Ossian was passed on to Painting, and the only subjects delineated were melancholy figures of men and women holding a harp by the banks of a torrent or sighing among the heather. It was from Ossian Lamartine borrowed that love of his for the woods and of solitude which has inspired several of his finest *Méditations* and *Harmonies.* The emptiness of the life he led in the country, the impossibility of finding nourishment for his heart and activity, the perusal of the great writers of melancholy, the ennui that consumed him, threw him into a profound sadness. He says himself : " The narrow limits within which my moral life was compressed in this aridity and isolation of my surroundings, the intensity of my thoughts for ever exploring within me the void of my existence, the throbbings of my heart consuming away without real nutriment and revolting against the cruel

---

[1] Lamartine, *Entretien*, cxxi., p. 9.

[2] "Ossian ! Ossian ! when in younger days I dreamed of the mists and mountains of Inistore, when thy verses in my heart and my harp in hand, I plunged into the trackless woods of winter."

deprivation of the air and light and love I was athirst for, ended by crippling me, wasting not my mind only but even my body, and producing languors, spasms, despondencies, disillusions, cravings after death, which I took to be sicknesses of the body, but which were only symptoms of the unhealthy condition of my soul."

Such was Lamartine's state of mind when he met Elvire in Savoy and was smitten with her charms. She was older than he, and fearing she would quickly lose his love and restrained by no religious belief, she proposed to the poet that they should die together, and the author of the *Méditations* and the *Harmonies* fell in with the wild suggestion with a weakness surprising in such an intellect. One day when walking with Elvire by the Lake of Bourget, the latter said to him: "Oh! let us die; yes! let us die. . . . Look at the pure waves, so clear and deep and silent, that prepare a bed of sand for us, where none will come to wake us and cry 'Away!' . . . Oh! let us die in this intoxication of soul and nature, which will make us feel naught in death but its voluptuousness. . . . Oh! let us die, and stifle the doubtful and gloomy future in a last sigh which will surely leave on our lips only the unmitigated savour of complete reunion." These words produced so deep an effect upon the poet that he replied: "Yes! let us die,"—and with this purpose knotted the ends of a fisherman's net eight times round the young woman's body and his own, "closely pressed together as in a winding-sheet." He then lifted her in his arms to throw her along with himself into the waters, but just as he was about to take his leap, he noticed that her overwrought feelings had made his companion lose consciousness; this sight restored him to his senses and he gave up the mad project.

This determination of Lamartine's to throw himself into the waves of the Lake of Bourget with the woman he loved would seem to be a reminiscence of the *Nouvelle Heloïse*; in that book Saint-Preux is also tempted to hurl himself into the Lake of Geneva with Mme. de Walmar, to end his life in her arms. Lamartine, like Saint-Preux, was in a false position; Elvire was, like Julie, a married woman, and was only for the time being away from her husband, who was to summon her to rejoin him in a few weeks' time. At the end of his life, which was so cruelly tried, Lamartine again had thoughts of suicide on more than one occasion, but was kept from carrying out his purpose by his religious beliefs. "I should have died long ago a thousand times over in Cato's fashion, if I were of Cato's religion, but I am not; I adore God in His all-wise purposes. . . . To die is to desert, and I cannot be a deserter." Amélie said the same to René in the novel to dissuade him from suicide: "For a man of your character, it is so easy to die! Believe your sister, it is more difficult to live!"

From these facts which I have borrowed from the lives of Lamartine, Byron, Chateaubriand and Goethe, we see clearly that literary imitation has played an important rôle in their melancholy and even in the attempts at suicide made by some of them. The two female writers who have rivalled these great authors in talent, Mme. de Staël and George Sand, likewise felt the fascination of suicide in their youth, under the influence of melancholy reading. An enthusiastic admirer of *Werther*, Mme. de Staël wrote an apology of suicide in the fourth chapter of her work on "The Influence of the Passions on Happiness" (*L'Influence des Passions sur le Bonheur*); in it she developed the doctrine that a man should not survive the loss of love. "It is only men," she writes, "capable of killing themselves that can with any shadow of prudence try this great road of happiness. . . . Passionate souls that surrender themselves to Nature's promptings must needs keep this resource in their mind's eye, that they may not be undone by calamity and even more in the midst of their efforts to avoid it." George Sand in her turn derived from her perusals of the romances and poetry of melancholy a similar disgust of life and longing for death; she wrote that man is superior to the animals because it is in his power to kill himself. "I read *René*," she says, "and was singularly moved by it. I felt myself crushed by disgust of life. . . . I caught through my imagination all the maladies of the soul described in that sad, sad poem. Then came Byron directly afterwards to deal a still ruder shock to my poor brain. . . . Shakespeare's *Hamlet* and Jaques finished me. . . . My melancholy became gloom and my gloom a fixed sorrow. From that to settled disgust of life and longing for death is but a step. . . . I fell into a very serious mental malady,— the fascination of suicide."

The thought of suicide became with George Sand a fixed idea, which obstinately possessed her mind, and as she said herself, "bordered very close at times on the confines of monomania." Water attracted her with a mysterious charm ; she would follow the banks of a stream, stopping before the deep places and telling herself with a feverish gaiety, "How easy it would be! I should only have to take a single step!" The sight of water magnetized her; "the nervous phenomenon, for I cannot define the thing more precisely, was so marked, that I could not so much as touch the parapet of a well without a strong trembling and a painful effort before I could move away in the opposite direction. After long struggling against this possession by suicidal thoughts, she at last thought herself cured, when one day she was obliged to cross a ford on horse-back ; in the very middle she was seized with the giddiness of death and roughly urged her horse towards a deep place, to drown herself there, with a nervous laugh and a cry of delirious exultation. But the horse carried her to the bank and saved her life in spite of herself; she got off with a wetting. This momentary immersion in the river freed her for good of her longings for a watery grave, though the fascination of suicide still persisted under other forms. At one time she would feel a strange emotion in handling weapons and loading pistols, at another the laudanum bottles, which she was constantly touching when preparing lotions for a sick grandmother, gave her fresh fits of dizziness. Eventually she cured herself of her mania by taking more sleep and by the reading of the Greek and Latin classics.[1] Still the cure was not definite, for after her rupture with Alfred de Musset, she was again haunted by the idea of suicide. M. Rocheblave, who has published George Sand's diary and her letters to Musset and to Sainte-Beuve, says her correspondence furnishes many and singularly convincing proofs of the existence of these suicidal tendencies. That she did not yield to the temptation is due to the fact that she grew out of the absolute scepticism into which she had fallen in her youth, after a first period of mysticism, into a belief in God and a future life. "Now that I no longer feel those bitter doubts," she writes, "under whose influence the perilous thought of annihilation comes to be one of an irresistibly voluptuous attractiveness, now that I have proved the eternal rest I spoke of just now to be illusory, in one word, now that I believe in an eternal activity beyond this life, the thought of suicide is but a momentary temptation and one easily overcome by a little reflection." [2]

A large number of George Sand's Novels bear traces of her preoccupation with ideas of suicide. Suicides are plentiful in her books,—of lovers, of husbands, of married and unmarried women, even of maidservants. Stenio kills himself, Juliette, in *Leone Leoni*, throws herself out of a window, Jacques destroys himself. The particular form of suicide George Sand assigns by preference to her heroes is death by drowning, the one she had chosen for herself. In *Lélia*, Stenio throws himself into a lake. In *Indiana*, Noun, the lady's-maid, commits suicide,[3] and Indiana herself, by dint of pondering on Noun's death, makes "an abortive trial of the voluptuous delight of suicide"; she is on the point of throwing herself into a river, but is saved by Ralph who drags her back. Later on in the book, Ralph himself has his fancy haunted by the idea of suicide;

[1] *Histoire de ma vie*, 4th Part, ch. vi.

[2] George Sand, *Histoire de ma vie*, 5th Part, ch. viii., p. 300.

[3] The scene which precedes Noun's death deeply impressed Alfred de Musset. The *Revue des deux Mondes* of Nov. 1, 1878, published a copy of verses he composed after reading the scene in question.

he begs Indiana to die with him ; he asks her if she has not a preference for some other form of suicide than drowning ; for himself, he knows no spot where suicide would be finer than in a waterfall. Indiana consents, putting her hand in Ralph's to seal the bargain ; they start on a long journey to find a place where they may drown themselves in the waters of a cascade.

Of all pictures, that of double suicide is perhaps the most dangerously seductive, firing as it does the imagination of young men and women always ready to admire and copy acts and sentiments that rise strikingly above the commonplace. *Indiana* has not only made many a wife unfaithful, but has suggested to lovers the notion of dying together. It was George Sand's Novels, and above all her *Indiana*, that suggested to Dr Bancal the mad idea of killing himself along with his mistress, Mme. X——, a married woman. An album was found upon him, into which he had copied quotations from different novels, and particularly the passage in *Indiana* where Ralph expresses the wish to die with the woman he loves. The Doctor, who attempted to kill himself after killing his mistress, was brought to trial before the Assize Court, and the report of the case has been published in the *Gazette des Tribunaux*. From the examination I have made of this report there appears to be proof positive that this double suicide, or to speak more exactly, this murder followed by attempted suicide, was copied from *Indiana*, down to the smallest details. Thus, just as Indiana grasps Ralph's hand to seal the bargain, when she agrees to the project of dying with him, so Mme. X—— presses Bancal's hand as a sign of consent and to show her willingness to die at the Doctor's hand. In George Sand's Romance the hero and heroine unite love and mysticism together ; immediately before destroying himself, Ralph gives utterance to pious sentiments. " This supreme hour," he says, addressing Indiana, " is one for religious meditation and prayer. The action we are about to commit, not being the result of any crisis of momentary aberration, but the reasoned outcome of a determination arrived at with feelings of calm and deliberate piety, we should bring to it the holy absorption of a Catholic in presence of the Sacraments of his Church." This association of love and mysticism was an imitation borrowed from German literature and German suicides. Bancal and Mme. X——, copying *Indiana*, imitated its mystical phraseology as well. Bancal wrote to his mother : " I see Eternity open before my eyes with as much calmness and delight as if I were watching one of those fair spectacles of Nature I have sometimes been privileged to enjoy." Both the Public Prosecutor and the Counsel for the accused were at one in recognizing that the main determining motive of the crime was to be found in the wildness of ideas and sentiments Bancal had derived from reading the Novels of the Romantic School. The charge set forth how Dr Bancal's head had been turned by " that distracted type of Literature in which disgust for active life, contempt of ordinary duties, negation of all simple and modest virtues, are extolled as so many evidences of a strong and peculiarly favoured organization." Bancal's advocate sought to diminish his client's responsibility by throwing some of it on Romantic Literature ; " If I am to look," he said, " for the source of these wild, eccentric notions, shall I not find it in Romanticism, in those antisocial books and dramatic representations that lead the imagination astray ? "

This wish to die together experienced by lovers when threatened with separation, a thing more cruel to them than death itself, is a sentiment deep-rooted in the human heart. We find it in Plautus.—" Oh ! might we die together ! " exclaim in one play of the Latin poet two lovers at the moment of enforced separation. Indeed the same longing to die together is sometimes expressed by melancholy lovers apart from any fear of coming separation. Even consummated love is not always gay.

> " Medio in fonte leporum,
> Surgit amari aliquid," [1]

---

[1] " In the mid fount of love's delights there rises a bitter drop."

says Lucretius (bk. iv. 8, 1127). Some men take love in melancholy wise, just as others take their wine sadly. This type of sentimental melancholy, so dear to the Novelists and Poets of the Romantic School,[1] is found long ago in Tibullus, but it has developed into a veritable disease of the imagination among the Romantics. " In the days of my youthful indiscretions," writes Chateaubriand in his *Mémoires d'Outre-tombe,* " I have many a time desired not to survive my present happiness; there was a degree of felicity in the first flush of success that made me long for annihilation."

Suicide for love was a rare phenomenon among the Ancients, and was looked upon as an act of feebleness and despair; it is so described by Sophocles, Euripides and Virgil. In the *Antigoné* of the first-named poet, Haemon kills himself on the tomb of his destined bride, without cursing either the gods or his fellow-men; his father inveighs bitterly against his weakness. In the *Æneid* Dido destroys herself under the empire of the grief and despair that overwhelm her. With *Werther,* and the Novels generally of the Romantic School, suicide becomes argumentative and philosophical; it is ennobled, extolled as a sublime act, as a sign of moral superiority; lovers claim the *right* to kill themselves, and deliberately defend suicide as justifiable. " When a man's life is disadvantageous to some, a burden to himself, useless to all," says Jacques in George Sand's story, " suicide is a perfectly lawful act." " Let us quit life together," cries Ralph to Indiana. " Let us return to God. . . . The God we adore, you and I, has never destined man to so many miseries, without giving him the instinct to escape them; and truly what makes, to my idea, the chief superiority of man over the brute is his knowledge where lies the remedy for all his woes. This remedy is suicide."

These sophistries are repeated in the Romances of Eugène Süe and Frédéric Soulié, who have always had and still have many readers. Suicide is depicted as the

---

[1] We find the same also in Leconte de Lisle and in Sully-Prudhomme.

logical outcome and termination of a love drama. Even with Novelists like Stendhal of a somewhat hard and cold type, the hero dwells complacently on the idea of suicide and is intoxicated with its fascination. " Again and again," says the author of *Rouge et Noir*, "the idea of suicide presented itself to him. The thought was full of charm, and brought a delicious sense of repose."[1] These writers seem to think love inseparable from suicide, that a hero of romance is bound to kill himself when love fails him, that Love is the sole end and obligation of life, that suicide is at once a right and the supremest gratification of amorous desire.

With *Chatterton*, this type of suicide was combined with hatred of society and literary vanity. " I possess the right to die," cries Alfred de Vigny's hero. . . . " I swear it before you and I will uphold it before God." Lamartine, who was on terms of close intimacy with de Vigny, tells us that the author of *Chatterton* regretted later on ever having written this play;[2] " he only forgave himself this glorious error after having courageously expiated his fault. Great poets are bound to choose their subject heedfully. *Werther* had led to suicides of imagination; *Chatterton* was responsible for suicides of scepticism." Not to mention the furious onslaughts in society found in the Play, how disastrous must have been the impression produced on the younger members of the audience by this invocation to death : "Oh! Death, angel of deliverance, how sweet is thy peace! I had every reason of old to adore thee, but not strength enough to win thee. . . . If only men knew! if only they knew what bliss I feel . . . they would not hesitate so long." And to duly depict the bliss of dying, Chatterton throws into his face a look of holy abstraction and divine happiness.[3]

---

[1] *Le Rouge et le Noir*, ch. xlix.—" I was saved from suicide," says Stendhal, " by political curiosity, and also no doubt by the fear of hurting myself."

[2] Lamartine, *Entretien*, xcv. p. 329.

[3] A. Barbier states that the author of *Chatterton*, who depicts in such lively colours the happiness of dying, had personally a profound terror of death, and relates how the day before his end he cried out to his friends, who had come to

Novelists and Poets have so often described the bliss of dying with the one beloved, that by dint of extolling this imaginary felicity, they have set the fashion of double suicides. " To die with the object of my love had long been the dream of my imagination," were the words of Dr Bancal, whose crime I have spoken of above. Alfred de Vigny celebrated the death of two lovers who killed themselves at Montmorency in these beautiful lines :

> " Qui passèrent deux jours d'amour et d'harmonie,
> De chants et de baisers, de voix, de lèvre unie,
> De regrets confondus, de soupirs bienheureux,
> Qui furent deux moments et deux siècles pour eux." [1]

But in doing so, he little thought his description would stir to madness the fancy of a young student half a century afterwards; yet here are the facts, admitting of no doubt as to its being so.

On January 25th, 1888, a young man of twenty-three and a woman of thirty, married and the mother of several children, got out of a carriage at the door of a villa in the suburbs of Constantine. Two hours later, two shots were heard, followed by two more and a loud scream. Some of the neighbours ran up at the noise, burst into the house and found themselves confronted with an appalling sight. Half undressed, propped against a sofa near the bed, lay the young man, with a shot wound through the cheek and throwing up torrents of blood ; he still held in his hand a five-chambered revolver, four chambers of which had been emptied. His whole body was shaken by

see him, "Do not let me die." Undoubtedly Alfred de Vigny is a poet of high and noble character. His pessimism arises not merely from personal grievances ; he felt keenly the nothingness of life, the cruelty of Nature, the physical and moral ills that crush humanity. But to these more general motives of pessimism were added also personal ones,—poverty, a woman's treachery, disappointed ambition, all of which made him suffer cruelly. If he wrote the antisocial drama of *Chatterton*, this was due to the chagrin caused him by the Revolution of 1830, which forced him to resign his post under Government.

[1] " Who passed two days of love and harmony together, of songs and kisses, voices and lips joined in one, of regrets intermingled and happy sighs ; two days !—two moments, nay ! two centuries for them."

a nervous trembling, and he kept asking for a weapon or a dose of poison to put him out of his pain, screaming and calling "Madeleine! Madeleine!"

In front of him on the bed was stretched the young woman, dead, her right temple pierced by two balls. The expression of the face was calm, as if she were asleep; the eye showed nothing of that fixed terror-struck look almost always observed in cases of death by violence.

The young man was a student of Law, intelligent and well-educated, of whom M. Paul Bourget and M. Funck-Brentano have given good reports. "I can see him now," M. Bourget said, "that young fellow, with his bright eyes and his mobile, clever face, such as he used to be when he attended my chambers two years ago. He used to bring me critical essays, fragments of novels, which showed good hope of a fine talent in the future." But incoherent, feverish, ill-regulated reading had sown disorder in his mind. After displaying in early years profound religious feeling, he fell into the most absolute scepticism. Uniting the study of the Positivist philosophers with a passionate love of Poetry, he became at one and the same time a sceptic and an enthusiast, a romanticist and a pessimist. The condition of moral negation into which he had fallen overwhelmed him with sadness and inspired him with thoughts of suicide. Believing nothing and seeking emotions only to taste and analyze them, he lost, in the midst of his dreamy reveries and physiological and psychological analyses, all healthiness of soul, rightmindedness and strength of will. Imagination and sensibility alone remained ardent and still greedy after fresh excitement.

It was while in this state of mind that he met Mme. X——, a virtuous mother of a family till then, but romantically inclined. He applied himself, like a hero of psychological romance, to set the strings of passion vibrating in her heart, and succeeded in his endeavour. Then, after beginning in a mere spirit of curiosity, he ended by getting caught himself and found his own breast fired by the love he had kindled. Next he proposed to

Mme. X—— to fly with him, but the scheme not having taken effect, they formed the plan of dying together.

When the Presiding Judge at his trial pointed out to the prisoner the odiousness of his conduct, his answer was that double suicide for love was not disgraceful, but heroic. "When passion is extreme, it becomes hallowed by its very intensity. . . . I had often told her how the *Lovers* of Alfred de Vigny were admired, who died together, how beautiful it would be to die like that and what wonder and admiration we should excite. We came at last to look upon our death as hallowed by the mere fact of our passion for one another.—'The one thing that afflicts me,' she kept saying, 'is the disgrace.'—'Why! we shall be admired for it,' was my emphatic answer." It was by suchlike sophistries drawn from Plays and Novels that the young student perverted his own sense of right and wrong and the unhappy lady's at the same time.

Ever since the *Nouvelle Heloïse*, passion is glorified, hallowed in Novels and Plays. Love is depicted as a virtue, and lovers think themselves more virtuous in proportion as they are more fondly enamoured.

Mme. de Staël declared Rousseau made a passion of virtue ; it would be truer to say she made a virtue of passion. A disciple of Jean Jacques, Mme. de Staël admires passion as if it were a virtue, and exalts love into a duty, a sublime self-sacrifice. In *Delphine* she makes the hero of the Romance say : "Your true and highest duty is to love me . . ., believe me, there is virtue inherent in love, virtue even in that absolute surrender and sacrifice of oneself to a lover you condemn so strongly. In her *Lettres sur les écrits de J. J. Rousseau*, Mme. de Staël also proclaims that love is the origin of virtue ; "when the object of worship is virtuous, a lover soon grows to be virtuous too."

In the Romances of George Sand, passion instantly ennobles the lover, even when it is a guilty love in the eyes of society. In the Preface to the famous *Dame aux Camélias*, Alexandre Dumas writes : "I do not deny the existence of these fatal, irresistible passions, that no law can combat, no reasoning overcome. Love at this height of power is almost identical with virtue."

The Student of Constantine referred to above told the Court on his trial that Mme. X—— asked him to let her die with him, when she noticed the butt of a revolver projecting from his pocket, which he had bought to kill himself with. A similar situation is found in Balzac's *La Femme de trente ans* ("A Woman of Thirty"): "You would wish to kill yourself under my roof?" asked Mme. d'Anglemont of Lord Grenville.—"Oh, no! not alone," he answered in a soft voice.—"What then! perhaps my father?"—"No! no!" he cried in a half-strangled tone. "Have no fear; my fatal resolve is gone. The instant I came in, as soon as ever I saw you, I felt brave enough to say no word, to die alone." At these words Julie rose and threw herself into Arthur's arms, who through his mistress's sobs, could distinguish two words charged with passionate emotion, "to know happiness and die," she cried, "Oh, yes! oh, yes!"[1]

In Alexandre Dumas' Play, Antony speaks in a similar vein: "I would fain have our two hearts beat in concert at the last, our last sighs mingle. Dost understand? a death as soft as sleep, a death happier than any life?" To which Adèle replies: "Yes! yes! to die with thee! an eternity within thy arms! have pity, and kill me!"

In *Christine*, Dumas makes another hero of the drama declare:

> "Que je serais heureux si j'expirais ainsi;
> Si je pouvais mourir alors que je la touche
> D'un poison lentement épuisé sur ta bouche:
> Et passer dans tes bras et les yeux sur tes yeux,
> Du sommeil à la mort et de la terre aux cieux."[2]

---

[1] Another point of resemblance. The heroine of the judicial drama and the heroine of the literary drama are the same age, thirty. In the course of the proceedings a friend of the prisoner's told the *Juge d'instruction* that the accused had been deeply impressed by reading Balzac's Novel, *La Femme de trente ans.*

[2] "How happy should I be, could I die so; if I could die draining a poison slowly drawn from thy mouth, and pass within thy arms and my eyes on thine, from sleep to death and from earth to heaven."

The Play of *Hernani* ends with a double suicide. Doña Sol poisons herself, and hands the half-emptied phial of poison to Hernani, with the words :

> " Ne te plains pas de moi, je t'ai gardé ta part . . .[1]
> Je suis bien pâle, dis, pour une fiancée ?
> Calme-toi, je suis mieux.—Vers des clartés nouvelles
> Nous allons tout à l'heure ensemble ouvrir nos ailes.
> Partons d'un vol égal vers un monde meilleur." [2]

Over-excited by the burning phrases that hallow passion and suicide, young men and women yield more frequently than they used to the fascination of death and are literally intoxicated by Novels and Plays inspiring them with a taste for Death. In former days double suicide was a rare crime in the South of France ; now it is common. I have noted no less than three double suicides at Marseilles in the course of a few weeks, and I have found the chief cause to be the terrible state of over-excitement induced by romantic reading. In one case, the young woman having survived her wounds, I was able to question her. I asked her if she were not in the habit of reading a great many Novels. She told me with a smile, as of one who sees her thoughts guessed, that her lover battened upon them. In another case, the lovers were both dead, but the young man's mother told me how her son used to read a fresh novel every day, and was constant in his attendance at the Theatre. The Opera of *Lucia di Lammermoor*, which he had witnessed three evenings running had intoxicated his imagination ; during the three months immediately preceding his suicide, his mother heard him for ever singing passages from the opera in question relating to Lucia's death and Edgar's suicide.

[1] Joseph Chénier, in one of his dramas, represents a woman whose lover has just taken poison as saying :
" Pour ton Elisabeth tu n'as rien réservé "—" For your Elizabeth you have kept none back."

[2] " Nay ! grudge me not, I have kept your share intact. . . . I am pale, very pale, am I not, for a bride ? Fear not, I am better now.—Toward new splendours we are soon, and together, to spread our wings. Let us away and fly side by side to a better world."

In former days the man who died with his fiancée, as a rule respected her virtue. At the trial of one Ferrand, a youth of eighteen, who desirous of dying with the girl he loved, killed her but failed to kill himself, it was brought out in evidence that she was a virgin. The same statement could not so often be made nowadays.

Young profligates who end in suicide are not simply and solely victims of their own evil passions, Romances and Poetry are often in part responsible for their ruin, drawing as they do a seductive picture of suicide as the finale of an orgy. Great Poets, no less indeed than Byron, de Musset and Baudelaire, have extolled this type of suicide. Byron sang the beauty of debauch, and himself lived a Don Juan life at Venice. Death which by right should awake only serious thoughts is mixed up by him with scenes of wild dissipation. He was fond of drinking from a skull and used to coquet with death as he did with love.

Following Byron's example, Alfred de Musset continued to mingle in his poems love and impiety with murder and suicide. Don Paez, after assassinating a rival, poisons himself along with his mistress and dies in her arms, and the piece ends with a declaration of absolute disbelief. In *Portia*, Dalté kills his mistress's husband, kicks the corpse out of the way and goes for a sail in a gondola with the object of his affections. Rolla, after a life of dissipation, poisons himself and dies in the middle of an orgy. Paul Bourget has described in *Le Disciple* the fascination exercised over young men by the Poetry that idealizes wild profligacy and infidelity.

Musset clearly realized the bond existing between infidelity, profligacy and suicide. He had suffered not a little from the anti-religious education he had received, and showed the ravages it might commit in the souls of young people in his *Confession d'un Enfant du Siècle*. His earliest reading had been in the licentious Romances of the Eighteenth Century, which initiated him into the mysteries of profligacy and free thinking. " I devoured them," he says, "with unspeakable bitterness and grief, with a broken heart and a smile on my lips. . . . Yes! you are right, I cried, you only have the courage to declare the only true thing is debauchery, hypocrisy, vileness. Be my friends." . . . "Who will ever dare," he says in another place, "to tell all that went on in schools and colleges? Men doubted every truth, young men went further and denied every truth. It was a sort of universal denial of all things in heaven and earth ; we may call it disenchantment, or if you will hopelessness." Musset suffered more than is generally supposed from this eclipse of hope. No doubt it was a result of his mistress's faithlessness that, unable any longer to believe in love, he conceived a disgust for life and society in general, but this was not the sole and only reason for his melancholy. Young people reading his poems see only an expression of love, its aspirations and disappointments, in them ; grown men find a more noble sorrow there, a sorrow caused by the Poet's loss of Faith. In a great number of passages the Poet notes as a deep poignant pain the loss of all belief in higher things.

"Une croix en poussière et le désert aux cieux."[1]

Not only has he cursed Voltaire in *Rolla*, he has cursed Goethe and Byron too, reproaching them bitterly with having destroyed hope in him. He cries : "Forgive me, ye mighty poets, who are now a handful of ashes and lie beneath the soil! forgive me, ye who are demigods, and I only a suffering child. But while writing all this, I cannot help myself but curse you." He cursed Byron and nevertheless imitated him ; for he confessed himself, "my greatest defect was my copying everything that struck me, not because of its beauty but because of its strangeness."[2]

M. Faguet and M. Jules Lemaître do not understand

---

[1] M. Jules Lemaître assures us Priests admire Musset ; and I have observed the fact myself. A good and excellent Priest and a man of much good sense, who had read Musset for the first time when sixty years of age, told me he had been charmed with him.

[2] *La Confession d'un Enfant du Siècle*, 2nd Part, ch. iv.

how Musset can reproach Voltaire with Rolla's suicide :
'Think what we may," says M. Faguet, "of the doctrines
of the Encyclopædists, they can justifiably enough answer
in this case that they are only responsible for the mistakes
of men of sense and not for the calamities of mere nin-
compoops."[1] Rolla a *mere nincompoop*! Musset says of
him :

> "C'était un noble cœur, naïf comme l'enfance,
> Bon comme la pitié, grand comme l'espérance . . .
> Jacque était grand, loyal, intrépide et superbe. . . ."[2]

Certainly I cannot profess to agree with much of this
panegyric. But Rolla was not a *mere nincompoop*, he was
a proud-hearted profligate, to whom Musset lent his own
powers of imagination and his own sensibility.

Musset is perfectly justified in charging infidelity with
leading to debauchery and eventually to suicide ; he has
told us himself that debauchery was the "first conclusion
from those principles of death" which he had acquired
from the hopelessness derived from "a corpse-like and
loathsome literature." He was right again when he says
in his apostrophe to Voltaire :

> "Penses-tu cependant que, si quelque croyance,
> Si le plus léger fil le retenait encor,
> Il viendrait sur ce lit prostituer la mort? . . ."[3]

All who have studied the causes of suicide, whether
physicians or magistrates, know that religious beliefs do
preserve men from this crime.[4] Rolla asks himself why
he is going to die :

---

[1] Faguet, *Études littèraires sur le XIXe siècle*, p. 269.

[2] "'Twas a noble heart, simple as childhood's self, gentle as pity, lofty as
hope. . . . Jacque was great and true-hearted, intrepid and superb. . . ."

[3] "But think you, if any faith, if the slenderest thread of belief yet held him,
he would come to this couch to prostitute death?"

[4] See the *Dictionnaire des Sciences Médicales* of Dechambre under *Suicide* ;
Nouveau dictionnaire de médecine of Jaccond, under same.—Doctors, themselves free-thinkers and materialists, recognize as an indisputable fact that
religious feeling is the best safeguard against suicide.

his father, "Die! die! soon as ever you can." I have heard a father say, speaking of a profligate son, "He!— he would like to stick a knife into my back!" In fact there is no single good feeling left to turn the profligate from the idea of suicide. Besides, the constant abuse of pleasure inspires a feeling of disgust towards life. Two mere boys, scarcely fifteen years of age, but who had already indulged in a life of dissipation, confessed when on trial for a criminal offence that the abuse of pleasure had made them conceive a disgust at existence generally.[1] Then again, indolence and pride co-operate with dissipation in urging the profligate along the road to suicide. He hates work, and thinks he does not hold a position in society commensurate with his merits; then if with these ideas in his head, he lets himself be intoxicated with a poetical picture of the bliss of non-existence, he is irresistibly drawn towards suicide. This was exactly the case of Tony Auray, profligate, indolent, disappointed in his schemes of ambition, too proud to work, who forms the design of self-destruction after dissipating his patrimony and taking toll of life's enjoyments, like Rolla:

> " Il prit trois bourses d'or et durant trois années,
> Il vécut au soleil sans se douter des lois . . .
> Le monde souriait en le regardant faire,
> Et lui qui le faisait, disait à l'ordinaire,
> Qu'il se ferait sauter quand il n'aurait plus rien." [2]

Tony Auray did not take three years however to dissipate his little patrimony; a few months were enough. Alfred de Musset's hero wishes:

> " Ressaisir la vie
> Au manteau virginal d'un enfant de quinze ans." [3]

---

[1] *Gazette des Tribunaux*, 23rd September 1886.

[2] " He took three purses of gold and for three years' space he lived in the sunshine without a thought of the laws. . . . The world smiled as it watched his ways of life, and he the while was wont to say, he would end all with a pistol when he should have nothing left."

[3] " To get a fresh lease of life, grasping the maiden robe of a fair girl of fifteen."

Similarly it is a girl of fifteen that Tony Auray seduces and entices from her father's custody. De Musset makes Rolla a sceptic; his apostrophe to Voltaire is no work of supererogation. Tony Auray also was an absolute unbeliever.[1]

These suicides of weary profligates were also known in Antiquity; learned and literary men of the Roman decadence deemed them poetical and induced others to do the same by their example. While Seneca's disciples would end their days like Zeno the Stoic, while perusing a treatise of morality or talking philosophy with their friends, the followers of Epicurus would kill themselves after an orgy. Excess of indulgence, satiety of pleasure, fear of pain, will lead to suicide just as effectually as melancholy. The highest good consisting for the Epicureans in "pleasure," when this failed, they would kill themselves. In Cleopatra's day, at Alexandria, there was even a Society formed of "Companions of the Tomb" or "Inseparables in Death," whose members, after exhausting all the pleasures of life in a series of orgies, were in the habit, when lassitude supervened, of putting an end to their lives.—These suicides of literary affectation and blasé profligacy were equally common among the Romans of the Silver Age. Petronius, the most licentious poet of the Court of Nero, voluntarily quitted life, when he began to fear his influence with the Emperor was at an end. He was the recognized arbiter of elegant society and its pleasures; " he devoted the day to sleep, the night to the duties of society and pleasure." Having excited the jealousy of the other courtiers by surpassing them all in the arts of wanton and luxurious living, he was denounced, and fearing to lose the Emperor's favour, and unwilling "any longer to bear this load of fear and hope," he opened his veins, the fashionable mode of suicide at that time, and calmly awaited death listening to the recitation of pleasant songs and merry verses.

A certain witty indecency has always been one of the

[1] Byron wrote at Venice: " I will use up the mine of my youth to the last shred of its ore. And then . . . good-night ! I have lived and I am satisfied."

characteristics of the French mind and above all of the Parisian. Gay and blithe with Brantôme, Marot, Rabelais, Règnier, La Fontaine, Voltaire, Diderot, Désaugiers, Béranger, it has grown melancholic and turned to debauchery in contemporary literature. Poets have thought to assimilate the genius of Byron and Musset by giving philosophical airs to profligacy and displaying a morbid preference for scenes of lust and blood. The mere titles of Baudelaire's Poems, *L'Amour et le crâne, La Fontaine de sang, Un Voyage à Cythère, Le Vin de l'assassin,*[1] etc., are enough to show this predilection for tales of blood and wild dissipation. He was right in naming his poems *Les fleurs du mal,* for indeed they are morbid and unhealthy enough. For him,

" La débauche et la mort sont deux aimables filles."[2]

In the Middle Ages also death formed a subject for poetry and painting; to intensify the impression produced by means of contrast, poets and painters set side by side in their books and pictures scenes of gloom and scenes of licence. These contrasted effects enshrined a moral purpose; they were intended to remind the favourites of fortune that life is fleeting, that death lay in wait for them and that they must prepare to die. It was in the early years of the Renaissance that the idea of Death grew into a refinement of sensual enjoyment and a motive of erotic poetry. Boccaccio prefaces the *Decameron* with a description of the Plague of Florence,—another way of saying, *Vita brevi fruamur* (" Life is short ; come let us enjoy "). Thoughts of death are salutary for believers but perilous for doubters, only stimulating in the sceptic a thirst for immediate enjoyment. The Epicurean and Freethinker throws himself with savage impetuosity on pleasure, because he sees it will soon elude his grasp. During the Plague of Athens and again during that of Florence, a

[1] " Love and the Skull," " The Fountain of Blood," " A Journey to Cythera," " The Murderer's Wine."
[2] " Debauchery and Death are two sweet maids."

feverish pursuit of pleasure was observed.[1] This is why writers, who seek sensations, for the sake of trying to describe them afterwards, bring the idea of death into close connection with that of licentious enjoyment. In a recent book entitled, *Du sang, de la volupté, et de la mort* ("Blood, Lust and Death"), M. M. Barrès writes: "My imagination is stirred by this atmosphere of death and ephemeral joys of the flesh. . . . A marvel that is in process of disappearing, this is the feature that adds a feverish delight to every pleasure. To be perishable, this is the supreme grace. To see our mistress within our arms waning away each day, this rounds the pleasure we have of her with an incomparable melancholy. No intensity of sensation is adequate in which is not intermingled the idea of Death."[2] "A fig for Love without the spicy condiment of Death," says a character in Renan's *Abbesse de Jouarre.*

By this profanation of Death, turning it into a refinement of sensuality, Literature has developed morbid tastes among the reading public and provoked not a few suicides. In fact, it is even more dangerous to coquet with Death than it is with Love; such trifling always ends badly. Here is an instance in proof of what we say. Not long ago while examining the official reports of suicides for the Department of the Seine, I found appended to one of them the following printed advertisement : "To all who are disappointed, disillusioned, sceptical,—a new sensation offered by the magnetico-spiritualistic visions of Death in his cave." The prospectus was illustrated with pictures of skeletons and death's heads and similar horrors, which "disillusioned sceptics" were invited to come and see. The particular "sceptic" in question on receiving this curious document, had visited the show in search of a

---

[1] Physicians have noted that venereal diseases are more common during troublous times following on great public calamities, because at such periods populations abandon themselves to every kind of excess, to escape the terrors weighing upon them. See *Nouveau dictionnaire de médecine* of Jaccond, under word "*Syphilis.*"

[2] M. Barrès, *Du sang, de la volupté et de la mort,* p. 124.

stimulant to his blasé imagination; once there, he had been bitten by the fascination of death, and had ended by committing suicide.

This poetry in which Death, Lust and Wanton Living are extolled is fit only for neurotic patients and men of half disordered intellect, and appeals only to ill-balanced minds, taught by it to associate the ideas of voluptuousness and death together. I have myself known students whose heads had been turned by reading these erotic and pessimistic poets and who had attempted to destroy themselves in consequence.

M. Bourget, discussing in his famous Novel *Le Disciple* the effects of unhealthy reading on Robert Greslou, specially mentions *Les Fleurs du mal*, *Rolla* and Stendhal's Romances, as having upset his conscience. The hero of the story is himself a copy of the hero of a Novel of Stendhal's, Julien Sorel. The criminal of Constantine, already more than once referred to, is more nervous than Julien Sorel, less master of himself, but he is like him, inquisitive of new sensations, and intermingles the idea of death with that of love. Stendhal's hero plans to kill himself after a last kiss. " I give her," he says, " one last kiss . . . and I kill myself . . . my lips will touch her cheeks before I die." [1]

The motives leading to suicide have since *Hamlet* and in the period from *Werther* to *Rolla* gradually lost every note of elevation and become more and more contemptible. We understand how Hamlet was profoundly sad after his father's murder and his mother's marriage with the murderer, how he was driven distracted by these fearful discoveries, and how crushed under his load of pain, he becomes a victim to hallucinations and pretending to be mad in order to secure vengeance for his father's death, he goes mad in very truth. But Werther and René have not the same reasons for being weary of life; their sorrows come merely from their disillusionment and their amorous dreams. When we come to *Chatterton*, disappointed love

---

[1] Stendhal, *Le Rouge et le noir*, ch. xlix.

is no longer the sole motive for suicide; it is combined with sentiments of hatred against society and wounded literary vanity. In *Rolla*, it is simply the natural termination of a life of debauch.

By throwing a glamour over dissipation and Bohemianism, Romance and Poetry are responsible for the existence of a host of profligates and Bohemians, who supposing the Café and the Brothel to be the road to fame, have found their way to wretchedness, disease, the hospital and the dead-house. By dint of continually hearing a predilection for debauch and a love of idleness extolled as artistic tastes and enemies of the "bourgeois" spirit, these literary and artistic charlatans come to a bad end, believing all the while that a life of dissipation must conduct them to success, that true elegance must be found in a never-ending search after new and violent sensation, and verve in the stimulation of strong drink. All they actually find, to use Lucretius' expression, is "a life bowed under an ignominious yoke, ruined fortunes, crushing debts, duties forgotten, and honour sick and staggering to its fall,"[1]—and, I may add to Lucretius' catalogue, "health undermined, a mind distracted, a heart weary and sad and longing only for death. The unhappy poet who for his part also sought intoxication in a great number of "flagons," left his genius behind in the wine cup:

> "J'ai perdu ma force et ma vie
> Et mes amis et ma gaîté ;
> J'ai perdu jusqu'à la fierté,
> Qui faisait croire à mon génie."[2]

He curses the dissipation he had not strength of mind to fight against :

> "Ah ! malheur à celui qui laisse la débauche
> Planter le premier clou sous sa mamelle gauche !"[3]

---

[1] Lucretius, Bk. iv. v. 1115 and following.

[2] "I have lost my vigour and my life, my friends and my gaiety ; I have lost even the pride that made me believe in my genius."

[3] "Ah ! ill-starred the man who lets debauch plant the first nail under his left breast ! "

In another place, speaking of the prostitute, he declares :

> " Deux anges destructeurs marchent à son côté,
> Doux et cruels tous deux, la mort, la volupté." [1]

Young men who are too ready to believe in the poetry of debauch and idleness and the efficacy possessed by alcoholic stimulants in supplying literary inspiration, may also recall with advantage the regrets Baudelaire has expressed in his *Œuvres posthumes* for the ill use he had made of his time, and his too great devotion to intoxicants.

Women are nowadays beginning to destroy themselves no less than men. Generally so timid, they have ceased to have any fear of death ; on the contrary, it attracts them and the thought of everlasting rest flatters their imagination. Young women end their life after dining merrily with their girl friends ; they tell each other of their intention, see to the necessary preparations together, go out and buy the charcoal at the same time as the provisions required for their farewell meal, and sit down to table laughing and singing. I read in the Official Report of a case of suicide how the " concierge " (house-porter), was obliged to get up in the night to silence a party of women who were supping together and singing at two o'clock in the morning. Next morning " the songs had ceased," and the " concierge " found the women dead ; they had asphyxiated themselves by means of charcoal fumes.

Literary vanity often forms one of the motives leading to suicide. Speaking of a Poet who killed himself along with a married woman in 1811 at Potsdam, Mme. de Staël makes a judicious remark applicable to more than one suicide : " Does not the man seem rather like an author, who lacking genius desires by means of a terrible catastrophe to produce the effects he cannot attain in Poetry ? " The suicide of passion is often enough theatrical, and desperate men rehearse like actors the part they are

---

[1] " Two Angels of Destruction march at her side, sweet and cruel both of them, Death and Desire ! "

going to play! Mme. P——'s death being very slow in coming, almost seven hours, Bancal wrote down hour by hour each incident of his victim's death agony, and the sensations he himself experienced. Before killing Mme. X——, the Student Ch—— read her a copy of verses he had written for her. Before destroying himself, Werther reads a Tragedy of Lessing's. Escousse, author of a drama played at the Porte Saint-Martin Theatre, carefully arranges his suicide with Lebras, as if it were a piece they were going to play, such as the melodrama he had collaborated with his friend in writing for the Gaîté. He invited him to repair to the place fixed for their suicide, much as he might have summoned him to a theatrical representation. "I expect you at half past eleven," he tells him; "at that hour the curtain will rise;[1] mind you come, that we may hurry up the catastrophe." Before collaborating in this funereal piece, he had prepared this paragraph for insertion in the newspapers: "I wish the newspapers which announce my death to append this statement to their notice:—'Escousse killed himself, because he felt he had no place here, because he lacked vigour every step he took forwards or backwards, because love of fame did not sufficiently dominate his soul, *if soul there is.*'" He had likewise prepared some time previously in view of his death, some verses he wished to pass off as composed impromptu at the moment of his death. They were found later among a heap of old papers, scored with erasures and corrections. We give them for what they are worth:

> "Adieu, trop inféconde terre,
> Fléaux humains, soleils glacés!
> Comme un fantôme solitaire,
> Inaperçu j'aurai passé;
> Adieu, palmes immortelles,
> Vrai songe d'une âme de feu,
> L'air manquait, j'ai fermé mes ailes,
>   Adieu."[2]

---

[1] This phrase appears to be a reminiscence of Werther, who says: "The curtain rises, we pass over to the other side, and that's all!"

[2] "Farewell! too unfruitful earth, human scourges, icy suns! Like a

By sanctifying passion, dissipation, the cult of self, the search after super-refined sensations and scepticism, Literature has disseminated the taste for death, for egoistic feelings are always incapable of attaching human beings to life. The dreamy, sentimental melancholy of Romanticism became yet more bitter and gloomy among the writers that followed Flaubert, Leconte de Lisle, Pierre Loti, Mme. Ackerman, because it has ceased to be consoled by any sort of belief and augmented by a deep sense of the sadness and sorrows of life. The general impression left from the perusal of these pessimistic writers is that life is not worth living, and I have myself had occasion repeatedly to notice this scorn of life expressed in the letters of students and teachers. A short time since one of the latter, before committing suicide, wrote the following lines : " I die by my own act, for I have come to the conclusion that life is not worth the trouble we take to enable us to live it. Time to smoke a cigarette, and all is over. Is life worth as much as a good cigarette?" When teachers have such an idea of life, is it surprising if their pupils share it? "I wish to be buried without religious rites," writes a lad of sixteen. "I die an atheist, having never believed in a God, and refusing to believe in immortality. After death, annihilation. (Feb. 1897.)" Underlying all this despair that leads to suicide is the idea that life is a poor business, and annihilation preferable. The same notion it is which nowadays induces parents who commit suicide to kill their children at the same time. Yet this pessimistic view of life is quite reconcilable with a love of life's pleasures. Schopenhauer managed quite well to make his pessimism go along with the cultivation of sensual gratifications. On the contrary, other pessimists, convinced that life is not worth living, end it once for all. As the result of reading Schopenhauer's works, Mainländer turned pessimist and hanged himself on March 31st, 1876.

lonely phantom, I shall have passed away unnoted ; farewell ! laurels of immortality, true dream of a fiery soul ; air failed me and I closed my wings, farewell ! "

Any book expressing contempt for life and vaunting the advantages of death may inspire a disgust for existence and a preference for death. The Philosopher Hegesias demonstrated with so much eloquence that life is an evil, "that King Ptolemy, they say, forbade him to treat of this question in his public teaching, because several of his hearers killed themselves in consequence." (Cicero, *Tusculan Orations*, Bk. I., § 34.) The same fact is recorded by Plutarch (*Of Love and Natural Charity*) and by Valerius Maximus (Bk. VIII., ch. ix., § 3). Underlying the thought of suicide is always a comparison between the advantages of life and those of death, and a conviction that the latter outweigh the former. Every pessimistic conception of life, if unaccompanied by faith in God and a future state, provokes despair and leads directly to suicide. The duty then of all Writers is to make their fellow-men love life rather than despise it, and to make life loved they must give it a moral aim.

Nor does suicide find its victims exclusively among persons of cultivated mind. Novels, by filling girls of the lower classes, working girls and domestic servants, with romantic ideas, inspire them with disgust at their modest position in life, and from that to disgust at life itself is but a step. From novel reading they acquire a habit of indulgence in impossible dreams; they too would fain be heroines, they are humiliated by their subordinate situation and the necessity of living with coarse and uneducated relatives, and when they do not take to evil courses, generally end in suicide. It would hardly be credited how many melancholic servant maids there are and working girls afflicted with the spleen. Laundresses, shoemakers' daughters, by no means escape the curse of the Century. "My daughter," a shoemaker told a Police Commissary, in reply to his questions as to the motives of the girl's suicide, "my daughter was a great reader, and this gave her melancholy thoughts. She envied the lot of those who are no more. She considered Death a deliverance, though she had nothing whatever to complain of in the life she led. We are well off; she was an excellent work-woman and gained an ample livelihood." The unhappy father, while recognizing the fact that novel-reading gave his child sad thoughts, could not account for her having shot herself with a revolver on retiring to bed; he failed to see that she was suffering from being only a shoemaker's daughter.

Everything grows democratical in these days,—suicide included. Saint-Marc Girardin wrote in his *Cours de littérature dramatique*: "Suicide is not a malady of simple-minded, simple-hearted folk, but of the highly educated and philosophically inclined." M. Caro in ' his *Études morales* says the same. Both are wrong. It is quite a mistake to think it is a special malady of the highly cultured reflective classes; it is equally a disease of working men, coachmen, locksmiths, carpenters, stone-masons and the like. I am acquainted with very few cases of suicide among contemporary philosophers. Suicide is supposed to be frequent among those who practise the liberal professions; but for myself, I have always found the opposite to be the case. Instances of suicide on the part of Advocates, Magistrates, Engineers, Priests, are very rare. In 1896, out of 1549 suicides in Paris, I only find seven committed by persons exercising the liberal professions. Some of these were (I have read the official reports) determined by illness or madness; amongst others, an Advocate destroyed himself from grief because he was compelled to put his wife, who had become insane, in an asylum. Suicides of workmen, of girls of the lower classes, of young clerks and shopmen and of domestic servants are, on the other hand, very frequent. Suicide is not, as it was at the beginning of the Nineteenth Century, an aristocratic vice; it has become a popular one, with the diffusion of novel-reading.

To give a few examples:

A young maid-servant destroys herself by means of charcoal fumes, after writing, "I am terribly weary of existence in this world. My life is gloomy and useless.

I am killing myself to escape its vexations."—Another girl of eighteen throws herself under the wheels of a locomotive, which crushes both legs, without killing her. When questioned as to the motive of her act, she answers, "I wished to destroy myself, because I have had enough of life ; it is too sad altogether."—In a large number of Official Reports recording the suicides of young servant girls, who have destroyed themselves by hanging, inhalation of charcoal fumes or drowning, I read how they thought it degrading to serve others, how life was a burden to them. They had repeatedly proclaimed their intention of killing themselves, and bid farewell to their family and friends with a host of sentimental phrases borrowed from Novels and Romances. A young maid-of-all-work, hating her position, leaves her place and prepares to put an end to herself, writing a long letter to her father to ask him to distribute souvenirs to her relations and friends ; she concludes the letter with the following words : "I only ask one favour, dear father, that you place flowers on my tomb and on my coffin. I should dearly have loved some for my death, but as I did not wish to be seen in the streets about here, I have foregone this last pleasure."

On November 2, 1893, at six in the morning, one Nizolli, a young Italian workman of twenty, cutter in a shoe-factory at Marseilles, the son of a school-mistress, attempted to commit suicide. A witness, who had run in at the sound of the shots, found him lying dressed on his bed, wounded in four places with revolver bullets ; one wound was near the breast-bone, two below the left breast, and a fourth in the groin. He was an industrious workman, regular in his conduct and affectionate towards his parents and relations. His day's work finished, he used to devote his evenings to reading Novels and Poetry, often robbing himself of sleep for the purpose. His aunt, a school-teacher at Marseilles, told me all this reading had excited him very greatly and had made him conceive a disgust for life and a hatred of society. In his room were found copies of verses which he had composed and two letters. In one of these addressed to his aunt, he asked her forgiveness for the pain he was about to cause her, prayed her not to think harshly of him, and told her that the small sum of money he left behind, which she would find in his purse, would serve "to pass Charon's boat with." In the other letter, addressed to his parents, he explained the motives of his suicide. It runs as follows:

"MY DEAR PARENTS,—It is books have been my ruin. Seeing man is bound to slip in the mud, why make him acquainted with the mountain summits? why inspire him with hopes of a life full of enchantment?

"Cursed be all books! Ah! if only the makers of novels knew the harm they do! From my earliest years, I have thought possible a life consecrated to all that is true and noble, I have dreamed of a life such as we read of in Romance. Now, disgusted and exhausted, I see I can never attain the chimæra my youthful brain set before it as its aim; but now, I cannot, I cannot slip into the mud. And as man is a brute with instincts more vile than any other animal, as life is a hell upon earth, I prefer to find rest in the tomb. Forgive me the pain I am going to cause you. I would not give it you, if I could help it, but I am only twenty and life is a burden to me.

"I kiss your hands fondly.

"Farewell for ever!"

The young Italian in question survived his attempted suicide. On leaving the hospital, where he was cured of his wounds, he sold all his novels, for which he had conceived a horror, used the money in buying a bicycle, and started for America.

Called upon to account for her son's suicide,—he was apprenticed to a gilder on leather, and sixteen years of age,—his mother stated to the police: "Our son was gloomy and often told us he was sick of the workshop; he lost his temper at the most innocent remark. Two days ago he flew into a passion and declared we should never see him again after a week's time. He was in the habit of reading a great many Novels, and these probably turned his head. Yesterday evening he came home from work more gloomy than ever. After dinner he retired to his room. We thought he had gone to fetch a book, but a moment later we heard a shot; we rushed into the room and found our boy stretched on the floor with a bullet through the right temple." The same fate had befallen these two young workers in leather [1] as befell Don Quixote, whose head was turned by reading books of Chivalry. " Our Hidalgo buried himself so deep in books; he spent the whole day in reading from morn to eve and the night from eve to morn; and so by dint of reading and watching he dried up his brain to such a degree that he presently lost his wits. His imagination was filled full of all he read in the books,—enchantments, disputes, challenges, battles, wounds, declarations of love, degradations." To abolish the cause of Don Quixote's madness, they burned his books; to recover his reason, the young Italian we have spoken of sold his collection of novels, bought a bicycle and started for America. When parents notice their son entertaining gloomy thoughts pointing in the direction of suicide, they should find out what he reads, discover if he is not in the habit of perusing Novels and Poetry of a melancholy, romantic type, and if this is so, locking up his bookcase and turning him out into the fields. A little travel would be all that is required very often to restore health and sanity to many a young victim ·of melancholia. But parents, absorbed in their daily tasks, have no notion as to the reason of their child's sadness, till one day, to their profound astonishment, they learn that he has committed suicide. Such was the case with a Paris bookseller, who in February 1895 found his son, a lad of seventeen, with a pistol bullet through his head. Questioned as to the motive for the suicide, the unhappy

[1] Working shoemakers as a rule profess very advanced political and social opinions. This revolt against society I attribute to the disproportion existing between their position in life and the one their ambition would have them fill; moreover, all sedentary occupations are provocative of dangerous day-dreams.

father told the Police Commissary: "My son, who has never been away from home, had everything he needed to be happy; but he suffered from melancholy, he had the spleen."

Of course all the young people who put an end to themselves are not imitating Werther or copying Indiana. Many of them do not so much as know the names of Goethe or George Sand; they are driven to suicide solely by the working of the passions and their own neuropathic constitution. But there are others, who finding themselves similarly situated to Werther, are so deeply impressed by reading the Novel as to be irresistibly drawn to imitate the hero's suicide. Side by side with physiological and psychical suicides, there are also *literary* suicides, determined by a *morbid* sentimentality derived from Romances which defend and draw a seductive picture of suicide. The play of *Romeo and Juliet* again is well calculated to inspire a young man with a longing not to survive the dear being he would fain have made his bride. Literature has so widely disseminated this idea, that two lovers ought to die together when they cannot live together, that M. Saint-Marc Girardin approves Romeo's suicide: "Which of us," he says, "would consent to see Romeo survive Juliet or Juliet Romeo?" Literature has yet further contributed to spread the mania of suicide by representing a voluntary death not merely as a poetical but as a religious act. "I am about to rejoin my Father and your Father," Werther declares; "I will carry my sorrows to the foot of His throne,· and He will comfort me till you come. Then, I will fly to meet you, I will seize you and will be for ever united with you in presence of the Eternal, in kisses without end."

Literature would be better inspired not to teach men these lessons of contempt for life and love of death. Human reason is too weak to bear shaking with sophistries in excuse of suicide. Life contains enough sadness without Novelists and Poets increasing its intensity by instilling a morbid and precocious melancholy. It is no part of their duty to make lads of twenty despair of life, to add to real sorrows the weight of imaginary grievances, and make men melancholy before their time. To tell young people life is not worth living is to destroy their illusions and turn them into useless whimperers,—and seeing contempt for life often ends in Epicureanism,—very often to make them selfish Epicureans.

No such reproach can be levelled at our Classical literature. No one has ever dreamed of holding Corneille, Molière, La Fontaine, Boileau or Racine responsible for the suicide of their readers. While some of the most celebrated authors of the Romantic School, Chateaubriand, Lamartine, George Sand, Alfred de Musset, Sainte-Beuve, Théophile Gautier and others, have either made attempts at suicide or have been constantly assailed by thoughts tending in that direction, no Classical writer has felt, or at any rate succumbed to, any such temptation. True Molière, Boileau and Chapelain on one occasion conceived the mad idea of jumping into the Seine, but this was after a dinner where the wine had been flowing freely, causing a temporary aberration of reason. Voltaire has denied the authenticity of the story, but there is no doubt about it; it is related by Racine *fils* himself in the Memoir he wrote of his father. "This famous supper," he says, "incredible as it may appear, really occurred. Happily my father was not there. The wise Boileau, who was, completely lost his head, like the rest. The liquor having produced in all the guests a fit of the severest moral disquisition, their lucubrations on the miseries of life and the maxim of the Ancients which declares that 'the best happiness is not to be born, and the second best to die soon,' caused them to adopt the heroic resolution of starting off at once to throw themselves into the River. Thither they promptly repaired and were very near carrying their purpose into effect, when Molière represented to them that so noble a deed should not be buried in the darkness of night, but deserved to be performed in open day. At this they stopped short, and looking at each other ejaculated, 'He is quite right.' To which Chapelain added:

'Yes! gentlemen, don't let us drown ourselves till to-morrow morning, and meantime suppose we go finish the wine that's left.' Next day they looked at it in a different light, and thought it best after all to go on bearing the miseries of life."[1] With the exception of this one youthful folly, which also goes to prove the influence exercised by literary memories during intoxication, our great Classical writers have never felt any temptation in this direction. Neither is any defence of suicide to be found in Virgil, who assigns those who have attempted their own life a place in Hell:

> "Proxima deinde tenent mœsti loca, qui sibi letum
> Insontes peperere manu, lucemque perosi
> Projecere animas. Quam vellent æthere in alto
> Nunc et pauperiem et duros perferre labores!"[2]

What especially characterizes the Classical writers is their good sense, their "sweet reasonableness," the balance of their faculties. These great minds are of a sound and healthy genius, well balanced, of a robust and vigorous moral constitution. Nor did they show any lack of sensibility or imagination, as the Romantics have alleged. Who had a more tender heart than Racine? Who possessed a more brilliant imagination than Corneille? Are not Pascal, and Bossuet himself, as remarkable for the force of their imagination as for the depth of their sensibility? Are they not at one and the same time poets, orators and philosophers? Who can deny the most graceful gifts of fancy and the most exquisite endowment of sensibility

---

[1] Andrieux wrote a Comedy based on the incidents of this famous supper under the title of *Molière avec ses amis* ("Molière and his Friends"). He made La Fontaine one of the party, but as a matter of fact he was not there.

[1] "The next in place, and punishment, are they
Who prodigally throw their souls away;
Fools, who repining at their wretched state
And loathing anxious life, suborn'd their fate.
With late repentance now they would retrieve
The bodies they forsook, and wish to live,
Their pains and poverty desire to bear,
To view the light of heaven, and breathe the vital air."
From Virgil, *Æneid*, vi. ll. 434-437. Dryden's translation.

to La Fontaine and Fénélon? But these great writers
distrusted sensibility and fancy as regular guides, they
preferred the sure government of reason. Boileau was
never weary of telling the poets :

"Aimez donc la raison. . . ."[1]

One of his friends, finding him one day absorbed in the
search for a rhyme, advised him to go and get a *Rhyming
Dictionary.* "No! no!" was Boileau's answer, "rather
get me a *Reasoning Dictionary* ;" he thought far more of
the justness of the sentiment than of the sonority of the
words or the perfection of the rhyme. How many poets
and romance writers of the present do just the opposite ;
"So much the worse for the sense!" Flaubert used to
say, "rhythm before everything!" Corneille, Descartes,
Pascal, were so enamoured of reason they made it part
and parcel of love ; "Love and reason," Pascal was wont
to say, "are one and the same thing." The modern view
is that love and *unreason* are one and the same thing ;
nay! more, that love is proved by suicide and even by
crime, that he is no lover who is not ready to kill himself
or others. Good sense, now deemed a vulgar, commonplace quality, was admired above all else by the great
Writers of the Seventeenth Century, who declared good
sense to be master of the house of human life, and
imagination the "foolish virgin" of the establishment.

"Que toujours le bon sens s'accorde avec la rime,"[2]

was Boileau's axiom. Corneille claimed with satisfaction
in his Preface to *Otho* to have endowed his characters with
propriety of conduct and displayed good sense in all their
sentiments. In this school the young men and women of
the Seventeenth Century learned to love reason and distrust
the enticements of sensibility and imagination. Suicides
of passion were rare at that period. When women had
love disappointments, they entered a Convent and never

---

[1] "Love reason therefore. . . ."
[2] "Let good sense ever chime in with the rhyme."

dreamed of throwing themselves into the Seine. They sought consolation in listening to the sermons of Bourdaloue and Bossuet. Sound reasoning faculties exercised the same fascination over Princes as grace and beauty. It was by her prudence and rectitude of mind that Mme. de Maintenon seduced Louis XIV.; it is well known how the King would ask her advice in the words, "What thinks your reasonableness of the matter?" In the Seventeenth Century good sense was more admired than wit; and the same is true of the greatest writers of Antiquity; there is more wit in Ovid and Martial than in Virgil or Lucretius. Louis XIV. himself preferred good sense to wit; the fanciful, brilliant wit of Fénélon frightened him. At the present day, on the contrary, to how many books and plays may Gresset's line be applied :

"De l'esprit, si l'on veut, mais pas le sens commun !"[1]

Quite forgetful of Boileau's advice :

"Il faut même en chanson du bon sens et de l'art,"[2]

modern Literature, no great admirer of Boileau, has put plenty of art into its Novels and Plays, but not so much common sense.

But if

"Raison sans sel est fade nourriture,
Sel sans raison n'est solide pâture,"[3]

as Jean Jacques Rousseau puts it.

The Eighteenth Century, sensualistic as it had become both in theory and practice, yet remained in Literature faithful in its preference for good sound reason. A critic having reproached Gresset with wanting wit, the latter who was not really at all wanting in this quality, replied : "I had rather lack wit than good sense." A modern writer on the other hand would far rather want good sense than wit; the reasonable author is thought a commonplace,

---

[1] "Wit, if you will, but no common sense !"

[2] "Even for a song good sense and art are needful."

[3] "Reason without salt is vapid stuff; salt without reason is not solid food."

mediocre creature, a "bourgeois" mind, a Philistine. Novelists like to see a small spice of insanity in their readers and do their best to insinuate it into their minds. What a contrast the fine sound sense in Voltaire, Buffon, d'Alembert, Montesquieu! J. Chénier agrees with Boileau when he writes :—

> "Qu'est-ce que vertu? Raison mise en pratique.
> Valeur? Raison produite avec éclat.
> Esprit? Raison qui finement s'exprime.
> Le goût n'est rien qu'un bon sens délicat,
> Et le génie est le raison sublime."[1]

Nowadays, according to the latest theories, genius is a nervous complaint and virtue the same, men of talent and saints are victims of degeneracy, hysteria, neurasthenia or epilepsy. In former days health of body and mind was the object aimed at,—"mens sana in corpore sano," "a healthy mind in a healthy body." Now the way to fame is through nervous disease, a disordered imagination, an inordinate sensibility.

In the school of the great Classical authors of the Seventeenth and Eighteenth Centuries, all with the exception of Rousseau, men of sound and sensible intellect, writers run no risk of stultifying their judgment with apologies for suicides of passion ; by contact with them reason is fortified, sensibility moderated, imagination cooled. Jean Jacques Rousseau is the only great Writer of the Eighteenth Century who approves of suicide. True, it may be urged that the defence he makes of suicide in the *Nouvelle Heloïse* is followed by a refutation ; but in a letter to Voltaire, on the occasion of his Poem on the Earthquake of Lisbon, he allows that man has a right to kill himself. D'Holbach is of the same opinion in his book *Le Système de la Nature*. On the other hand suicide is condemned by Voltaire (*Dictionnaire Philosophique*, under "Cato"), by the Encyclo-

---

[1] "What is virtue? Reason put in practice. What is valour? Reason displayed under brilliant circumstances. Wit? Reason gracefully expressed. Taste is nothing else but a delicate good sense, and genius is reason at its sublimest height."

pædists and by Montesquieu. The last-named, it is true, had written its apology in the *Lettres Persanes* (*Letter* 76), but he condemned it in the *Esprit des Lois* (bk. xiv. ch. x.); he even approves of the Law branding suicide as a crime, except always in England, where he believes this form of death to be the result of a disease due to the climate!

Nay! more, not only do the Classical authors avoid any suggestions of suicide; they are actually a cure for morbid cravings in that direction, as I have shown by the example of George Sand. But beginning with Jean Jacques Rousseau, Literature has changed its character; imagination and sensibility have come to the front at the expense of reason in Romance and Poetry;[1] inordinate sensibility, morbid imagination, false sentiment, there you have Rousseau and the Literature he inspired. The most famous writers of the Nineteenth Century, Chateaubriand, George Sand, Victor Hugo, all have too much imagination and not enough good sense. Their style is too full of tropes; some of these are superb, but others again are in bad taste. Sainte-Beuve relates how Bernardin de Saint-Pierre, when asked his opinion of Chateaubriand, answered that his imagination was too strong for him.[2] Not a doubt about it, imagination and sensibility are fine faculties, the primary preconditions of Poet and Novelist; an author must himself feel deeply to move readers or spectators. But exaggerated sensibility and over-strung imagination, uncontrolled by reason, are prejudicial to literary sanity

---

[1] These reflections do not apply to the Historians, Moralists, Literary Critics or Philosophers of the Nineteenth Century. We have had historians of the very first rank ; A. Thierry, Guizot, Thiers, Mignet,—Michelet himself, in spite of many whimsicalities of imagination, may be set side by side with the historians of Antiquity. Cousin, Roger-Collard, Jouffroy, Caro, J. Simon are all Philosophers of distinguished merit. Our literary critics, Villemain, Sainte-Beuve, D. Nisard, Saint-Marc Girardin, Caro, Patin, Boissier, J. Lemaître, Brunetière, Faguet, Larroumet are not less remarkable for the acuteness of their powers of moral observation than for the justness of their literary judgments. In all these writers imagination and sensibility are duly controlled by reason ; one only ! Michelet, has allowed his fancy to run away with him and thereby spoiled his great talent.

[2] *Chateaubriand et son groupe*, p. 203.

no less than they are to bodily health. To be convinced of the fact, it is only needful to visit a lunatic asylum and read the works of Doctors Magnan, Dagonnet, Ball, Féré, on the causes leading to mental complaints. Before their time a Theologian (Theologians have many points of contact with specialists in insanity), Malebranche, had pointed out the dangers of inordinate imagination in *La Recherche de la Vérité*. "It is no defect," he writes, "to possess a brain adapted for picturing things rigorously and receiving distinctly very clear and very vivid images of the smallest objects. . . . But when the imagination dominates the soul and, without waiting for the orders of the will, its impressions are called up by the mere action of the brain as affected by external objects, . . . it is then manifestly a bad rather than a good quality, and indeed almost a form of insanity." Men who are slaves of their imagination do not see things as they really are, they exaggerate and overestimate them, and consequently fail to appreciate them at their true value; they are subject to illusions, visions and hallucinations; they are restless, agitated, unstable, eccentric, irritable, the *genus irritabile vatum* ("the irritable tribe of bards"); they lack deliberation, balance, judgment.

Literary health, just like physical, is a matter of the equilibrium of the faculties; it implies a due compromise between imagination and reason, sensibility and good taste. This accord of the faculties is found in Classical literature; it does not exist in Romantic, which is marked by the predominance of imagination and sensibility over reason. Thus Goethe himself used to say, "I call classical whatever is healthy, and romantic whatever is morbid."

Romanticism plumed itself on being in opposition to common sense; it sought out by preference the exceptional, the odd, it poetized melancholy, consumption, and suicide and crime arising out of amorous passion. In his notice on Gérard de Nerval, who went mad and hanged himself from the bars of a vent-hole of one of the old Parisian street lamps, Théophile Gautier tells us how

his wild extravagancies appeared quite matters of course
to the other members of the early Romantic school, his
friends. "In those days," he says, "of literary eccentricity,
among the paroxysms of originality, the voluntary or involuntary outrages on propriety that were every day occur-
rences, it was extremely difficult to appear extravagant;
every folly seemed plausible, and the least eccentric among
us would have been deemed a fitting occupant for a cell
in a lunatic asylum." Théophile Gautier himself, who
ended in Epicureanism, began as a pessimist; in early
years his sick imagination craved,

> "Dans l'immobilité savourer lentement
> Comme un philtre endormeur l'anéantissement." [1]

He longed for annihilation like a disciple of Buddha, or
a precursor of Schopenhauer; he composed the *Comedy of
Death*, taking delight only in mournful images and associating with them, as often happens in like circumstances,
the most voluptuous fancies. At twenty he had arrived,
he declares, "at such a degree of surfeit as to be no longer
tickled by anything that was not out of the way and
difficult;" [2] he was already enamoured of a literature
highly-spiced, gamey, decadent, in preference to healthy
writing, he had already contracted morbid tastes, in spite
of the pure surroundings amid which he lived. "I rotted
away," he says, "little by little of my own inward corruption, without a sign being visible externally, like a medlar
on straw; in the bosom of that worthy, pious, saintly
family, I was idle to the pitch of downright wickedness."

Sainte-Beuve, who later on became a genial Epicurean
like Gautier, likewise began by being a disciple of Werther,
"an amateur, radical Werther," to use M. Guizot's phrase.
Before developing into the judicious critic, so replete with
delicate appreciation and sound sense, of the *Causeries
du Lundi* and the *Nouveaux Lundis*, he was the morbid-
minded poet, whom he has described in the book entitled,

---

[1] "In immobility to relish annihilation languorously, like a philter that lulls
to slumber."

[2] *Mademoiselle de Maupin*, ch. v.

Vie, poésie et pensées de Joseph Delorme. "His soul," he says, "presents henceforward only an inconceivable chaos, where monstrous fancies, vivid reminiscences, criminal visions, great thoughts strangled in their birth, wise resolutions followed by mad actions, pious aspirations succeeded by blasphemies, dance and toss confusedly against a background of despair." Remembering in later years this early period of storm and stress, Sainte-Beuve delivered the following judgment on the Romantic School, where he had learned the art of groaning, lamenting and despairing at twenty : " In this school, to which I belonged from the latter part of 1827 down to July 1830, nobody had any sound judgment whatever,—neither Hugo, nor Vigny, nor Nodier, nor the brothers Deschamps ; I did more or less what all the rest did during this period, I put my judgment in my pocket and gave free play to my imagination."

The want of taste, so frequent among the Romanticists, is nothing but a want of judgment. Is it not, for instance, a defect of taste and judgment on the part of Chateaubriand to recount his own sister's incestuous passion, on the part of Lamartine to describe in minute detail his own mother's physical charms ? Does not the flood of *Confessions*, which since Rousseau has inundated Literature, point to a lack of tact, of judgment? "If it is a fault to talk often of oneself, it is a piece of effrontery, rather a form of insanity, to be praising oneself at every instant " (Malebranche).

And not only were the Romantic writers, notwithstanding the great talent and genius of some of their number, wanting in judgment, but not a few of them were affected by nervous complaints and even mental infirmities. Jean Jacques Rousseau, who was the true promoter of the Romantic movement, suffered from the " mania of persecution," particularly during the last years of his life. Several of his books show manifest traces of insanity ; Voltaire drew attention to the fact. When Rousseau published *La Profession de foi du Vicaire savoyard* (" The Savoyard Vicar's Confession of Faith "), one of his best works, Voltaire exclaimed, in mingled astonishment and delight: "Oh! Rousseau, you write like a madman and act like a scamp, but you have just spoken like a wise man and a good one. Read, my friends, and let us greet truth and morality wherever they show out, even amid ill sentiments and aberration of mind." Rousseau's insanity has been described by Dr Môbius, Dr Chatelain, Dr Krafft-Ebing ; [1] there is no room left for doubt.

Nor was Rousseau the only Romantic writer touched with mental disease ; Byron, also an Author of a high genius, was as ill-balanced in mind as he. Taine declares he was half mad. As a boy he used to fight with his mother, and the pair of them, after a furious quarrel, would run to the chemists, each anxious to discover if the other had not been there to buy poison to commit suicide with. One day he seized a knife from the table to stab himself in the breast, and it had to be taken from him by force. His wife believed him mad and had him examined by the doctors ; and he himself entertained the dread of "dying at the top," like Swift.[2] In a letter written in 1811 he says, "I think I shall end by going mad." Stendhal, who knew Byron personally and lived several weeks with him, declares that on some days he was actually mad.

Of course I do not maintain for a moment that all the writers of the Romantic school were victims of insanity. But notwithstanding my admiration for the genius of some of them, I am bound to allow the existence in several of a diseased imagination and morbid sensibility predisposing them to suicide. In Chateaubriand, who resembled Rousseau in so many respects, imagination and sensibility were undoubtedly diseased, and, as we have said, he made an attempt at self-destruction in his early days.—George

---

[1] See also an article by M. Brunetière on *La Folie de J. J. Rousseau* in the *Revue des Deux Mondes* of February 1st, 1890. Sainte-Beuve believed, but on insufficient grounds, that Rousseau had put an end to his own life in a fit of madness (*Chateaubriand et son groupe*, p. 107). As a matter of fact, Rousseau died of an attack of serous apoplexy.

[2] The "Great Dean" had dreaded for years the fate of insanity which eventually overtook him. "Young . . . tells how he once heard Swift say, 'I shall be like that tree : I shall die at the top.'" (Translator.)

Sand too had troubles of sensibility and will, she says so herself. "I was, I am perhaps still," she writes, "a victim to excessive sensibility, refusing all restraints of reason, especially at its crisis."

In more than one passage in the *Histoire de ma vie* are to be found traces of actual mental disorder. As a girl she had hallucinations and had conceived the fancy of an imaginary god she called *Corambo*, whom she adored as an actually existing deity, and paid regular worship to on a rustic altar. She was possessed for many years with the idea of suicide; I have related above how on one occasion she tried to drown herself. Dr Brissaud, Professor in the Faculty of Medicine in the University of Paris, who has made a special study of mental and nervous diseases, and with whom I have discussed the psychical condition of George Sand, assured me of the existence in her case of a nervous disorder, giving me details I think it better not to repeat out of respect for the woman and her genius.

Alfred de Musset, for all his brilliant talents, did not escape a degree of nervous disorder that at times bordered close on actual dementia. His *Nuit de Décembre* leads me to believe he suffered from hallucinations and the nervous phenomenon known by the name of "duplication of self":

"Du temps que j'étais écolier,
Devant ma table vint s'asseoir
Un pauvre enfant vêtu de noir,
Qui me ressemblait comme un frère. . . ."[1]

Again it would seem to be the result of a fit of introspection when De Musset wrote:

"Mais n'est-il pas un heure dans la vie,
Où le génie humain rencontre la folie?"[2]
(*La Coupe et les Lèvres.*)

---

[1] In the days when I was a schoolboy, there came and sat at my desk a poor lad clothed in black, who was like me as a brother. . . ." If we are to believe Dr Moreau of Tours, the same nervous phenomenon would seem to have been exhibited in Goethe's case also. He is said one day to have seen his own "double" coming to meet him.

[2] "But is there not an hour in life, when human genius is near akin to madness?"

On more than one occasion during his life the Poet was tempted to commit suicide. In *La Confession d'un enfant du siècle* ("Confession of a child of the Century"), he relates how he conceived a longing to kill his mistress and himself afterwards, and how he concealed a table knife under the pillow for this purpose. In his *Lettre à Lamartine* he says he twice over put a weapon to his naked breast. More than once he wished to kill himself along with George Sand. " If you renounce life," he writes to her, " remember the oath you swore ; do not die without me." In a letter of George Sand's to Dr Pagello, the companion of the Poet declares she has fears for Alfred de Musset's reason. "Once," she writes, "three months ago, he was like a madman all night long, seeing phantoms all about him, and at the present moment he is complaining of a nameless and causeless malady, and declaring he is on the point of death or madness." De Musset was endowed with a nervous organization of so fine and feminine a delicacy, that it threatened to break down under the strain of disappointed love; so impressionable was his nature, he declares, that the sight of a woman set him trembling, and he suffered from very serious nervous crises. He is so well aware of the want of energy that characterizes him that he has said himself in his Poems :

> " Mes premièrs vers sont d'un enfant,
> Les seconds d'un adolescent,
> Les derniers à peine d'un homme." [1]

Less nervously constituted than Alfred de Musset, and uniting to the highest lyrical genius much sound sense, even in Politics,[2] Lamartine had yet been so impression-

---

[1] " My first verses are a child's, my second a youth's, my last hardly those of a man."—De Musset is not the only poet who had this childish nature. The character of poets whose imagination and sensibility are not counterbalanced by reason, closely resembles the childish character of women of a nervous idiosyncracy. Coppée says of Verlaine that he was a child all his life (Preface by Coppée prefixed to the Selected Poems of Verlaine).

[2] Before M. Thiers, Lamartine had pointed out in his *Entretiens* that Italian Unity would lead to German Unity later on, and that this would be disastrous to France.

able in his younger days as to have many times turned his thoughts to suicide. When he was sent to school at Lyons, "my impressions were so keen and so unhappy," he writes, "that ideas of suicide, a thing I had never heard spoken of, assailed me strongly. I can remember passing whole days and nights pondering by what means I could be done with a life I could no longer endure." [1] He says of Raphaël, who is no other than himself, that he possessed "a sensibility so exquisite it came near being a disease."

At the period when Sainte-Beuve was publishing the poems of Joseph Delorme, Lamartine said of him : "He was a young man, pale-faced, blond-haired and delicate-looking, morbidly excitable, a poet with all a poet's tearful sensitiveness." Sainte-Beuve too had felt the temptation to suicide,—by drowning, like Lamartine and George Sand :

> "En me promenant là, je me suis dit souvent :
> Pour qui veut se noyer la place est bien choisie ;
> On n'aurait qu'à venir un jour de fantaisie,
> À cacher ses habits au pied de ce bouleau,
> Et comme pour un bain, à descendre dans l'eau." [2]

Victor Hugo was never possessed like the other great poets of the Nineteenth Century with the idea of self-destruction, for all his prodigious imagination, which exaggerated everything and was prejudicial to justness of judgment. He was safeguarded against the temptation by the family life he led and the love he bore his children. Nevertheless, judging by an Ode in Book V. of the *Odes et Ballades*, even he would seem to have on one occasion conceived the purpose of dying after a disappointment in love :

> "Tu m'oublieras dans les plaisirs,
> Je me souviendrai dans la tombe." [3]

---

[1] Lamartine, *Les Confidences*, bk. vi.

[2] "Walking there I have often said to myself, for any who wishes to drown himself the place is well chosen ; he would only have to come some day of fancy, to hide his clothes at the foot of yonder birch, and as if for a bathe to slip into the stream."

[3] "You will forget me in a life of pleasure, I will remember in the tomb."

Nor are the celebrated Novelists of the Nineteenth Century less sensitive and emotional than the Poets. We learn from the entrancing Memoirs of Mme. Octave Feuillet how excessively nervous her famous husband was.[1] Almost all the heroines delineated in his Romances are nervous women. If their story often ends in suicide, this is not, as M. Brunetière points out, because suicide " is the highest manifestation of human will," but because women of a nervous temperament, incapable of bearing the pains of disappointed love, kill themselves by a sudden, unforeseen impulse that leaves little room for deliberate volition at all. In some very rare cases, suicide may be " the highest manifestation of human will," but with nervous women it is on the contrary a manifestation of weakness of will and of morbid over-excitement of the nerves, frequently an unpremeditated, almost automatic, act.[2] Moreover, in spite of the decency and elegance of style of Octave Feuillet's Novels, I cannot think his fair readers' reason is likely to be fortified by the delineation of these hare-brained heroines of his who kill themselves out of disappointed love. The painter of these fierce and desperate passions, who was yet at bottom, like Racine, a Christian moralist, lavishes over-much admiration on these society ladies with their reckless loves, who hide under an aristocratic exterior very vulgar passions. I think it is a mistake to call him, as some do, " a Musset for family reading "; he might more appropriately be described as a Racine among Novelists. There is the same grace of style, the same pictures of passionate womanhood, the same tragic catastrophes of crime and suicide.

Nor are the naturalistic Novelists one whit less nervous, as a rule, than the great idealistic author I have just

[1] An ill-natured article by Jules Janin "occasioned a veritable disturbance of his health." The temporary failure of his *Belle au Bois Dormant* ("Sleeping Beauty") "came near killing him." The sight of Rubens' *Descent from the Cross* impressed him so deeply it nearly made him fall down from excess of emotion and caused him hallucinations. He used to say the view of a high mountain seemed to weigh down his brain.

[2] Dr Magnan, *Les Dégénérés*, p. 144.

named. Guy de Maupassant said of Flaubert: "Ever on the quiver and impressionable to a degree, he used to liken himself to a skinless man, through whom the slightest touch sent a shudder of pain. . . . Sometimes he reached such a state of nervous exasperation he would have liked to destroy the whole human race." It is well known how excessively nervous the brothers de Goncourt and Alphonse Daudet were. "Our work," wrote one of the de Goncourt brothers, "and this I suppose is the heavy price it has to pay, is based on nervous disease. . . . Critics may say what they please, they can never prevent my brother and me being the Saint John Baptists of modern sensibility (*Journal des Goncourt*, vol. vi.). In his medico-psychological study on Émile Zola, Dr Toulouse writes: "There exists then a certain nervous want of balance, an exaggerated susceptibility to emotion, which provokes, under the influence of very slight excitations, altogether disproportionate and painful reactions." [1] Maxime du Camp has shown us that Flaubert was epileptic. The latter's nephew, Guy de Maupassant, who made an attempt at suicide, died of general paralysis, that is to say a mental disease, and one that must not be confounded with forms of paralysis resulting from cerebral hæmorrhage.

I do not believe with some physiologists, Dr. Moreau (of Tours), Dr. Lombroso, M. Jules Soury, M. Max Nordau, Dr. Charles Richet, that genius is a form of nervous complaint or of epilepsy. According to them the man of genius is a diseased, an abnormal being, an epileptic; "it is very seldom," says M. Richet, "that on studying near at hand the life of any large number of superior men, we do not find in their mental organization and intellectual processes something defective, morbid, pathological, bringing them into connection with the insane. . . . I will never advise a woman to marry the son of a man of genius. . . . The great and powerful genius of inventors, discoverers, creators and disseminators of original ideas,

[1] Dr Toulouse, *Émile Zola*, p. 166.

embitter his pain by the same means. Poets, Novelists and Artists in general complain very bitterly of the miseries of life, because they feel them more deeply than other people on account of their sensitiveness. In the Official Report of the suicide of a poet that occurred some four years ago, I find the following evidence given by a neighbour: "He always appeared to me to be very highly strung; he used often to talk to me in an animated strain of the miseries of life; but I merely looked upon his laments as the expression of a poetical spirit. Possessing senses more delicate than other men, being more sensitive, more imaginative, more impressionable, poets, artists, suffer much more keenly; this sensibility, which is one of the conditions of their talent, is the torment of their life unless they know how to moderate it by the help of judgment. Besides, yielding naturally to the pleasure of developing exclusively the faculty that is the cause of their superiority, they lose the proper equilibrium and harmony of the faculties. But directly a faculty becomes unduly exaggerated, it produces irritability and nervous troubles. "Whatever is excessive, is faulty," Lamartine says with remarkable scientific precision; "whatever is not harmony, is disorder in our organization. . . . If there existed equality, equilibrium, harmony among all their faculties, if sensitiveness were counterbalanced by reason, imagination by judgment, enthusiasm by good sense . . . these men strong and able in a single faculty would become strong in all, and their special superiority, which now constitutes their misfortune, would be changed into a universal superiority that would make the glory of humanity."[1]

There is in every man, and still more in every woman, a tendency to self-pity, to an inclination to accuse fortune of cruelty, to curse life,—which is indeed often exceedingly hard. Religion and spiritualistic Philosophy, schools of good sense as they are, preach resignation. "Blessed·are those who suffer," they repeat, "for one day they shall be

[1] Lamartine, *Entretien*, xcii., on Tasso.

consoled." But young men and women, who neglect religious consolations, to feed on poetry and romance of a melancholy type, quickly lose the faculty of resignation. These poems and tales flatter what Plato calls "the part of our soul, thirsty for tears and lamentations, that would fain surfeit itself with these." [1] This tearful part of our soul must be kept in check and not suffered to contemplate for too long the tears and lamentations of the poets, for " the sentiments of others infallibly become our own, and often encouraging and fortifying our sensibility with the sight of other men's sufferings, it is very difficult to moderate them in the case of our own." The melancholy poetry of the Nineteenth Century has killed resignation and largely increased the number of suicides. The best means whereby to moderate our griefs is not to heed them overmuch, to get out of ourselves, to try and think of something else, to avoid becoming absorbed in contemplation of the sad side of life and the reading of pessimistic poets who, as a matter of fact, while affecting in their writings a sombre despair, by no means despise the pleasures of life, like that gay pessimist Schopenhauer.

Maladies of imagination and sensibility being essentially infectious, it is obvious that young men and women, already so impressionable naturally, will become still more nervous when brought into contact with writers having an excess of these very qualities and constitutionally predisposed to neuropathic troubles. It is impossible to compose a book of History, Philosophy, Ethics, Literary Criticism, without a healthy judgment. But what is impossible to a Historian, Philosopher, Moralist or Critic, is possible for a Poet and a Novelist. Imagination and sensibility may be very highly developed while the judgment is exceedingly feeble, and inasmuch as imagination and sensibility are what Poet and Novelist need above all else, they may preserve their talent unimpaired, even when their reason has gone astray. In their case reason may falter without their talent being lessened. To name dead authors only, Tasso, Rousseau,

---

[1] Plato, *De Republica*, bk. x.

Edgar Allan Poe, Gérard de Nerval, Maupassant, have been noteworthy writers, when they were all the time sufferers from cerebral disorders. Atrophy of the reasoning faculties does not hinder a Poet's or Novelist's play of fancy or their keen sensibility, or prevent them from strongly impressing their readers by the exercise of these faculties. We may even go further, and say that with some writers the fancy seems to gain added vigour in proportion as the judgment weakens. In Rousseau's *Confessions*, in his *Dialogues*, in the *Rêveries d'un promeneur solitaire*, we find pages of entrancing charm side by side with others giving clear evidence of the author's mind being affected by the "mania of persecution." "There is no doubt the mental equilibrium of de Nerval," writes Théophile Gautier, "had long been disturbed, before any of us were aware of the fact. It was the more difficult to guess, as never was style more clear and limpid, in one word more reasonable, than that of Gérard. Even when disease had incontestably attacked his brain, he still preserved intact all the high qualities of his intellect. No fault, no error, no blunder betrayed the disorder of his mental faculties. To the last he remained impeccable. He was thus long able to hide a condition no one thought of suspecting. Dark sayings now and again would make us open our eyes in wonder, but these he would explain in a fashion so ingenious, learned and profound, that our admiration of his genius was only increased." Just as fever will give a keener vividness to the glance, a diseased nervous system gives increased brilliancy to the imagination and sensibility of the Novelist and enables him to exercise a more lively influence over his readers who are dazzled and stirred by his flights of fancy.

Seeing then how in Novelist and Poet talent may be allied with nervous disease or even mental aberration,[1]

---

[1] Among musicians nervous and cerebral troubles are even more frequent, because their talent has an even more sensuous origin. Schumann was attacked by lypemania (melancholy madness) and attempted suicide; Paganini died of general paralysis. Chopin was morbidly nervous. I myself knew personally the specialist in mental disease who attended Gounod.

we may readily understand how dangerous the reading of works of imagination, when it becomes exclusive, is for young people and women who read nothing else; the inordinate, sometimes morbid, sensibility of the Writer is communicated to his readers. For an educated man, who is acquainted with maladies of the mind, the morbid character of neuropathic Authors is obvious in their works; but youthful readers fail to notice this and readily fall under its pernicious influence, for it is through imagination and sensibility that literature acts upon them. A high-wrought writer works them to the same pitch of exaltation as himself. A fiery imagination fires them in turn. An emotional sensitiveness stirs the same emotions in them and inflames their fancy. Whence comes the prodigious influence Jean Jacques Rousseau has exerted over his innumerable host of readers, if not from the passionate character of his writings? " I could never write," he declared himself, " except by virtue of passion." Wisdom bores the majority of mankind, and good sense sends them to sleep, while paradox and passion enchant them.

Under the influence of Rousseau and his disciples Literature has become *passionate*. With a large number of Romance-writers and Poets, to think is to feel, to write is to note down sensations; like Byron's Manfred, they think to enlarge the domain of their intellect by increasing the rage of their sensations, declaring with him, " a new sensation is revealed to me, it has enlarged the domain of my thoughts." George Sand, copying Manfred, makes Lélia say, " I was ever increasing my powers from day to day, and heightening my sensibility beyond measure." In the Seventeenth and even in the Eighteenth Century, writers formed collections of thoughts, maxims, reflections; Pascal composed his *Pensées*, La Rochefoucauld his *Maximes*, La Bruyère his *Caractères*, Vauvenargues his *Réflexions et Maximes*, Duclos his *Considérations sur les mœurs*. Nowadays it is collections of sensations that are published. Novels, poems are but analyses of sensations; *meditations* are quite out of fashion. With the one exception of M. Sully-Prud'homme, who composes philosophical poems, thinkers are *raræ aves* among Poets. Works of literary Criticism, books of Travel and even of History, are nothing now but books of impressions, sensations. Thus we find such titles as *Idées et Sensations* by the brothers de Goncourt, *Sensations d'histoire* by Barbey d'Aurévilly, *Sensations d'Oxford, Sensations d'Italie* by P. Bourget, *Sensations de littérature et d'art* by Byvanck. A critic, who nevertheless possesses the gift of moral perspicacity and might well carry on the tradition of our great Moralists, M. Jules Lemaître, yielding to the fashion of the day, gives us his *Impressions de Théâtre*. It seems as though the part of the Writer is no longer to set men thinking but feeling. It is no longer to reason he addresses himself, but to the senses and imagination. Sensation takes the place of sentiment, and fancy of reason. Literature becomes painting, music, photography. "I would have described Sodom very willingly and the Tower of Babel with enthusiasm," says Théophile Gautier. "I am not working for the "prix Montyon" of virtue, and my brain performs to the best of its ability its function of "dark room."[1] Novelists and Poets are ready to describe all sensations, and particularly those of physical love and smell!

Succeeding *impressionist* literature, we have *impressionist* painting, not to mention *impressionist* justice among juries and *impressionist* politics among deputies. The *sensations of a juryman* have been written already, and there is nothing to prevent the *sensations of a deputy* being issued before long, for just as the modern jury bases its verdict on the *impressions* of the trial, the Chamber keeps Ministers in office or turns them out according to the *impressions* of the sitting. Authors, painters, jurymen and deputies, all blindly follow their impressions without ever checking them by reason. Paris has grown as impressionable and hypersensitive as a nervous woman. With many people who call themselves Christians, religious sentiment itself is

---

[1] *Th. Gautier*, by E. Bergerat.

only a craving for religious emotion, and even some formal apologies for Christianity consist rather of a series of æsthetic and mystical impressions than of arguments and reasons.

To augment their sensibility, we see writers resort to drink as a stimulant. This method had already been tried in Antiquity. " The poet Æschylus," Plutarch says, " used to compose his tragedies by the help of drink, when he was sufficiently warmed with wine. And Lampias our grandfather always showed himself more eloquent, incisive and fertile in invention after drinking."[1] To excite their faculties, novel writers and poets of our own day have had recourse not to wine only, but to alcohol, absinthe, opium or hashish. Hoffman had hallucinations, which he systematically provoked by stimulants, and which helped him to write his *Contes fantastiques.* " His poetry was a disease," Heine said of him ; and Heine himself was a neuropathic subject and suffered from locomotor ataxy. Edgar Allan Poe used to drink to rouse his imagination, and arrive at the visions and hallucinations he turned to account in writing his *Tales of Mystery.* He was picked up in the street suffering from *delirium tremens,* and carried to a hospital, where he died. Baudelaire who took him as his model and translated some of his works, sought inspiration in opium and hashish, and died of general paralysis. In 1845, the " Club of Hashish-eaters " (" Le Club des Haschidins ") was founded in Paris, frequented by literary men in search of hallucinations. Dr. Maurice de Fleury, who knew Guy de Maupassant personally, tells us that the famous Novelist in question had for years given himself up to the abuse of artificial stimulants of thought, whereas he of all men ought to have refrained from such things, having several insane persons among his ancestors in the direct line.[2] The Doctor having complimented him on the talent he had displayed in the delineation of

[1] Plutarch, *Table-Talk.*
[2] Maurice de Fleury, *Introduction à la médecine de l'esprit,* p. 138. F. Alcan, Paris.

delight! To be the object of a young man's affection, a young man elegant and high-born like a hero of romance, becomes the longing of novel-reading workgirls as much as it is of society young ladies. Their thoughts turn away from the working-man who might marry them, because of his dirty clothes, his horny hands and his face blackened by the grime and coal dust of the factory. Novels create in these poor girls a romantic, nonsensical state of mind that is their undoing, for they never say anything of the beauty of family life, of household joys, and the happiness of working together for a common end ; instead of throwing a halo of poetry over the poor and toiling folk of humble life, writers (excepting Coppée and René Bazin) prefer to idealize the follies of idle libertines of the great world. Seduction and suicide are the end of these silly dreams of love and luxury and pleasure.

If the number of suicides has so largely increased as it has in the last hundred years, this is in great part due to the fact that the number of novel-readers has been much augmented. In former days Novelists wrote for a small number of readers. Now Novels circulate everywhere, in the work-room as much as in the drawing-room, in the garret no less than in the boudoir. I have quite lately read in the Official Report of a case of suicide how an old woman wishing to leave a remembrance to a neighbour, made her a present, before proceeding to kill herself by means of charcoal fumes, of a big bundle of newspaper novels for her daughter. A fine present truly! I heard the other day a peasant woman say to her husband, who was going to the market town, " Bring me back *Crime d'amour* " (" A Crime of Love "). To read her *feuilleton* the cook lets the joint burn, the lady's-maid neglects her ironing, the housewife forgets her duties. Year by year, and month by month, we see hundreds, thousands of new Novels published, while the old ones are re-edited. No Newspaper is without its *feuilleton*, no Review but has its Serial, and God knows there are enough Newspapers and Reviews. The *feuilleton* is what makes the success of the paper, and the Serial Story that sells the Review. There are even some Newspapers and Reviews that publish several *feuilletons* and several Serials running concurrently.

It is a well-known fact that suicide is much more uncommon in the country than in towns. One cause of this difference arises from the circumstance that country women read few Novels, while women in the large towns read a great many. In a Report addressed to the Minister of the Interior, the Préfet of the Department du Léman states that in 1812 "melancholia is much more common at Geneva than anywhere else" in Switzerland, and assigns as the chief cause of this the excessive reading of romances which Jean Jacques Rousseau had brought into fashion.[1] Refusing to work for the Montyon prize of virtue, modern Novelists are working for the Morgue. In their eagerness to find subjects for picturesque description everywhere, they have written up and embellished everything, adultery, profligacy, drunkenness, low life, seduction, suicide, crime and amorous passion ; everything has been idealized and made to look poetical,—except good health, hard work, conjugal love and family affection.

While admitting that *Werther* had been the determining cause of a great number of suicides, Goethe maintained it was not right to make the writer responsible "because one of his works, misunderstood by narrow intellects, has, when the worst is said, purged the world of a dozen or so fools and rascals, incapable of anything better than extinguishing altogether the feeble remains of their wretched light."[2] This Olympian scorn for the readers of *Werther* who have put an end to themselves seems to me far from being a satisfactory or sufficient answer. In the first place, suicide is not always a mark of folly and weak-mindedness, seeing that Chateaubriand, Lamartine, George Sand and Goethe himself, all made attempts at suicide. Besides, if it were permitted to Writers to purge the world of narrow intellects and extinguish the light of life in scantily

---

[1] *La folie de J. J. Rousseau*, by Dr Chatelain, p. 151.
[2] *Entretien de Goethe et d'Eckermann*, p. 267.

Horace, Cicero, Seneca, Tacitus, with the commentaries of MM. Boissier, Patin, Gréard, Berger, Nisard, Martha, and you will be surprised at the pleasure and profit you will derive from the task. If as the result of some disappointment in love, the idea of suicide crosses your mind, remember how a woman, George Sand, cured herself of the temptation to suicide that possessed her by a perusal of the Greek and Latin Classics.

Love the Poets, but those only who have given more heed to loftiness and correctness of thought than to sonority of words and splendour of imagery; prefer gold to tinsel. Reject erotic and mystic verse; prefer that which elevates the soul, philosophical and religious poetry. Never forget that the greatest poets of France are still those of the Seventeenth Century, Corneille, Racine, Molière and La Fontaine; read them, re-read them, they are never wearisome. But do not read without due pre-caution the pessimistic poets and novelists of the Nineteenth Century, who endowed with an abnormal sensitiveness and a morbid imagination, feel too vividly the sadness and sorrows of life and express their dismal convictions with a heart-rending emphasis that kills all proper resignation. To read their despairing outcries makes life a vale of tears. To enjoy life, or at worst to endure it, a literature that inspires hope and courage is indispensable.

Do not despise the Moralists. I know they are not generally appreciated at your age, and are reserved to be read in old age. But never be frightened at their grave title of Moralists; you will find their works full of charm, you will not experience a single instant of weariness with Montaigne, Pascal, La Bruyère, La Rochefoucauld, Vauvenargues, Joubert. Montaigne is as delightful as Plutarch, Pascal is heart-stirring, La Bruyère entrancing, Joubert charming. Among contemporaries, you have literary critics, who are at bottom moralists full of wit and good sense, D. Nisard, Saint-Marc Girardin, Bersot, that tender heart and character of antique mould, Caro so odiously vilified, Jules Lemaître, Brunetière.

Read also the Historians, who are almost all men of weighty and judicious intellect. What marvellously balanced geniuses,—Tacitus, Bossuet, Montesquieu! History possesses the merit of taking us out of ourselves, making us forget our private griefs, carrying us into the mighty past, interesting us in the sufferings and the advances of humanity.

In the society of these chosen spirits you will run no risk of catching the "disease of the century"; you will find them a tonic to reason and will. They too have known sadness in its nobler aspects; they too have felt pity for the sufferings of humanity and above all for its moral infirmities; they too, in spite of their religious faith or philosophic creed, were terrified by the awful mysteries of life. What weight have the declamatory outcries of Werther and René, tormented as they were by sexual craving, beside the melancholy utterances of Pascal and Jouffroy? Who has felt tenderer pity for the sufferers of the lonely and poor than Racine and Fénélon, who exposed themselves to disgrace in order to draw Louis XIV.'s attention to them? Who has had more compassion for animals than La Fontaine, and who has better appreciated the charm of solitude? These great men, being men of sense, did not rise in revolt against God, because He has made life so short and so full of wretchedness. If they had love disappointments, they did not turn their thoughts to suicide, like those melancholy, love-sick beings who blow out their brains when they fail to seduce their friend's wife; they realized there are sufferings more noble and more poignant than any due to a woman's indifference or the unsatisfied cravings of passion:

> "Les beaux chagrins que les chagrins d'amour,
> Nous passons tous par là, c'est l'affaire d'un jour." [1]

Do not take too seriously the melancholy of our modern poets and novelists; often it is more literary than real, the

[1] "Oh! a fine sorrow truly,—disappointed love! Why, we all go through it; 'tis the affair of a day." Victor Hugo, *Ruy-Blas*.

less, because some organisms have made a victorious resistance to their attacks.   Similarly some minds, more sensible than others, resist the perusal of *Werther*, of *René*, of the Plays and Novels that defend suicide ; but we cannot therefore declare these books to be innocuous.   I believe I have proved by incontestable evidence that they have actually determined, among readers predisposed to succumb to their teaching, no small number of self-sought deaths.

CHAPTER XI.

CRIME DETERMINED BY PASSION, AND THE CONTAGION OF NOVELS OF PASSION AS AFFECTING IT.

" Songeons à cette épouvautable communication de crimes qui existe entre les hommes, complicité, conseil, *exemple, approbation,* mots terribles qu'il faudrait méditer sans cesse. . . . Où sont les bornes de la responsabilité ? " [1]—T. DE MAISTRE.

(Soirées de Saint-Pétersbourg, 3ᵉ édition.)

WHEN in 1848 scenes of Revolution were being re-enacted in Paris, a Historian, looking on at a parody of a Revolutionary procession defiling past, exclaimed : " Look ! my History of the Great Revolution passing before my eyes." Investigating as a Magistrate the motives of crimes of passion, I have in the same way frequently had occasion to observe how these crimes are imitations of Romances, nothing more nor less in fact than Literature in action.

In August 1881, the Assize Court of the Seine adjudicated on the case of a young man, Bernard by name, whose mother was "concièrge" to M. L——, a member of the French Academy ; the individual in question, whose head was turned by Novel reading, had tried to penetrate at night into the room of Mlle. D——, his master's granddaughter, to kiss her in her sleep. The girl's mother, who slept in the next room, awakened by the sound of his steps, got up, and was stabbed by Bernard with a knife in several places.

The questions of the *Juge d'instruction* elicited the fact that the young man was in the habit of lying in bed

1 " Only think of the appalling intercommunication of crimes existing between man and man,—complicity, advice, *example, approbation,* terrible words we should never cease to ponder over. . . . Where are the limits of responsibility ? "

part of the day reading Novels, accounts of crimes and famous trials. In his room were found the *Idiot*, the *Péché d'une Vierge*, the *Assassinat d'une fille*, the *Crime de la Comtesse*, the collected numbers of the *Tribunal illustré*, besides poems entitled *Visions, Peines de cœur, Renaissance de l'amour*.[1] Questioned about his favourite reading, he said he was very fond of love stories. It was shown that he had a great repugnance for manual labour of all kinds, and that when he was not reading Novels, he would do nothing but talk about the stage, actresses and so forth, or enlarge on the love he felt for Mlle. D—— During the preceding year he had stolen a petticoat belonging to the child and had carried it with him to his sleeping room. Bernard was not recognized by Mme. D—— at the moment of his attempt, but was driven subsequently to confess his guilt, which however he tried to account for by saying he had done what he had in a fit of somnambulism, urged on by an irresistible impulse. This statement was found to be untrue ; he had never been a somnambulist, though he described exactly the phenomena of sleepwalking. "I had read all about it in my books," he told Dr. Lassègue, who examined him and found him to possess a highly nervous temperament, an intellect at once subtle and exceedingly weak, and a morbidly excitable imagination. It is on suchlike nervous temperaments, combining a too excitable imagination with weak powers of mind, that romantic books make a deep impression. And many children and many young people display this type of physical and moral organization.

In 1886 the Assize Court of the Pas-de-Calais had to deal with two young men, belonging to a well-to-do peasant family of that Department, Henri and Clément Muchembled by name. His imagination fired by romantic reading, Clément fell violently in love with a girl of the neighbourhood of his own age. Having quarrelled with her, he made up his mind to punish her and took his

---

[1] *The Idiot, A Maiden's Sin, A Courtesan's Murder, The Countess's Crime, Illustrated Police News, Visions, Pangs of the Heart, Renaissance of Love.*

cousin Henri into his confidence. The two youths, who had read a great many novels and used to call each other by the names of *Flying Stag* and *Great Serpent*, borrowed from Fennimore Cooper's stories, determined to murder the girl and then start for America, the land of *The Last of the Mohicans*. They bought big knives, which they wore for several days in leather sheaths, very proud, they declared, at feeling themselves armed. Surprising the poor girl in a wood, they stabbed her with their knives in seventeen places.

Examination brought out the fact that before starting for the ambuscade they had prepared, the lads had drawn up under the title of *A Terrible Drama* an account of the crime they were about to commit; in it they described themselves as victims to melancholy, weary of life and disgusted with the world, and after recounting the girl's murder, they proceeded to describe their own suicide.

In July 1881, the Assize Court of the Department of the Seine had before it a youth named Lemaître, fifteen years of age, who had murdered a little boy of six. He had taken him up into his bedroom, tied his hands behind his back, thrown him full length on the bed, then cut his throat and opened his abdomen. At first blush this crime seems the act of a madman; but Drs. Motet and Legrand du Saulle, who examined the youthful criminal, found no symptoms of mental derangement. Dr. Legrand du Saulle protested in his report against "the sort of literature that familiarizes the public with Crime and raises a kind of pedestal for those who appear before the Criminal Courts." The lad Lemaître had devoured this species of literature; of good abilities he had attracted notice at the Communal School by his quickness, but also by his conceit. He used to keep himself apart from his schoolfellows during play-time, and at night was for ever reading in his own room novels and dramas of the Criminal Courts. On leaving school, he ran loose in the streets and in places of ill repute; placed in various employments, he robbed his masters to buy novels and theatre tickets. The Judge

having asked him how he spent his days, he replied : " I
used to read a great deal, lying on my bed ; I went to the
theatre, where I saw the *Chevaliers du Brouillard* played.
My afternoons I used to spend in the Jardin des Plantes,
taking a book with me there, the *Dame de Montsoreau* or
the *Orphelins du Pont-Notre-Dame.*" [1] *The Judge :* "What
theatre used you to frequent ?—*The Prisoner :* " I took
stalls at the *Opéra Comique,* the *Ambigu* or the *Châtelet.*
I used always to choose the best seats."

When in prison, he asked "whether the Papers spoke
of him and if his photograph was on sale the same as
Menesclou's was." On his trial, he struck a theatrical
attitude, describing his crime without a trace of emotion,
unmoved and looking the spectators quietly in the face.
He said a Somnambulist had prophesied he would be
famous.

Penitent criminals very often confess that their fall was
due to bad books. A certain A——, son of a Captain in
the Custom-house service, who was condemned to death
for murder, said : " I want to tell young men the causes
that have undone me, to make them see how, going from
bad to worse, I have come at last to the foot of the
scaffold. . . . Youthful profligates, believe a dying man ;
I began like you by being merely a loose liver, but from
sin to sin I have become a murderer. Bad books have
been my ruin." Not a Governor or Chaplain of a gaol,
not a Magistrate, but has received similar avowals.

" It is the reading of novels more than anything else
that has brought me here," said the youth Ronat, who
murdered the forewoman at his place of employment. . . .
I had been warned of the harm these books might do
me, but I did not believe a word of it ; yet this was the
beginning of all my ruin. They made me see life as
something quite different to the reality ; I indulged in
altogether impossible fancies."

Lachaud who defended the murderer Tropmann, said in

---

[1] *The Knights of the Mist, The Lady of Montsoreau, The Orphans of the
Bridge of Notre Dame.*

the course of his speech in which he drew a sketch of the accused's character and examined into the motives of his crime: "His head was turned by bad books, a kind of reading highly injudicious and dangerous for him ; his preference was for dismal stories, crammed with calamities and where horror is piled on horror. He told a witness he loved to read the *Juif Errant* ("Wandering Jew") of Eugene Sue. Tropmann admitted to the Abbé Crozer that novel reading was at the bottom of his profound demoralization. "By dint of living in this imaginary world, he had lost all notion of justice and honour, and was fairly enamoured of those gallows-birds who regain the advantages of a virtuous and reputable existence by lavishing about them the fruits of a life of crime, and die in the odour of philanthropy after making a handsome income by the judicious use of knife and poison."[1]

In the Gouffé case, it was proved that novel reading of a certain kind had done much towards depraving the character of the girl Bompard.

Criminal Court stories giving an account of famous crimes are exceedingly popular ; they are published in *feuilleton* form by the small halfpenny Papers and penetrate to every corner of the country. Advertised by big, coloured posters representing a scene of murder or orgy, they familiarize the minds of children, girls and women with ideas and pictures it would be wiser to keep them in ignorance of. On every dead wall in Paris we see murdered men, tortured children, women taking part in scenes of wild revelry ; and these pictures one and all are engraved on the minds of the passers-by.

All who know the susceptibility of a child's brain to impressions and the powerful effect a moral shock may produce, must recognize that a lascivious picture may profoundly stir the imaginations of young people, and especially of girls at the period of puberty. I have drawn attention in the preceding chapter to the great influence exerted by the first books read ; still deeper is the mark

[1] *Souvenirs de la petite et de la grande Roquette*, vol. ii. p. 228.

of heart in preference to greatness of birth, but it is not
so wise to imagine a good heart is more likely to be found
in a servant-girl than in a young lady of birth and breeding.
Novelists are merely misleading their readers' judgment
when they advise young men to look for a wife in the
kitchen, and girls to choose their fiancé from the stable
or the workroom. Already in *Astrée* we have seen great
ladies accepting the love of their inferiors. "How,
Madam," says Léonide to Galatée, "should you ever love
a shepherd? Do you not remember who you are?"—
"Oh! yes, Léonide, I remember," she returns, "but you
must also know that shepherds are men as much as Druids
or Knights." If we find dependents lifting their eyes to
their masters' daughters and the latter not scandalized by
the audacity of the "earth-worm in love with a star," it
is often to the reading of romantic literature we must
attribute the fascination. At the trial, the presiding Judge
said, addressing Mlle. Lemoine: "You used to read a
great many novels?"—*The accused:* "Yes! sometimes,
but without my mother's knowledge." *The Judge:* "You
told the *Juge d'instruction* your mother did know."—
The accused: "Oh! no; she knew I was in the habit of
reading stories appearing as *feuilletons* in the papers, but
I always hid the others from her." Urged to declare how
she had received her coachman's offers of love, she replied:
"F—— is the first man who ever spoke words of love
to me; I was unfortunate enough to believe him, and
abandoned myself to him. . . . Afterwards, I was divided
between shame at having sacrificed my honour to a
servant and the happiness of having raised to my own
level a man who, according to social conventions, was in
an inferior position to mine." Becoming pregnant, she
was not at all affected by the scandal of the thing, hoping
to force her mother to consent to the wished-for marriage
with the coachman. "This was the only means," she said,
"of bringing my romance to a fitting termination. I
wished to make a man happy, as my mother had made
my father." However, her mother on discovering her

daughter's condition, dismissed the coachman, and after vain attempts to bring about abortion, ended by killing the child before birth.

The "Procureur Général," who prosecuted, and M. Lachaud who was Counsel for the defence, were agreed as to the fact that the young woman had been ruined by reading novels. "I see with regret," the former declared, "how the Drama and the Novel are making themselves felt in judicial cases." In a recent trial at the Assize Court at Paris there was another girl, of mournful celebrity, who had to defend herself at one and the same time against a crime and a passion described as being unbridled. To prove the reality of the latter, and doubtless in the hope of interesting and softening the Court, her letters were read aloud, their ardent style painting the force of this irresistible passion. Well! these passionate epistles were not the girl's own at all; she had copied them in the most barefaced way from a not over-decorous Play of the period. Like her predecessor, Angelina Lemoine plagiarised, in order to lend a halo of poetry to her infatuation.

I have often noted in criminal proceedings how seducers are in the habit of lending novels to girls they are trying to lead astray, and how they very soon attain their ends by this means. On August 24th, 1860, the Assize Court of the Bouches-du-Rhône tried for abduction of a girl under age, a certain Treuil,- a commercial traveller, a married man of thirty-seven, who had enticed from her home a girl belonging to a highly respectable family of Marseilles. To pave the way to seduction, the man had made her read a number of trashy novels.—Vitalis, a retired bookseller, who was condemned to death and executed at Marseilles, was ruined himself (he admitted as much) and had ruined his accomplice, Marie Boyer, by persistent reading of novels. In Marie Boyer's bedroom were found a host of novels, conspicuous among the number being *Vierges folles*, *Mlle. de Maupin*, *Mœurs galantes de Marseilles*.

is no feeling we can experience without a sort of recollection of having read about it somewhere; all the veils of the heart have been rent asunder. The Ancients would never have made their soul in this way a theme for fiction; they kept it as a sanctuary into which even their own eyes would have feared to pry." [1] La Fontaine, by way of apologising for the light-heartedness of his tales, said very justly : " If there is anything in our writings likely to make a deep impression on men's minds, this is certainly not the light-hearted gaiety of these tales, which only touches the surface of things. I should be much more afraid of a gentle melancholy, into which the most chaste and modest of romances are likely enough to plunge us, and which goes far towards paving the way for love." [2]

It was the reading of a Tale of Romance that proved the undoing of Francesca da Rimini. " If you so greatly desire," she says in the *Inferno*, " to learn what was the first root of our love, we were one day reading by way of pastime the adventures of Lancelot and how he was smitten with love; we were alone and quite without distrust. Again and again the words made our eyes encounter and our faces change colour. . . . The book and he who wrote it were for us another Galahad (pandar); that day we read no more."—It was by reading sentimental books with Charlotte that Werther strove to touch her heart. " Ah! my friend," writes Werther . . . " how many times in the middle of some passage in an enthralling book have our hearts, Lotta's and mine, understood each other ! " It was while reading with Werther some of Ossian's songs that Charlotte came very near giving herself to him, like Francesca da Rimini in *Dante*. Their hearts were melted ; Werther interrupted the reading and threw down the·book, then seized Lotta's hand and bathed it in tears. Lotta rested her head on the other arm and covered her eyes with her handkerchief; the agitation of both was extreme. They felt their own wretchedness in the hero's destiny,

---

[1] Mme. de Staël, *De l'Allemagne*, 2nd Part, ch. xxviii.
[2] La Fontaine, Preface to the second edition of the *Contes*.

they felt it with one heart, and their tears intermingled.
. . . Their burning cheeks touched.   The whole world
disappeared from their eyes ; he took her in his arms and
pressed her to his heart. . . ."   Charlotte had strength
of mind enough to recover herself, and running to her
room barricaded the door ;—but she was only just in
time.

Old Brantôme, not an author likely to be suspected of
prudery, says in his *Vies des dames galantes*, that he would
be a very rich man, if only he had as many hundreds of
crowns " as there be fair women, whether of the great
world or ladies of religion, the which the reading of
Amadis hath undone."   He goes on : " How many young
maids in the schoolroom have been undone by reading this
same tale (of Teiresias) I have but now related, and that
of Biblis, of Conus, and many more of like sort writ in the
Metamorphoses of Ovid."

Who can tell the number of imitators fathered by the
history of Abelard and Heloïse?   Even in their lifetime
young lovers took them as a model ; " our follies," writes
Abelard to Heloïse, " have penetrated even to the holiest
places ; our sin has scandalized a whole kingdom, the tale
of it is read and delighted in.   We are the consolation of
young folk that go astray as we did, and whoso offends
after us, deems his offence so much the less."

The three Latin poets who have applied their genius to
the delineation of love, Ovid, Catullus and Propertius, themselves recognize the danger inherent in their erotic strains.
"Touch not the poets of love," Ovid says in the *Remedia
Amoris*! . . .   Who can read unscathed your verses,
Tibullus, or yours, sweet singer whom your fair Cynthia
alone inspired."—Catullus is himself conscious of the
aphrodisiac effects his verses possess : " My verses," he
says, " are spicy and gay, they stir desire."   Propertius in
his Sixth Elegy devotes to the infernal gods the man who
first filled Roman homes with obscene paintings.

Forgetting how powerful is the impulse to imitation
found among young men and women, particularly in

but under the reign of Romanticism it became a disgrace
to be well and hearty. The canons of Romantic literature
decreed that a woman should be pale, "pale as a fair
evening of Autumn," while for a young man it was poetical
to be as white as a consumptive. Either would have
blushed to show a fresh, rosy face.[1]

Fiction has repeatedly brought into fashion particular
modes of dress and particular colours. After *Werther*,
young men adopted the sky-blue coat and yellow breeches
the hero of Goethe's story wore the first time he danced
with Lotta. Byron, liking to have his neck free, wore no
cravat, or if he did left it untied ; and his devoted admirers
followed suit. After d'Urfé, pale green[2] became the rage.
George Sand made olive-green universally admired, the
colour she gave to a Creole beauty in one of her Novels.

If the hero of the Novel a young girl reads has blonde
hair, she longs for a fair husband ; if he is dark, she prefers
a dark man. Mme. Laffarge tells us in her Memoirs how,
after reading a Novel as a young girl the hero of which was
a deaf-mute, she had been silly enough to long to be loved
by a deaf mute. "A story written with considerable
feeling and talent," she says, "impressed me vividly. In
this interesting work, the hero Anatole follows the
woman he loves wherever she goes, saves her life, surrounds
her with the tenderest marks of a passionate affection,
writes to her, gets her to love him, without making an
attempt to come near her. At the end of five or six
hundred pages, after Anatole has won the adoration not
only of the object of his affections, but of all his fair
readers as well, he is discovered to be deaf and dumb."
While she was reading the Novel in question, Mme.
Laffarge, a girl at the time, used to be followed in her
walks by a mysterious young man, who only succeeded
in expressing his admiration at a distance by means of

---

[1] Ovid gave the same advice long ago in his *Ars Amoris* ! "Palleat omnis
amans," he says,—"Every true lover should be pale."

[2] In French céladon, the name of the colour being derived from Céladon,
the sentimental swain who is the hero of *Astrée*.—(TRANSLATOR.)

burning glances ; very soon she found herself hoping this unknown lover would turn out a deaf-mute like Anatole, she longed for this infirmity and eagerly looked for traces of it in his face, his melancholy mien and sad eyes.

I quote this case to show to what a degree a girl may be impressed by romantic books. We can now readily understand how her mind must be stirred by romances where the lover is always handsome, amiable, witty, high-born, tender, passionate and elegant, while the poor husband is depicted in the blackest colours. While the lover has every good quality, every merit and every distinction, the husband is represented as plain, common-place, tiresome, always full of his work at providing the household expenses. All these flattering portraits of the lover, these grotesque caricatures of the husband, are a bad training for a girl in realizing the beauty of marriage and family life ; while they set the woman who is married but misunderstood by her husband dreaming of this ideal adorer, who will know how to appreciate her, if others do not, and console her for the vulgarities of a husband's affection. An ideal love with a high-born and distinguished adorer, one to match with a hero of romance, this is what she craves. She longs for such a lover, lets her curiosity play round him, and would fain know him in more than fancy. She is unfaithful in her thoughts, till she can become so in very deed and act.

In Novels love is the one and only business of all the characters ; so the fair readers of such books are shocked if their husband fails to spend all his time in adoring them and busies himself primarily about his proper business. At the least disappointment, on discovering the smallest defect in their husband, they conclude he is quite different from the ideal lover, a man quite incapable of a noble passion.

Tacitus, drawing a picture of Roman decadence under the Empire, described "the very Capitol burned by the hands of citizens, sacred things profaned, adultery in the noblest families." We too in France have seen the Hôtel de

Ville burned, not by the enemy, but by the hand of French citizens, we see sacred things profaned every day, family, country, army insulted, adultery spreading in all ranks of society. This increase of adultery I attribute very largely to the reading of countless novels, all defending adultery. By making adultery poetical, novels do what the tales of Mythology did in ancient times, sanctifying as they did the passions. In a Comedy of Terence, a young profligate encourages himself in vicious courses by the example of Jupiter seducing Danaë. "Why!" he exclaims, "what a mighty god did, should not I a weak mortal do? Yes! truly, I have done it, and with right goodwill." Adultery cannot be a crime, as it is only copying from divine beings. "What man," says Plato not without reason, "will not excuse himself the evil he has done, once he is persuaded the heroes do and have done the same things? . . . These reasons constrain us to abolish all these fictions, for fear they give young men too great a facility for doing wrong." Notwithstanding his admiration for Homer, Plato is obliged to allow that the description of Jupiter's amours is not of a kind to inspire young people with a wise moderation. Imitation of evil is a much more rapid process than that of good. Without holding themselves bound to imitate what is good, men make bad examples their warranty for imitating what is evil. "The example of Alexander the Great's chastity," Pascal says, "has never made so many men continent, as that of his drunkenness has made intemperate" It is no disgrace not to be as virtuous as he, while it seems excusable if we are not more vicious.

Inasmuch as Novelists write especially for young people and women (husbands and fathers having but little time for reading and preferring History to Romance), they always assign the contemptible rôle to these latter, to gratify their favourite audience. Parents are all Gérontes and Orgons, husbands all Sganarelles and George Dandins, ready-made dupes. In Novels every husband and father is a tyrant who is for safeguarding his wife against adultery or his daughter against seduction. When Saint-Preux, abusing the hospitality offered him and the confidence reposed in him, is waiting for his pupil in her bedroom to dishonour her, he thinks he hears a noise and fearing to see his enterprise fail exclaims: "Can it be your cruel father?" (*Letter* liv.) In the Preface to the *Nouvelle Heloïse*, Rousseau does not dissemble the fact that he wrote the Romance particularly for women, and he invites them all, respectable and disreputable alike, to read it. "This Collection," he says, "with its Gothic tone suits women better than books of Philosophy; it may even be useful to some who, in an ill-ordered life, have still preserved some love of honourable living." He admits a girl is undone if she reads a single page of this Novel, yet he encourages her to go on at once with its perusal; "as she has begun, she had better finish, she has no more risks to run."—Rousseau who professed that when he composed the *Nouvelle Heloïse* as a book for women, he was writing a work of morality, nevertheless acknowledges in his *Confessions* that its perusal had hardly tended to make them more moral. He declares that "women were so intoxicated by the book and its author, there were few of them, even in the highest circles, I could not have made a conquest of, if I had tried." On the publication of *Atala*, Chateaubriand was like Rousseau overwhelmed with feminine attentions and declarations of love.

Wives who torment their husbands with scenes of jealousy often derive their over-excitability from Novels depicting men unfaithful to the marriage vow; finding husbands deceiving their wives in books, they instantly rush to the conclusion their own is doing the like to them. In his book on *La Folie lucide* ("Lucid Madness"), Dr Trélat relates how a husband, complaining to him of the scenes of furious jealousy his wife used to indulge in, attributed this entirely to her novel reading propensities. "One fault I always had to find with her," the husband declared, "was finding novels lying about in every corner . . . these books unduly excited her imagination."—The same Dr. Trélat also gives instances where furious jealousy on the husband's side was awakened by novels describing the adultery of wives. The husband, naturally predisposed to jealousy, when he comes to read romances in which he finds the wife deceiving her husband, believes his fate to be the same. The Tales of Boccaccio and La Fontaine, which make bachelors laugh, often make husbands thoughtful and sad. One wife, whose husband had become furiously jealous, said that for two days running she had seen Boccaccio's Tales in her husband's hands and that he was for ever studying them.

By providing a stimulant to their sensibility and imagination, without providing any nourishment for reason, novels over-excite and enervate young readers, especially those of the weaker sex. They set them dreaming and prevent their thinking, carrying them away to the land of chimæras instead of developing their critical powers and correcting the want of exactitude and precision which so often characterizes them.

In his pamphlet dealing with the Chorinski trial, the famous specialist in mental disease, Morel (of Rouen) states that the accused, a brilliant young officer in the Austrian service, who poisoned his wife in complicity with the elegant Canoness Julia von Ebergegny, had debauched his mind by the reading of romances of passion. The Doctor, having gone to visit him in prison, the accused wanted to tell him the story of his life, which surpassed, he declared, anything he had ever read in novels of wild adventure, his favourite form of reading.

For a romantic writer like Jean Jacques Rousseau, who joined a most highly-strung imagination to a temperament of fire, and who, to use his own expression, "simply adored the sex," to write a Novel is only an indirect way of making love. In the same way for young people of either sex, at the age when love is the main preoccupation of the mind, to read a Novel is only another mode of the same thing. Novels intoxicate young people, because they set fair-faced, flattering phantoms dancing before their eyes, phantoms with brown hair or blonde, and eyes of black or blue.

I am ready to admit that Novel-reading is not exclusively the delight of young people and of women. "Beside a scanty fire and by a flickering light," says Chateaubriand, "sure of being undisturbed, we melted in pity over the fictitious woes of a Clarissa, a Clémentine, a Heloïse, a Cecilia. Novels are the sacred books of the unhappy and unfortunate; true, they feed us on illusions; but after all are these more numerous in them than in real life?" Bishop Huet of Avranches used to declare Paradise was without a doubt "reading a novel in a lounging chair." Saint Francis de Sales was extremely fond of d'Urfé's novels; Cousin the philosopher delighted in the perusal of those of Mlle. Scudéry. But there are Novels *and* Novels. The Fiction of to-day bears but little resemblance to that of the Seventeenth Century, which formed the delight of Bishop Huet and Saint Francis de Sales. Nor have their fair readers much in common with the women of the same century, who fed on Nicole and would have enjoyed putting Bourdaloue's sermons to steep, the better to assimilate them. Reading the romances of Mlle. Scudéry and Mme. de Lafayette was a pleasant and harmless enough amusement, so long as the fair readers' solid reason remained mistress of their imagination,—the "foolish virgin" of the establishment. The conditions are altered nowadays, when both in Novels and Life, imagination encroaches dangerously on reason.

The Literature of imagination has its *raison d'être*, provided always we do not limit our diet to it. Novel-reading is like dram-drinking, it is a liquor which taken in a small dose gives an agreeable fillip, but which on too frequent repetition produces intoxication and becomes a veritable poison. There are too many Novels; we are inundated with them. Those capable of reading them without risk have no time to read them at all, while those who would be doing better to read something else, read nothing but fiction. The majority of Novel-readers, male and female,

parents or what not, the pair belong to each other by a law of nature, by a right divine, spite of all human enactments and conventions." This right of love, and right of adultery, are allowed by Schopenhauer, as a consequence of the natural duty of reproduction. The German Philosopher argues that women are vaguely conscious that while betraying their duties towards the individual, they are the better fulfilling those they owe the species, which has rights of infinitely superior stringency.[1] A husband who revolts at his wife's unfaithfulness to him is merely an egoist selfishly preoccupied by his own paltry individual interests. But passion, representing the interest of the human species, is rightly paramount over the egoism of the husband. If onlookers at dramas of passion are so indulgent as they are towards amorous extravagances, this is because, Schopenhauer tells us, they feel that the destinies of the species take precedence of those of the individual.

Stendhal, repeating this sophistical argument of Chamfort's, writes : " A woman belongs of right to the man who loves her and whom she loves better than life itself." The right is conferred by Nature, and no social convention can abrogate it. Stendhal belongs to the sensualist school of the Eighteenth Century.[2]

Inspired by suchlike naturalistic theories, Michelet has claimed the right of love even for fishes,—their natural right to love before coming to the frying-pan : " Let them love,—and then come what may ! If we must kill them, kill them. But let them have lived first." [3]

Romanticism, notwithstanding all its lyrical aspirations, ends by coming to the same conclusions as Naturalism. It too, with pathetic accents glozing over a coarse sensual-

---

[1] Schopenhauer, *Méditations*. (French Translation, Alcan, Paris, pp. 103, 123.)

[2] Stendhal expresses his own true sentiments in *Le Rouge et le Noir* when he puts these words in Julien Sorel's mouth : " There is no such thing as natural right ; the word is nothing but a piece of old-fashioned foolishness. . . . Before law, there is no natural right whatever but the lion's strength or the need of the creature that is hungry, or cold,—in one word *need*, *necessity*."

[3] Michelet, *La Mer*, p. 341.

ity, appeals to the *right of love*, and even the *right of adultery*; it proclaims that passion must be obeyed, as being at once the voice of God and involved in the order of Nature, declaring "there can be nothing criminal, where sincere love finds place."[1]   The Abbé Prévost[2] began by making love a right; Rousseau constituted it a duty and a virtue; it was left to Romanticism to consecrate it a Religion. All these writers have persuaded women they may love without being blameworthy, that in doing so they are only following the Laws of Nature. Accordingly we find this excuse based on the "Laws of Nature," constantly recurring in the letters and in the mouths of adulteresses. Mme. Weiss, who deceived her husband and afterwards poisoned him, wrote to her lover: "Crimes against human laws I do not heed; it is only crimes against Nature that revolt me. I adore Nature!" The Abbé Grégoire states that the licentious clergy of the Eighteenth Century were not backward even at that date in invoking in the same way the Laws of Nature. Nature is the enemy of morality and the laws; it is to hold Nature in check that moral and social laws are made. And so Novels, which recognise no other rights but those of Love, are always urging their readers to follow the Laws of Nature.

The Ancients said: "There is a husband Fate reserves for each woman."[3]   Romanticism declares: "There is a sister-soul Providence reserves for each woman, and this sister-soul is seldom the husband's. If the woman finds it under the features of a lover, she belongs to him of right. 'Tis God Himself who commands love, brings lovers together, predestines them one for the other. Did not that Supreme Providence, that is everywhere, in spite of man's conventions, preside over the union of Benedict and Valentine?" If love runs low, if the heart is seized by another passion, again it is God that calls it to another vocation, and by consequence inconstancy is an act of

---

[1] George Sand, *Jacques.*   [2] Author of *Manon Lescaut.*
[3] Fragments of Euripides.

After all this sort of language is nothing new, it is Tartuffe's likewise, who uses the very same metaphors :

"J'aurai toujours pour vous, ô suave merveille,
Une dévotion à nulle autre pareille."[1]

Tartuffe prides himself on not copying mere worldly lovers :

"Dont la langue indiscrète, en qui l'on se confie,
Deshonore l'*autel*, où le cœur sacrifie."[2]

This religion of love has not only been celebrated by Poets and Romance writers, it has also been preached by a Historian, Michelet, by the Socialists, Fourier and Enfantin, and by a Philosopher, Renan. In his naturalistic and mystical style, Michelet makes woman at one and the same time a sick patient and an "altar," and love a "communion." "What is Woman," he asks, "if not our living temple, our sanctuary, our altar, on which burns the fire of God ? "—Fourier, similarly exalting love into a religion, regrets that the Philosophers have not established priests and pontiffs of this Cult.—Renan for his part writes, that we are wrong to lament the weakening of religious beliefs, for he says, beliefs change shape and we shall always have the religion of love. In this religion of love there are likewise sacraments, a communion, a priesthood. The lover of the *Abbesse de Jouarre* is represented as a messenger from Heaven, a priest ; if the nun repulses him, she is offending God; by remaining virtuous, she fails in nobility of conduct. "You will miss a woman's true greatness," they tell her, " . . . the true God will be angry with you, even if the monks' God is glad . . . proud virtue is a vice in a woman ;

---

[1] " I shall ever have for thee, thou sweet and tender marvel, a devotion like unto no other."

[2] "Whose indiscreet tongue, unworthy of its trust, dishonours the *altar*, where their heart makes *sacrifice*."—Molière would seem to have borrowed these expressions from Corneille, who says in *Théodore* (Act v.) :

"Et je n'ai pas moins qu'elle à souffrir d'un supplice
Qui profane l'autel où j'ai fait sacrifice."

—"And 'tis my lot no less than hers to suffer a punishment that profanes the altar where I have made sacrifice."

you think to enter into Eternity more nobly with your inflexible attitude ; a mistake, believe me ; you will be less noble." The Abbess yields to please God ; and her brother absolves her, with the words : "It was a Sacrament, and the most august of all, the mystery of that night, when you accepted his love an hour before dying."

This language, stranger than Tartuffe's, only makes a man of sense smile, but its effects are by no means harmless on the minds of young men and women ; by confusing love with virtue and piety, it warps their mind. But, as we know, perversion of heart is often the result of perversion of mind ; sophistries, clothed in brilliant phrases, are the most powerful agents of corruption. Two great Writers, who have disseminated many sophistries by their books, Jean Jacques Rousseau and George Sand, have themselves been the first to allow that Sophistry is often more dangerous to society than Crime, because it may be the father of an endless series of bad actions. In the *Nouvelle Heloïse*, Claire says to Julie : "I hate bad maxims even more than bad actions." [1] George Sand, deploring the faults into which her inordinate love of independence had dragged her, cried : " Cursed be the men and the books that have helped me on in this by their sophistries." [2]

If she was right in cursing the sophistries of other Writers who contributed to lead her astray, she would not have been far wrong in regretting likewise the sophistries she disseminated in her own Novels. I have already instanced several crimes, that of Dr. Bancal and that of Mlle. Lemoine amongst the number, that were in great part inspired by Novel reading. Who can tell the number of women who have fallen into adultery as the result of reading *Indiana, Jacques, Valentine, Lélia*? It is no squalid and disgraceful adultery that we read of in romantic Novels, but a proud adultery that walks with head erect and a picturesque aureole around the brow, trampling underfoot the narrow

---

[1] *La Nouvelle Heloïse*, 1st Part, Letter xl.—In Part 3, Letter xviii. is devoted to refuting the sophistries that are made to excuse adultery.

[2] *La veritable histoire d'Elle et Lui*, by M. de Lovenjoul.

This fatality of passion is at the bottom of George Sand's first novels. "What have I done here below either good or ill?" cries Stenio in *Lélia*. . . . "I have only obeyed the organization given me." If man is obliged to succumb to his organization, if he cannot resist passion, the fault is not in him; "the fault is God's, who allows humanity thus to go astray," says Lélia, who is a fatalist. Pretty nearly all the heroes of romance are the same. So soon as Nature speaks, they haste to hear her voice, because they know they cannot do otherwise; and in this they are only yielding to the irresistible impulses of heart and temperament.

In the Novels of Stendhal, Balzac, Mérimée, Flaubert, Dumas *fils*, Zola, the same mischievous doctrine of fatality is found. According to these authors, there is nothing beyond certain physiological fatalities; adultery is nothing more nor less than a matter of opportunity, of circumstance, of a sofa handy! Heart, and still more temperament, have sudden calls, which nullify at once all moral responsibility. The heroes of romance are victims of their nerves, of the current of their blood; they are no longer their own men, they are the slaves of the passion that devours them and the appetites that master them. Fatality crushes them to the earth; passion is with them as irresistible as the cravings of hunger and thirst. In these sensual and determinist Novels, the greatest weaknesses are precipitated by the smallest physical causes, by a storm, by an excess of electricity in the atmosphere, by penetrating odours. Odours, perfumes! what a part they play in feminine frailty! The analysis and influence of odours fill a large place in tne poems of Baudelaire and the Novels of Zola. Baudelaire is the Poet, Zola the Novelist, of sensations of smell. Nor is it always the delicate perfumes only that are made the subject of their analysis.

Stendhal explains mankind exclusively by physiology. His philosophy is that of Helvetius, d'Holbach, La Mettrie, who derived all the faculties from sensation. For him soul is temperament; "there is no such thing as morality."

In his eyes Free Will is a contradiction, is an absurdity.[1] The aim of life is the cultivation of sensations, and Love itself is merely one of these. When Mlle. de la Mole, in *Rouge et Noir*, takes count of the love she feels for Julien, what does she find in it? why! a group of sensations! " I have the bliss to be in love, she said to herself one day, with a transport of incredible joy; I am in love, in love, no doubt of it! At my age, where should a girl, young, pretty and clever, find *sensations*, if not in Love?"[2]—"In all her life, never had a sensation so purely delightful, so deeply moving, stirred Mme. de Rénal."—Julien looks upon his love for Mlle. de Mole simply as a means of tasting the keenest pleasures, which the most elegant civilization has united in her person.—Sensualist to the core, Stendhal is a determinist as well. According to him, women are incapable of virtue; the resistance they offer is only a farce; when they make laments at having been ravished, it is a lying pretence. How many young men, corrupted by these sophistries, which are psychological mistakes, have endeavoured to put in practice this theory of seduction, and have ended as criminals! Stendhal may say what he pleases, but there are women who resist so firmly that they will let themselves be murdered rather than yield. Such women are met with even among savages.[3] I have seen cases myself where a young girl, who had been violated, fainted away with grief and shame. It is impossible to recount all the cases of rape I have become acquainted with as a Magistrate; I will content myself with quoting two. A girl of eighteen, having gone on board ship at Gaëta to cross to Marseilles, was ravished on the voyage by the Mate. To save his comrade, the Captain made the sailors all swear to say nothing, and the girl herself not to divulge the violence that had been offered her.—In another case, a lady, who had been the

[1] *De l'amour*, ch. v.—See also *L'Art et la vie de Stendhal*, p. 406.
[2] *Le Rouge et le noir*, ch. xii.
[3] Livingstone, *Exploration of the Zambesi*, p. 153. Cameron, *Across Africa*, p. 58.

victim of an attempt at rape, conceived so fierce a passion of indignation against her assailant, that she killed him some days afterwards.—This reminds me of the heroism of the wife of a Gallic chief, who was ravished by a Roman Centurion, and had him murdered in consequence; before embracing her husband, she threw down the Centurion's head at his feet.[1] Women resist so stoutly, that it is shown by judicial investigation that their bodies are covered with bruises and injuries. Indeed prisoners' charged with rape sometimes admit the vigorous resistance they have encountered. History is full of stories of women who have killed themselves to escape violation or shame.

The influence exerted by Stendhal on contemporary Literature and public Morality has been considerable and pernicious; and it still continues. Balzac, Mérimée, Taine, Bourget, Zola[2] have all been bitten by this Writer's psychology, and have copied from his Novels. M. Bourget has borrowed of him the expression " state of soul," which occurs so frequently in his books. Nevertheless, in spite of his admiration for the Author, he admits freely he has known *Le Rouge et le Noir* " produce under certain circumstances in the brains of young people an incurable intoxication."[3] He has recovered himself, but how many other readers have remained fatally affected, unable to eliminate from their minds the poison of suchlike sophistries! Among the causes leading to the degradation of mind and heart in Robert Greslou, Bourget specially mentions the influence of this book *Rouge et Noir*.

Balzac's Novels, like Stendhal's, are sensualistic and determinist. He too has put a great deal of bad physi-

---

[1] The incident is related by Livy, lxxxviii. § 24, and by Valerius Maximus, lvi. ch. i. No. 2.

[2] Balzac said, speaking of the *Chartreuse de Parme*, that it was a book in which the sublime is conspicuous on every page. Stendhal was the master of Mérimée, who wrote a highly appreciative notice of him. Taine, who borrowed from Stendhal his theory of heredity, and environment in place and time, calls him " the greatest psychologist of the present and of preceding centuries."—" He is our father, the father of all of us, like Balzac," Zola writes.

[3] Bourget, *Essais de psychologie contemporaine*, p. 309.

ology into his books. In his *Physiologie du Mariage*, he draws his inspiration from Broussais and recommends the use of mustard-plasters and the application of leeches to make women virtuous. If Balzac really supposes female virtue depends on the application of leeches, it follows he believes women not to possess Free Will.[1]

A similar vein of sensualistic and determinist philosophy is found in Mérimée. It is his belief in the fatality of passion and temperament that makes him relate with cool irony the outbreaks of ferocity and lubricity of the human animal.

Belonging to a family of doctors, Flaubert explains the moral solely and entirely by the physical ; he discredits the possibility of human beings reacting effectively against physiological influences. The heroes and heroines of his Novels are mere playthings of physiological necessity.

A disciple and a nephew of Flaubert, Guy de Maupassant, is likewise a believer in physiological fatality. The love he describes in his Novels is primarily physical love ; and he accounts for female adultery on purely physiological grounds.

Again it is mankind from the physiological side that M. Zola studies in his books. His ideas are revealed in the very titles of some of these. In the *Bête Humaine*, he sits at the feet of Dr. Lombroso. In the *Rungon-Macquart* series, he is inspired by Dr. Prosper Lucas, the author of a very remarkable treatise on heredity. Only, whereas Dr. Lucas reconciles heredity with free will, Zola rejects the latter doctrine altogether.[2] Considered exclusively from the physiological point of view, men and women cease to be moral beings, free and responsible ; they are mere *animals, male and female*, with their *young ones*. And these very words are continually occurring in the pages of the great Naturalistic Novelist.

It may cause some surprise if I include George Sand

---

[1] *Physiologie du Mariage*, p. 129.

[2] In *Cosmopolis*, M. Bourget also exaggerates the part played by heredity in suicide, believing that even the form it takes is hereditary (p. 449).

among Novelists who believe in the fatality of passion
and the all-powerful influence of physiological inheritance.
Still, when she is recounting her frailties in the *Mémoires
de ma vie*, she finds excuses for her conduct in heredity,
telling us of her mother's lapses.

It might be thought that the grave problem of moral
freedom and the reconciliation of its existence with physiological heredity should not intrude in these light Works,
written as they are merely to amuse. But, seeing how the
ideas and preoccupations of a period penetrate everywhere, and that the problem of Free Will and Heredity
very largely arrests the attention of contemporary society,
we find this most serious, complicated and important subject treated in Novels, on the Stage, even in Newspapers,
and by no means always by the most competent hands.

Alexandre Dumas *fils*, who pays much attention to
moral and social questions, is too fond of seeking their
solution in physiology; he admits as much in his Preface
to *L'Ami des femmes*. Not a few of his books are dedicated to doctors. He has small belief in Free Will; he
thinks that virtue and vice are in the blood and that
education can do nothing against physiological fatality.
In *L'Affaire Clémenceau*, the hero of the story claims to
find justification in the transmission of a blood naturally
inclined to sensual love. Dumas is convinced that beings
exist of fatally perverse tendencies, whom society should
"kill in a corner like mad dogs." The Court a shambles,
the judge a butcher, the brand of justice a pole-axe, this is
the determinist theory in matters of Criminal Law. He
delights in exhibiting the animal side in men (*Visite de
noces*), and in women (*La Femme de Claude*). Read the
portrait he draws of the sensual woman, you might
imagine yourself reading that of the female criminal by
Dr. Lombroso. He loves to strip woman bare, to wash
her dirty linen in public, to show the seamy side of her
nature, to account physiologically for Love, Jealousy and
Adultery. He concludes his delineation of the sensual
woman with the words, "Here we have the animal!"

Physiology has led the Novelists of the Naturalistic School to Pathology, the portrayal of alcoholic dementia, epilepsy, and hysteria,—all of them studies of intense interest, when carried out by competent scientific men, such as Drs. Charcot, Magnan, Féré, Motet, Brouardel, Garnier, Dejerine, Ballet, Brissaud, etc., but entirely without scientific value, when pursued in fanciful tales of fiction, apart from clinical or any other form of direct observation of the patients. But if these claims of the Novel to treat of Physiology and Pathology are useless to Science, they may easily disturb readers' consciences, by representing exceptions as the general rule, and by setting forth as scientific truths what are nothing more than hypotheses rejected by the best qualified savants. Thus Dr. Lombroso's theory of the "born Criminal," which Zola has reproduced in *La Bête humaine*, is rejected by MM. Tropinard, Manouvrier and Magnan. While Novelists are crying that Science repudiates moral responsibility, the greatest scientists, Pasteur, Claude Bernard, J. B. Dumas, Chevreul, Armand Gautier, and so on, believe in human freedom of choice, which they find perfectly reconcilable with the doctrine of heredity.

Novelists who are the victims of nervous diseases have actually encouraged these, in order to be the better able to describe them, and because they were sick themselves have believed all humanity sick, incapable of governing its passions, and bound hand and foot to the fatality of its own instincts.

Such advances have this idea of fatality made of late years, that one Author, M. Henry Rabusson, in his Novel *Roman d'un Fataliste*, recently published in the pages of the *Revue des Deux Mondes*, has made his chief character a Magistrate of determinist convictions. The Magistrate in question is well aware of the opposition existing between his theories and the duties he has to perform, and I will not contradict him when he thus pronounces judgment on himself: "I shall always remain a bad Magistrate."

At the present day, when Novelists of other countries

give instead some other instances of crimes committed
under the same influence. A few years since, I was
present at the trial before the Assize Court of the
Bouches-du-Rhône of one Cornou and saw him condemned to death. He had insured his young servant-
maid's life and afterwards killed her to get hold of the sum
insured, 100,000 francs (£4000). The prisoner in question,
a retired tramway conductor, had read with passionate
interest a large number of works of Darwinian philosophy.
Transferring to social life the zoological laws of Darwinism,
he became convinced that Society, no less than Nature,
was governed by the laws of the Struggle for Life and
Natural Selection. After his sentence, on being visited
in prison by the Protestant pastor, he told the latter he
had wished to put these doctrines in practice and that he
had been beaten in the struggle for life that he had had to
sustain. "I recognize the fact," he said, "that Society is
stronger than I am and strikes me down ; I am one of the
defeated in life's struggle." Previously, during the trial,
just as the sentence of death was pronounced, I had seen
him approach the Advocate General and say to him : "No
ill-feeling, sir ! we have fought, and you have won ; I bear
you no ill-feeling ! " When the Pastor, wishing to awake
his remorse, spoke to him of his conscience, he replied :
"Conscience ! Conscience is a mere product of education
and heredity."—"But," added the Pastor, "have you no
conscience of right and wrong ? "—" Right and wrong,"
returned the condemned man, "are only relative notions ;
what is right in France, is wrong in China, and what is
wrong here, is right there." Intelligent, but at the same
time extremely vain, he loved to display the extent of his
reading, which had been the means of his ruin. Literary
vanity showed in all he said. Before sentence, he declared :
"My Counsel and myself have prepared a scheme of
defence which defies refutation." After his condemnation,
while anxious to do justice to his Counsel's abilities, he
said he was sorry he had not read the notes he had himself
prepared, as he was persuaded they would have produced

a greater effect. When his appeal was refused and he realized that the death sentence would be executed, he threatened he would make a scene on the day he should be led to the scaffold, adding : " I'll make some talk in the records of Justice."

Another instance of the rapidity with which the Darwinian theories of the Struggle for Existence and Natural Selection penetrate amongst working-men is afforded by the trial of the Anarchist Ravachol. The Presiding Judge said to the accused: " There was premeditation in your case. You said under examination on June 9th : ' I wish to succeed and triumph over all obstacles. The hermit was the obstacle ; so I put him out of the way.' " The prisoner replied : " Yes, sir ! that is so." *The Judge :* " Subsequently you saw the coachman again some days later, on June 26th, and took his conveyance once more ; what was your object ? "—*Ravachol :* " I wished to find out whether he had given any information to the Police ; if he had told, I had a dagger and a revolver, and my intention was to put him out of the way."—*The Judge :* " It seems you put anybody out of the way who annoys you, very readily ? "—*Ravachol :* " Yes ! it is a necessity with us, it is a necessity of existence, of everybody's existence." This and all the prisoner's answers revealed no less corruption of mind than perversity of feeling ; his intellectual depravity was obviously due to the books he read. The Judge having said to him : " You commit murder to satisfy your passions ; what can you expect Society to do for a man who displays such sentiments ? "—" It is I who have a claim on Society," was the answer ; " Society ought to keep me. It is no wonder men use any and every means to be happy, as Society abandons us. . . . It is all the fault of Society ; it is a phenomenon arising as the result of the situation of workers, who are dying of hunger in the midst of the wealth they have themselves produced." The *phenomenon* the man spoke of was the murder of an old man, whom he had killed in order to rob him. These are the terms in

be the penalty you inflict on me, it is of small concern to me, for looking on this assemblage with the eyes of reason, I cannot help seeing you as mere atoms adrift in matter, reasoning away because you possess a prolongation of the spinal marrow, and cannot bring myself to acknowledge any right in you to judge your fellows." [1]

The Anarchist Étiévant when before the jury of the Department Seine-et-Oise read aloud a formal statement, in which he repudiated moral responsibility, and this statement was lavishly distributed by his companions amongst working-men.

Taine likewise believed for a long time in the innocuousness of metaphysical theories, but in the latter years of his life, taught by experience, he was in the habit of saying : " I ought never to have written philosophy except in Latin for the initiated ; the risk is too great of hurting one's fellow-creatures." [2] If Taine acknowledges we may do harm with books of philosophy, what havoc must not be wrought by novels, where man is represented as being an irresponsible animal ! No doubt there is a wild beast in every man, and we must remember to muzzle it. But nothing is more dangerous than to wantonly display the bad sides of human nature without at the same time showing what constitutes its greatness. If a man thinks of himself as an irresponsible brute, he will act the brute, never fear. If, on the other hand, he conceives a high idea of his own nature and destiny, if he feels and realizes his responsibility, he will respect himself and be afraid of deteriorating and growing like the "beasts that perish."

The Novelists of the Naturalistic school who are so fond of poking fun at spiritualistic beliefs, are even ready to repeat Pascal's saying : he who would play the angel, often plays the beast. True alas ! that to aspire to a too lofty ideal does not prevent woeful backslidings. Still, the man who from playing the angel falls to playing the beast, has at any rate been an angel for a while ; and even in his

---

[1] *Gazette des Tribunaux*, 11th Jan. 1894.
[2] *Les Débats* of 6th March 1893, article by M. du Vogüé on Taine.

degradation regrets his former high estate and would fain recover it. But he who believes himself pure animal and nothing else, makes no effort at all to reach a higher plane; he goes peacefully to sleep in the mud, and there is no awakening for him. Novels which animalize man are degrading; robbing him of all sense of his dignity, they corrupt his very nature.

Unfortunately, these novels of the physiological and determinist type have penetrated everywhere and disseminated even in country districts a degrading conception of human nature. Their evil influence now makes itself felt among peasants no less than amongst workmen. The following saying was quoted to me the other day as coming from a Provencal peasant: "A peasant," he said, "is a machine, who opens the ground to put manure into it, till the day when he lies down in it to become manure himself." We have long been in the habit of contrasting the corruption of great cities with the innocence of the country. But with the wide diffusion of naturalistic romances and revolutionary journals, the corruption of peasants will soon be greater than that of working men in the towns, if it is not so already. Brutal passions no longer finding a counterpoise in religious faith, but on the contrary being encouraged by novels that bring man down to the level of the beasts, do actually produce veritable brute beasts. Pornographic tastes and habits of drunken debauchery have greatly developed in country places. Parents sing obscene songs before their own children. A friend of mine one day said to a peasant, a married man and the father of a family, who made it his amusement to seduce girls: "You have a daughter yourself; if someone were to seduce her, would you like that?" —"Of course not," the man replied, "but there! what matter, if she did not make me a young 'un!" If crimes against morals are more frequent in the country than they used to be, I believe this may be partly attributed to the influence of pornographic novels. The profligacy thus provoked leads to sterile marriages, practices to procure

young workman who had stolen from a bookseller's shop-front, a copy of this very book (Voltaire's *La Pucelle*), the title of which had enticed him. Men of mature age and of a cold temperament can read without risk the erotic verses of Voltaire, Ovid, Catullus, Martial, and find in thém pleasant strokes of wit and interesting pictures of life and manners ; their age and disposition are a sufficient protection. They experience, says Bayle, "what physicians and surgeons find, who by dint of handling sores and being exposed to evil smells form a habit of not being incommoded by such things." But for young people it is as difficult not to be corrupted by erotic Novels and Poetry as to touch fire without being burned.

Of what use all the efforts of parents to keep obscene images from the eyes and thoughts of their children, if these very things are flaunted in the streets? All the lessons of teachers, all the good advice of parents, must remain barren, if children are to find unhealthy stimulus in the public ways. It is the duty of Society to protect young people by removing all causes of corruption out of their reach; it fails in this duty when it does not second the efforts made by fathers of families in the same direction. Juvenal wrote: "Let nothing that may wound eyes or ears penetrate the dwelling where childhood lives. . . . What! miserable man! you are in agonies of fear lest your hall, fouled by a dog's excrement offend your friend's eyes when he enters your house, lest your porch show stains of mud . . . yet you pay no heed that your home show pure of all stain, free from every vice, in your boy's eyes?" May we not address the same vigorous expressions to the representatives of public order, and say: "What! you remove with scrupulous care the filth of the streets, but you leave in the windows of booksellers' and photographers' shops, in street kiosks, and on railway bookstalls, books and journals, whose very titles are an abomination; you allow songs to be sung in cafés which cannot but corrupt the mind. You make unheard-of efforts to cleanse the streets and remove everything that can vitiate the atmosphere, and you let young people's minds inhale all the while a poisoned air. Why do you not lavish the same care on the soul as on the body? If the moral atmosphere young people breathe is wholesome, it will give them health and strength; if it is vitiated, it will poison them. Moral sanitation is just as important as physical.

Nor are the revolutionary Papers the only ones to bring bad novels within the reach of young people and the working classes, Newspapers calling themselves conservative often publish novels in *feuilleton* form which tend to upset society by their sophistries, and disseminate bad behaviour by their naturalistic descriptions.

I have shown above how man's evil instincts find encouragement in materialistic and fatalistic doctrines, and how Crime is the inevitable outcome. The disciple, in M. Bourget's Novel of that name, is quite justified in writing as he does to his master, who has taught him the doctrines of materialism and irresponsibility: "There exists between you, the illustrious master, and me, your pupil, now accused of the most despicable crime, a tie that men can hardly comprehend, one that you do not yourself realize, but which *I* feel at once binding and unbreakable. I have lived with your thought and by your thought so passionately and so completely at the most decisive epoch of my existence."

Still, in these cases Crime is not glorified. It remains to me to show how Fiction, after poetizing disease, death, suicide, adultery, selfishness, has come at last, like the Anarchists, to glorify Crime.

The glorification of Crime has been the capital folly of Romantic Literature. Jean Jacques Rousseau said he "could not conceive what pleasure is to be found in picturing and fashioning the character of a villain . . ., in throwing the most fascinating glamour over him." Yet just this has been the great delight of the Romanticists.

The glorification of Crime was after all only a plagiarism from English and German Literature, which had brought brigands and corsairs into fashion. "In Germany," Goethe says, "we got drunk in every shape and form, on wine, beer, love and blood-thirsty dreams." Schiller was still in this period of young intoxication and wild thoughts, when he composed *The Robbers*, which gave birth in Germany and France to a host of dramas, the heroes of which were bandits. "My thoughts were held in check," Schiller writes; "they exploded in the creation of a monster (the Robber Chief), such as never existed in this world. My only excuse is, I wanted to paint men two years before I knew them." Alfred de Musset copied Schiller's *Robbers* in his *La Coupe et les Lévres*. Victor Hugo in the same way made banditti into heroes and saw never a scoundrel but among Kings, Priests and Ministers of the Crown. Authors of the Romantic school assigned admirable virtues to murderers, courtesans, brigands and lackeys; in fact they created monsters. "Monsters are the fashion," George Sand used to say, "come let us make monsters."—"She used to hatch her Romances with a facility almost equal to mine," Musset declared, "choosing the most dramatic subjects, parricides, rapes, murders, down to common pocket-picking."—"At that period," George Sand herself states, "the strangest things were done in Literature. The eccentricities of Victor Hugo's genius had intoxicated young men. . . . Chateaubriand was voted not romantic enough. . . . Impossible titles were at a premium and disgusting subjects preferred."[1]

The Romantics went out of their way to find "energetic" characters in the gaols. George Sand saw in the inhabitants of the bagnio men "full of power." Tremnor, who murdered his mistress, is depicted in Lélia as a superior being; Alexandre Dumas accumulates crime upon crime in his Novels and Plays; "it is a wager of wickedness, a primitive fanfaronade of villanies."[2]

In this Literature nothing is thought so fine as a good dagger-thrust; the dagger is a sort of fetish. Charles de

---

[1] George Sand, *Histoire de ma vie*, 4th Part, ch. xv.
[2] Weiss.

Rémusat, who for all this was a man of wit and taste, speaking at this time of the dénoûment of *Emilia Galotti*, where a father is shown killing his daughter who had let herself be seduced, exclaims admiringly : " 'Tis a fine bit of dagger play ! " These Romantic heroes always have a dagger handy, wearing it as an ornament when they don't want to use it. Antony uses a dagger by way of a seal. In *Christine*, Sentinelli employs a dagger to open a clasp with. Byron's heroines carry daggers like his corsairs. Balzac laments because the Parisians hang up the dagger as a curiosity on a gilt nail ; he would rather see them wear it in their belts and know how to use it.

These monsters of Literature, brigands, murderers, poisoners, poetized by Romances, have in turn produced monsters of the Criminal Courts, robbers and murderers like Lacenaire, adulterous wives and husband poisoners like Mme. Laffarge. The crimes of Lacenaire and Mme. Laffarge were essentially *romantic* crimes. The cakes this woman gave her husband were drugged with arsenic and Romanticism. We have only to read her *Memoirs* to see she was merely an echo of George Sand's Novels ; indeed she admits she had read her stories with enthusiastic admiration, and particularly *Indiana*. These studies had developed in her such a high degree of romantic exaltation that she positively refused to marry a young man who sought her hand previously to M. Laffarge, because he had declared his love in such a commonplace way she had found it impossible to throw any romantic glamour over the affair; she longed to be loved, to be adored madly. Marriage moreover seemed a very prosaic thing to her, and she strove to put it off all she could. After marriage, she had for her husband the scorn a heroine of romance never fails to feel, upbraiding society for having invented the slavery of wedlock. Unable to overcome the disgust her husband inspired her with, she put in practice the advice she had read so often in prose and verse :

"Tu peux tuer cet homme avec tranquillité."[1]

---

[1] "You can kill this man with a quiet conscience."

Indeed in Romantic Novels and Romantic Dramas the adulterous wife and her lover never dream of anything but murdering the unhappy husband. "Oh! if only you knew," says Antony, "how often I have fallen asleep thinking of the fellow, my hand upon my dagger . . . and I have dreamed of gallows and scaffold . . . Duty, virtue, empty words! . . . A murder will make you a widow. . . . I am ready to undertake murder ; a crime stands between you and me,—well! I will commit the crime."—In Balzac's *La Femme de trente ans*, Lord Grenville says to Mme. d'Anglemont: " I have repeatedly counted over too carefully all the ways and means of killing the man (her husband) to be able to go on resisting the temptation, if I remained with you," to which the woman replies with equal coolness, " I have entertained the same idea myself."

If after a first crime, a second is required, the hero of romance does not hesitate to commit it ; it is only the first crime. that counts,—or rather it scarcely does count and the second even less. " To have committed, to win you, rape, assault and adultery, and to keep you to stick at another crime? . . . To lose my soul for such a trifle. . . . No, no! you are mine . . . I am carrying you off; woe to the man who stops me ! "

Romanticism, having begun by defending suicide, was not slow to go on to the glorification of murder. Werther kills himself rather than kill Albert. Antony does not put an end to himself, in spite of his melancholy, but he murders Adèle. Dumas' plays fired young men's and women's fancies, and just as Werther gave rise to *Wertherism*, Antony produced *Antoninism*.

In the pages of Romantic Literature, lovers who rest content with adultery and boggle at the husband's murder, are ashamed of their weakness, but console themselves by tickling their imagination with the refreshing thought of the murder they dare not commit. " If now and again," says one of them, " I refresh my mind by the thought of a crime, theft or murder, or both together, I find myself quite incapable of committing it in sober reality. The

Countess is a wonderful creature who might well claim our pity, and a man is not an Othello for wishing to be."

Men of culture have left off by this time reading Eugène Sue's novels; but he was widely read formerly, at the time when the *Journal des Débats* brought them out, and the people, working men and women, still devour them greedily. But on every page we find the sentiment expressed that "to complete a truly great, a frenzied passion, a warm and ardent passion, a crime is a necessity."

The author who most ardently admired crimes of passion was Stendhal, of whom I have already spoken, and must speak again. This Novelist, who despised humanity and called his father an "old villain," when he failed to send him money enough, professed the liveliest admiration for crimes of passion. The aim of life, for him, was pleasure; happiness lies only in the satisfaction of the passions, and "energy" is only expressed in crimes of passion. He has summed up his life in the words: "I have written, I have loved, I have lived."

On the occasion of a crime of passion committed in 1699 by the wife of a Counsellor in the *Parlement* of Aix, some ladies challenged the Abbé Gastaud, Advocate in the same *Parlement*, to compose a funeral oration over the accused. The Abbé accepted the challenge, and the ladies locked him up in a room, telling him he would not be released until the funeral oration was finished. The Abbé finally came out with a harangue, in which he drew a seductive picture of the woman guilty of this crime of love, of her greatness of soul, the vigour of her passions, the strength of mind with which she had conceived and prepared her crime for three long years! This panegyric of amorous strenuousness, which was merely a *jeu d'esprit* at the time, a society diversion, has since Stendhal grown into a literary theory. In the eyes of these admirers of strenuousness, Love that does not run to crime is no true love at all. Unless it is a fever, a fury, a homicidal frenzy, it is without vigour or beauty; but if it rises to the level of crime, ah! then it is grand, glorious, admirable. Murders due to jealousy delight Stendhal. "Last night," he writes in his *Promenades dans Rome*, "two murders took place. A young butcher, a mere boy, stabbed his rival. . . . The second murder occurred near St Peter's, among the Trasteverini. This is another dangerous quarter, they say,—but in my eyes superb; energy is to be found there, the quality of all others most lacking in the Nineteenth Century." Stendhal despises France, because in his day crimes of passion were rare in that country; he dislikes his fellow-countrymen, because they do not know how to kill either themselves or other people from love. "Hardly do the Newspapers," he exclaims regretfully, "tell us the story of a bare yearly half-dozen Othellos; Frenchmen, by the gradual perfecting of their ways of life, are attaining refinement and elegance, but they are losing energy. At Rome, on the contrary, none of those limitations and constraints exist, none of those modes and conventions, which in other countries are known to science as usages of society, or even as decency and virtue." At Rome, they know how to hate a rival, and how to wreak vengeance on him. At Rome, a husband knows how to kill his wife's lover and have done with it; "and this is why Rome is the finest place in all Italy."[1] In France men of position are incapable of flying in a fury and avenging a wrong; working men may punch each other's heads, but this is the utmost to be expected. The Romans carry knives, and use them. Only let a knife thrust be delivered by a Roman, even for some motive that has nothing to do with love, and instantly Stendhal is full of boundless admiration for the murderer's "energy." He never gives a moment's consideration to the victim's sufferings and those of his family;

---

[1] Chateaubriand however, who lived for years in Rome, says in his *Mémoires d'outre-tombe*, "tragic love adventures have ceased to fill the lives of the great Roman ladies."—Taine, who travelled in Italy, understood better than Stendhal the true nature of this Italian "energy"; "it is," he says, "merely a tendency towards violent and dangerous acts . . . passion and blood suffuse their eyes simultaneously, and in an instant they are back in primitive ferocity; they are downright savages." (*Voyage in Italie*, vol. i. p. 315.)

all his sympathies go out to the murderer.   The sight of blood was agreeable to him.   One day he saw a workgirl of Civita Vecchia stabbed to death, and was struck by the superbly picturesque effect produced by the fine colour of the blood on well-gartered stockings and a well-made leg."

At the very time Stendhal was making himself miserable over the inferiority of France as compared with Italy in the matter of knifing, a crime of passion was committed in the Pyrenees by a working cabinet-maker ; this event he saluted with a cry of enthusiasm, and wrote that "the murderer had more soul in him than all the poets of the period put together, and more wit than most of these gentlemen."   These poets, who according to Stendhal had less soul and less wit than the murderer, enjoyed the names of Delavigne, Lamartine and Victor Hugo.   All the same the murderer was a common criminal who, wounded by the indifference his mistress manifested towards him, first shot her with a revolver, and then cut her throat.   We shall see from the account he gave of his crime before the Assize Court, that this bully was also a coward.   "Then," (on Thérèse refusing to go out with him), "then," he says in his narrative, "I fire a pistol shot at her and miss ; I seize her by the arm, saying, 'turn round,' and at the same moment fire a second shot.   She falls down and her headkerchief covers her eyes.   I want to kill myself. . . .   But, before firing, I notice there is no blood near Thérèse's body and I say to myself, 'perhaps she is only swooning ?' . . .   I raise the kerchief that hid her eyes, and found them open.   I say to myself, 'Alas! I am done for now, and *you will survive me to make fun of my death*!'   No! it is not fair.   I will confess all ; I take my knife, the coward's weapon (I had no other), and cut her throat with it.   I was horrified at my own act. . . .   I covered up her face so as not to see it. . . .   Presently, obeying a natural instinct of order and cleanliness, I wipe my knife, shut it and put it back in my pocket.   I then let off a pistol shot in my own mouth, but without my being aware of it, the weapon was loaded with powder only."

This commonplace malefactor's mind was unhinged; he was on the brink, in fact, of madness, under the form of the mania of persecution. It was the dread of his mistress's mockery that turned him into a homicidal maniac; in Stendhal's eyes he is a model of "energy and tenderness!"

Nor is it only the murderer out of jealousy who rouses Stendhal's admiration; the thief gives him pleasure too. "When I am stopped by thieves," he says, ". . . I feel a great passion of anger against the Government and the Parson of the parish. As for the thief, I like him, if he is a man of energy, for he amuses me."[1]

What Stendhal calls energy or strenuousness is the letting loose of cruelty and sensuality, the violence of passion deaf to reason. Directly passion is restrained and reason comes in to regulate the senses, "energy" disappears. If a girl refuses to quit her father's house and disgrace her name by eloping with a lover, Stendhal writes, "she had character enough to fly with him." To have character, it would seem a girl must lose all sense of honour and modesty.[2]

Stendhal's paradox as to the beauty of crimes of passion has been reiterated, cultivated and enlarged by the most celebrated writers of the Romantic School; and at the present time is to be found in the Novels of M. M. Barrès. M. Barrès adores Spain, because it shows "the most violent life of nervous energy ever given to man to live," because its bull-fights breathe "the intoxicating force that exhales from slaughter," because the Spaniard knows how to be at one and the same time of high-strung soul and ferocious cruelty, at once mystical and savage, and "loves to see blood, to bite and tear."[3] M. Barrès, it is plain enough,

[1] The quotation is borrowed from a book entitled, *L'Art et la vie de Stendhal*, p. 406.

[2] Nevertheless in a Collection of great French Writers dedicated to young people this Novelist has been included, a man who says in one of his Prefaces, "I write for a mere poor hundred readers . . . not hypocrites, and not *moral*. I cannot understand why they should style 'the apostle of energy' an author who spends his time in analysing his sensations and makes the end and aim of life consist in the search after pleasure."

[3] M. Barrès, *Du sang, de la volupté et de la mort.*

copies Stendhal, but Stendhal himself was an imitator of
Saint-Evrémond. Everywhere plagiarism,—*O imitatores,
servum pecus* (" Ye plagiarists, a servile crowd "). As long
ago as the Seventeenth Century, Saint-Evrémond complained they did not know how in France to love with
the same energy as in Spain, vaunting the fury and fierce-
ness of Spanish love and deeming love in France to be of
far too reasonable a sort. " Though naturally enough," he
· wrote, " Love never has very well defined rules and regula-

say that in France
nd either in the way
it produces. What
just escapes being
worth living without

ve extravagant and
erary *doctrinaires* of
confined to frantic
ers are sensual and
lves with dreaming
the enjoyment of
care not to do any
ake others commit.
matic authors who
passion, came the
on, with their glori-
sacres of the Terror,
Commune and the
ling bombs. Even
logists ; Dostoiewski
f the secret Societies
f madness, as Littré
ome idea, almost a
e populace has been
hich the murderer is
and the prostitute
school ; he admired
erer," he said, " is a

brave man." Well! he has made converts, and has had his admirers male and female, especially the latter; not a few women wrote to him to express their admiration in passionate letters. The same thing happened to Pranzini. These examples show how dangerous are the Romances that poetize criminals and lend a factitious intellectuality and tragic grandeur. Descriptions of murder are particularly dangerous when they are joined with the delineation of voluptuous sensations. This association of sanguinary and voluptuous images, which constitutes *Sadism*, has been drawn in glowing colours by a number of Writers, who have thus been instrumental in spreading this form of sexual perversion. It is well known that in certain individuals voluptuous sensations provoke cruelty and *vice versâ*; voluptuous ideas awake sanguinary ones, and sanguinary ideas voluptuous ones. The Princes who have been most prone to debauchery have been cruel Princes. It has been proved that soldiers, after a battle, have experienced when pillaging fierce sexual appetites. I am much inclined to believe that the sight of blood, shed in the games of the Circus, tended strongly to excite among the Romans voluptuous cravings. Physicians who have studied sexual perversions, say that debauchees delight in picturing women bathed in blood to their imagination. Dr Krafft-Ebing, Professor of Psychiatry at the University of Vienna, quotes several cases from amongst his patients showing the connection existing between voluptuous sensation and the craving to shed blood or to see it shed. He gives the instance of a young man "whose imagination was continually haunted by ideas of bloodshed which produced in him feelings of voluptuous pleasure. . . . Frequently other cruel fancies beset him. For instance he would picture himself playing the part of a tyrant mowing down the populace with grape shot. Or he would find his mind filled with pictures of the scenes that would occur if an enemy were entering a conquered city, violating, torturing and carrying off virgins."[1] I am

[1] *Psychopathia sexualis*, p. 98.

of opinion that a similar state of mind existed in certain poets, notably in Baudelaire, Musset and Byron, all of whom found pleasure in writing poems at once sinister and voluptuous, where murders follow scenes of love-making. Byron's poems are full of descriptions of battles followed by the ravishing of women; it is to heighten the voluptuousness that he first wallows in a butchery. In Musset's early poems, dagger thrusts and pistol shots alternate with kisses. Baudelaire goes farther still; he says in the preface of his book :

> "Si le viol, le poison, le poignard, l'incendie
> N'ont pas encor brodé de leurs plaisants dessins
> Le canevas banal de nos piteux destins,
> C'est que notre âme, hélas ! n'est pas assez hardie. . . ."[1]

The fact is familiar that profligates sometimes strangle the women they have abused, and this not solely to escape the law by putting the witness out of the way, but because they experience a highly agreeable sensation in killing them in this way. Verzeni, who strangled several women after violating them, said these murders caused him "an intensely voluptuous sensation"; barely did he touch his victims' necks before he experienced sexual excitement.[2] Probably Vacher and other stranglers of women were similarly affected. Baudelaire would seem to have been possessed by a like picture of a murdered woman and he has written a poem on the subject entitled, *Une Martyre* ("A Martyr").

> "Dans une chambre tiède où, comme en une serre,
>   L'air est dangereux et fatal, . . .
> Un cadavre sans tête épanche, comme un fleuve,
>   Sur l'oreiller desaltéré,
> Un sang rouge et vivant. . . ."[3]

Baudelaire ends the poem with the question whether

---

[1] "If rape, poison, dagger, arson, have not yet embroidered with their pleasing patterns the dull canvas of our petty destinies, it is because, alas ! our soul is not bold and brave enough. . . ."

[2] *Psychopathia sexualis*, p. 89.

[3] "In a heated bedchamber where, as in a greenhouse, the atmosphere is dangerous and sinister . . . a headless corpse pours out like a river over the soaked pillow a red and living blood. . . ."

the murderer has eventually succeeded in assuaging his appetite for voluptuous sensations :

> " L'homme vindicatif, que tu n'as pu vivant,
>   Malgré tant d'amour, assouvir,
>   Combla-t-il sur ta chair inerte et complaisante
>   L'immensité de son désir ? " [1]

Taine tells us that Byron said one day : " I should be curious to experience the sensations a man must have when he has just committed a murder." [2]   In a Novel of Dostoiewski's, Raskolnikoff has the same longing to feel the sensations of a murderer. Plagiarism again ! There is never a literary eccentricity that is not copied from Literature to Literature. Wholesome ideas are disseminated slowly and with difficulty, but the infection of extravagant follies always spreads rapidly. Fiction has been so successful in arousing the taste for perverse sensations that at the trial of the Student Ch——, a witness came forward to depone how he had heard the accused express the very same wish as Lord Byron, " I should like to procure myself the sensations of a murderer."   Remembering the insignificant wound which the accused had given himself in the cheek, instead of aiming at the temple, and the fact that he refrained from firing the fifth chamber of his revolver, which remained undischarged to the end, we are led to suppose he had wished to kill his victim after dishonouring her, to gratify his craving for literary and perverse sensations, and mingle love and death together, like the heroes of Romance. [3]

---

[1] " The revengeful man whom you could not, in spite of all your love, satisfy when alive, did he surfeit on your still and uncomplaining flesh the immensity of his desire ? "

[2] *Histoire de la Littérature anglaise*, 8vo ed., vol. iii. p. 532.

[3] On April 23rd, 1898, two foreign students, one a Bulgarian, the other a Russian, living in the University district of Paris, shot themselves with revolvers. The first died, the second survived his wound, and declared he had tried to commit suicide in search of a new sensation. These strange words, showing to what a degree Literature, by turning young men's thoughts to the search and analysis of sensations, upsets their minds, were reported to me by the Police Commissary's Secretary of the Val-de-Grâce, who enquired into the affair. The Police Commissary himself told me he was terrified by

Literary vanity combines with the most perverted sensualism in all the forms these crimes of passion take. Before killing Mme. C——, Ch—— read her a copy of verses he had composed for her. After the murder, he is proud of his pseudo-romantic escapade, the memory of which he hopes to utilize in a psychological Novel. One of his *quartier latin* friends writes to him : "You talk of pride ; ah ! yes ! you can and you ought to be proud. . . . Write to us. . . . Tell us of the state of your mind. . . . All, men and women, the whole quarter is with you and for you. . . . You will be a great man, never fear, great heart, after being a great agonizer (you see I invent a word) ; you must write us Literature from your point of view."

To make a novel out of the murder of the woman he had killed, a married woman and the mother of three children, is the idea that filled the mind of this young murderer of literary tendencies and of his friends. He is to become famous by writing down as a tale the fine love tragedy he has brought about. A love adventure is to be utilized to supply copy !

Men who prey on women's hearts feel no repugnance, in their consuming self-conceit, to admit the public to their amorous confidences, and even to those of others. The most illustrious of our Novelists have not avoided this pitfall. Rousseau composed his *Nouvelle Heloïse* out of recollections of his love for Mme. d'Houdetot, the details of which he made public in his *Confessions.* Goethe divulged in *Werther* his liaison with Charlotte Buff and Kestner, making a friend of the latter's declare "it is a dangerous thing to have a friend an author." In *René,* Chateaubriand did not fear to relate the incestuous passion of his sister Amélie. The great Lamartine, who with a marvellous poetic genius combined a sound good sense that is rare among poets, failed to guard himself from

the continual increase in the numbers of suicides in the *Quartier latin,* and that he had noticed that those who killed themselves by means of charcoal fumes took a pleasure in describing their sensation down to the minutest details. In the Russian student's rooms was found a note-book filled with maxims from Schopenhauer, Spinoza and other philosophers.

written, also sought fame in crime. He had a fervent
admiration for Lacenaire; "he is a magnificent fellow," he
declared, "a powerful individuality. . . . Shall I end like
him? When I cross-question my conscience, I elicit the
reply, ' It may be so.' Poet, thief, murderer,—a noteworthy
progression. And I tell myself softly,—in a whisper: I
am half-way on the road already."

The authors of crimes of passion, who very often are
great readers of novels, draw attention to themselves by
their literary pretensions; they write poetry, in which they
allude to favours they have not received, or else avenge
themselves for the slights they have suffered by satirical
verses. In the letters they write, they love to harp on the
so-called " right of love," a phrase they have borrowed from
some novel. One Foucou, who was tried some few years
ago at the Assize Court of the Bouches-du-Rhône, wishing
to seduce a young married woman, who would not accept
his advances, declared: " When you love a woman, that
woman ought to be yours." Young men who commit
suicide together with their mistresses often write the
history of their amours with copious detail. I have
myself read a number of these highly circumstantial
accounts. It is evident that, their heads stuffed with
romantic books, they experience a craving to themselves
compose a dramatic novel. One of these conceived the
quaint idea of filling a bulky note-book for his mother's
perusal with a minutely detailed narrative of his amours;
without a thought of the impropriety of his confidences,
he described for his mother's benefit the bliss he had felt
in possessing his mistress a few hours before dying along
with her.

Another thing frequently observed in the authors of
crimes of passion and even among common murderers, is
a great affectation of sensibility, borrowed from the books
they have read. It was Jean Jacques Rousseau, as everybody knows, who brought sensibility into fashion, being
endowed with extreme sensibility himself. He was melted
to tears with the utmost facility. Almost every page of

his confessions speaks of his tears and sobs ; in the Second
Dialogue he says of himself : " As to moral sensibility, I
have never known anyone so much its slave as myself.'
He thought himself very virtuous, because he always spoke
of virtue in a melting mood ; he mistook a love of virtue
for virtue itself.   Sensibility has been deemed, since
Rousseau wrote, a sufficient passport to virtue, and the
world has plumed itself on its sensibility as if that included everything.   Necker, who like all his contemporaries, fell under the influence of his fellow-countryman,
wrote : " I care not whether or no there is a moral aim
in the novel or story that has made me shed so many tears, ·
for I cannot be so stirred without becoming a better
man." [1]   But a readiness to feel emotion and shed tears is
not necessarily a proof of goodness.   Rousseau himself, who
could not mention children without the liveliest emotion, put
his own in the Foundling Hospital.   Mme. de Luxembourg,
who attracted much attention by her extreme sensibility,
killed her step-daughter by inches.   The sentimental
Bernardin de Saint-Pierre was anything but a good man.
Sensibility is not true pity.   In the Revolution time, men
who would weep in the theatre over imaginary sufferings,
used to look on indifferently as the heads fell under the
executioner's hand.   By dint of shedding tears over fictitious
misfortunes, none are left to expend on real ones.   It is no
uncommon thing to hear murderers talk about their sensibility.   Hermione says of herself in the play : " Hermione
possesses sensibility, Oreste virtue."

Here are some passages from letters I have read written
by a murderer, afterwards executed.   He freely admits it
is impossible to conceive a more horrible crime than his,
but endeavours to find extenuating circumstances in the
mental sufferings his victim had made him endure.   " These
can be realized," he says, " only by one who has suffered as
I have, and who possesses a just and sensitive heart such as
mine."   Maintaining he had been driven to the crime by
his mistress, he goes on to say he had devoted all his being

[1] Manuscript by M. Necker, *Sur l'attendrissement*, p. 43.

unfortunate cat I cruelly murdered. There's something for you to explain, my philosophic friends."—The widow Gras, who was guilty of such an atrocious crime, used to pick up and take care of wounded birds.—Women of pleasure who care little for their family, are as a rule deeply attached to animals. Ovid tells us his mistress was devoted to a parrot. Juvenal says Cynthia was inconsolable at the death of a sparrow. It is no uncommon thing to see women ill-treat their children and lavish the greatest attention on their cats.—I have myself noted a case where a mother used her children vilely, but kept seven pet dogs ; she would stint her children of food to increase the dogs' allowance. Juvenal speaks of Roman ladies who would willingly have sacrificed their husbands to save their favourite lap-dog's life. I believe women of the same sort might be found in Paris at the present day. Bright feminine eyes that fill with tears at the death of a dog, a cat or a canary, are dry when a husband dies.

"La mort d'un passereau leur fait verser les larmes." [1]

"Il n'aurait pas marché sur une mouche à terre,
Mais s'il l'avait trouvée à dîner dans un verre,
Il aurait assommé cinq on six de ses gens." [2]

Sensibility then and affection for animals we see are no sufficient proof of the possession of a tender heart. The Student Ch——, though endowed with extreme sensibility, accepted readily enough the sacrifice of Mlle. G——'s life, entirely indifferent to the grief her death must necessarily cause her husband and children and the disgrace such a scandal must bring upon a respectable family. This morbid sensibility was not solely due to his temperament, he owed it largely to the books he read. "I read enormously," he said, "particularly the poets." He read romances no less passionately ; "I wept over *Obermann*

---

[1] "The death of a sparrow makes them shed tears."—GILBERT.

[2] "He would not have stepped on a fly on the ground, but had he found one in his glass at dinner, he would have killed five or six of his servants."—ALFRED DE MUSSET.

and *René*. . . . The mere play of my intelligence had consumed in me the solid stuff of my will. The more I meditated, the more I felt myself off my balance." All this reading of novelists and poets had already inordinately stimulated his sensibility and imagination, when he devoted himself to the perusal of the analytical romances of Stendhal, Balzac M Bourget. In this school of literature he acquired a craving for sensation and analysis pushed beyond all bounds; he watched himself live, like the hero of a psychological romance, analysing every sentiment and every emotion and composed a novel on *The infinitesimal Dispersion of the Heart*! This craving for sensation and analysis inordinately indulged, a thing that dries up the heart and destroys the brain, completed the derangement of his nerves and imagination, and he was now ripe for suicide, crime or madness. " I had a dread of going mad," he said; " one day I felt myself irresistibly drawn to seize a knife lying on a block, and had to fly to escape the temptation. My condition had become pathological."

M. Bourget began by protesting against the notion of throwing upon Literature and more especially on novels of analysis any share of responsibility for the intellectual and moral perversity of the criminal of Constantine. "It is very easy," he said, "to make Literature responsible for the moral obliquities painfully elaborated in this man's mind by ten years' efforts, and malevolence has not missed its opportunity to do so,—as if Literature had ever exercised the smallest influence over souls not previously prepared to meet it half way." [1] "Why, my good sir!" Stendhal

Preface by M. Paul Bourget prefixed to *Causes Criminelles* of 1888 by Bataille. M. Bourget's objection being only a reproduction of Ovid's and M. Jules Lemaître's, which I have already answered, I think it unnecessary to repeat my reply here; it is to be found on pp. 420, 406. M. Bourget has himself in more than one of his books drawn attention to the fact that reading is capable of exerting no small influence, inasmuch as he attributes the moral degradation of several of his heroes to effects of Literature. Thus in his *Crime d'amour*, he makes one character say: "School life and modern Literature befouled my mind before I knew what life was. The same sort of reading set me against Religion at fifteen."

wrote as long ago as 1850, referring to this problem of literary responsibility, " a book is a looking-glass travelling on the highway. At one moment we see it reflect the blue skies, at another only the mire and mud of the road-way. And the man who carries the looking-glass on his back you choose to call immoral! His mirror shows mire, and you blame the mirror! Rather blame the state of the track where mud is allowed to accumulate and still more the road-inspector, whose neglect lets water collect and mud-holes abound." [1]

To begin with, we may tell Stendhal and M. Bourget that it is degrading Literature to make it a mere looking-glass, reproducing indiscriminately blue sky and roadside mud. The mirror does not select, but the Writer must; the mirror reflects, it does not think. Because there is filth in the human heart, is the Novelist bound, like the mirror, to reproduce the filth? [2]

This mania for endless analysis is especially dangerous for young men who require activity, enthusiasm and generous beliefs. It is not well to live too self-centred a life, preoccupied with the analysis of one's own sentiments and sensations. This worship of the *ego*, so much in fashion nowadays, leads to a ferocious selfishness, an aridity of heart, a predilection for violent emotions, a contempt for morality.

This same habit of ruthless analysis overstimulates a morbid sensibility; by dint of too constant observation,

---

[1] Stendhal, *Le rouge et le noir*, ch. xlix.

[2] Literature is not so much the " mirror " of society as the expression of its aspirations, regrets and hopes. The pastoral poems of Fontenelle, Florian, Gesner, do not represent the manners of the Eighteenth Century, but its ideals. The Army officers in Scribe's plays show admirably the contemporary attitude of mind in France, where men living under a peacefully-minded Prince, re-gretted the excitements of war and admired the gallant soldiers of the Revolution and the Empire. The domination of the middle classes sees the outburst of Romantic Drama, drawing its inspiration from the dramas of the Great Revolution and rousing the desire for fresh Revolutionary dramas. Literature then is not simply a reflection of life and habits of life ; it provokes changes in ideas and sentiments, and is thus a powerful factor in the formation of habits of life.

men grow nervous, over-impressionable, the "slave of circumstance." "By too much self-study and too little self-discipline, a man becomes a sort of moral *écorché*,[1] a bundle of nerves, a creature wounded by every pin-prick, defence-less, skinless, bleeding ; "[2] he loses the finest of all qualities, manly energy, and turns his soul into a woman's. "When Nature has given you a man's soul, your affectation is to be like a woman," wrote Euripides.[3]

Chenedollé, who had formed the habit of self-analysis and of noting down his most trifling impressions, soon found that it is not good for a man to observe his own sensations too exactly, to give himself up to his own thoughts and griefs ; "by doing so he eats out his heart, and ends by killing himself or going mad." To counteract this danger, he set himself for three months to dig in his garden all day long ; "only by this means could I gain a little rest for my sick fancy, which was gone astray from Nature's beaten tracks."—In the article he wrote on Sautelet's suicide, Armand Carrel stated how his friend was endowed to the highest degree with the faculty of analysing rapidly and perspicaciously whatever emotions he felt, and penetrating deeply into the secret recesses of others' hearts ; he said further that he was animated by the liveliest curiosity, and the wish to try every experience life has to offer.—"John Stuart Mill maintained that self-introspection and the advance of psychological analysis have a disintegrating effect, which added to disillusion springing from too much knowledge, leads to melancholy. We see too clearly the working of the springs of action and the true basis of character and feeling." (Guyou, *L'Irréligion de l'Avenir*.)

The Student Ch—— so fully realized the dangers inherent in unlimited analysis that after his condemnation, think-ing in prison over the causes of his ruin, he declared : "I

---

[1] An artist's lay-figure showing the human figure flayed, so as to display the anatomy of the muscles.

[2] *Idées et sensations*, by the Brothers Goncourt.

[3] Euripides, *Fragments*, vol. ii. p. 374.

promised myself, if ever I became a father, I would guard
my children against self-analysis." M. Bourget says himself in the Preface I have just quoted from, that the
criminal of Constantine " was the victim of that dangerous
spirit of analysis which goes on continually from bad to
worse in some of the new generation till it lays waste
utterly heart and mind." No doubt, "this morbid sort of
literature has no great hold over healthy minds," as
Michelet says, who regrets " to see in our century so much
genius wasted in this dismal form of romance, devoted to
sounding our wounds and sharpening their pain."[1] But
how many of these robust minds are there, minds inacces-
sible to bad influences? Michelet himself allows that a
young woman who has been " prematurely ripened, spoiled,
bitten by the worm of mysticism and religious ambiguities,"
has ceased to be wholesome-minded, and is all ready to
be corrupted by Fiction.

Not less manifest is the influence of the Novel of analysis
in the case of Mme. Weiss than in that of Ch——. This
woman, who tried in concert with her lover, the Engineer
R——, to poison her husband, found pleasure after her
condemnation in writing an account of her life and her
crime, in making an elaborate analysis of her own personality, its variations and states of mind. " M. R——," she
wrote, "awoke in me a woman I did not know existed, a
woman of violent passions but passive submissiveness ; he

---

[1] Michelet, *L'Amour*, p. 275.—Nisard has expressed similar regrets to
Michelet's : " All the imagination, wit and style that are wasted on his ingenious but rash experiments, might perhaps turn to the glory of France, if she
were to take a sudden disgust for Novels and send all these pens back to work
more worthy of the Nation that holds the sceptre of things intellectual."
(D. Nisard, *Histoire de la Littérature française*, vol. iv. p. 576.) The Ancients
preferred History to Fiction ; the history of public life seemed to them more
interesting than any pictures of private could be. They found more profit and
pleasure in reading the lives of great Captains, Philosophers and Legislators
than in perusing the story of a servant maid in love or a profligate's adventures.
There were only two writers of fiction among the Romans, Petronius and
Apuleius, and neither is exactly a praiseworthy author. *We* can count them
by thousands. The populace is more deeply interested in the tale of the
Wandering Jew or of Rocambole than in the history of their own country.

changed my whole existence, changing at the same time my entire inner nature. . . . I loved him as the arbiter of my thoughts, my intellect, my person, of every fibre of my being, as the beloved master in whom I was annihilated body and soul." In some letters written by the accused woman which were impounded by the police, were found hints of the novels of analysis she was in the habit of reading. " I have read *Cruelle Énigme*," she writes, "the plot is just the same as in *Cœur de Femme*,—sensual love and intellectual inspired at one and the same time in the same woman by two different men. I do not myself see much enigma in the situation; if one is the lover but is incapable to playing the male, why the other. ·. . ." Analysing her love, she tells her lover in a letter it is at once intellectual and sensual,—" My body cannot live without yours."—In prison also she wrote a great deal. Speaking of her husband, who notwithstanding the crime she had attempted against him, still loved her, she said : " He pitied me, for he knows better than any one that the woman who displayed herself in me during the past twelve months, was not the same who made his home happy for five years." [1]   Bracing her courage to commit suicide by the thought that her death would relieve her husband and children of the shame of her being in gaol, she is surprised by her own hesitation and her desire to live, " so I give the idea the slip like a coward," she writes ; " I set to work and this rids me for the time being of the consciousness of my own personality, and I stick stolidly at it." " Suicide," she declared, " is the strength of those who have no strength remaining, the hope of those who have no hope left, the sublime courage of the vanquished. I have no home now, no husband, no soul ; I am death's, and death's only. My double death wrings my heart " (she had just lost a little girl who had been allowed her as a companion), " and I can no more, I will no more ! To the

---

[1] Indeed, as a matter of fact, her husband told the Court that during the first years of marriage she had been a devoted and pious wife, reading her Bible every morning.

rescue, Death, for pity's sake! Come, come, come!" After a fruitless attempt to strangle herself during her preliminary detention, she eventually poisoned herself, during the night subsequent to her condemnation, with strychnine, wrapped up in a cigarette paper hidden in the hem of her pocket-handkerchief.

The analytical Novel is useful, by way of a scrutiny of conscience, for teaching men to know themselves,—but on two conditions, that we do not base our gratification exclusively on sounding all the depths of wretchedness possible to weak and degraded natures, and secondly, that we do not take pleasure in depicting vice without a thought of its enormity. It is a dangerous thing to teach men to despise human nature and believe themselves the slaves of their temperament; it is an ugly thing to study mankind with perverse and malevolent inquisitiveness, altogether leaving the good side out of account. The writer of the Novel of analysis makes it his first business to lower mankind in their own estimation, and to make a profound study of the causes of woman's frailty and man's wickedness. This type of Novel, as it is written nowadays, is at bottom only the sequel of Eighteenth Century Romances, the stories of Crebillon *fils* and Laclos, doctors in profligacy.

In fact M. Bourget actually quotes as models of analysis the *Liaisons dangereuses*,[1] *Le Rouge et le Noir*, a book in which roués give instructions in the art of seduction, and *Mademoiselle de Maupin*, where a form of unnatural love is depicted. The true Psychology is to be found in Pascal's *Pensées*, La Rochefoucauld's *Maximes*, La Bruyère's *Charactères*, the Comedies of Molière and the Sermons of Bossuet and Bourdaloue. It is not the science of the human heart, as these great men understood it, that is the subject of the analytical Novel. Its real interest lies in the psychology of Love, and this psychology is found in much greater perfection in the Tragedies of Corneille and Racine, in the Comedies of Marivaux, and the Romances of Mme. de Lafayette, than in the licentious Novels of the

Preface to *Terre Promise*.

Eighteenth and Nineteenth Centuries. Even in the most passionate of Racine's female characters, love is described with decency before the final error ; in contemporary novelists it is analysed before, during and after the woman's fall, without a shadow of reticence.

In an article in the *Semaine littéraire* of Geneva of October 30th, 1898, M. Philippe Godet, who has had opportunities, both as instructor and friend, of seeing a great number of young men at close quarters, declares that a certain psychological Novel (I refrain from giving the title) has done an irreparable amount of harm to young readers. "This is an actual fact, and I have the proofs before me ! The book, with all its culture, has wrought havoc that I have seen with my own eyes." No doubt whatever there *are* psychological Novels which by virtue of elevation of thought and refinement of sentiment, do more good than harm. Nothing can be finer or more moral than Mme. de Lafayette's *Princesse de Clèves*, while several of Octave Feuillet's books, *Monsieur de Camors*, *Sibylle*, *La Morte*, are at once works of art and wholesome reading. In the same category may be reckoned M. Paul Bourget's later Novels, the *Terre promise* and *Cosmopolis*. The same cannot however be said of some earlier books from the same pen, such as *Crime d'amour*, *Mensonges*, *Cruelle Énigme*, in which mere sensuality masquerades under the name of sensibility. The heroes and heroines of these works live at the mercy of their own sensations ; "it is all a pack of dirty abominations," as the Abbé Taconet says in *Mensonges*. It was Rousseau who first taught Novel Writers to cloak sensuality under the guise of sentiment, to throw a halo of poetry over sensibility. Long before the Abbé Taconet, Bourdaloue had seen where sensibility often leads to. "Sensibility of the heart," he says, "is not a crime in itself, but it is the beginning of a great many ; it so easily changes into sensuality."[1]

It was the crime committed by the Student Ch——

[1] Bourdaloue, *De la charité chrétienne et des amitiés humaines.*

490 CRIME DETERMINED BY PASSION, AND CONTAGION

whose mind had been corrupted by the books he read, that awoke in M. Paul Bourget the sense of literary responsibility and wrought the moral transformation so conspicuous in his more recent works. It was of the unhappy criminal of Constantine he was thinking when he wrote in his *Sensations d'Italie*, p. 58 : "Our analysts heat their brains to prove the ever-changing complexity of human personality,[1] what a poor boy I really cannot remember without unfeigned compassion called the *Infinitesimal dispersion of the heart*,"—this is the title Ch—— gave to a Novel of analysis he proposed to write. It was while thinking of the harm wrought by doctrines which destroy moral belief, that M. Bourget wrote his noble preface to the *Disciple*.

This question of responsibility preoccupies him more and more ; responsibility of the Writer towards his readers, responsibility of the father towards his natural son, responsibility of the man who has lived a profligate life towards a fiancée of spotless and unsullied purity, all these responsibilities are dwelt upon in his later Novels.

The numerous examples I have quoted suffice to teach us what we are to think of the opinion of those who say Novels libel life without corrupting it.[2] Yes, truly! Novels often enough libel society, representing it as worse than it really is. Even in the Eighteenth Century, society was less vicious than society Novels. In the same way at the present time our society is good for something better than most Novels make out. Such pictures libel French society in the eyes of foreigners, who, judging us by our Novels, form a low opinion of our morality. But they forget that Novels exaggerate the vices of society, to amuse their readers, and because vice lends itself more readily than virtue to picturesque effects. These delineations of vice

---

[1] M. Bourget belongs to that group of analysts who have substituted for the unity, the identity of the *ego*, the multiplication of the *ego*. This last doctrine, which approves itself to him as a great psychological verity, is in my opinion a great psychological error, and a view utterly destructive of all moral responsibility.

[2] Cuvillier-Fleury.

do indeed libel society, but they corrupt it as well, because
suggesting the pursuit of a similar line of conduct.

Stendhal claims for the Novelist the right to paint mire
and mud.   From mire to filth is only a step, and one that
has been often taken.   Is there any real necessity why the
Novelist should concentrate all his attention on ugly and
repulsive matters?   Is beauty not as real as ugliness?
Why is no place to be found in Novels for poetry, grace,
pure sentiment?   The realities of the muck-heap and the
Criminal Court are not the only truths.   The merit and
charm of a story does not surely depend on the delineation
of obscenity and crime, and the use of coarse phrases.   It
shows a want of good taste and moral sense to seek inspiration exclusively among debauchees, criminals, drunkards,
prostitutes and adulteresses.   It is dangerous to devote
every energy to the representation of scenes of wantonness
and cruelty, for fear of stirring up a spirit of emulation.
There is in every man a wild heart full of lubricity and
cruelty, whose perverted instincts are put to sleep by
education, but are always ready to awake at the call of
bad example.

The Novelist professes to chasten morals by exhibiting
vice in all its hideousness.   But we do not ask the Novelist
to teach morality, we only ask him not to flaunt vice
abroad.   Every sort of exhibition and delineation is not
judicious ; and there are moral maladies it is as imprudent
to expose in books as it is in the street.   Do they hope
to improve morals by making a public spectacle of vice?
Are they not aware that lasciviousness is stimulated by
lascivious pictures?   What would be said of a physician
who should make his patients breathe a vitiated atmosphere, in order to teach them the value of fresh air?

Nor are Novels always a faithful picture of society,
because very often they depict exceptional characters.
The brother and sister who love each other like René and
Amélie with incestuous passion, are quite exceptional
beings.   The young man, who enamoured of a married
woman he cannot seduce, kills himself out of despair, like

Virgil and Horace, forged a will in conjunction with certain Roman *equites*; and the historian accounts for his crime by saying, " he had committed the error of supposing poverty the greatest of all ills."[1] In the same way the married woman who lets herself be overpersuaded by novels that Love is the greatest of all good things and that it is allowed her to seek it outside marriage, such a one is not far from forgetting her duty to her husband. Hence the Novelist who has led his fair readers into unfaithfulness to the marriage vow must bear a share of responsibility for the lapses of women intoxicated by the sophistries to be found in his pages? The Author who, by means of his paradoxes as to the beauty and nobility of crimes of passion, has corrupted his reader's mind and driven him to commit an act of violence, seems to me morally an accomplice in the murder he has made him do.

Writers who disseminate antisocial paradoxes, are averse, I know, to hearing their responsibility proclaimed; after assailing everything, family, law, religion, they then claim for themselves the privilege of irresponsibility. But Magistrates, who hear literary sophistries, that have been their undoing, from the mouths of prisoners in the dock, are appalled by all the mischief that may be done by words whether written or spoken. In the Weiss affair, for instance, the Engineer R—— claimed from his mistress that she should poison her husband as the only indisputable proof of her love for him. After long hesitating at such a crime, Mme. Weiss made up her mind to do it solely and entirely that she might not refuse her lover the testimony of affection he demanded. After her condemnation, realizing the harm she had got from the sophistries that are so common in novels and how these had corrupted her mind, she wrote in her autobiographical memoranda, that her crime had been one " of error not of malice prepense, and that she had been blinded by cunning sophistries."[2]

Another way in which the Novelists seek to escape

---

[1] Tacitus, *Annals*, Bk. xiv. § 40.
[2] *Archives d'anthropologie criminelle*, 1891, p. 427.

responsibility is by saying that a work of literature, if written with talent, can never be harmful. "Directly a writer has talent," Zola says, " I hold everything is lawful for him ; . . . for me no books are obscene but those ill-conceived and badly executed."[1] But talent does not abrogate responsibility, it really increases it. Are we to say that Voltaire's *Pucelle* is not an obscene book, because it is written with talent? In a Novel, as in every work of art, there are two different things,—the form and the matter. The form may be good and elegant, but the matter as bad as can be, just as a poisoned draught may be offered in a beautifully chiselled cup. There are Novelists who possess a great deal of talent, and very little morality. The artists of the Renaissance, who had the highest development of the æsthetic sense, often lacked moral sense ; their number included murderers, thieves and forgers. Nor were the Italian artists the only ones to have many dealings with the law ; the Belgian, Flemish, Dutch painters who came to Rome soon adopted Italian ways. A high æsthetic sense then by no means necessarily implies a high moral tone. Talent only makes Novels more dangerous, when their motive is unwholesome. Coarse lubricity will revolt a delicate mind, while elegant naughtiness will corrupt it almost unconsciously. " The coarseness you eliminate would horrify, if it were openly displayed ; and the skill shown in concealing it only tends to attract the fancy in a more delicate fashion, and one that is only the more dangerous, the better disguised it appears." (Bossuet.) Talent then is no excuse, it is an aggravation of the offence. The Novelist is subject to the laws of Morality like the rest of mankind, even when he possesses, or thinks he possesses, great talents ; he is not justified in using these to the detriment of society. He may not choose to compete for the " prix Montyon " of virtue, but at any rate he should not work for the Morgue and the Criminal Courts.

Novel Writers object that preoccupation with morals clips

[1] Zola, *Documents littéraires*, 2nd ed., p. 386.

said Hermios, ". . . poor me! they were for pulverising me in atoms, but now . . . now they make me out an animal. . . . Last of all comes Empedocles, and turns me into a plant!"[1] If only he will make his characters men endowed with conscience and will and not plants and animals governed slavishly by their instincts, if he will re-establish in Fiction that most dramatic of struggles, between duty and passion, the Author will at the same time avoid the risk of encouraging crimes of passion by affording it the excuse of physiological necessity, and rendering his work more literary and more moving.

As modern Novelists study the text-books of Medicine and Physiology, an acquaintance with which is necessary for a proper knowledge of man, let them remember that the great lesson to be learned from these studies is the recognition of human weakness. Medicine teaches us that not only is the flesh weak, but the reason weak and fragile too, that very little is needed to confuse and lead it astray, and that every writer who has any sense of responsibility towards young people, women and the masses, should avoid every sort of unwholesome stimulation, harmful phrase and chance of offence. Goethe did not think so; "even for a child," he said, "there is no need to be over-anxious about the effect a book or a play may have upon him."[2] My own opinion is exactly the opposite; I do not think we can be too anxious. Victor Hugo,[3] who has always had a proper respect for children, was better inspired than Goethe when he wrote: "Poets, ever keep a moral purpose before your eyes. Never forget that perhaps children may read you. Have pity on the flaxen heads. We owe even more respect to youth than to old age."

Absence of any evil intent is not enough to prevent a book's being harmful, or to relieve the Author from the responsibility of the mischief he causes. There is a classi-fication of crimes in Literature no less than in Penal Law,

---

[1] Plutarch.   [2] *Entretiens d'Eckermann*, p. 268.
[3] Victor Hugo, *Littérature et philosophie mêlées*, p. 14.

there is wilful murder, and there is manslaughter by mis-
adventure. To kill a man by carelessness or failure to
observe regulations is a fault the Law very rightly punishes.
Absence of criminal intention does not eliminate moral,
nor even penal, responsibility. Man living among his
fellow-men is bound to think of the consequences of his
acts, and is liable to punishment if he causes another's
death by his carelessness. I have myself had to try a
landowner, who to keep his wine sound added a deleterious
substance to it which poisoned those who drank it; the
man had no intention of killing anybody, yet he was
condemned for involuntary manslaughter. Similarly the
Writer who mixes in his Tales sophistries that pervert
the mind and lead his readers into suicide, adultery and
crime, is guilty of an offence for which he is directly
responsible. When M. Bourget's *Disciple* commits a
crime, which is the logical consequence of the master's
teaching, the latter is morally responsible for the crime
he has led up to, and the disciple's mother is justified in
blaming the master for the mischief that has ensued.

However, Novelists are not always the only persons
responsible for the consequences arising out of their
books. Often it is schoolmasters and parents that are
to blame, because they set young people to read, or let
them read, Novels never intended for them. If a child
wounds itself with a gun its parents have allowed it to
handle, it is not the gunsmith who is responsible for the
accident, it is the parents who have acted unwisely.
Moral nourishment ought to be adapted to the mind,
just as physical nourishment should be to the stomach.
Such and such an article of food is suitable to the stomach
of an adult, but is unsuitable to that of a child. A glass
of wine which helps a grown-up man's digestion, will
upset a boy's. A man can bear strong drink, but children
require milk.

I would ask if teachers and lecturers, led away by their
admiration for the genius of Ovid, Tibullus, Propertius,
are not sometimes unwise in lavishing unqualified

panegyric in the presence of young people on a poetry that inculcates the art of loving, trifling, drinking, counting all women alike, even servants, that idealizes not merely physical love, but even homosexual love. In a study on Ovid, after extolling the beauties of the *Ars Amoris*, a literary critic exclaims, addressing young men : "Hear the master and imitate him."[1] I have heard lectures given at the Sorbonne, before young women, on La Fontaine's and Boccaccio's *Contes*. *Non erat hic locus*,— "this was not the place." The Lecturers, who are after all men of wit and intelligence, Members of the Institute, would have done well to remember a sentence in La Bruyère : "We may speak well, truly, *and* on a fitting occasion." It is surely an offence against this last condition to treat *risqué* subjects before girls coming for instruction to the Sorbonne ; these have other and better things to do than to read La Fontaine's and Boccaccio's *Contes*. I have often had occasion to note, in both Civil and Criminal cases, how young women and young men had been ruined by the reading of erotic Poets and Novelists. In the trial of M. and Mme. S——, Maître Betolaud brought out the fact that the young woman had been corrupted by reading Ovid's *Ars Amoris* and Théophile Gautier's Novel *Mademoiselle de Maupin*.[2] This study of Novels and erotic poetry gives young people a taste for profligacy, and the precocity so fostered prepares the ground, it may be for suicide, it may be for crimes of passion.

Lads of fifteen to eighteen who experience fierce outbursts of disappointed love and furious jealousy at an age when they should be playing prisoner's base, have not the strength of mind to master their passions. If they still retain some measure of self-restraint, they kill themselves, unable to bear the pangs of baulked love. If, on the other hand, they let themselves be led into entanglements with unworthy women, they will steal to satisfy their caprices

---

[1] Study by Jules Janin on Ovid prefixed to the *Ars Amoris*, p. 62.
[2] Bataille, *Causes criminelles* for 1880, p. 85.

and end in murder. Such, for instance, was the fate of the young Ducret, who belonged to a highly respectable family. At thirteen, he began to read a great many erotic novels and poems; he fell in love with a young girl, and spent his time in writing sentimental poetry. At seventeen he started for Brussels to rejoin the object of his young affections. Turned out of the house, he came back to Paris on foot; subsequently he returned a second time to Brussels to see the girl again, and in order to get money, resorted to smuggling and begging, and finally robbed his employer. A passion for another girl next seized him; this love not being returned, he felt such poignant unhappiness that he tried to kill himself. To stifle his pain, he gave himself to a life of profligacy, frequented the public dancing-rooms and took to drinking. Having lost his employment, in a moment of intoxication he strangled an old woman, intending to rob her; seized with a sudden remorse, he abandoned the proceeds and went and gave himself up to the Police. A copy was found on him in his own hand-writing of Victor Hugo's fine lines on *Conscience*, and it was this that seems to have dictated his final action, his unprompted confessions and remorse. If the Courts have before them a constantly increasing number of youthful thieves and murderers, this must partly be attributed to the precocious development of profligacy at the present day. I was myself on the bench at the trial of a young Graduate on a charge of inciting children under age to immorality; he kept a bar, it appears, where he welcomed girls of tender years. His mistress was a *divorcée*, the daughter of an Officer of Rank, who had been brought up at Saint-Denis.

If only teachers, who think more of the form than of the matter of Authors they comment on, would better realize the necessity of distinguishing the intellectual training from the moral education they should give their pupils, they would spare them a great deal of nonsense and their parents many bitter disappointments. The smallest solecism from a pupil makes them gasp with

horror. Let them show the same indignation against the
lapses of Writers who turn Literature into a forcing-house
of sensuality.

Erotic reading directly stimulates sexual precocity.
But, from the point of view of morals no less than of
health, it is advisable to retard the manifestations of the
sexual instinct. Continence is a saving of force, while
precocity of the passions destroys both physical and moral
vigour, diminishes intellectual activity, weakens family
affection and exaggerates selfishness. A youthful profligate, heedless of his parents and family, careless of his
honour, may easily grow capable of any and every breach
of decorum, any and every baseness, to satisfy his evil
passions.

Not that the Novelist's responsibility abrogates in any
way that of the reader. One of the most important of
moral obligations is a fitting choice of books; these must
be appropriate for the age, sex, temperament and upbringing of readers. Such and such a book may be quite
inoffensive for one person, yet highly dangerous for another.
Montesquieu, surprising his daughter in the act of reading
the *Lettres Persanes*, told her : "Let it alone ; 'tis a book
of my young days, never intended for yours." The same
books are far from making the same impression on all
readers. Novels which charm the fancy of a grown-up
man without disturbing his equilibrium, will stir the heart
of a young woman and upset her mind. The very same
romance of passion which is harmless for a man and wife
of middle age, nay! which may even be good for them as
warming their dulled imagination, will be mischievous to a
young man by throwing fuel on the fire of his passions.
The impression produced by books varies according to our
mental predispositions, and should therefore be chosen
with a view to these. The same work may have a bad
effect at one time, yet an exactly opposite one at another.
Again novel-reading is different in the results it produces
according as it is pursued in moderation, by a mind
occupied with serious studies, which only resorts to it for

a momentary diversion, or as it becomes the regular mental food of youthful intellects. Constant and exclusive reading of works of fiction, affording as they do merely emotions, sensations, impressions, teaches young people neither to think nor act. Age moreover modifies the influence exercised by books. A novel which only wearies a man of mature age, may dangerously inflame the imagination of a young man. In 1803 Napoleon I. thought Rousseau tedious, whereas in his young days the *Nouvelle Heloïse* had turned his brain. It was after reading this Author that in May 1806, at Valence, he took a disgust for life and wished to die.[1] *Werther* seemed extremely tiresome to La Harpe and Geoffroy. The latter wrote in 1812 : " There is a certain German Romance, that in former days appeared well adapted to turn young people's heads. . . . Yet so diffuse is it, so stuffed with empty nonsense, that nowadays its only effect is to make a man die of weariness, instead of love." Nevertheless we have seen instances, already quoted in the preceding Chapter, to show that for years after Geoffroy's criticism, *Werther* continued to make young men die, not of weariness at all, but of love and despair.

Believe me, it is a mistake for young men and young women, in whom sensibility and imagination are more developed than reason, to seek in the books they read only a stimulus to the former faculties. But what are we to think of Politicians who found libraries for the people as a means of influencing their constituents, and who to attract readers and gain votes, put licentious novels side by side with books of political propaganda ? I have seen boys and girls of fifteen and sixteen come for these books. And what are we to think of the Municipal Libraries, in which the interests of party introduce electoral agents of little or no education as administrators, men who use the funds in purchasing pornographic novels and authorizing schoolboys to come and read them ?

Public taste too shares the responsibility for this literary dissipation. Being all for "light literature," it stimulates

[1] Chuquet, *La Jeunesse de Napoléon*, p. 15.

authors to meet this demand. Pornographic novelists
would not be so numerous, if the public did not read
their books, if it preferred more solid literature. " I could
write serious books well enough," Martial says; " but I
prefer amusing ones; it is all your fault, dear reader, you
who read and sing my verses in every street in Rome."

CHAPTER XII.

CRIME DETERMINED BY PASSION, AND THE CONTAGION OF PLAYS OF PASSION AS AFFECTING IT.

> "Les mauvais exemples sont contagieux même sur les théâtres ; les feintes représentations ne causent que trop de véritables crimes. . . ."
> (*Sentiments de l'Académie française sur le "Cid."*) [1]

THE influence exerted on Morals by the Stage has been discussed in Antiquity by Plato, Aristotle and Aristophanes, in the Seventeenth Century by Theologians, Nicole and Bossuet, in the Eighteenth by Philosophers, Voltaire, Rousseau, d'Alembert. I propose myself to study it as a Magistrate and a Moralist, by the light of proceedings in the Criminal Courts. In Modern days documents and close reasoning are the chief things looked for, for no estimate is worth much that is not based on established facts. So long as the proofs are withheld, enquiry makes little or no progress, and we are left to wander in the domain of individual opinion. If the everlastingly debated question of the influence exerted on Morals by the Stage remains still undecided, this is because both sides alike, those who admit such influence and those who deny it, omit to furnish any proof, any decisive document, to support their contention ; neither advance beyond mere generalities.

Moreover, I think the question has been badly put. In fact, all those who have studied the influence of Stage plays on Morals have declared it good or bad as the case may be *absolutely*, without making any distinction between good plays and bad plays, without drawing attention to

---

[1] " Evil examples are infectious even on the Stage ; fictitious representations are only too apt to lead to veritable and actual crimes. . . ."
(Opinions of the " French Academy " on the *Cid.*)

the fact that the impression produced by a piece varies according to the age, sex, education and intelligence of the spectators. For some the Stage is invariably pernicious ; it is a mere school of corruption. For others, it is invariably beneficial,—a school of morality. The former declare :

> " Les dogmes qu'il contient, les lecons qu'il renferme,
> Loin de nous corriger, de nous rendre meilleurs,
> Séduisent l'innocence et corrompent les mœurs." [1]

The latter are no less absolute in affirming the contrary, and stoutly maintain the Stage to be an academy of virtue, a lay sermon.

> " La scène est une école où l'on n'enseigne plus
> Que l'horreur des forfaits et l'amour des vertus." [2]

According to Voltaire " genuine Tragedy is a school of Virtue, and the only difference between the purified Stage and the recognized Works on Morality is that in Tragedy the teaching is exhibited in action, that it is interesting and is displayed heightened by the charms of an Art, which surely was invented in old times for no other end but to instruct the earth and bless the sky." [3] D'Alembert again, in his *Letter to Rousseau*, opines that the Stage " is Morality put in action, its precepts reduced to concrete examples ; Tragedy shows us the calamities produced by the vices of mankind, Comedy the ridicule attaching to their less heinous faults, the two together place before our very eyes what Morality exhibits only in an abstract fashion and as it were afar off."

The truth seems to me to lie midway between these two extremes. There are good plays and bad plays ; there are Comedies which correct our faults by making us laugh at them ; there are Tragedies which educate by

---

[1] " The dogmas it contains, the lessons it includes, far from chastening us and making us better, seduce our innocence and corrupt our morals." Le Brun.

[2] " The Stage is a school where no longer now is anything taught but horror of sin and love of Virtue." Hauterive.

[3] Voltaire, *Dissertation sur la tragèdie.*

combining moral emotions with literary. But there are
also on the other hand Comedies which demoralize the
crowd by exciting their mockery of holy things, and there
are Dramas which by poetizing free love, adultery and
even crimes of passion, encourage them. The Stage may
purify or corrupt morals, elevate or degrade men's minds,
according to the use Dramatic authors make of their
talents, according to the ideals they set before them,
and their own moral idiosyncrasies.

The Stage then is a school of good or of bad morals
according to the play put upon it. My object, therefore,
is to inquire by the help of judicial documents, reports
of criminal proceedings and my own reminiscences as a
Magistrate, under what circumstances and to what audience
the Stage exerts a good, bad or indifferent influence, and
what are the plays that encourage Vice and crimes of
passion by the alluring pictures they draw of their delights
and by the sophistries they give currency to in order to
excuse their indulgence.

Writers who dread the reproach of immorality maintain
there are no such things as immoral plays, only badly
written plays; or else they quiet their conscience by
declaring the Stage has not the smallest influence on
morals and the character of the people at large. My own
opinion on the contrary is that the Stage exerts very
considerable influence, that the exaggerated love of
theatrical emotions makes a People "theatrical." It must
enjoy emotions in everyday life like those of the Stage,—
whether political, judicial or religious. Life seems tiresome, if it is not full of stir and movement, love seems
insipid, if it is not tragic; Politics, the Administration of
Justice, are interesting only in virtue of dramatic incidents.
A People that has once acquired this passion for the
Theatre, will have the Theatre everywhere, at the Law
Courts, in the Chamber of Deputies, in Church; it transforms a criminal trial into a judicial drama, a political
debate into a parliamentary drama, a religious ceremony
into a theatrical representation, history into a series of

awakened in them during its progress, are not effaced
directly they have left the theatre ; the spectacle remains
engraved in their minds, in their ears and eyes, and the
images thus called up are powerful enough to stir the
desire to imitate what has been seen.

At a Commission of Inquiry held at the "Conseil d'État,"
under the presidency of M. Vivien, on the management
and improvement of the Theatres and the Censorship of
Plays, Jules Janin insisted on the necessity of a prohibitory
censorship, relating the following anecdote in support of his
contention. Visiting one day one of the Paris prisons, he
was much impressed by what the Governor told him : "I
read," the latter said, "your notices in the paper, but I can
tell without that what sort of pieces are on at the Theatres ;
if a bad play has been staged, I discover the fact immediately by the number of young offenders who come here." [1]
A mother, whose son had turned out badly, told Philarète
Chasles her boy had been demoralized by theatre-going,
"that this had broken down his physical strength, got into
his head and taken away all taste for work." [2] Mme.
de Stael relates in her book on Germany [3] how young men
who saw Schiller's *Robbers* on the stage, were filled with
enthusiasm for the character and life of the Robber Chief,
and longed to imitate their hero. They revolted against
conventional society and hurried to the woods to lead
the life of bandits. "Their attempts at revolt were only
ludicrous," says Mme. de Staël ; "but for all that tragedies
and romances have far more importance in Germany than
in any other country. Everything is taken seriously there,
and the perusal of such and such a book, or the witnessing
of such and such a play, exercises an influence over life and
all its destinies."

Nor is it only in Germany that books and plays may
exert a determining influence over life. The passion for
the Theatre is even stronger in France than in Germany.

[1] *Histoire de la censure théâtrale*, by Hallays-Dabot, p. 331.
[2] *Études contemporaines*, p. 96.
[3] *De l'Allemagne*, 2nd Part, ch. xvii.

The Stage has acquired a high degree of importance in Paris and the great provincial towns. Conversation turns on the last new piece and the play of the actors, and Parisians are more familiar with the names of players than of Generals. An actress is more popular than a Commander-in-Chief, and the favourite Comedian of the hour enjoys an enormous prestige. We might well suppose ourselves back in the days when the Romans of the Decadence would be crowding to the Theatre, though the Barbarians were at the Gates, and when more than one city was captured while the populace was wildly applauding the actors' efforts. The Roman People asked for bread and the Games. A section of the Parisian population asks only alcohol and Stage-plays.

I have shown in the preceding Chapter how readers are drawn on to copy the heroes of novels by a kind of infectious imitation. And the influence of the Stage is even greater than that of books. Not only is the Theatre an amusement for the idle, a refined pleasure for the cultured, it is also, according to the nature of the pieces played, a school of good or bad manners and morals, a pulpit preaching just ideas or mischievous fallacies; it moulds the spirit of the audience, forms public opinion, paves the way for moral, social and even political reforms. With Corneille, the Stage is a school of heroism; with some other dramatic Authors, it is a school of depraved morals, adultery, profligacy and even murder.

The Stage stirs all passions, the noblest as well as the basest. It teaches love, piety, patriotism, just as it teaches hatred and revenge; its lessons include the sacrificing of love to duty, as they do that of duty to love. There are good plays, which elevate the mind and strengthen the will; there are bad plays, which enervate the mind and weaken the will. There are dramatic authors, who are true painters of character, clear-minded psychologists, moralists, politicians and philosophers; there are others, who are no more than public entertainers, flatterers of the populace and artists in pornography. Everything depends

On the boards it is not merely words appealing to the reader's intellect; it is living passion speaking to the eyes of the spectator, sounding in his ears, communicating itself to him in every feature and look and gesture of the actors, in every illusion and piece of stage effect, while each spectator's individual emotion is further increased by that radiated from all the rest. In an empty house or one only partly filled, a play produces only half its proper effect. If the benches are full, the emotion of the audience is enormously increased; a sort of electric current runs through the crowd and sets all hearts quivering. Montesquieu, though far from being a man of sensitive heart or hot head, writes that the *Sémiramis* and *Atrée* of Crébillon threw him into "transports worthy of the Bacchantes." Lord Byron tells us that a piece of Alfieri's, *Myrra*, actually moved him to tears, making him sob, he declares, "with an anguish, a terror, that very few specimens of the poetic art have ever occasioned me." If men of genius, like Montesquieu and Byron, are stirred so forcibly by dramatic fictions, we can easily understand how they may upset the imaginations of young people, of women, and generally of persons of more sensibility than solidity of mind. Horace quotes the case of a spectator whom a tragedy turned into a madman, while Lucian relates how an excellent actor, named Archelaus, having played the *Andromeda* of Euripides before the citizens of Abdera, in the middle of an exceptionally hot summer, several of the audience left the Theatre in a state of high fever, their imaginations all on fire with the Tragedy. Fancying themselves now Andromeda, now Perseus, now Medusa, they could not stop declaiming the Poet's verses and going through the piece the same as Archelaus had done. In fact, the Tragedy had brought on an excess of *Euripidomania*. It was the sight of Euripides' play of *Telephus* that decided Crates to embrace the life of a cynic.[1] Bayle, who mentions the mad fit of imitation on the part of the men of Abdera just referred to,[2] adds with no small

[1] Patin, *Eschyle*, p. 135.　　[2] In his *Dictionary*, under "Abdera."

sagacity : "The mind is subject to epidemics, just like the body. . . . Let a heresiarch or fanatic arise, whose infectious imagination and vehement passions are adapted to impress others, he will in a very short time infatuate a whole countryside or at any rate a very large number of persons."

Passion is infectious. In its criticisms of the *Cid*, the French Academy undoubtedly judged Corneille's play with an unfair degree of harshness, but it was quite justified in the remark that "strong passions well expressed often produce in those who see them as spectators some part of the effect they make on those who represent them in actuality ; . . . fictitious presentments only too frequently lead up to veritable crimes, and the danger is great in amusing the masses with pleasures which may one day cause public calamities."

Much has been written in the last few years on this tendency to imitation, awakened by reading about criminal acts or seeing them represented on the Stage.[1] The famous *savant* Chevreul was one of the first to draw attention to it in his pamphlet on *La Baguette divinatoire et les tables tournantes* ("The Divining Rod and Table Turning"). "I have no doubt," he says, "that the sight of certain actions, or even the knowledge gained of them merely by reading, leads certain individuals to perform the same acts, by reason of a tendency to movement thus mechanically determining them to an act which they would never have thought of apart from a circumstance foreign to their will, and to which instinct would never have led them." I have repeatedly seen instances coming under my cognizance as a Magistrate, where this observation of M. Chevreul's found confirmation.

So great is the force of example it creates a sort of contagion, a species of epidemic. Those who find themselves in a situation identical with that of the author of a crime, feel themselves almost irresistibly drawn on to

[1] See the Works of M. Tarde and Dr. Aubry, as also ch. x. of my book *Le Crime et la Peine*, headed *Le Crime et l'imitation* ("Crime and Imitation").

sophical reflections will be thrown off their balance by the passions they see dramatized before their eyes and experience feelings akin to those of the heroes of the play. The representation of *Phèdre*, a performance which will interest the most rigid moralist in a very high degree (everybody knows that the great Arnaud was a great admirer of this play and considered it highly moral), may produce disastrous effects upon a young woman, who will be shocked and corrupted by the spectacle of so shameless a passion. Habitués of the *Comédie Française* and the Odéon go to the Theatre in search of a literary gratification, a psychological study, an exact knowledge of human passions and human character. The illusion which the representation affords them is never so strong as to prevent their judging the piece and its author's intention, appreciating the truth of the delineation and the logical sequence of the situations. Reason is never overset, and they either do not yield themselves at all to the author's imaginative spell, or if they do so for an instant, very soon recover their habitual mental attitude. Once at home again, when the emotion stirred by the play has had time to cool, they escape the influence of the bad examples and sophistical maxims of the piece. Far different are the impressions experienced by young people, by women, by the uneducated, whose imagination and sensibility much exceed their powers of judgment; they do not criticize the play, they feel it, identifying themselves with its heroes and making its sentiments their own. For them a play is no fiction, it is a drama they live out themselves; they are not spectators, but actors; when present at a play of passion, it is not so much psychological instruction they look for as a series of excuses and encouragements for the indulgence of their own passions. This is just what Goethe found; "Young men," he declared, "saw in my piece a banner, under which their fiery passions could flaunt the day with impunity."

The number of those who go to the Theatre to judge of the merits of a play is very limited. The majority of spectators go there in search of emotions, to feel rather than to think.   The success of a piece depends on the interest it arouses, the emotions it gives rise to.   With the exception of a small minority of men who live by the head, the main part of every audience, including almost all the women and young men, live by the heart and imagination; they find pleasure only in emotion, and frequent only those plays which stir their feelings.

It is never the delineation of quiet goodness that rouses an audience; no doubt it elevates the mind, but then it does not pique the curiosity or excite any burning interest, it is too unexciting.   Men of sense and masters of their passions, women who are able to find love and happiness in marriage, are no heroes for the boards. What the public likes is frenzied passion, imagination run mad; what it does not appreciate on the stage is reasonable love and domestic bliss.   It finds virtue dull, and reproaches authors who write idylls for it with putting no wolves in their pastorals; it likes wolves.   It is to suit this taste of their patrons, to divert their audiences [1] and supply them with a due stock of thrilling emotions, that Dramatic Authors search the records of Crime for good telling horrors to set spectators shuddering with terror and pity, and pile up in their dramas adultery, jealousy, revenge, murder, poisoning and suicide.   Criminals abound in every play.   The public appears to find no pleasure in a piece unless it sees some of the characters either as murderers or suicides.   Death is the main-spring of the modern Theatre.   Many sittings of the Assize Courts would be needed to judge all the criminals of the tragic stage, and a whole row of tables to hold as "pièces de conviction" all the daggers, ropes, cups of poison employed by heroes of the theatre to stab, strangle and poison their victims.   Every variety of crime is found on the Stage,

---

[1] "For my own part," Corneille himself says, "I hold with Aristotle and Horace that our arts only end in amusement."   Dedication to *La Suite du Menteur.*—In the Preface to *Bérénice,* Racine also declares the sole aim of the stage to be to please.

Criminal dock use less ferocity of language to announce their purpose. Lacenaire alone,—and he was the author of several tragedies,—proclaimed in melodramatic style : "Society will have my blood, but in my turn I shall have society's." Your Stage heroes on the other hand are for ever repeating, till one is tired of hearing it, that *they want blood*; they are continually figuring in their imaginations the pleasure they are going to enjoy in shedding a rival's blood, or slaying an unfaithful wife.

In *Zaïre*, Orosmane exclaims :

> " . . . et ma main dégouttante
> Confondrait dans son sang le sang de son amant." [1]

Even the female characters love to set blood flowing ;

> " Dans ton perfide sang, je puis tout expier . . .
> Revenez tout convert du sang de l'infidèle," [2]

cries Hermione, intoxicated with jealousy and the lust of vengeance.

Phèdre again declares :

> "' Mes homicides mains, prêtes à me venger,
> Dans le sang innocent, brûlent de se plonger." [3]

The sentiments found in the mouths of the heroes of Tragedy, stripped of the splendour of the verse that enshrines and transfigures them, are identical with those we note among the heroes of the Criminal Courts ; savage lust of vengeance is what inspires both and drives them to the commission of the most atrocious deeds. Always excepting Bérénice, almost all the female characters of the Stage who are forsaken avenge their wrongs ; Hermione,

---

[1] " . . . and my dripping hand should mingle with her blood her lover's gore."

[2] " In thy traitorous blood I can expiate all offences . . . return drenched in the deceiver's gore."

[3] " My murderous hands, ready to wreak my revenge, burn to plunge in innocent blood."

Roxane, Phèdre, Médée, all do so. Like the vitriol throwers of the present day, Hermione and Roxane utter horrid threats of death against Pyrrhus and Bajazet, which they go on repeating *ad nauseam* :

"Bajazet doit périr, dit-elle, ou l'épouser."[1]

To punish Pyrrhus, Hermione urges Oreste to slay him, and when she sees him hesitate, forms the project of going herself to stab him to death. Her frenzied fancy pictures the pleasure she is sure to find in shedding the traitor's blood :

"Quel plaisir de venger moi-même mon offense . . .
De retirer mon bras teint du sang du parjure ! "[2]

Just like the female criminals who are tried at the Courts of Assize, the heroines of the Stage show refinements of cruelty in the forms their vengeance takes, and they love to make a hated rival suffer doubly in actually witnessing the faithless lover's death pangs.

Hermione pushes her savage lust of vengeance so far as to wish to kill her involuntary rival's child, and Pyrrhus himself is odious enough to threaten Andromaque with the ultimatum, " Marriage or Astyanax' death ! "

The same vindictive fury animates a large number of Corneille's heroines ;

"L'esclave le plus vil qu'on puisse imaginer,
Sera digne de moi, s'il peut t'assassiner,"[3]

is what Pulchérie says to Phocas.

Lastly, yet another point of resemblance with ordinary female criminals who often kill themselves after killing others, the heroines of the Stage too make their own suicide the sequel of murder :

---

[1] " Bajazet must perish, she declares, or marry her."

[2] "What pleasure to avenge my wrong myself . . . to withdraw my arm dyed with the perjured traitor's gore ! "

[3] " The vilest slave you can imagine will be a worthy mate for me, if he can but murder you."

The man who has a peaceful home of his own, sheltered
from every storm, likes to watch in others the tempests of
a tortured heart and harrowed senses and the rage of unbridled passion. The most virtuous wife does not object
to a picture of guilty love. A pessimist will account for
the fact by saying that she is a trifle weary of her virtue
and longs to win the enjoyment, though only in make-
believe, of a criminal passion. But it is more correct to
say that this attraction towards what is wrong arises
mainly out of curiosity. For the most part of men and
women life is so flat and prosaic that the representation
of a love drama, abounding in tragic situations, shakes
them up and stirs their minds in an agreeable fashion :

"Le jeu des passions saisit le spectateur,
Il aime, il hait, il pleure, et lui-même est acteur."[1]

If the hero suffer, the spectator suffers with him, if he
is happy, he is happy too,—so closely does he identify
himself with him ; the young man falls in love with the
heroine of the piece, the young girl with the hero. Both
come to see, then love to inflame their own affection
by so infectious a sight; they leave the theatre with senses
on fire and imagination blazing, with never a thought
but of high-wrought passions. "I learned to bewail Dido,"
wrote Saint Augustine . . . "if they tried to deprive
me of this reading, I should bewail at having nothing to
bewail. . . . I felt likewise an inordinate passion for the
spectacles of the theatre, because I found therein a lively
picture of my own miseries, and because they served as
a train to kindle the fires that consumed me."[2] Passion
represented on the boards soon communicates itself to
the younger members of the audience, who are fired by
seeing lovers plead their passion on the stage, long for
the possession of the object of their affections, and win
it at last, making them desire the same happiness. M.
Jules Lemaître accounts for Racine's abandonment of

---

[1] "The play of passions seizes the spectators ; he loves and hates, and weeps,
and is an actor himself." L. Racine, *Epître à M. de Valincourt.*
[2] *Les Confessions de Saint Augustine,* bk. v., bk. iii., ch. ii.

poetic composition after *Phèdre* by the terror the infectious nature of passion caused him: "When he saw
the character of Phèdre as interpreted by Mlle. Champmeslé,
he realized for the first time all there is of contagion residing in the presentment of love-sickness on the stage."[1]
Nor is it only love-sickness that is communicated by
theatrical representation; all love is contagious, as Bossuet
pointed out in his *Réflexions sur la Comédie.* Some may
think he treats the Stage from a too limited point of view
and a too ascetic standpoint; but his psychological and even
physiological reflections (for Bossuet had been a profound
student of Physiology) are admirable for their acuteness and
good sense. He depicts, just as a Physiologist of the present
day might do, the infectious nature of those theatrical representations, "which set all the pit aflame and all the
boxes, . . . which excite youth to love," which set the
fire of passion coursing "in all veins," and penetrating
"to the marrow of the bones." Again and again he uses
the word "contagion" to express the communication of
passions to the audience by their representation on the
stage: "Do you really and truly imagine," he says, "that
the subtle *contagion* of a dangerous evil always demands
a coarse and unworthy object? . . . To think that Saint
Augustine did not deplore in Comedies this play of the
passions and the *contagious* expression of our moral
weaknesses."

Corneille professes to believe that "love in misfortune
only excites pity and is better adapted to purge this
passion in us than to set us longing for it. "There is no
man," he says, "who, on leaving the house after seeing a
performance of the *Cid*, ever really wished to have killed,
like the hero, his mistress's father, in order to enjoy similar
favours."[2] Corneille is mistaken, the delineation of love
in calamity does not repel, and every spectator would
like to change places with Rodrigue:

"Tout Paris pour Chimène a les yeux de Rodrigue."[3]

---

[1] Jules Lemaître, 8th Series, p. 81.   [2] Corneille, Preface to *Attila.*
[3] "All Paris for Chimène has the eyes of Rodrigue."

But Corneille, by way of answer to the two stringent criticisms of Bossuet, might have pointed out that, if the Stage only offered types of lovers such as Chimène and Rodrigue, it would not be a very dangerous institution, for the lesson they teach is no other than that duty must come before love.

Ovid likewise observed the infectious character of the presentment of love on the stage. A young man, he says, docile enough to the advice I offered him, by which to free himself from his love, was all but cured; "but the *infectious* sight of some lovers brought on a sad relapse. . . . All ye who would fain cease to love, *avoid contagion*. . . . He who looks upon another's wounds finds himself wounded too."

At the end of the *Symposium*, Xenophon described long ago, with full precision of physiological detail, the impression produced on the audience by the representation of a love drama. "They heard Bacchus ask Ariadné," he writes, "if she loves him, and Ariadné swear she loves none but him. . . . When finally the guests saw them hold each other embraced . . . those that were not married took an oath to marry straightway, and those that were, sprang into the saddle and away to their wives to be happy in their turn."

If the representation of a love drama had no worse effects than to rekindle conjugal affection and inspire a wish to marry in single men, all would be well. But alas! it often leads to irregular liaisons, ending in desertion, it provokes in young people a dangerous precocity in matters of sex, and paves the way to the fall of a certain number of married women. There is no need, in order to safeguard the morality of the young, to inspire them with a horror of love and the stage plays that depict it; it is advantageous indeed to hold out a loving marriage as the end they should aim at. But it is unwise too soon to display before their eyes an ardent presentment of love's ecstasies; too early an initiation into the science of the passions is sure to inspire them with a desire to supplement theory with practice. Young men, whose nature lays them open only too much to amorous impressions, need something to distract their attention by the suggestion of a different line of thought. It would be greatly to the advantage of their well-being, both physical and moral, as well as of their education, to postpone their initiation into the turmoils of the heart. But the representation of love on the stage has exactly the opposite effect, it accelerates the blossoming of love. I have likewise frequently had occasion in criminal proceedings to observe the fact that young girls who had been taken to the theatre at too early an age readily succumbed to seduction and had, without hesitation, abandoned friends and family to go off with some Lovelace or other, under the excitement of a play that had stirred their imaginations. Seeing how on the stage Passion is an excuse for everything, how it is always noble and always admired, even when it tramples underfoot every duty, they had come to believe there was nothing higher than passion, nothing more important, more poetical and more ennobling. If they had not found love follies invariably excused and glorified on the boards, they would have thought a little more of their parents, their honour and their future, and a little less of their seducers,—who were only very commonplace profligates after all.

The Literary Critics consider it a mark of great progress the ever greater place Dramatic Authors assign in their pieces to the delineation of love. In his parallel between the Ancients and Moderns, Perrault reproaches the former with having known nothing of gallantry. Under the influence of the romances of Chivalry and the habits of gallantry customary at Courts, dramatic writers have acquired the custom of representing all their heroes as in love and reckoning gallantry a merit. Boileau himself, who in his Dialogue on the heroes of romance made fun of those heroes that never have a word to say of anything but love, and who had no personal knowledge of the

passion owing to an accident in his boyhood,[1] declares
the *Jerusalem Delivered* would be tiresome without its
descriptions of the loves of Renaldo and Tancreda,
"*Fabula nulla est sine amore Menandri*,"—"No pleasing
piece of Menander's is without Love." Love being part
of life and the stage a copy of life, its representation on
the boards cannot well be prohibited, if only the dramatic
author does not devote himself to the portrayal of sensual
love, and refrains from declaring that love is virtue, is
superior to all laws, is the chief end of life, that true love
will not stop short at crime,—sophistries that lead the way
to seduction, adultery, and crimes of passion.

The modern Stage is the apotheosis of Love. It is only
in Corneille's Tragedies and in Racine's *Bérénice* that the
hero sacrifices Love to Duty. The rule is nowadays, Duty
must be sacrificed to Love. On the boards Passion is
always noble, even when it is savage, mad and criminal.
This was not the case among the Greeks. Less importance
and less dignity were attached to love in the Greek theatre,
because women did not frequent it ; the dramatic poets of
Antiquity wrote for men. Modern Authors on the contrary write above all for women, and seeing the latter are
interested chiefly, nay ! almost exclusively, in the delineation of love, they compose dramas of love expressly for them,
plays in which Passion is represented as a divine force,
entitled to rank above honour and duty. Manzoni used
to say all this picturing of passion effected was to increase
the dose of love there is in the world, and as this dose is
already infinitely stronger than it should be, Dramatists
would be doing humanity a great service, if only they
would use their talents to describe and so reinforce other
sentiments, such as courage, patriotism, piety, good-nature
and generosity. In so doing they would but be imitating
the greatest Greek Poets, Æschylus and Sophocles. There
is no love in Æschylus and very little in Sophocles ; there
is a great deal in Euripides, but Aristophanes blames him
for the fact. In one of his pieces he makes Æschylus say

---

[1] This accident has been recorded by Racine *fils* in his Memoirs of his father.

to Euripides: "I will show them neither Sthenebœa nor shameless Phædra, and I am not aware I have ever put a woman in love on the stage."—*Euripides:* "But what harm have my Stheneboeas done to Athens?"—*Æschylus:* "You are to blame that honest wives of honest citizens have drunk hemlock."—*Euripides:* "Did *I* invent the tale of Phædra?"—*Æschylus:* "No! 'tis a true story, but it is a poet's duty to hide what is infamous, and not display it on the scene."[1]—The calamities of Royal Houses, and of the Fatherland, appeal to Æschylus as more interesting than the fury of a jealous lover or the sorrows of a woman whose passion is not returned. Corneille was of the same opinion, when he said: "The dignity of Tragedy demands some great interest of State or some passion nobler and more virile than Love, such as ambition or revenge, and should foreshadow greater calamities than the loss of a mistress." In *Esther* and *Athalie*, Racine has likewise shown that fine Tragedies can be written without love. Alexandre Dumas *fils*, who gave so large a place to love in his earlier Comedies, discovered in due course there are higher thoughts than sexual preoccupations, for he makes Claude say to his disciple: "Man of twenty, who have it may be forty years still to live, what mean you by coming here to talk of love sorrows? . . . And your God you must find again? And your conscience you must re-establish? And your Country you must re-make?" The young men of Greece and Rome, who found something else on their stage than outpourings of passion, had fewer thoughts to throw away on their mistresses and more to devote to their Country. The effect of the excessive, all but exclusive, importance given nowadays by the theatre to passion, is to throw into the shade nobler and more elevated sentiments. Surely it is an inordinate limitation of an audience's intellectual faculties to concentrate the whole of their attention upon the relations of the sexes. Something more of variety is demanded in the subject matter of our plays.

[1] See *Tusculans*, bk. iv. §§ 32, 33.

ness, modesty, resignation, good-nature, sweet reasonableness, are in no way incompatible with love. There is more
than one kind of love. It is hardly to be desired there
should be many women in the world who love, knife or
revolver in hand ; this sort of love is within the reach of
the most commonplace of womankind. It is for having
loved after this fashion that so many female criminals
appear in the dock between two gendarmes at the Police
Courts and the Assizes. Another type of love altogether,
bearing no resemblance to the frenzied passion of such
women, is no less true and far nobler and deeper.

Sensual love is not so common in women as in men.
The physical craving is less insistent in the female. The
number of passionately amorous women is not large. The
maternal instinct is much more highly developed in them
than the sexual. " Give me a child, or I die," Rachel
said to Jacob. If dramatic authors so often depict feminine
love as sensual, this is because it is sensual love that en-
genders crimes.

Above all it is the romantic Stage which, by poetizing
the love that kills either others or itself, has disseminated
among the public this idea that the murderer from love is
a great heart, a noble character. According to the Writers
of this school, a hero cannot really be in love, unless he is
ready and willing to stab his mistress or his mistress's
husband to death at a moment's notice. In Corneille's
plays, a lover proves his love to the woman he has failed
to marry by heroically saving her husband's life. On the
romantic Stage, on the contrary, the lover finds no better
way to prove his love for his mistress than by offering to
murder her husband. According to this school, so long as
love stops short of murder, its sincerity may legitimately
be doubted ; to ensure recognition, it must have set blood
flowing. If the lover does not become a furious madman,
ready to stab a husband and strangle a rival, he is not
judged to be in earnest ; his only method of proving the
sincerity of his passion is to commit a series of follies and
crimes. Woe to the stage hero who possesses common

sense or common morality; he ceases at once to inspire interest, if he shows any respect for human life. The audience, and especially the female part of it, seduced by these pictures of guilty love, deem the man worthy of all admiration who sacrifices everything to love; a hero who stops short of this last extravagance will fail to please them, as being too reasonable and cool-headed. The Stage must have frenzied passions, delirious madness, daggers, blood, to show.

The same fallacy has spread from the theatre to society at large,—the fallacy that love is not really deep, unless it is capable of every reckless extravagance and savage crime. Yet nothing can be more unfounded than such a belief; criminality in love proves only violence and excitability of temperament, in no sense energy of character. The brutes kill their rivals and the females of their species who repulse them, and yet they are quoted as models of what love should be. Why, therefore, extol as energy on the stage the brute force of the lover who kills? With the one exception of Oreste, Racine has attributed suchlike criminal frenzies of love only to violent and weak-willed women; Bajazet, Xipharès, Britannicus, deeply as they are enamoured, are not madmen.

Every day the Courts of Assize have to adjudicate in crimes committed by madmen in love, who have little or nothing poetical about them. For instance, in 1891 the Assize Court of Meurthe-et-Moselle condemned to death a man named Meunier, a custom-house officer and time-expired soldier, who from motives connected with love had twice been guilty of arson and three times of murder, and had actually killed his own son. Left a widower with two children, Meunier had fallen in love with Marie J——, his Captain's sister, and asked her in marriage. His demand was refused, although he was liked and respected by his superior officers, on the ground of his being a widower, father of two children, and without fortune. To get money, he robbed a priest and set fire to his house, and the priest and his maid-servant were burned to death. Marie J——, still persisting in her refusal to marry him, Meunier threatened to kill himself at her feet; and subsequently, in order to make her as poor as himself, he set fire to the house she lived in, with the idea that she would consent to marry him, when she found herself houseless. Finally, seeing that his two children were another obstacle to his marriage, he made up his mind to put them out of the way, and began by killing the elder, a boy of eight, smothering the child on a bed underneath an eider-down quilt. Finding Marie J—— still set against him and thinking her brother was encouraging her in her refusal, he determined to be revenged and shot him with a gun, shattering his right arm and right leg. When the Presiding Judge questioned him about the murder of his son, Meunier answered: "Ah! but I was very fond of him for all that, my little lad!"—*The Judge:* "What! and yet you murdered him!"—*The Prisoner:* "What would you have? It was for love of the young lady. I was mad." He received the sentence of death with a smile, and curling his moustache, observed: "Well and good! Still, it's not what every man would have done, to die like this, for a woman." On his way to the scaffold, he remarked further: "I am no common criminal. Ah! women, women! For love of a girl, to kill one's own offspring! A man who had never been in trouble with anybody, and was always well conducted. . . . I am ready as soon as you are. A good Frenchman is not afraid of death. A good soldier like me will not turn coward."

It is no uncommon thing to see prisoners who have done murder from motives of love or jealousy, proudly admit the crime they have committed; they are like heroes of the playhouse, vain of their misdoings. The fact is, by encouraging a habit of living in an atmosphere of passion, the Stage makes men love and admire the passion it is so ready to depict, and weakens the sense of duty by rendering the authors of crimes of passion interesting. In this way the horror a murder should by rights inspire is transformed into pity, and the acmé of the dramatist's skill and triumph is to draw these tears of pity not for the victim but the murderer. To elicit sympathy for the victim would be too commonplace. It is to the criminal the modern playwright strives to direct pity and compassion, and not without success ; the audience appreciates his motives, bewails his hard fate and sympathizes in his sufferings, his anger and his revenge. The stage presentment of a crime of passion produces the same effect as a piece of skilful special pleading, that by laying stress solely on the extenuating circumstances assures the acquittal of the accused. The dramatic author makes the criminal interesting by bringing him near us, accounting for him, showing how he has been little by little driven to crime by a passion we all share with him, and how he struggled against it, suffered and succumbed. The fact is, when we see a fellow-creature in pain, no matter how guilty he may be, we cannot but feel some sympathy for him.

So in his answer to Rousseau, Marmontel seems to me to have singularly exaggerated the moral good effects of the Stage when he says, speaking of dramatic authors : " What is the evil passion they have flattered ? . . . What is the vice they have encouraged ? . . . All pernicious tendencies are condemned on the Stage ; all deadly passions inspire horror ; all unhappy weaknesses meet with pity and abhorrence. The Stage does what Sparta did, where to keep children from drunkenness, they used to show them drunken Helots."[1] Possibly the sight of drunken helots may have taught the Spartans sobriety. But the delineation of passion, embellished as it is by the charm of poetry and the actor's talent, entirely fails to inspire the same repugnance as intoxication ; the sight of a man proud in his love does not produce the same disgust as that of a drunkard does ; the presentment of his happiness or even of his sufferings is seductive rather than the reverse.

Women, whom love drives into crime, are objects of our admiration on the Stage. M. Legouvé calls them " sublime

[1] *Mercure de France*, Nov. 1758.

murderesses ";[1] M. Jules Lemaître says "these angels of assassination" are, in his eyes, adorable.[2] Such is the magic of dramatic poetry, which gives an aureole of sanctity to murderers from love, that the crimes of Hermione, Roxane, Phèdre, Médée do not inspire us with the slightest horror. We sympathize with Hermione who has Pyrrhus stabbed, and with Roxane who has Bajazet strangled. Racine makes us take an admiring interest in Phèdre, who is stained both with incest and perjury. M. Saint-Marc Girardin and M. D. Nisard, those two Nestors of the University, find nothing unjustifiable in the murders of Pyrrhus and Jason, and declare that if they had had to judge Hermione and Médée as prisoners at the bar of the Assize Court, they would not have hesitated to acquit them. "When these women, so basely betrayed, find means of revenge," writes Saint-Marc Girardin, "we applaud the well-deserved act of punishment. . . . Yes! against Jason anything is lawful; and if Medea's soul *is* thirsty for the traitor's blood, and she takes his life, if I were on the jury no man should ever make me pronounce the woman guilty. I excuse, nay! I approve and support the outraged wife who avenges her wrongs."[3] Yet this Fury, whom the famous Critic excuses and approves, has had her rival done to death with hideous tortures, has killed her own father, and would fain have burned Corinth to the ground, to ensure her father's and her rival's death. In her thirst for vengeance, she regrets her rival has no children that she might destroy them.[4] Finally, with hellish cruelty, she slaughters her own children as a means of taking vengeance on their father. Yet, supposing this unnatural mother to be brought up at the bar of the Court of Assize, M. Saint-Marc Girardin would have no hesitation, as a juryman, in acquitting her! We can scarce wonder

---

[1] *Revue Bleue*, 11th Oct. 1890.   [2] *Ibid.*, 2nd Aug. 1884.

[3] *Cours de littérature dramatique*, vol. iv. p. 306.

[4] " Que n'a-t-elle pas déjà des enfants de Jason,
    Sur qui plus pleinement venger sa trahison ? "

"Why has she not already children by Jason, on whom more fully to avenge his treachery?"

now that juries so often acquit the authors of less odious crimes of passion, and by this mistaken clemency make such crimes so common as they are.

Nor is M. Saint-Marc Girardin the only literary Critic who has approved of the vengeance of passion. In his study on Hermione, D. Nisard does not hesitate either to declare that "her revenge is quite justified."[1] M. G. Merlet again, in his remarks on Corneille as a dramatist, cannot refrain from admiring "the art of the Poet that can ennoble crime by the very intrepidity of its daring, and endow it with an inexplicable air of grandeur." In his observations on *Rodogune*, Corneille congratulates himself on having framed the character of Cléopâtre, who hesitates at no crime necessary to punish a rival and maintain her own power. "All her crimes," he says, "are fraught with such a high-souled grandeur, that while we detest her actions, we cannot but admire the source from which they spring."

"To ennoble crime," "to endow it with an air of grandeur," to make the murderer interesting and the female prisoner saintly,—is this a useful task? Here is an instance, which I borrow from a criminal trial, to prove the danger of familiarizing the minds of an audience with notions of crime and the pictures it evokes, of minimizing the horror it should inspire and setting up a false ideal by ennobling the crime of murder. On Nov. 16, 1860, the Assize Court of the Bouches-du-Rhône tried for attempted murder a man named P——, a tailor of Marseilles, of Italian origin and an enthusiastic admirer of Alfieri's tragedies. This man had become the lover of a married woman, and had tried to murder her husband out of jealousy. When he was arrested and taken to the Police Station, he asked for a glass of water, and the officer having told him to wait a moment, the prisoner exclaimed that he was surprised to see how civilization was understood in France. A moment later, the same officer having looked hard at him, the man said : " There is no need for you to stare at me so; I am more to be

[1] D. Nisard, *Histoire de la Littérature française.*

vengeance and treachery they would see represented and as it were realized on the Stage;[1] and in this opinion he was at one with Plato. Judicial experience confirms the correctness of view of these two great Philosophers. Here is another example in support of their contention. On Nov. 2, 1884, a child of thirteen, Joseph Wentzeis, appeared at the bar of the Assize Court of the Department of the Cher. The boy, apprenticed to a Confectioner at Bourges, had been dismissed on account of his improprieties of conduct and the amorous advances with which he pestered a young servant girl, who, so he said, showed herself more hard-hearted than her predecessor. He made up his mind to be avenged on his former master; with this end he carefully sharpened a long knife, posted himself one evening at a place where his master was bound to pass and plunged the weapon in his breast. At his trial he stated he had conceived the idea of his vengeance from reading a novel called *La Belle Julie*, the hero of which is a boy of fourteen, who commits a murder under similar conditions. If the mere account of a crime can impress a child's brain so vividly as to set him upon copying it, how much more perilous for a young brain must be the representation of a crime on the stage, where we hear the cries of fury of the guilty hero and see his face inflamed with angry passion. Here lies the danger of melodramas and those judicial dramas which adorn the boards of the Minor Theatres.

Not that all Melodramas without exception are bad'; "Long live the Melodrama where Margot has wept!" Musset says: There are Plays of this kind that do not offend either against morals or good sense. MM. Weiss and Sarcey did not despise the *genre*; and at any rate a good Melodrama is better than a bad Tragedy. But it is a perilous thing to set the people weeping over virtuous convicts and laughing at the sallies of witty murderers. In a great proportion of these Melodramas written for the masses, convicts are represented as such prodigies of

---

[1] Aristotle, *Politics*, bk. iv. ch. xv. § 7.

virtue as to make the hulks admired and society an object
of contempt, while murderers sparkle with wit and intellect.   It is seldom these Plays do not contain, besides
the usual crop of murders, seduction, adultery and even
rape.   The witty murderer is almost always an elegant
seducer, a Don Juan of the finest manners ; he proclaims
his love in lyrical accents, and invokes the sacred rights
of passion.   If the woman is married and endeavours to
resist him, he lifts her from her feet and carries her off
amid the frenzied applause of the house, the young men
envying the seducer, the female part of the audience the
victim.

Schiller first brought amorous brigands into vogue, Byron
passionate corsairs, Victor Hugo chivalrous bandits; melodrama has idealized the "comic murderer."   All these
ruffians are at once ferocious and tender-hearted, devils
and angels, men full of bitter laughter and biting irony,
greedy of blood and love.   The hero of Schiller's Play,
Moor, takes an anarchist's joy in firing powder magazines.
"Do you hear," he cries, "the powder magazine explode,
stifling in the bed of pain the mother and her new-born
babe?   Do you see yonder tongues of flame lick the cradle
of her first-born? . . . There is the nuptial torch, and
the marriage songs."[1]   All these literary bandits, half
satyrs, half murderers, turn the heads of young men, who
take them for models and long for a life like theirs, made
up of orgy and revolt.   Only one thing could avail to
deter them from this false hero-worship, fear of justice,
terror of the police, but in melodramas they see criminals
invariably escaping the officers of justice and getting the
laugh of them.   Not only are murder, theft, rape, adultery,
prostitution and vagrancy, put upon the boards, but Justice
is mocked at and the Police flouted, the fine part being
always assigned to the murderer, and the contemptible
one to the Magistrate.   How can we suppose such sights
likely to inspire respect for Law and Justice ?

Plays   have   actually   been   written   with   Cartouche,

[1] Schiller, *The Robbers*, Act v. Sc. 3.

of vice. After turning into derision marriage and respect for the marriage vow, chastity, paternal authority, social law and obligation, the Stage trifles with Crime, holding up for popular admiration types like Robert Macaire, the sneak-thief, the go-between, the night-hawk, and suchlike. When *Robert Macaire* was played for the first time in 1835, Jules Janin wrote with much good sense : "Beware of Robert Macaire, he is already chosen first favourite by the crowd ; they love, admire, and applaud him ; they call him friend, and would lend him a knife at any moment if he wanted it. Beware, I say ; Robert Macaire is the popular hero." And Jules Janin was quite right ; Robert Macaire has served as model to Lacenaire and many another young stage-struck criminal, the sort who indulge in buffoonery just before and directly after a murder, and accompany a foul blow with a bad joke. After assassinating Germeuil to steal his money, Robert Macaire loses none of his assurance ; he is proud of his crime, and thinks it a clever thing to have done. To hold up a criminal to admiration, to make him inter- esting, to extol his ability and skill, is debauching the spectators' minds, stifling their sense of right and wrong, and their feeling of indignation against crime. Such plays destroy all respect for human life ; I may go further and say, they destroy all respect for the legal punishment of crime. Indeed, it is a far commoner sight nowadays than ever before to behold youthful murderers walk to the scaffold laughing and joking. This is only another theatrical pose borrowed from melodramas, where criminals are represented cracking jokes with the executioner ; they wish in their turn to die like stage heroes, and the spectacle of their cynical indifference still further corrupts the crowd, who learn from it to feel contempt for the last penalty of the law. When Campi was led to the scaffold, he affected to brazen it out, and exclaimed, on first catching sight of it, "And that's all, is it ?" . . . On the morning of his execution, Prado stripped off his prison clothes, and put his own on again with a smile, red socks, patent-leather shoes, and all ; he horrified the chaplain who attended him by his appalling coolness. When the priest offered him a glass of liquor to give him courage, Prado retorted : " Courage, my dear sir; why ! I have more than you have ; you are all shaken, but I'm not, though I'm on my way to the shambles to be axed."

In the Police and Assize Courts in Paris and the large towns, we often see youthful prisoners trying to provoke the hilarity and surprise of the public by cynical answers and mocking comments on the proceedings ; they are posing in fact for the Newspaper Reporters, who are only too ready to print their vapourings. These stagey misdemeanants, who seek to win notoriety by their insolently cynical attitude, are often habitués of the cheap theatre, wags whose proper place is in the pit or "gods" of a penny-gaff. In no country in the world does a greater tendency exist to make fun of the law, the police, the defenders of society generally. This want of proper respect arises from a variety of causes,—the frivolity of the Parisian's character, his love of raillery and *blague*, the violence of language indulged in by the Press, the frequency of revolutions, placing men in power who are not invariably fitted for its exercise. But there is no doubt those theatrical pieces in which the public is taught to laugh at authority, and find diversion at the expense of Magistrates and Policemen, are not unconnected with the loss of proper respect referred to. These more or less witty jokes may very well supply actors and artists generally and other educated minds with a little harmless amusement, but they are far from being equally inoffensive for the crowd and for young people who take these gibes in dead seriousness.

Nor does the Stage appear to me to have been much better inspired in poetizing the Paris *gamin*, who is more often than not only a young blackguard, haunting taverns, associating with thieves, on familiar terms with girls of the streets, and with indecent songs for ever on his lips. Victor Hugo persists, in spite of all this, in making him

The Stage is unwholesome when it makes a mock of marriage, when it poetizes free love and puts passion above the laws. It would seem, to judge by plays, that marriage is never based on love, that conjugal love is not really love at all, because it rests on a basis of mutual respect as well as mutual sympathy; it is supposed to be impossible for husband and wife to love each other, because they are reasonable beings and not a sort of lunatics. In Plays, as in Novels, husbands are almost invariably tyrants, ruffians, coarse-minded vulgarians, while lovers are represented as tender-hearted, high-minded, sweetly sympathetic creatures. "The public," Voltaire says, "always takes the side of the hero lover as against the husband who is no hero,"—the reason being that the Stage has accustomed people to laugh at the husband and the marriage tie. The best of our Dramatists only laugh at the misfortunes, which are not really laughable at all, of the husband who is dishonoured by his wife. Molière's Comedies are full of witticisms on the subject. The Ancients saw nothing diverting in the calamity of an outraged husband; nor do other Nations find anything so very agreeable in the lot of a father who has reason to doubt the paternity of his children, whereas on the French stage a wife's wickedness merely makes the husband ridiculous.

This dread of ridicule, which under the conditions of our modern society falls so unjustly on the outraged husband, has much to do with acts of revenge on the latter's part. I have found on many occasions, in criminal cases, that the unfortunate husband suffers so keenly from the fear of ridicule as to be almost driven mad by it. He fancies he sees his neighbours, and even passers-by in the street, laughing at him, till at last in his exasperation he becomes a murderer.

Few and far between are the Plays that undertake to defend marriage and the husband's rights. Dramatic authors as a rule have scant respect for these latter, holding the lover's to be superior. There are even pieces, the *Enfant malade* for instance, in which the husband, like George Sand's *Jacques*, surrenders his wife to her lover, after receiving a confession of her adulterous passion. These sentimental declamations are even more disastrous to good morals than the Comedies that make fun of conjugal mishaps.

Attacks have not ceased to be directed against marriage, even since the re-establishment of the law of Divorce. The author of *Les Tenailles* claims that Divorce should be granted on the demand of either man or wife separately, which reduces marriage to mere concubinage. The kind of love represented on the contemporary Stage is identical with that desired in actual life, that is love without duty. People no longer marry to found a family, and devote themselves to their children, self-devotion and serious undertakings are by no means relished. Everybody marries for his own gratification, hopes for a small family, and has as few children as possible,[1] and is ready to sacrifice these by obtaining a divorce in order to run after other women. The fact is ignored, as M. Jules Lemaître puts it wittily and feelingly, that "in marriage there is. not only the bed, there is the cradle and the hearth as well";[2] but men think only of the bed and give no thought to the other two. Can it be supposed that these Plays, in which marriage is profaned and its aims and objects misrepresented, are exactly adapted to inspire women with elevated sentiments? We may say of the Theatre, which teaches the wife to despise marriage and claims for her the right of love apart from duty, what Martial said of Baïæ: "She went there a Penelopé and left it a Helen."

---

[1] Women come to Magistrates to lay complaints to the effect that their husbands will not have children, not even a single one.   One of my colleagues even tells me he received such a complaint from a peasant woman.   It is not merely that in a great many families only one child is desired, but that there are households where they don't want any at all.   Among the ancient Germans, whom we wrongly think of as barbarians, "to limit the number of children .   . was looked upon as a crime." Tacitus, *Germania*, § 19.

[2] Jules Lemaître, *Impressions de théâtre*, 10th Series, p. 201.

which Gresset long ago exposed in his play of *Le Méchant*:

> " La parenté m'excède, et ces liens, ces chaînes . . .
> Tout cela préjugé, misères du vieux temps . . .
> Tous ces noms ne sont rien, chacun n'est que pour soi . . .
> Tout ce qui vit n'est fait que pour nous réjouir,
> Et se moquer du monde est tout l'art d'en jouir." [1]

In the Eighteenth Century, the Marquis d'Argenson wrote, "The fashion of marrying will pass away." This scorn of marriage has now spread to the democracy like everything else; "free unions" grow more and more common in the large towns, where the morals of the stage tend to supersede those of religion.

The Stage delights to turn parental authority into ridicule, as it does marital. Young people might reasonably be supposed most in need of instruction, but the Theatre reserves all this for the parents; in the majority of Plays it is the children who give lessons to their elders. The father who is for stopping a love intrigue on his daughter's part is always a barbarian, and the girl is taught to deceive him with the help of a soubrette. Can anyone imagine it a good way to teach a young girl respect for her father, to let her listen to such advice as her waiting-maid gives her mistress Lucinde in *L'Amour médecin*. "Come, come!" she tells her, "you must not be such a goose as to let them do whatever they please with you; we may surely resist a father's tyranny a bit, if we can do it honourably. What would he have you do? Are you not old enough to be married? Does he think you are made of marble?" [2] On the Stage, a girl who obeys her

---

[1] " I am sick of the claims of family, those ties and chains of former days. . . . 'Tis all prejudice, a wretched inheritance from of old. . . . All these names mean nothing, each man is only for himself. . . . All living things are created only to give us pleasure, and to jest at the world is the sole art of enjoying it."

[2] Bayle allows the fact "that there is nothing more likely to inspire coquetry than these plays, because they are for ever ridiculing the pains that fathers and mothers take to oppose love entanglements on the part of their children." (*Nouvelles de la République des Lettres*, March 1684, vol. i. p. 204.)

father is a fool ; it is a sign of wit and cleverness if she can
raise a laugh at her parent's expense.   On the Stage, the
husband a girl's parents wish to give her is invariably a
simpleton, while the man of her own choice, whom her
family do not approve of, possesses every good quality.
The *Ecole des Femmes* makes fun very properly of the
pretensions of jealous greybeards who wish to marry
young girls, but the latter may easily learn from that play
a string of tricks and stratagems they will afterwards have
no scruples in employing themselves in imitation of what
they have witnessed on the boards.   The *Ecole des Maris*
again, a diverting and instructive piece enough for men
thinking of matrimony, appears to me scarcely a school of
virtue for young girls, who see Isabelle, while pretending
to embrace her guardian, extending her hand behind her
back for Valère to kiss, and later on going to her fiancé's
lodgings.   No doubt Regnard in the *Folies Amoureuses* and
Beaumarchais in the *Barbier de Séville* are quite right in
setting the public laughing as Molière did in the *Ecole des
Femmes* at the expense of fond old men and amorous
guardians.   But it is certain the girl who sees on the stage
how the *ingénue* flouts Arnolphe, or Albert, or Barthole,
to the huge delight of the audience, will be learning a
lesson of trickery and persiflage she will turn to good
advantage against her lawful protectors ; and it will be
strange if it does not suggest the thought that she too
may dupe her guardian, and choose a husband without
consulting her family.   I am not wandering from my
subject when I blame all Plays liable to make women and
girls lose their sense of modesty, for this is at the root
of all crimes of passion, making the unmarried girl more
open to seduction and the married woman more accessible
to adulterous temptations.   But seduction leads its victim
speedily to desertion, pregnancy, abortion, infanticide,
vengeance on the seducer who has forsaken her, while for
the married woman adultery may have consequences no
less terrible.

The mother is as a rule better treated on the Stage than

grows weaker among the people, it would be more and more perilous to let them look on at Vice triumphant. I am aware literary Critics have protested against this punishing of Crime on the Stage, declaring it is not needful in order to make us hate Vice. They invoke in support of their contention several passages of Corneille, who said : "(Virtue) invariably attracts our love, however unfortunate; Vice our hatred, however triumphant . . . just as the portrait of an ugly woman cannot be really beautiful, and there is no need to announce that the original is an unattractive person to prevent her being loved, so is it in our delineation of Vice; when Crime is painted in its true colours, and its faults well and accurately portrayed, there is no necessity to exhibit its ill success at last, in order to warn people against imitating it."[1] There is much truth in Corneille's reflection; the essential duty of a Dramatist is to paint Vice and Virtue under their true colours. The faithful delineation of Vice suffices to inspire disgust for it in choice souls, but not in the common herd. *Nil nisi turpe juvat*,[2] says Ovid. Doubtless there is some exaggeration in this aphorism, but there is a good deal of truth as well; evil has an attraction of its own, and the representation on the stage of adultery, far from inspiring disgust, only inspires a wish to do the like in the minds of most spectators.

"Discitur adulterium, dum videtur."[3]

Nor must it be forgotten that Art can and does embellish Vice, and makes even the criminal interesting.

"Il n'est pas de serpent et de monstre odieux,
Qui par l'art imité ne puisse plaire aux yeux."[4]

It was to correct this ill effect arising from the portrayal of evil that on the Classical Stage the criminal is always

[1] Corneille, Epistle prefixed to *La Suite du Menteur.*
[2] " Nothing but what is vicious gives delight."
[3] "Adultery is learnt by being seen."
[4] "There is never a snake or odious monster that may not, when limned by art, give pleasure to the eyes."

punished, if he does not first punish himself. Hermione, Oreste, Phèdre, Œnone, and the rest, punish themselves by ending their days at their own hands. "We must take good heed," declares the Académie Française,[1] " to accustom neither the eyes nor ears of the people to actions they should know nothing of, and not to teach the audience now cruelty, now dishonesty, unless we teach it at the same time that these vices are punished, and unless on going home from the theatre it carries away at least a little fear as well as a great deal of satisfaction." Corneille, who had originally been of an opposite opinion, afterwards shared the views of the Academy ; he wrote, we are bound "to end a dramatic poem by punishing the bad actions done in the course of the piece and rewarding the good." . . . The success and final triumph of Virtue, in spite of hindrances and dangers, stimulates us to adopt it, while the ill success and disastrous issue of crime or injustice may very well serve to increase the natural horror we feel for them by making us dread a similar calamity.

Doubtless there are crimes of such enormity, of such an odious character, there is no need, in order to inspire a horror for them, to show their punishment on the stage, or even to make the criminal feel remorse. Cléopâtre, Athalie, Néron, display no remorse. Yet crimes of passion are always interesting on the Stage. Accordingly Racine, who well understood the danger of such delineation—for did he not eventually give up the stage altogether?—was careful to diminish it as far as possible by duly punishing Crime. Here, indeed, is what he writes in the Preface to *Phèdre*: "I cannot make bold to assert this to be the best of all my Tragedies. . . . What I can say is, I have written no other in which Virtue is more displayed than in this. *The smallest faults are severely punished in it.* The mere thought of Crime is regarded with as much horror as Crime itself. This is, strictly speaking, the aim every man who works for the public should set before him."

Molière, to punish Tartuffe, goes so far as to make the

[1] *Les sentiments de l'Académie française sur le " Cid."*

for every desire ought to be satisfied."[1] To believe these admirers of Don Juan, it would seem a man must be high-minded and intellectual, a being of lofty ideals, an elegant, brilliant creature, a gentleman, in order to play the part of a seducer. They quite forget that neither high-minded-ness, intellect, nor elegant manners are indispensable for the rôle; it is enough to be false, sensual and evil-minded. There are village Don Juans, no less than drawing-room Don Juans—Don Juans of the stable and the kitchen no less than of the boudoir.

Nor is the Stage content merely to make seduction poeti-cal and palliate guilty love; like the Novel, it has made Love into a virtue.

> " Par ses principes faux, les crimes déguisés
> Sous le nom de vertus sont metámorphosés."[2]
>
> (LE BRUN.)

The chief of all causes of corruption is the transforma-tion of Vice into Virtue. To picture, for instance, as a virtuous woman a girl who lets herself be seduced, and as an honourable man a Tutor who abuses the confidence her parents place in him to wrong his pupil, is to transform vice into virtue, and corrupt the morals of other young men and women, who may find themselves in the same situation as Julie and Saint-Preux. To read of a heroine who makes assignation with her lover in her father's house, after indulging in much moral sermonising, and who preaches Virtue after yielding to Vice,—such an ex-ample perverts and darkens the consciences of young girls, whose mind is uncritical and their reason not firmly based.

Modern Literature does not always properly distinguish between honourable and guilty forms of love. It pro-claims *all* passion to be fine and noble, declaring that Love is proved not by its quality, but by its violence.

" Qu' importe le flacon pourvue qu'on ait l'ivresse,"[3]

---

[1] Théophile Gautier, *Histoire de l'art dramatique*, 5th Series, p. 16.

[2] " By its false principles, crimes disguised under the name of virtues have their very nature changed."

[3] " What matters the bottle, provided we get drunk."

was what Musset said ; and Théophile Gautier writes to the same effect in *Mademoiselle de Maupin* : " All my life I have troubled about the shape of the bottle, never about what it held." In a play of Alexandre Dumas, Mme. Aubray says : " We must love, no matter whom, no matter what, no matter how, provided only we do love." To put on the same footing all sorts of love, to cease to distinguish between the love of a good wife and the love of a prostitute, is to give up all distinction between what is noble and what is base, is to give up loving woman from any side but that of mere form, without a thought of any moral qualities. In that case, Love ceases to be a moral sentiment, it becomes an " intoxication," which may be experienced by the coarsest of mankind. Modern Society, which speaks of the morals and manners of the Middle Ages as barbarous, is very far from showing on the Stage the same types of chivalric love. In the Middle Ages, to pleasure his lady, the Knight was bound to fight for God and the oppressed, and he proved his love by his valour ; the stage hero of the present day proves it by his sensuality and extravagant behaviour.

The man who allows passion to tyrannise over him to the point of forcing him to satisfy it by crime, should surely be looked upon as a degraded being, who has lost all nobleness and beauty of character, as one deprived of pride, energy, and moral sensibility. The Stage, on the contrary, like the Novel, has given currency to the fallacy that the man of passion is nobler and greater than the man of self-restraint.[1] The woman again most commonly represented on the Stage is the woman who possesses no self-restraint, but gives herself up to the promptings of fierce, sensual love. It would seem as if no other sort of love existed ; yet it is the lowest of all kinds of love, and the one most nearly approximating to brute instinct. Corneille is the only Tragic poet who has represented women as able to govern their passions. For this reason he has been blamed for making his women too heroic. This reproach affected

[1] This fallacy is to be found even in M. Séailles, *Le Génie dans l'art*.

a freedman of Maxime's, who is stirring up his master to betray his friend, and the other two by a female attendant. Corneille's real sentiments are to be sought in the fine lines:

> " Nous n'avons qu'un honneur, il est tant de maîtresses ;
> L'amour n'est qu'un plaisir, l'honneur est un devoir." [1]

Corneille declared the great use of Poetry consisted in " the sentences and reflections that may be ingeniously thrown in here and there and everywhere." [2] With this idea in mind, he has filled his Tragedies with the noblest thoughts in glorification of honour, patriotism, religious courage, clemency and the like qualities. His maxims of this kind would form an admirable body of morality.

Racine's Plays are of a less moral tone than Corneille's. [3] Still he never makes Love into a virtue of and for itself. In the Preface to *Phèdre*, he takes care to draw attention to the fact "that the frailties of love are there represented as true frailties "; he is at one with Boileau, who would wish:

> " . . . que l'amour de remords combattu
> Paraisse une faiblesse et non une vertu." [4]

Aware of the criticisms made by Nicole on the Tragic poets, to the effect that they strip the passions of all that is blameworthy about them and paint them up to look charming, Racine wishing, he says, "to make out a case for Tragedy in the eyes of numerous persons famous for their piety and learning, who have condemned it in these latter days," set to work to depict Phèdre's passion " with colours that accentuate its deformity and make it odious."

---

[1] " We have but one honour, let mistresses be as many as they may ; Love is only a pleasure, honour a duty."

[2] Dedication of the *Suite du Menteur*.

[3] "Corneille is more moral, Racine more natural " (La Bruyère). Corneille is more moral because he represents men such as they ought to be, Racine more natural because he represents them such as they are. There is the same difference between Corneille and Racine as between Sophocles and Euripides ; Sophocles himself used to say : " I represent personages as they should be, and Euripides as they are " (Bayle's *Dictionary*, under " Euripides").

[4] " . . . that Love combated by Remorse should appear a weakness and not a virtue."

It is only since the days of Jean Jacques Rousseau and the Romantic school that guilty love has ceased to be a weakness, and become a virtue.

From the glorification of love to the rehabilitation of the courtesan by love is only a step.   When Corneille put on the stage Théodora, virgin and martyr, condemned to the punishment of prostitution, the public found the play too licentious for its taste, and Corneille attributed its failure " to the idea of prostitution which the public could not stomach," he says, " though perfectly aware it would have no practical effects, and while to lessen the horror it inspires I used every artifice art and experience could supply me with."   Voltaire criticised Corneille in lively terms for having ventured to deal with such a subject. " He does not appear," he declares, " to have thrown any sort of veil over this revolting subject, for he employs in the Play the words prostitution, shamelessness, and speaks of the girl as abandoned to the soldiers' lusts."   Who would have expected an attack of modesty like this from the author of the *Pucelle*?   But Voltaire, who allowed himself sufficient licence of obscenity in his books, understood at any rate the necessity for decency on the Stage. He was far from foreseeing a day when the language of the boards would be as free as that of books, and dramatists, preferring to pander to the evil instincts of the crowd rather than to respect their audience, would accustom the latter to listen to obscenities, in which prostitutes would be excused, made poetical and rehabilitated on the Stage.

In several Comedies of the Eighteenth Century we already find " kept women " among the *dramatis personæ*. But the author does not claim special interest and sympathy for them ; he merely draws them as they are.   In the Eighteenth Century the Stage never dreamed of rehabilitating the courtesan by Love, of making Love into a purifying virtue.   It was in the Nineteenth that the courtesan invaded the Theatre, as she invaded society.   According to the notions of the modern Stage, Love washes away all stains, effaces all blemishes ; the instant a woman of gallantry falls really in love with one of her many lovers, society must melt over her affecting case, and the jury freely acquit her, if she takes vengeance for his forsaking her.

The modern Stage is in accord with the modern Novel in attributing the most elevated sentiments to courtesans, holding them to be devoted, heroic, sublime, and declaring that passion transfigures them and that their love is more desirable than that of honest women. According to Balzac, "the humility of the courtesan in love[1] shows moral splendours which bring her very near the angels." But Balzac forgets that the inclination to submit to humiliating acts is often a form of sexual perversion, known as *masochism*, and that this craving for humiliation, self-abnegation, may go so far as a systematic cultivation of rough and cruel treatment from the object of love,—a phenomenon frequently observed among hysterical and weak-minded persons.—In Eugène Sue's Novels, which are still eagerly read by the people, by youths and working girls, the prostitute has the candour and delicacy of a virgin.—In George Sand's *Lélia*, Pulchérie glories in her prostitution and sets herself above the matron, the mother of a family ; the true prostitute in the eyes of the author of *Consuelo* is the wife and mother who consents to remain with a husband she does not love. In Plays where Kings, Queens, Ministers of State, Priests and Magistrates, are dragged through the mire, we see courtesans rehabilitate their virtue by passion, and attain a new maidenhood by love. In his preface to *Angelo*, Victor Hugo declares that, if he has brought a courtesan on to the boards, it is because he wished to protest against the scorn felt by society for her, " to prove to the world that tears will wash away the worst stains, and how unjust is mankind, how absurd the act of society, when they brand the courtesan with their contempt." The same feeling is shared by George Sand ; according to her, we condemn the courtesan only through a survival "of that insurmountable power of social vanity

---

[1] The *Courtisane amoureuse* (Harlot in Love), is also the subject of a tale by La Fontaine.

that is called *honour*." [1] We are a long way here from Corneille and the cult of *honour* that appealed to him. Michelet himself, who possesses so much wit and intellect, so much imagination and sensibility, but alas! so little sound sense, has also suffered himself to be melted at the thought of the " Saints and Virgins of Prostitution " who are thirsting for honour.[2] Under the influence of the Romantic School and particularly of George Sand,[3] this tenderness and respect towards prostitutes has passed into Russian Literature.   In Dostoiewski's "Crime and Punishment," we see Raskolnikoff falling on his knees before the prostitute Sonia.

In the name of good sense and good morals, the dramatists, Émile Augier and Th. Barrière, have endeavoured to supply a correction in a series of vigorous pieces such as *Le Mariage d'Olympe*, *La Contagion*, *Les Filles de Marbre*, to this unhealthy rehabilitation of the courtesan.   But, on the other hand, by setting the public to weep over the *Dame aux Camélias*, Dumas has made her interesting and, painting her under the most alluring colours, has made her a popular favourite.   In the contest between the courtesan Marguerite and Duval senior, the hero's father, the author's sympathies are on the side of the Dame aux Camélias, and draw the sympathies of the audience in the same direction.   The spectator says of Marguerite what Musset says of Manon :

" Tu m'amuses autant que Tiberge m'ennuie." [4]

Nor does the Dame aux Camélias merely interest him ; he finds her touching and sympathetic, and longs to meet someone like her.   Since the date of Dumas' famous

[1] *Lélia.*

[2] Michelet, *La Femme*, p. 412.

[3] A great Russian lady has just completed a Biography of George Sand, writing under the pseudonym of Vladimir Karénone.   In it she shows that George Sand exercised a very important influence over the Russian writers, Tourgueneff, Dostoieffski, Tolstoï.—Dostoieffski, a man of extremely nervous and impressionable temperament, like almost all writers of imagination, relates how he had fever a whole night long, after reading a novel of George Sand's.

[4] "You amuse me as much as Tiberge wearies me."

play, all categories of courtesans have invaded the Stage. The total of plays dealing with courtesans is beyond counting, and these women have the same importance on the boards they have in Parisian life. This sympathy for fallen women, first awakened by the Stage, sows no little trouble in families, stirring up as it does imitators of Duval among young men, and sham copies of Marguerite among the members of her class.

Courtesans, themselves, have not been slow to appropriate, for their own purposes, this literary fallacy about rehabilitation by Love; they all set up for being *Dames aux Camélias* and subjects for rehabilitation! And young men, on their side, readily fall under the dangerous fascination of the paradox. The Lady of the Camellias is an exception; but the average young man takes the exception for a general rule. Thus a character in one of M. Bourget's Novels says: " Phrases read in his young days about the redemption of prostitutes by love . . . recurred to his memory; the divinest figure of a courtesan transfigured by Love, that has ever been drawn, the Esther of Balzac, had strongly coloured his youthful dreams, and in natures like his, in which literary impressions precede the others, those of actual life, suchlike dreams never fade entirely from the heart."[1] Who has not known young men, fascinated by the poetical delineation of the courtesan, scorn the pure love of marriage, take some vulgar prostitute for a new Dame aux Camélias, and allow himself to be led by her wherever she may wish to drag him, into breaking trust, into theft and forgery, merely to please her and gratify her caprices? If so many unhappy young men come to the bar of the Correctional and Assize Courts, it is because their senseless passion for an unworthy object, to the true baseness of which literary paradoxes have closed their eyes, has made them lose every redeeming quality, love of family, honour and conscience.

The influence of the same sophistical fallacies makes itself felt again in the verdicts of acquittal recorded in

[1] Bourget, *Mensonges*, p. 460.

favour of women of pleasure accused of having thrown vitriol over their lovers. Juries chosen from among the spectators of the Dramas that throw a halo of poetry around the courtesan and female criminal, take *au grand sérieux* mere passing liaisons, formed first in the streets or at public balls; they see in women of gallantry, forsaken by their lovers, Hermiones deserving of all indulgence and pity. I have known juries acquit prostitutes who had killed their lovers. Encouraged by such impunity, women of pleasure mutually excite each other to take vengeance on the lovers of a night who leave them for other charmers. One of these women said to one of her friends, offering half a bottle of vitriol she intended for her lover : " Take some, come, have your revenge, too." And they do revenge themselves, in the most cowardly and cruel way, and this for the most frivolous motives, because they are jealous, because they have been refused a pecuniary *douceur* they had claimed ; they demand marriage, though still frequenting the public balls every night, and juries constantly acquit these throwers of vitriol, so unworthy of the interest of any sensible man. They commiserate the lot of women of pleasure guilty of crimes of passion, but quite forget to feel pity for the fate of the man who is killed or blinded for life.

The type of Play that rehabilitates the courtesan appears to me to bear a large share of the responsibility for the excessive complaisancy of modern juries towards crimes of passion, and the consequent frequency of such offences. The French, more slavish admirers of the literary fashion of the day, more unstable in their sentiments, than other peoples and less bound by tradition, have little force to resist mischievous paradoxes. They worship dramatic talent to the verge of superstition, without a thought as to the use it is put to, or the consequences that result from it; they have a frantic admiration for the Writer in vogue, even when by his sophistries he is imperilling both family life and society at large. We find husbands taking their wives to see Plays in which adultery is glorified, and

enemies of society, bandits, courtesans, and criminals. It is an ungrateful task to insist on the mistakes of great Writers who occupy deservedly a high rank in the Literature of the Nineteenth Century. I deny neither their talent, nor the genius of some of their number, but observing that the fallacies they have disseminated have had, and still have, disastrous consequences, I hold it my duty to say so. *Amicus Plato, magis amica veritas.*[1] We may apply to the Romantic Stage, where there is plenty of talent, but a lack of good sound sense, the phrase of Tacitus: *urendo clarescit,*—"it enlightens by consuming." In fact, we are such eager admirers of whatever blazes brightly, and so indifferent to the consequences of the conflagration, that we are something like people whose attention, when their house is being set on fire, is occupied about the look of the torch employed and the engaging air of the incendiary.[2]

Again, the modern Stage has done no little harm by representing man as a passive, sensitive, irresponsible being. In many Plays of the day, the characters declare themselves carried away by fatal, irresistible accesses of passion. What a highly convenient excuse for Vice is supplied by such a belief in the irresistibility of temptation! Men find it so much to their interest to think themselves irresponsible that they seize the excuse with avidity. Not a few women yield to passion, because they have been taught by Plays the creed that it is impossible to resist Love. Possibly they might have resisted it, if they had thought they could; but conviction of the impossibility of such resistance at once paralyzed their will. The fact is, successful resistance to passion depends upon strength of the will, and strength of will, in turn, depends upon belief in such strength.

The Classical stage, on the contrary, counteracts the danger involved in the delineation of crime and passion by the moral elevation of its thought, its firm conviction of the power of will, and the responsibility of the

[1] "Plato is my friend, but Truth is a dearer friend."   [2] Joubert, *Pensées.*

individual; it believes by strength of will men can resist
passion, and that if they fail to do so, they are to blame.
In Corneille's plays, such noble words as *duty*, *honour*,
reason, *will*, are of continual occurrence.   What a contrast
with the sensualistic and determinist Stage of our own
day!   Corneille's heroes and heroines are not men and
women who believe themselves irresponsible and incapable of resisting the dictates of their own passions; they
are tender hearts, but brave ones, sustained by their fine
sense of honour.   Corneille possesses in the highest
degree the sentiment of human freedom, and he gives his
heroes the same.

Poet of the will, he gave it its due share even in love;
in his Dedication of his play *La Place Royale*, he writes:
"'Tis from you I learned that the love of an honest man
must ever be voluntary."   In one of his last Tragedies
(which we do wrong in neglecting, as we do in similarly
neglecting La Fontaine's later Fables, where such fine
things are to be found), in Pulchérie namely, we find yet
another picture of a Love which rests upon the basis of
Will and Reason.

> "Je vous aime, Léon, et n'en fais point mystère,
> Des vœux tels que les miens n'ont rien qu'il faille taire.
> Je vous aime et non point de cette folle ardeur,
> Que les vœux éblouis font maîtresse du cœur . . .
> Ma passion pour vous généreuse et solide
> A la vertu pour âme et la raison pour guide." [1]

I admit that Racine, who is Jansenist in tendency, shows
less of the feeling for human freedom than Corneille, but
I think M. Jules Lemaître exaggerates this difference when
he says: "Racine's plays, in contradistinction to those of
Corneille, leave us under the impression of an overmastering Destiny there is no escaping." [2]   Louis Racine long

---

[1] "I love you, Léon, and make no mystery of it; vows such as mine have
nothing that need be hid.   I love you, and not with that foolish ardour that
dazzled vows make mistress of the heart. . . .   My passion for you, firm-based
and generous-hearted, has virtue for its soul and reason for its guide."

[2] J. Lemaître, *Les Contemporains*, 2nd Series, p. 182.—M. P. Janet only
goes so far as to say that in Racine the part played by free will is of minor
importance.   (*Revue des deux Mondes*, 15th Sept. 1875.)

ago showed the baselessness of this reproach in the extremely interesting Memoirs he wrote of his father's life: "So far was my father from teaching the doctrine of determinism that he has placed its expression in the mouth of the odious Œnone." Phèdre rejects indignantly the excuse based on the *fatal* nature of passion which her nurse whispers in her ear in the lines:

> " Vous aimez, on ne peut vaincre sa destinée . . .
> La faiblesse aux humains n'est que trop naturelle." [1]

Phèdre on the contrary does not believe in any such impossibility of fighting against her destiny:

> " Qu' entends-je? Quels conseils ose-t-on me donner?
> Ainsi donc jusqu'au bout tu veux m'empoisonner?" [2]

She knows she is to blame for her conduct; she feels remorse, and says so:

> " Je cédais au remords dont j'étais tourmentée,
> Qui sait même où m'allait porter ce repentir? . . .
> J'ai voulu devant vous, exposant mes remords,
> Par un chemin plus lent descendre vers les morts." [3]

Remorse is the proof of freedom and responsibility. A woman who is driven into crime by an irresistible power, feels no remorse. I have myself seen, and watched, and questioned, murderers, who under the empire of a morbid condition that annihilated their responsibility, had killed their mother or tried to kill their father; they felt no remorse, declaring they had been driven into their crimes by an irresistible force. Nor can I share the opinion of M. Jules Lemaître, who thinks that Phèdre, tortured by the pangs of remorse, is perfectly innocent, because she

---

[1] "You are in love; none can fight against his destiny. . . . Frailty is only too natural to human beings."

[2] "What do I hear? What advice is this they dare give me? Will you to the last persist in poisoning my mind?"

[3] " I was yielding to the remorse that I was tormented by; who knows even where this repentance was to lead me to? . . . I was fain before you, making show of my remorse, by a longer road to descend to the dead."

is a victim of inevitable destiny, and that she is "truly, in spite of her incestuous infatuation, as chaste as Hippolyte."

Though she accuses Venus of having kindled the flame of her passion, still Phèdre reproaches herself for having yielded to it ; she recognizes that she should and could have resisted it, and that she is blameworthy in having wished to make Hippolyte share her guilty love.   She tells him as much in the lines :

> " Ne pense pas qu' au moment que je t'aime
> Innocente à mes yeux je m'approuve moi-même." [1]

When Thésee returns, she upbraids her nurse for having opposed her projected suicide :

> " Sur mes justes remords, tes pleurs ont prévalu." [2]

She still thinks of killing herself to escape her shame, with no fear of the inheritance of dishonour she will be leaving her children :

> " Le *crime* d'une mère est un pesant fardeau,
> Je tremble qu'un discours, hélas ! trop véritable,
> Un jour ne leur reproche une mère *coupable*. . . .
> Mes *crimes* désormais ont comblé la nature,
> Je respire à la fois l'inceste et la posture !" [3]

Thus, in Racine's Tragedies, Passion, no matter how violent, is never *fatal*, irresistible.

Dr. Despine has maintained that Molière intended in Tartuffe to depict the *fatality* of vice.   But Molière believed so firmly in free will that he admits the possibility of repentance on Tartuffe's part. (Act v. Sc. 8.) The indignant words of Cléanthe against hypocrisy, which express Molière's own opinions, presuppose a belief in responsibility for wrong-doing.   Indignation is thrown away against a vice that is *fatal*.   Tartuffe would only be

---

[1] " Think not that at the very time I love you still, innocent in my own eyes, I approve myself of my own conduct."

[2] "Over my well-founded remorse your tears won the day."

[3] "A mother's *crime* is a grievous burden ; I tremble lest report, alas ! only too well founded, some day reproach them with a *guilty* mother. . . . My crimes henceforth have passed the bounds of Nature, I breathe at once incest and deceit ! "

an object of pity if his vices could not be referred to him as the responsible agent, and Orgon would be justified in speaking of him as "that poor fellow!" Indignation implies belief in responsibility. Without indignation, high comedy would be an impossibility.

The modern Stage, on the contrary, is, as a rule, fatalistic. Its heroes, who are guilty of crimes of love, are not in the least ashamed of their wrong-doing, throwing the responsibility for it on nature and society. The prisoners at the bar of our Assize Courts take them as models and follow suit. They make no excuses, they accuse society; they make no claim of extenuating circumstances, they refuse any such to society, which baulks their passions. They demand their acquittal as a right,— a right the jury very often accord,—saying like some stage hero :

> "Je pardonne à l'amour les crimes qu'il fait faire." [1]

Modern juries are only too ready to believe in the fatality of passion, like the heroes of the Romantic and the Naturalistic stage. Victor Hugo, who for all that has written some noble verse on Conscience and Remorse, has made Hernani a fatalist :

> " . . . Je me sens poussé
> D'un souffle impétueux, d'un destin insensé . . .
> Agent aveugle et sourd des mystères funèbres." [2]

In a large number of modern Plays, when a wife is guilty of adultery, it is the fault of Nature, or the fault of Society, or very likely the husband's fault; everybody is

---

[1] "I pardon Love the crimes it makes men commit."

[2] "I feel myself driven by an impetuous breath, a wild destiny . . . an agent, blind and dumb, of the funereal mysteries."—Poet of the Conscience and Human Responsibility in *Les Châtiments*, *L'Histoire d'un crime*, *La Légende des Siècles* and *Les Misérables*, Victor Hugo is the poet of fatality in his Plays, in *L'Année Terrible* and *La Pitié suprême* ; according to him, only the elements are to be accused for the crimes men do :

> "Je le dis, l'accusé pour moi c'est l'élément . . .
> Hélas ! la faute en est au veut, ce noir passant,"

—"I own it, the guilty party for me is the element. . . . Alas ! the blame lies with the wind, this passing night of gloom."

to blame, husband, laws, society,—always excepting the guilty woman! Some husbands actually dare not reproach their wives with their unfaithfulness, because they believe such conduct to be fatally predetermined, and this character of fatality makes it excusable. Like Jacques, the fatalist husband in George Sand, they say: "None can answer for the movements of the heart, and it is no sign of weakness to yield passively to its impulses." In Flaubert's Novel, Madame Bovary's husband, when informed of his wife's unfaithfulness, tells her lover, "'tis the fault of destiny"; and the very lover himself cannot help thinking so very good-natured a husband contemptible.

The Plays of Alexandre Dumas *fils* again are fatalistic. Mme. Aubray rightly interprets the author's thoughts, when she says : " Evil-natured, guilty, hard-hearted wretches! Nay! there are no such people, only sick men and blind men and madmen." This physiological fatalism Dumas learned from his physiological studies, far too superficial as these were. So far is Physiology from necessarily leading to any negation of moral responsibility, that the most illustrious Physiologists, whose names I have already mentioned (p. 451), and to whom we may add Flourens and Gall, admit the existence of free will. But Dumas, like so many other Writers who make only a summary study of scientific and philosophical problems, had allowed himself to be unduly impressed by the influence, no doubt very important, exercised by temperament and heredity, to the neglect of the action, not less surprising, of the will and ideas.

M. Paul Hervieu's Plays appear to me no less fatalistic in tone than Alexandre Dumas'. In his *Les Tenailles*, a married woman who has taken a lover, because she has been unable to obtain a divorce, does not look upon herself as in any way blameworthy, but only as unfortunate, and the Author seems to be of the same opinion. When the woman in question informs her husband that the child of their married life is not really his, and the husband in his turn wishes for a divorce, she refuses, and on the

In Euripides, as in Racine, Phèdre knows herself guilty and responsible for her sin. " I was well aware," she says, " of the shame attaching to this conduct and this passion ; I knew a woman who abandons herself to such a love to be an object of horror to all mankind." When her nurse is for calming her scruples by telling her it is no sin to yield to Cypris, who governs gods and men, Euripides' Phèdre rejects the argument with indignation. " Odious words !" she cries, " be silent, let me hear no more of such shameful talk."

Shakespeare's plays are still less fatalistic in tone than the Tragedies of Antiquity. " 'Tis in ourselves that we are thus or thus. Our bodies are gardens ; to the which our wills are gardeners, . . . we have reason to cool our raging motions, our carnal stings, our unbitted lusts," writes the great English Poet (*Othello*, Act i. Sc. 3). The same author has drawn an admirable picture of remorse. Macbeth is no monomaniac, no epileptic, as M. Taine has described him, but a criminal tortured by remorse. Remorse,—I have known an instance in my own experience, —is capable of producing hallucinations.

It was Diderot who first brought physiological fatality on the Stage in *Le Fils naturel*, and he was followed in the same line by the Romanticists and Naturalists of later days.

In the majority of modern plays there is no longer any struggle between passion and duty, and no traces of remorse. Having ceased to believe in responsibility, slaves like the beasts that perish to their mere instincts, the heroes of the modern Stage are no longer free creatures, divided between the attraction of passion and the protests of conscience, over-riding by force of will the temptations of the senses, or bewailing their faults and rising to higher things by virtue of repentance ; they yield to passion without a struggle, no longer blushing for their sins, incapable either of energy or remorse. Losing moral beauty, the Stage of to-day is like to lose æsthetic beauty as well ; all inward struggle being annihilated, the dramatic interest

is sadly lessened. Passion is dramatic only on condition
of its being at struggle with conscience and will. Louis
Racine judiciously points out that, if Phèdre yielded without any remorse to her shameful passion, the audience in
its indignation at her conduct would never consent to
listen to her.   A fatalistic passion, which pursues its gratification without a struggle or one pang of remorse, is a
mere pathological case, interesting only to the physician.
What is enthralling on the stage is passion at deadly feud
with the will, the contest in Chimène's heart between love
and duty, the combat in Zaïre between love and religion,
the struggle of Will against Destiny or against the sexual
instinct. Will is not only the foundation of Morality, it
is the basis of the Drama.   It is this that makes the hero
interesting, dramatic ; he appeals to the audience only in
virtue of his struggles, his resistance to the passions and
circumstances that are bearing him down.   In one word,
without will there can be no struggle, no moral activity,
and without such activity no drama.   To exaggerate in a
Play the violence of passion and to suppress the will is to
lower the interest of the action ; nay ! more, it is to make
the spectators doubt their own freedom of will, and so
diminish their power of free action.   Further, it is to make
juries, chosen as they are from these spectators, doubt the
justifiability of legal penalties.

Pity for the authors of crimes of passion is an excellent
sentiment, but only on condition that it does not degenerate into silly sentimentality ; that it does not absolve
the guilty of all healthy consciousness of their sin, and
does not disorganize society by letting criminals off scot-
free.   There is a marked tendency nowadays towards a
certain false sentimentality ; people weep over murderers,
but quite forget their victims' sufferings ; lavish all their
pity on lovers who turn assassins, but keep none for husbands poisoned by their wives, and lovers blinded by in-
furiated vitriol throwers.   This extravagant commiseration
for criminals is an unhealthy sign, confounding as it does
crime with disease, voluntary vice with involuntary mis-

of the Play. Endued with all the glamour of Poetry, delivered with fire and spirit by talented actors, applauded by the public, they offer a specious show that dazzles such of the audience as are lacking in solid judgment or who share the passion of the heroes on the stage ; they seize eagerly on these phrases to supply an excuse for their own evil passions. Cicero relates the fact that Cæsar had for ever on his lips the passage of Euripides' *Phœnissæ*, which says : " If ever justice may be violated, 'tis to win empire ; in all things else we must be just." [1] Of course it was not this false maxim that first gave Cæsar the idea of violating justice to win empire, but it may very well have strengthened him in his purpose. " The man who used to quote this maxim," says Schlegel, " was a standing proof in himself of how dangerous it might be in its results." M. Patin adds further : " It is indeed a thing by no means free from danger to give by a sententious turn of phrase to an evil thought the apparent authority of a general truth, and so prepare axioms all ready to be used in the defence of crime." [2]

The danger that may result from the sophistries and wrong-headed maxims of the Stage is not so serious, when these are directed towards criticism of the conditions of government. Great political crimes are not infectious like crimes of passion. Everybody has not a kingdom to conquer, a power to usurp, but everybody is liable to feel the passions arising out of love, jealousy, anger and revenge. This is why Tragedies, like Corneille's, that deal with affairs of State, political ambitions, patriotic sentiments, do not offer the same risk as those in which the only question is one of crimes of passion, as in Racine's earlier Plays. Phrases justifying passion and revenge are more infectious than the other kind, being apt to corrupt the minds of a far larger number of any given audience.

The Stage is a school of Love ; but no less is it one of hate and vengeance, by reason of the examples of these passions it displays before the eyes of all, and the fallacies

[1] *De officiis*, iii. 21.   [2] Patin, *Eschyle*, p. 60.

it expresses, all tending to justify Revenge. Corneille and Racine excel in the delineation of feminine revenge. In Corneille's Plays, which show much more variety than Racine's, we find every form of such vengeance : revenge of the forsaken wife (Médée), revenge of the ambitious woman (Rodogune), revenge of the mother (Marcelle in *Théodore*). What Racine loves to describe is more especially the revenge of the jealous woman. His Plays likewise abound in lovers, rivals, jealous and outraged husbands, all of whom find means to avenge their wrongs. In any given audience visiting a theatre there will be found jealous lovers, betrayed husbands, forsaken wives, who have not hitherto conceived the thought of revenge, or who, having conceived it, have repelled the temptation. But little by little they lose their repugnance to violence, when they hear the passion of revenge extolled in noble verse that wins the hearty applause of the house. The beauty of the Poetry quite hides the baseness of the sentiment. When passions, even the meanest, are expressed in the grandest diction, they take on a look of nobility that masks their really odious nature. Seeing the heroes of the Stage breathing these sentiments of hatred and revenge, impressionable spectators cannot but feed their souls on the same class of ideas, and are only too ready to make their own the excuses the Poet puts in the mouths of his characters.

Aristotle held that the Stage purges our passions, by making them more refined and pure.[1] I hold an exactly contrary opinion,—that by giving an extraordinary intensity to our passions, it makes these more violent and less pure. If the theatrical representation of a passion awakens the germ of the said passion in the heart of a man who has not hitherto felt it, it cannot surely fail to strengthen and inflame it yet further in the heart of a man who is already under its influence on entering the house. Seeing *Othello* on the boards, a spectator who is already jealous will feel his jealousy increased by contact with its manifestation on the part of Shakespeare's hero, and his

---

[1] Aristotle, *Poetics*, Preface by Barthélemy Saint-Hilaire, p. xxix.

But—why does he write at all in that case? The truth is that Authors, that *genus irritable vatum*, do not like to hear their responsibility spoken of, and that the very people who criticise everything, Religion, Legislation, the Administration of Justice, cannot bear to be criticised themselves. " No literary work can involve danger," d'Holbach used to declare, appealing to Hobbes's opinion, who likewise maintained " that no harm can be done to mankind by setting out ideas before them." La Mettrie and Grimm spoke in a similar strain.[1]

The theory of murder advocated in *La Femme de Claude* is not merely that of the hero of the play, but the deliberate conviction of the Author as well. Dumas advises the husband to kill the adulterous wife in defiance of the dictates of Divine and human law, which forbid such an act. The writer of *La Femme de Claude* who, in his youth, drew such alluring pictures of great sinners of the fairer sex became, in his riper years, their most savage adversary, and expressly authorizes marital vengeance to the annihilation of rights of law. He constitutes him Grand Justicier and slayer of women; he tells the husband, already blinded by anger and jealousy, to take the place of the judge, who at any rate is calm and unprejudiced, to take a gun and shoot down his wife like some noxious beast. In the Play in question, Claude threatens to kill his wife, if she lays her hand upon Antonin or Rebecca, if she attempts to hinder his task, if she becomes an obstacle in the way of what God bids him do ; in a word, it is the deliberate apology of murder. Who can fail to perceive the danger of repeating, again and again, a series of representations where the audience is to be numbered by thousands, among whom there will certainly be some injured husbands included: " Kill your guilty wives, the Laws allow you to do so,"—which is not true. Unfortunate husbands are already urged quite strongly enough by their

---

[1] D'Holbach, *Système de la nature*, 2nd Part, chaps. xii. and xlii.—La Mettrie, *Discours préliminaire* ; Grimm, *Correspondance Littéraire*, January 1772.

anger to exact some terrible punishment, without its being needful for the dramatic author to further encourage this craving for revenge.

Dumas gives the husband an absolute right to kill his wife, in contradiction to the Law which denies him any such privilege, adding : " She is not your wife ; she is not a woman at all ! She is no part of the Divine conception of humanity, but an animal, pure and simple ! She is the beast of the land of Nod, the helpmate of Cain. Kill her ! " But it wants more than a figure of speech to change a human being into a " beast," a noxious animal we have the right to kill without further form of law. Already, in *L'Affaire Clémenceau*, the hero of the Novel kills his wife, with the words : " I have slain the monster." But in civilized societies, " monsters," that is to say criminals, are judged by the representatives of society, and not by their self-styled victims.   In Courts of Law, an interval elapses between the criminal act and the delivery of judgment, disinterested witnesses are heard by impartial judges ; the prisoner is properly defended, and light is thrown on the case by the comparison of conflicting evidence. But if the plaintiff is to be himself both judge and executioner in his own case, if trial, witnesses, defence, judicial impartiality are all to be abolished, it is not Justice that is done but an act of vengeance that is wreaked,—to speak plainly, a murder that is committed.

The Classical Stage abounds also in heroes and heroines who avenge their wrongs with their own hands. But we never find them claiming the right of vengeance, and representing murder as an act of justice. In *Horace*, it is true, this confusion occurs. Horace (Horatius) having just killed his sister, Procule asks him :

> " Que venez-vous de faire ? "—" Un acte de justice ;
> Un semblable forfait veut un pareil supplice," [1]

answers Horace. But the King reasserts the truth in the words :

[1] " What have you done ? "—" An act of justice ; such a crime deserves no less a punishment."

taken love of Religion; Nobles and Priests guillotined out
of an ill-understood love of Liberty. It is equally unreasonable to shoot the adventuress in Augier's Play from love
for the sanctity of family life. All the Author needs do is
to hold her up to scorn and detestation by means of a
faithful portrayal of her ignominy. To go further, to
murder, is to go beyond all bounds. Scorn and contempt
are enough. A human being cannot be put out of the
way like "a noxious beast," "a vibrio[1] in human shape,"
"a kind of vermin"; and it is not permissible to raise the
cry, "Down with *Olympe*! death to the *Wife of Claude*!
death to the *Foreign Woman's* husband!" merely in order
to win a literary triumph.

After slaughtering on the boards with revolver shots
or dagger thrusts adulteresses and adventuresses, Dramatic
Authors, always on the look-out for new effects, have now
adopted the doctrine of forgiveness. Bound to be ever
oscillating between these two doctrines, the Stage, which
craves perpetual variety, passes from one to the other.
Literary dogmas are like fashions; directly one of them,
that of the right of vengeance for instance, grows hack-
neyed, the opposite doctrine of the beauty of forgiveness
reappears, as it has at the present moment. These
dogmas of the Theatre almost invariably show a lack of
proportion and moderation; and audiences are mighty
simple when they take them seriously, and look to the
Stage for examples to copy in everyday life.

To sum up, after pointing out the dangers liable to
result, for certain sections of the audience, from the stage
representation of crimes of passion, I do not conclude the
Stage must be abolished. I only advocate its reformation,
to bring it into better accord with moral truth and legal
requirements, and the banishment of antisocial fallacies
from the boards. An exact reproduction of the life of
passion and its tragic consequences is not necessarily immoral. *Frou Frou*, for instance, is not only a most remarkable Play, but a highly moral spectacle, bringing into relief

[1] A species of infusoria.

with striking vividness and truth the terrible results of adultery. The portrait so finely drawn in it of the Parisian woman of fashion, frivolous and pleasure-loving, incapable of a single serious thought, nervous, more or less hysterical, in the medical sense of the word, rushing into adultery at the call of a mere sudden infatuation, is the companion picture to the Romantic country wife, described for us by Flaubert in *Madame Bovary*.

The study I have penned above is not a piece of special pleading against the Stage, but against the corruptions of the Stage. Side by side with Plays that do harm, are others that do good. Anyone who is present at a representation of *Cinna*, *Horace*, or *Polyeucte*, leaves the Theatre with feelings more generous, more patriotic, and more Christian than he entered it with. The Stage then is not bad in itself, as was thought by Nicole, Bossuet, and Jean Jacques Rousseau ; it may enlighten or pervert the public conscience, according to the use it is put to. Nothing is better than a good play. " Tragedy," Napoleon I. declared warmly, " stirs the soul, elevates the heart, can and ought to create heroes. In this respect it may well be France owes to Corneille some parts of her noble deeds ; therefore, gentlemen, if Corneille were alive, I would make him a Prince."[1] He added that noble Tragedy was the school of great men, and that it was the duty of Sovereigns to encourage it and extend its influence. And without doubt a people that loved Corneille's plays, would become great in chivalrous courage, patriotism, and moral elevation. Its soldiers would grow braver ; and women no less than men would find literary gratification and moral advantage in his Tragedies. A young girl runs no risk of imitating Chimène. A wife, who has made a marriage " of reason," and presently meets the man she would fain have wedded, will not be tempted by any words of Pauline's to forsake her husband and fly with a lover. Nothing can be better than Corneille's plays, teaching as they do honour, duty, the power of will, the subordination of sensibility to reason.

[1] *Mémorial de Sainte-Hélène.*

crimes of passion, makes excuses for adultery, idealizes free love and turns marriage into ridicule. His bounden duty is never to make virtue look ridiculous or vice attractive.

Again, the Stage would do well to follow another piece of advice given by Voltaire: "It is allowed, of course, to bring villains on the Stage, but it is a finer thing to see good people there."[1] The boards have been so glutted with adulteresses, harlots, criminals of love, it would be an agreeable novelty to show a few honest men and virtuous women there for a change. The public would find the same pleasure in looking at them that George Sand experienced in writing *La Petite Fadette* and *La Mare au Diable*, after *Lélia* and *Indiana*. "In this literature of mystery and iniquity that talent and imagination have brought into fashion," she wrote, "we like the mild and gentle characters better than the scoundrels, with all their dramatic intensity." I am entirely of her opinion. It is not true that nobility of sentiments is any less literary than baseness of instincts, or that vice and crime are the only things really interesting. Pénélope and Andromaque appeal more to our sympathies than Clytemnestre and Phèdre. Antigone and Iphigénie are more touching than Hermione. *La Petite Fadette* is better worth having than *Indiana*. The character of Burrhus is finer, even from the dramatic point of view, than that of Pyrrhus. Moral beauty is more, not less, literary than moral ugliness.

The magnanimity of Augustus forgiving his would-be assassin, the patriotism of old Horatius preferring the safety of his country to his son's, are more dramatic sentiments than the fury of some jealous husband. The tears of admiration Corneille drew from the eyes of the great Condé are more truly moving than those shed over some sorrow of disappointed love. There are other passions as interesting as Love, and more noble. There are other calamities greater and more tragic than broken hearts. Why must our dramatic writers go out of their way to

[1] Voltaire, *Commentaire sur Corneille*.

represent what is morally repulsive, under pretence of seeking after truth? Noble sentiments are just as true as ignoble. Adulterous wives and harlots and criminals do not make up all the world. Why should not the beautiful have the same artistic value in Literature as it has in Painting and Sculpture? Literature is no whit less fitted than the *Fine Arts* for the representation of what is fine and noble. To think otherwise is surely not very flattering to Letters.

The Ancients, whose sense of beauty was more highly developed than ours, also appreciated better than we do the charm of noble sentiments on the Stage. *We* prefer the delineation of guilty passion. We want women possessed by furious passions, and find the Furies adorable. These we prefer to good women of gentle, timid nature, who express their love with modesty and refinement. A married woman, of virtuous character, ready to devote herself to death to save her husband's life, would seem insipid to us ;[1] a young man as chaste as Euripides' *Hippolytus* we should vote ridiculous. Why will not the Stage paint types of pure love, instead of preferring to represent the frantic, sensual-minded love that often makes a murderer of a man? A would-be bride, divided between her love and her duty towards her parents, a Christian wife repulsing the man she would have preferred to wed, are surely more truly interesting than a woman who is simply amorous and yields to her sensual impulses unresistingly. The struggles of Conscience against Instinct are surely more moving than the delineation of physical love and the description of feminine frailties.

The Ancients, who knew nothing of the theory of *Art for Art's sake*, thought it no degradation to Literature to say :

> "Omne tulit punctum qui miscuit utile dulci."
> "ET PRODESSE VOLUNT ET DELECTARE POETÆ."[2]

---

[1] Racine contemplated at one time restoring the Tragedy of the Ancients, and treating this theme of Alcestis.

[2] "He bore away every suffrage who united the useful with the pleasing."
"Fain would our Poets be at once profitable and delightful."

its aureole; it is not nearly so poetical as on the Stage.

At the period when Romanticism was trying to beautify Crime, a vigorous Poet, too much neglected nowadays, Népomucène Leminier, raised a protesting voice against this orgy of literary crimes:

> "La poésie, institutrice
> Des dogmes, des lois et des mœurs,
> Au vil crime, à son noir supplice
> N'accorde point de lâches pleurs.
> Elle doit, en fille des temples,
> N'exalter que les beaux exemples,
> Qui seuls touchent les nobles cœurs.
> Quelle contagion étrange
> Nous pousse à vouler dans la fange
> Les couronnes des doctes sœurs! . . .
> C'est propager les mœurs vandales,
> Qu' exhumer, des vieilles annales,
> Les monstres jadis trop fameux." [1]

In a society where the taste for the Play-house is so universal, where the people frequents the cafés far more than the Churches and picks up its morality at the Theatre, it is not well for the Stage to rival the Assize Courts and feed the imagination of the populace on pictures of blood. The latter must not be shown too many crimes, nor its thoughts allowed to dwell too much on hideous subjects. Taine has judiciously noted how evil an impression is left behind by such things; that "the true heroes" of Literature are persons of the highest culture and the most perfect works from the point of view of art identical with the most beneficial from the point of view of morality. This author, who as a young man had shown himself indifferent as to the consequences of any doctrines

---

[1] "Poetry, fair teacher of dogmas, laws and manners, must not accord the tears of a cowardly compassion to vulgar crime and its grim punishment. She is bound, like a priestess of the Temples, to exalt none but noble exemplars, the only ones that touch noble hearts. What strange infection impels us to roll in the mire the crowns of the learned sisterhood! . . . 'Tis to encourage the manners of Vandals, to exhume from ancient story monsters shamefully notorious in olden days."

that might be advanced in books, was much exercised, when age had ripened him and experience brought wisdom, about the harm Literature was capable of producing, and like La Bruyère made the criterion of literary merit depend upon the amount of good likely to be effected. Théophile Gautier himself said : "What is good and honourable is so dramatic and so fine ! It is to goodness and honesty, to virtuous emotion, we must come back sooner or later, if we wish to draw legitimate tears. You may try as you will after a factitious dramatic interest in cries and tears and posthumous rehabilitations of vice . . ., calm and innocent emotion will always carry the day against the most artfully presented exaggerations. . . . Boldly strike this noble cord in the human heart, and instantly you will know by its all-powerful vibrations the imperishable, eternal character that belongs to it."[1]

Knowing as I do from my judicial experience that literary monsters are quite capable of producing monsters of the Criminal Courts by awakening evil instincts in the younger members of an audience, I would beg Dramatic Authors to introduce rather oftener on the Stage characters guilty neither of crime nor suicide. If the merit of the Dramatist consists in giving strong emotions and nothing else, I can understand d'Alembert's having likened Tragedy to the execution of a criminal. Besides, if that is so, the Poet is eclipsed by the executioner, for the guillotine gives emotions still stronger than the latter. But Dramatic Art should not consist merely in violently stirring the spectator's emotions. When Aristotle said Tragedy has for aim to excite pity and terror, he was unduly restricting its domain.

I do not fail to recognize the advantage there may be in rousing the pity of an audience. History relates several incidents proving that the Stage from this point of view is a school of humanity. When Athens was taken by Lysander, the victors debated whether they ought not to raze the city. Whilst they were still deliberating, a Musi-

[1] Th. Gautier, *Histoire de la Littérature dramatique*, vol. v. p. 264.

Rostand, Brieux, and the like, are healthy and vigorous works.

Above all the Dramatist should be asked not to transform evil into good and good into evil, and to remember that sophistry does even more harm than passion. "Woe unto them that call evil good, and good evil; that put darkness for light, and light for darkness; that put bitter for sweet, and sweet for bitter!" (Isaiah). It is perverting the people to say Love is a virtue, Adultery submission to natural law, and to declare mankind has a right to happiness and a right of revenge.

When Divine and Human Law both tell a man, "Thou shalt not kill," it is not permitted the Dramatist to say to the husband of an unfaithful wife, "Kill her," and to the woman who has been forsaken by her lover, "Kill him." Inasmuch as society is instituted in order to replace individual vengeance by legal punishment, the Stage is assuming a heavy responsibility when it purposes to replace legal punishment by revenge. To corrupt the minds of the audience, and teach them that Love is identical with virtue and admirable in its frenzies and its crimes, is to unchain the passions of mankind and pave the way to manslaughter.

It is perverting the female portion of an audience to show them one type, and one only of feminine love, viz., the sensual, and to represent it as incapable of control. It is not by insisting on the impossibility of mastering love that women are to be taught chastity. Nor in fostering the belief that the sexual instinct cannot be restrained, has the naturalistic Stage even the excuse of sheltering this doctrine of the fatality of passion behind a scientific truth, for no serious treatise on Physiology is to be found affirming this irresponsibility of passion.[1]

[1] In a recent work on the Sexual Instinct (*L'Instinct Sexuel*, Paris : F. Alcan), Dr Féré, on the staff of the Bicêtre Asylum, pens the following remarks, the more worthy of attention as coming from a scientist of determinist ways of thought : "The present work aims at putting in a conspicuous light the necessity of self-control and personal responsibility in connection with sexual activity, no less from the point of view of hygiene

Woman is not merely an organism, a womb ; she is above
all else a living soul, possessed of a conscience and a will,
which save her from any such irresistible fatality.

To restore good taste and good sense on the Stage, it is
not enough for Dramatic Authors to be willing and ready ;
the co-operation of the public is likewise requisite.   If the
public will leave off admiring Vice and crimes of passion,
theatrical managers will stop providing such fare.   In any
case, audiences should bear in mind that the heroes of
the Stage are not models to imitate, but subjects for
observation ; that Roxane, Médée, Hermione, Phèdre,
are as little examples for women to copy, as Pyrrhus,
Oreste, Othello, are for men.

than from that of morals " (Preface).   Dr Féré adds, further, that " it is in
the name of the psychology of animals, subject to the madness of the regularly
recurring period of rut, and not of the psychology of civilized mankind, that
the irresistibility of sexual impulses is affirmed " (p. 30).   An animal in virtue
of his organs, man is free in virtue of his mental endowment.   Literary
fallacies are often nothing more nor less than scientific mistakes.

to take into consideration the change of character often produced by passion. Under the empire of a violent and unfortunate love, of a devouring jealousy, a man hitherto gentle and good-natured may become irritable and ill-conditioned; the man who was industrious loses all taste for work; the man whose disposition was gay and merry-hearted is attracted by melancholy and despair. An individual of energetic temperament, when deceived by a wife he fondly loved, grows excitable and nervous, and may be seen crying like a child or positively bellowing with rage. Under the influence of the passion dominating him, the man feels his own character altering and may ask himself in alarm, like Racine's hero:

"Par quel trouble me vois-je emporté loin de moi?"[1]

The man who is thus carried away by passion far out of the bounds of his natural disposition, is deserving of our pity, more particularly when he is young, that is to say when his heart is full of generous feelings and his head empty of ideas and experience.

Clemency towards women accused of crimes of passion is also obligatory in the majority of cases for physiological and psychical reasons. Woman is a womb; *tota mulier in utero* ("the whole woman is in the womb"), Van Helmont declared. Of course such a definition is manifestly incomplete, for if woman is a womb, she is likewise a brain, a heart and a soul. At the same time there is no doubt the important reactions the womb exercises on the nervous system should be taken into account. The physiological functions to which women are subject, menses, pregnancy, lactation, menopause, frequently determine cerebral troubles. There exists a close connection between the condition of the organs of generation and the condition of the brain. Every woman's physiological and psychical life gravitates round the great fact of maternity.

There are many hysterical subjects, in the medical sense of the word, among such women as are guilty of

[1] "By what trouble do I see myself carried away far from my own self?"

crimes of passion. Now, as everybody knows, hysterical women cannot bear annoyance or contradiction without weeping and stamping; they often have fits of crying and despair arising out of the most trivial motives. To give an instance: a working-man scolds his wife for not keeping his dinner hot, and the woman, of a very nervous temperament and feeling his reproaches keenly, answers, "Now I'll never get your dinner ready again; you won't find me when you come home this evening;" so saying, she seizes a bottle of laudanum and drains it. It is obvious that a woman of a disposition like this, incapable of enduring a word of reproach, cannot quietly submit to a lover's treachery, or a husband's unfaithfulness. Jealous wives who make scenes, scream, smash the crockery and lead their husband a life, are of objectionable character only because they are of unsound temperament; they are called ill-tempered and ill-conditioned, when they are only really in ill-health.[1] The spirit of contradiction that is common with such women is a symptom of their nervous diathesis;[2] and this nervousness, making the patient irritable, excitable, hot-tempered and violent may be determined not alone by heredity, but by long continued suffering, by a great sorrow, by the death of a child.

The character of the woman who is guilty of a crime determined by passion is often of a high-strung, romantic type, the result of a neuropathic temperament inherited from her ancestors. Mme. Weiss was of ill-balanced mind, a nymphomaniac in fact. The widow Gras was hysterical. Marie B—— was the daughter of a woman who had been under treatment as insane, and the niece of a man who died out of his mind; at fifteen, she had already made two attempts at suicide. "From my earliest youth," she told

---

[1] It is only in virtue of an exaggerated and unjustifiable generalization from numerous, but still exceptional, instances, that Michelet arrived at his description of Woman as a pathological subject.

[2] This spirit of contradiction is exactly portrayed in this line of Terence :

"*Nolunt ubi velis ; ubi nolis, cupiunt ultra,*"

—"They will not when you will ; when you will not, they will and must."

had defended her honour as sturdily as she defends her purse, she would never have fallen. In that admirable work *Don Quixote*, Cervantes has drawn attention to this fact in a very witty fashion. A woman comes before Sancho to lay a complaint of having been ravished by a shepherd. Sancho condemns the offender to pay twenty ducats to the complainant; then, when she has left the Court, he tells the shepherd : " Run, friend, run after that woman ; get her to give you your purse back again, and if she won't, make her, and come back to me both of you." Before long " the shepherd and the woman appear again, locked tightly in each other's arms, she with lifted petti-coats holding the purse between her legs, he trying might and main to get hold of it ; but this he could in no wise succeed in effecting, so well did the good woman defend its possession. ' Justice ! ' she kept screaming at the top of her voice, ' justice ! justice, just look, your worship, at the effrontery of the blackguard, who's trying to take the purse from me again. . . .'—' And has he taken it ? ' asked Sancho. ' Taken it ! ' she cried ; ' nay ! he would have to tear out my life first. . . .'—' I admit I'm fairly beaten,' said the countryman . . . and he let go." Then Sancho, ordering the purse to be restored to the woman, addressed her thus : " My sister, if only you had defended yourself this morning with as much strength and courage as you have just shown in defending your purse, ten men together would never have succeeded in ravishing you." [1]

While fully recognizing that the girl who is weak enough to allow herself to be seduced is deserving of much pity, Society cannot for all that give her the right to say to the

---

[1] *Don Quixote*, ch. xlv.—Muyart de Vouglans relates how a Judge put Sancho's sentence in practice. He condemned a young man, whom a woman accused of rape, to pay her a certain sum for damages and compensation ; then he gave the man leave to rob the woman of the money he had just given her. But the young man was quite unable to do this, so vigorous was the resistance the woman offered. Seeing which the Judge ordered the woman to give the money back, telling her she might very well have defended her person as successfully as her money, if she had been so inclined. (*Institutes au droit criminel*, vol. ii. p. 358.)

seducer : " Marriage or death ! " A society in which the citizens should do justice on one another, and Jealousy and Revenge could do murder with impunity, would cease to be a civilized community at all. No man can be Judge at once and interested party in his own case, still less Judge, interested party and executioner ! Among civilized Peoples, it is the State that dispenses Justice. The plain citizen, man or woman, has no right to take the place of the State, to condemn to death or blindness, to invent new forms of punishment, to pronounce sentence in the tribunal of private judgment and carry the same into effect. A woman can no more say to a man, " Marry me, or die ! " than a man can say to a woman, " Be mine, or die ; Love or Death ! " If by the instrumentality of its representatives, Society were to give private vengeance the right to wound or kill, Society would be pronouncing its own doom. To allow Jealousy and Revenge to inflict suffering, to burn the features and destroy the eyes, to stab the breast, would be to set Society back on a level below primitive barbarism. It would be something worse than the *lex talionis*, " an eye for an eye, a tooth for a tooth "; it would be a still more savage law,—an eye blinded for reparation refused, a broken skull for a marriage missed. The duty of Juries is to secure respect for human life and not to encourage murder ; but to acquit a woman who has killed her lover is to authorize individual vengeance.

The pity a Jury feels for the woman who has been forsaken and has taken revenge into her own hands springs from genuine good-nature, but after all sentimentality is not the proper frame of mind for giving judgment. Pity, like every other sentiment, must be governed by reason. Besides, a Jury ought not to lavish all its commiseration on the love sorrows of women, who are so open to temptation ; let it keep a little for the victims. For eyes burned out after horrible torments, heart and lungs pierced by bullets, are spectacles no less deserving pity than female hearts transfixed by the mythological arrows of Love.

pose to curb passion. Apart from exceptional cases, where a man is deprived of Will and Reason by disease, he has the power as well as the obligation of self-restraint. As Dr. Magnan says, "the superior centres situated in the frontal region regulate and moderate the appetites and instincts which have for organic base the vast region lying behind the vertical parietal division." [1] Writers who maintain the passions to be irresistible take no account of the force of will [2] and abstract ideas. The high ideas of Duty and Justice, love of the ideal, enthusiasm for moral beauty, feeling of personal dignity, horror of sin and fear of remorse, all these sentiments, unknown to the brutes, form a counterpoise in man to the passionate instincts, and make him a responsible being. Man has been called a reasoning animal, a religious animal, a metaphysical animal, an imitative animal, a tool-inventing animal; he might also be defined as a *responsible* animal. Responsibility is the most salient characteristic of human nature. Society is the organization of civil and penal responsibility.

There are some both amongst physicians and moralists who liken Love to a fever or a form of madness. Huet, Bishop of Avranches, used to say Love was a fever, that was cured by copious bleeding. Dr. Sauvages of Montpelier, in the Eighteenth Century, looked upon Love as a disease, and wrote a treatise on the Prognostics and Therapeutics of Love. It is not a mere metaphor when Poets speak of "the fires of Love," "the fever of Love," "the flame that burns the heart." In some cases Love actually produces fever; it is not simply a figure of rhetoric when Phèdre declares:

"Je sentais tout mon corps et transir et brûler." [3]

Still, though Love may become a pathological condition, it is not so normally; it is a physiological condition, and

---

[1] Magnan, *Recherches sur les centres nerveux*, 2nd Series.

[2] Will power even contributes to ward off and cure diseases. To wish to get well is the beginning of a cure. *Pars sanitatis velle sanari fuit* (Ovid),— "a part of the cure was the wish to be cured."

[3] "I felt my whole body freeze and burn at one and the same time."

one in the regular order of Nature, being directed to assure the conservation of the species. It is only in exceptional instances it brings about disturbances of the circulation and nutrition, and a true delirium, a state of melancholia accompanied by stupor.

We cannot make of Love an excuse for irresponsibility and assimilate it to a mental disease by any insistence on characteristics common to both, such as fixity of idea, obsession of the mind combined with precordial oppression. It is perfectly true that Love, like neurosis, contracts the intellectual horizon, that the lover thinks exclusively of the person loved, that his attention is entirely concentrated on her beauty, that the place where she lives, the air she breathes, the clothes that touch her body, are the whole universe for him. But then mental obsession is not necessarily a sign of insanity. The Scientist has all-absorbing ideas, he is always thinking of the object of his special studies. The inventor only arrives at a great discovery by the concentration of all his thoughts on one and the same subject. We all know the answer a man of science gave in reply to the question, " How were you led to hit on this discovery ? "—" By constantly thinking about it," was the answer. Thus we see fixity of idea, which characterizes the psychical condition of the lover, is not a sign of insanity.

Every fixed idea determines certain acts, provokes the activity of certain impulses. This is the normal play of the intellectual life, and is perfectly reconcilable with responsibility, because it abrogates neither Conscience nor Will. All passions are absorbing and constraining, but we do not regard them as morbid states involving irresponsibility. Every passion consists in a predilection, a concentration of thought on the object of the passion in question. The ambitious man has a fixed idea,—power ; the miser a fixed idea,—money. The nobler passions are likewise fixed ideas ; the ardent patriot has a fixed idea,— the greatness of his native land ; the Missionary has a fixed idea,—the conversion of Pagan tribes ; the Saint concen-

feigned as the Clermont-Ferrand Specialist thought. The new experts declared that the accused was shamming stupidity; he pretended he could not distinguish a fifty-centimes piece from a five-francs piece; that he knew neither his age nor the year when he drew for exemption from military service; that he could not count. They added that they found on him none of the characteristic stigmata of degeneration. The Court eventually condemned him to two years' imprisonment.

Specialists when called in by Justice are in the habit of reading up the particulars of the case, finding much very valuable information, especially in the examinations and cross-examinations of the accused and the depositions of witnesses, bearing upon the character, antecedents and family of the prisoner, and the way in which the crime was committed. But I consider that in their Report the doctors should confine themselves to the medical aspect of the case,—a thing which they do not always do, sometimes basing their conclusions on such or such a piece of evidence. In my opinion they are here going beyond their proper province. A short time since, in the Court over which I preside, we had to examine into the mental condition of a prisoner who had tried to commit a murder under the influence of jealousy. The Specialist made his conclusions depend on a fact alleged by the accused, but not established under examination. If, the expert said, this fact is true, the prisoner is responsible; if it is inaccurate, he is irresponsible. We held, my colleagues and myself, that the Specialist ought to have confined himself to the medical aspect, and enquired whether the accused presented physical and psychical characteristics that were abnormal or morbid, and ordered a fresh medical examination, which is at present being made.

For prisoners who are neither mad enough to be shut up in Lunatic Asylums nor yet sane enough to be declared responsible for their actions, there should be Institutions occupying an intermediate position between Asylum and Gaol. To pronounce them irresponsible and leave them

at large is to compromise the public safety ; to condemn
them to punishment is to violate justice.[1]

But if Love is not normally a morbid state of mind and
body, it may become so. Side by side with normal, physiological love there is abnormal, pathological love. As Littré
says, in his *Dictionary of Medicine*, Love " is the source of
aberrations which the specialist and professor of Medical
Jurisprudence are called upon to forestall or to interpret,
in order to find out if they have been carried out under
normal conditions or those of mental alienation." The
question is a very delicate one to decide. It is the
Physician, deeply versed in the study of mental diseases,
who must adjudicate in this matter ; all Physicians do not
possess the needful competence. In very delicate cases
my advice to *Juges d'instruction* is to have the persons
accused examined by the Parisian Specialists in Mental
Disease, who have exceptional competence, and get them
transferred by the Court to the Prefecture of Police, where
they can be conveniently examined by the doctors. In the
Walroff affair the Chamber of Prosecutions of the Court of
Aix ordered an examination of the accused by MM. Brouardel, Motet, and Garnier, and the prisoner was transferred
to Paris. In such circumstances the question of expense is
a secondary one. The all important point is that Justice
should not run the risk of condemning a man who is
afflicted with disease, and so irretrievably disgracing both
him and his family.

I tremble every time I see a question of responsibility
referred to a Jury, because they have never made the
special studies indispensable for a decision. Sometimes
we find them proclaiming as irresponsible prisoners whom
the Specialists in Medical Jurisprudence declare responsible, sometimes affirming the responsibility of persons
who are undoubtedly irresponsible. Juries take as a

---

[1] See Gilbert Ballet, *Annales medico-psychologiques*, 1895, p. 271.—Also *Les
Dégénérés*, by Drs. Magnan and Legrain, 214. Since 1863 there has existed in
England, at Broadmoor, an Asylum for Criminal Lunatics. This expression,
Criminal Lunatics, is a misnomer, for Lunatics cannot be criminals *qua*
criminals, inasmuch as they are irresponsible.

forms of partial insanity, the patient may be responsible
for crimes having no connection with the particular aberration that possesses them.   "A man who is driven mad by
conjugal jealousy and who commits murder under the influence of this delirium is irresponsible," says M.Charpentier;
"but he is responsible if he is guilty of forgery or swindling,
because there is no connection between those offences and
morbid jealousy."[1]   Along with MM. Fabret, Morel, Grie-
singer, Magnan, I believe on the contrary that partial delirium is invariably bound up with a general disturbance
of the reason, a diseased condition of the brain, and that
accordingly it *ipso facto* implies irresponsibility.

Dr. Lassègue, insisting very justly on the predisposition
to suicide arising from temperament, declares there is no
relation of cause and effect between an act of suicide and
the motive to which it is attributed, that the man who
kills himself through disappointed love was predisposed to
suicide before the disappointment occurred, and that the said
disappointment is not the main cause of his suicide.[2]   The
fact of such predisposition is undeniable.   Seeing all men
who have disappointments in love do not kill themselves
or others, we are justified in supposing some persons are
more than others predisposed to suicide and crime.   The
predisposition to suicide is nothing more nor less than an
organization more than usually sensitive to grief and less
able to bear it, and consequently eager to escape it,—
ferroque avertere dolorem (and to avert calamity by the
steel).   The biological cause of suicide is excess of suffering ; persons driven to desperation say so themselves in
the writings they leave behind.   "My grief is too heavy,"
writes one despairing woman, "I cannot bear it any more.
I am going to seek a remedy in death.   When you receive
these lines, all that is left of your poor Marie will be
ashes."—"I cannot live separated from X——," writes
another, "my pain is so deep I had rather die."

It is a great mistake to suppose, as Stendhal did, that

[1] *Congrès de médecine mentale de Lyon*, 1891, p. 183.
[2] *Gazette des Hôpitaux*, 1865.

what characterizes the author of a crime of passion is energy; anger, jealousy, desire of vengeance, seize upon nervous, irritable individuals, incapable of self-government, upon children and women. Such irritability is a sign of weakness and not of energy. The man who cannot endure his mistress's unfaithfulness without losing his wits, is not an energetic man, but a weak one. He who, transported with fury at the sight of a rival, yields to the impulse to strike him is not a strong man either. Nor is the forsaken woman, who weeps and screams and stamps, tears out her hair, and would like to tear out her false lover's eyes, a woman of energy, but the reverse. Energy does not consist in flying in a passion, yielding to every impulse of the blood and the nerves, submitting to physiological influences of every sort, without power to resist. Persons of this violent sort are at bottom weaklings, the slaves of impulse, victims of debility of will. Here is a recent instance of morbid jealousy determining a fixed idea of suicide, as related by the victim of jealousy involved, a working cabinet-maker, a man of intelligence quite capable of analyzing his own feelings : " I thought I was losing my wits altogether. So confused were my ideas I thought my head was going to burst, my brain was boiling so. What came of these thoughts? The result was a madman's notion, one of those ideas that occur only to lunatics, and I cannot get rid of it. My whole life flashed through my mind in those few seconds, and I could see nothing all through it but disappointment and ill fortune; an evil genius seemed to have consistently pursued me, and before this black picture, the fatal idea occurred to me to escape it all by death."—We give another example of the same thing : " I am utterly incapable of any kind of work, in one word, I do not know what I want or what I don't want. . . . I am all at sea, and utterly unstrung. One fixed idea possesses me, which has pursued me for years,— and that is suicide. Hence my dejection and cowardly self-abandonment."

Morbid jealousy is capable of inspiring the most extra-

ordinary acts.   A jealous woman, of hysterical temperament and cunning to the last degree, will invent a thousand
fables, a thousand false charges, each more ridiculous than
the other, to punish her husband, or whoever it is that
excites her enmity.   To give an example: a wife cut
herself in a number of places with a knife, and then
accused her husband of giving her the wounds she had
to show.   An enquiry was held, and the woman retracting
the charges she had made, told the Commissary of Police:
" I was mad yesterday; I love my husband dearly, but I
am jealous, and I wanted to kill myself."   We see what
prudence, what discernment, are needful for the Magistrate
who receives such complaints, in order to discriminate their
truth or falsity.   It is not enough to know the Criminal
Code to be a good Magistrate; a good Magistrate must
know human nature and the female heart; he must be a
psychologist and a specialist in insanity.[1]   A jealous
woman, with a highly nervous, ill - balanced temperament, again, is very ready to believe her husband wishes
to get rid of her by poison, so as to be free to take a
mistress or marry a second wife.   A prey to the mania of
persecution in its completest form, she will bring the most
unfounded charges against her husband, and will do it in
perfect good faith.

[1] A knowledge of mental diseases should be required on the part of all
Magistrates, and a course of study on these subjects instituted with this express
purpose in all the Faculties of Law.   Such a course of lectures does exist in
Paris, under the direction of Dr. Dubuisson ; but it ougnt to be made compul-
sory and more comprehensive.   For want of such acquaintance with mental
diseases, the Members of the Bench and *Juges d'instruction* are unable to
treat cases where examination by a Specialist in insanity is called for.   Irresponsible lunatics are condemned to punishment as being responsible for their
actions.   According to Dr. Magnan, in the Paris Courts alone 50 insane
persons are condemned on an average every year.   Between 1885 and 1890, 281
insane patients, 76 of these suffering from general paralysis, have been received
in the Asylums of the Department of the Seine within short periods after their
condemnation in a Court of Law.—Again, in certain civil matters of great
importance, such as the annulling of testamentary dispositions on the plea of
insanity, the science of mental diseases is equally indispensable for Magistrates ;
the testator being dead, these latter are deprived even of the information
procurable by medico-legal examination.

These false charges, brought by victims of jealousy, are frequently the result of pure hallucination.

One T——, a working plumber, married to a very good and respectable woman, became exceedingly jealous of her. He was a man of nervous, excitable disposition, and the relations between husband and wife soon grew strained. Suspicious and ready to take offence, he used to play the spy on her, and ended by believing she was in the habit of committing acts of bestiality. His wife, insulted and ill-treated, was forced to leave her husband's roof and sue for a divorce. On Dec. 5. 1897, the husband hid himself in the corridor of the house where she was working, and on her arrival accosted her with the words: "I want to know what you went to R—— Street for?" On her refusing to answer, he drew a bottle of vitriol from his pocket and threw the contents in his wife's face. The corrosive fluid only just touched the intended victim, but burned more seriously a young girl who was in the corridor at the moment. The culprit instantly took to flight, but was arrested next day. He made a determined resistance, and was found to be in possession of a sword-bayonet freshly sharpened. Questioned as to why he carried such a weapon, he replied it was to defend himself against a possible attack on the part of his wife's lover. Before the Court he bore himself more as accuser than accused. His examination brought out the fact that he had always shown a certain strangeness of character. There had been insanity in his family too. His paternal uncle lost his reason in 1870; he had two sons serving with the colours, and receiving no news of them he started out to join them. His behaviour appearing strange, he was taken for a spy, arrested and shot. The accused in the present case, on being examined by a professor of Medical Jurisprudence, was found to be suffering from morbid jealousy, and to be dominated by insane ideas combined with hallucinations, and incapable of controlling his actions.

A change in the character is often a sign of mental derangement. In a case directed against a husband, who

stimulates his violent tendencies and brings on an enfeeblement of the brain, diminishing his responsibility.
On March 27. 1897, the Assize Court of the Department
of the Puy-de-Dôme condemned to three years' imprisonment one Joseph Passavy, a mason, who under the influence of jealousy and intoxication had killed his wife's
lover.   Exasperated by his wife's misconduct and her
lover's insolence, who boasted openly of his relations with
her, the unfortunate husband gave way to heavy drinking,
and intemperance and grief combined led to intellectual
enfeeblement. One day, when excited by drink, he yielded
to the anger he felt against his wife's lover and murdered
him.   In prison he suffered from hallucinations of sight
and hearing, seeing great splashes of blood on the walls
of his cell, being unable to sleep and refusing food.   After
being transferred to the Insane Asylum at Clermont, he
recovered his health and asked to be tried at the Assizes,
so as to establish his innocence. His demand was granted,
after he had undergone examination by three Doctors of
Moulins, who declared him to be responsible for his actions.
They found that he presented no signs of degeneration, and
was normally constituted.

Advocates have made inordinate use in Criminal Court
cases of irresistible impulses, which they attribute instinc-
tively to every accused person who has committed a crime
under stress of passion.   But, while we must resist these
systematic views which would make irresponsibility almost
universal, we are equally bound to admit there are cases
where, under the influence of a morbid condition, prisoners
have in very truth succumbed to impulses they could not
master.   The Law recognizes the existence of irresistible
impulses; "There is neither crime nor misdemeanour,"
says Article 64 of the Penal Code, ". . . when the accused
has been constrained by a force he was incapable of resisting."   In such cases the irresponsibility is self-evident,
and acquittal a duty.   Physicians in Insanity, exercised
by the unjust reproach so often brought against them of
seeing madmen everywhere, do not always see their way

in these cases to declare clearly and boldly for absolute irresponsibility, and give their voices for extenuated or partial responsibility.[1] But disease is more than an extenuation, it is a justification. Physicians should not allow themselves to be intimidated by the frivolous criticism of ignorant people, who blame them for seeing insanity where they cannot perceive it themselves. The general public, never having studied mental diseases, entertains utterly mistaken notions about madness, supposing it to exist only in conjunction with wildly disordered thoughts and incoherent words, and entirely ignorant of the terrible power of hallucinations and the irresistible impulses they provoke. Consequently it may very well fail to see insanity in cases where specialists know it to exist.

If some medical authorities on insanity err on the side of timidity in their conclusions, others, inordinately exaggerating the importance of exceptional cases, are so rash as to assert that Jealousy is a genuine form of madness, bound to involve irresponsibility. Dr. Paul Moreau (of Tours) looks upon Jealousy as an actual monomania, and writes: "A passion that is at once violent, exclusive, and dominant, that forcibly interferes during its continuance with the exercise of moral freedom, must involve irresponsibility.[2] If this theory were correct, every prison would have to be shut up, and Gaols transformed into Lunatic Asylums; for all crimes are committed under the

[1] Dr. Coutagne of Lyons was quite justified in telling his colleagues at a medical Congress : " A declaration of extenuated irresponsibility must not be suffered to burke a thorough-going diagnosis."—The Physicians of former days lent themselves so readily to raillery, that Poets, from Horace, Ovid, Juvenal and Martial down to Molière, have overwhelmed them with epigrams that always find an echo in the heart of patients who have not been cured, or in parents, who make the doctors responsible for the death of a beloved child. Journalists, Novelists and Dramatic Authors are endeavouring nowadays to rouse public opinion against the physicians who are specialists in insanity, but their criticisms are unfounded. No doubt, among doctors as among members of any other profession, incompetent and untrustworthy men are to be found. But can anybody suppose that among Barristers there are none but Berryers and Dufaures, or that all Magistrates possess the character of a Matthieu Molé and the knowledge and acumen of a d'Aguesseau?

[2] Dr. Paul Moreau (of Tours), *La Folie Jalouse*, p. 105.

is wounded by a look or a smile cannot make a man irresponsible. In breaking off engagements, a thing so apt to lead to quarrels, self-love plays a not inconsiderable part, and young men have been known to kill their fiancée on the ground that they have been insulted when they were sent about their business and laughed at.

True Love is allowed to be a strong reason for admitting extenuation ; [1] but we must not delay to add that all crimes of passion are not crimes of Love. Crimes of true Love, of high-strung and lofty passion, are rare. In most crimes of passion there is plenty of brutality and jealous frenzy, of alcoholism and base avarice, but very little Love, and often none at all. True Love is not often met with. To tell a woman, " I will kill you, if you do not submit," is a sort of love exceedingly like rape. Love and concupiscence are two different things ; and concupiscence may be extremely strong without Love having anything to do with

[1] This extenuation of guilt may be attained by a special application of the Bérenger Law. The penalty for assassination being still often over severe, the Presiding Judge of Assize, by breaking up the questions laid before the Jury, gives them the power of diminishing it. Instead of putting before the Jury the question : "Is so and so guilty of having on such and such a date and at such and such a place committed wilful murder on the person of so and so?" he may break up the charge of murder and put the two following questions : 1. "Is so and so guilty of having on such and such a date, at such and such a place, wilfully offered violence and wounded so and so?" 2. "Did the said violence cause death?"—It is certainly to be regretted that a Jury, in order to diminish the penalty, should be obliged to eliminate an undisputed fact ; it would be better to admit the system of "extenuating circumstances in a high degree." But what is far more regrettable is acquittal, which is a scandal and an encouragement to crime. A penalty, no matter how much softened, would be a satisfaction to conscience and a sufficient deterrent ; it is not the length of the imprisonment that is the important point, but the principle of condemnation. Our Legislators have made a mistake in rejecting the system of "extenuating circumstances" altogether, under the pretext of not weakening the hands of Justice in the repression of crime ; this is much more likely to happen by reason of acquittals, which Jurymen agree to because they recoil at pronouncing an over severe sentence.—I fail to understand why Virgil in the Sixth Book of the Æneid, puts in Tartarus, without making any distinction between them, all the victims of Love alike, equally the noblest and the basest ; Evadné is found side by side with Phaedra, Laodamia with Pasiphaé. A Judge should not follow Virgil's example ; he ought to distinguish the less guilty, graduate punishments and make them proportionate to the offence.

the matter. Crimes of rape and criminal offences are determined by the violence of concupiscence and nothing else. The males of animals, no less than men, maltreat and kill the females of their species that resist them. Love which tries to win possession with knife and revolver is only a counterfeit of Love; for true Love is the very opposite of brutality, it does not hurt and curtail the liberty of the person loved, but rather submits and sacrifices itself to the will of the object of its affection.

Crimes of debauchery are not crimes of love. Prisoners who have killed a woman who resisted their attempts, are often heard trying to excuse themselves by saying, " I was madly in love . . . I loved her to madness." Yet cross-examination will reveal the fact that these madmen of love had other intrigues on hand at the same time or spent the night before with another woman. A farmer, owning his own land, a brutal, dissipated fellow, who made it his amusement to seduce the young farm-girls he hired for agricultural work, and used to abandon them when he had made them mothers, was so exasperated at the resistance one of them made to his attempts, that he lay in wait for her one evening in a lonely place and with a blow of his bill-hook very nearly severed her head from her body. As his victim lay on the ground, he threw himself savagely upon her and struck five more times with the bill-hook. On the Presiding Judge at his trial reproaching him with his abominable cruelty, he made the same answer,—he was mad with love !

Debauchery makes men especially commit monstrous crimes. In 1891, for instance, of 571 persons accused of rape and criminal assaults on minors, 567 were men and only four women. The report of the Ministry of Justice issued in 1895, giving the facts observed for 1892, notes an increase in the number of rapes and criminal assaults on children. Little girls are torn, bitten, disembowelled, strangled, thrown into the water. Vile debauchees attack them like wild beasts. Studying these abominable crimes at close quarters, crimes of which the details cannot be

jealousy, often tries to excuse his crime by giving it the character of a crime of passion; he feigns jealousy, spreads some scandal about his wife's behaviour, attributes some guilty intrigue to her.

Prostitutes and their bullies quarrel, fight and kill one another very often from jealousy, after indulging in alcoholic excesses. In Paris, a section of the female population lives by prostitution, whether from inadequate wages or through idleness, and a section of the working-class population lives in chronic alcoholism. In this world of gay women and drunkards, suicides and crimes of passion are extremely common.

Just as there are crimes of passion falsely so described, there are suicides of passion in the same category. For instance, I find the formal report of a Commissary of Police classifying as a suicide for love that of a rag-picker, a widower of sixty-four, who had entered into relations with the widow of a cobbler and was thinking of marrying her. The man was a drunkard, who used to spend his wages, ten francs a day, in drink. One day, drinking with a comrade, he said to the latter: "I am going to ask Mme. X—— to marry me, and if I don't succeed, I shall hang myself." Next day he was found hanged. In a case like this it was Intemperance surely rather than Love the Commissary should have attributed the man's suicide to.—To give another instance. In September 1896 at Paris, the Commissary of Police notes the suicide of a workman, a widower of fifty, and father of three children, who in despair at his mistress having deserted him, swallowed the contents of a phial of vitriol. On being carried to the Hospital and there questioned by the Commissary, he gave the following account of himself: "I had been living for two years with the woman X——, when she left me a few days ago. This gave me the deepest grief, and I tried to end my days." Now this suicide might certainly seem to be attributable to despair arising from disappointed love. But it appeared on further enquiry that the man and his mistress were in the habit

of constantly getting drunk together and quarrelling per-
petually, that one day the woman, having been beaten
rather harder than usual, ran away and left her lover,
and that the latter, vexed at her departure, redoubled
his potations; for the three days preceding his suicide,
he never left off drinking.

Alcoholism has made appalling progress in Paris, and
developed to an incredible degree the worst instincts
of profligacy and violence. While I was Judge at the
Correctional Tribunal of the Department of the Seine, I
found fully a half of all offences might be attributed to
drunkenness. At every sitting we had to judge prisoners
who under the empire of alcoholism had committed public
outrages on decency and serious acts of violence. These
drunkards, who attack, like brute beasts, the members of
the Police force, their neighbours, their comrades, give way
to the same violence towards their wives and mistresses,
under the influence of jealousy and strong drink. Alcoholism naturally leading to ideas of suicide and murder,
the drunkard tells his wife, "I am going to kill you, and
myself afterwards." It is impossible from a distance to
form any idea of the brutish degradation of a section of
the Parisian population due to alcoholism. Habits of intoxication have now extended to women. Drunken women
quarrel with their lovers, and in the paroxysm of their
anger throw themselves out of window. If they survive
the fall, they never fail to falsely accuse their lover of
having pitched them out.

In crimes of passion so called, love sorrows are often
further complicated with questions of money. Murder
or suicide results, not only because the heart is too full
of love, but because the purse is too empty of coin.
Women who avenge their desertion by murdering the
faithless lover, invariably describe themselves as the
victims of Love. Nevertheless there are Ariadnes whose
grief is appeased by money, and whose despair only takes
violent shape if the rupture is not duly accompanied by
metallic arguments to comfort wounded feelings.—How

her, that she might always have him by her side and enjoy his fortune.   When the young man, who received the contents of a cup of vitriol right in the face, learned the motive of his mistress's act, the moral grief he felt was even more cruel than the physical pain caused by the acid. He told the *Juge d'instruction*, " When I received the vitriol in my eyes, I uttered not cries, but howls, it is impossible to describe the agonies I suffered.   Well! when I knew it was my mistress who had burned me so cruelly, I experienced an unspeakable pang and heartache, which still causes me atrocious sufferings.   Still, these are perhaps less keen than what I felt, when I realized that so much unkindness and cruelty can be hidden in the heart of a woman I had never done anything but good to.   I did not sleep a wink for thirty nights, and I only wonder a man can survive such grief and pain.   Now I am blind.   I could have understood her killing me ; but she has shown far greater cruelty in letting me live on in the condition she has reduced me to, and with the future that is before me." So atrocious was the woman's wickedness that previous to the discovery of her guilt, she had installed herself at her lover's bedside, to nurse him better, as she pretended, but in reality to counteract the medical treatment and prevent his cure.   All this time, and after her arrest, she carefully studied the fluctuations of the Money Market.

Adultery and greed of money are also very often associated.   Men of mature years, who marry young wives, are often obliged in order to win the consent of the latter, to make provision for them in the marriage contract.   This provision being contingent on the husband's death, the wife kills the husband, so as to enter into immediate possession of the advantages in question and enjoy them along with her lover.   It is the over-hasty proceedings of the adulterous wife and her lover the sooner to enjoy the husband's fortune that usually betray them. The lover, if he is a workman or a farm-labourer, gives up working, goes shooting, visits the public-house, launches into expenditure that attracts attention, helps the wife in the proceedings she takes with the Notary in order to get in her husband's succession.—The master, well on in years, who gives pecuniary advantages to his housekeeper in his will runs similar risks to those attending the old husband of a young wife. I have myself known the case of such a servant, who after sharing her master's bed, got up to strike him dead and then set fire to the house that he might perish in the flames.

Again it is a mistake to regard as crimes of passion all the murders committed by husbands who, separated from their wives, beseech the latter to renew cohabitation with them, and on their refusal kill them, and then try to kill themselves. Love is not the determining factor in these crimes ; the truth is, the husbands, having come to the end of their resources, wish to renew cohabitation, in order to get hold once more of the administration of their wives' fortunes.

In Paris money difficulties are so pressing, that both in suicides and crimes of passion, the pecuniary question often plays as important a part as passion itself. Take the instance of a young woman who had two lovers, one whom she loved, the other who loved her and paid the piper. The latter, discovering what was going on, broke off the connection. His mistress in despair committed suicide by means of charcoal fumes, after writing the following letter to the man she loved : " I wished to write to you before dying. My *friend* is leaving me ; he has found out I had you too ; all is over between us, he told me. After this, why should I go on living? I should have to look out other protectors and go on the loose ; it isn't worth the trouble, really. Receive a last kiss from your darling, and farewell ! From one who is going to die loving you fondly." There are also a certain number of women who kill themselves when they suffer love disappointments complicated with money difficulties, or when money failing them, on the death of their lover, they cannot make up their minds to work. " A certain G——," says a Police report, " lived for several years with the Baron X——, who died three months

carried out under dramatic circumstances which prove the
motive to have been rather a wish for notoriety than the
despair of a broken heart.   Before shooting their lover,
girls will make public announcement of their intentions,
declaring, " The Newspapers will be full of it."

This longing to attract attention is common among
hysterical subjects, inducing them sometimes to play the
comedy of a pretended suicide.   Till within the last few
years hysteria was supposed to be an exclusively female
complaint.   But it is now established that men may suffer
from it.   Though much more common in large towns, it is
also seen in the country.   The responsibility of hysterical
patients must be estimated according to the degree of
hysteria.   Pronounced hysteria may involve complete
irresponsibility, slight hysteria a considerable diminution
of responsibility.   Women even slightly affected in this
way, while generally showing lively spirits and brilliant
parts, possess little will power, and are liable to sudden
impulses and bursts of anger, which they find it extremely
difficult to control.

The Works of Specialists in Mental Disease demonstrate
the necessity of extending the sphere of irresponsibility,
and that among the authors of crimes there are more victims
of disease than used to be supposed.   Magistrates multiply
medical examinations in doubtful cases, in order to have
the assistance of mental science.   But, on the other hand,
its professors must beware of blindly following a system,
and must guard carefully against exaggeration.   They
must not confound vice voluntarily acquired with involuntary disease, or regard habits of profligacy and
drunkenness leading to the frenzies of jealousy and anger
as fatally determined consequences of temperament, as
Dr. Buchner would have us believe.

We must not suffer Science falsely so called to set itself
up in contradiction with Law and Conscience, or melt
in foolish commiseration over the Criminal who is really
responsible for his vices, telling him as Jocasta might
Œdipus: "Alas! alas! unhappy man, for this is the only

name I can give you, and I will call you no other.
Guilty I could never name you. 'Tis not you are
guilty; 'tis your brain that is malformed, 'tis the society
that has reared you. Virtue and vice are products as
much as sugar and vitriol."[1]

Man is irresponsible only if he is corporeally and
mentally unsound. But mental disease and irresponsibility are exceptional. The general rule is health and
responsibility.

The study of mental diseases has led a certain number
of medical Specialists in Insanity to deny moral responsibility altogether, even in persons of sound mind. But
Pinel, Baillarger, Morel of Rouen, Foville, Brière de Boismont, Legrand du Saulle, Lassègue, Tardieu, Delasiauve,
Fournet, Fabret, Dagonnet, etc., have on the contrary
made madness consist in the loss of free will, and have
admitted irresponsibility only in the case of men suffering
from disease.

Crimes of passion falsely so called should not be allowed
to benefit by the pity and indulgence inspired by crimes
of Love. Even Love itself, though it may extenuate guilt,
must never be suffered to justify crime. The victims of
Jealousy and amorous Vengeance have as good a right
to find protection in the Law as those of greed or
hate. Whether due to passion or not, Crime is always
Crime.

[1] This formula, enunciated as a profound scientific truth, was employed for
the first time by Balzac, in his *Peau de Chagrin*, being placed in the mouth of
an intoxicated vagabond. (*Édition Charpentier*, 1845, p. 69.)

and perhaps kill a rival.   Love outside of marriage cannot
then be counted on to purify humanity, to teach women
purity and sincerity, and men goodness and gentleness.
For Love makes adulterous wives who poison their
husbands, unnatural mothers who forsake their children
to go off with a lover, fathers who ruin their family to
satisfy a mistress's caprices, girls who let themselves be
seduced and kill their parents with grief and shame.   How
many men has Love made forgetful of every tie, of honour,
friendship, country, family!   How many employés cheat
their masters, how many subordinate officials commit
breaches of confidence and forgeries, for the sake of
winning some woman's love!   Under the sway of passion,
doctors abuse their patients, priests their penitents, high
functionaries young women employed in their offices.[1]
"For how many unhappy women," said Bourdaloue, "has
not the necessity to petition an immoral Judge been a
snare and a temptation?"

Poets and Novelists, therefore, strangely deceive themselves when they represent Love as a means of purification,
an instrument of rehabilitation, when they exclaim with
George Sand, "Think you, a love or two sufficient to
exhaust and wither a strong soul? . . . 'Tis a fire that
tends ever to rise higher and higher, purer and purer."
But it is a fire that likewise tends to sink lower and lower,
to burn blacker and blacker and flicker out in mire and
blood.   If it burns outside the domestic hearth, it destroys
everything, and leaves a heap of ruins in the family and in
society.

What purifies mankind is not passion, as the Poets and
Novelists assert, but love of country, love of humanity,
pity for the poor and for little children, respect for unhappy women who gain their bread so painfully, goodness
and friendship systematically pursued.   These sentiments
do not originate in a chance meeting, the exchange of a

---

[1] The Head of an Academy told me of a certain Department of his institution, in which a large number of governesses had been ruined by Politicians
whom they had visited to obtain recommendations.

glance, a physical impression ; they come from the soul, and are felt only by upright hearts.

Doubtless the Poets have done well in displaying the moral transformations Love brings about sometimes. But Love is not enough to transform a criminal into a hero. A scamp in love remains a scamp still. Love does not purify him, it only makes him more ready for crime. Just as in a noble soul all is noble, in a base soul all is base, even Love. Pascal, depicting the beauties of Love, has written : " A man is elevated by this passion, and becomes all greatness." But a man may be lowered also by the same passion, and become all baseness. Humanity is still far from the ideal Love that Poets sing of. Love seldom turns men into angels, though it often changes them into brutes ; it makes more madmen than sages, more murderers than heroes. It often makes lovers cowardly and cruel, friends hypocrites and traitors, women adulteresses and poisoners, husbands monsters of jealousy and murderers. Love may be the charm of life, if it is in due accord with reason and the laws of society ; but it becomes its torment and its shame when it claims to be superior to duty. To make Love accord with duty, that is to bring it into harmony with marriage, is the surest way to escape the tragic consequences that are so apt to follow from an irregular situation.

He who places himself in a false position cannot tell where he is going ; he is taking a leap in the dark, into the surprises and catastrophes of life, into pain and suffering, and maybe into the road that leads to suicide and crime. He wishes to stop, but cannot always succeed, for he is hurried on by the force of circumstances, which drag him where he never thought to go at the commencement of his passion. One step outside the path of duty may bring a man, and still more a woman, to the Morgue, the gaol or the hospital, for the first slip leads to others, each more serious and more tragic than the last. The girl who yields to love without marriage is running blindfold to meet calamity that is surely lying in wait for her, though

have reserved her love for an honest man, who would have made her his lawful wife.

To place oneself in a false situation is to run the risk of loss of repose and honour, both one's own and other people's. The "situation à trois," which leads up to so many comic scenes on the Stage, is often fertile in tragic incidents when it comes to real life ; it is responsible for Werther's suicide and Saint-Preux's intention of drowning himself along with Mme. de Wolmar. How many young men, who expected to find nothing but simple happiness in a young married woman's friendship, have glided like Goethe's hero unawares into the temptation of murdering the husband ! They thought at first merely to enjoy the distraction of a harmless flirtation ; but presently their heart was touched, they learned to love and could not bear to live without the object of their affection, they grew jealous of the husband. At length, one day, like Werther, they awake horrified at the murderous thoughts that cross their minds from time to time. "When I thus lose myself in my reveries," Werther says, " I cannot help the thought : Why ! if Albert were to die, you would be ! . . . she could . . . I pursue my wild fancy, till it brings me to the brink of an abyss, and I draw back shuddering." Others, under similar circumstances, do not draw back on the brink of crime.

How many married women, who wished at first to draw the line at a refined affection, have fallen eventually into adultery and from that into even greater sins ! At the first commencement of the attraction she feels for another than her husband, the married woman who yields to it recoils with horror at the mere thought of attempting her husband's life. But before long her character becomes modified, her indifference towards her husband becomes hatred, and if her husband, by his jealousy and suspicions, becomes an obstacle interfering with her passion, the idea of suppressing the said obstacle presents itself to her mind and is not rejected.

It was of this lightning rapidity with which unforeseen

consequences arise out of a false situation that Ovid exclaims at the beginning of the *Remedia Amoris* :

" Principiis obsta, sero medicina paratur." [1]

The tempests of the heart are like the tempests of the sea, beginning with a wind that at first only whitens the waves; presently the gale increases, the waves roll in heights and hollows, and soon "the sea can no more continue calm, and its waves dash on the shore with salt and turbid foam." [2] Passion becomes violent, exacting, imperious, because it was not resisted at first; if once allowed to grow, it gets beyond all mastery.

The Latin Poet who taught the Roman youth the Art of Love, surprised to find amorous idylls ending in sanguinary dramas, seeks to quench the fire he has kindled : "Why," he says, "suffer a lover to squeeze his neck in a noose, and hang himself from the top of a lofty beam ? or that another plunge in his inwards a murderous weapon ? . . . Begin by flying idleness ; idleness gives birth to love and feeds it, once it is born. . . . Work therefore, and you will be saved. Sloth, sleep prolonged beyond measure . . . play, long hours spent in drinking, rob the soul . . . of all its energy. . . . Country life and the cares of farming are also a source of agreeable distractions for the heart. . . . Devote yourself likewise to the exercises of the chase. . . . Above all, fly far away ; no matter what the ties that restrain you, fly, undertake travels of long continuance . . . prolong your absence till your love has lost its strength and the fire has ceased to smoulder under the ashes. . . . Assume the exterior seeming of a perfect tranquillity, and this artificial calm will become real." This last piece of advice reveals Ovid as a great psychologist, for to simulate a feeling tends to produce it.[3] *Frequens*

---

[1] " Withstand the first beginnings ; it is too late afterwards to exhibit drugs."

[2] *Æneid*, bk. xii. 528 ; *Isaiah*, ch. vii. 28.

[3] Specialists in Mental Diseases point out even that the pretence of madness will sometimes lead to actual madness (Magnan, *Recherches sur les centres nerveux*, 2nd Series, p. 561).

the health of mind and body, the unsatisfied craving for love may lead to melancholia, cerebral troubles and wasting diseases. Love matches, which were formerly common in France, have become rare events, though they are still numerous in England, Germany, Switzerland and Sweden. The stress of life in large towns, the love of luxury and comfort among women, make marriage difficult. For the same reasons in the large towns French people marry at a later age than in England and in Sweden. These late marriages contribute towards the growing demoralization of society, for the men cannot wait for the legal union, but form temporary liaisons, which often turn out ill. Besides, when it comes to marriage, they are already exhausted by pleasure. Marriage grows less and less common; hence so many bachelors on the look-out to seduce young work-girls or married women. Also marriages being less frequent, many girls unable to marry, are tempted to take to a life of gallantry. If marriages were more numerous, not so long deferred, and above all ratified under better conditions, there would be fewer girls seduced and then forsaken, avenging their wrongs with revolver and vitriol, fewer unfaithful wives poisoning their husbands, fewer deceived husbands killing their wives in jealous fury. I may add there would likewise be fewer crimes against children.[1]

The Physiologists, who are most unjustly accused of immorality,[2] terrified at the ravages caused by the corrup-

[1] There are to be found married people who make martyrs of their children; but it is especially in irregular unions that the children are ill-treated. Love of children is not so natural and universal a sentiment as is generally supposed. It is not the Chinese only who kill their children, especially the girls, with the utmost readiness. Among the Romans, the father had the right to kill weakly children, and to expose his children, if he pleased, whether weakly or not; if he considered he had too large a family, he got rid of the surplus by exposing them. At the present day, the selfishness of irregular liaisons and divorce have undermined the love of children; working-men who are divorced readily abandon their children along with the mother. Irregular unions are afraid of children; the more honourable under such circumstances are content not to wish for any, the more unscrupulous take measures against them.

[2] The English authorities have just seized several books by distinguished Physiologists, notably that of Dr. Féré on *La Pathologie des Émotions*.

tion of morals in modern times, declare it urgent, in order
to raise the moral level of Peoples, to recommend continence to bachelors and faithfulness to married people.
While a certain proportion of Novelists, Poets and Dramatic
Authors boast the superiority of free love and make excuses
for adultery, Physiologists, speaking in the name of hygiene,
are found in agreement with morality, and reserve their
praise for pure morals and legitimate marriage. While
one section of modern Fiction flatters the evil instincts of
the crowd, exalts the pleasures of incontinence, and overwhelms chastity with mocking epigrams, declaring it at
once ridiculous and impossible, Science more enlightened,
more moral and more careful of the true interests of
society, proclaims the advantages and the possibility of
continence for bachelors, and the necessity and sanctity of
marriage; it teaches that it is the chaste races that make
strong and fruitful races.[1] In his book on Love, Michelet,
who had much acquaintance with the Physiologists and
appreciated them highly, judiciously pointed out that the
Novelists and devisers of Utopias, who had written so
much on Love but had hardly been successful in their
treatment of it, would have done better to consult History,
and even Natural History. History, in fact, teaches that
marriage has powerfully contributed towards the progress
of Humanity. Natural History shows that the higher
animals tend towards stability in their loves; that the
widow who remarries keeps the impress of the first
husband, and may bear children who resemble him.

Encouragement of the religious sentiment is another
means of diminishing the number of crimes arising out of
passion. Darwin, who visited the primitive savage populations of Tahiti and New Zealand, noted that a system of
profligacy, unparalleled in any other part of the World,

[1] International Congress held at Brussels in 1889 on means of guarding
against Syphilis and other Venereal Diseases.—Krafft-Ebing, *Psychopathia
Sexualis*; Dr. Ribbing, *L'Hygiène sexuelle*; Dr. Surbled, *La Vie de Jeune
Homme*; Dr. Féré, *L'Instinct sexuel*; Dr. Herzen of Lausanne, *La Question
des mœurs*; Dr. Maudsley, *Crime and Insanity*, p. 272.—Darwin was a great
admirer of chastity (*Descent of Man*).

and infanticide resulting from the system in question, had almost entirely disappeared under the influence of the Christian Missionaries. Taine compares Christianity to "the great pair of wings indispensable to lift man above himself." "Without it," he says, "man becomes again voluptuous and callous ; cruelty and sensuality are rampant." [1]

I have again and again observed during my career how men and women have been saved from suicide by religious belief. God is the great Consoler of forsaken women. The dread of appearing before Him, after doing an act He forbids, restrains many desperate women who are sorely tempted to end their own life. George Sand relates that she was cured of the temptation to commit suicide by reading the Classical Writers, and by her return to the belief in a future life, which she had lost. Despair, as the etymology of the word itself declares, is the loss of hope. The heroes of Goethe, Byron, Musset, who end in suicide, are all sceptics. In *Lélia*, George Sand makes Stenio, who commits suicide, a profligate and an atheist. Don Juan mingles impiety with debauchery, and is for forcing the poor man into atheism. Mephistopheles says of himself, "I am he who denies."

Wherever the religious sentiment is preserved, crime diminishes; where it is weakened, crime increases. Suicide was very rare in the Middle Ages ; it first began to be more frequent in the Eighteenth Century, when the religious sentiment was weakened. Religious Faith is an even better preservative from Suicide than from Crime, because the Believer, after committing a crime, hopes to escape punishment, and to have time to become reconciled with God, whereas after suicide he must appear immediately before His Presence. This is why in countries where there are many murders, in Spain and Italy for instance, there are but few suicides. In papers left behind by suicides, of which I have read a very large number, I

[1] Darwin, *A Naturalist's Voyage* ; Taine, *Revue des Deux Mondes*, June 1, 1891, p. 493.

found ample proof that they had lost all belief and merely hoped to find repose in annihilation.

M. Jules Lemaître does not believe that Religious Belief is any better preservative against suicide and crime than scepticism. He makes fun of Octave Feuillet because he represents an atheistical hero in one of his Novels as swallowing a phial of opium, and an atheistical woman as poisoning her rival, a married woman, that she may marry the latter's husband, who is her lover.[1] For all my admiration of his fine talents, I am bound to say I think M. Jules Lemaître is wrong, no less than M. Barrès, who in the Preface of a recent work "offered to sundry Collegians of Paris and the Provinces," attributes the numerous suicides of young men to the mistake they make in taking life too seriously. To guard their comrades against the contagion of suicide, M. Barrès advises them to be "ardent and sceptical." I think myself he would have been wiser to advise them to have moderation and faith. Of course all Atheists do not end in suicide and murder, there are sceptics as incapable of either one or the other as any believer; a happy nature, a good education, the love of science, are all preservations against vice. There are even lay Saints, like Littré. But to say that men, and still more women, are not better preserved from suicide and crime by religious Faith than by scepticism, is an assertion contrary both to judicial and medical experience.

Women have even greater need than men of spiritual beliefs, to sustain their unstable will and moderate their nervous sensibility. Faith alone can make of this being, naturally so weak, a strong character in virtue of education. My own researches show there are fewer suicides of widows than of widowers determined by grief at the death of their mates. Moreover, I have noted several cases of suicide of fathers in despair at the death of their children, but never one of a mother. If widows and mothers, though more sensitive of pain and less strong to bear it, kill themselves more rarely than widowers and

[1] J. Lemaître, *Les Contemporains*, 3rd Series, p. 28.

fathers, this is because they find strength and consolation in religious sentiment and the hope of another life, in which they will see their children and husbands again. If the proportion of women in the total number of suicides has been increasing for some years past, it is because women are beginning to lose their beliefs, by contact with free-thinking husbands and fathers.

It is true at the same time that religious beliefs are not always sufficient to preserve women from suicides of love, because love is sometimes combined in one with mysticism.

It is no profanation of the Religious life to deem it may be a consolation for disappointed love. Devoid of faith, poor girls who have been seduced and abandoned, let themselves fall into despair or a life of profligacy. Would it not be far preferable to see them entering a Convent, where little by little their sorrow would be appeased, and give place to the desire to occupy their energies and their craving for love in loving the orphan and the pauper!

The precocity young people of to-day show for dissoluteness being a cause of their equal precocity in suicide and crimes of passion, parents could arrest the latter by a better system of upbringing, by a stricter surveillance of the books they are allowed to read, the companions they go with, and the plays they see. Racine, junior, tells us his father never talked of theatrical pieces before his children, and that once having been asked to give lessons in elocution to a young Royal Princess of fifteen, he was so deeply shocked to hear her recite a passionate declamation of love from the part of Hermione that he refused to continue the lessons. Nowadays, there are parents who take their children to see downright indecent plays.

There would be fewer girls seduced and unfaithful wives, if parents would leave off teaching their daughters habits of luxury above their social position and fortune. Unable to realize in marriage the ideals they have dreamed or to continue their luxurious ways of living, girls suffer from the disappointment and disillusion; they will not marry, but prefer a rich lover, who will one day forsake them, to a husband in modest circumstances, who would have loved them all their life long, but who would have made them blush to be seen with him,—or else, if they do marry, they suffer from their husband's vulgarity of mind and manners, and take to bad courses.

Young men would be less precocious in profligacy, if parents did not themselves encourage them to amuse themselves, saying young folks must " sow their wild oats." The young men of our large towns are so ready to acquire habits of dissipation at an early age, that they take mistresses at fifteen or sixteen, whence come quarrels and jealousies that end in suicide or knife thrusts.

Parents again would often be saved their children's suicide after a love disappointment, if they did not oppose a projected match solely because the girl their son is in love with, though possessed of every quality of heart and mind and body, has not just quite the fortune they would have wished for.

Suicides of passion being only possible through an excess of sensibility and a lack of energy to bear suffering, how many calamities would parents avoid, if only they taught their children to moderate their sensibility and to strengthen their will! How many acts of despair would they prevent if they taught them early to master and moderate their nervous susceptibilities! Disgust of love, despair following on a love disappointment, are often indeed the consequences of a too impressionable nervous system and too weak a will; there is a very close connection between pessimism and nervosity![1] Suicide, insanity, crime, are marks of failure of will and a disordered sensibility. Incapacity in a man to moderate and govern the affection or emotional element of his nature I call slavery, Spinoza says. To master the nerves, to develop the will power, is the best preservative against suicide, insanity, and crime.

[1] Dr. Régis, *La Médecine et le Pessimisme contemporain.*

pulses to suicide and murder are of common occurrence among "degenerates," among hysterical subjects and epileptics. Of this I have observed several cases, particularly among women. Numerous examples are to be found in the books of Specialists dealing with Mental Diseases.[1]

Again, parents might do much to guard their children against crimes of passion by exercising proper surveillance over the books they read. Literature has a great deal to do with suicides and crimes of passion among young people. To discover the reason, it is not enough to say : " Look for the woman ; " we must often rather look for the book. The choice of books to be read and plays to be witnessed is not indifferent to the health of the mind any more than the choice of food is to the health of the body. The moral and physical health of young people depend largely on the nourishment they take and the air they breathe.

No less than parents, writers of Fiction and Drama have a part of the responsibility for the frequency of suicides and crimes of passion. Many of them have no suspicion of the fact ; for as a rule men fail to recognize all their responsibilities. They think themselves responsible only for their own faults, forgetting the share of responsibility they must bear for the faults of others, children, friends, pupils, readers, spectators. Every word we utter, every act we do, exercises some influence over the words and acts of other people. In the moral order as in the physical nothing is lost altogether. Each man is born for the salvation or the ruin of some of his fellow-creatures,— and the Author more than anybody. Literature, which could do so much good by disseminating healthy thoughts and lofty sentiments, does incalculable harm by destroying the moral sense of readers, by throwing a glamour over profligacy, sexual perversions, adultery, suicide, double suicide and revenge of passion.

I have given numerous instances of suicide and double

---

[1] Drs. Bourdin and Carrière have written special studies on suicidal and homicidal impulses among " degenerates."

suicide after an orgy, copied from the poems of Musset and Alfred de Vigny ; I have quoted the words of young men who, having survived attempts of this sort, declared how double suicide had appeared to them something heroic and poetical. Seeing that suicide is infectious and this dramatic end to a sensual passion appeals so highly to the imagination of the young, it is the bounden duty of Poets not to present such images to them, invested with all the glamour of verse. So many young men are to be found, weakened in mind and body by debauchery, overwhelmed with debts, in revolt against the paternal authority, incapable of resuming honest work, that when Poets offer them suicide after a scene of orgy as a means of escape from all these embarrassments, the unfortunates will inevitably yield to the temptation. There would undoubtedly be fewer debauchees and suicides, if Poets and Novelists did not persist in representing profligates as noble hearts athirst for the ideal. Don Juan, who admits no truth but this : 2 and 2 make 4, and 4 make 8, they describe as devoured by thirst after the infinite. As a matter of fact, this thirst after the infinite is merely a thirst for pleasure ; this hunger after the ideal is merely the pursuit of sensual gratification ; the ideal of Don Juan is Mathurine, Elvire, Charlotte, and the like. Sganarelle, who knows his master thoroughly describes him as "a true Sardanapalus, a hog of Epicurus, a downright brute." It is only in Novels that profligates have noble hearts and philosophic minds. In actual fact, they are candidates for ruin, for suicide and crimes of passion ; the authors of the dramas of Parisian life are often enough simply "men about town."

If any young man is inclined to think a life of Bohemianism alluring, let him read Murger's life, written by one of his friends ; there is not a sadder book in Literature. A considerable proportion of Murger's letters given in the volume are dated from the Hôpital Saint-Louis, where he made several stays,[1] and several of his friends are noted as

[1] Murger sought inspiration in coffee ; " some nights," he declares, " I have taken as much as six ounces of coffee." This abuse of coffee brought on terrible

having died in the same hospital. Murger's own death was " terrible," his friend says.

Poets would spare their readers the commission of many follies, if only they put them on their guard against the temptations of sensual love, which is full of hatred and vindictiveness, and showed them the superiority of spiritual love. The great Poets of Love, Dante, Petrarch, Lamartine, have nowhere celebrated sensual love in their verses.[1]

The higher form of Love is that in which the consideration of the moral and intellectual qualities plays as important a part as the value attached to physical qualities, and affection and esteem are added to desire. A People that should cling only to physical beauty and neglect moral and intellectual, would be on the verge of decadence and a return to primitive barbarism.

Erotic Writers think to excuse themselves by declaring that their own life is honest and respectable. Thus Ovid said :

> " Mores distant a carmine nostro,
> Vita verecunda est, Musa jocosa mihi " ; [2]

and Martial repeated the same apology, writing :

> " Lasciva est nobis pagina, vita proba est." [3]

But the strictness of the Erotic author's life in no way removes the danger of his writings. Free Love and the liaisons based on it almost invariably terminating in a rupture, and this often leading to acts of revenge, Literature might likewise prevent many suicides and crimes of passion, by bringing married love into fashion. This is asking a great deal, I allow ; but Literature has so much

---

attacks of purpura. In the Life of Murger referred to we find nothing but accounts of dismal poverty and continual begging for employment and money. Nothing can be more melancholy than his love affairs, nothing less poetical. The woman he loved best deceived him with one of his intimates a week after the tie was first formed.

[1] Lamartine, it is true, wrote in his youth two volumes of erotic poetry ; but he burned them subsequently.

[2] " My character is very different from my verse ; my life is modest, only my muse sportive."

[3] " Wanton are my pages, but my life upright."

power that it could, if it would, throw a halo of poetry over honourable love. Did it not in the Eighteenth Century, by the pen of Jean Jacques Rousseau, bring into fashion the practice of mothers suckling their own children, till Society ladies, dining out, would have their babies brought to them at dessert, to give them the breast there and then? Nothing is impossible to Poets and Novelists. They have turned into ridicule Mankind's two greatest blessings, health and virtue; they have found health less poetical than disease, life less picturesque than death, virtue more tiresome than vice; they have embellished melancholy, phthisis, perversions of the sexual instinct, Sapphism, Sadism, Masochism, adultery, suicide, double suicide and crimes of passion. I ·hold they are equally capable of idealizing health, reason, temperance, hard work, and pure love, which are just as poetical as folly, idleness, intemperance, and profligacy.

We may apply to the type of Literature that embellishes Vice and makes Virtue look ugly the verse of the Latin Poet:

" Dat veniam corvis, vexat censura columbas." [1]

It would make the crow white and the dove black, and so in everything. Instead of teaching the beauty of modesty, the value of temperance, the dignity of married love, it holds up for the reader's imitation and admiration orgy, suicides, and crimes.

But surely the Writer's task is not to make men melancholy, desperate, vindictive, and criminal, to supply excuses for passions that are always on the look-out for some piece of sophistry to palliate their heinousness, to silence conscience, that tiresome, unfortunate judge. Society being based on family life and this on marriage,[2] is it too much

---

[1] " While it is lenient to the crows, censure falls heavy on the doves."

[2] In Egypt and Syria, Mussulmans of the higher classes, recognizing that Polygamy is a principle of disintegration for the family and the State, are going back to Monogamy, in spite of the fact that Mahomet allows them to take a number of wives. I have this information from a Mussulman judge at the High Court of Cairo and a former *Procureur Général* at the Court of Alexandria.

to require the Novelist not to write that "the marriage vow is an absurdity imposed by society?"[1]   Men are apt enough already in their search after the forbidden fruit and the refinements of vice,[2] without its being needful to draw an alluring picture for their benefit of criminal passions. Poor humanity is sufficiently tempted by nature to indulge in profligacy and evil passions, without its being needful to make it still more licentious and revengeful by sensual stimulations and direct appeals to its vindictiveness.   The mission of Literature would rather seem to consist in softening down what there is in us of instinctive savagery ; to subordinate the animal part of human nature to the rational, to give the spiritual the mastery over the in- stinctive, the social over the brutish, to make the passions submit to reason and social well-being, to modify the bestial element and curb it beneath the yoke of law,— this is the end and aim of human life.   Has Literature any right to keep mankind from this aim, to destroy this ideal, to excite his worst instincts?

The very object of organized society being to ensure respect for women and children and human life, is Literature fulfilling its social mission by teaching contempt for all these things?   If Novelists who represent woman as an invalid, inferior creature, did not with a curious inconsist- ency incite the husband to kill the unfaithful wife, who is in their eyes irresponsible, there would most certainly be fewer crimes of marital vengeance.   Literature has no right, merely in order to supply readers with strong emotions, to make acts of revenge more frequent.   Murders are common enough for it to be quite unnecessary to further increase the number.   Literature should be an instrument of life

---

[1] G. Sand, *Jacques.*

[2] *Nitimur in vetitum semper, cupimusque negata.*—" We are for ever striving after forbidden pleasures, and longing for joys denied us " (Ovid).—Savage Peoples resemble civilized in their constant efforts to increase pleasure by the perverse refinements of fancy.   A missionary was explaining to a cannibal, who was going to eat a human head, how odious it was to kill a man in order to eat a head that thinks.   "That is just why," retorted the cannibal, " it is so delightful to eat it."

and progress, not of death ; it has no right whatever to set itself up in revolt against the decrees of Law and of Morality. The Writer's duty is not to counteract the efficacy of the laws of the land, to disseminate antisocial fallacies about fatality, the irresistible character of passion and the rights of love which is on a par with virtue and superior to legality, about the justifiability of suicide, the beauty of crimes of passion, the paramount claims of vengeance. These are sophistries one and all that make villains, suicides and murderers.

No one has ever thought of attributing to the Literature of the Seventeenth Century any share of responsibility for suicides and crimes, because it was never its habit to disseminate sophistical fallacies or to flatter the evil instincts of the crowd ; it always refused to draw a line of separation between æsthetics and morals. At that period Literature was better than society, and tended to raise its moral level. To-day, sick as society is, the Literature of imagination, with some very honourable exceptions, is worse than society, and helps, along with Politics, to corrupt it still further. If it will not make men wise, it should at any rate not turn them into madmen and criminals.

Authors who pervert the public conscience with sophistries and unhealthy imaginings, fail to consider how weak is human nature and how rapid the progress of mental infection. Just as a whole flock may be infected with scab by a single sheep being attacked, so a whole group of readers may be demoralized by a single book. Nor is it only weak minds that fall under the contagion of example and of sophistry. The same influence is felt by intelligent men, of high sensibility but feeble will. Young men, women,[1] persons of nervous temperament, very easily catch up the ideas and sentiments of those around them and of the writers that stir them keenly. Paradoxes readily seduce them ; and they find it hard to resist ingenious sophistries. Their unreasonableness quickly spreads from

---

[1] G. Sand, in spite of all her talent, espoused in succession all her friends' ideas, even the most paradoxical.

ideas to actions. "Frailty, thy name is woman!" says one of Shakespeare's characters. It would be more correct to say, "Frailty, thy name is humanity!"—for indeed the "stronger sex" is as frail as the weaker; in fact, it commits a far greater number of suicides and crimes.

I will not go so far as to say with Taine: "Reason is not natural to man, nor universal in humanity. . . . Strictly speaking, man is insane, as the body is sick, by nature; the health of our minds like the health of our organs is only a frequently achieved piece of luck, a happy accident." [1] A condition of health, not of disease, is the general rule; but human reason is very frail. The greatest minds were on the borderland of madness. Napoleon I. said to Pinel that between a man of genius and a madman, there was not the thickness of a sixpenny bit, and added with a smile, "I must take care to keep out of your hands." [2] Man is not insane by nature, but he very easily becomes so. Many men, and still more women, live in a condition of half madness, on the confines of madness. Writers should thoroughly realize this frailty of human reason, and never forget that sophistry is far more catching than sweet reasonableness.

It is not the delineation of evil, if done with proper reserve, that constitutes a Work immoral; the Book may still be chaste, if its inspiration is lofty, and evil is described only to be branded as hateful. In spite of the coarseness of his language, Juvenal is chaste. Lucretius remains chaste throughout the physiological description of love. A book is immoral when the author's object is to rouse sensuality by an alluring picture of vice.

No less than Authors, the "powers that be" should remember this frailty of human nature, so as to secure surroundings favourable to the health of mind and body, not permit the Press to stifle the sense of shame and excite antisocial passions, and exercise a stricter surveillance than at present over the works displayed in the street

---

[1] Taine, *L'Ancien Régime*, 10th edition, pp. 314, 312.
[2] Pinel, *Physiologie de l'homme aliéné*, p. 40.

kiosques and in booksellers' windows, over municipal and popular lending libraries, and over the minor Theatres, where anything and everything may now be said and sung.[1]   It is a matter of the greatest social importance to preserve the sentiment of modesty intact ; besides its being the charm and ornament of womanhood, it is the safeguard of domestic peace.   Woman's chastity is the most solid foundation of family life and public peace.   It is by good character more than by mental achievements that women serve the interests of society and contribute to its progress.   Female corruption destroys the family, and the disorganization of the family leads directly to the decadence of Nations.   Is it not Horace who said : " Our Age, so fertile in crime, began by degrading marriage, the conception of children, family life ; hence all the ills that have fallen upon People and Land." [2]   Montesquieu has spoken in the same strain : " So many ills are connected with the loss of virtue in women, their whole soul is so much degraded in consequence, this main support being removed brings so much else down in ruin, that in a popular State we may well look upon public incontinence as the worst of calamities and a sure sign of impending revolution." [3]

Habits of intemperance contributing so largely as they do to the frequency of suicides and crimes of passion, society again might diminish the total of these by taking effective measures against drunkenness.[4]   Opportunity

---

[1] The author of *La Censure sous Napoléon III.* (The Censorship under Napoleon III.) calls for the abolition of the Censorship on the ground that it is, according to him, more preoccupied with preventing political allusions than indecencies ; " all that highly trained pornography can invent has appeared on the Stage,—*doubles entendres*, naughty puns, *risqué* situations, suggestive farces, have for years received the official authorization of the Censors."—Valerius Maximus attributes the austere discipline that was maintained among the inhabitants of Marsilia (Marseilles) in Ancient times to the strict surveillance they exercised over performances in the Theatre (bk. ii. ch. vi. § 7).

[2] Horace, *Odes*, bk. iii. 6.

[3] Montesquieu, *Esprit des Lois*, bk. vii. ch. viii.

[4] According to Dr. Magnan, of every 100 men admitted into the Insane

makes the tippler, just as it makes the thief; so that if there were fewer dram-shops, there would be fewer drunkards, and as a result fewer lunatics and criminals. Among Nations where alcoholism has been systematically combated, a decrease has been witnessed in insanity and crime. In Norway, for instance, the proportion of alcoholic sufferers in the total of insane patients fell as low as 4·4 per cent. in 1893; suicides which numbered 109 annually for every million inhabitants up to 1850, decreased to 65 in 1896. The total of criminals which stood at 180·3 annually for every million inhabitants fell to 142·1 in 1894.[1]

The authorities again might largely diminish the number of crimes of passion, if they would cease attracting working men to large towns, which are hot-beds of amorous stimulation,—if they would only leave them in the country. The poets, Horace, Juvenal, Boileau, have described the inconveniences and noisiness of great towns. But from the moral and social point of view, the accumulation of human beings in big towns leads to mischief very much more serious than any of the inconveniences alluded to by the poets. Feeble intellects (and there are many such) are easily led astray by the exciting influence of the revolutionary and pornographic Press, by political and literary sophistries, by the performances given at the minor Theatres, by the songs sung at the *Café-concerts*, and the demoralizing sights of the streets. In large towns parents cannot exercise a proper supervision over their children, nor masters over their servants; hence so many irregular *liaisons* that turn out badly, so many suicides of girls who have been seduced and find themselves pregnant. Marriage is less frequent in towns and longer delayed

Asylums of the Department of the Seine, more than 35 have been brought there by alcoholism; of every 100 women, more than 12 (*Recherches sur les centres nerveux*, 2nd Series, p. 46).—According to Dr. Rochard, what alcoholism costs France annually (cost of the alcohol, loss of work, expense of treatment, etc.) would amount to a sum of at least a milliard and a half of francs—£60,000,000.

[1] *Archives d'anthropologie criminelle*, Nov. 15, 1899, p. 689.

than in the country, where the number is far smaller of seductions and illegitimate births, as well as of suicides and crimes of passion. By encouraging agriculture, by reducing the land tax, labouring men might be kept in the country districts.

Another source of demoralization which Society might do away with is the temptations to profligacy to be found in the public streets, in the taverns, at the public balls and minor theatres, which are nothing more nor less than marts for prostitution.

It is a great mistake, in my opinion, to hold civilization responsible for the increase of crime; it is rather the apathy of governments and the incapacity of legislators that should be blamed. The Philosophers of the Eighteenth Century, d'Holbach, Grimm, Helvétius, Jean Jacques Rousseau have exaggerated the influence of Laws and Governments, asserting morals to be the creation of Laws and Constitutions.[1] Nowadays, on the contrary, the effect of Laws is over much ignored, and the maxim *quid leges sine moribus?* ("what are laws without conduct?") for ever on men's lips. What strikes everyone is the influence of temperament, the force of heredity; everything is accounted for by temperament, —the virtue of women, the eloquence of orators, the sensibility of poets, idiosyncrasies of mind and character, even political opinions and philosophical systems.[2] The influence

---

[1] Montesquieu alone, with his wide and comprehensive mental outlook, has fully appreciated all the factors, social, religious, philosophical, political, physical, and physiological, that contribute to the formation of character and morals.

[2] M. Faguet writes: "A Philosopher, however eminent, setting out his system, is only a man who is explaining his own character, and perhaps his temperament." (*Études sur le xixe siècle*, p. 268.) When Descartes explains his system to us, he is explaining his thought and not his temperament. With the same character, Philosophers may have different systems; the characters of Malebranche and Condillac are very much alike, their systems quite different. With different temperaments, Philosophers may hold identical doctrines; Maine de Biran, Jouffroy, and Cousin had not the same temperament, and yet their philosophical systems are alike. M. Boissier, Permanent Secretary of the Académie Française, that refined scholar who has passed his life in the intimacy of Cicero, Virgil, Horace, Juvenal, and Tacitus, instead of accounting for Mme. de Sevigné's virtue by her high education,

exercised by temperament is actually very great, and has been recognized by spiritualistic Philosophers, by Theologians, by our Moralists, even by our great Poets of the Sixteenth Century, by Corneille, Molière, and La Fontaine, the last named having even noted the effects of temperament as affecting the genius of the English Writers (Bk. xii. Fable 23). Quite right to insist on the influence of temperament; but it is spoiling a truth by exaggeration to make too much of it, and ignore entirely the effects arising from laws, government, religion, and literature. Laws and Governments are not unimportant factors in the formation of character and morals. The Laws of Moses, of Manu, of Solon, of Lycurgus, have powerfully contributed to form the character, sentiments, and ideas of the Jews, Hindus, Athenians, and Spartans. Bad Laws, bad Governments, corrupt morals; good Laws, and good Governments, improve them. Increase of drunkenness and indecency, licence of Press and Stage, are not inevitable consequences of civilization; they may be counteracted by judicious laws. The advance of civilization does not necessarily involve the advance of intemperance and pornographic literature.

It is bad laws that make bad morals,[1] and it is bad morals that lead to so many suicides,[2] and so many

---

her right-mindedness, her Christian faith and tender affection for her children, attributes it merely to the coldness of her temperament. He supports his contention by the witness of her cousin Bussy, a spiteful tattler if ever there was one, who inspires Michelet with no confidence in his trustworthiness, and who was known, Saint-Simon tells us, "for the vanity of his mind and the baseness of his heart." Moreover, he had been wounded in his self-love because his fair cousin had repulsed his advances, and as a matter of fact afterwards retracted the satirical portrait he had drawn of her.

[1] Among bad laws I count the Law of 1880, which abolished the control of drinking shops,—the Law of 1881, which declared the impunity of the Press,—the Law of 1884, which re-established divorce, in other words, the disorganization of the family,—the Articles of the Civil Code which systematize the irresponsibility of the seducer, requiring a formal document to authenticate the paternity of an illegitimate child, and consequently declaring inoperative recognition resulting from the actual avowal of the father or from his letters, and forbidding enquiries into the question of paternity.

[2] In the Statistics I have given of suicides due to passion, I have included

crimes,—not the progress of civilization. Repeal bad laws, make the people moral, leave them the sentiment of Religion, which is a pillar of morality and a safeguard against suicide and crimes of passion, combat alcoholism and pornography, organize the responsibility of the Press, ensure the execution of justice by a better selection of jurymen, protect women and children by declaring the seducer responsible for the wrong he does, and you will greatly diminish the number of suicides and crimes determined by passion.

Poor humanity which is largely composed of weak and feeble creatures, slaves of mere passion and instinct, would rapidly sink back towards sheer animality, if Government, Legislation, Literature and Religion did not set before its eyes an ideal of Justice and Morality, and help it on the upward path towards the attainment of this ideal.

only suicides resulting in death. But attempted suicides are still more numerous, though it is difficult to get at the precise number. The majority of Police reports relating to mere attempts at suicide are not communicated to the Central Criminal Bureau of the Department of the Seine; they remain arranged in classes at the First Office of the First Division of the Prefecture of Police, or else among the special Records of the Prefect of Police, when they have to do with families of position. Lastly, the Police Commissaries do not even invariably draw up reports at all; they often purposely omit doing so at the request of relations or in cases of small importance. Hence the Statistics of the Ministry of Justice only exhibit a portion of the facts. The real truth is even more terrible than what appears in the official reports. Under the influence of alcoholism, debauchery, sophistical and erotic literature, materialism of ideas and manners, politics that protect drink shops, or in other words, poison shops, the population becomes brutalized, impoverished and corrupt; the race degenerates, and its numbers diminish. Legislative reforms, that might raise the moral level of the people, are barred by electioneering considerations. In spite of the ever-increasing total of madmen, suicides, broken intellects and criminals for which alcoholism is responsible, in spite of the campaign conducted against this scourge of humanity by the Academy of Medicine, the "Institut," Moralists, Economists and Criminalists, no repressive Law is ever passed, because the drink-sellers are the best electoral agents.